ASPEN PUBLISHERS

Wage and Hour Answer Book
2008 Edition

by Littler Mendelson's Wage and Hour Practice Group

Complying with the Fair Labor Standards Act's minimum wage, overtime, and recordkeeping provisions is no easy task. To help employers avoid costly penalties, Littler Mendelson's *Wage and Hour Answer Book* provides comprehensive explanations of the requirements along with real-world detailed examples that simplify the complex issues of overtime pay, hours worked, and other calculations. In addition, the *Wage and Hour Answer Book* includes up-to-date citations to controlling regulations and case law, insightful discussions of gray and evolving areas, and tips and precautions that can be applied immediately to avoid noncompliance.

Highlights of the 2008 Edition

The 2008 Edition of the *Wage and Hour Answer Book* brings the reader up to speed on the latest regulatory and case law developments as well as opinions of the Department of Labor. Revised material includes the following:

- Analysis of the Fair Minimum Wage Act of 2007.

- Updated 50-state survey of minimum wage laws following an increase in state legislation and passage of the Fair Minimum Wage Act of 2007.

- New interpretations of the definitions of "administrative," "executive," and "professional" employees.

- Updated 50-state survey of overtime requirements.

- The circumstances under which an insurance adjuster may be considered an exempt, white-collar employee.

- Explanations of permissible and impermissible deductions from salary to maintain exempt status.

- New interpretations of what can be included in an employer's calculation of an employee's "regular rate of pay" for overtime purposes.

- New strategies for dealing with misclassified employees.

- Recent interpretations of the disciplinary docking rules.

Wolters Kluwer
Law & Business

- Additional analysis of enforcement actions under the Davis-Bacon Act.

- Updated information about the Department of Labor's enforcement of the FLSA.

10/07

For questions concerning this shipment, billing, or other customer service matters, call our Customer Service Department at 1-800-234-1660.

For toll-free ordering, please call 1-800-638-8437.

Wage and Hour
Answer Book

ASPEN PUBLISHERS

Wage and Hour Answer Book

2008 Edition

Littler Mendelson, P.C.
Wage and Hour Practice Group

Wolters Kluwer
Law & Business

AUSTIN   BOSTON   CHICAGO   NEW YORK   THE NETHERLANDS

This publication is designed to provide accurate and authoritative information in regard to the subject matter covered. It is sold with the understanding that the publisher is not engaged in rendering legal, accounting, or other professional services. If legal advice or other professional assistance is required, the services of a competent professional person should be sought.

—From a *Declaration of Principles* jointly adopted by
a Committee of the American Bar Association and
a Committee of Publishers and Associations

Printed in the United States of America

ISBN 978-0-7355-6604-0

1 2 3 4 5 6 7 8 9 0

About Wolters Kluwer Law & Business

Wolters Kluwer Law & Business is a leading provider of research information and workflow solutions in key specialty areas. The strengths of the individual brands of Aspen Publishers, CCH, Kluwer Law International and Loislaw are aligned within Wolters Kluwer Law & Business to provide comprehensive, in-depth solutions and expert-authored content for the legal, professional and education markets.

CCH was founded in 1913 and has served more than four generations of business professionals and their clients. The CCH products in the Wolters Kluwer Law & Business group are highly regarded electronic and print resources for legal, securities, antitrust and trade regulation, government contracting, banking, pension, payroll, employment and labor, and healthcare reimbursement and compliance professionals.

Aspen Publishers is a leading information provider for attorneys, business professionals and law students. Written by preeminent authorities, Aspen products offer analytical and practical information in a range of specialty practice areas from securities law and intellectual property to mergers and acquisitions and pension/benefits. Aspen's trusted legal education resources provide professors and students with high-quality, up-to-date and effective resources for successful instruction and study in all areas of the law.

Kluwer Law International supplies the global business community with comprehensive English-language international legal information. Legal practitioners, corporate counsel and business executives around the world rely on the Kluwer Law International journals, loose-leafs, books and electronic products for authoritative information in many areas of international legal practice.

Loislaw is a premier provider of digitized legal content to small law firm practitioners of various specializations. Loislaw provides attorneys with the ability to quickly and efficiently find the necessary legal information they need, when and where they need it, by facilitating access to primary law as well as state-specific law, records, forms and treatises.

Wolters Kluwer Law & Business, a unit of Wolters Kluwer, is headquartered in New York and Riverwoods, Illinois. Wolters Kluwer is a leading multinational publisher and information services company.

ASPEN PUBLISHERS SUBSCRIPTION NOTICE

This Aspen Publishers product is updated on a periodic basis with supplements to reflect important changes in the subject matter. If you purchased this product directly from Aspen Publishers, we have already recorded your subscription for the update service.

If, however, you purchased this product from a bookstore and wish to receive future updates and revised or related volumes billed separately with a 30-day examination review, please contact our Customer Service Department at 1-800-234-1660 or send your name, company name (if applicable), address, and the title of the product to:

ASPEN PUBLISHERS
7201 McKinney Circle
Frederick, MD 21704

Important Aspen Publishers Contact Information

- To order any Aspen Publishers title, go to *www.aspenpublishers.com* or call 1-800-638-8437.

- To reinstate your manual update service, call 1-800-638-8437.

- To contact Customer Care, e-mail *customer.care@aspenpublishers. com*, call 1-800-234-1660, fax 1-800-901-9075, or mail correspondence to Order Department, Aspen Publishers, PO Box 990, Frederick, MD 21705.

- To review your account history or pay an invoice online, visit *www.aspenpublishers.com/payinvoices*.

Wolters Kluwer
Law & Business

Preface

Wage and hour laws have near-universal application to U.S. employees. As such, wage and hour laws are or should be of near-universal concern to all types of employers. The Fair Labor Standards Act (FLSA) and its amendments dictate minimum wages, regulate the payment of overtime, set forth narrowly construed exemptions, and proscribe the use of child labor. All of the wage and hour statutes contain recordkeeping requirements, set forth enforcement guidelines, and provide for damages or penalties for noncompliance. Wage and hour statutes, combined with a collection of federal regulations and case law, present employers with a daunting array of information and rules on wage and hour issues. Investigations of and litigation regarding wage and hour issues are common and can be costly for employers that have made mistakes in applying the laws to their employees. In fact, nationwide investigations by the Wage and Hour Division, and especially class action lawsuits by plaintiff's lawyers, have increased dramatically in recent years.

Wage and Hour Answer Book is a comprehensive reference for personnel and payroll managers, human resources professionals, consultants, advisors, attorneys, and anyone who employs and/or compensates a covered employee. It addresses significant concepts in wage and hour law, such as:

- Coverage of employers and employees
- Computation of hours worked
- Exemptions
- Minimum wage
- Overtime pay
- Litigation issues in wage and hour law
- Child labor restrictions
- Recordkeeping obligations

The 2008 Edition provides new insights into wage and hour compliance in light of the recent passage of the Fair Minimum Wage Act of 2007 and

Department of Labor interpretations of the FLSA and additional material on such significant issues as recent cases on compensable time, exempt employees' salary requirements, the new duties test for white-collar employees, limitations on salary deductions, and being able to use the "window of corrections" opportunity to reimburse employees when improper deductions have been made and restore the ability to use the salaried employee exemption.

Wage and Hour Answer Book, 2008 Edition, gives authoritative and concise answers to both broad and specific questions under the wage and hour laws, including:

- What employees are covered by the Fair Labor Standards Act (FLSA)?

- Are independent contractors excluded from FLSA coverage?

- Can deductions from pay be made in overtime workweeks?

- What requirements must an employer satisfy to make deductions for board, lodging, and other facilities?

- How does a deduction that is treated as part of wages impact the calculation of overtime?

- Does time spent performing work that the employer has not requested be performed count as hours worked?

- When are rest and meal periods considered compensable hours worked under the FLSA?

- Is time that an employee spends traveling compensable working time?

- When can employees claim that time spent in training is compensable?

- What is an employer's basic overtime obligation under the FLSA?

- What is the regular rate of pay for overtime calculation purposes?

- Which supplemental payments must be included in an employee's overtime pay computation?

- What types of payments are excluded from an employer's calculation of the regular rate?

- Are 401(k) and profit sharing contributions from the employer excluded from the regular rate?

- Are stock options excluded from the regular rate?

- What is premium pay and how does it affect the calculation of overtime pay?

- How is overtime calculated for piece-rate employees?

- How is overtime calculated for commissioned employees?

- How is overtime calculated for employees paid a fixed rate for a fluctuating workweek or a day rate for a fluctuating workday?

- Under what circumstances can employers satisfy their overtime pay obligations by providing employees with compensatory time off?

- How can public sector employers limit or control the use of compensatory time off by employees?

- What factors determine whether an employee is exempt as an executive, administrative, or professional employee?

- Can an employee lose his or her exempt status?

- What drivers are exempt from overtime requirements?

- When are retail employees paid with commissions exempt from overtime?

- How does a Wage and Hour Division investigation of an employer come about?

- What should an employer do when the investigator appears at the employer's place of business?

- What statute of limitations applies to collecting back pay pursuant to the FLSA?

- Can the statute of limitations be tolled by employer misconduct?

- Can employees agree to waive their FLSA rights to minimum wage and overtime?

- What are liquidated damages, and when will an employer be required to pay liquidated damages to an employee under the FLSA?

- When is a violation of the FLSA a willful violation?

- What civil money penalties can be assessed against an employer that violates the FLSA's minimum wage and overtime pay provisions?

- How can an employer avoid liability under the FLSA?

- Can employers waive defenses to wage and hour claims by employees?

- Can employers be liable for damages to employees working for a contracted entity?

- When is an 'independent contractor' really an employee for wage and hour purposes?

- Where can wage and hour litigation be initiated and maintained?

- How can employees sue their employer as a class for alleged FLSA violations?

- What types of employee activity are protected by the FLSA's anti-retaliation provisions?

The detailed explanations and convenient resource materials presented here will provide an essential guide to all aspects of wage and payroll administration.

About the Authors

Littler Mendelson is *The National Employment & Labor Law Firm.*® With over 600 attorneys practicing in 43 offices coast-to-coast, Littler is the largest law firm in the United States to represent management exclusively in employment law and labor relations.

The firm was founded in 1942 to represent employers in public- and private-sector labor issues. Its attorneys quickly gained a reputation as aggressive problem solvers, handling precedent-setting labor relations cases in the food, trucking, and lumber industries. With the passage of the Civil Rights Act of 1964 and subsequent legislation involving a wide range of workplace issues, employers' needs expanded—and Littler responded.

Littler attorneys are experienced in the many subtleties of employment law. Yet we provide clients with the added value that comes from our understanding of how companies do business. As a law firm, Littler Mendelson has represented more than 50,000 employers in virtually every industry. We have an extensive track record of representing major corporations on both a regional and national basis in employment litigation and related matters. As a result, we are knowledgeable on issues affecting small companies as well some of the world's largest corporations.

One of Littler's premier practice groups is the Wage and Hour Practice Group. With a nationwide employment practice that extends into practically every state, attorneys in Littler's Wage and Hour Practice Group are uniquely qualified to defend clients against state wage and hour claims, wherever clients do business. Littler attorneys throughout the country handle hundreds of state wage and hour cases each year, creating a huge knowledge base through which attorneys share solutions to the particular problems each client faces.

The attorneys in the Wage and Hour Practice Group who contributed to the 2008 edition of the *Wage and Hour Answer Book* include:

- R. Brian Dixon (Co-Chair of Littler's Wage and Hour Practice Group), Shareholder (San Francisco)

- Donald W. Benson, Shareholder (Atlanta)

- Melodie K. Craft, Shareholder (Dallas)

- Barry Y. Freeman, Shareholder (Cleveland)

- Van A. Goodwin, Shareholder (San Diego)

- Gerald T. Hathaway, Shareholder (New York)

- Grady B. Murdock, Shareholder (Chicago)

- Angelo Spinola, Of Counsel (Atlanta)

- John T. Stembridge, Associate (Atlanta)

- Michelle Stevenson, Special Counsel (Sacramento)

Acknowledgments

The authors would like to gratefully acknowledge the contributions of Littler shareholder Susan A.P. Woodhouse, Esq., Executive Editor of Littler Publications and Kristen Countryman, Managing Editor of Littler Publications.

Invaluable assistance was also rendered by the librarians at Littler including Joanne Block, Cynthia Brown, Bria O'Brien and Yarka Odvarko whose tireless efforts are always much appreciated but rarely acknowledged.

Thanks, too, to editor Joanne Mitchell-George, whose attention to detail enhanced the quality of the book. We also acknowledge senior manuscript editor, Bernie Johnston, whose careful sheperding of the publication helped it to be published in a timely manner.

Contents

Contents

Contents

List of Questions

Chapter 1 Introduction and Overview of the Fair Labor Standards Act and Amendments

Chapter 2 Determining Coverage Under the Fair Labor Standards Act

Employer-Employee Relationship

Joint Employment Relationship

Chapter 3 Minimum Wage Issues

Overview

Uniforms

Tip Credits

Deductions from Wages

Deductions for Board, Lodging, and Other Facilities

Professionals

Computer Employees

Public Sector Employees Who Are Executives, Administrators, or Professionals

Outside Salespersons

Chapter 5 Exemptions from Minimum Wage, Overtime Pay, Child Labor, and Recordkeeping Obligations

Exempt Minors

Recordkeeping for Exempt Employees

Chapter 6 Computation of Hours Worked

Hours Worked Defined

Incidental Activities

Training Time

Special Public Employee Issues

Exercise Time

Chapter 7 Overtime Pay

Regular Rate

Basic Rate as an Alternative to Weekly Calculation of the Regular Rate

Chapter 8 Employer's Recordkeeping Obligations

Chapter 9 Child Labor Restrictions Under the FLSA

Fluctuating Day Rate Plan

Belo Contracts

Chapter 11   Government Contracts

Employer Defenses

Chapter 13 Investigations by the Wage and Hour Division

Chapter 14 Penalties for Violations of the FLSA

Chapter 15 Migrant and Seasonal Agricultural Worker Protection Act

General Concepts

Chapter 1

Introduction and Overview of the Fair Labor Standards Act and Amendments

The purpose of this book is to provide a broad discussion of federal wage and hour law. This chapter presents an overview of topics discussed more fully in other chapters of this book. Chapter 2 explains in detail which employees fall within the coverage of the Fair Labor Standards Act (FLSA), including the meaning of joint employer relationships and independent contractor status. Other chapters focus on how employers calculate hours worked (Chapter 6), the intricacies of overtime regulations (Chapter 7), and employees who are so-called exempt employees under the FLSA (Chapters 4 and 5). The federal law permits several methods for determining how employees' pay may be calculated (Chapter 10) and contains special requirements for government contracts (Chapter 11). Some special issues pertaining to wage and hour investigations, litigations, and penalties are discussed in depth in Chapters 12, 13, and 14. Chapter 15 explains the protections afforded to migrant and seasonal agricultural workers.

Introduction

Q 1:1   What is the Fair Labor Standards Act (FLSA)?

The FLSA is the primary federal law covering minimum wage, overtime pay, child labor, equal pay, and recordkeeping requirements of employers in both the private and public sectors. [29 U.S.C. §§ 201–219] It is enforced by the Wage and Hour Division of the U.S. Department of Labor (DOL), which has regional and field offices throughout the United States.

The purpose of the FLSA, which was adopted in 1938, was to aid recovery from the Great Depression. The Act was intended to create monetary penalties for employers by requiring premium payments to employees for long hours of work. This gave employers reason to distribute work among employees and to hire more employees.

Not all employees are covered by the FLSA. The employer, its type of business, or its employees may fall outside the coverage of the Act. In addition, the employer, its type of business, or its employees may be exempt from coverage or may be protected by specific constitutional provisions. Other federal laws may permit employers to maintain wage and hour policies that differ from what the FLSA typically mandates.

Q 1:2   What does the FLSA regulate?

The FLSA sets a minimum wage that must be paid to all employees covered by it and requires that most hourly, nonexempt employees be paid overtime for all hours worked above 40 hours in a workweek. The FLSA also prohibits oppressive child labor for businesses with activities related to interstate commerce and mandates that employers maintain certain types of records and reports on covered employees.

Q 1:3   What is not regulated by the FLSA?

The FLSA does not regulate every aspect of wage payments. For instance, the FLSA does not address severance pay, vacation or holiday pay, methods of paying employees, or methods of giving notice of termination of employment. Some of these issues are regulated by state law.

Q 1:4   What effect do state wage and hour laws have on the FLSA?

The FLSA does not completely prevail over state law; it sets a minimum standard for all covered employers. States are free to enact laws affording more protection for employees than is provided by federal law. The FLSA does not dictate how many hours an employee may work, only what employees must be paid if they work more than 40 hours in a week. Many states' laws address areas not covered by the FLSA, such as the timing and method of paying employees, what constitutes wages for purposes of paying terminated employees, and when and how final paychecks must be delivered to terminated employees. The general rule is that employers must follow whichever law is more favorable to employees. Practically, this means that employers often must follow a combination of state and federal law.

A number of states have set a minimum wage exceeding the federal minimum wage, have different provisions regarding overtime pay, and have more stringent child labor laws. Such laws supersede federal law for covered employers when they are more favorable to employees.

As an example of unusual state laws, consider Florida's minimum wage and hour law, which requires an undefined amount of "extra" pay for manual workers employed by the day, week, month, or year when they work more than ten (10) hours in a day. The extra pay can be waived by written contracts setting a higher or lower number of hours. [Fla. Stat. § 448.01]

This statute, however, does not apply to hourly workers. [Quaker Oats v. Jewell, 818 So. 2d 574, 575 (Fla. Dist. Ct. App. 2002)] To illustrate, in *Quaker Oats* a group of hourly employees sued their employer for failing to pay overtime on a daily basis after working in excess of ten hours per day. The employees also sued for breach of contract, because the employee manual at one time stated that the employer would pay overtime for hours worked in excess of eight hours per day. [818 So. 2d at 574, 575] The court not only held that Florida Statute section 448.01 does not apply to hourly workers, but it also ruled that policy statements in an employee manual generally do not create enforceable contract rights. [818 So. 2d at 575, 578]

For Florida state workers, a workday is defined as eight hours. [Fla. Stat. § 110.219]

Coverage

Q 1:5   What organizations are subject to the FLSA?

The FLSA applies only to organizations that have employees who are engaged in interstate commerce, produce goods for interstate commerce, or handle, sell, or work on materials moved in or produced for interstate commerce and have annual gross sales of $500,000 or more. [29 U.S.C. § 203(s)(1)(A)] Employees of firms with dollar sales of less than $500,000 still may be covered in any workweek in which the employees are individually engaged in interstate commerce, production of goods for interstate commerce, or an activity closely related or directly essential to the production of such goods. Some enterprises are covered by the FLSA regardless of their dollar volume: hospitals (i.e., institutions primarily engaged in the care of the sick, aged, mentally ill, or disabled who live on the premises); schools for children who are mentally or physically disabled or gifted; preschools, elementary and secondary schools, and institutions of higher education; and federal, state, and local government agencies. [29 U.S.C. § 203(s)(1)(B), (C)]

Q 1:6   Who is covered by the FLSA?

The FLSA distinguishes between employees who are not covered by it and those who are exempt from minimum wage, overtime pay, child labor, or recordkeeping requirements.

To be covered by the FLSA, an employee must be: (1) an employee under the FLSA definition; (2) engaged in the production of goods for commerce or employed by an employer in an enterprise engaged in commerce or in the production of goods for commerce; and (3) located within the geographical area covered by the FLSA. Employers in the United States, including the District of Columbia, and in Puerto Rico and other U.S. territories, such as Guam and American Samoa, are covered by the FLSA, but the Act applies only to work actually performed in these locations, regardless of the employee's citizenship.

For an employee to be covered by the FLSA, the employee must be engaged in interstate commerce on a regular and recurring, not sporadic, basis. [29 C.F.R. §§ 776.3, 776.25] For example, the interstate nature of goods may cease when they are unloaded on the receiving room floor if the goods are placed in stockpile inventory before being used or sold. Employees handling the goods after placement in inventory may not be engaged in interstate commerce.

Exempt employees are those who fall outside one or more provisions of the FLSA. *Nonexempt employees* are protected by the Act's requirements. For example, an employer will be held liable for failing to pay overtime to employees who are not exempt from the Act's overtime provisions. The burden of proving that an exemption applies to an employee always falls on the employer trying to claim that the employee is exempt.

The FLSA does not apply to employees who are not covered by it. Employees who are exempt from the FLSA are technically covered by it but are exempt from certain portions—most notably, overtime pay—because of the types of jobs they perform. For example, exempt white-collar employees generally fall into one of four categories: executive, administrative, professional, or outside sales personnel. Federal regulations establish tests for determining whether an employee falls under any of those categories. (Chapters 4 and 5 address in more detail what it means to be an exempt employee.) Employees also may be exempt from minimum wage or child labor provisions (see Chapters 3 and 9).

An *employee* is "any individual employed by an employer," and an *employer* is "any person acting directly or indirectly in the interest of an employer in relation to an employee." [29 U.S.C. § 203(d), (e)(1)] *Employ* is merely defined as "suffer or permit to work." [29 U.S.C. § 203(g)] Independent contractors are not considered employees and thus are not covered by the FLSA. Employers cannot, however, simply label employees as independent contractors in order to avoid FLSA compliance. Under the FLSA and the Portal to Portal Act, *employer* has the same meaning [29 U.S.C. § 262(a)], but as used in the Walsh-Healey Public Contracts Act (Public Contracts Act) or the Davis-Bacon Act, *employer* refers to a contractor or subcontractor covered by such an act. [29 U.S.C. § 262(b)] See Chapter 11 for details about the Walsh-Healy Public Contracts Act and the Davis-Bacon Act.

Q 1:7   Can two employers be liable for a jointly shared employee?

Yes. An employer may be liable for wage payments to employees shared with another employer. A *joint employment relationship* exists when there is an arrangement between employers to share an employee's services. [29 C.F.R. § 791.2(b)]

An exception to the general rules on joint employer status was created by the 1985 FLSA amendments and public sector regulations. [29 C.F.R. § 553.227] Public safety employees (i.e., firefighters and law enforcement officers) may voluntarily accept employment from independent third-party employers for special duty work during off-duty hours. These hours of special duty work need not be counted as compensable hours worked for the public sector employer. However, the independent employer must be truly independent, and the public safety employee must be free to accept or reject the special assignment (see Chapter 2).

Q 1:8   When does an employment relationship exist?

Courts use an "economic reality" test to determine whether an employment relationship exists. [*See* Real v. Driscoll Strawberry Assocs., Inc., 603 F.2d 748, 754–55 (9th Cir. 1979) (finding "sub-licensees" of strawberry plots to be employees, not independent contractors, because company was able to fire them at any time, no special skills were used to tend berry patches, and activities were found to be essential to company's operation rather than an independent enterprise); Bailey v. Pilots Ass'n for Bay & River Del., 406 F. Supp. 1302, 1306–07 (E.D. Pa. 1976) (finding that apprentice-pilot was an employee during apprenticeship because he substituted for hired hands and was working, not training, during time spent as deckhand)] That is, courts look at all of the circumstances of the employer's business and the work performed by the employee, considering the employer's ability to hire and fire the employee, degree of control, ability to set wages, and maintenance of employment records. [Watson v. Graves, 909 F.2d 1549, 1553–57 (5th Cir. 1990)]

Q 1:9   Who is not covered by the FLSA?

The FLSA excludes from its coverage (1) family members of an agricultural employer and (2) government employees who are not subject to the civil service laws and who hold elective public office or are selected personal staff, policy-makers, or immediate advisors to elected officials. [29 U.S.C. §§ 203(e)(2)(C), 203(e)(3)] Most congressional employees are covered by the FLSA, but employees of state and local governments typically are not.

Individuals who volunteer for interstate, state, and local public agencies are not covered by the FLSA provided they are not performing services for which they are employed by the agency and provided the individuals are not compensated or are paid only "expenses, reasonable benefits, or a nominal fee." [29 U.S.C. § 203(e)(4)(A)]

Another exclusion, which is not found within the text of the FLSA itself, is for trainees.

Students working as summer interns are not considered employees for FLSA purposes when they are participating in training programs that are "designed to provide students with professional experience in the furtherance of their education and training and are academically oriented for their benefit." [Wage & Hour Opinion Letter, FLSA1988 (Jan. 1988)]

Other bona fide volunteers, whether individuals or members of civic organizations, may provide services without compensation. For example, the DOL recognizes that parents may help out at their children's schools or volunteers may assist the Red Cross or help out at hospitals without running afoul of the FLSA. [Wage and Hour Division Field Operations Handbook § 10b03(c)] However, volunteers who perform work for a private employer other than a charitable organization likely are covered by the FLSA.

Q 1:10   Must all work be performed on the employer's premises to be covered by the FLSA?

No. Work need not be performed at a particular facility, such as a factory or a hospital, to bring it within the coverage of the FLSA. However, employers must obtain a certificate from the DOL before certain types of work may be performed in an employee's home. [29 C.F.R. § 530.3] Industries singled out are those manufacturing knitted outerwear, gloves and mittens, buttons and buckles, handkerchiefs, embroideries, and jewelry, as long as no health or safety hazard is involved. [29 C.F.R. § 530.101] Generally, manufacturing women's clothing at home is prohibited unless the employee is unable to work at the employer's place of business because of age, physical or mental disability, or responsibility for caring for an invalid in the home. [29 C.F.R. § 530.4] State laws may further restrict homework and, in such cases, would supersede federal regulations.

Administration

Q 1:11   Who is responsible for administering the FLSA?

The DOL Wage and Hour Division administers the FLSA by enforcing minimum wage rates, recordkeeping requirements, and child labor restrictions and by imposing penalties.

Q 1:12   How is the FLSA enforced?

Under the FLSA, the DOL, through its Wage and Hour Division, may initiate an investigation or inspection. The Wage and Hour Division may investigate and gather data on the wages, hours, and other employment practices of an industry subject to the FLSA. Within its investigative authority, the Wage and Hour Division has the power to conduct an investigation into whether an employer is subject to the FLSA and whether the Act is being violated. Investigations typically begin when a complaint is filed by an employee or when the DOL targets a specific industry for investigation. The DOL need not disclose to the employer the reason for the investigation.

The Wage and Hour Division does not need probable cause to believe an employer has violated the FLSA in order to conduct an investigation. In conducting an investigation, the Wage and Hour Division investigators may inspect places and records, question employees, and investigate any "facts, conditions, practices, or matter" that the investigator deems necessary for determining whether the FLSA has been violated. [29 U.S.C. § 211(a)] Typically, the investigation period extends back two years for a business that has not previously been investigated. If an establishment has been investigated previously, the investigation normally extends back two years or to the beginning of the period not covered by the prior investigation, whichever period is shorter. [Wage and Hour Field Operations Handbook § 51a05(b)]

The Wage and Hour Division investigator usually will not need a warrant or subpoena to inspect an employer's records, unless the employer categorically refuses to allow the inspection. For example, the U.S. Supreme Court has found that the DOL may inspect an employer's payroll records without a search warrant, but the employer retains the right to challenge in federal court the validity of the subpoena. [Donovan v. Lone Steer, Inc., 464 U.S. 408 (1984)] In *Donovan*, the DOL served a subpoena on an employee of a motel and restaurant to have an "officer or agent" of the company with personal knowledge of the company's records bring payroll and sales records to DOL offices in Bismarck, North Dakota. The company refused to comply with the subpoena and filed suit in federal court, claiming the subpoena amounted to an unlawful search and seizure under the Fourth Amendment. Ultimately, the Supreme Court found, contrary to the district court, that serving a subpoena in a public lobby is not a Fourth Amendment violation, but the employer still may challenge its reasonableness.

Federal regulations permit the Wage and Hour Administrator to enter into agreements with state agencies to conduct FLSA inspections and investigations.

The Wage and Hour Division investigators are not limited to investigating violations of the FLSA; they may also investigate violations of the other statutes it oversees, such as the Davis-Bacon Act [40 U.S.C. §§ 3141 *et seq.*] and the Service Contract Labor Standards Act [41 U.S.C. §§ 351–358].

Once the investigation is complete, the investigator has a conference with the employer to discuss the investigator's findings. If the investigator finds violations, he or she reviews what violations were found and how to correct them. The investigator attempts to get the employer's agreement to comply with the FLSA in the future and remedy past violations of minimum wage or overtime pay requirements found by the investigator. If the employer refuses to comply, the DOL Solicitor may initiate a court action to recover amounts owed for the alleged violations.

Minimum Wage Rates

Q 1:13 What is the minimum wage?

The Fair Minimum Wage Act of 2007 was signed into law on May 25, 2007 as part of the U.S. Troop Readiness, Veterans' Care, Katrina Recovery, and Iraq Accountability Appropriations Act, 2007. This revision of the FLSA provides that the FLSA's mandated minimum wage will gradually increase in three increments to: (A) $5.85 an hour, beginning on the 60th day after enactment of the Fair Minimum Wage Act of 2007 (July 24, 2007); (B) $6.55 an hour beginning 12 months after the 60th day (July 24, 2008); and (C) $7.25 an hour, beginning 24 months after the 60th day (July 24, 2009). Previously, the minimum wage rate was $5.15 per every hour worked.

Employers must pay all nonexempt employees at least this much per hour. Employees under age 20 may be paid a minimum wage of at least $4.25 per hour during the first 90 consecutive calendar days of employment with an employer, but an employer may not terminate the employment of any employee in order to hire an employee at the youth minimum wage. Recently, more and more states, including Arkansas, Iowa, Kentucky, Nevada, New Hampshire, New Mexico, and Vermont, have increased their minimum wage rates. Traditionally, California, Connecticut, Delaware, Hawaii, Illinois, Maine, Oregon, Rhode Island, and Washington, as well as the District of Columbia, had minimum wage rates higher than the federal rate. These higher rates supersede the federal minimum wage. See Table 3-1 for a listing of the minimum wage rates for each state and the District of Columbia.

Q 1:14 Must all employees be paid on an hourly basis?

No. Nonexempt employees may be paid on an hourly basis or on a salary, commission, or piecework basis, but under any payment method the employee must be paid at least the minimum wage for each workweek. For example, under the FLSA a restaurant may apply its servers' tips toward their minimum wage earnings, except that at least $2.125 per hour must be paid in wages by the restaurant in addition to the tips. If a server fails to earn at least the minimum wage under this system, the employer must pay the employee the difference needed to bring his or her compensation up to the minimum wage.

Additionally, employers are permitted to substitute for cash payment compensation in the form of board, lodging, or other facilities. There are restrictions on the employer's ability to substitute food or lodging for cash wages, and the employee must voluntarily accept this form of payment. Some states have imposed their own requirements before an employer can compensate employees in kind.

Overtime Pay

Q 1:15 What *is overtime pay*, and how is it computed?

Under the FLSA, an employee must be paid his or her regular rate of pay plus an additional half of the regular rate for all hours the employee works in excess of 40 hours in a workweek. The workweek must be based on a seven-day cycle, and it does not matter which days count as the beginning and ending days. Some state laws are more stringent than the FLSA and may place different requirements on employers for purposes of computing overtime.

The FLSA does not place limitations on the number of hours persons over age 16 may work. State laws may differ.

Q 1:16   What constitutes an employee's regular rate for overtime purposes?

When calculating overtime, the employer must determine what the regular pretax hourly rate is. The regular pretax hourly rate is based on all of the employee's "remuneration for employment" [29 U.S.C. § 207(e)], which includes hourly wages, salary, commissions, in-kind payments such as meals and lodging, and bonuses based on the employee's work quality or quantity. This rate must be calculated separately for each workweek.

The regular pretax hourly rate is determined by dividing all of the employee's regular compensation for that week by the number of hours worked. The overtime rate, therefore, is the regular rate plus an additional half of the regular rate.

State law may dictate a different method of calculation. For example, in California a nonexempt salaried employee's regular rate is calculated by dividing the salary for the workweek by the maximum number of normal hours of work per week, which typically is 40. The employee must be paid at one and one-half times the resulting hourly rate for all overtime hours.

Q 1:17   When is overtime pay not required?

A nonexempt employee need not be paid time and one half for work performed on Saturdays, Sundays, or holidays, unless the employee will have worked more than 40 hours for the workweek. An employee need not be paid overtime for vacation or severance pay, and paid-leave time and paid holidays do not have to be counted as hours worked when calculating required overtime pay for a workweek.

Recordkeeping

Q 1:18   What kinds of records are required by the FLSA?

Employers subject to the FLSA must keep records for all covered employees—exempt and nonexempt—on employee wages, hours, and other conditions of employment required by the DOL regulations (see Chapter 8). No specific form or format is required for the records. More restrictive state or federal regulations take precedence over the FLSA's requirements.

As an example of unusual state requirements, consider Wisconsin law, which mandates that an employer maintain time records for all employees, both exempt and nonexempt employees for three years. [Wis. Admin. Code § 272.11] A fine of $10 to $100 per employee per day may be imposed for a violation. The state adopted the definitions in the Fair Labor Standards Act for salaried exempt employees but did not exempt them from the recordkeeping standards. The director of the Labor Standards Bureau has stated that he believes Wisconsin is the only state that has this "twist" to this issue.

Posting

Q 1:19   What kind of notice must employers give employees regarding the FLSA?

As with other state and federal statutes—most notably the federal antidiscrimination laws—employers are required by the DOL to post a notice in a conspicuous place specifying employees' rights under the FLSA. The notice lists information about overtime pay, child labor, minimum wage, and employees' rights under the Act. A copy can be obtained from any office of the Wage and Hour Division. States may have their own required notices, which must be posted in addition to the federal notice. (See appendix A for a list of federal DOL offices and state agencies administering state wage and hour laws.)

Child Labor

Q 1:20   What restrictions does the FLSA place on child labor?

The FLSA regulates employment of persons under age 18, prohibiting "oppressive child labor" and imposing penalties for violations. Many state laws are more restrictive than the FLSA with respect to child labor and should be followed in such cases.

Generally, the FLSA provides that:

1. Persons under age 16 cannot be employed, except that 14- and 15-year-olds may work in specific positions in retail, food service, and gasoline service businesses;

2. A person must be at least 16 years old to work in a hazardous agricultural occupation; and

3. Persons under age 18 may not work in hazardous nonagricultural professions.

[29 U.S.C. § 203(l); 29 C.F.R. § 570.2]

The FLSA's restrictions on oppressive child labor differ when the employer is the child's parent or a person who stands in the parent's place. In such cases, children under age 16 may be employed by their parents in occupations other than manufacturing, mining, or an occupation deemed particularly hazardous or detrimental to the health or well-being of children ages 16 to 18. [29 C.F.R. § 570.126] This provision has been interpreted not to permit employment of children by a corporation, even if the parent owns most of the stock. [Lenroot v. Hazelhurst Mercantile Co., 59 F. Supp. 595, 600 (D. Miss. 1945), *rev'd on other grounds*, 153 F.2d 153 (5th Cir. 1946)] In *Lenroot*, a 13-year-old was working as a labeler, attaching the company's brand names to crates used to ship vegetables. [59 F. Supp. at 597] Despite the fact that the minor's father owned most of the stock in Hazelhurst Mercantile Co. and was president of the corporation and manager of the packing shed, the court held the minor was not "employed in agriculture" under the FLSA, since the job performed by the 13-year-old was part of an independent commercial enterprise involving tomatoes and cabbage grown on other farms as well as on the defendant's own farm. [59 F. Supp. at 599–600]

A parent who operates a farm may employ a child under age 16 on the farm, even in an occupation the Secretary of Labor determines to be particularly hazardous for the employment of children under age 16. [29 U.S.C. § 213(c)(2)]

Enforcement

Q 1:21   How are employers that violate the FLSA penalized?

The FLSA provides four avenues for redressing violations:

1. Criminal prosecution by the Department of Justice for willful violations. Employers may be fined up to $10,000 for a first offense and fined up to $10,000 and/or imprisoned for subsequent offenses, in addition to civil penalties.

2. Civil suit by individual employees to recover unpaid wages or for injunctive relief from an employer's retaliation for an employee's complaint under or testimony related to the Act. The employee may recover back pay and an equal sum as liquidated damages, which together may be referred to as double damages. The employee also may recover attorneys' fees.

3. Civil action by the Secretary of Labor to recover minimum wages or overtime on behalf of employees.

4. An action by the Secretary of Labor seeking injunctive relief halting current unlawful acts or enjoining further withholding of minimum wages or overtime.

(Chapter 14 covers penalties for FLSA violations in detail.)

Suits brought by employees for FLSA violations may be brought in state or federal court. Most courts agree that the employee bears the burden of proving by a preponderance of the evidence all the elements of his or her claim, including that he or she was employed within the meaning of the Act, was engaged in activities covered by the Act, the fact that the employer violated the Act, and the amount allegedly owed.

Courts have not required employees to bring forth documentary proof, and an employer's lack of proper records required by the Act does not shift the burden of proof to the employer; however, when the employer has not kept required records on hours worked, the employee's recollection is more likely to be given great weight.

Q 1:22 Must employees arbitrate their claims under the FLSA if they have signed a valid arbitration agreement with their employer?

Probably. In *Circuit City Stores, Inc. v. Adams* [532 U.S. 105 (2001)], the United States Supreme Court ruled that the Federal Arbitration Act applies to employment-related contracts (except those involving workers engaged in transportation of foreign or interstate commerce) and, therefore, employees who sign valid arbitration agreements may be compelled to arbitrate their claims against their employers, including statutory claims. Consistent with this opinion, the Southern District of New York has ruled that employees who sign valid and enforceable arbitration agreements with their employers may be compelled by the employer to arbitrate claims they subsequently bring under the Fair Labor Standards Act. [*See, e.g.,* Martin v. SCI Management L.P., 296 F. Supp. 2d 462 (S.D.N.Y. 2003); Ciago v. AmeriQuest Mortgage Co., 295 F. Supp. 2d 324 (S.D.N.Y. 2003)]

Chapter 2

Determining Coverage Under the Fair Labor Standards Act

The pervasive scope of the Fair Labor Standards Act (FLSA), its complexity, and the significant liability that can befall employers that fail to comply with its provisions make it crucial to understand to whom and under what circumstances the Act applies. In short, this problem can be termed one of coverage. The main import of determining coverage under the FLSA is to ascertain what obligations, if any, an employer may have with respect to payment of minimum wage and/or overtime pay to employees. Coverage of employees under the FLSA is determined either by the type of work performed by the individual employee (individual coverage) or by the dollar volume or type of work performed by the employer's organization (enterprise coverage).

Before 1961, coverage under the FLSA was determined solely by reference to the type of work performed by the individual employee. In order for an employee to be covered, the employee had to have been engaged in interstate or foreign commerce or in the production of goods for interstate or foreign commerce. This method of determining coverage is called the *individual employee test*.

Unlike the current situation, the volume or type of business of the employer did not determine coverage. When Congress amended the FLSA in 1961 and 1966, however, it significantly expanded coverage by adding an alternative method of determining coverage, called the *enterprise test*. Under the *enterprise test*, an employee is covered if he or she is employed by an enterprise engaged in commerce or in the production of goods for commerce. [29 U.S.C. § 203(r), (s)]

Since there are two methods of determining coverage under the FLSA, all employees of a business conceivably could be covered under the enterprise test. However, even if that is not the case, one or more employees may still be covered under the individual employee test.

To determine coverage under the FLSA, it is important for employers, legal practitioners, and human resources professionals to understand the meaning of the technical terms used by the FLSA and how they have been interpreted by the Department of Labor (DOL) and the courts in various situations. Additionally, the existence or degree of coverage may depend in many instances on factors such as whether an individual is employed by a government employer or, conversely, by an employer in the private sector. Resolution of the issue of coverage may also depend on status distinctions such as whether one is considered an employee under the FLSA versus an independent contractor, trainee, or volunteer. Therefore, defining terms and drawing distinctions—which are critical to resolving the central question of coverage—are the focus of this chapter.

Covered Employees

Q 2:1   What employees are covered by the Fair Labor Standards Act (FLSA)?

Employees covered by the FLSA include: (1) employees engaged in interstate or foreign commerce or in the production of goods for interstate or foreign commerce (*individual employee test*) and (2) employees of an enterprise engaged in commerce or the production of goods for commerce (*enterprise test*). An employee who fails to meet the individual employee test for coverage may still be covered by the FLSA under the enterprise test. Likewise, an employee of an employer that fails to meet the enterprise coverage test may still be covered by the FLSA under the individual coverage test. The net result of these two tests is that, in practice, there are very few employers whose employees are not covered by the FLSA.

Q 2:2   If an employee meets the requirements of either the individual employee test or the enterprise test, does this necessarily mean that the employee is owed minimum wage and overtime pay?

No. There are exceptions from the minimum wage and overtime pay requirements, called *exemptions,* delineated by the FLSA. If an employee falls under one of these exemptions, the employee is not subject to or may be only partially subject to minimum wage, overtime pay, or recordkeeping require-ments under the FLSA. This is true even though coverage may otherwise appear to exist under one of the two tests. If an employee is exempt from the FLSA, the employer is not bound by its provisions with respect to that employee.

Exemptions are generally based on the nature of the work performed. For example, executives, administrators, professionals, and outside salespersons are four categories of employees partially exempt from coverage under the FLSA, provided they meet certain standards set forth in the FLSA's implement-ing regulations (see Chapter 4). Under these partial exemptions, if an employee qualifies for an exemption, then he or she would be excluded from the FLSA's overtime pay guarantees. Additionally, domestic companion employees are completely exempt from the FLSA, and consequently are excluded from the FLSA's minimum wage and overtime pay guarantees.

Q 2:3   What is the definition of *commerce* under the FLSA?

Under the FLSA, *commerce* means "trade, commerce, transportation, trans-mission or communication among the several States or between any State and anyplace outside thereof." [29 U.S.C. § 203(b)] In analyzing the question of FLSA coverage under the individual employee test (see Q 2:1), the operative terms are *interstate commerce* and *foreign commerce*. Under the enterprise test (see Q 2:1), the operative term is simply *commerce*. Therefore, an understanding of *commerce, interstate commerce*, and *foreign commerce* is integral to ascertain-ing the existence or nonexistence of coverage in a given case.

Q 2:4   What are the definitions of *interstate commerce* and *foreign commerce* under the FLSA?

Although the FLSA specifically defines *commerce*, it does not define *interstate commerce* or *foreign commerce*. However, it can be strongly inferred that if an employee is engaged in commerce as defined by the FLSA, or the production of goods for commerce, that employee is engaged in interstate or foreign commerce or the production of goods for interstate or foreign commerce. That is, if the language "trade, transportation, transmission, or communication among the several states or between any state and any place outside the state" defines commerce, this language would also seem to encompass the definitions of interstate commerce and foreign commerce. Thus, it is probably safe to say that if an employee is engaged in commerce or the production of goods for com-merce, he or she is by necessity engaged in interstate commerce or foreign commerce or the production of goods for interstate or foreign commerce. Consequently, unless the employee is otherwise exempt, he or she would, generally speaking, be covered by the FLSA.

Similarly, the FLSA expressly provides that if an enterprise is engaged in commerce or the production of goods for commerce, employees of that enter-prise are covered. The conclusion that *commerce* includes interstate or foreign commerce is greatly strengthened by the language of FLSA Section 203(s). In defining under what circumstances an enterprise is engaged in commerce for the purpose of determining whether employees of that enterprise are covered, Congress has provided that two or more employees must be "engaged in commerce," in "the production of goods for commerce," or in "handling, selling, or otherwise working on goods or materials that have been moved in or produced for commerce by any person." [29 U.S.C. § 203(s)]

Q 2:5   Can it be assumed that all nonexempt employees who are engaged in interstate or foreign commerce are covered by the FLSA?

Not necessarily. An employee's duties may only occasionally constitute engagement in interstate or foreign commerce. This is not sufficient for coverage under the FLSA. Rather, for an employee to be individually covered, engagement in interstate commerce by that employee must be regular and recurring, not merely sporadic. [29 C.F.R. § 776.25; Mabee v. White Plains Publ'g Co., 327 U.S. 178 (1946)]

Since coverage under the individual employee test is determined by the type of work performed by the individual employee, it is helpful when considering whether coverage exists under that test to identify the primary duties of the employee in question. The following are examples of types of employees who are likely to be individually covered under the FLSA:

1. *Communication and transportation workers.* If their duties relate only to intrastate as opposed to foreign or interstate communication and transportation, however, these workers are not entitled to coverage under the individual employee test. They may still be entitled to coverage under the enterprise test, notwithstanding that their own particular duties do not encompass engagement in interstate or foreign commerce. That is, if their employer's business involves engagement in commerce or the production of goods for commerce on a regular basis, they are covered.

2. *Employees who handle, ship, or receive goods moving in interstate commerce.* An example of such an employee is a longshoreman who unloads goods off a ship that has arrived in port from another state or a foreign country or even from another destination in the same state if the goods will, in turn, be transported to another state or country after they are unloaded from the ship. The interstate nature of goods may cease, however, when they are unloaded on the receiving room floor of a business if the goods are first placed in stockpile inventory before being used or sold. [*See* Walling v. Jacksonville Paper Co., 317 U.S. 564 (1943)] Therefore, employees who handle the goods after they have been placed in stockpile inventory may not be entitled to coverage, at least under the individual employee test, regardless of how much the goods may have moved prior to being inventoried. [*See* Russell v. Cont'l Rest. Inc., 430 F. Supp. 521 (S.D. Md. 2006) (employee of restaurant was not engaged in commerce as serving out-of-state patrons did not implicate interstate commerce, and handling produce did not move goods interstate as

employee handled goods after restaurant purchased goods for its own use)]

3. *Clerical or other workers who regularly use the mail, telephone, or tele-graph for interstate communication or who keep records on interstate transactions.* These types of employees can be contrasted against employ-ees who may frequently use the phone or mail as part of their primary job responsibilities, but use them only for intrastate business purposes or only sporadically for interstate or foreign business transactions. The latter employees are not covered individually, although the enterprise test may provide coverage.

4. *Employees who regularly cross state lines in the course of their employment.* An example would be long-haul truck drivers. [*See also* Bowrin v. Catholic Guardian Soc'y, 417 F. Supp. 449 (S.D.N.Y. 2006) (employee who crossed state lines two-to-four times a month made frequent enough crossings to cause the employee to be covered by the FLSA; however, other employees who crossed state lines once or twice a year were not covered under the FLSA as their interstate activities were de minimis)]

Q 2:6   If an employee is not directly engaged in the production of goods for interstate or foreign commerce, can he or she still be covered under the individual employee test?

As stated in Q 2:1, for an employee to be entitled to FLSA coverage under the individual employee test, the employee must be engaged either in interstate or foreign commerce or in the production of goods for interstate or foreign commerce. [29 U.S.C. § 203(s)] Certainly there would seem to be no problem with classifying employees such as auto workers, factory workers, and others who are directly involved in the manufacture of goods that will be shipped out of the state squarely into the latter category of employees engaged in the production of goods for interstate or foreign commerce. This category, however, is substantially broader than it may appear on its face.

The FLSA regulations specify that production of goods for commerce in-cludes "any closely related process or occupation directly essential" to the production of goods for interstate or foreign commerce. [29 C.F.R. § 776.17(a)] In other words, an employee need not be engaged in interstate or foreign commerce or in the production of goods for interstate or foreign commerce per se to be covered under the individual employee test. Many occupations are directly essential to the production of goods for interstate or foreign commerce. For example, employees who are engaged in making tools, machinery, or component parts necessary for the manufacture of goods that will be shipped out of state are clearly engaged in occupations directly essential to the produc-tion of goods for interstate commerce. The same is true of employees who are involved in the production of certain chemicals, plastics, steel, aluminum, or other materials essential to the production of the ultimate product to be shipped in interstate commerce. Employees who make a product that their employer never sells out of state, but that will be used by in-state customers to help ship their products out of state, would also be individually covered by the FLSA and entitled to its protections.

The list of processes or occupations that are arguably closely related or directly essential to the production of goods for interstate or foreign commerce is limited only by the imagination. Therefore, when determining if an employee is covered under the individual employee test, an employer must consider how expansive the concept "engaged in the production of goods for interstate or foreign commerce" is. If an employer doubts whether FLSA coverage applies in a given case, the prudent course of action is to consult expert legal counsel or the Department of Labor (DOL) to avoid the consequences of an erroneous determination.

Q 2:7 What is the definition of *enterprise* under the FLSA?

The FLSA defines *enterprise* as "related activities performed (either through unified operation or common control) by any person or persons for a common business purpose." [29 U.S.C. § 203(r)] Although one company or a sole proprietorship may easily constitute an enterprise under this definition, the concept of enterprise is an elastic one and can also encompass more than one particular business or corporation. Therefore, merely establishing and maintaining separate corporations does not prevent coverage under the FLSA if the "separate" corporations perform related activities for a common business purpose.

> **Example 1.** Assume that a holding company establishes three separate divisions, each of which has its own separate corporate identity, articles, bylaws, officers, and board of directors under applicable state law. Assume further that while Company A is directly engaged in interstate commerce and/or the production of goods for interstate commerce, Companies B and C merely provide support services to Company A, such as data entry, computer programming, job training, and maintenance. Regardless of the fact that Companies B and C are not engaged in interstate commerce, they are likely to be construed as part of an overall enterprise that is engaged in interstate commerce. Accordingly, the employees of all three corporations would be entitled to coverage under the FLSA and, concomitantly, all three "employers" would be deemed a single enterprise for purposes of the FLSA. Thus, all three companies would be obligated under the enterprise test to abide by applicable FLSA provisions such as payment of minimum wage and overtime to all nonexempt employees. [*See* Reich v. Japan Enters. Corp., 91 F.3d 154 (9th Cir. 1996) (third corporation in nightclub group was part of enterprise where all corporations performed related activities for a common business purposes, and there was overlapping ownership and control among the corporations)]

Moreover, even several corporations or other business entities that do not share common ownership could collectively be deemed an enterprise under the FLSA if their activities are related to fulfillment of a common business purpose and they have a unified operation. Common ownership of separate corporations is only one way, although it is the most usual way, of finding common control.

> **Example 2.** Three nonprofit corporations (with only overlapping ownership) would constitute one "enterprise" for coverage purposes where they engaged in related activities, had common control of performance, and operated for a common business purpose. This occurred in *Archie v. Grand Central Partnership, Inc.* [997 F. Supp. 504 (S.D.N.Y. 1998)], where three interrelated nonprofit corporations created one enterprise for the purpose of serving homeless and formerly homeless persons.

Enterprise coverage rests on activities performed for a common business purpose. Therefore, such coverage may not extend to religious, educational, or similar activities of organizations operated on a nonprofit basis where such activities are not in competition with other businesses. Thus, while there is no general exclusion for nonprofit organizations as such, a charitable or education organization may not qualify as an "enterprise" for FLSA purposes if the services it provides are not services provided for a business purpose. [Wage & Hour Opinion Letter, FLSA1999-2120 (Mar. 1999)]

Q 2:8   When an enterprise is engaged in commerce or the production of goods for commerce, is that alone sufficient to conclude that all nonexempt employees of that enterprise are entitled to benefits under the FLSA?

No. For employees to be covered under the enterprise test, the enterprise that employs them not only must be engaged in commerce or the production of goods for commerce but also must make a minimum amount of yearly revenues. As of April 1, 1990, most businesses became subject to minimum wage and overtime requirements at a threshold level of $500,000 in annual gross revenues. Before April 1, 1990, most employers with gross revenues of $250,000 or more in a 12-month period were covered by the FLSA. Additionally, before that date, laundries and construction companies were automatically covered by the FLSA, regardless of the amount of their gross revenues. As of April 1, 1990, laundries and construction companies are covered under the FLSA if they meet the $500,000 revenue test. It is important to note, however, that the Wage and Hour Division's interpretation is that employees of construction companies and laundries are grandfathered in and remain entitled to minimum wage and overtime because they existed prior to imposition of the $500,000 minimum revenue requirement. Furthermore, any enterprise that was covered before April 1, 1990 (i.e., any enterprise with over $250,000 per year in gross revenues) remains partially covered. The minimum wage then was $3.35 per hour.

The increase in the minimum revenue threshold from $250,000 to $500,000 as of April 1, 1990, means that fewer small companies and businesses are burdened by the FLSA requirements under the enterprise coverage provisions. Additionally, employees of hospitals, nursing homes, and public employers (with some exceptions; see Q 2:13 and Chapter 5) continue to be covered under the enterprise test, regardless of the gross receipts of these employers. This has been the case since the FLSA's enactment.

In computing gross revenues, an employer should use annual gross income or receipts, exclusive of excise (sales) taxes at the retail level (which are separately accounted for). An employer should use a rolling four-quarter test; that is, look at the last four complete calendar quarters to see if the $500,000 threshold has been exceeded. [29 U.S.C. § 203(s); 29 C.F.R. §§ 779.258–779. 269] Revenue for purposes of the revenue test, however, does not include income derived from contributions, pledges, and donations that are used in furtherance of the charitable activities of a nonprofit organization. [Wage & Hour Opinion Letter, FLSA1999-2109 (Jan. 1999)]

Finally, an employer should not assume that because an employee is employed by a small establishment or because revenues are less than $500,000 per year, there is no minimum pay or overtime pay requirement. Individual employee coverage must nevertheless be considered, and the Wage and Hour Division will likely assert coverage based on the employee's handling of interstate mail, telephone calls, credit card transactions, or receipt of interstate shipments or merchandise.

Q 2:9   Can a private not-for-profit organization be excluded from the FLSA because it is not an "enterprise"?

Yes, it is possible. For example, a private not-for-profit organization may not qualify as an "enterprise" because, exclusive of its donations, pledges, and other charitable donations (which are used in furtherance of the charitable activities of the organization), it does not have at least $500,000 in annual revenue. However, such an exclusion may have no real effect, because employees of the not-for-profit organization could still be covered if they engage regularly in interstate commerce or in the production of goods or materials for interstate commerce. [Wage & Hour Opinion Letter, FLSA1999-2109 (Jan. 1999)] [*See also* Bowrin v. Catholic Guardian Soc'y, 417 F. Supp. 449 (S.D.N.Y. 2006) (holding certain employees of nonprofit organization who worked at four residential homes for children were covered employees under the FLSA as four residential group homes were enterprise; as to the employer's other activities and home services, there was no enterprise coverage; however, certain of employer's other employees were still covered under the FLSA as their work involved more than de minimis interstate movement when they transported residents across state lines)]

Q 2:10   When is an enterprise engaged in commerce or in the production of goods for commerce?

An enterprise is engaged in commerce or in the production of goods for commerce when two or more employees are engaged in: (1) interstate or foreign commerce; (2) producing goods for transportation in interstate or foreign commerce; or (3) handling, selling, or otherwise working on goods or materials moved or produced for interstate or foreign commerce by any person. [29 U.S.C. § 203(s)]

Q 2:11 Does FLSA coverage apply to employees of states and political subdivisions who work in areas of traditional governmental functions?

Generally, yes, although this was not always the case. In 1976, the Supreme Court ruled that the minimum wage and overtime compensation provisions of the FLSA were not constitutionally applicable to the operations of the states and their political subdivisions in the areas of traditional governmental functions. [National League of Cities v. Usery, 426 U.S. 833 (1976)] According to the Court, these functions included, but were not limited to, the operation of schools and hospitals, fire prevention, police protection, sanitation services, maintenance of public health, and the operation of parks and recreational facilities. The rationale of the Court's decision was to minimize federal interference with state sovereignty, particularly in areas that had been traditionally regulated by states and municipalities. In addition, in the wake of the *National League of Cities* decision, federal regulations were issued stating that libraries and museums were considered traditional governmental functions yet, inexplicably, the operation of a railroad or local mass transit system and the generation and distribution of electric power were not considered traditional governmental functions. Unfortunately, the line between what constituted a traditional government function and what did not seemed to be blurred, if not arbitrary. Consequently, litigation arose over the definition of traditional versus nontraditional functions.

In 1985, the Court reversed its decision in *National League of Cities* by a 5-4 vote in *Garcia v. San Antonio Metropolitan Transit Authority.* [469 U.S. 528 (1985)] Justice Blackmun, the swing vote in both decisions, changed his vote in *Garcia*, believing that the "traditional governmental function" test had proven vague and unworkable. Notwithstanding the expressed fear of several dissenting justices that *Garcia* would detrimentally alter constitutional principles by leaving state sovereignty at the mercy of the federal political process, *Garcia* carried the force of law and resulted in a dramatic expansion of FLSA coverage. In November 1985, President Reagan signed a bill extending the FLSA's coverage to include the traditional governmental functions that had formerly been considered exempt from its provisions. In January 1987, final regulations implementing the amendments were published. [29 C.F.R. 553]

The Wage and Hour Division estimated that approximately 11 million employees across the country were swept within the coverage of the FLSA's wage and hour provisions as a result of *Garcia*. Of these employees, however, approximately 3.5 million were teachers who fell within the professional employee exemption. Without the teachers, 7.5 million employees became covered by the FLSA's wage and hour requirements as of April 15, 1986. Many of the 7.5 million had not been covered during the preceding 10 years. In post-*Garcia* decisions, various federal courts have held that it would be unfair to apply *Garcia* retroactively and impose liability for back pay, because *Garcia* overruled what had been clear precedent and the courts wished to avoid imposing any undue financial burden on local governments.

Employer-Employee Relationship

Q 2:12   Aside from employees who qualify as exempt from coverage under the FLSA, are there any other individuals who are not covered by the FLSA?

Yes. Only employees are covered by the FLSA. There are several classes of individuals who are not considered employees covered by the FLSA's requirements. Individuals within these classes are considered excluded from coverage, whereas other individuals who are employees are not entitled to benefits because they are considered exempt (either totally or partially) from FLSA requirements.

The FLSA applies only when an employer-employee relationship exists. Under the FLSA, *to employ* means "to suffer or permit to work." [29 U.S.C. § 203(g)] The definition of employee is very broad, and generally an employment relationship is easily created. For example, individuals who render services to an employer are deemed employees when the benefits of such services accrue to the employer and where the employer could have discovered who was rendering the services through reasonable diligence. Indeed, if an employer does not know or have reason to know that work is being performed, the work time may be compensable under the FLSA even if the work was not authorized or requested. [29 U.S.C. §§ 203(e), 203(g); 29 C.F.R. §§ 785.6, 785.7, 785.11] The FLSA is remedial social legislation from the Great Depression; therefore, employees may not waive the requirements of the statute, even assuming they would agree to do so.

Courts and the DOL often judge whether an employer-employee relationship exists by examining the "economic reality" of the situation. Factors to consider are whether the alleged employer: (1) has the power to hire and fire; (2) supervises the employee work schedules or the terms of the relationship; (3) determines the rate and method of payment; and (4) maintains employment records. [Bureerong v. Uvawas, 922 F. Supp. 1450, 1467 (C.D. Cal. 1996)] The purpose of the inquiry is whether the employee is economically dependent upon the employer.

Remember that there may be more than one employer to consider. In *Preston v. Settle Down Enterprises, Inc.* [90 F. Supp. 2d 1267 (N.D. Ga. 2000)], a Georgia federal district court, agreeing with the Ninth Circuit determined that temporary employment services and their consultants were joint employers for the purpose of determining FLSA qualifying terms of employment.

Welfare and workfare relationships also have precedent applicable to these situations. In *Johns v. Stewart* [57 F.3d 1544 (10th Cir. 1995)], participants in a general assistance and emergency work program sponsored by the state were held not to be employees of the state agency because the work component of the program was only one aspect of a comprehensive assistance program for the poor, the totality of which weighed against a finding of employee status. On the other hand, the court in *Archie v. Grand Central Partnership, Inc.* [997 F. Supp. 504 (S.D.N.Y. 1998)], held that program "trainees" were actually employees entitled to minimum wage. There, a nonprofit corporation ran a work program for formerly homeless persons in which participants worked 40 hours per week for 20 weeks for a minimal stipend. The program used participants to perform various services of the corporation and its related corporations, such as food service or clerical activities, and the corporation was able to use the program labor to underbid competitors for revenue-generating services such as recycling. In light of the benefits to the program, these "trainees" were held to be employees. On the other hand, a work therapy program sponsored by the Salvation Army did not create an employment relationship with a program participant who was admitted to the Salvation Army treatment center for counseling, guidance, and therapy, including work therapy designed to reaccustom the participant to working hours and working skills. The purpose of the therapy was clearly rehabilitative in nature and there was no promise of any payment or compensation. In fact, program participants were required to apply for public assistance and turn over those benefits to defray the costs of the program. [Williams v. Strickland, 87 F.3d 1064 (9th Cir. 1996)]

Generally speaking, prison work program participants and prisoners required to provide work services or labor during their incarceration, even if paid at low rates for their labor, are not considered employees. [Gambetta v. Prison Rehabilitative Indus. & Diversified Enters. Inc., 112 F.3d 1119 (11th Cir. 1997) (inmates who work in state prison industries are not covered by the FLSA); Danneskjold v. Hausrath, 82 F.3d 37 (2d Cir. 1996) (FLSA does not apply to prison inmates who provide services to the prison); Burleson v. California, 83 F.3d 311 (9th Cir. 1996) (prison laborers fulfilling state's hard-labor requirement for inmates were not employees under the FLSA)]

Q 2:13 Which individuals, if any, who work in the public sector are excluded from FLSA coverage?

In 1985, Congress added to the FLSA an exclusion for individuals who work in the legislative branch of a state or one of its political subdivisions and who are not subject to civil service laws. [29 U.S.C. § 203(e)(2)(C)(i), (e)(2)(C)(ii)(v)] Under this provision, virtually all non-civil service employees working for state legislatures, county commissions, or city councils are excluded from FLSA coverage. However, those who work for state or local legislative libraries, by statute, and employees of school boards, according to the DOL, do not fall within this exclusion and are covered by the FLSA. [29 C.F.R. § 553.12(b) and DOL commentary]

Anyone who is not subject to the civil service laws of the state, political subdivision, or agency that employs him or her is not considered an employee and is excluded from the minimum wage and overtime pay requirements of the FLSA if that person *also*:

1. Holds a public elective office of that state, political subdivision, or agency;
2. Is selected by the holder of such an office to be a member of his or her personal staff;
3. Is appointed by such an officeholder to serve on a policymaking level; or
4. Is an immediate advisor to such an officeholder with respect to constitutional or legal powers of his or her office.

[29 U.S.C. § 203(e)(2)(C)]

Clearly, officials such as state governors, legislators, city mayors, and council members fall within the foregoing exclusion because they hold public elective office of a state or political subdivision of a state. Determining when staff members of elected officials are excluded, however, can be more problematic. [29 C.F.R. §§ 553.10, 553.11]

The Tenth Circuit federal court of appeals has ruled at least twice that deputy sheriffs of publicly elected officials fall within the personal staff exclusion and hence are not covered by the FLSA. [Biggs v. Logan County Bd. of County Comm'rs, 211 F.3d 1277 (10th Cir. 2000); Nichols v. Hurley, 921 F.2d 1101 (10th Cir. 1990)] The *Nichols* court outlined several factors that should be considered when determining if a public sector employee is subject to FLSA coverage:

1. Whether the elected official has plenary powers of appointment and removal;
2. Whether the person in the position at issue is personally accountable only to that elected official;
3. Whether the person in the position at issue represents the elected official in the eyes of the public;
4. Whether the elected official exercises a considerable amount of control over the position;
5. The level of the position within the organization's chain of command; and
6. The actual intimacy of the working relationship between the elected official and the person filling the position.

The court noted that the county had demonstrated, with respect to the first four factors, that the sheriff and his deputies had the type of relationship that should render the deputies subject to the personal staff exclusion. The court rejected the position of the DOL that the deputy sheriffs should not be excluded from coverage. Since a federal court and the DOL took diametrically opposed positions on the issue of whether there should be an exclusion in this case, it is obvious that this is an area with little or no guarantee that an assumption that the personal staff exclusion applies will be the right assumption.

Another gray area of public sector employment concerns the exclusion from coverage of persons appointed by elected officials to serve as policymakers or as immediate advisors. Only those policymaking appointees who actually formulate policy, distinct from those who apply policy, are excluded from coverage under the FLSA. To be classified as an immediate advisor, the advisor must advise on constitutional and legal aspects of the elected official's office. [29 C.F.R. § 553.11(d)] This exclusion is most likely reserved for attorneys.

Q 2:14 Are independent contractors excluded from FLSA coverage?

Yes. As noted in Qs 2:12 and 2:13, an individual who is not considered an employee is excluded from FLSA coverage. Independent contractors are not considered employees and are therefore not covered. The FLSA definition of employee, however, is substantially broader than the common-law concept. Again, to employ under the FLSA simply is to suffer or permit to work, and if an employer (including a supervisor) knows or has reason to know that work is being performed, the work time may be compensable under the FLSA even if it has not been authorized or requested. [29 U.S.C. § 203(e), (g); 29 C.F.R. §§ 785.6, 785.7, 785.11] In view of the FLSA's very expansive definition of employee, many workers who would be considered independent contractors for purposes of ordinary tort or contract law are nevertheless deemed employees for purposes of coverage under the FLSA.

Therefore, an employer should be particularly careful when dealing with independent contractors. Situations often arise in which individuals are identified and treated as independent contractors, subcontractors, contract workers, or consultants, but under the FLSA they are considered employees eligible to receive the minimum wage and overtime pay and for whom an employer has recordkeeping obligations. [Usery v. Pilgram Equip. Co., 527 F.2d 1308 (5th Cir. 1976)] In fact, it is not uncommon for a written contract to designate an individual as an independent contractor, but such designations by the parties are not definitive and not controlling. [Mitchell v. Strickland Transp. Co., 228 F.2d 125 (5th Cir. 1956); Mitchell v. Cowley & Bros., Inc., 292 F.2d 105, 42 Lab. Cas. (CCH) ¶ 31,131 (5th Cir. 1961); 29 C.F.R. § 778.316]

Q 2:15 How does an employer determine whether an individual is an employee or an independent contractor for FLSA purposes?

The Wage and Hour Division and the courts consider a number of factors in determining employee or independent contractor status. [Wage & Hour Opinion Letter, FLSA1969-1029 (Sept. 1969); Wage & Hour Opinion Letter, FLSA1986-1662 (June 1986)] No one factor alone is controlling; rather, the economic reality of the overall situation must be analyzed. This economic reality test focuses on how much the individual economically depends on the business with which he or she is associated. [Cobb v. Sun Papers, Inc., 673 F.2d 337 (11th Cir. 1982); Weisel v. Singapore Joint Venture, Inc., 602 F.2d 1185 (5th Cir. 1979)] The factors set forth in *Cobb* and *Weisel* include the following:

- The extent to which services rendered by the individual are an integral part of the principal's business;

- The permanency of the relationship between the individual and the principal;

- The amount of investment in facilities and equipment by the individual;

- The opportunities for profit and loss by the individual and method of compensation;

- The degree of independent business organization and operation by the individual;

- The degree of independent initiative, judgment, or foresight exercised by the individual who performs the service;

- Performance of the same or similar services by the individual for third parties in addition to the principal;

- Employment of the individual by the principal in any other capacity;

- Comparison of the relationship to other independent contractor operations of a similar nature in the industry; and

- The right of either party to terminate the relationship on short notice without penalty.

More recent case law has set out a shorter test to measure the degree of the alleged employee's economic dependence on the alleged employer as a way of determining who is an independent contractor or employee. The factors considered for economic dependency include: the degree of control exercised by the alleged employer, the extent of the relative investments of the alleged employee and the alleged employer, the degree to which the alleged employee's opportunity for profit and loss is determined by the job, and the permanency of the relationship. [Freund v. Hi-Tech Satellite, Inc., 185 Fed. Appx. 782 (11th Cir. 2006) (cable installer was independent contractor and not employee as details of how installer carried out work left to installer, installer had special skills, installer was paid by job rather than by hour and so installer was largely able to control his profit and loss, and relationship was not permanent as installer was allowed to accept installation jobs from other companies); Johnson v. Wyandotte County Unified Gov't, 371 F.3d 723 (10th Cir. 2004) (security officers of housing project were independent contractors, despite limited opportunity for profit and loss as little control was exercised by housing project and the providing of security was not an integral function of the housing authority); Metzler v. Express 60-Minute Delivery Serv., Inc., 3 Wage & Hour Cas. 2d (BNA) 1737, 1997 WL 397467, at *28 (N.D. Tex. 1997) (courier delivery service drivers who were not economically dependent on the service were independent contractors); *but see* Schultz v. Capital Int'l Sec., Inc., 466 F.3d 298 (4th Cir. 2006) (security guards were employees and not independent contractors as they were economically dependent on the business they served and had little control over the manner of their work, little opportunity for profit or loss, were dependent upon individual skill, and were supplied almost every piece of equipment they used)]

Circuits vary on their use of the listed factors. Some use as few as "four factors" while others use "five factors" and some use as many as "six factors." [*See* Freund v. Hi-Tech Satellite, Inc., 185 Fed. Appx. 782 (11th Cir. 2006) (applies six-factor test); Schultz v. Capital Int'l Sec., Inc., 466 F.3d 298 (4th Cir. 2006) (applies six-factor test); Brickey v. County of Smyth, Va., 944 F. Supp. 1310 (W.D. Va. 1996) (applies four-factor test); Metzler v. Express 60-Minutes Delivery Serv., Inc., 3 Wage & Hour Cas. 2d (BNA) 1737, 1997 WL 397467 (N.D. Tex. 1997) (applies five-factor test); Johns v. Stewart, 57 F.3d 1544 (10th Cir. 1995) (applies five-factor test); Johnson v. Unified Gov't of Wyandotte County/Kansas City, 371 F.3d 723 (10th Cir. 2004) (applying five-factor test); Cahill v. City of New Brunswick, 99 F. Supp. 2d 464 (D.N.J. 2000) (applies six-factor test)]

Since all of the foregoing factors must be evaluated in determining whether an individual is an employee or independent contractor and no one factor is controlling, the determination appears to be far more an art than a science. It is prudent to err on the side of caution when there is doubt and to classify an individual as an employee rather than an independent contractor. An erroneous conclusion that the individual is an independent contractor and a consequent failure to provide minimum wage and overtime pay could prove costly to employers if they are successfully challenged by employees or the DOL. Employers have the advantage of seeking an opinion from the DOL and labor counsel before making a definitive determination. In addition, a finding of employee status under other laws and by other agencies (such as unemployment compensation, workers' compensation, tax, Social Security, or ERISA-covered benefit plans), though not absolutely controlling, can have a deleterious domino effect under the FLSA, and vice versa.

While courts typically apply all of the factors that they list in evaluating whether an individual is an independent contractor, one court failed to apply all factors it listed. Specifically, in *Johnson v. Unified Government of Wyandotte County/Kansas City* [371 F.3d 723 (10th Cir. 2004)], the court listed the following factors to consider in evaluating whether someone is an independent contractor: "(1) the degree of control exerted by the alleged employer over the worker; (2) the worker's opportunity for profit or loss; (3) the worker's investment in the business; (4) the permanence of the working relationship; and (5) the degree of skill required to perform the work." The court also noted that another factor commonly applied is "the extent to which the work is an integral part of the alleged employer's business." In ruling that the plaintiffs were independent contractors, however, the court only considered the first, second, and fifth factors. Moreover, though the second and fifth factors were neutral or in favor of finding the plaintiffs to be employees, the court found that the first factor weighed so heavily in finding independent contractor status that the court of appeals let such a finding stand.

In any event, it may be useful to consider some hypothetical examples and to analyze what status should be accorded to an individual.

Example 1. An individual is hired for the first time by the owner of a realty company solely to wash the windows of the building where the business is located. Assume there is a one-year contract, which can be terminated on 60 days' notice; the work will be provided on an "as needed basis;" and the window washer will be paid by check. The window washer has his own truck and equipment, and the owner defers to his expertise, giving very little in the way of instructions, except that he would like the windows cleaned inside and out. It would be fairly safe to conclude that even under the FLSA's broad concept of employee, this individual is an independent contractor. Most, if not all, of the factors from *Cobb* and *Weisel* favor independent contractor status. The services rendered are not an integral part of the realty business, and there is no permanency to the relationship between the window washer and the owner. Moreover, there appears to be no investment by the realty business in the window washer's equipment, and there is opportunity for the window washer to sustain profit or loss from his own business. The method of compensation is simply by check and does not involve company stock, benefits, pensions, or other types of consideration. There is a high—if not exclusive—degree of independent business organization, operation, and judgment to be exercised by the window washer (not the owner), and the window washer probably performs similar services for others. The individual is not being used in any capacity other than that of window washer, and he seems to bear the same relationship to the owner as others who provide similar services do to other business owners. Finally, either party can terminate the relationship on 60 days' notice. If this window washer is not considered an independent contractor under the FLSA, it is difficult to conceive of anyone who would be an independent contractor.

Example 2. Assume that the realty company owner described in Example 1 engages the services of a photographer to take photographs of property for the company. Assume further that the service can be terminated on notice by either party, but the relationship has continued for several years, and that the photographer works once a week for several hours with the owner and/or office manager. In this situation, the individual performing services appears more like an employee than the window washer in Example 1. All of the factors do not necessarily militate in favor of deeming the photographer an employee; however, given the very broad definition of *employee* under the FLSA and the presence of several factors indicating an employment relationship, it is more likely that the photographer would be considered an employee for FLSA purposes. Unlike the window washing service, photographing property is an integral part of the owner's business. Certainly, the relationship has a higher degree of permanency than the short-term relationship existing between the window washer and the owner. One critical question is whether the photographer uses some of the owner's equipment and facilities, such as a computer and office space. Moreover, because the photographer works in tandem with the owner and/or members of the owner's staff, the degree of independent organization, initiative, and judgment exercised on the part of the photographer may be somewhat compromised. In addition, does the photographer perform similar services for others, does he have any investment stake in the company, or is he employed by the owner in any other capacity? The wrong answer in just one area will likely lead to the photographer's being deemed an employee entitled to coverage under the FLSA. This is particularly true in light of what is almost a presumption that an individual is an employee under the FLSA's very broad interpretation of that term. Therefore, as a rule of thumb, it is wise to assume that far more factors indicating an independent contractor relationship are necessary to conclude that such a relationship exists.

Q 2:16   Are students or trainees excluded from coverage under the FLSA?

It depends. Whether students or trainees are employees under the FLSA, and thus included within its coverage, depends on all the circumstances of their educational or vocational activities on the premises of the employer. If the following criteria apply, students or trainees are *not* employees within the meaning of the FLSA and are therefore excluded from coverage:

1. The training, even though it includes actual operation of the facilities of the employer, is similar to training that would be given in a vocational school.
2. The training is primarily for the benefit of the students or trainees.
3. The students or trainees do not displace regular employees, but work under their close observation.
4. The employer that provides the training derives no immediate advantage from the activities of the students or trainees, and on occasion the employer's operations may actually be impeded.
5. The students or trainees are not necessarily entitled to a job at the conclusion of the training period.

The employer and the students or trainees understand that the latter are not entitled to wages for the time spent in training. [Williams v. Stickland, 87 F.3d 1064 (9th Cir. 1996); Wage & Hour Opinion Letter, FLSA1995-1986 (July 1995)]

During the last decade, the DOL has continued to address the issue of interns and students in opinion letters. The DOL clarified, for example, that the payment of a stipend, but not wages, to an intern does not create an employment relationship so long as the stipend does not exceed the reasonable "approximation of the expenses incurred" by the interns or students involved in the program. [Wage & Hour Opinion Letter, FLSA1996-1986 (May 1996)]

An illustrative case of an employer misclassifying students as nonemployees is *Archie v. Grand Central Partnership, Inc.* [997 F. Supp. 504 (S.D.N.Y. 1998)], where the court concluded that "trainees" of a nonprofit corporation servicing the homeless were actually employees entitled to minimum wage, because they were used for the classic purpose of employees—to make money. The nonprofit corporation in question operated to provide direct services to homeless and formerly homeless clients, outreach services, and revenue-generating services in the community. The nonprofit corporation also operated a work program for some of its formerly homeless clients. Participants in this program would work 40 hours per week for 20 weeks for a small weekly sum. Participants performed clerical work, food services, and other work that supported all of the services and programs of the nonprofit corporation, including revenue-generating services. By using this cheap labor, the corporation was able to underbid competitors for revenue-generating contracts. Though the "trainees" were allegedly being trained for a return to regular employment, none of the services provided training similar to that provided in vocational schools. Furthermore, the "trainees" performed job functions, with minimal supervision, otherwise performed by regular employees, the performance of which benefited the corporation and not the "trainee." Thus, the program participants were actually employees and they should have been paid at least minimum wage for their work.

Q 2:17   Are volunteers excluded from coverage under the FLSA?

Sometimes, yes. The FLSA's regulations only define the term "volunteer" in the public sector. The term *volunteer* means "an individual who performs hours of service for a public agency for civic, charitable, or humanitarian reasons, without promise, expectation, or receipt of compensation." [29 C.F.R. § 553.101(a)]

There is a difference between volunteers in the public sector and volunteers in the private sector. Volunteers at state and local government agencies are not considered employees under wage and hour law and are therefore not covered by the FLSA even if they are paid a nominal fee or expenses. In the public sector, a regular employee cannot volunteer to perform for an employer the same type of services that he or she regularly performs. For example, if a nurse at a public hospital attempts to "volunteer" to perform nursing services after his or her regular shift is completed or on a day the nurse is not otherwise required to work, FLSA coverage would apply. Thus, the nurse would be entitled to minimum wage and overtime benefits—the latter to the extent that the extra work results in a total of more than 40 hours in a particular workweek. On the other hand, an employee of a public employer can volunteer to perform the same type of work for a *different* public sector employer. In that situation, there would be no coverage under the FLSA for the employee's work for the other public sector employer. [29 U.S.C. § 203(e)(4)]

The DOL states that when a public employer has a practice or requirement of hiring only from its pool of volunteers and advises job applicants of this practice, or where the volunteers expect or anticipate future employment after a period of "volunteering," such circumstances raise a question as to whether the individuals are bona fide volunteers or, instead, trainees who would be covered under the FLSA.

Finally, an official Wage and Hour Opinion Letter dated April 19, 1995, explains the technicalities of allowing public employees to volunteer to do other work for their government employer either during or after their regular working hours. When employed in a different job capacity, employees were allowed to volunteer as firefighters for a municipality; however, any such volunteer time occurring during their regular work hours was considered to be at the request of, directed, or controlled by their employer and was considered to be compensable (a general rule followed by the Wage and Hour Division). However, the fact that the firefighters were paid for the "volunteer" work that occurred during their regular working hours did not adversely affect their unpaid volunteer status when performing the same volunteer firefighting duties outside their regular working hours. [Wage & Hour Opinion Letter, FLSA1995-1954 (Apr. 1995); *see also* Wage & Hour Opinion Letter, FLSA1995-1955 (Apr. 1995)]

Until recently, volunteers were virtually nonexistent in the private sector. However, the DOL has recently issued opinion letters analyzing volunteers in the private sector. The DOL appears to have revised its earlier position that volunteers are limited to very narrow functions. The general rule for private sector volunteer work is that "[t]ime spent in work for public or charitable purposes at the employer's request or under his direction or control, or while the employee is required to be on premises is working time." However, time spent "voluntarily in such activities outside of normal working hours is not hours worked" if the volunteer activities are not "the same or similar to the activities the employee is employed to perform." [Wage & Hour Opinion Letter, FLSA2005-33 (Sept. 2005)] Therefore, the rule for volunteering in the private sector is that the volunteer work must be outside normal working hours and an employee can never volunteer to work in a job similar to the employee's normal job. If a regular employee in the private sector attempts to "volunteer" services that he or she normally performs for his or her regular employer, there is no exclusion and the FLSA's minimum wage and overtime pay requirements are applicable. [Wage & Hour Opinion Letter, FLSA2000-2218 (May 2000) (ambulance drivers and EMTs employed by a corporation that contracted with an ambulance company to provide drivers and EMT services could not "volunteer" to provide those same services to the ambulance company in the same week that they provided contract services via the contract company)]

There are other fine points regarding the FLSA's treatment of volunteers. First, the DOL has changed its policy concerning parents volunteering in their children's classrooms if they are employed in their children's classrooms. This new policy, grounded in the Clinton administration's effort to get parents more involved in their children's education, allows parents to volunteer in their children's classrooms, provided they do not expect to be compensated for the time and they were not coerced into volunteering. [Wage & Hour Opinion Letter, FLSA1995-1959 (Aug. 1995)] Second, federal regulations specify that whether two agencies are treated separately for statistical purposes by the Bureau of the Census in the Census of Governments is a factor supporting the conclusion that two agencies in the same state or local government constitute the same public agency for the purpose of determining for whom the volunteers work. [29 C.F.R. § 553.102] There are no restrictions on the type of services that may be provided on a voluntary basis by private individuals to public agencies if the private individuals are not otherwise employees of the public agency.

Q 2:18 Can private organizations have "volunteers" who are excluded from FLSA coverage?

Yes. A related question is whether private corporations may use volunteers without running into FLSA problems. Individuals who volunteer or donate their services for public service, religious, or humanitarian objectives without contemplation of pay are not considered employees of the religious, charitable, and similar not-for-profit organizations that receive their services. [Wage & Hour

Opinion Letter, FLSA1999 (Sept. 1999)] In addition, for-profit organizations like hospitals or nursing homes may have non-employee "volunteers" who perform activities of a charitable nature, so long as the hospital or nursing home does not derive any immediate economic advantage from the activities of the volunteers and there is no expectation of compensation. [Wage & Hour Opinion Letter, FLSA1995-1962 (Sept. 1995)]

Even not-for-profit or charitable organizations using volunteers, though, cannot have volunteers displace regular employees. For example, unpaid persons who are used in a "volunteer" capacity to supplement an existing workforce at a local theater created to bring not-for-profit productions to the public at lower cost are not "volunteers" for purposes of the FLSA. By utilizing volunteers in the same job function that regular employees would normally perform, the theater created an employer-employee relationship with the unpaid "volunteers," making them fully subject to the requirements of the FLSA. [Wage & Hour Opinion Letter, FLSA1998-2081 (Sept. 1998)] Similarly, when an organization provides benefits to volunteers—cash, meals, gift certificates, etc.—the organization runs the risk of converting the relationship from a volunteer relationship to an employment relationship. Food banks receive different treatment under the 1998 Amy Somers Volunteers at Food Banks Act, under which individuals who volunteer at food banks are excluded from the definition of "employee," even if those individuals receive food from the food bank. [29 U.S.C. § 203(e)(5)]

As outlined in Q 2:17, it is also clear that a not-for-profit organization must be very careful about allowing employees to serve as "volunteers" after hours. The DOL has been very clear that while an employee may perform volunteer work for events sponsored by his or her employer, the work must be outside normal working hours, it must be truly voluntary, and the work must not be the same or similar to the work the employee is paid to perform. [Wage & Hour Opinion Letter, FLSA2005-33 (Sept. 2005)] Problems occur when, for example, a non-profit organization that trains puppies to be seeing eye dogs for the visually impaired allowed its employees to volunteer to be a part of the puppy foster home program. Time spent on the program by an employee would be compensable activity. [Wage & Hour Opinion Letter, FLSA1999-2109 (Jan. 1999)] In another opinion letter, the DOL advised that employees of an organization that provides care and support services to disabled persons could not "volunteer" to serve as chaperones and companions on overnight outings planned for the disabled clients of the organization. [Wage & Hour Opinion Letter, FLSA1999 (Sept. 1999)]

Joint Employment Relationship

Q 2:19   What is a joint employment relationship under the FLSA?

If there is more than one entity employing a single employee, a joint employment relationship may exist. *A joint employment relationship* exists under the FLSA when:

1. There is an arrangement between employers to share an employee's services;

2. One employer is acting directly or indirectly in the interest of the other employer in relation to the employee; or

3. The employers are not completely disassociated with respect to the employment of a particular employee and may be deemed to share control of the employee, directly or indirectly, by reason of the fact that one employer controls, is controlled by, or is under common control with the other employer.

[29 C.F.R. § 791.2(b)]

Examples. A joint employment relationship exists when an ambulance company that has no drivers or EMTs contracts with a separate corporation that employs EMTs to provide driving and EMT services to the ambulance company. [Wage & Hour Opinion Letter, FLSA2000-2218 (May 2000)]

A joint employment relationship was also found to exist between two hospitals, a nursing home, and a combined nursing home and hospital where each entity had its own human resources department, employee handbook, payroll system, retirement plan, and tax I.D. number. The DOL concluded that because there was a shared president and Board, the HR staff provided common support, and there were shared employment policies, there was a joint employment relationship. [Wage & Hour Opinion Letter, FLSA2005-15 (Apr. 2005)]

A joint employment relationship was found to exist between a nursing referral agency and hospital where nurses used equipment provided by hospital, the referral agencies generally assigned nurses to one hospital, hospital evaluated performance of nurses, and nurses performed work integral to hospital's operation. [Barfield v. New York City Health & Hosp. Corp., 432 F. Supp. 2d 390 (S.D.N.Y. 2006)]

A joint employment relationship was found to exist between a security firm and the individual being guarded where both shared control over guards and both were involved in hiring and discipline/discharge of guards. [Schultz v. Capital Int'l Sec., Inc., 466 F.3d 298 (4th Cir. 2006)]

Q 2:20   If a joint employment relationship exists and one employer fails to comply with the requirements of the FLSA, is liability assessed against the other employer?

Yes, because joint employers are subject to joint liability. For example, when an employer uses the services of a temporary employment agency that furnishes employees, a joint employment relationship occurs. The employer that uses the temporary employee's services would almost certainly be considered a joint employer of that employee along with the agency itself. Therefore, liability could be assessed against the employer using the services of the temporary employee for the hours worked for the user-employer if the primary employer (the employment agency) failed to comply with the FLSA minimum wage and overtime pay requirements. In other words, the DOL or individual plaintiffs could bring an action against an employer that engaged in no wrongdoing under the FLSA, purely by virtue of that employer's joint employment relationship with the employer that committed the violation. [Wage & Hour Opinion Letter, FLSA2000-2218 (May 2000); Wage & Hour Opinion Letter, FLSA1969-960 (Mar. 1969)] However, the user-employer would not normally be a joint employer with any other client-employers of the temporary agency, so one user would not normally be liable for hours worked at another company in the same workweek even if the employee went over 40 hours in total.

Liability can also be assessed when there are joint employers of a single employee, such as in employee leasing. It behooves anyone considering employee leasing to be aware of this potential liability, as well as the benefits.

It becomes particularly important for employers to realize when they are in a joint employer relationship and thus vulnerable to the actions of another employer. In most situations, an employer cannot control (or even be aware of) the actions of another that fails to comply with the FLSA requirements. An employer that is considering a joint employment relationship should insist on an indemnity agreement with the other employer, which provides that the other employer will indemnify in the event it fails to comply with the FLSA.

Q 2:21 Are there any exceptions to the rules of joint employer liability?

Yes. An exception to the general rule on joint employer status was created by the 1985 FLSA amendments and public sector regulations. [29 C.F.R. § 553.227] Public safety employees (i.e., firefighters and law enforcement officers) may voluntarily accept employment from independent third-party employers for special duty work during off-duty hours. The hours of work performed for the third-party employer need not be counted as compensable hours worked for the public sector employer. However, the independent employer must truly be independent, and the public safety employee must be free to accept or reject the special assignment. This exception to joint employer status applies even if the public sector employer sets up restrictions and terms and conditions under which special assignments may be offered and accepted, and even if a local law or regulation requires the independent employer to hire employees of the jurisdiction in which the special assignment or duty is to be conducted. An example would be a requirement by city ordinance that promoters of parades or civic center events must provide security for the events and can use only sworn off-duty law enforcement personnel, with a minimum dollar amount set for hourly wages. The city can maintain a referral list of volunteers, ranked in order of preference, such as by seniority. The off-duty officers must be free to accept or reject the assignment, but if the officers accept the assignment, departmental rules on dress and use of firearms may be used.

Chapter 3

Minimum Wage Issues

This chapter surveys the various circumstances in which an employer may deduct income from, or receive credit to, an employee's compensation. (Minimum wage issues affecting government contractors are discussed in Chapter 11.)

Overview

Q 3:1   Is there a difference in wage requirements for overtime versus nonovertime weeks?

Yes. The minimum wage requirement does not have to be met through the payment of an hourly wage rate. The only requirement is that all compensation for a given workweek average the applicable minimum wage rate (presently $5.85 per hour; $6.55 effective July 24, 2008). [29 U.S.C. § 206(a)] Under the *Klinghoffer* rule, if an employee works 40 or fewer hours in a workweek, the employee does not have to be compensated for each hour of working time as long as the average compensation per work hour equals the applicable minimum wage rate. [United States v. Klinghoffer Bros. Realty Corp., 285 F.2d 487 (2d Cir. 1960), *aff'd on reh'g*, 285 F.2d 493 (2d Cir. 1961)] If an employee works more than 40 hours in a workweek, some compensation at least equal to the minimum wage must be found to apply to each hour of work up to and above 40 with an additional half of the regular rate owed for each hour of overtime. [29 C.F.R. §§ 778.315, 778.317]

Q 3:2　For what time period is minimum wage compliance tested?

The minimum wage (and overtime pay) must be calculated on the basis of a workweek, which is any seven consecutive 24-hour periods starting on any day and at any time, that is consistently applied for the future. Employees working for the same employer may have different workweeks. [29 C.F.R. § 778.105] The beginning and end of the workweek may be changed if the changes are intended to be permanent in nature and if the purpose of the changes is not to evade minimum wage or overtime pay under the workweek concept. A week in which the minimum wage or overtime is underpaid cannot be averaged with prior or subsequent weeks in which excess wages are paid. [29 C.F.R. §§ 778.103, 778.104] Since the minimum wage requirement does not require an hourly wage rate, the statutory requirement can be fulfilled through various compensation plans, including an hourly wage rate; fixed weekly, biweekly, semimonthly, or monthly salaries; piece rates; commissions; or a combination payment plan.

Q 3:3　Can unions waive Fair Labor Standards Act requirements?

Not usually. The Ninth Circuit has held that "the minimum wage and overtime provisions of the [Fair Labor Standards] Act are guarantees to individual workers that may not be waived through collective bargaining." [Local 246 Util. Workers Union of Am. v. S. Cal. Edison Co., 83 F.3d 292 (9th Cir. 1996)]

Q 3:4　What is the general effect of employer-required purchases or deductions from payroll?

Although the Fair Labor Standards Act (FLSA) may permit an employer to make payroll deductions or require employees to be properly outfitted or equipped for work, if any credit or deduction related to these requirements has the effect of reducing the minimum wage and overtime pay due an employee in cash, the employer may have violated the FLSA. Thus, this chapter is concerned with instances in which the Wage and Hour Administrator has said that deductions or job requirements are really costs associated with having a job that are primarily for the benefit of the employer and cannot be used to avoid minimum wage and overtime requirements. [29 C.F.R. §§ 531.3(d), 531.28]

Deductions from wages for merchandise, tools, and protective clothing may create a problem. For example, for the purchase of tools, protective clothing, or other items required by the employer or the nature of the job, neither payroll deductions nor cash transactions, in any amount, that take an employee's wages below the minimum wage or cut into overtime pay may be made. Payroll deductions for cash register shortages, check errors, damages, personal loans, and similar items that are not deductions to recoup prior wage advances may not cut into an employee's minimum wage. On the other hand, even if an employee is paid at or near the minimum wage, a payroll deduction of the reasonable cost of voluntary employee purchases of merchandise such as meals, lodging, or other facilities may be made, or a separate voluntary cash transaction in any amount may be made. [29 C.F.R. § 531.32; Wage & Hour Opinion Letter, FLSA1962-102 (June 1962) (voluntary arm's-length cash transactions are preferable to payroll deduction)]

Q 3:5   Does federal wage and hour law override more stringent state laws?

No. Various federal, state, and local governmental entities may enact wage and hour laws or adopt regulations that address the minimum wage issues discussed in this chapter. If these laws and regulations do not contradict the requirements of the FLSA, they supersede the Wage and Hour Administrator's interpretation of the FLSA, which is expressed in the various regulations discussed in this chapter. [29 C.F.R. § 531.26]

Uniforms

Generally, if an employer requires an employee to wear a uniform, the cost of purchasing and maintaining it must not cut into the minimum wage or overtime pay due the employee. This, however, is primarily an issue for employers that pay at or near the minimum wage.

Q 3:6   What constitutes a uniform?

Although there is no authoritative rule governing whether an employee dress code necessarily constitutes a requirement that an employee wear a uniform, the Wage and Hour Division has indicated that when an employer requires employees to wear a general type of street clothing that permits variations, that clothing is not considered a uniform. If, however, the employer requires that a specific type or style of clothing be worn, for instance, a tuxedo shirt and slacks of a distinctive style or quality, that clothing is a uniform, and the cost of procuring and maintaining it may not cut into the minimum wage or overtime pay due the employee. [Wage & Hour Opinion Letter, FLSA1978-1519 (July 1978)]

Q 3:7   If an employer provides a uniform, can it deduct the cost of the uniform from the minimum wage and overtime pay due an employee?

Uniforms, like other nonfacilities described in Q 3:27, are regarded as a business expense of the employer, whether they are required to be worn by law, by the nature of the business, or by the employer. If an employee is paid more than the minimum wage, the employer may require the employee to bear the cost as long as it does not cut into the minimum wage or overtime compensation due to the employee.

Example 1. Assume that an employee is paid $6.20 per hour in a 30-hour workweek and the minimum wage is $5.85. The employer can legally deduct from the employee's wages, or have the employee reimburse the employer, $10.50 ($0.35 × 30) for uniforms.

As discussed further in Q 3:32, deductions for uniforms may not be made before the regular rate is calculated for overtime purposes.

Example 2. If the employee in Example 1 works 40 hours, the employer would have $14 ($0.35 × 40) "padding" above the minimum wage. If the employee works more than 40 hours (overtime), $14 would still be the maximum that could be deducted for the uniform.

[Wage & Hour Opinion Letter, FLSA1997-2013 (Jan. 1997)]

Q 3:8   May an employer reimburse an employee for a uniform's cost over the life of the uniform?

An employer may reimburse an employee for the purchase price of a uniform over a period of time, as long as during any workweek an employee's wages and overtime due at the end of the pay period, less that part of the cost of the uniform not reimbursed, are not reduced below the minimum wage.

Example. An employee who is paid $5.90 per hour during a 40-hour workweek, which includes an additional 5 cents per hour as reimbursement for the cost of the uniform, would be due $236 ($5.90 × 40), or a minimum of $234 ($5.85 × 40) at the end of the week. If during the first workweek the employee must purchase a $20 uniform, the actual discretionary wage available to the employee is only $216 ($236 − $20), which is $18 less than the minimum cash wages that must be paid to the employee ($234 − $216). This reimbursement plan would, therefore, violate the FLSA. In these circumstances, the employer must reimburse the employee in full by the end of the pay period for the required uniform purchase.

[Wage & Hour Opinion Letter, FLSA1976-1445 (Aug. 1976)]

Q 3:9   May an employer require a prospective employee to purchase a uniform?

Yes. As discussed in Q 3:8, however, the applicant must be fully reimbursed for the cost of the uniform by the end of the first pay period to the extent the purchase would cause a minimum wage violation. [Wage & Hour Opinion Letter, FLSA1974-1327 (June 1974)]

Q 3:10   Does an employer need to reimburse an employee for the cost of laundering uniforms?

If the cost of laundering uniforms cuts into an employee's minimum wage and overtime pay, the employer must reimburse the employee for the cost of maintaining the uniforms. The employer may either wash the uniforms for the employee, making no deductions for the actual cost, or pay the employee the equivalent of one additional work hour at the minimum wage rate—$5.85 per workweek. (For ease in enforcement, the Wage and Hour Division presumes that employees spend an average of one hour per workweek maintaining their uniforms.) If uniforms are of wash-and-wear material and may be cleaned with the employee's regular laundry, a one-work-hour laundry reimbursement is not required. For uniforms that require daily or special laundering because of heavy soiling or usage, or that require ironing, dry cleaning, or patching and repairs because of the nature of the work, however, a uniform maintenance reimbursement is required. These amounts apply regardless of the length of the day an employee works and therefore are applicable to part-time employees. If the employee can demonstrate that the maintenance costs are higher, or if the employer can establish that they are lower, the reimbursement amounts are fixed accordingly. [Wage & Hour Opinion Letter, FLSA1974-1327 (June 1974); Wage & Hour Opinion Letter, FLSA1981 (July 1981)]

Tip Credits

Employers may pay tipped employees a reduced minimum wage that when combined with a tip credit is at least equivalent to the minimum wage due a nontipped employee. A tip credit may be taken based only on tips actually earned by a tipped employee in a given workweek, among other requirements. If a tipped employee does not earn tips in a given workweek, the employer generally must pay the employee the minimum wage in cash, with some exceptions for board, lodging, and other facilities that may be treated as cash equivalents.

Q 3:11   What is a tip?

A tip is a gratuity or gift that an employee receives in cash, by check, or by credit card from the customer for services performed. It does not include gifts in forms other than money. According to Wage and Hour Division Fact Sheet No. 015 (1998), if tips are charged on a credit card, the employer may pay the employee the tip, less the percentage the employer must pay the credit card company on each sale; however, also according to the Wage and Hour Division, this charge on the tip may not reduce the employee's wage below the required minimum wage and the tip must be paid to the employee no later than the employee's regular pay day even if the employer has not yet been reimbursed by the credit card company. As the charged gratuity only becomes a tip after the employer liquidates it and transfers the proceeds to the employee, the employer retains the legal right to deduct the cost of converting the credited tip to cash. Because a tip must be given at the sole discretion of the customer, a mandatory service charge is not a tip. For instance, a service charge added to a customer's check for large parties or banquets is not a tip. Nor are gratuities that an employee must turn over to the employer considered tips, since only tips that an employee receives "free and clear of any control by the employer" may be counted in applying the tip credit. To the extent that the employer pays its employees from these "nontips," it may do so to satisfy the minimum wage and overtime requirements of the FLSA applicable to nontipped, nonexempt employees, but it may not take a tip credit. [29 C.F.R. §§ 531.52, 531.53, 531.55, 531.56; Wage & Hour Opinion Letter, FLSA1997-2018 (Jan. 1997); Gillis v. Twenty Three E. Adams St. Corp. dba Miller's Pub, 11 Wage & Hour Cas. 2d (BNA) 766 (2006)]

Q 3:12   Who is a tipped employee?

An employee who customarily and regularly receives more than $30 per month in tips is a tipped employee for purposes of the minimum wage and overtime requirements. The month used to determine the amount of tips need not be a calendar month (e.g., January 1 through January 31), as long as the recurring monthly period begins on the same day of the calendar month (e.g., January 12 through February 11). This is so whether or not the employee receives tips as part of a full-time or part-time occupation, and even if the employee regularly and customarily is paid tips but occasionally does not meet the plus-$30-per-month requirement because of "sickness, vacation, seasonal fluctuations or the like." If, however, the employee receives tips only occasionally—for instance, on holidays—the employee is not a tipped employee. (Employees who regularly and customarily receive tips include servers, bellhops, counterpersons, and service bartenders. Janitors, dishwashers, chefs, and laundry room attendants may not be considered tipped employees. [Wage & Hour Opinion Letter, FLSA1996-1983 (June 1996)]

The plus-$30-per-month requirement must be met for each employee, including new employees, and not for a category of employees (e.g., waitresses). If an employee does not work a full month because he or she starts or is terminated before the month is complete, the amount earned for that time may be prorated to determine whether the plus-$30-per-month requirement is met. [29 U.S.C. § 203(t); 29 C.F.R. §§ 531.56–531.58]

Q 3:13   What is a tip credit, and how does it work?

Under FLSA Section 203(m)(1) and (2), an employer may take a tip credit for the difference between the current minimum wage ($5.85; $6.55 effective July 24, 2008) and the minimum cash wage set for tipped employees as of the date FLSA Section 203(m) was revised, which was $2.125. Therefore, with a minimum wage for nontipped employees of $5.85 per hour, an employer may take a tip credit of $3.72 per hour ($5.85 – $2.13). When the minimum wage increases to $6.55, the tip credit will be $4.42 per hour. Because the tip credit may not exceed the amount of tips actually received by the employee, however, if a tipped employee does not earn $3.72 ($4.42 effective July 24, 2008) per hour in tips for a given workweek, the employer must make up the difference in cash wages or in board, lodging, and other facilities. In order for an employer to avail itself of the tip credit, it must have first explained to the employee that a tip credit will be used and how it works. In addition, the employee must be permitted to keep the tips free of any control by the employer except for valid tip-pooling arrangements. If the employer does not meet these requirements, it is not entitled to a tip credit and must meet the minimum wage and overtime requirements in the same way that it does for nontipped employees. [29 U.S.C. § 203(m); 29 C.F.R. § 531.52]

Q 3:14 What if a tipped employee works overtime in a given workweek?

Generally, an employee who works more than 40 hours in a workweek may be entitled to overtime pay, or one and one-half times the regular rate, for the hours worked in excess of 40. A tipped employee's regular rate is determined by adding the tip credit plus cash wages plus any mandatory service charge collected by the employer and paid to the employee and dividing by the total number of hours worked. [Wage & Hour Opinion Letter, FLSA1997-2045 (Aug. 1997)] As discussed in Qs 3:32 and 3:33, the regular rate also includes board, lodging, and other facilities and may include bonuses or commissions, which are discussed in Chapter 7. Any amount of tips an employee receives in excess of the tip credit need not be included in the regular rate.

Example 1. Assume an employee earns $500 in tips by working 45 hours in a single workweek and that the minimum wage is $2.13 for tipped employees and $5.85 for nontipped employees. An employer may take a tip credit of $3.72 ($5.85–$2.13), since the employee has earned at least that amount in tips. If the employee also receives $20 in mandatory service charges, this amount would be part of the regular rate but would not be considered a tip. Therefore, the employee's total cash wages would be calculated as follows:

Cash wages ($2.13 × 45)	$95.85
Tip credit ($3.72 × 45)	$167.40 (The total tips earned, $500, is not part of the regular rate.)
Mandatory service charge paid to employee	$20.00
Total straight-time compensation ($95.85 + $167.40 + $20)	$283.25
Regular rate ($283.25 ÷ 45)	$6.29
Overtime pay due (0.5 × $6.29 × 5)	$15.73
Total cash wages due ($95.85 + $20 + $15.73)	$131.58

The Wage and Hour Division takes the position that the tip credit taken by an employer may not be increased during an overtime week

Example 2. Assume that an employer takes a $3.72 tip credit during a 40-hour workweek and pays the employee a minimum cash wage of $2.13. An additional $2.93, or half time (0.5 × $5.85), must be paid in cash for each overtime hour. The tip credit cannot be increased in an overtime week to offset the total of $5.06 ($2.13 + $2.93) in cash that the employer must pay for each overtime hour.

[29 C.F.R. § 531.60; Wage & Hour Opinion Letter, FLSA1977-1475 (July 1977); Wage & Hour Opinion Letter, FLSA1997-2045 (Aug. 1997); Wage & Hour Opinion Letter, FLSA1976-439 (July 1976); Wage & Hour Opinion Letter, FLSA1904-1904 (Feb. 1998)]

Q 3:15 What if the employee works dual jobs as a tipped employee and as a nontipped employee at the same establishment?

A tip credit cannot be attributed to nontipped hours worked by an employee who works dual jobs, one of them at a nontipped occupation. For example, a hotel waiter who also works at the hotel as a maintenance person must be paid according to the hours worked at each separate occupation. Wages for hours spent doing "side-work" or completing other duties related to the tipped occupation, however, such as folding napkins or filling salt and pepper shakers for the server's tables, need not be computed separately from tipped hours. [29 C.F.R. § 531.56] If tipped employees of an eating establishment routinely perform maintenance tasks or spend a substantial amount of time performing general preparation work, cleaning, or maintenance not related to the server's own tables, it is the Wage and Hour Division's interpretation that no tip credit may be taken for the time spent performing such duties. [Wage and Hour Division Fact Sheet No. 015 (1998) (not entitled to the same deference as a regulation); *see also* Dole v. Bishop, 740 F. Supp. 1221, 1228 (S.D. Miss. 1990) (finding that waitresses spent a substantial amount of time before the restaurant opened cleaning bathrooms and other general areas of the restaurant and preparing food, duties that were not incidental to their tipped duties and that were therefore compensable at the full statutory minimum wage).]

Q 3:16 Are there valid tip-pooling arrangements?

Although the FLSA states that all tips must be retained by the employee for the tip credit to apply, employees who regularly and customarily receive tips may pool them and share them with other tipped employees. Valid tip-pooling arrangements include instances in which a waiter splits his or her tips with a busboy or all tipped employees account to the employer for the amount of tips received and the employer then redistributes the tips on some basis mutually agreed upon by the tipped employees. Employees who are not regularly and customarily tipped, such as cooks and dishwashers, may not be included in the tip-pooling arrangement. Only those tips that are in excess of tips used for the tip credit may be taken for a pool. Tipped employees cannot be required to contribute a greater percentage of their tips than is customary and reasonable. If tips are redistributed pursuant to an invalid tip-pooling arrangement, the money paid loses the characteristic of a tip and is a form of straight-time pay that may be required to be included in computation of the regular rate. [29 U.S.C. § 203(m); 29 C.F.R. § 531.54; Wage and Hour Division Fact Sheet No. 015 (1998)]

An issue has arisen as to whether an employer that does not claim a tip credit can violate the tip-pooling restrictions of the FLSA. It is the Wage and Hour Division's position that a violation could occur if such pooling deprives an employee of any amount of tips actually received and the employer does not pay a sufficiently high cash wage to reimburse the employee for losses due to tip pooling. [Wage & Hour Opinion Letter, FLSA1989 (Oct. 1989)]

> **Example.** Assume the minimum wage is $5.85, and an employee is paid a $6.70 hourly wage and earns $10 per hour in tips, $3 of which is diverted by the employer to other employees via an invalid tip-pooling arrangement. There could be a minimum wage violation of $2.15 per hour ($6.70 − $5.85 = $0.85; $3.00 − $0.85 = $2.15). The employee actually receives $13.70 ($7 in tips plus $6.70 in wages, but according to the agency is due $15.85 ($10 in tips actually received plus the minimum wage of $5.85).

Although the Wage and Hour Division's interpretations are entitled to deference, a court could decide to take another approach. One court has held that the validity of tip pools is not an issue if the employer does not claim a tip credit. [Platek v. Duquesne Club, 961 F. Supp. 831 (W.D. Pa. 1994)]

Deductions from Wages

Both minimum wage and overtime pay must be paid in cash or with a negotiable instrument like a check, with some exceptions. These wages must be paid free and clear, with no portion that would cut into the minimum wage being kicked back to the employer or a third person for the employer's benefit. [29 C.F.R. § 531.35] One exception is that the reasonable cost or fair value of board, lodging, and other services customarily provided by the employer may be treated as a monetary equivalent to wages for purposes of computing the minimum wage due an employee. In addition, tax deductions required by law, as well as court-ordered garnishment or voluntary payments to a third party, may be treated as equivalent to a wage payment. Deductions that do not fall within these categories are not prohibited under the FLSA, but they may be made only to the extent that they do not cut into or reduce wages below the minimum wage or take any part of overtime pay due an employee. Therefore, deductions not permitted under the FLSA primarily are of concern to employers that pay employees at or near the minimum wage.

Deductions can generally be placed into three categories:

1. Board, lodging, and other facilities;
2. Items that have not been deemed facilities; and
3. Deductions authorized by the employee or required by law.

The type of deduction made is important for two reasons: it determines whether the reasonable cost or fair value requirements of FLSA Section 203(m) apply, and it determines whether the deduction may be made before or after the regular rate is calculated for overtime purposes. To the extent that any deductions for board, lodging, and other facilities cut into the minimum wage, they may do so only up to the amount of their reasonable cost or fair value. In addition, these items are treated as wages and therefore must be calculated as part of the regular rate. Deductions for items that have not been deemed facilities may be made, regardless of their reasonable cost or fair value, as long as the deduction does not reduce the cash wages paid to the employee below the minimum wage or cut into overtime requirements. Finally, the reasonable cost/fair value requirements do not apply to deductions authorized by the employee or required by law. Moreover, like the deductions for board, lodging, and other facilities, these deductions may cut into the minimum wage due an employee and they are not made until after the regular rate is computed. [29 C.F.R. §§ 531.3, 531.40]

Deductions for Board, Lodging, and Other Facilities

Q 3:17   What requirements must an employer satisfy to make deductions for board, lodging, and other facilities?

An employer that makes deductions for board, lodging, and other facilities must meet the following requirements to obtain a credit for these furnished items:

1. The board, lodging, and other facilities must be customarily furnished by the employer for the employee's benefit. [*See, e.g.*, Marshall v. Truman Arnold Distrib. Co., 640 F.2d 906, 909 (8th Cir. 1981) (holding that at-the-station living quarters provided to gas station attendants were primarily for the benefit of the employees even though the employer obtained an incidental benefit of crime deterrence)]

2. The employee must have been informed of the amount that would be deducted and must have voluntarily and without coercion accepted the facility. Whether a facility is voluntarily furnished depends on the nature of the employee's job, whether the facilities are an integral part of the job, and whether the employer placed any additional restrictions on the employee that could be deemed coercive. [*See* Lopez v. Rodriguez, 668 F.2d 1376 (D.C. Cir. 1981) (holding that an employee's voluntary acceptance of employment as a live-in maid indicated her voluntary acceptance of board, lodging, and other facilities, absent other evidence of employer-imposed restrictions); *see also* S. Pac. Co. v. Joint Council Dining Car Employees, 165 F.2d 26 (9th Cir. 1947), *cert. denied*, 333 U.S. 838 (1948)]

3. A collective bargaining agreement must not prohibit board, lodging, or other facilities from being included as part of the wage. [29 U.S.C. § 203(m)] This part of the FLSA directly covers only those collective bargaining agreements entered into by certified employee representatives pursuant to the National Labor Relations Act. Other collective bargaining agreements are separately ruled on by the Wage and Hour Administrator. [29 C.F.R. § 531.6]

4. The employer must be able to substantiate the reasonable cost or fair value, or have obtained such a determination from the Wage and Hour Administrator. [Donovan v. New Floridian Hotel, 676 F.2d 468 (11th Cir. 1982)]

[29 C.F.R. § 531.30]

Q 3:18   What is the difference between a reasonable cost and a fair value determination?

The FLSA distinguishes between the reasonable cost of board, lodging, and other facilities furnished to an employee and the fair value of such facilities furnished to defined classes of employees and in defined areas. The reasonable cost is the actual cost of furnishing the facilities, whereas the fair value can be some other value such as average cost or average value of the board, lodging, or facilities. If the fair value is greater than the reasonable cost, the employer may request that the fair value be used in lieu of the actual or reasonable cost. [29 U.S.C. § 203(m); 29 C.F.R. § 531.33(a)]

Q 3:19   Who makes the reasonable cost or fair value determination?

An employer may make the reasonable cost calculation on its own, or it or a group of employers may petition through administrative procedures that a reasonable cost or fair value determination be made by the Wage and Hour Administrator. In addition, the Wage and Hour Administrator may on his or her own motion or on the petition of an interested party make the determination. Interested parties include employees or their designated bargaining representative. [29 C.F.R. § 531.4(b)] The petition for a reasonable cost determination must include the following:

1. The name and location of the employer's place or places of business;
2. A detailed description of the board, lodging, or other facilities furnished by the employer or employers, whether or not these facilities are customarily furnished, and whether or not they are alleged to constitute wages;
3. The charges or deductions made for the facility or facilities by the employer or employers;
4. An itemized statement of the actual cost to the employer or employers of the facility or facilities, if known;
5. The cash wages paid;
6. The reasons for which the determination is requested, including any reasons why a determination is unnecessary; and
7. Whether an opportunity to make an oral presentation is requested, and if it is, a summary of the presentation.

[29 C.F.R. § 531.4(b)]

In addition to the requirements listed above, a petition to determine the fair value of facilities furnished to a defined class of employees must include the following:

1. A proposed definition of the class or classes of employees involved;
2. A proposed definition of the area to which any requested determination would apply; and
3. Any measure of the "fair value" of the facilities that may be appropriate in addition to the cost of such facilities.

[29 C.F.R. § 531.5(b)]

The Wage and Hour Administrator makes a preliminary determination of the reasonable cost or fair value and publishes a notice of proposed determination in the Federal Register for public comment. [29 C.F.R. § 531.4(a)]

Because an employer has the burden of proving, with proper records, the reasonable cost of the board, lodging, and other facilities it furnishes, failure to properly substantiate the reasonable cost of the deductions and to separate permissible from impermissible deductions (i.e., profits) may result in denial of the credit for the facilities provided. [*See, e.g.*, Donovan v. New Floridian Hotel, 676 F.2d 468, 475 (11th Cir. 1982); Donovan v. Williams Chem. Co., 682 F.2d 185, 190 (8th Cir. 1985) (burden is on the employer to substantiate, through records it has kept, the reasonable cost of lodging provided); *see also* 29 C.F.R. §§ 516.27(a), (b)] (See Chapter 8 for discussion of an employer's recordkeeping obligations.)

Q 3:20 How does an employer calculate the reasonable cost of deductions?

The reasonable cost of board, lodging, or other facilities is not more than the actual cost to the employer of providing those items. The reasonable cost is computed by adding: (1) the cost of operation and maintenance; and (2) the depreciation value of the facility, plus a reasonable allowance for interest (5.5 percent or less) on the depreciated amount of employer-invested capital. These cost and rate determinations assume "good accounting practices" that have not been rejected by the IRS. Reasonable cost does not include any profit made by the employer or affiliated person. [29 C.F.R. § 531.3] One court has held that the reasonable cost may be determined by the contractual amount of the facility voluntarily agreed to by the employer and employee. [*See, e.g.*, Marshall v. Truman Arnold Distrib. Co., 640 F.2d 906, 909 (8th Cir. 1981)]

Q 3:21 What does the requirement that board, lodging, and other facilities be customarily furnished mean?

Board, lodging, and other facilities that are customarily furnished by an employer may be treated as the monetary equivalent of wages for purposes of computing the minimum wage due an employee in cash. If the facilities are provided free of charge to its employees, an employer can take a credit against required wages, or if the employer furnishes facilities for a charge, it can make a charge equal to the reasonable cost or fair value of the facilities. Facilities are customarily furnished by the employer if they are regularly provided to the employee or if it is the customary practice in a given industry in a similar community for employers to provide such facilities. Thus, employee discounts at retail establishments on occasional employee purchases may not be treated as wages because they are not customarily provided. Facilities are not customarily furnished if they are provided in violation of federal, state, or local law. [29 C.F.R. § 531.31] For example, if lodging provided does not comply with housing code requirements for heating or violates permit requirements due to over-crowding, an employer may not be entitled to a reasonable-cost payroll deduction during the period of the violation. [Soler v. G & U, Inc., 768 F. Supp. 452 (S.D.N.Y. 1991)]

Q 3:22   Apart from board and lodging, what *other* facilities may be deducted from wages or, in the alternative, considered an addition to employee wages?

Under the FLSA, wages include the reasonable cost to the employer of providing board, lodging, and other facilities. The Wage and Hour Administrator has interpreted other facilities to mean "something like board and lodging." The following items have been deemed to fall within this category:

- Meals furnished at company restaurants or cafeterias or by hospitals, hotels, or restaurants to their employees;
- Meals, dormitory rooms, and tuition furnished by a college to its student-employees;
- Housing furnished for dwelling purposes;
- General merchandise furnished at company stores and commissaries (including articles of food, clothing, and household effects);
- Fuel (including coal, kerosene, firewood, and lumber slabs), electricity, water, and gas furnished for the noncommercial personal use of the employee; and
- Transportation furnished to employees between their homes and work when the travel time does not constitute hours worked compensable under the FLSA and the transportation is not an incident of, and necessary to, the employment.

[29 U.S.C. § 203(m); 29 C.F.R. § 531.32(a)]

Q 3:23   Is there a limit to the amount that may be deducted for board, lodging, or other facilities?

No. There is no limit on deductions for reasonable-cost board, lodging, or other facilities, whether the deductions are made during an overtime or non-overtime workweek. In an overtime workweek, however, the amount of over-time paid is not considered in determining whether a deduction cuts into an employee's minimum wage. Thus, the total cash wages paid to an employee, plus the reasonable cost of the facility, must at least be equivalent to the minimum wage

> **Example.** Assume that an employee works at an hourly wage of $5.85 for a 40-hour workweek, earning a total of $234, and, as an addition to wages, the employee receives lodging at a reasonable cost to the employer of $30 per week. The employee must be paid a minimum in cash of $204 ($234 − $30). Effective July 24, 2008 when the minimum wage increases to $6.55 an hour, the employee would have to be paid $232 ($262 − $30).

[29 C.F.R. §§ 531.36, 531.37]

Q 3:24   What is an unlawful deduction?

Deductions for board, lodging, and other facilities are unlawful only if they are provided at a profit to the employer and the profit reduces the employee's cash wages below the minimum wage. Thus, only a deduction for the reasonable cost, excluding profits, of the board, lodging, and other facilities may cut into an employee's minimum wage. Deductions for amenities other than board, lodging, and other facilities are unlawful only when they cut into the minimum wage. [29 C.F.R. § 531.36]

Q 3:25   May an employer make deductions for cash shortages?

Employees are not considered to have received their wages if they are not paid the minimum wage free and clear. This means that direct or indirect kickbacks to an employer are prohibited. [29 C.F.R. § 531.35] For instance, an employer may not require an employee, either involuntarily or "voluntarily," to sign an agreement to be indebted to the employer for cash shortages. [Mayhue's Super Liquor Stores, Inc. v. Hodgson, 464 F.2d 1196 (5th Cir. 1972)] In addition, deductions for bad or uncollected customer credit card charges or for gas purchases by customers who fail to pay are prohibited. [Brock v. Phillips, 27 Wage & Hour Cas. (BNA) 935 (M.D. Fla. 1986)] However, deductions down to the minimum wage may be made.

Q 3:26   May an employer make participation in a meal credit plan a condition of employment?

The Secretary of Labor has interpreted the FLSA to require that employee meals that are customarily furnished under FLSA Section 203(m) be voluntarily accepted. A meal plan that is made a condition of employment could not be voluntarily accepted. All courts may not agree, however. The Eleventh Circuit has permitted employers to take a meal credit as long as the meals are regularly provided. [*See* Davis Bros. v. Donovan, Inc., 700 F.2d 1368 (11th Cir.), *reh'g denied*, 708 F.2d 734 (11th Cir. 1983)]

Deductions for Other than Board, Lodging, and Other Facilities

The minimum wage is the baseline for the permissibility of a deduction. Thus, it is not required that the deduction fall within the category of board, lodging, and other facilities or that only the reasonable cost be deducted, as long as the deduction does not reduce the amount of cash wages due the employee below the minimum wage. A deduction is illegal only when it cuts into the minimum wage.

Q 3:27   What items are not regarded as facilities?

Items that are *not* facilities include, but are not limited to, the following:

1. Shares of capital stock in an employer company, representing only a contingent proprietary right to participate in profits and losses or in the assets of the company at some future dissolution date. [29 C.F.R. § 531.32(b)]

2. Scrip, tokens, credit cards, "dope checks," coupons, and other mediums of payment that cannot be immediately converted into cash. (An employer may, however, provide an employee with scrip or coupons that may be exchanged for board, lodging, or other facilities during a given pay period. The reasonable cost of these items may be included as part of the wage, since the scrip or coupons are used only as indicators of cost. An employer may not credit to itself unused scrip or coupons and may not charge an employee with the loss or destruction of the scrip or coupons.) [29 C.F.R. § 531.34]

3. Facilities furnished to the employee at a profit to the employer or an affiliated person. [29 C.F.R. § 531.33] An affiliated person is defined in the regulations as a spouse, child, parent, or other close relative of the employer; a partner, officer, or employee in the employer company or firm; a parent, subsidiary, or otherwise closely connected corporation; or an agent of the employer. [29 C.F.R. § 531.33(b)]

4. Facilities furnished primarily for the benefit or convenience of the employer, including items such as:
   a. Safety caps, explosives, and miners' lamps (in the mining industry);
   b. Electric power (used for commercial production in the interest of the employer);
   c. The cost of building construction completed by and for the employer;
   d. Company police and guard protection;
   e. Taxes and insurance on the employer's buildings that are not used for lodgings furnished to employees;
   f. "Dues" to chambers of commerce and other organizations used, for example, to repay subsidies given to the employer to locate its factory in a particular community;

g. Transportation charges when such transportation is an incident of, and necessary to, the employment (as in the case of maintenance-of-way employees of a railroad);

h. Charges for rental, purchase, repair, or laundering of uniforms when the nature of the business requires employees to wear a uniform;

i. Medical services and hospitalization that the employer is required to furnish under workers' compensation acts or similar federal, state, or local laws;

j. Tools of the trade that the employer requires its employees to provide; [29 C.F.R. § 531.35];

k. Meal expenses on long-term trips that can be considered business-related expenses; [*see* S. Pac. Co. v. Joint Council Dining Car Employees, 165 F.2d 26 (9th Cir. 1947), *cert. denied*, 333 U.S. 838 (1948) (holding that meals customarily furnished to railway dining car waiters for consumption on their own time were not primarily for the benefit of the employer)];

l. Damage to or theft of the employer's property caused by the employee or other individuals, even if it is the result of the employee's negligence; [Brennan v. Veterans Cleaning Serv., Inc., 482 F.2d 1362, 1369–70 (5th Cir. 1973) (holding impermissible and for the employer's benefit a deduction that cut into the employee's minimum wage for the cost of repairing damages to the employer's truck resulting from the employee's drunk driving, even though the employee voluntarily agreed to such an assignment)];

m. Financial losses due to customers' or clients' failure to pay bills; and

n. Disciplinary deductions.

[29 C.F.R. §§ 531.3(d)(2), 531.32(c), 778.307; Wage and Hour Division Fact Sheet No. 016 (1998) (note that items 4l and 4m were cited in Wage and Hour Division fact sheet and are not as authoritative as the other lettered items, which are cited in the regulations)]

Q 3:28 What if an employer makes deductions from wages for items not deemed to be board, lodging, or other facilities?

Deductions for items other than board, lodging, or other facilities are considered unlawful deductions only if the deductions would reduce an employee's wage in a given workweek below the minimum wage or reduce the overtime pay due an employee. Thus, if an employee receives at least the minimum wage in cash free and clear after the deduction, the FLSA has not been violated.

Example. Assume that an employee is paid at an hourly rate of ($X + $0.20) where the minimum wage is $X. The maximum amount that the employer may deduct from the employee's wages in a 40-hour workweek for items that are not facilities (see Q 3:27) is 20 cents per hour. In an overtime workweek, the deduction cannot exceed the amount that would be permitted in a nonovertime workweek, that is, $8 per week (40 hours × $0.20).

When an employer furnishes an item that does constitute board, lodging, or other facilities at a profit, the profit cannot reduce the employee's cash wage below the minimum wage. In the example, the profit could not exceed 20 cents (plus the full amount of any deductions for items that are not deemed facilities). [29 C.F.R. § 531.37(a)]

Deductions Authorized by Employee or Required by Law

Q 3:29 What deductions may be authorized by the employee or are required by law?

Social Security and Medicare taxes, state unemployment insurance taxes, and other federal, state, and local taxes are included as wages and therefore may cut into the minimum wage received in cash by the employee without violating the FLSA. The employer must not make any tax or Social Security and Medicare deductions in excess of the amounts required by law. In addition, although an employer may make a deduction from an employee's wages for tax reporting applicable to reported tips, such a deduction may not be made from a tipped employee's tips. [Wage & Hour Opinion Letter, FLSA1997-2018 (Jan. 1997)] In addition, these deductions may be made only after the regular rate is computed. When an employer is required by court order to garnish an employee's wages, these deductions are considered equivalent to payment to the employee, provided that neither the employer nor any person acting on its behalf derives any profit or benefit from the transaction and the garnishment does not exceed the restrictions imposed by Title III of the Consumer Credit Protection Act. [15 U.S.C. §§ 1671–1677] Restrictions on wage garnishment are further regulated by Part 870 of Title 29 of the Code of Federal Regulations.

If an employee voluntarily assigns or authorizes a sum to be paid to a creditor or third party for the benefit of the employee, the employer may make the deductions, provided that neither the employer nor any person acting on its behalf derives any profit or benefit from the transaction and the payment is not part of a plan to evade the requirements of the FLSA. When properly made, these deductions are considered equivalent to payment to the employee. Permissible voluntary assignments include sums paid for the following:

- U.S. savings stamps or U.S. savings bonds bought on the employee's behalf;
- Union dues paid pursuant to a bona fide collective bargaining agreement;
- Employees' store accounts with companies independent of the employer;
- Insurance premiums paid to independent insurance companies when the employer is under no obligation to supply the insurance and derives, directly or indirectly, no benefit or profit from it; and
- Voluntary contributions to organizations or societies that do not otherwise benefit the employer.

[29 C.F.R. §§ 531.39, 531.40]

Q 3:30   May an employer make a deduction for a debt an employee owes to the employer that cuts into the employee's minimum wage?

If an employer has made advances to an employee free and clear, either as a loan or as a payment to a third party at the request of the employee, the amount of the advance may be deducted from the minimum wage due the employee. In such circumstances, the employee has had free use of the money and therefore received it free and clear. [*See* Brennan v. Veterans Cleaning Serv., Inc., 482 F.2d 1362, 1369 (5th Cir. 1973) (permitting an employer to deduct amounts expended by the employer at the employee's request to pay the employee's traffic fine)] The employer must not derive any profit or benefit from the transaction; however, individual state wage payment laws may affect when employee debts can be recovered by an employer.

Effect of Enforcement Policy on Deductions

Q 3:31   Can Wage and Hour Division enforcement policy affect wage deductions?

The Field Operations Handbook published by the Wage and Hour Division was amended June 30, 2000, in an effort to bring some consistency to the sometimes-inconsistent interpretation and enforcement practices of the different regional offices that make up the Wage and Hour Division with respect to how to handle deductions from pay.

In nonovertime weeks, where fewer than 40 hours have been worked, deductions from an employee's wages may be made for any purpose so long as the minimum wage is still received on average for all hours worked. [FOH § 30c16] Of course, state laws may be more stringent and there may be minimum prevailing wages set under such laws as the Davis-Bacon Federal Government Construction statute, the Service Contract Act, or contractually noticed wages such as under the Migrant and Seasonal Agricultural Worker Protection Act (see Chapter 15). If so, those laws or provisions will still apply so long as they are more stringent in their requirements.

In an overtime week (where more than 40 hours have been worked) the rules are different. [FOH § 32j08] The Wage and Hour Division's current enforcement policy, effective June 2000, is that wage deductions are not permitted in overtime workweeks unless the following conditions are met:

1. *Deductions are for particular items according to an agreement or understanding between the parties.* The agreement must be reached before the employee performs the work that becomes subject to the deductions. The agreement must be specific concerning the particular items for which the deductions will be made, and the employee must know how the amount of the deductions will be determined that are included in the agreement (such as cash register shortages). The employee must affirmatively agree or assent to the employer's deduction policy. Although the employees' assent to the policy may be written or unwritten, the employer bears the

burden of proof that an employee has agreed to the deduction policy. Thus, it makes sense for employers to put this understanding in writing.

2. *Only bona fide deductions, made for particular items, are permitted.* Deductions that are otherwise prohibited by other laws or authority (federal, state, or local) are not bona fide. For example, if a state law prohibits any deductions from employee wages for tools and similar items or equipment that are business expenses of the employer, the Wage and Hour Division would not allow any such deductions in that state in an overtime workweek (or in any workweek), regardless of whether the minimum wage was paid (net after the deductions). Deductions for amounts above the reasonable cost to the employee for furnishing a particular item to an employee for his or her benefit are also not bona fide (such as furnishing items to employees "at a profit" or deductions for substandard housing). Deductions from wages where no prior agreement exists as to particular items are never permitted in an overtime workweek.

3. *The regular rate of pay must be based on the stipulated wage before any deductions are made.* Deductions for items that do not directly benefit the employee and that reduce an employee's rate of pay to below the highest applicable minimum wage are illegal unless the law establishing the particular minimum wage allows the specific deductions. In overtime weeks (where overtime requirements apply), deductions may be made according to an agreement that reduces the effective hourly rate down to the highest required minimum wage, but only from the first 40 hours in the week. Time and one-half the full regular rate (predeductions) must be paid for all statutory overtime hours above 40.

It should be noted here that the Wage and Hour Division is now effectively enforcing state laws that set higher minimum wages than the federal law, as well as other federal wage-related laws, and finding violation of these other laws also to be a violation of the Fair Labor Standards Act overtime pay requirements. For example, if a forestry worker subject to a $9.00 prevailing wage determination under the Service Contract is paid $10.00 per hour ($1.00 above the legally required wage rate of $9.00) and works 50 hours in a particular workweek, the most that may be deducted from this worker's wages for that week pursuant to a prior agreement covering specific deductions (such as purchase of a saw) is 40 × $1.00 ($40.00). Statutory wages due net after deductions [40 × $9.00 = $360.00] plus [(10 × 1.5) × $10.00 = $150.00 overtime] or $510.00 total minimum wage and overtime pay. The foregoing is the Wage and Hour Division's stated enforcement policy, but it may be subject to legal attack since it appears to go beyond the published regulations and even attempts to enforce the wage laws of individual states.

Effect of Deductions on Calculating Regular Rate for Overtime Purposes

This section only alerts employers to the impact the facilities they may choose to provide will have on overtime pay. The overtime requirements of the FLSA are discussed in Chapter 7.

Q 3:32 How does a deduction that is treated as part of wages affect the calculation of overtime?

Overtime pay is calculated based on an employee's regular rate of pay. When payments are made to employees in the form of board, lodging, and other facilities, these items are considered part of wages and their reasonable cost or fair value must be included in the regular rate. The deduction may be made for these items only after the regular rate is computed. In addition, deductions required by law, voluntary payments by an employee to an employer or third party, and disciplinary deductions must not be made before computing the regular rate. An employer may impose disciplinary penalties, for instance, when an employee is late for work. Unlike deductions required by law and voluntary deductions, disciplinary deductions may not cut into an employee's minimum wage. [29 C.F.R. § 778.307]

The regular rate does not include payments to an employee that are not intended to be treated as compensation for hours worked. For instance, the following items are excluded from the regular rate because they are not provided as part of the employee's compensation:

1. The actual and reasonably proximate amount of expenses incurred by the employee on the employer's behalf and for the sole convenience of the employer, including:

    a. Business travel and accommodations, temporary home-to-work travel when an employer relocates before an employee can find a new home, and home-to-work travel on occasional days when an employee reports to a different work site (expenses that are for the sole benefit of the employee, however, such as the cost of traveling to and from work must be included as part of the regular rate if the cost is reimbursed by the employer) [29 C.F.R. § 778.217] (see Chapter 7 for a more detailed discussion of calculating the regular rate),

    b. Purchase, repair, laundering, and replacement of uniforms,

    c. Supplies, tools, and materials, and

    d. Supper money when the employee occasionally works overtime;

2. Sums paid to the employee for the rental of his or her truck or car;

3. Loans or advances made by the employer to the employee;

4. The cost of conveniences such as parking spaces, restrooms, lockers, on-the-job medical care, or recreational facilities;

5. Facilities that would not increase the overtime pay of an employee by more than 50 cents per week on the average for overtime weeks worked, as long as there is an agreement between the employer and employee as to this exclusion; and

6. One meal per day.

[29 U.S.C. § 207(e)(2); 29 C.F.R. §§ 531.37(b), 548.304, 548.305, 778.116, 778.216, 778.217, 778.224, 778.304, 778.305, 778.307]

Q 3:33   How is the regular rate computed when an employer provides board, lodging, and other facilities as an addition to wages?

In an overtime week, the reasonable cost of board, lodging, and other facilities must be included in the regular rate when computing overtime pay.

Example. An employee who is paid an hourly wage of $5.85 normally works a 40-hour workweek, earning a total of $234. As an addition to wages, the employee receives lodging at a reasonable cost to the employer of $30 per week. If the employee works four overtime hours, the total straight-time pay of $257.40 ($5.85 × 44 hours), plus $30 for lodging, is divided by the total number of hours worked ($287.40 ÷ 44) to obtain the regular rate ($6.53 per hour). Overtime pay is $13.06 ($6.53 × 0.5 × 4 overtime hours). The employee would then receive a total payment of $270.46 for the week: $257.40 in straight-time wages ($5.85 × 44) plus $13.06 as the overtime premium. In addition, the employee is deemed to have received $30 as the value of the lodging provided to him or her, but that is not a cash payment. [See 29 C.F.R. §§ 531.36, 531.37(b)]

Q 3:34   Are there any exceptions to the requirement that employee meals must be included as part of the regular rate?

Yes. Upon agreement between the employer and the employee, the employer may omit from the computation of overtime the cost of one daily meal—and only one—customarily furnished by the employer. If the employer customarily furnishes more than one meal per day, all meals must be included within the employee's regular rate. Thus, if the employer provides two meals per day, it cannot take advantage of the one-meal-per-day rule by deducting the cost of one meal from the regular rate. However, if the employer furnishes one meal per day and occasionally furnishes "supper money" when the employees work overtime, the cost of the meal and supper money may both be excluded from the regular rate. [29 C.F.R. §§ 548.3(d), 548.304]

Q 3:35   What salary deductions are allowed for violations of safety rules?

Until the 2004 amendments to the DOL regulations, Wage and Hour policy provided that an employer could not reduce the future wages of a salaried employee because he or she committed "serious misconduct" or for violation of a "significant disciplinary policy." The regulations only permitted partial-day salary deductions for violations of a major safety rule. The 2004 amendments now allow an employer to deduct from the pay of exempt employees for "unpaid disciplinary suspensions of one or more full days imposed in good faith for infractions of workplace conduct rules." [29 C.F.R. § 541.602(5)]

According to the court in *Kelly v. City of New York & the New York Police Department*, [2000 WL 1154062, 6 Wage & Hour Cas. 2d (BNA) 753 (S.D.N.Y.

2000)] examples of major safety violations that would permit a partial-day deduction include:

- Discipline for sleeping on duty or being away from your post, if it poses a threat to fellow workers;
- Discipline for threatening and harassing a fellow employee because it poses a threat to fellow employees;
- Discipline for compromising a corruption investigation because it put the officer who reported the corruption at risk;
- Discipline for a scheme of breaking into drug dealers' apartments, stealing money from drug dealers, and giving false testimony in proceedings against drug dealers;
- Discipline for requesting that fellow officers provide false testimony; and
- Discipline for losing a gun, misusing a gun, and interfering with police activities.

Examples of actions that the court concluded were not major safety violations include:

- Solicitation of bribes where no evidence existed of fellow officers being put at risk;
- Being charged with murder of a suspect where the murder charged was dismissed;
- Failure to make reports when a subordinate discharges his firearm;
- Solicitation of prostitution, unauthorized off-duty employment, illegal gambling, patronization of unlicensed premises, intoxication while off-duty, cheating on the sergeants' exam, failure to report in sick, insurance fraud, improper fraternization with recruits, and arrests for driving while intoxicated off-duty.

[Kelly v. City of N.Y.& the N.Y. City Police Dep't, 2000 WL1154062, 6 Wage & Hour Cas. 2d (BNA) 753 (S.D.N.Y. 2000]

State Minimum Wage

Q 3:36   Must an employer comply with the state minimum wage rate?

Yes. Employees who are covered under both the federal minimum wage and the minimum wage law of the state in which they are working must be paid whichever minimum wage rate is higher.

Table 3-1. State Minimum Wage Rates

Alabama	No state minimum wage law
Alaska	$7.15
Arizona	$6.75
Arkansas	$6.25

Table 3-1. (cont'd)

California	$7.50; $8.00 effective January 1, 2008
Colorado	$6.85
Connecticut	$7.65 or 0.5% more than the federal minimum wage rounded to the nearest cent, whichever is greater
Delaware	$6.65; $7.15 effective January 1, 2008
District of Columbia	$7.00; $7.55 effective July 24, 2008
Florida	$6.67
Georgia	$5.15, applicable to employers with more than $40,000 in sales or 6 or more employees, unless employer and employess are subject to the FLSA; $6.55 effective July 24, 2008.
Hawaii	$7.25
Idaho	$5.85; $6.55 effective July 24, 2008
Illinois	$7.50; $7.75 effective July 1, 2008
Indiana	$5.85; $6.55 effective July 24, 2008
Iowa	$6.20 ($5.85 during initial 90 calendar days of employment); $7.25 effective January 1, 2008 ($6.35 during initial 90 calendar days of employment)
Kansas	$2.65, unless employer and employees are subject to the FLSA
Kentucky	$5.85; $6.55 effective July 1, 2008
Louisiana	No state minimum wage law
Maine	$7.00
Maryland	$6.15; $6.55 effective July 24, 2008. Effective October 2007, employers with state contracts subjected to higher minimum wage ranging from $11.30 in the Washington-Baltimore area to $8.50 in rural counties.
Massachusetts	$7.50; $8.00 effective January 1, 2008
Michigan	$7.15; $7.40 effective July 1, 2008
Minnesota	$6.15 if annual receipts are $625,000 or more (large employer), $5.25 if annual receipts are less than $625,000 (small employer), and not otherwise subjected to the FLSA
Mississippi	No state minimum wage law
Missouri	$6.50; $6.55 effective July 24, 2008
Montana	$6.15; $6.55 effective July 24, 2008
Nebraska	$5.85; $6.55 effective July 24, 2008
Nevada	$5.85 if health benefits; $6.33 if no health benefits are provided
New Hampshire	$6.50; $6.55 effective July 24, 2008; $7.25 effective September 1, 2008.
New Jersey	$7.15

Table 3-1. (cont'd)

New Mexico	$5.85; $6.50 effective January 1, 2008; $6.55 effective July 24, 2008; $7.50 effective January 1, 2009
New York	$7.15
North Carolina	$6.15; $6.55 effective July 24, 2008
North Dakota	$5.85; $6.55 effective July 24, 2008
Ohio	$6.85
Oklahoma	$5.85; $6.55 effective July 24, 2008
Oregon	$7.80
Pennsylvania	$7.15 for employers with 10 or more employees (large employers) and $6.65 for employers with less than 10 employees (small employers) and effective July 1, 2008, $7.15 for small employers
Rhode Island	$7.40
South Carolina	No state minimum wage law
South Dakota	$5.85; $6.55 effective July 24, 2008; $7.25 effective July 24, 2009
Tennessee	No state minimum wage law
Texas	$5.85; $6.55 effective July 24, 2008
Utah	$5.15 unless employers and employees are subject to the FLSA
Vermont	$7.53
Virginia	$5.85; $6.55 effective July 24, 2008
Washington	$7.93
West Virginia	$6.55 for employers with 6 or more employees at one location who are not subject to the FLSA; $7.25 effective July 1, 2008. The state minimum wage is not applicable to an employer if 80% of its employees are subject to the FLSA.
Wisconsin	$6.50
Wyoming	$5.15 unless employers and employees are subject to the FLSA

Some states, such as Oregon and Washington, adjust the state minimum wage rate annually for inflation.

In May 2007, Maryland became the first *state* to pass a "living wage" ordinance. Under the law, employers with state contracts will generally have to pay workers a minimum amount of $11.30 in the Baltimore-Washington urban corridor and $8.50 an hour in rural counties where the cost of living is usually lower.

Many municipalities have enacted "living wage" ordinances. For example, in Santa Cruz, California, the living wage is $12.00 per hour without benefits, otherwise it is $11.00 with health benefits. Employers in Santa Fe, New Mexico, with more than 24 employees must pay their employees at least $9.50 per hour, increasing to $10.50 on January 1, 2008.

Chapter 4

White-Collar Exempt Employees

This chapter discusses what it means for an employee to be exempt as a white-collar employee from certain requirements of the Fair Labor Standards Act (FLSA). Once coverage under the FLSA is established, the next area to examine is whether the employee must be paid minimum wage and overtime, or whether the employee is subject to one of the many FLSA exemptions. The most common exemptions are the so-called white-collar exemptions. Employees who are considered executive, administrative, or professional employees (including certain computer personnel) and outside salespersons are exempt from the FLSA's overtime requirements if specific conditions are met.

Employers may transform an exempt employee into a nonexempt employee by taking certain actions prohibited by Congress and the courts. For instance, making deductions from employees' salaries for partial-day absences may destroy the employees' exempt status. These and other issues relating to the white-collar exemptions under the FLSA are addressed in detail in this chapter.

Q 4:1　What does it mean to be *exempt* under the Fair Labor Standards Act (FLSA)?

To be *exempt* under the FLSA means to be excluded from one or more of the FLSA's requirements, such as minimum wage or overtime. The most common usage of *exempt* refers to an employee who is not entitled to the payment of overtime for some or all of the employee's hours over 40 per week. The FLSA distinguishes between employees who are not covered by it (see Qs 2:12–2:18) and employees who are exempt from certain portions of it, such as its minimum wage and overtime requirements based on their status as white-collar exempt employees (see Qs 4:8–4:50).

Q 4:2　What are the *white-collar exemptions*?

The *white-collar exemptions* are those exemptions from the FLSA's minimum wage and overtime pay requirements for the so-called "white-collar" occupations: executive (see Qs 4:8–4:12), administrative (see Qs 4:13–4:26), professional (see Qs 4:27–4:43), computer employees (see Qs 4:44–4:45), and outside sales employees (see Qs 4:47–4:50). [29 U.S.C § 213(a)(1)]

Q 4:3　Have there been any changes to the white-collar exemptions?

Yes. With the publication of proposed regulations in March 2003, employers and labor attorneys had considerable hopes that clarification of what are known as the salaried white-collar employee exemptions would finally be issued. [29 C.F.R. pt. 541] After considerable debate, the final regulations were published on April 20, 2004, and looked considerably different from the original proposed regulations. The official commentary, regulations, economic review, and related documents published by the DOL are 536 pages long. Depending on the point of view heard, it is far from clear whether the final regulations help employers or employees more, or whether they do anything to stop the groundswell of collective actions filed during the last few years.

Q 4:4　Now that the new regulations are in effect, do the old regulations have any relevance?

Yes. Many states also have wage-hour laws that provide for "white-collar" exemptions tied into the old DOL regulations. Some of these states are now using the DOL's new regulations, while others have opted to stay with the old regulations in whole or in part. Cases decided under the old regulations, which construe the same terms that appear in the new regulations, will continue to be important references.

For example, Illinois does not follow the new DOL regulations. Instead, under Illinois SB 1645 (effective April 2, 2004), the exemption for white-collar employees is applied under the FLSA regulations as they existed on March 30, 2003, with one exception. The salary levels contained in the new DOL regulations (e.g., $455/week) will be applied to the Illinois overtime exemption for white-collar employees. Oregon's white-collar regulations [Or. Rev. Stat. § 653.020(3); Or. Admin. R. § 839-020-0004(25), (29), (30), Or. Admin. R. § 839-020-0005], patterned after the old DOL regulations, remain in effect for covered employees, except that the salary levels in the new DOL regulations will apply. Pennsylvania's white-collar regulations [34 Pa. Code §§ 231.81 *et seq.*], which were substantially similar to the old DOL regulations, also remain in place.

Q 4:5   Under the old regulations, what factors determined whether an employee was exempt as an executive, administrative, or professional employee?

The two factors that determined whether an employee was exempt as an executive, administrative, or professional employee were the employee's duties and the employee's salary. Each of these classifications had a "long" and a "short" test for evaluating exempt status.

Q 4:6   What is the new minimum salary level?

The new regulations set a minimum of $23,660 per year ($455 per week; $910 biweekly; $985.83 semimonthly; $1,971.66 monthly). This is quite an increase from the $22,100 minimum annual salary that was required under the proposed regulations. These cash equivalent payments do not include room and board or benefits.

The DOL estimates that the new regulations will enhance the pay of 6.7 million American workers, including many who are currently exempt, who receive less than $23,660 per year. Many retail and service establishments with assistant managers or administrators under the minimum salary level can expect to be affected. Choices will have to be made between increasing salary payments or converting to hourly wage status.

Q 4:7   Has the primary duty test changed under the new regulations?

The new regulations basically rephrase, with some new nuances, the old short test under which an employee's actual job duties must be looked at in detail to determine whether his or her primary duty involves the exercise of managerial, high-level administrative, or professional functions. Indeed, the DOL stated in its preamble that the new "standard duties task" is "equally or more protective than the short duties test currently applicable to workers who earn between $23,660 and $100,000 per year."

Executives

Q 4:8 What made an employee an *exempt* executive employee under the old regulations?

Determining executive status depended more on an employee's duties than on his or her title. To be exempt, executives had to meet either the short test or the long test. The long test was obsolete even before the 2004 amendments because the salary was so low, $155 per week, that it resulted in payment below the minimum wage. Important factors in finding an employee to be an executive employee were the amount of time spent in managerial duties, the amount of discretion the employee had, and the number of employees supervised by or directed by the executive. [Former 29 C.F.R. § 541.1]

Short test. To qualify as an exempt executive employee under the short test, an employee had to be paid at least $250 per week on a salary basis, the employee's primary duty had to be management of an enterprise or a department or subdivision of the enterprise, and the employee had to regularly direct two or more other employees. [Former 29 C.F.R. §§ 541.1(f), 541.118, 541.119(a)]

Managerial duties included the following:

- Interviewing, selecting, and training employees
- Setting and adjusting employees' rates of pay and hours of work
- Directing employees' work
- Maintaining employees' production records for use in supervision or control
- Appraising employees' productivity and efficiency for the purpose of recommending promotions or other changes in their status
- Handling employee complaints and grievances and disciplining employees when necessary
- Planning the work
- Determining the techniques to be used
- Apportioning the work among workers
- Determining the type of materials, supplies, machines, or tools to be used (or merchandise to be bought, stocked, and sold)
- Controlling the flow and distribution of materials or merchandise and supplies
- Providing for the safety of employees and the property

[Former 29 C.F.R. § 541.102]

Long test. To qualify as an exempt executive employee under the long test, an employee had to be paid at least $155 per week on a salary basis. As was also required under the short test, the employee's primary duty had to be management of the enterprise or a department or subdivision of the enterprise, and an exempt employee had to customarily and regularly direct the work of two or more other full-time employees, or the equivalent. The long test required exempt executives to customarily and regularly exercise discretionary authority. Under the long test, an executive employee's nonexempt work could not exceed 20 percent of his or her weekly hours, nor more than 40 percent of weekly hours in a retail or service establishment. There was no restriction under the long test on time spent on nonexempt work for executives in charge of independent establishments or physically separate branches or who owned at least a 20 percent interest in the business (see the new regulations, Q 4:12). [Former 29 C.F.R. §§ 541.104–541.107, 541.112–541.114]

Federal regulations excluded "working foremen" from the executive exemption. During a strike, however, bona fide executives could perform nonexempt work provided they performed exempt work before the strike and they were not paid less than the salary required under the short test ($250 per week) during the strike. [Former 29 C.F.R. § 541.115; Wage and Hour Division Field Operations Handbook § 22c03]

Additionally, executives could perform nonexempt work during an emergency without having the time count toward the limitations on nonexempt work. The old regulations state that "when conditions beyond control arise which threaten the safety of the employees, or a cessation of operations, or serious damage to the employer's property, any manual or other normally nonexempt work performed in an effort to prevent such results is considered exempt work and is not included in computing the percentage limitation on nonexempt work." [Former 29 C.F.R. § 541.109(a)]

Higher-level fire department and law enforcement officers could fall within the executive exemption under the FLSA. [Wage & Hour Opinion Letter, FLSA2005-40 (Oct. 2005); *see also* West v. Anne Arundel County, Md., 137 F.3d 752 (4th Cir. 1998) (finding fire department-employed EMS captains and field lieutenants qualified for the executive exemption)]

Q 4:9   What are the basic requirements of the new executive exemption?

New regulations establish that, for an employee to fulfill the executive exemption, all of the following requirements must be met:

1. The employee must receive a salary of at least $455 per week;

2. The employee's primary duty must be managing the enterprise or managing a customarily recognized department or subdivision of the enterprise;

3. The employee must customarily and regularly direct the work of at least two other full-time employees or the equivalent; and

4. The employee must have the authority to hire or fire other employees, or have his or her suggestions and recommendations regarding the hiring, firing, advancement, promotion, or any other change of status of other employees be given particular weight.

[29 C.F.R. § 541.100(a)(1)–(4)]

In addition to the examples of management duties listed in Q 4:8, the new regulations also include: (1) planning and controlling the budget; and (2) monitoring or implementing legal compliance measures. The preamble to the revised final regulations explains that several public comments recommended that the list of management activities be expanded to include activities that are not supervisory but are still within the purview of management duties. Therefore, the DOL added these two activities as examples to reflect its agreement that management activities are not limited to supervisory activities. It is the DOL's position that the executive exemption and the definition of *management* were not previously limited to "supervisory" functions before the update but rather included all activities that could be properly described as management, including budgeting and implementing legal compliance measures. Thus, the new language in the regulations is a clarification and not a change from the old regulations. [Wage & Hour Opinion Letter, FLSA2005-19 (Aug. 2005)]

The new regulations provide, as did the old regulations, that the performance of nonexempt work during an emergency will not affect an employee's exempt status. [29 C.F.R. § 541.706] The performance of occasional tasks that cannot practicably be performed by nonexempt employees will also not affect an employee's exempt status. [29 C.F.R. § 541.707]

The regulations also contain a new discussion of what the phrase "concurrent duties" means: the performance of exempt and nonexempt work by an executive. Concurrent performance of exempt and nonexempt work does not disqualify an employee from the executive exemption if the executive employee's primary duty is the performance of work that meets the executive exemption requirements. The performance of exempt and nonexempt work by an employee is a particular challenge for an employee who, for example, might be a working manager. [29 C.F.R. § 541.106] The regulations use an assistant manager in a restaurant as an example of an employee who might perform exempt and nonexempt work. The manager might serve customers and stock food but also supervise the day-to-day activities of employees. Whether such an employee meets the primary duty test when the employee performs concurrent duties is determined on a case-by-case basis. Generally, exempt executives make the decision regarding when to perform nonexempt duties and remain responsible for the success or failure of business operations under their management while performing the nonexempt work. In contrast, the nonexempt employee generally is directed by a supervisor to perform the exempt work or performs the exempt work for defined time periods. An employee whose primary duty is ordinary production work or routine, recurrent, or repetitive tasks cannot qualify for exemption as an executive. [29 C.F.R. § 541.106(a)–(c)]

According to the DOL, the new discussion of concurrent duties is a clarification of the DOL's previous position that exempt executive employees can spend time performing exempt duties at the same time they are performing nonexempt duties and that the performance of such nonexempt work does not preclude the exemption if an employee's primary duty is management. The DOL believes that the new regulations are consistent with case law under the prior existing regulations, which make it clear that the performance of both exempt and nonexempt duties concurrently or simultaneously does not preclude an employee from qualifying for the exemption. Numerous courts have determined that an employee can have a primary duty of management while concurrently performing nonexempt duties. [Wage & Hour Opinion Letter, FLSA2005-19 (Aug. 2005)]

Q 4:10   What does "directing the work of two or more employees" mean?

An executive must direct the work of two or more full-time employees or the equivalent of two full-time employees (e.g., four part-time employees who generally work half time) in order to be an exempt executive employee. The supervision of two or more employees may also be divided between two or more executive employees. So, for example, two executive employees may share supervisory responsibility over a department of 10 employees. But the shared supervision must be substantial. An employee who assists a manager only in the manager's absence will not be an exempt executive. [29 C.F.R. § 541. 104(b)–(d)]

Q 4:11   What is meant by "particular weight" as required for the new executive exemption?

The fourth element of the new executive test, which requires an exempt executive to have the authority to hire or fire other employees or have recommendations given "particular weight," is a significant change. Even the DOL states, in its preamble to the new regulations, that the requirement may now result in disqualifying from exempt status some individuals who qualified previously. This requirement may be troublesome for public sector employers such as cities, counties, and school boards. The final rules state that factors to be considered in determining whether an employee's recommendations regarding employment status are given "particular weight" include: (1) whether it is a part of the employee's job duties to make such recommendations; and (2) the frequency with which such recommendations are made, requested, and relied upon. The duty requirement is not fulfilled by an employee who makes occasional suggestions. Fortunately, the DOL stated that an employee's recommendations may still be deemed to have "particular weight" even if a higher level manager's recommendation has more importance and even if the employee does not have the authority to make the ultimate decision as to another employee's change in status. [29 C.F.R. § 541.105]

Likewise, in its preamble commentary, the DOL stated that an executive does not have to possess full authority to make the ultimate decision regarding an employee's status, such as where a higher-level manager or a personnel board makes the final hiring, promotion, or termination decision. These words may prove to be important in future lawsuits, with the DOL noting that its guidance was intended to help in special situations that frequently exist in the public sector where unionization or civil service laws require major employment decisions to be made by board or committee or by the highest level manager.

Regarding large private sector organizations, the DOL did not provide further guidance of what might be considered sufficient decisions or recommendations with "particular weight" regarding "change in status" of an employee. However, the DOL in its preamble did recommend review of the Supreme Court's decision in *Burlington Industries, Inc. v. Ellerth* [524 U.S. 742 (1998)] for guidance on other possible activities that would be included in the phrase "change of status."

Regulations acknowledge that "working foremen" often present difficult situations to categorize and that they may still qualify for exempt status if their primary duty is management and they otherwise fulfill the requirements of the exemption. [29 C.F.R. § 541.106(a)–(c)] Thus, the new regulations provide little guidance in this regard.

Q 4:12   Can part owners of businesses now qualify for exempt status?

Yes. Under the new regulations, an employee in the private sector who owns at least 20 percent of the business in which he or she is employed and is "actively engaged in the management of the business" may qualify for exempt status and the salary basis test need not be met. [29 C.F.R. § 541.101]

Administrative Exemption

Q 4:13   How was an exempt administrative employee defined under the old regulations?

Employees who fell under the administrative exemption performed widely varying jobs. It was difficult to articulate any broad definition for an exempt administrative employee, and employers were required to show that each employee met each requirement of the exemption for the exemption to apply. That is why job duties mattered more than job title.

Short test. Administrative employees had to be paid a salary of $250 per week and their primary duty had to be to perform office or nonmanual work relating to management policies or general business operations. They also had to customarily and regularly exercise discretion and independent judgment. [Former 29 C.F.R. §§ 541.2, 541.206, 541.207]

Long test. The employee had to spend 80 percent or more of his or her time performing office or nonmanual work related to management policies or general business operations of the employer or the employer's customers and had to regularly exercise discretion and independent judgment. No more than 20 percent (40 percent for retail) of the employee's time could be spent on nonexempt activities, and the employee had to be paid a minimum weekly salary of $155. There was also a requirement that the employee: (1) regularly and directly assisted a proprietor or an executive or administrative employee; (2) worked under only general supervision along specialized or technical lines requiring special training, experience, or knowledge; or (3) executed under only general supervision special assignments and tasks. [Former 29 C.F.R. §§ 541.2, 541.206] Under the old regulations, these requirements resulted in three general types of administrative employees: (1) executive and administrative assistants; (2) staff employees; and (3) employees who perform special assignments. [Former 29 C.F.R. § 541.201] These distinctions are not made in the new regulations.

Q 4:14   What positions did executive and administrative assistants hold?

Executive and administrative assistants typically held positions such as executive assistant to the president, confidential assistant, executive secretary, assistant to the general manager, administrative assistant, assistant manager, or assistant buyer. The old federal regulations explained that these positions typically were found in large corporations. An exempt administrative assistant's primary duty still had to be "office or nonmanual work directly related to management policies or general business operations of his employer or his employer's customers." [Former 29 C.F.R. § 541.201(a)(1); 29 C.F.R. § 541.2(a)(1)] (See Q 4:25.)

Q 4:15   Do the new regulations provide better guidance on how to apply the administrative exemption?

The administrative exemption, which is by far the most difficult of the white-collar exemptions to apply, has little new guidance in the new regulations. The new regulations establish that in order for an employee to be an exempt administrative employee all of the following requirements must be met:

1. The employee must receive a salary or compensation on a fee basis of at least $455 per week (see Q 4:40);

2. The employee's primary duty must be the performance of office or nonmanual work directly related to the management or general business operations of the employer or the employer's customers; and

3. The employee's primary duty includes the exercise of discretion and independent judgment with respect to matters of significance.

[29 C.F.R. § 541.200(a)(1)–(3)]

Q 4:16   What is work that is "directly related to the management or the general business operations" of an employer?

The new regulations give examples of the type of general work that is directly related to management or general business operations of an employer: (1) tax, finance, accounting, auditing and budgeting; (2) quality control; (3) purchasing and procurement; (4) advertising, marketing, and research; (5) safety and health; (6) personnel management, human resources, employee benefits, and labor relations; (7) public relations and government relations; (8) computer network, internet, and database administration; and (9) nonlegal and regulatory compliance. In a nutshell, administrative work is the work performed by employees who have a proactive role in running the business. [Wolfslayer v. IKON Office Solutions, Inc., Civ. Action No. 03-6709 (E.D. Pa. 2005)]

Q 4:17   What does it mean to "exercise discretion and independent judgment with respect to matters of significance"?

The new regulations provide the following examples to assist in determining whether an employee meets the requirements of the duties test to exercise "discretion and independent judgment" with respect to matters of significance. According to the DOL, an employee can exercise discretion and independent judgment if the employee:

1. Has authority to formulate, affect, interpret, or implement management policies or operating practices;
2. Carries out major assignments in conducting the operations of the business;
3. Performs work that affects business operations to a substantial degree (even if the employee's assignments are related to operations of a particular segment of the business);
4. Has authority to commit the employer in matters that have significant financial impact;
5. Has authority to waive or deviate from established policies or procedures without prior approval;
6. Has authority to negotiate and bind the company on significant matters;
7. Provides consultation or expert advice to management;
8. Is involved in planning long- or short-term business objectives;
9. Investigates and resolves matters of significance on behalf of management; and
10. Represents the employer in handling complaints, arbitrating disputes, or resolving grievances.

[29 C.F.R. § 541.202(b)]

The DOL concluded that continuing to use the requirement that an exempt administrative employee's primary duties include the use of "discretion and independent judgment" was preferable to implementing new criteria. The new regulations continue the requirement that discretion and independent judgment must be exercised "with respect to matters of significance." [29 C.F.R. § 541. 202(a)] The new regulations state that employees can exercise discretion and independent judgment even if their decisions are reviewed by a supervisor, or if more than one employee performs the same duties. [29 C.F.R. § 541.202(c), (d)] However, employees do not exercise discretion and independent judgment merely because the employer will experience financial losses if the worker fails to perform the job properly. [29 C.F.R. § 541.202(f)]

The new regulations did little to clarify the "production exception," which has been one of the most heated areas of litigation in recent years. The new regulations state that an exempt administrator must perform work directly related to assisting with running or servicing the business, as distinguished, for example, from working on a manufacturing production line or selling a product in a retail or service establishment. [29 C.F.R. § 541.201(a)] Trying to draw a fine distinction, the DOL stated in its preamble that "we do not believe that it is appropriate to eliminate the concept entirely from the administrative exemption, but neither do we believe that the dichotomy has ever been or should be a dispositive test for exemption." "The Department believes that the dichotomy is still a relevant and useful tool in appropriate cases to identify employees who should be excluded from the exemption," with the DOL noting that the production worker test is just one factor and is not controlling. Therefore, in light of past court decisions going in different directions on production versus staff issues, the new regulations provide no clear answers. [29 C.F.R. § 541. 202(b)]

For example, real estate closers who were employed by a law firm were found to be entitled to overtime, where the closers had functional, rather than conceptual roles, and did not contribute to the firm's strategy, did not craft policies, and did not attempt to draw new business to the firm. The closers were found to be nonexempt "production" employees because they applied existing policies and procedures on a case-by-case basis to prepare documents for closings, to oversee closings, to distribute checks and to complete any post-closing activities. [Relyea v. Carman, Callahan and Ingham, L.L.P., 2006 U.S. Dist. LEXIS 63351 (E.D.N.Y. 2006)]

Q 4:18   Is there new guidance on specific administrative occupations?

After some long-running court controversies, the new regulations do clarify the parameters under which insurance claims adjusters and financial services employees (such as loan officers, credit managers, and financial advisors) may be considered exempt. Likewise, human resource employees may be exempt if they formulate or implement policies. However, the final regulations specifically state that recruiters or hiring office employees may not be exempt if they merely screen applicants and are applying routine or standardized policies. [29 C.F.R. § 541.203(e)] The new regulations state that quality control inspectors, comparison shoppers, and public sector inspectors and investigators will not generally qualify as exempt employees. [29 C.F.R. § 541.203(h)-(j)] New sections added to the regulations clearly state that "blue collar" workers are entitled to overtime. [29 C.F.R. § 541.203(a)–(h)]

Q 4:19   What is the meaning of the new term "team leader"?

The administrative exemption regulations contain a new section that discusses "team leaders." [29 C.F.R. § 541.203(c)] "An employee who leads a team of other employees assigned to complete major projects for the employer (such as purchasing, selling, or closing all or part of the business, negotiating a real estate transaction or a collective bargaining agreement, or designing and implementing productivity improvements) generally meets the duties requirements for the exemption," even if the employee does not directly supervise the other employees on the team.

Q 4:20 Are paralegals exempt administrative employees?

Under both the old regulations and the new regulations, the Wage and Hour Division determined that the duties of paralegals do not involve the exercise of discretion and independent judgment of the type required by the regulations in order to qualify for the administrative exemption. Rather, paralegal employees appeared to fit more appropriately into the category of employees who applied particular skills and knowledge in preparing assignments. As such, these employees were not deemed to be exercising independent judgment. [Wage & Hour Opinion Letter, FLSA2005-54 (Dec. 2005); Wage & Hour Opinion Letter, FLSA1998 (Mar. 1998); Wage & Hour Opinion Letter, FLSA1995 (Apr. 1995)] See Q 4:35.

Q 4:21 What duties does a staff employee perform under the administrative exemption?

Under the old regulations, staff employees acted as advisors to management or were in charge of a functional department. Positions often fitting under the administrative exemption as staff employees were tax experts, insurance experts, sales research experts, wage-rate analysts, credit managers, purchasing agents, personnel directors, investment consultants, foreign exchange consultants, and statisticians. [29 C.F.R. § 541.201(a)(2)] The new regulations do not use this term. However, such employees may qualify as exempt employees under the terms of the new regulations. [29 C.F.R. § 541.203]

Q 4:22 Does the number of employees who are engaged in the same work affect whether the employees are exempt?

No. The new regulations specifically state that many employees can perform the same type of work of the same relative importance and all can be exempt so long as each meets the requirements of the exemption. [29 C.F.R. § 541.202(d)]

Q 4:23 Are field service technicians exempt administrative employees?

No. Field service employees are employees who are sent out to different sites to assess problems with equipment their employer manufactured. For example, an employer that manufactures large-scale conveyor belts and systems will send out field service employees to assess and fix problems with the conveyor belts which have already been placed in the field. Field service employees, although they may be highly skilled technicians, do not qualify as exempt because their duties do not involve "the comparison and evaluation of possible courses of conduct and the making of decisions after the various possibilities have been considered," meaning that although they have some leeway in reaching conclusions, they do not exercise a sufficient amount of independent judgment. Moreover, field service employees generally do not qualify as professional employees because their training generally does not require an advanced degree. [Wage & Hour Opinion Letter, FLSA2000 (July 2000)]

Q 4:24 Are insurance claims adjusters exempt administrative employees?

It depends. The new regulations provide that "[i]nsurance claims adjusters generally meet the duties requirements for the administrative exemption, whether they work for an insurance company or other type of company, if their duties include activities such as interviewing insureds, witnesses and physicians; inspecting property damage; reviewing factual information to prepare damage estimates; evaluating and making recommendations regarding coverage of claims; determining liability and total value of a claim; negotiating settlements; and making recommendations regarding litigation." [29 C.F.R. § 541.203(a)]

Insurance adjusters who handled automobile damage claims, nonautomobile property damage claims, and personal injury claims were found to be exempt employees where they were required to do practically all of the things the regulations consider to be exempt work. The adjusters used their discretion to determine whether or not a loss was covered, to set reserves, to determine who was liable, and to negotiate with the insured or his lawyer. In *In re Farmers Ins. Exch. Claims Representative Overtime Pay Litig.*, the court of appeals rejected the distinction drawn by the district court, which found certain adjusters to be nonexempt based on the size or type of the claim. [481 F.3d 1119 (9th Cir. 2007)]

The complication is that not all claims adjusters perform these types of duties. For example, one court recently determined that GEICO (Government Employees Insurance Company) adjusters do not interview witnesses and physicians, they do not make recommendations regarding coverage of claims, they do not determine liability, and they do not make recommendations regarding litigation. They therefore do not perform the majority of the duties included in the description of "insurance claims adjuster" found in the new regulations. As a result, they cannot be automatically classified as exempt employees. The court found that the new importance of computer software to the work of adjusters has reduced the discretion and judgment they exercise. Although the court agreed that the computer does not, and cannot, exercise discretion and independent judgment for the adjuster, "it cannot be denied that the auto damage adjusters' duties today involve applying 'well-established techniques, procedures or specific standards described in manuals or other sources' [29 C.F.R. § 541.202(e)] and that the computer program aids in compliance with those standards. . . ." [Robinson-Smith v. Gov't Employees Ins. Co., 323 F. Supp. 2d 12 (D.D.C. 2004)]

The DOL recently issued an opinion letter that contains an extensive analysis of the new claims adjuster regulation. The opinion letter concluded that senior-level claims specialists who are assigned to handle complex cases, who conduct independent investigation of accident scenes, who hire and interact with medical and vocational providers, and who handle claims in litigation and arbitration meet the new administrative exemption. But the "junior"-level adjusters are not exempt because the work of junior claims handlers is supervised, and they are assigned only routine other cases. [Wage & Hour Opinion Letter, FLSA2005-25 (Aug. 2005)]

Q 4:25   What are some examples of exempt and nonexempt administrative employees?

Planners

When employees engage in work that is ancillary, or supportive, to the employers' principal production activity, those employees are administrative employees. For example, where the company's principal production activity is generating electricity, an employee whose primary duty is creating plans for maintaining equipment and systems is considered to be engaged in work that is ancillary, thus related to the general business operations of the employer. [Renfro v. Ind. Mich. Power Co., 370 F.3d 512, 517–18 (6th Cir. 2004)]

Employees who worked in a shipyard were properly classified as administrative employees because their duties, which included evaluating work scope requirements, providing guidance to ensure work schedules were met, and ensuring that adequate information was relayed to craft workers, required use of judgment and discretion on a daily basis and were intellectual in nature, not requiring manual labor. [Cowart v. Ingalls Shipbuilding, Inc., 213 F.3d 261, 266 (5th Cir. 2000)]

Information Technology

An employee who was responsible for the computer system of the employer was not engaged in production of the employer's product but instead worked in one of the supporting administrative functions enumerated in the regulations (computer network). His duties also entailed work of substantial importance to management, and he was thus an exempt administrator. The exempt duties were ordering replacement parts, recommending purchases, installing and repairing software and equipment, investigating problems, and implementing solutions. [Koppinger v. Am. Interiors, Inc., 295 F. Supp. 2d 797, 802 (N.D. Ohio 2003)]

Business Analysts/Consultants

Where an employee's duties entailed communication between management and employees, coordinating project plans and plan deadlines, and coordinating, conducting, and following up on issues raised in weekly conference calls, the court found these duties were not the product IKON offered to the public and thus were related to the general business operations of the employer. [Wolfslayer v. IKON Office Solutions, Inc., 10 Wage & Hour Cas. 2d (BNA) 500 (E.D. Pa. 2005)]

Employees who supply reports and file government forms are not necessarily engaged in production work unrelated to management and general business operations of the employer, even though these may be the very products the employer is in business to produce. For example, a human resources consultant who generated reports for clients as well as suggested problem solutions and ways to improve was performing work directly related to the general business operations of the employer. [Piscione v. Ernst & Young, L.L.P., 171 F.3d 527, 538–39 (7th Cir. 1999)]

Clerical Employees

The old regulations generally classified clerical employees as those who do not perform work directly related to management policies or general business operations. [29 C.F.R. § 541.205(c)(1)(2003)] However, there are instances where clerical employees with significant responsibilities have been found exempt.

An executive secretary who helped the company president transfer his office to another location, managed his personal checking account, screened telephone calls, and worked with a team of executive assistants performed work related to the general business operations of the employer. [Seltzer v. Dresdner Kleinwort Wasserstein, Inc., 356 F. Supp. 2d 288 (S.D.N.Y. 2005)]

But an administrative assistant who processed checks for deposit, paid company bills, disbursed petty cash, prepared invoices, processed expense reports, monitored grants, maintained expense accounts, and performed office support functions such as screening calls, sending faxes, and monitoring mail did not perform tasks directly related to general business operations, as the duties were more related to "day-to-day" functions of the organization. [Wage & Hour Opinion Letter, FLSA1998 (June 1998)]

Manager/Security Guards

A manager of security and safety performed duties that were of substantial importance to management and the operation of the business where he advised management and made recommendations on building design, feasibility of security systems, guard services, and budgetary items, even though management did not always follow his suggestions. The employee was exempt even though he performed field work and carried valuables at times. [White v. All Am. Cable & Radio, 656 F. Supp. 1168 (D.P.R. 1987)]

Union Vice President

An employee who handled employee grievances and workers' compensation claims and served on the company-union staff committee and generally ensured the company followed the collective bargaining agreement was not engaged in production work; rather, his duties were of substantial importance to management and had a direct relationship to general business operations. [Douglas v. Argo-Tech Corp., 113 F.3d 67, 72 (6th Cir. 1997)]

Administrative Assistants

An administrative assistant who processed accounts payable and receivables, kept the master community event calendar, managed office equipment and supplies, filed, coordinated executive schedules, assisted the board of directors, assisted in preparing a monthly newsletter, oversaw volunteers and the hospitality assistant, and performed various duties as requested by the executive director was not exercising discretion and independent judgment. [Wage & Hour Opinion Letter, FLSA1997 (Oct. 1997)]

An administrative assistant whose job duties entailed data entry of accounts payable and receivable, word processing, maintaining workers' compensation/insurance paperwork, reception, and ordering of routine office supplies was not an exempt administrator under the new regulations because she did not exercise discretion and independent judgment. [Wage & Hour Opinion Letter, FLSA2005-8 (Jan. 2005)]

But an administrative assistant whose workers' compensation responsibilities occupied 28 of her 45-hour workweek, who exercised substantial independent judgment with respect to the company's employee manual, and who exercised discretion in matters affecting secretaries in her work area was an exempt administrative employee. [Szymula v. Ash Grove Cement Co., 941 F. Supp. 1032, 1036–38 (D. Kan. 1996)]

Bookkeepers/Accounting Clerks

While Certified Public Accountants will likely qualify as exempt under the professional exemption, bookkeepers may, at times, qualify under the administrative exemption, providing their duties require the exercise of discretion and independent judgment with respect to matters of significance.

Where an accounting clerk was responsible for managing an insurance fund (including marketing, billing, and collecting) and general administrative duties such as coordinating seminars and meetings and training employees, the employee exercised discretion and independent judgment and was exempt. [Callahan v. Bancorpsouth Ins. Servs. of Miss., Inc., 244 F. Supp. 2d 678, 687 (S.D. Miss. 2002)]

An accounting and credit manager whose duties included approving the release of orders on credit hold, making recommendations concerning extension of credit and discounts, and overseeing the work of another employee, was an exempt administrative professional, even though he spent more than 50 percent of his time in nonadministrative bookkeeping and clerical functions. [Hills v. W. Paper Co., 825 F. Supp. 936, 938–39 (D. Kan. 1993)]

But a bookkeeper who worked without immediate supervision performing duties of preparing bills and bank deposits, recording receipts, handling petty cash, checking prices, recording inventories, and working with financial reports and books, but who did not have the authority to sign payroll checks and where preparation of reports was dictated by a monthly deadline, was not an exempt administrative employee. [Clark v. J.M. Benson Co., 789 F.2d 282 (4th Cir. 1986)]

Office Managers

When an office manager is responsible for supervising the work of two or more full-time employees, the employee may be exempt under the executive exemption. In many cases, these employees may also be exempt administrative employees.

An office manager responsible for supervising incoming work and directing it to proper departments, prioritizing projects, and assisting the supervisor, who performed manual labor only 5 percent of the time, exercised discretion and independent judgment and was exempt. [Cowan v. Tricolor, Inc., 869 F. Supp. 262 (D. Del. 1994)]

An office manager who prepared payroll, workers' compensation reports, tax returns, and sales tax reports and supervised the work of other employees was an exempt administrative employee. [Lott v. Howard Wilson Chrysler-Plymouth, Inc., 203 F.3d 326 (5th Cir. 2000)]

Q 4:26   Do employees working at educational establishments qualify for an administrative exemption?

Yes. The educational establishment exemption is a specific administrative exemption that applies to employees who meet the salary test and who have as their primary duty administrative work in an educational institution. This work is defined as "directly related to academic instruction or training in an educational establishment or department or subdivision thereof." [29 C.F.R. § 541.204(a)(1), (2)]. An "educational establishment" is a public or private school, grades K–12, and may also include some pre-K programs. It includes schools for special-needs children. Examples of exempt educational employees include principals and assistant principals, department heads, and academic counselors. [29 C.F.R. § 541.204(c)(1)]

Professionals

Q 4:27   What made an employee a *professional employee* under the old regulations?

The exemption for *professional employees* was limited to traditionally recognized professions such as law and medicine in which the acquisition of the necessary knowledge required prolonged academic study. An essential criterion for finding an employee to be an exempt learned professional was the need for an academic degree in a field directly related to the employee's occupation. [Former 29 C.F.R. §§ 541.300, 541.301(e)(2)] Also included was an artistic exemption in fields such as music composition and performance and acting (see Q 4:41).

Short test. Under the short test, professional employees had to be paid at least $250 per week and had to perform work, which required the consistent exercise of independent judgment and discretion due to advanced knowledge or teaching or which required invention, imagination, and talent in a recognized field of artistic endeavor. [Former 29 C.F.R. § 541.3]

Long test. The long test required a minimum salary of $170 per week, work requiring advanced knowledge or work that is creative or involves teaching, the consistent exercise of discretion, performance of predominantly intellectual and varied work, and a 20 percent limit on nonexempt activities. [29 C.F.R. § 541.3]

The following professions were generally found to fulfill the requirement for a "prolonged course of specialized intellectual instruction and study":

- Registered nursing (not licensed practical nursing)
- Accounting (not bookkeeping)
- Actuarial computation
- Engineering
- Dental hygiene (with four years of study)
- Architecture
- Teaching
- Work in the physical, chemical, and biological sciences, including pharmacy and medical technology

[29 C.F.R. § 541.301(e)(1)]

Q 4:28   What are the new requirements for the professional exemption?

To qualify for the learned professional exemption, an employee's primary duty must still be the performance of work requiring advanced knowledge in a field of science or learning customarily acquired by a prolonged course of specialized intellectual instruction. This primary duty test includes four elements:

1. The employee must receive a salary or compensation on a fee basis of at least $455 per week (see Q 4:40);
2. The employee's primary duty must be to perform work requiring advanced knowledge;
3. The advanced knowledge must be in a field of science or learning; and
4. The advanced knowledge must be customarily acquired by a prolonged course of specialized intellectual instruction.

[29 C.F.R. § 541.301(a)]

The phrase "work requiring advance knowledge" is intended to define work that is predominantly intellectual in character and that includes work requiring the consistent exercise of independent judgment and discretion. [29 C.F.R. § 541.301(b)] The requirement that a learned professional employee exercise judgment and discretion on a consistent basis sets a higher standard than that in the administrative exemption, where an employee need only have as a primary duty work that requires the exercise of some discretion and independent judgment with respect to matters of significance. [29 C.F.R. § 541.200(a)(3)] The phrase "customarily acquired by a prolonged course of specialized intellectual instruction" restricts the exemption to professions where prolonged academic training is a standard prerequisite for entrance into the profession. The best prima facie evidence that an employee meets this requirement is possession of the appropriate academic degree. Before 2004, the Wage and Hour Division repeatedly took the position that work that can be performed by employees with education or training below the college level would not be work of a bona fide professional level within the meaning of the old regulations. Such work, even teaching or instructing, does not require the consistent exercise of discretion or judgment and would not be predominantly intellectual and varied in character so as to permit the application of the exemption. [Wage & Hour Opinion Letter, FLSA1997-1462 (Mar. 1997); Wage & Hour Opinion Letter, FLSA1986-1645 (Mar. 1986); Wage & Hour Opinion Letter, FLSA1986-1659 (May 1986)] Both the old and the new regulations allow this requirement by the occasional employee who has substantially the same knowledge level and performs substantially the same work as degreed employees, but who attained the advanced knowledge through a combination of work experience and intellectual instruction. Thus, for example, the learned professional exemption is available to the occasional lawyer who has not gone to law school, or the occasional chemist who is not the possessor of a degree in chemistry. [29 C.F.R. § 541.301(d)]

The comments to the new regulations also clarify that jobs that only require a two- or four-year degree in any field of study as a prerequisite for entrance into the field will not qualify for the learned professional exemption. [69 Fed. Reg. 22150 (Apr. 23, 2004)]

Q 4:29   Are nurses considered exempt employees?

Under the new regulations, registered nurses continue to be considered as qualifying for the professional employee exemption if they are salaried, while licensed practical nurses are not to be considered exempt. [29 C.F.R. § 541. 301(e)(2)] However, registered nurses who are paid by hospitals and other employers at an hourly wage rate based on industry norms and competition are not exempt.

Q 4:30   Are physician assistants considered exempt employees?

The new regulations update the DOL's position on physician assistants by stating that those who graduated from a program accredited by the Accreditation Review Commission on Education for the Physician Assistant and who are certified by the National Commission on Certification of Physician Assistants generally meet the educational requirements for the learned professional exemption. [29 C.F.R. § 541.301(e)(4)]

Q 4:31   Is an ultrasound technologist an exempt professional employee?

No. Ultrasound employees perform work that requires use of skills and procedures that do not require a four-year degree in a professional discipline. The duties include positioning of patients for ultrasound testing, keeping patient records, and visual inspection of equipment. Thus, although they have specialized training and exercise independent judgment, ultrasound employees are best described as "skilled nonexempt technicians." [Wage & Hour Opinion Letter, FLSA2000 (Nov. 2000)] Although this opinion was issued before the new regulations, the new regulations do not seem to contradict the opinion because the new regulations specify that registered or certified medical technologists who have successfully completed three academic years of pre-professional study in an accredited college or university plus a fourth year of professional course work in a school of medical technology approved by the Council of Medical Education of the American Medical Association generally meet the duties requirements for the learned professional exemption. [29 C.F.R. § 541.301(e)(1)]

Q 4:32   Are funeral directors and embalmers considered exempt employees?

Under the new regulations, funeral directors and embalmers may now also be considered exempt, if certain requirements are met. Licensed funeral directors and embalmers who are licensed by and working in a state that requires successful completion of four academic years of pre-professional and professional study, including graduation from a college of mortuary science accredited by the American Board of Funeral Service Education, generally meet the duties requirements for the learned professional exemption. Absent state licensing, the DOL will not recognize exempt status. [29 C.F.R. § 541.301(e)(9)]

Q 4:33   Are chefs considered exempt employees?

The learned professional exemption is not available to cooks who perform predominantly routine mental, manual, technical, or physical work. However, a chef whose primary duties require "invention, imagination, originality, or talent" may be considered exempt under the creative professional employee test. Chefs (such as executive chefs and sous chefs) who have attained a four-year specialized academic degree in a culinary arts program generally meet the duties requirement for the learned professional exemption. [29 C.F.R. § 541.301(e)(6)]

Q 4:34   Are athletic trainers considered exempt employees?

Athletic trainers who have completed four academic years of pre-professional and professional study in a program accredited by the Commission on Accreditation of Allied Health Education Programs and are certified by the National Athletic Trainers Association qualify for the learned professional exemption in the new regulations, which is a change in the DOL's position after considerable litigation. [29 C.F.R. § 541.301(e)(8)]

Q 4:35   Are paralegals considered exempt professional employees?

Generally not. Under both the new and the old regulations, paralegals are generally not considered to be exempt professionals because an advanced specialized academic degree is not required to enter the field. Many paralegals have a four-year degree, but many certification programs require only two years of study. The professional exemption is available to those paralegals who possess an advanced specialized degree in another professional field and apply advanced knowledge in that field in the performance of their paralegal duties. [29 C.F.R. § 541.301(e)(7)] For example, a paralegal with a degree in chemistry might use this knowledge in assisting on patent cases. [*See* Wage & Hour Opinion Letter, FLSA2005-54 (Dec. 2005); Wage & Hour Opinion Letter, FLSA2005-9 (Jan. 2005) (stating that the new regulations preclude exemption absent a specialized advanced degree in another profession that is used in performing paralegal duties)]

Q 4:36   Are social workers considered exempt employees?

It depends. According to the DOL, a job that requires a social worker with a master's degree may be exempt if paid at least $455 per week, but case workers who merely have a bachelor's degree in "social sciences" do not have the specialized academic training necessary to meet the professional exemption. [Wage & Hour Opinion Letter, FLSA2005-50 (Nov. 2005)]

Q 4:37   Will other occupations be included in the learned professional exemption category in the future?

The DOL also opens the door in a separate section of the new regulations to future accreditation and certification agencies under which learned professional exemptions may possibly be created. Similar to those recognized under 29 C.F.R. Section 541.301(e)(1), (3), (4), (8), and (9), organizations may develop similar specialized curriculums and certification programs that, if they become a standard requirement for a particular occupation, may indicate the occupation has acquired the characteristics of a learned professional. It may take considerable litigation to establish a new job as an exempt, learned professional occupation. An alternative to always consider is requesting a detailed opinion letter from the Administrator of the Wage and Hour Division on which an employer or group of employers, such as those covered by a trade association or accreditation agency, may rely.

Q 4:38   Are physicians and lawyers exempt professionals?

Yes. Under both the old and the new regulations, doctors and lawyers are exempt professionals. The exemption applies to "any employee who is the holder of a certificate permitting the practice of law or medicine or any of their branches" and who is actually practicing medicine or law. [29 C.F.R. § 541. 304(a)(1)] Furthermore, doctors and lawyers are exempt regardless of their wage arrangements. A practicing lawyer or doctor (including an intern or resident) is exempted from the salary requirement on an hourly or daily basis without losing exempt status, unlike executives, administrative employees, and other learned and creative professionals. [29 C.F.R. §§ 541.304(d); Wage & Hour Opinion Letter, FLSA2005-34 (Sept. 2005)]

Q 4:39   Are teachers exempt professionals?

Yes. The exemption for professional employees applies to any employee whose primary duty consists of teaching, tutoring, instructing, or lecturing in an educational establishment. [29 C.F.R. § 541.303] The FLSA's salary requirements for exempt employees do not apply to teaching professionals. [29 C.F.R. § 541.303(d)]

The exemption extends beyond traditional primary and secondary school teachers, to include, but not be limited to:

- Regular academic teachers;
- Teachers of kindergarten or nursery school pupils;
- Teachers of gifted or disabled children;
- Teachers of skilled and semi-skilled trades and occupations;
- Teachers engaged in automobile driving instruction;
- Aircraft flight instructors;
- Home economics teachers; and
- Vocal or instrumental music instructors.

The employees who are engaged as teachers but also spend a considerable amount of their time in extracurricular activities such as coaching athletics or moderating or advising debate or speech clubs are engaged in teaching, as such activities are "a recognized part of the schools' responsibility in contributing to the educational development of the student." [29 C.F.R. § 541.303(b)]

Teachers who possess a teaching certificate qualify for the exemption "regardless of the terminology (e.g., permanent, conditional, standard, provisional, temporary, emergency, or unlimited) used by the State to refer to different kinds of certificates." A teacher who is not certified may be considered for the exemption provided that such individual is employed as a teacher by the employing school or school system. [29 C.F.R. § 541.303(c)]

Teachers are also excluded from the salary requirement. [29 C.F.R. § 541. 303(d)] While this exclusion appeared very clear in the old regulations, at least one federal court opinion interpreted this exemption to mean that teachers (and, by extension, doctors and lawyers) were exempt from the minimum salary requirements used to define salaried or professional status, but held that they had to still receive a salary. This opinion appeared to be an aberration. [Page-Wood v. Michigan, 849 F. Supp. 1200 (W.D. Mich. 1994) (although teachers were not required to receive any particular salary to be exempt, failure to maintain salaried status as a result of improper deductions for unpaid leave caused the exemption to be lost)]

Q 4:40   Are professional and administrative employees who are paid on a fee basis still exempt?

Yes. Professional and administrative employees paid on a fee basis may retain their exempt status. Employees are paid on a fee basis when they are paid an agreed sum for one job irrespective of the time required to complete the job, a payment structure that resembles piecework payments. But, unlike the case with piecework payments, the job must be unique and cannot be merely a series of jobs which are "repeated an indefinite number of times and for which payment on an identical basis is made over and over again." Additionally, payment cannot be based on the number of hours worked. Under the old regulations, the pay arrangement had to amount to at least $170 per week to professional employees or $155 per week to administrative employees. [Former 29 C.F.R. § 541.313(a), (b)] Under the new regulations, the employee is tested by determining the time worked on the job and whether the fee is at a rate that would amount to $455 per week if the employee worked 40 hours. For example, an artist who was paid $250 for a painting which took 20 hours to complete would meet the minimum salary requirement because the artist would have been paid $500 for 40 hours of work. [29 C.F.R. § 541.605]

Q 4:41   What requirements did artistic professionals need to meet to be exempt under the old regulations?

Under the exemption for artistic professionals in the old regulations, an employee had to be performing work in a recognized field of artistic endeavor, such as music, writing, theater, or the plastic and graphic arts. The old regulations required the work to be "original and creative," as opposed to work that could be performed by anyone with general manual or intellectual ability and training. [Former 29 C.F.R. § 541.302]

Musicians, composers, conductors, and soloists were considered to be engaged in original and creative work within the sense of this definition. In the plastic and graphic arts, the requirement was generally met by painters who, at most, were given the subject matter of their paintings. It was similarly met by cartoonists who were merely told the title or underlying concept of a cartoon and then had to rely on their own creative powers to express the concept. It would not normally be met by a person who was employed as a copyist, an animator of motion-picture cartoons, or a retoucher of photographs because it was believed that such work was not properly described as creative in character. [Former 29 C.F.R. § 541.302(c)(1)]

Q 4:42 What is the minor change to the "creative professional" exemption?

The other prong of the professional exemption is the exemption for creative professionals. The new regulations rephrase the definition. An exempt, creative professional's primary duty must be work in a recognized field of artistic or creative endeavor. An exempt creative professional's work must require "invention, imagination, originality or talent." [29 C.F.R. § 302(a)] The exemption has changed little other than adding the term "originality" to the duties test and by deleting any reference to the "plastic" arts. Therefore, the new test applies to an employee whose primary duty is the performance of work requiring invention, imagination, originality, or talent in a recognized field of artistic or creative endeavor. [29 C.F.R. § 541.302]

Q 4:43 Are journalists and commentators considered exempt employees?

In the new regulations, the DOL dealt with journalists and on-air personalities who have been the subject of considerable litigation. The new regulations provide that employees of newspapers, magazines, television, and other media are not exempt creative professionals if they only collect, organize, and record information that is routine or already public, or if they do not contribute a unique interpretation or analysis to a news product. However, journalists may qualify as exempt creative professionals if their primary duty is performing on the air in radio, television, or other electronic media; conducting investigative interviews; analyzing or interpreting public events; writing editorials, opinion columns, or other commentaries; or acting as a narrator or commentator. [29 C.F.R. § 541.302(d)] Previously, there had been much confusion and debate over whether print journalists fell under the professional exemption. Because a directly-related college degree is not a standard requirement to become a journalist, the learned professional exemption did not apply. The only journalists to qualify as exempt professionals were those whose duties were found largely to be creative. [29 C.F.R. § 541.302(d); *see* Reich v. Newspapers of New England, Inc., 44 F.3d 1060, 1076–78 (1st Cir. 1995) (newspaper writers, photographers, and editors were not exempt as artistic professionals or under learned professional exemptions); Wang v. Chinese Daily News, Inc., 435 F. Supp. 2d 1042 (C.D. Cal. 2006) (reporters were not exempt as their jobs depended primarily on intelligence, diligence and accuracy)] In the newspaper field, only writing that was "analytical, interpretative or highly individualized" was considered creative. Editorial writers, columnists, critics, and "top flight" writers of analytical and interpretative articles fell within this category. General reporting and newswriting were not considered artistic. [29 C.F.R. § 541. 302(f)(1), (2)]

In the field of broadcast journalism, decisions have reached differing results regarding exempt status. For instance, in *Freeman v. National Broadcasting Co.* [80 F.3d 78 (2d Cir. 1996)], the court rejected the DOL's application of the long test to the artistic professional exemption and found that highly skilled and creative news writers and producers for NBC were exempt professionals. The court also noted that, despite technological advances affecting news organizations since the 1940s, little had changed in the regulations classifying employees of news organizations. For this reason, little deference was due the DOL's interpretation of the regulations. [*Id.* at 84–87]

On the other hand, the Fifth Circuit held that general-assignment television news reporters, news producers, directors, and assignment editors were not exempt because their work was dictated by management and did not depend on invention, imagination, or talent. [Dalheim v. KDFW-TV, 918 F.2d 1220, 1228–32 (5th Cir. 1990)]

In the newspaper industry, general-assignment reporters, journalists, and other employees working for small community newspapers with circulations of less than 4,000 are exempt. [29 U.S.C. § 213(a)(8)] Circulation figures for a group of community newspapers can be aggregated for purposes of finding the employees to be nonexempt. [*See* Reich v. Gateway Press, Inc., 13 F.3d 685, 697 (3d Cir. 1994)] In *Gateway Press,* the company published 19 weekly newspapers in the Pittsburgh area. Although each newspaper was geared toward a different market and ran its own news items, the court found that the newspapers constituted one newspaper based on the fact that each newspaper was engaged in a similar activity—providing local news to the area it served—each newspaper ultimately was controlled by the central office, and each newspaper, although it contained local news at the front of the paper, contained identical feature stories, editorials, and advertisements. [*Id.*]

Computer Employees

Q 4:44 Has the computer employee exemption changed with the new regulations?

Not in a substantial way. The exemption for computer professionals continues relatively unchanged in the new regulations. Such employees may be classified as exempt if they meet the duties requirement and are paid (on either a salary or fee basis) $455 per week or at a rate of $27.63 per hour or more. Such employees may also be placed under the administrative or professional exemptions. [29 C.F.R. § 541.400(b)]

Computer systems analysts, computer programmers, software engineers, and other skilled computer workers may be considered exempt professionals under the FLSA, even though they are paid on an hourly basis. [29 C.F.R. § 541.400(a), (b)]

To fit under the computer professional exemption, an employee's primary duties must consist of the following:

1. The application of systems analysis techniques and procedures, including consulting with users, to determine hardware, software, or system functional specifications;

2. The design, development, documentation, analysis, creation, testing, or modification of computer systems or programs, including prototypes, based on and related to user or system design specifications;

3. The design, documentation, testing, creation, or modification of computer programs related to machine operating systems; or

4. A combination of these duties, the performance of which requires the same level of skills.

[29 C.F.R. § 541.400(b)]

The new regulations omit the requirement in the old regulations that an exempt computer professional's job requires the consistent exercise of judgment and discretion. [Former 29 C.F.R. § 541.3(b)] The new regulations also omit the requirement that an exempt computer professional's work requires the "theoretical and practical application of highly specialized knowledge in computer systems analysis, programming and software engineering." [Former 29 C.F.R. § 541.3(a)(4)] Whether these omissions will affect the scope of the exemption is unclear.

Q 4:45 What are some examples of exempt computer professionals?

Not everyone in an employer's information technology department will qualify for the computer professional exemption. A classic example of a computer employee who is not exempt under the computer exemption is a help desk employee. The Sixth Circuit Court of Appeals recently ruled that the help desk employees were not eligible for the exemption for computer professionals. The help desk employees took calls from employees who were having problems with their computers. The employee responded to these help desk inquiries to determine the nature of the problem, to "troubleshoot" it to determine how to proceed, and to repair the problem if possible. The employees also installed software on individual workstations and installed provided software patches.

The court pointed out that there was simply no evidence that a help desk employee "consults with users, to determine hardware, software, or system functional specifications." Instead, the employee "consults with users" for purposes of repair and user support, not to determine what "hardware, software, or system functional specifications" the power plant will employ, as a systems analyst might. Likewise, when a help desk employee does "testing," he or she is testing things to figure out what is wrong with a workstation, printer, or piece of cable so that it can be restored to working order. The employee is not doing the type of testing that is involved in creating a system, determining the desired settings for a system, or otherwise substantively affecting the system. Indeed, he or she is merely ensuring that the particular machine is working properly according to the specifications designed and tested by other employees. Maintaining the computer system within the predetermined parameters does not require "theoretical and practical application of highly-specialized knowledge in computer systems analysis, programming, and software engineering." [Martin v. Ind. Mich. Power Co., 381 F.3d 574 (6th Cir. 2004)]

The new regulation specifies that the computer employee exemption does not apply to employees engaged in the manufacture or repair of computer hardware and related equipment. Trainees or entry-level employees who lack the expertise and skill necessary to work independently and without supervision are not covered by the exemption. [29 C.F.R. § 541.401]

Computer personnel may also be considered exempt administrative employees if they meet the salary test and they have duties that meet either the executive or administrative duties test. In *Priest v. Ribelin*, the court found that a computer systems manager whose duties consisted of maintaining her employer's information system, serving as a liaison with the user group and system vendor, training staff members on using the system, troubleshooting, and performing audits was an exempt administrative employee. [Priest v. Ribelin Lowell & Co. Ins. Brokers, Inc., 24 Fed. Appx. 760, 2001 WL 1579998 (9th Cir. 2001)] Under the new regulations, systems administrators who meet all of the requirements of the administrative exemption may now be classified as exempt administrative employees. [29 C.F.R. § 541.201(b)]

It is relatively rare for computer personnel to be exempt learned professional employees, because possession of a directly-related bachelor's degree, such as a bachelor's degree in computer science, cannot be shown to be necessary for the performance of many computer-related jobs.

Examples of the Application of the Computer Exemption Under the Old Regulations:

A programmer was an exempt computer professional employee, both under the old and the new regulations, because the employee designed programs, did intensive research and analysis of data to develop the programs, participated in project planning, coded and tested programs, and performed on-going maintenance of a program. His duties also met the requirement under the old regulations that his primary duty entail the consistent exercise of discretion and judgment. [Bergquist v. Fidelity Info. Servs., Inc., 399 F. Supp. 2d 1320 (M.D. Fla. 2006), *aff'd per curiam*, 197 Fed. Appx. 813 (11th Cir. 2006)]

Where an employee served as a liaison with an end-user group, trained staff members on using the system, was responsible for troubleshooting and performing accuracy audits, recommended appropriate updates to hardware, software, technical, and floor plan configurations to ensure efficiency, and determined the most cost-effective methods of accomplishing such updates, the court determined the employee was exempt. [Priest v. Ribelin, Lowell & Co. Ins. Brokers, Inc., 24 Fed. Appx. 760, 761 (9th Cir. 2001)]

A consultant who determined how a company could best use computer hardware and software while providing on-site computer consulting services to end-user clients, working with the employer's clients to evaluate how they could best use old computer hardware and software by identifying the clients' needs and requirements for software inventory, was an exempt employee. [Hagadorn v. M.F. Smith & Assoc., Inc., 1999 WL 68403 (10th Cir. 1999)]

However, an employee whose duties included maintaining the computer workstation software, troubleshooting and repairing, preparing network documentation, installing hardware and cable, and moving computer workstations was not an exempt computer professional. The employee did not decide or recommend equipment replacement needs, write reports, or recommend purchases, and had no degree beyond high school. [Martin v. Ind. Mich. Power Co., 381 F.3d 574 (6th Cir. 2004)]

And, an employee who installed computer systems and provided customer training on the installed software was found to be nonexempt under the computer professional exemption by the Department of Labor. The employee in question provided training on specialized software, manipulated software settings and specifications to fit customer needs, debugged software, performed troubleshooting, converted dates, tested modems, and followed up on customer concerns. [Wage & Hour Opinion Letter, FLSA1999 (Aug. 1999)]

Public Sector Employees Who Are Executives, Administrators, or Professionals

Q 4:46   Are there any special rules applicable to public sector employees?

The new regulations seem to mirror the regulations that were released on August 19, 1992. The regulations provide an exception for public employers from certain provisions of the regulations that require that exempt employees be paid on a salary basis. This exception provides that no otherwise exempt public employee will be denied exempt status if the employee is paid according to a pay system established by statute, ordinance, regulation, or public policy under which the employee accrues personal leave and sick leave and that, absent the use of such accrued leave (because the leave has been exhausted or by the employee's choice), requires the public employee's pay to be reduced (leave without pay) for absences—for personal reasons or because of illness or injury—of less than one workday. [29 C.F.R. § 541.710]

In *McCloskey v. Triborough Bridge & Tunnel Authority* [903 F. Supp. 558 (S.D.N.Y. 1995)], the court held that the partial-day docking rule, as it applied to public sector employers before the 1992 amendments to the regulations which permitted partial-day docking for absences for personal reasons and due to illness, was invalid. Moreover, the provisions of the salary-basis test that provide that salary status is lost when deductions are made for absences caused by jury duty, attendance in court as a witness, or temporary military duty were also found to be invalid as applied to public sector employers. These provisions of the salary requirements were not changed in 1992 or in the new regulations.

Outside Salespersons

Q 4:47   What requirements did an outside sales employee have to meet to be exempt from the FLSA's minimum wage and overtime pay provisions under the old regulations?

Under the old regulations, the exemption from the FLSA's minimum wage and overtime pay provisions applied to any employee:

1. Whose primary duty was making sales or soliciting orders or contracts for services;

2. Who was customarily and regularly engaged away from the employer's place of business in making sales, or in taking orders or contracts for services or for the use of facilities; and

3. Whose responsibilities did not include spending more than 20 percent of his or her hours in a workweek on nonexempt work. Any work that was incidental to or done in conjunction with the employee's sales or solicitation did not count as nonexempt work.

[Former 29 C.F.R. § 541.5]

Courts have considered various factors as indicative of an employee's status as an exempt outside salesperson:

- Wage payments based largely on commission for drivers who also serve as sales employees [Hodgson v. Krispy Kreme Doughnut Co., 346 F. Supp. 1102 (M.D.N.C. 1972)]

- Autonomy in conducting daily business [Hodgson v. Krispy Kreme Doughnut Co., 346 F. Supp. 1102 (M.D.N.C. 1972)]

- A contract designating the employee as a salesperson, and establishing commissions as the basis for payment [Jewel Tea Co. v. Williams, 118 F.2d 202 (10th Cir. 1941)]

In the past, there had been legislative attempts to exempt some inside sales employees. In 1998, the House of Representatives passed a bill that would have granted exempt status to certain inside sales employees. Although the bill did not make it out of committee in the Senate, the House bill recognized that large numbers of inside sales professionals perform sales jobs from the office that, before the advent of computers and facsimile machines, required travel to the customer.

Q 4:48   Has the 20 percent nonexempt work limit been deleted under the outside sales exemption?

Yes. The primary change in the new regulations for outside sales employees is that the old 20 percent limit on nonexempt work performed by other nonexempt employees (which was almost impossible to understand and apply) has now been eliminated. The new regulations simply apply the "primary duty test" used with the other exemptions. The outside sales exemption continues to require that an employee's primary duty be to make sales or solicit orders or contracts for services and that the employee customarily and regularly work away from his or her employer's place of business in making sales or obtaining orders or contracts for services for which a consideration will be paid by the client or customer. [29 C.F.R. § 541.500] Also, there continues to be no salary, fee, or other compensation requirement for outside sales employees.

Q 4:49   How should sales calls from home be treated?

The new regulations continue to require that sales must be made away from the employer's place of business, such as at a customer's place of business or customer's home. The regulations state that a person whose primary duty is making sales via mail, telephone, or the internet does not qualify for the outside sales exemption and that any fixed site, whether home or office, used by a salesperson as a headquarters is considered the employee's place of business. Therefore, the employee making sales calls from home is not conducting sales away from his or her place of business as required under the outside sales exemption. [29 C.F.R. § 541.502]

Q 4:50   Can mortgage loan officers be exempt as outside salespersons?

Yes, if they otherwise meet the outside sales exemption requirements. The DOL has concluded that mortgage loan officers or loan originators who have as their principal duty the sale of mortgage loan packages can be exempt as outside salespersons if they are "customarily and regularly engaged in work away from the employer's place of business." [Wage & Hour Opinion Letter, FLSA2006-11 (Mar. 2006)]

General Concepts

Q 4:51   What about employees whose job duties may fall under more than one white-collar exemption?

Under the old regulations, an employee had to satisfy the requirements of the strictest of the two or more categories. The old regulations provide, by way of example, a situation in which an employee performs executive and outside sales work. In such a case the employee would have to meet the executive's salary requirements, and the amount of time spent on nonexempt work could not exceed 20 percent of the employee's own time (executive) or 20 percent of the hours worked in a workweek by nonexempt employees of the employer (outside sales), whichever is smaller. This means that an employee cannot spend more time on nonexempt work than is permissible under any of the categories making up the combination. In addition, any work that is exempt under one category does not count as nonexempt time for purposes of defeating an employee's exempt status under another category. [Former 29 C.F.R. § 541.600] The new regulations permit combination or tacking of white-collar exemptions when employees' duties do not all fit within one category (executive, administrative, professional, outside sales). Work that is exempt under one of the categories will not defeat the exemption under another category. [29 C.F.R. § 541.708]

Q 4:52 May an employer have different payment arrangements for employees within the same job classification?

Yes. Before the amendments, employers regularly classified some employees as exempt from overtime and some as eligible for overtime, and recent DOL opinion letters clarify that this is a permissible practice. For example, the DOL recently concluded that an employer was permitted to pay full-time nurse practitioners a salary but pay part-time and casual nurse practitioners on an hourly basis. The DOL said, "[H]aving some employees within the same job classification who perform the same duties but who are paid on a different (hourly) basis does not affect the status of any other exempt employees paid on a salary basis." [Wage & Hour Opinion Letter, FLSA2005-20 (Aug. 2005)]

Q 4:53 What does it mean to be paid on a salary basis?

Once an employee meets the duties test as an executive employee, the employee must also meet the salary test before being exempt from overtime as a white-collar employee. Employees who meet the administrative or professional duties test must be paid a salary or a fee. Employees who meet the computer professional duties test must be paid a salary or a fee, or at an hourly rate of not less than $27.63 per hour. The salary test involves both a minimum salary payment and a payment of that minimum level on a regular basis for all weeks where work is performed, without regard to quality or quantity of work performed. In other words, the employee must receive the same predetermined compensation in every week the employee performs any work.

The weekly salary requirement for an employee to qualify as exempt moved from $155 per week under the long test and $250 per week under short test to $455 per week under the new regulations. Any employee now earning less than $455 per week, with some limited exceptions for outside sales, must be paid overtime for hours worked in excess of 40 in any week.

Q 4:54 What does it mean to be a highly compensated employee?

The new regulations include an additional exemption for highly compensated employees who have as their primary duty any "identifiable" executive, administrative, or professional function. [29 C.F.R. § 541.601(a)] The exemption applies only to those employees earning more than $100,000 per year. Some particulars of the pay requirement are as follows:

1. Employees must earn at least $455 per week, paid on a salary or fee basis;
2. The $100,000 amount may include nondiscretionary bonuses, commissions, and other nondiscretionary compensation paid during the year;

3. The employer may make up shortfalls in employee earnings by making a final payment within one month after the end of the 52-week period;

4. The amount can be prorated for newly hired or terminated employees who do not work a full year; and

5. The amount does not include credits for board, insurance and retirement contributions, and fringe benefits.

The highly compensated employee must also customarily and regularly perform office or nonmanual work. The exemption expressly excludes nonmanagement, production-line and maintenance workers, and carpenters, mechanics, operating engineers, longshoremen, laborers, and other employees engaged in work involving repetitive operations with their hands, no matter how highly paid they might be. [29 C.F.R. § 541.601]

Q 4:55   What are the rules for payment "on a salary basis" to an exempt employee?

To be paid on a salary basis, an employee must receive the predetermined compensation each week without regard to the number of hours worked, and the amount of salary cannot be "subject to reduction because of variations in the quality or quantity of work." [29 C.F.R. § 541.602(a)]

An employee will not be considered to be paid on a "salary basis" if the employee's weekly compensation is reduced (in partial- or full-day increments) because of absences required by the employer, because of the business operations of the employer, or because no work is available. For example, an employee whose pay is reduced when he or she works fewer than the employer-required 37½ hours per week is not paid on a salary basis. [Wage & Hour Opinion Letter, FLSA2005-1 (Jan. 2005)]

The general rule for payment on a salary basis is that an employee gets his or her predetermined compensation in any week in which an employee performs any work. [29 C.F.R. § 541.602(a)] An employee need not be paid any salary for any week in which the employee performs no work.

Q 4:56   Are there any exceptions to the salary payment rules for exempt employees?

The new regulations set out seven exceptions to the requirement that an exempt employee be paid his or her full salary for any week in which he or she does any work:

1. An employer may deduct from an employee's salary for absences of one or more full days for personal reasons, other than sickness or disability.

2. An employer may deduct for one or more full days when an exempt employee is absent because of sickness or disability and the deduction is made pursuant to bona fide plan, policy, or practice of paying wage-replacement benefits.

3. When an exempt employee is absent from work for less than one week for jury duty, as a witness, or for military duty, the daily compensation received from the government may be offset against the employee's salary.

4. An employer may make partial-day deductions from salary for violation of a major safety rule.

5. An employer may make deductions for one or more full days as discipline for violation of workplace conduct rules. The comments to the new regulations indicate that disciplinary suspensions apply only to violations of workplace conduct rules, and not to performance or attendance rules.

6. An employer may make deductions for full days in the initial or last week of employment.

7. An employer may make partial-day deductions for reduced or intermittent leave under the FMLA.

[29 C.F.R. § 541.602(b)(1)–(7)]

Q 4:57   How do the regulations clarify employer pay practices?

The new regulations and subsequent DOL opinion letters outline a number of permissible and impermissible practices with respect to the meaning of "payment on a salary basis" to exempt employees.

- Taking deductions from exempt employees' accrued leave accounts is permissible for partial-day absences due to personal reasons or illness or injury. But the employer may not reduce an exempt employee's salary for partial-day absences when there is no accrued leave, unless the reduction is for one of the specific reasons for which partial-day deduction can be made, such as violation of a major safety rule or intermittent or reduced schedule leave under the FMLA (see Q 4:56). [Wage & Hour Opinion Letter, FLSA2005-7 (Jan. 2005)]

- It is permissible to require exempt employees to keep track of and record their hours. For example, a practice that requires employees to inform their supervisors about the reasons for their absences and to give advance notice if they plan to arrive for work after a specified hour does not violate the salary basis test. [Wage & Hour Opinion Letter, FLSA2005-5 (Jan. 2005)]

- It is permissible to require exempt employees to keep a particular schedule, work a specified number of hours, and make up time if the hours were not met so long as there is no deduction from the employee's predetermined salary if the employee does not work the required hours. [Wage & Hour Opinion Letter, FLSA2006-6 (Mar. 2006)]

- It is permissible to pay employees additional compensation, such as bonuses and additional pay based on hours worked beyond the normal workweek. For example, where employees are required to work 35 hours per week, but are allotted compensatory time off for any hours worked in addition to the 35-hour minimum, the salary test is not violated. [Wage & Hour Opinion Letter, FLSA2004-14 (Oct. 2004)]

Q 4:58   Which pay practices violate the salary test?

The regulations and comments also give examples of pay practices that will violate the salary test. These include:

- Deductions for partial-day absences due to attendance at parent-teacher conferences.
- Deductions of a full day's pay for weather-related closures if the employer closes the office. If an employee chooses not to come to work for a day due to inclement weather, a one-day deduction can be made. [Wage & Hour Opinion Letter, FLSA2005-41 (Oct. 2005)]
- Deduction of three days' pay for absences for jury duty.
- Deductions from the salaries of exempt employees for the loss, damage, or destruction of the employer's property, even if the employee agrees to the deduction in writing. [Wage & Hour Opinion Letter, FLSA2006-7 (Mar. 2006)]

Q 4:59   When do partial-day salary deductions invalidate employees' exempt status?

The DOL regulations indicate that, in almost all circumstances, an employer may not make a deduction from a salary for a partial-day absence. A regular practice of making improper deductions can jeopardize an employee's exempt status. The courts, however, have come to differing conclusions regarding how much regular deductions from salary for personal absences of less than one day affect employees' exempt status. In *Abshire v. County of Kern* [908 F.2d 483, 487 (9th Cir. 1990), *cert. denied*, 498 U.S. 1068 (1991)], the court found that such deductions are impermissible and render an employee nonexempt under the FLSA. The employees at issue in *Abshire* were fire department battalion chiefs. [*Id.* at 484] Although deductions were not actually made, the fact that the employees were "subject to" deductions rendered them nonexempt. Other federal courts have followed this rationale. [*See, e.g.*, Kinney v. District of Columbia, 994 F.2d 6 (D.C. Cir. 1993) (finding that firefighters were not exempt given the fact that they were subject to partial-day deductions); Martin v. Malcolm Pirnie, Inc., 949 F.2d 611, 615–17 (2d Cir. 1991), *cert. denied*, 506 U.S. 905 (1992) (company's policy permitting docking of professional employees' pay for partially missed workdays was enough to destroy the employees' exempt status and entitle them to overtime)]

The Supreme Court did not conclusively settle matters when it decided *Auer v. Robbins*. [519 U.S. 452 (1997)] The Court held that the "mere possibility" of an employer's making an improper deduction from a salaried employee's pay does not defeat the employee's exempt status. Rather, the Court relied on the interpretation given by the DOL that the salary-basis test is not met when the employer has an "actual practice" of making deductions from exempt employees' pay or when there is a "significant likelihood" of the employer making such deductions.

Employers that wish to protect the exempt status of white-collar employees should review their personnel policies and practices so that exempt employees will not suffer a deduction nor be subject to lost pay for less than a day's absence from work.

Q 4:60 Can an hourly rate be used to calculate an exempt employee's total compensation for the week?

An exempt employee's earnings may be computed on an hourly, daily, or shift basis without losing exempt status if the arrangement also includes a guarantee of at least a minimum of $455 per week regardless of the number of hours, days, or shifts worked. [29 C.F.R. § 541.604(b)] However, there must be a reasonable relationship between the number of hours, days, or shifts worked and the guaranteed amount versus the amount actually earned. The reasonable relationship test will be met if the weekly guarantee is roughly equivalent to the employee's usual earnings at the assigned hourly, daily, or shift rate for the employee's normal scheduled workweek. For example, if an employee who normally works four or five shifts each week at $150 per shift is guaranteed $500 for any week in which he or she performs any work, this arrangement does not violate the salary basis requirement. The example given in the regulations does not discuss the actual number of hours worked per shift or per week. [29 C.F.R. § 541.604(b)] The better and safer approach is to continue to use a salary. An employer can pay by the hour for hours of work beyond the normal or scheduled workweek, or allow the use of compensatory time for such hours of work. [29 C.F.R. § 541.604(a)]

Q 4:61 Is it permissible to pay more than the base salary?

The salary basis regulations also provide that the exemption is not lost if an exempt employee who is guaranteed at least $455 per week on a salary basis also receives additional compensation based on hours worked beyond the normal workweek. The additional compensation could be paid on any basis, such as a flat sum, a straight-time hourly amount, time and one-half, or on any other basis. An employer may also provide compensatory time off for the additional hours of work. [29 C.F.R. § 541.604(a); Wage & Hour Opinion Letter, FLSA2005-20 (Aug. 2005)]

Q 4:62 Can an exempt employee be paid extra compensation for performing nonexempt work?

Yes. If an employee has as his or her primary duty a duty of one of the white-collar exemptions, the employee may perform nonexempt work and receive extra compensation without jeopardizing the white-collar exemption. The caveat is that the employee's primary duty must be the performance of exempt work. [Wage & Hour Opinion Letter, FLSA2005-14 (Mar. 2005)] The converse, however, is not true. A nonexempt employee may not perform exempt work and be paid on a salary basis. If an hourly employee performs exempt work, the employee must receive overtime for the exempt work.

Q 4:63 Can an employer reduce an exempt employee's hours and salary during slow periods without forfeiting the exemption?

Yes. The new regulations provided that "[a]n employee will be considered to be paid on a 'salary basis' within the meaning of these regulations if the employee regularly receives each pay period on a weekly, or less frequent basis, a predetermined amount constituting all or part of the employee's compensation, which amount is not subject to reduction because of variations in the quality or quantity of the work performed." [29 C.F.R. § 541.602] The old regulations contained a similar provision. This raises the question: If an employee's salary is reduced when business is slow, is the "predetermined amount" requirement violated?

That issue was addressed in a recent federal court of appeals case involving Wal-Mart Stores. Full-time exempt pharmacists who worked for Wal-Mart claimed that their hours and salaries were reduced during the summer season—when the demand for prescriptions was relatively low. As a result, the pharmacists contended that they were no longer paid on a salary basis and were no longer exempt employees. The Tenth Circuit Court of Appeals ruled that Wal-Mart did not forfeit the exemption for the pharmacists when it reduced their hours and salary. The court said that a natural reading of "predetermined amount" is that it refers to the amount previously agreed on for the period for which the salary is to be paid, not an amount that had been agreed on for some earlier period. The regulations contain no explicit requirement that the salary set ("determined") for one pay period be continued to the next. According to the court, "an employer may prospectively reduce salary to accommodate the employer's business needs unless it is done with such frequency that the salary is the functional equivalent of an hourly wage." [*In re* Wal-Mart Stores, Inc., 395 F.3d 1177 (10th Cir. 2005)] The DOL has also issued opinion letters stating that the requirement that exempt employees receive at least a "predetermined amount" as salary does not preclude an employer from making occasional prospective salary reductions before the affected pay period in response to business needs. [*E.g.*, Wage & Hour Opinion Letter, FLSA1998-1905 (Feb. 1998)] Employers must appreciate that any change in employees' salaries raises some risk of losing exempt status and, at an ill-defined point, too-frequent changes will invalidate an employee's exempt status.

Q 4:64 How do leave-bank deductions affect employees' exempt status?

The new regulations and a number of Wage and Hour Division opinion letters have stated that employers may deduct paid leave from accumulated paid leave banks for absences of less than a day without destroying employees' exempt status. Many courts have followed this rationale. [*See* Barner v. City of Novato, 17 F.3d 1256, 1263 (9th Cir. 1994); McDonnell v. City of Omaha, 999 F.2d 293, 297–98 (8th Cir. 1993), *cert. denied,* 510 U.S. 1163 (1994); Lucero v. Regents of Univ. of Cal., No. C-91-3999 MHP, 1993 U.S. Dist. LEXIS 12208, at *30 (N.D. Cal. Aug. 23, 1993); Wage & Hour Opinion Letter, FLSA1997-2039 (July 1997)]

Employers that make deductions from exempt employees' leave banks by the hour should announce specific policies for dealing with employees who have no leave-bank or negative leave-bank balances. The policy should specify that although leave may be reduced in hourly amounts, the employee's actual pay will not be reduced for anything less than a full day's leave. Additionally, employers should be cautious when allowing employees to cash out their unused leave because such policies may contravene the salary-basis test if they permit deductions by the hour.

Q 4:65   What are the new disciplinary salary-docking options?

One of the areas in which the new regulations are more employer-friendly is deductions from salaries for disciplinary purposes.. However, employers must be careful to adopt and enforce "written" standards of conduct because only violation of written rules of general applicability can result in partial-week unpaid suspensions of exempt employees. [29 C.F.R. § 541.602(b)(5)] Under the new rules, employers will be able to dock the salary of an exempt employee for less than an entire workweek, as long as the deduction is in full-day increments, for inappropriate or illegal conduct. The DOL, in its preamble, stated the salary deductions should not be used for performance or attendance problems, but rather for "serious workplace misconduct." The DOL offered the following examples that would warrant docking the salary of an exempt employee:

1. Sexual harassment;
2. Violence;
3. Drug or alcohol violations; or
4. Violations of state or federal laws.

These rules are in addition to the pre-existing pay docking options for an employee in violation of a safety rule of major significance (which was almost never used). [29 C.F.R. § 541.602(b)(4)]

While stating that an employer's written policy need not include an exhaustive list of specific violations or a definitive declaration of when a suspension will be imposed, the written policy should be sufficient to put employees on notice that they could be subject to an unpaid disciplinary suspension. Additionally, the employer's policy must be applicable to all employees. A sexual harassment policy that is distributed to all employees and warns that disciplinary action up to and including suspension will result for violation of the employer's sexual harassment rules would be sufficient. It is recommended that employers review their policy statements and include references to the possibility of "suspension and disciplinary wage or salary deductions." The DOL stated that conduct that occurs off the work site should not preclude an employer from imposing a disciplinary suspension (of less than whole workweeks) as long as the employer has a bona fide work place conduct rule that covers such offsite conduct.

The Wage and Hour Division has found that a full workweek of disciplinary suspension does not violate an employee's exempt status because a salaried, white-collar employee need not be paid in any workweek in which the employee did not perform any work. [Wage & Hour Opinion Letter, FLSA1996-2006 (Dec. 1996)] Thus, an employer that is uncertain as to whether a particular disciplinary deduction is permissible may discipline the employee by suspension for a full workweek, regardless of the reason.

An employer can make disciplinary deductions for any reason from the pay of teachers, lawyers, and doctors because such employees are specifically excluded from the salary test. [Wage & Hour Opinion Letter, FLSA2001-4 (Feb. 2001)]

Q 4:66   What role do scheduling and timekeeping play in invalidating employees' exempt status?

In 1993, the Wage and Hour Division found that personnel policies that require employees to work specific hours, record the number of hours worked, and obtain permission before taking time off from work did not violate the salary-basis test. Similarly, requiring employees to work a 45-hour week and to make up lost hours is not a violation so long as the employee's salary is not reduced. [Wage & Hour Opinion Letter, FLSA2006-6 (Mar. 2006); Wage & Hour Opinion Letter, FLSA1993 (July 1993)]

Q 4:67   Is the "window of correction" still available for improper salary deduction?

Yes. The effect of improper salary deductions has been the subject of considerable litigation in recent years, with the courts of appeal going in different directions regarding the opportunity to correct deficient salary payments pursuant to the "window of correction." The new regulations state that an actual practice of making improper salary deductions results in loss of exempt status only:

1. During the time period the deductions were made;
2. For employees in the same job classification; and
3. For employees working for the same manager responsible for the improper deduction.

[29 C.F.R. § 541.603(b)]

Isolated or inadvertent improper deductions will not result in loss of exempt status if the employer reimburses the employee. [29 C.F.R. § 541.603(c)]

The "window of correction," now called the "safe harbor" provision, provides that exempt status will not be lost if the employer:

1. Clearly communicates a policy (it should be in writing) prohibiting improper salary deductions that includes a complaint mechanism;

2. Reimburses employees promptly when a salary payment deficiency is raised; and

3. Makes a good faith commitment to comply in the future.

The safe harbor can be lost if the employer willfully violates the policy by continuing to make improper deductions after receiving an employee complaint. [29 C.F.R. § 541.603(d)]

Under the old "window of correction," reimbursements could be made for improper deductions for "reasons other than lack of work." The old "window of correction" had been the subject of varying interpretations, most of which were quite narrow. One court had required that the impermissible deduction be inadvertent *and* done for reasons other than lack of work, although the language of the regulation reads otherwise. [Dole v. Malcolm Pirnie, Inc., 758 F. Supp. 899, 906–08 (S.D.N.Y. 1991), *rev'd sub nom.* Martin v. Malcolm Pirnie, Inc., 949 F.2d 611 (2d Cir. 1991)] In *Klem v. County of Santa Clara* [208 F.3d 1085 (9th Cir. 2000)], the court explained that the window of correction was not available to an employer that could not demonstrate an objective intention to pay its employees on a salary basis, such as where the employer had a practice and policy of noncompliance with the regulations relating to salary basis and made impermissible deductions from salary. However, a number of other courts relied on the plain language of the regulations and allowed reimbursements of improper salary deductions to be made even where the deductions were not inadvertent and were made based on standardized policies or procedures of the employer. Consider *Davis v. City of Hollywood* [120 F.3d 1178 (11th Cir. 1997)] and *Moore v. Hannon Food Service, Inc.* [317 F.3d 489 (5th Cir. 2003)], where reimbursement was allowed five days before trial.

Q 4:68 Has the DOL provided any guidance on employee use of manuals?

Yes. The use of manuals, lists, and tables arguably can reduce the independent judgment and discretion which is required for an employee to be an exempt administrative or professional employee. The new regulations conclude, however, that "the use of manuals, guidelines, or other established procedures containing or relating to highly technical, scientific, legal, financial, or other similarly complex matters that can be understood or interpreted only by those with advanced or specialized knowledge or skills does not preclude exemption." Thus, a certified public accountant would not lose the learned professional exemption simply because he or she is expected to follow the industries' Generally Accepted Accounting Principles. Going further, though, the DOL explained that the exemptions are not available for employees who simply apply well-established techniques or procedures described in manuals or other sources within closely prescribed limits to describe the correct response to an inquiry or set of circumstances. [29 C.F.R. § 541.704]

Q 4:69   Will the solicitor's office assist plaintiffs and their lawyers?

To address the concerns of unions and plaintiff-side critics, the Bush administration's DOL solicitor's office has recently announced establishment of the "Overtime Security *Amicus* Program" and is inviting attorneys who file lawsuits on behalf of workers under the new exemption rules to contact the solicitor's office, which will then consider whether to file a friend of the court brief in order for the DOL to articulate its position regarding the new regulations. The Solicitor of Labor stated that there had been "[a]n unprecedented misinformation campaign against the new rules [which] is creating confusion which could compromise the stronger worker protections in the new rules. We are taking extra precautions to [e]nsure that the intent of the new rules—to provide stronger, clearer overtime protections for workers—is reflected in the courts." [www.dol.gov/sol]

Chapter 5

Exemptions from Minimum Wage, Overtime Pay, Child Labor, and Recordkeeping Obligations

This chapter discusses exemptions from the minimum wage, overtime, child labor, and recordkeeping requirements of the Fair Labor Standards Act (FLSA) other than the white-collar exemptions discussed in Chapter 4.

Q 5:1 How can employees be *exempt* under the Fair Labor Standards Act (FLSA)?

Employees will be considered exempt if they are excluded from one or more of the FLSA's requirements, such as minimum wage or overtime. Chapter 4 examined the most common usage of "exempt," the white-collar exemptions. Employees may be completely exempt (see Qs 5:3–5:11) or partially exempt (see Qs 5:12–5:43) from the minimum wage, equal pay, and overtime requirements. There also are certain exemptions from the child labor provisions (see Q 5:44).

Q 5:2 What if an employee performs both exempt and nonexempt work?

Federal regulations apply workweek by workweek. Thus, employees may be exempt from FLSA requirements for one workweek but not for another. That is, an employee is exempt from the FLSA during the workweek in which he or she performs exempt work, and it is irrelevant that the employee may otherwise perform nonexempt work in all other workweeks. [29 C.F.R. §§ 780.10, 780.11]

If an employee performs both exempt and nonexempt work in the same week, the employee is not exempt during that workweek. [29 C.F.R. §§ 780.11, 780.602, 780.723, 784.115, 793.21] There is also a primary-duty provision under the white-collar exemption.

Additionally, an employee's exempt status is not lost because the employee performs work outside the scope of the FLSA. Generally, the FLSA applies to businesses: (1) whose employees are engaged in interstate commerce, produce goods for interstate commerce, or handle, sell, or work on materials moved in or produced for interstate commerce; and (2) have annual gross sales not less than $500,000. Individual employees of firms with less than $500,000 in gross revenues still may be covered in any workweek in which the employees are engaged in interstate commerce, production of goods for interstate commerce, or an activity that is closely related or directly essential to the production of such goods. If an employee engages in any work that is covered by the FLSA, that employee will be considered covered by the FLSA for the whole workweek. [29 C.F.R. § 776.3]

Completely Exempt Employees

Q 5:3   Which groups of employees are completely exempt from the FLSA's minimum wage, equal pay, and overtime requirements?

Certain classes of employees are completely exempt from the FLSA's minimum wage, equal pay, and overtime requirements. These classes of employees are:

1. Agricultural employees (see Q 5:4);
2. Seasonal amusement or recreational establishment employees (see Q 5:5);
3. Casual babysitters (see Q 5:6);
4. Domestic companions (see Q 5:7);
5. Seamen (see Q 5:8);
6. Switchboard operators (see Q 5:9);
7. Fishing industry employees, including employees engaged in offshore seafood processing (see Q 5:10); and
8. Employees working in a foreign country (see Q 5:11).

Q 5:4   Which agricultural employees are exempt from the FLSA's minimum wage, equal pay, and overtime requirements?

The minimum wage and equal pay requirements of the FLSA do not apply to employees in agricultural production if their employer did not employ more than 500 man-days of agricultural labor during any calendar quarter of the preceding calendar year. [29 U.S.C. § 213(a)(6)(A)] All agricultural employees—including those who are not exempt from the minimum wage and equal pay requirements—are exempt from the overtime pay requirements of the FLSA. [29 U.S.C. § 213(b)(12)] *Man-day* means "any day during which an employee performs any agricultural labor for not less than one hour." [29 U.S.C. § 203(u)]

The FLSA explains that "[a]griculture includes farming in all its branches and among other things includes the cultivation and tillage of the soil, dairying, the production, cultivation, growing, and harvesting of any agricultural and horticultural commodities. . .the raising of livestock, bees, fur-bearing animals, or poultry, and any practices (including any forestry or lumbering operations) performed by a farmer or on a farm as an incident to or in conjunction with such farming operations, including preparation for market, delivery to storage or to market, or to carriers for transportation to market." [29 U.S.C. § 203(f)] Given this definition, the Tenth Circuit has ruled that a worker who packages chicken feather pelts on a farm where the chickens are raised is an agricultural worker exempt from overtime. [Pacheco v. Whiting Farms, Inc., 365 F.3d 1199 (10th Cir. 2004)] The court explained that Whiting Farms bred and raised chickens for the feathers, which were used in making fishing lures. After the chicken pelts were skinned and trimmed, they were brought to the packaging department and were packaged on the farm. The packagers were responsible for stamping the backs of the pelts designating their grade, making a record of the pelts, and then delivering the pelts either to storage or to carriers for transportation to the market to fill an order. The court held that this packaging process constitutes secondary farming as if it was performed on the farm and was incident to or in conjunction with the farming operations. Accordingly, the packaging employees were exempt from overtime requirements.

The Fourth Circuit Court of Appeals recently ruled that the growing of Christmas trees qualifies for the agricultural exemption. The DOL had argued that, like forestry and lumbering, Christmas tree operations qualify for the exemption only if they are incident to or in conjunction with farming operations. The Christmas tree growers, on the other hand, contended that the raising of Christmas trees involves the "cultivation of an agricultural or horticultural commodity." Because Christmas trees are not processed into pulp or harvested as timber, the Fourth Circuit concluded that Christmas tree farming is not like forestry or lumbering and that the cultivation, growing, and harvesting of Christmas trees is agriculture. [Department of Labor v. North Carolina Growers Ass'n, Inc., 377 F.3d 345 (4th Cir. 2004)]

A person employed on a family farm is exempt from the FLSA's minimum wage, equal pay, and overtime provisions if he or she is the parent, spouse, or child of the employer or is otherwise a member of the employer's immediate family. Even if the employer uses more than 500 man-days of labor in a calendar quarter, the immediate family members remain exempt. Immediate family members include stepchildren, foster children, stepparents, and foster parents in addition to parents, spouses, and children. [29 U.S.C. § 213(a)(6)(B); 29 C.F.R. §§ 780.307, 780.308]

Commuting hand-harvest laborers are exempt from the FLSA's minimum wage, equal pay, and overtime provisions if they are employed on a piece-rate basis in a business that typically pays on a piece-rate basis, commute daily from a permanent residence to the farm where they are employed, and have been employed in agriculture for less than 13 weeks during the preceding calendar year. [29 U.S.C. § 213(a)(6)(C)]

Minors age 16 and under employed as hand harvesters are exempt from the FLSA's minimum wage, equal pay, and overtime provisions if they are employed on a piece-rate basis in an operation that typically pays on a piece-rate basis, are employed on the same farm as their parent or person standing in the place of their parent, and are paid at the same rate as persons over age 16 on the same farm. This provision is aimed at minors who are children of migrant workers but also may apply to minors who work for short durations without returning daily to their homes located on farms beyond commuting distance. [29 U.S.C. § 213(a)(6)(D); 29 C.F.R. § 780.320]

Q 5:5   Which seasonal amusement or recreational establishment employees are exempt from the FLSA's minimum wage, equal pay, and overtime requirements?

FLSA Section 213(a)(3) completely exempts any employee of an amusement or recreational establishment from the FLSA's minimum wage, equal pay, and overtime provisions if: (1) the establishment does not operate for more than seven months in any calendar year; or (2) during the preceding calendar year, its average receipts for any six months of the year were not more than one-third of its average receipts for the other six months. To meet the second part of the test at least 75 percent of the income must be received within six months, although the months need not be consecutive. [*See* Adams v. Detroit Tigers, Inc., 961 F. Supp. 176 (E.D. Mich. 1997)]

Businesses in this category are concession operators at amusement parks, beaches, and golf courses; swimming pools; summer camps; and ice-skating rinks. The business must be seasonal or recreational to fall within this exemption; the type of work performed by an employee is irrelevant.

Courts look at the work performed at distinct locations, as opposed to a company's entire operation, when evaluating this exemption. For example, in *Brennan v. Yellowstone Park Lines, Inc.* [478 F.2d 285 (10th Cir.), *cert. denied*, 414 U.S. 909 (1973)], the heterogeneous nature of distances between facilities and the different tourist facilities offered by the company did not lend themselves to a finding that Yellowstone Park Company, the owner and operator of the tourist facilities, was a single integrated unit subject to the recreational establishment exemption. The exemption would apply to employees at each individual tourist establishment; it would not apply to employees in the central office who perform functions serving several, or all, of the company's establishments at various locations in the national park.

The principal activity of the establishment must be amusement or recreational in nature for the exemption to apply. Specific establishments or employees found to be within the exemption include the following:

- A souvenir stand at a Civil War battlefield. [Wage & Hour Opinion Letter, FLSA1971-1170 (Apr. 1971)]

- Food and souvenir vendors employed by an amusement park, baseball park, racetrack, or state or county fair. [Wage & Hour Opinion Letter, FLSA1967-623 (June 1967)]

- An indoor year-round swimming pool operated by a town's park and recreation board if it meets the receipts test. The opinion indicated, however, that if public tax funds rather than admission charges were used to operate the pool, the exemption would not apply. The decision did not indicate whether a combination of funding from tax monies and admissions could fulfill the exemption if the receipts test was met. [Wage & Hour Opinion Letter, FLSA1974-1340 (Sept. 1974)]

- Lifeguards employed by a city to patrol public beaches, since the operation of a public beach is an amusement or recreational facility, even though the lifeguards performed off-season work such as maintenance and repairs. [Wage & Hour Opinion Letter, FLSA1975-1361 (Jan. 1975)]

- Summer camps operated for a maximum of 12 weeks in the summer. [Wage & Hour Opinion Letter, FLSA1968-903 (June 1968)]

The minimum wage, equal pay, and overtime provisions expressly apply to employees of private enterprises located in national parks, in national forests, or on land in the National Wildlife Refuge System, but the minimum wage and equal pay provisions do not apply to employers providing skiing and directly related services in these areas. [29 U.S.C. § 213(a)(3)] Employees of private enterprises providing services or facilities in national parks, national forests, or on land in the National Wildlife Refuge System under a contract with the Secretary of Interior or Secretary of Agriculture, including employees of employers providing skiing and related services, are partially exempted from overtime by a separate provision: they are exempted from overtime compensation except for hours worked in excess of 56 hours in any workweek, which must be paid at a rate of one and one-half times their regular rate of pay. [29 U.S.C. § 213(b)(29)]

Country or town clubs that are not open to the general public or whose membership fees are so high as to exclude the public do not qualify for the exemption; however, clubs that charge a nominal fee may qualify for the exemption. [Wage & Hour Opinion Letter, FLSA1967-600 (May 1967); Wage & Hour Opinion Letter, FLSA1975-1364 (May 1975)]

Q 5:6 Which casual babysitters are exempt from the FLSA's minimum wage, equal pay, and overtime requirements?

Anyone employed as a babysitter on a casual basis is exempt from the FLSA's minimum wage, equal pay, and overtime requirements. [29 U.S.C. § 213(a)(15)] Under federal regulations, *casual* means less than 20 hours per week, although a sitter may work more than 20 hours per week if the extra hours are for irregular or intermittent periods. [29 C.F.R. § 552.104(b), (d)] Anyone employed by an agency or employer other than the family using the babysitter's services is not considered exempt, because such employment is deemed to constitute a vocation rather than a casual activity. [29 C.F.R. § 552.109(b)]

Q 5:7 Which domestic companions are exempt from the FLSA's minimum wage, equal pay, and overtime requirements?

Workers employed to provide companionship services to infirm or aged persons are presently exempt from the FLSA's minimum wage, equal pay, and overtime provisions. Unlike the provisions on babysitters, the current provision on domestic companions contains no requirement that companions be employed on a casual basis to be exempt. However, the exemption does not apply to anyone who does not work in a private home. [29 U.S.C. § 213(a)(15); 29 C.F.R. § 552.109(a)]

Regulations define *companionship services* as services providing fellowship, care, and protection for a person who, because of age or physical or mental infirmity, cannot care for his or her own needs. Work that can and/or should be done only by a trained professional, such as a registered or practical nurse, does not fit within the meaning of companionship services. Time may be spent on household work related to the individual, such as taking care of that individual's laundry, but only a limited amount of time (20 percent of working time) may be dedicated to general household work before the exemption is lost. [29 C.F.R. § 552.6]

The exemption applies only to domestic companionship services provided in a private home. A private home is a fixed place or abode of a person or family. A residence used by a business enterprise for the purpose of supplying domestic/companionship services to the public is not a private home. [Wage & Hour Opinion Letter, FLSA1999-2134 (Apr. 1999)] A fact-specific case-by-case analysis will be applied to determine whether domestic/companionship services are provided in a private home. [Johnston v. Volunteers of Am., Inc., 213 F.3d 559, 565 (10th Cir.), *cert. denied*, 531 U.S. 1072 (2000)]

There is currently a dispute about whether the exemption applies to companions employed by third parties. DOL regulations specifically provide that the exemption covers companions employed by "an employer or agency other than the family using the companion's services." [29 C.F.R. § 552.109(a)] However, the Second Circuit Court of Appeals recently struck down these regulations in *Coke v. Long Island Care at Home, Ltd.* [376 F.3d 118 (2d Cir. 2004)].

The appeals court pointed to the legislative history of the FLSA coverage of domestic workers. Prior to 1974, domestic workers were exempt from the FLSA. However, this exemption did not apply to workers who were employed by third parties. In 1974, Congress amended the FLSA to broaden its coverage to include a new set of workers: employees performing "domestic services." However, this expanded coverage did not apply to "any employee employed on a casual basis in domestic service employment to provide babysitting services or any employee employed in domestic service employment to provide companionship services for individuals who (because of age or infirmity) are unable to care for themselves (as such terms are defined and delimited by regulations of the

Secretary of Labor)." [29 U.S.C. § 213(a)(15)] Subsequently, the DOL issued its regulations providing that the exclusion of companions from FLSA coverage applied both to companions employed by the families receiving the services and to companions employed by third parties. The Second Circuit could find no reason why a Congressional expansion of FLSA coverage could be used by the DOL to exclude from coverage companions who had previously been covered by the FLSA—those employed by third parties. The court refused to enforce the DOL regulations excluding companions employed by third parties from FLSA coverage. [Coke v. Long Island Care at Home, Ltd., 376 F.3d 118 (2d Cir. 2004)]

After the Court's decision in *Coke v. Long Island Care at Home*, the DOL issued an advisory memorandum justifying its interpretation of the application of the exemption to companions employed by the third parties. The DOL said it would continue to apply the exemption to companions employed by third parties, even in light of the Second Circuit's decision. [Wage & Hour Advisory Memorandum, FLSA2005-1 (Dec. 2005)] The parties to the *Long Island Care at Home* matter also appealed the case to the United States Supreme Court. The Court told the Second Circuit to reconsider its opinion in light of the DOL's advisory memorandum. [Long Island Care at Home, Ltd. v. Coke, 126 S. Ct. 1189 (2006)] On remand, the Second Circuit affirmed its earlier interpretation [462 F.3d 48 (2d Cir. 2006). The Supreme Court again reviewed the decision by the Second Circuit and reversed the circuit's decision and remanded for further proceedings. [127 S. Ct. 2339 (U.S. 2007)] The Supreme Court held that the DOL's regulation was valid and binding.

Q 5:8   Which seamen are exempt from the FLSA's minimum wage, equal pay, and overtime requirements?

Seamen working on foreign ships are exempt from the minimum wage, equal pay, and overtime provisions of the FLSA; seamen working on American ships are exempt from the overtime provisions only. [29 U.S.C. § 213(a)(12), (b)(6); 29 C.F.R. §§ 783.24–783.27]

Federal regulations define a *seaman* as someone who performs a service primarily to aid in the operation of a vessel as a means of transportation. Being employed on a vessel on navigable waters does not necessarily make a person a seaman, and the exemption is lost if the employee spends more than 20 percent of his or her time on work unrelated to duties as a seaman for a given workweek. [29 C.F.R. §§ 783.31, 783.33–783.37]

Employers must also be aware of more stringent state requirements, which are likely not preempted by the FLSA. In *Pacific Merchant Shipping Ass'n v. Aubry* [918 F.2d 1409 (9th Cir.), *cert. denied*, 504 U.S. 979 (1992)], the Ninth Circuit held that California's overtime provisions, which are more stringent than the FLSA's, apply to seamen who are exempt under the FLSA, because stricter state laws supersede the FLSA and because states may pass laws regulating maritime matters as long as the state laws do not conflict with federal law.

Q 5:9   Which switchboard operators are exempt from the FLSA's minimum wage, equal pay, and overtime requirements?

Switchboard operators of independently owned telephone companies with fewer than 750 stations, which are receiving and transmitting instruments served by telephone exchanges, are exempt from the FLSA's minimum wage, equal pay, and overtime requirements. [29 U.S.C. § 213(a)(10); *see* Southern Bell Tel. & Tel. Co. v. Davis, 202 S.W.2d 753, 754 (Ky. 1947) (defining *station* as telephone instrument)]

Q 5:10   Which fishing industry employees are exempt from the FLSA's minimum wage, equal pay, and overtime requirements?

Employees who are engaged in catching, taking, propagating, harvesting, cultivating, or farming any kind of fish, shellfish, crustaceans, sponges, sea-weeds, or aquatic animal or vegetable are exempt from the FLSA's minimum wage, equal pay, and overtime pay provisions, as are employees involved in processing, canning, or packing marine products when these tasks are done at sea in conjunction with fishing operations. [29 U.S.C. § 213(a)(5); 29 C.F.R. § 784.102]

Q 5:11   Which employees working in a foreign country are exempt from the FLSA's minimum wage, equal pay, and overtime requirements?

Anyone employed in a foreign country is exempt not only from the FLSA's minimum wage, equal pay, and overtime exemptions but also from the FLSA's recordkeeping provisions. [29 U.S.C. § 213(f)]

Partially Exempt Employees

Q 5:12   Can an employee be partially exempt from the FLSA?

Yes. There are two major exemptions: exemptions from the minimum wage requirements and exemptions from the overtime requirements. The following employees are exempt from the FLSA's minimum wage provisions:

- Learners (see Q 5:13)
- Apprentices (see Q 5:13)
- Workers with disabilities (see Q 5:14)
- Students in retail or service establishments (see Q 5:15)
- Students in agriculture (see Q 5:15)
- Students in institutions of higher learning (see Q 5:15)
- Students working for schools (see Q 5:15)
- Homeworkers in Puerto Rico and the Virgin Islands

- Employees in American Samoa
- Messengers

[29 U.S.C. §§ 206(a)(2), (3), 214]

Q 5:13   What is a *learner,* and what is an *apprentice?*

Learner generally is defined as "a worker who is being trained for an occupation not customarily recognized as an apprenticeship trade and for which skill, dexterity, and judgment must be learned." The worker produces little or nothing of value when initially employed. An employee can no longer be considered a learner once he or she has acquired 240 hours of training during the past three years. [29 C.F.R. § 520.201(b)]

The regulations define *apprentice* as a worker who is at least 16 years old, or older if state law sets a higher age, and "is employed to learn a skilled trade through a registered apprenticeship program." [29 C.F.R. § 520.201(d)]

An apprentice is different from a learner in that an apprentice is bound by a formal legal contract primarily to learn a skilled art or trade, usually over a time period of long duration. The master is obligated to instruct the apprentice and stands in the place of a parent or teacher. [Am. Jur. 2d *Employment Relationship* § 49]

Q 5:14   How are disabled workers exempt from the FLSA's minimum wage provisions?

The FLSA was amended in 1986 to allow for payment of disabled workers at a subminimum wage. The regulations require that such workers be paid at a rate based on comparative productivity, which should be proportional to the rate paid to nondisabled workers performing the same work in the same area. [29 C.F.R. § 525.1]

The Wage and Hour Division must issue special certificates allowing sheltered workshops to pay subminimum wages. Certificates are issued only when an individual's earning capacity is impaired to the extent that person is unable to earn the minimum wage. [29 U.S.C. § 214(c); 29 C.F.R. § 525.5]

The Wage and Hour Division considers the following factors before allowing disabled workers to receive subminimum wage:

- The nature and extent of the individual's disability as it relates to the individual's productivity;
- The prevailing wages of experienced nondisabled employees performing similar work in the vicinity;
- The productivity of the disabled workers versus productivity of the nondisabled workers; and
- Wage rates to be paid to workers with disabilities for work comparable to work performed by experienced nondisabled workers.

[29 C.F.R. § 525.9(a)]

Employers are required to submit to review of employees' wage rates at least every six months and must annually adjust wages paid to disabled workers to reflect changes in local wages being paid to nondisabled workers. [29 C.F.R. § 525.9(b)] Additionally, employers must be prepared to have their records inspected by the Wage and Hour Division, and they must maintain the following:

- Verification of the workers' disability;
- Evidence of the productivity of each disabled worker;
- Prevailing wages paid for nondisabled workers performing the same type of work in the vicinity as the work performed by the workers under the certificate;
- Production standards for nondisabled workers for each job being performed by workers with disabilities; and
- All records required under 29 C.F.R. Part 516, except for provisions relating to homeworker handbooks

[29 C.F.R. § 525.16]

Q 5:15   What rules apply to students exempt from the FLSA's minimum wage provisions?

The following rules apply to the employment of students at subminimum wages:

1. Full-time students of colleges, universities, junior colleges, and other postsecondary level institutions may be paid no less than 85 percent of the federal minimum wage for work performed in school. [29 U.S.C. § 214(b)(3); 29 C.F.R. §§ 519.12, 519.15]

2. Full-time students age 14 or older may be employed in retail or service businesses or in agriculture at 85 percent of the minimum wage, provided the employer obtains a certificate and employs no more than six full-time students, and provided further employment of the students does not curtail employment opportunities for other employees. The employer must file an application for a certificate to employ full-time students, and the certificate will not be issued for more than one year. [29 U.S.C. § 214(b); 29 C.F.R. §§ 519.1–519.3, 519.5–519.6]

Employment of students under all of these provisions requires obtaining certificates from the Wage and Hour Division.

Postsecondary institutions employing students at subminimum wages must comply with certain recordkeeping requirements, including maintaining for three years copies of student certificates. [29 C.F.R. § 519.17]

For employers to receive certificates permitting employment of students in retail, service, or agricultural occupations, all of the following conditions must be met:

1. Full-time students are available for employment at subminimum wage rates and granting the certificate is necessary to prevent curtailment of employment opportunities.

2. Employment of more than six full-time students by an employer will not create a substantial probability of reducing full-time employment opportunities for persons other than those employed under certificates.

3. There is no strike or lockout presently in effect at the farm or business.

4. The information on the application for a certificate is accurate and based on available records.

5. The farm or business requesting a certificate authorizing student employment for more than 10 percent of the total hours of all employees during any month without records of hours worked for students will be required to show on its application the practice of similar establishments.

6. The employer has no outstanding violations of any prior student certificate and has not seriously violated the FLSA, including the hazardous occupation provisions of the regulations.

7. The proposed subminimum wage must be at least 85 percent of the statutory minimum wage.

8. Issuance of a certificate will not result in reduction of the wage rate paid to current employees, including current student-employees.

[29 C.F.R. §§ 519.5, 519.15]

Q 5:16   Are there any exemptions to the FLSA's minimum wage requirement for employing youths that do not require a special permit from the DOL?

Yes. The FLSA allows employers to pay employees under twenty (20) years old a lower wage of $4.25 per hour for ninety (90) consecutive calendar days (not work days) after they are first employed. [29 U.S.C § 206(g)] Note that this rate is not increased by the Fair Minimum Wage Act of 2007, which increased the regular minimum wage rate.

Q 5:17   Who may be paid the youth minimum wage?

Only employees under twenty (20) years of age and only for the first ninety (90) consecutive calendar days after initial employment or until the employee reaches the age of twenty (20), whichever occurs first.

Q 5:18   Which employers are eligible to use the youth minimum wage?

Unless prohibited by state or local law, all employers covered by the FLSA may pay eligible employees the youth minimum wage.

Q 5:19   If a state or local law requires payment of a minimum wage greater than $4.25 per hour and does not make an exception for employees under age twenty (20), may an employer pay an employee under twenty (20) the youth minimum wage?

No. If a state or local law requires payment of a minimum wage greater than $4.25 per hour and does not make an exception for employees under age twenty (20), an employer may not take advantage of the federal youth minimum wage.

Q 5:20   Are employers required to provide special training to employees paid the youth minimum wage?

No. Employers are not required to provide any special training to employees paid the youth minimum wage. Additionally, an employer may not terminate the employment of an employee paid at the youth minimum wage simply because the ninety (90) day calendar period has passed or the employee turned twenty (20).

Q 5:21   Can an employer terminate the employment of an employee to hire someone to be paid the youth minimum wage?

No. The FLSA specifically forbids an employer from terminating employees to hire an employee to be paid at the youth minimum wage.

Q 5:22   Are any employees exempt from the FLSA's overtime pay requirements?

Yes. The following employees, who still must be paid the applicable federal or state minimum wage, may be entirely exempt from the FLSA's overtime provisions (but still subject to the FLSA's minimum wage and other provisions):

- Certain employees of radio and television stations in small communities
- Taxicab drivers
- Certain drivers and helpers making local deliveries compensated on a delivery payment plan [Qs 5:23–5:31]
- Employees of motor carriers and motor private carriers in interstate commerce (employees of local mass transit systems may be exempt if the interstate commerce requirement can be fulfilled) [Qs 5:23–5:31]
- Employees of railroads subject to Part I of the Interstate Commerce Act
- Employees of air carriers subject to Title II of the Railway Labor Act
- Salespersons, parts persons, and mechanics of auto, truck, or farm implement dealers and salespersons for trailer, boat, or aircraft dealers [Qs 5:32–5:33]
- Seamen on American vessels [Q 5:8]

- Agricultural employees and certain employees closely connected to the agricultural field; in this context, agriculture includes "farming in all its branches" such as cultivation and tillage of the soil; dairying; the production, cultivation, growing, and harvesting of agricultural and horticultural commodities; the raising of livestock, bees, furbearing animals and poultry; and any practice performed by a farmer or on a farm as an incident to or in conjunction with farming operations, such as the preparation of agricultural or horticultural commodities for market, the delivery of those commodities or products for transportation to market, and the operation and maintenance of ditches, canals, reservoirs, or waterways used for supply and storage of water for agricultural purposes

- Household domestics, such as service employees, who reside in the household

- House parents of nonprofit educational institutions

- Employees of motion-picture theaters

- Employees in certain forestry or logging operations

- Under FLSA Section 213(b)(20), employees of a public agency who are engaged in fire protection or law enforcement activities (including security personnel in correctional institutions) if the public agency employs fewer than five full or part-time firefighters or fewer than five full or part-time law enforcement officers. (For purposes of calculating the number of firefighters or law enforcement officers, volunteers are excluded. [*See* Cleveland v. City of Elmendorf, Tex., 388 F.3d 522 (5th Cir. 2004)]

- Employees of certain county elevators

- Employees involved in processing maple sap into sugar or syrup

[29 U.S.C. § 213(b)]

Q 5:23   Under what circumstances are drivers exempt from the FLSA's overtime requirements?

Drivers for whom the Department of Transportation (DOT) has power to establish qualifications and maximum hours of service pursuant to the Motor Carrier Act of 1935 are exempt from the FLSA overtime requirements. This is called the *motor carrier exemption.* To qualify for this exemption, a driver must be engaged in interstate commerce. Drivers are engaged in interstate commerce when:

1. Their vehicles cross states lines; or

2. They are transporting goods as a part of a continuing movement originating in or destined to a point in another state or country.

[29 U.S.C. § 213(b)(1); 49 U.S.C. § 31502]

The key factor in determining whether drivers are engaged in interstate commerce is the "character" of the employees' activities, not the proportion of time spent in activities directly affecting interstate safety. [Levinson v. Spector Motor Serv., 330 U.S. 649 (1947)] The guiding inquiry "is whether a particular employee's duties have a substantial effect on the safety of operation of motor vehicles transporting property in interstate commerce." [Sinclair v. Beacon Gasoline Co., 447 F. Supp. 5, 10 (W.D. La. 1976)]

Although courts have recognized a *de minimis* exception, that exception has force, at least as applied to drivers, only when the interstate-travel portion of the employees' work can be characterized as "infinitesimal." [Peraro v. Chemlawn Servs. Corp., 692 F. Supp. 109 (D. Conn. 1988)] As observed by one court, in those cases in which the *de minimis* exception has been applied, the employees had "spent less than one percent of their time in interstate travel." [Turk v. Buffets, Inc., 940 F. Supp. 1255, 1262 (N.D. Ill. 1996)] Thus, it was not determinative that employees spent more time in field service than in the transportation of property; "their interstate operations affected safety on the highways. . .even though they were not employed primarily as carriers." [Friedrich v. United States Computer Serv., 974 F.2d 409, 418 (3d Cir. 1992)] And, in the *Peraro* case, a federal district court found that a carpet-cleaning company's employees affected safety in interstate commerce although the percentage of time they spent driving interstate ranged among the employees from 6 percent to 46 percent. In short, "[t]he activities of one who drives in interstate commerce, however frequently or infrequently, are not trivial. Such activities directly affect the safety of motor vehicle operations." [Crooker v. Sexton Motors, Inc., 469 F.2d 206, 210 (1st Cir. 1972)]

Q 5:24   When does the DOT have jurisdiction over a driver?

The DOT has jurisdiction over drivers who actually drive across state lines. Additionally, the DOT has determined that it has jurisdiction over drivers who, during the four-month period preceding the analysis, could have been called upon to, or actually did, engage in interstate commerce. For example, when an interstate driver is sick or otherwise unavailable, an employer may use other drivers to cover his or her routes. If drivers who do not normally drive out of state are subject to being called to duty on an out-of-state route, they may still be regulated by the DOT and are eligible for the overtime exemption, at least for the four-month period during which they are subject to being called upon to drive out of state. [Wage and Hour Division Field Operations Handbook § 24e01(b)(2); Wage & Hour Opinion Letter, FLSA1998-1944 (June 1998)]

In August 2005, Congress changed the definition of *motor carrier* and *motor private carrier* in such a way that the motor carrier overtime exemption now applies only to commercial motor vehicles. *Commercial motor vehicles* are defined as trucks greater than 10,000 pounds, vehicles designated to carry more than 8 passengers for compensation, vehicles designed to carry more than 15 passengers, and vehicles used to transport hazardous material. Practically, this means that employees who had been subject to the exemption because, for example, the employee drove a company van in interstate commerce will no longer be exempt because the van does not meet the amended definition of a motor carrier over whom the Secretary of the Department of Transportation has the authority to regulate the hours.

Q 5:25   When may the motor carrier exemption from the FLSA's overtime requirements be lost?

The motor carrier exemption may be lost if a driver is no longer subject to being called to duty as an interstate driver or becomes eligible to be called on a seasonal basis only. For example, in *Reich v. American Driver Service, Inc.* [33 F.3d 1153 (9th Cir. 1994)], drivers for a company that engaged in interstate commerce on a seasonal basis only were not exempt during the off-season. Similarly, drivers who never, regardless of the bidding cycle or manpower shortages, actually took an out-of-state route, did not qualify because the exemption could not rest solely on the contention they were subject to being called for out-of-state duty. [Wage & Hour Opinion Letter, FLSA1998-1943 (June 1998)]

Q 5:26   Are drivers who drive only local routes exempt if they are transporting goods that are continuing in interstate commerce?

Yes. Although drivers may not actually cross state lines, it is still possible for them to be exempt from the payment of overtime if the intrastate deliveries they are making are a continuation of the interstate movement of the goods being delivered. Goods that are delivered within one state only may still maintain their interstate character where the in-state transportation forms a part of a practical continuity of movement across state lines from the point of origin to the point of destination. Practical continuity of movement is maintained where an out-of-state shipper has a "fixed or persisting transportation intent" beyond the terminal storage point at the time of shipment, such as where goods are special ordered by customers. In that instance, local (intrastate) drivers would be exempt because their local delivery would be a continuation of the interstate journey of the goods being delivered. [Wage & Hour Opinion Letter, FLSA1998-1943 (June 1998)]

Q 5:27   When is a fixed or persisting transportation intent present?

There may be a fixed or persisting transportation intent when:

1. Goods are delivered from interstate commerce to an employer's warehouse or distribution center to be delivered to customers to fill pre-existing orders and the out-of-state shipper knows that the goods will move through the local warehouse in a short period of time (72 hours or less).

2. Goods are stored at a warehouse or distribution center for a short period before delivery and are parceled for specific identified customers. (For example, in *Klitzke v. Steiner Corp.* [110 F.3d 1465 (9th Cir. 1997)], an in-state delivery driver for a laundry and uniform service was exempt, because half of the goods delivered by drivers were delivered pursuant to specific orders placed on behalf of customers on the local route.)

3. Goods are delivered pursuant to special orders; they are not intended for the company that receives the goods in the first place; and the transport to the ultimate customer is just another leg in their interstate journey. In *Foxworthy v. Hiland Dairy Co.* [997 F.2d 670 (10th Cir. 1993)], a local dairy delivery driver was exempt because dairy goods came from out of state to satisfy existing orders in the local market, although goods went through the employer's distribution center.

[Wage & Hour Opinion Letter, FLSA1999-2111 (Feb. 1999)]

Q 5:28 When is a fixed or persisting transportation intent lacking?

A fixed or persisting transportation intent is lacking when goods "come to rest." Goods that are ordered from out of state for delivery to multiple customers in-state and that are stored for an unspecified period of time, one to four weeks or more, are likely not continuing their interstate movement when they are delivered to their in-state destinations. [Wage & Hour Opinion Letter, FLSA1998-1943 (June 1998)] Also, the processing of goods will break the continuing interstate journey of goods. However, goods that are merely broken down into smaller volumes for local delivery may not be considered to have "come to rest" in the state before delivery; therefore, such goods, when delivered locally, will be continuing their interstate journey. For example, in *Middlewest Motor Freight Bureau v. ICC* [867 F.2d 458 (8th Cir.), *cert. denied*, 493 U.S. 890 (1989)], a company that received chemicals and related products in bulk from another state and delivered those products in smaller amounts within a single state was still engaged in interstate commerce.

Q 5:29 Is there a test to determine whether a fixed or persisting transportation intent exists?

Yes. A three-part test exists to determine whether there is a fixed or persisting transportation intent. The Interstate Commerce Commission formulated a three-prong test in *Ex Parte No. MC-48* [71 MCC 17, 29 (1957)] laying out the circumstances under which there is no fixed or persisting transportation:

1. At the time of delivery from out of state, there is no specific order being filled for a specific quantity of goods intended for a specific destination beyond the terminal storage;
2. The terminal storage is a distribution point from which specific amounts of goods are sold or allocated; and
3. Transportation of the goods within a single state is specifically arranged only after sale or allocation from storage.

[29 C.F.R. § 782.7(b)(2)]

When goods are transported though interstate commerce to a warehouse or distribution center, the exemption will not apply if there was no fixed destination for the goods when they reached the warehouse. If the goods will be sold at a later date, the exemption does not apply. This means that the goods received from another state must be allocated for delivery to their final destination before the goods reach the warehouse and must not remain at the warehouse for any extended amount of time, such as beyond a few days. [Wage & Hour Opinion Letter, FLSA1998-1943 (June 1998)]

Q 5:30   Are chainstore warehouse distribution systems operating in interstate commerce?

Yes. Dedicated distribution systems called "chainstore warehouses" are operating in interstate commerce, even if most or all of the deliveries take place within one state. "Transportation within a single state from a chain store warehouse to outlets of the chain, of goods brought into the state for sale at the outlets, is covered on traditional 'in commerce' grounds under the FLSA and is also transportation in interstate commerce under the Motor Carrier Act." An independent supplier can also be exempt under the chainstore warehouse concept where the independent supplier orders goods from other states to meet the needs of a group of affiliated retail stores. The supplier is presumed to be operating in interstate commerce when the warehouse serves the stores exclusively and is comparable to a chainstore situation. [Wage and Hour Division Field Operations Handbook § 24d02(d), (e)]

Q 5:31   What is the local delivery exemption to the FLSA's overtime requirements?

Drivers who make local deliveries can be compensated on a trip-rate or similar basis and be exempt from the overtime pay provisions of the FLSA. To qualify, drivers must be paid a trip-rate or a commission for the deliveries. The deliveries must be local in nature. The deliveries cannot be from one segment of the employer's business to another (such as transportation of the goods from a main plant to a sales outlet). Additionally, the plan must have the "general purpose and effect" of reducing the driver's hours below 40 per week. If an employer wishes to use this payment plan, it must petition the DOL for approval prior to implementing the plan. [29 U.S.C. § 213(b)(11); 29 C.F.R. § 551.1]

Q 5:32   What is the exemption for trailer, boat, or aircraft dealers?

An exemption from only the overtime pay provisions of the FLSA is provided for salespeople, partsmen, or mechanics primarily engaged in selling or servicing automobiles, trucks, or farm implements for a nonmanufacturing establishment primarily engaged in the business of selling such vehicles to ultimate purchasers. [29 U.S.C. § 213(b)(10)(A)] Also exempt are salespeople, but not partsmen or mechanics, primarily handling trailers, boats, or aircraft for a nonmanufacturing establishment primarily engaged in selling those vehicles. [29 U.S.C. § 213(b)(10)(B)]

Only a nonmanufacturing establishment primarily engaged in the business of selling vehicles listed to ultimate purchasers may take advantage of the exemption. Only establishments selling automobiles, trucks, or farm implements may utilize the exemption for partsmen and mechanics. They can also invoke the exemption as to salespeople, but so can dealers in trailers, boats, or aircraft.

By its terms, the exemption applies only to employees of a nonmanufacturing establishment "primarily" selling automobiles, boats, trailers, trucks, farm implements, or aircraft to ultimate purchasers. Establishments that are primarily engaged in nonselling activities—such as automobile or truck rental establishments, garages, or repair shops—do not qualify for the exemption merely because they may sell some motor vehicles, aircraft, or farm implements incidental to their principal activities. [Wage & Hour Opinion Letter, FLSA1967-660 (Aug. 1967), Wage & Hour Opinion Letter, FLSA1976-654 (Sept. 1967)] On the other hand, it would appear that an establishment that is primarily engaged in selling vehicles to ultimate purchasers does not lose the exemption merely because it sells some new vehicles for resale or because it disposes of traded-in vehicles by selling them to used-car dealers for resale.

In addition to requiring that an establishment must be primarily engaged in selling automobiles, trailers, trucks, farm implements, or aircraft to ultimate purchasers, the statute also requires that a salesperson, partsman, or mechanic must be "primarily" engaged in selling or servicing such vehicles to be exempt. Thus, the exemption does not apply to an employee who spends most of the working time in the performance of clerical duties and only a minor part in the selling or servicing of vehicles. [Gieg v. Howarth, 244 F.3d 775 (9th Cir. 2001)] The term "primarily," as used in this context, is interpreted as over 50 percent of an employee's time. [Wage & Hour Opinion Letter, FLSA1967-660 (Aug. 1967)]

Q 5:33   Are "service advisors" exempt from the FLSA's overtime pay requirements pursuant to the exemption for salesmen working for automobile dealerships?

Yes, under some circumstances. The FLSA exempts from overtime pay requirements "any salesman, partsman, or mechanic primarily engaged in selling or servicing automobiles, trucks, or farm implements, if he is employed by [a dealership selling such vehicles]." [29 U.S.C. § 213(b)(10)(A)] In interpreting this statute, the DOL issued a regulation defining "salesman" as "an employee who is employed for the purpose of and is primarily engaged in making sales or obtaining orders or contracts for sale of the vehicles." [29 C.F.R. § 779.372(c)(1)] Under this regulation, service advisors would not be exempt as a salesman in an auto dealership, as they are not selling vehicles. The Fourth Circuit, however, has ruled that this interpretation of the term "salesperson" by the DOL is unreasonable and therefore invalid. [Walton v. Greenbrier Ford, Inc., 370 F.3d 446 (4th Cir. 2004)] The court reasoned that the clear language of the FLSA "exempts any salesman 'primarily engaged in selling *or servicing automobiles*' from the overtime requirements." [*Id.* at 452] The court explained that Walton, as a service advisor, was required to greet customers, listen to their concerns about their cars, write repair orders, follow up on repairs, and keep customers informed about maintenance. He also suggested to customers additional services that needed to be performed and would prepare work orders. He was paid a salary as well as commissions for work orders that he wrote up. Thus, the court found that Walton promoted and attempted to sell goods and services provided by the dealership, sold the proper repairs and services responsive to customers' needs, and had a "key role" in the dealership's service operations. Accordingly, based on his duties, Walton was a salesman primarily engaged in servicing vehicles and was therefore exempt from the FLSA's overtime pay provisions.

Q 5:34   What are the other FLSA partial exemptions?

Under FLSA Section 207, the following employees may be partially exempt from the FLSA's overtime provisions:

- Employees working under certain collective bargaining contracts that guarantee certain weekly or total hours. [29 U.S.C. § 207(b)(2)]

- Employees processing or handling leaf tobacco. [29 U.S.C. § 207(m)]

- Cotton gin and sugar-processing employees under specific circumstances. Since January 1, 1978, this exemption is limited to 14 workweeks in a year and requires overtime pay for employment in excess of 10 hours in a day and 48 hours in a workweek. [29 U.S.C. § 213(i)]

- National park concessionaires. The 1977 amendments to the FLSA created a partial overtime exemption for concessionaires providing services or facilities in a national park or a national forest, or on land in the National Wildlife Refuge System, under a contract with the Secretary of the Interior or the Secretary of Agriculture, with employees to be paid at least the minimum wage rate for each hour worked and one and one-half times their regular rate of pay for all hours over 56 in a workweek. [29 U.S.C. § 213(b)(29)]

- The "7(k)" exemption for police and firefighters. FLSA Section 207(k), implemented by 29 C.F.R., Sections 553.201 through 553.223, allows public agencies to adopt a partial overtime pay exemption for employees engaged in fire protection or law enforcement activities (including security personnel in correctional institutions and including employees who are engaged in ambulance or rescue service activities that are substantially related to fire protection or law enforcement activities) who work tours of duty (see Qs 5:43, 7:81). These employees may engage in nonexempt work that is not related to fire protection or law enforcement activities as long as that work does not exceed 20 percent of the total hours worked during the workweek or applicable work period. [29 C.F.R. § 553.212] Additionally, when fire protection and law enforcement employees work special details in fire protection, law enforcement, or related activities on an occasional or sporadic basis at their option for a separate or independent employer, the extra hours worked will be excluded from calculation of hours for the purpose of determining whether overtime is warranted. [29 U.S.C. § 207(p)]

- Mass transit employees. FLSA Section 207(n) provides that the hours of employment of a mass transit employee do not include the time spent in charter activities if: (1) pursuant to a prior agreement the time is not to be so counted; and (2) such charter activities are not a part of the employee's regular employment.

- Employers that provide remedial education. A little known provision in the 1989 FLSA Act Amendments creates FLSA Section 7(q) [29 U.S.C. § 207(q)] and applies to employers that provide remedial education to employees who lack a high school diploma or educational attainment at the eighth grade level. If an employer provides remedial education to an employee, and the education does not include job-specific training, the employer may require the employee to participate in remedial education, which would be considered work time, for up to ten hours overtime in any workweek without the employee's being entitled to the additional half time for the overtime. The employee would still be entitled to receive straight-time pay for the ten overtime hours, but would not receive the half-time overtime. For example, if an employer is paying an employee $8 per straight-time hour, it would not have to pay him or her $12 per hour for the ten hours worked in return for the remedial education, but it would have to pay him or her the regular straight-time rate of $8 per hour. An employer can require and pay for up to ten hours of remedial education, not remedial education plus ten hours of other overtime work.

- Public court reporters. Under legislation enacted to clarify the application of the FLSA overtime provisions to court reporters employed by public entities, hours spent and pay received by a public sector court reporter preparing transcripts outside of his or her regular schedule are not included in hours worked or wages paid in his or her primary job for purposes of the overtime calculation. FLSA Section 207(o)(6) requires that the hours spent performing such duties be outside of the hours the employee performs other work for the public agency. Specific per-page payment rates must be fulfilled.

Q 5:35   What is the so-called 7(i) exemption?

It is actually a partial overtime pay exemption available to use for employees of retail establishments. The term *retail sales or service establishment* means "an establishment 75 [percent] of whose annual dollar volume of sales of goods or services (or of both) is not for resale and is recognized as retail sales or services in the particular industry." [29 C.F.R. § 779.411] To be eligible for this partial exemption, employees must receive earnings in excess of one and one-half times the minimum wage for each hour worked and more than half of the compensation from a representative period of not less than one month must be income from commissions. [29 U.S.C. § 207(i)] For example, a 15 percent mandatory service charge at a restaurant falls under this provision and would not be a tip or gratuity. (See Qs 5:36–5:41) Therefore, the present minimum that such employees can receive is $8.78 per hour ($9.83 per hour effective July 24, 2008).

Q 5:36   What is a "retail" establishment?

Disputes often arise over whether or not a facility or company is retail in nature, but, generally speaking, the exemption can be used in a broader range of companies than one might at first suspect, including pest control companies, air conditioning sales organizations, installation and service companies, funeral homes, cemetery sales, and restaurant servers or hotel banquet servers. [29C.F.R. §§ 779.312 *et seq.*]

Even a business such as a carpet-cleaning service may qualify as a retail or service establishment. In *Reich v. Delcorp, Inc.* [3 F.3d 1181 (8th Cir. 1993)], the court held that "under some circumstances a laundry could qualify as a 'retail or service establishment'" for purposes of FLSA Section 207(i) and thereby lawfully avoid paying overtime to its commission employees without violating federal overtime provisions. The court rejected the government's argument that the in-home carpet-cleaning business was part of the laundry industry and therefore could never qualify as a retail or service establishment.

A lease can also qualify as a "sale" for purposes of the retail sales or service establishment exemption. For example, one federal court of appeals recently ruled that automobile leases by a car dealer can be counted as sales for purposes of the 75 percent annual dollar volume requirement. [Gieg v. DDR Inc., 407 F.3d 1038 (9th Cir. 2005)] On the other hand, another appeals court held that fleet leasing is not a retail "sale" because of the wholesale nature of the transaction. [Acme Car & Truck Rentals, Inc. v. Hooper, 331 F.2d 442 (5th Cir. 1964)]

Recently, the DOL concluded that a private health club and fitness facility met the Section 207(i) exemption. [Wage & Hour Opinion Letter, FLSA2006-9 (Mar. 2006); Wage & Hour Opinion Letter, FLSA2005-53 (Nov. 2005)]

Q 5:37   Are employees covered by the retail sales or service establishment exemption if their commissions aren't based on sales?

Yes. By its terms, the Section 207(i) exemption applies to "any employee" of a retail or service establishment who meets the compensation requirements; the exemption is not limited to those employees who actually sell retail goods and services. For example, the Ninth Circuit Court of Appeals held that finance and insurance managers at a car dealership qualified for the exemption because their compensation was based on commissions, even though the commissions did not come from sales. [Gieg v. DDR Inc. 407 F.3d 1038 (9th Cir. 2005)] However, even though the employee's commission need not be based on sales, the employee's activities must be an integral part of sales business. For example, *Davis v. Goodman Lumber Co.* involved the applicability of the retail sales exemption to employees of a company that was primarily engaged in the retail sale of lumber but that also had a separate department that manufactured rollers for cotton mills. The court held that because manufacturing rollers for cotton mills was "separate and distinct" from the company's retail lumber yard, the retail and service exemption did not apply to the employees of the manufacturing business. [Davis v. Goodman Lumber Co., 133 F.2d 52 (4th Cir. 1943)]

In an opinion letter issued October 17, 1995, the Administrator of the Wage and Hour Division opined that employees of an automobile dealership classified as "detailers," who were paid on a flat-rate basis, qualified for the Section 7(i) exemption from the overtime requirements of the FLSA. Each detailer was paid a flat-rate hour, which is not an actual clock hour. Each job was assigned a certain number of hours for which the customer was charged, regardless of the actual time it took to perform the job. The dealership did not change the detailer's share per flat-rate hour if the charge to the customer was changed. The Administrator believed that the method of compensation represented commissions on goods or services for the purposes of Section 7(i) of the FLSA.

Q 5:38   Can sales to commercial establishments be considered retail in nature as are sales to individual's residences?

Yes, they can be, but one must always consider whether or not a sale to a commercial establishment is to the end user or is a sale for resale. Any item or service that is sold to a company for resale is not considered to be retail in nature. For example, contracting to install storm shutters on all the condominiums at a high rise construction project, where the condominiums will, in turn, be sold to individuals, would not be a retail sale. However, a sale directly to the individual condominium owner could be considered a retail sale, so long as installation costs are not a major part of the total sales price. That leads to a second concern: Construction activities are not considered retail in nature; therefore, if the sale to a construction project appears to be a part of a major renovation, or if sales and installation at new construction projects become more than 25 percent of an establishment's revenue, the retail nature of the sales can be lost. [29 C.F.R. § 779.321]

Q 5:39   Are insurance sales considered retail in nature?

Insurance sales are not considered retail in nature, at least by the Wage and Hour Division. In response to investigations of funeral homes and cemeteries, where the commission-paid salespeople would otherwise be considered to be working for a retail establishment, if the salespeople are handling an insurance product that allows customers to purchase future burial services and products, the Wage and Hour Division takes the position that the functions of the employees are not retail in nature. In other words, there is a "no tolerance" rule followed by the Wage and Hour Division in regard to insurance sales by an employee. Whether or not this position by the DOL would be upheld by the courts is questionable. The DOL's position is not always followed by the courts. In *Reich v. Cruises Only* [140 Lab. Cas. ¶ 34,017, 1977 U.S. Dist. LEXIS 23727 (M.D. Fla. 1997)], the DOL sued a travel agency in court. The court performed a detailed analysis on the retail concept and found that the travel agency dealt primarily with individuals and provided and sold services that would normally be considered retail in nature (e.g., personal trips on cruise lines). The fact that customers do not always visit the travel agency's offices was not a controlling factor. The court considered the Wage and Hour Division's position to be unreasonable.

Q 5:40   Where a service charge, such as at a restaurant or at a banquet, is automatically applied to the customer's bill, does all of this service charge have to be paid to the servers?

No. The service charge is revenue to the company and it may be used and divided any way that the company desires. If the employees receive at least $8.78 per hour ($9.83 per hour effective July 24, 2008) for all hours worked, and more than half of their total compensation for a prior representative period of at least one month and not greater than one year represents commission calculations, then the 7(i) exemption can still be used without that entire service charge being paid to the servers.

Q 5:41   What if a waiter or waitress performs other job duties during the same workweek in which they are performing 7(i) commission paid duties?

This presents a potentially difficult situation. Technically, an employer can have a 7(i) employee perform secondary job duties, which might be paid only on an hourly wage basis, or use the tip credit for an employee who receives gratuities. The problem is that the 7(i) exemption must be complied with for the entire workweek as a whole. In other words, adding all hourly wage rates and all commission payments together and then dividing by total hours worked, the employee's compensation for the whole week must equal at least $8.78 per hour ($9.83 per hour effective July 24, 2008) or more. Likewise, the secondary part of the 7(i) test (which is that more than half of total compensation for a representative period must come from commission calculations) can be affected if an employee performs a secondary job function a considerable number of hours. The situation could develop where the hourly wage rate determines more than half of total compensation in some months (or other representative periods), thereby voiding use of the exemption. For a tipped employee, the $3.72 ($4.42 effective July 24, 2008) tip credit as well as the $2.13 per hour paid in cash wages would be treated like an hourly wage payment for this second part of the 7(i) test. The bottom line is that if a 7(i) employee works a second job, the hours in the second job should probably be limited in order to avoid losing the 7(i) exemption.

Q 5:42   What are the other partial overtime exemptions?

The following are other partial overtime exemptions:

- *Nursing home and hospital employees; the so-called 8 and 80 employees.* An advance agreement with the employees may be obtained that no overtime is owed unless more than 80 hours are worked in a 14-day period, but overtime is owed after 8 hours per day. This is the only FLSA daily overtime pay requirement. [29 U.S.C. § 207(j)] Use of this exemption has been increasing because of the need for flexible scheduling of health care personnel in the face of managed care practices. Hospital employees include laboratory employees working in a hospital when the laboratory is an "integral part of the hospital" but do not include laboratory employees when the laboratory is operated independently of the hospital, because they would not be "engaged in the operation of a hospital." [Wage & Hour Opinion Letter, FLSA2000-2231 (Sept. 2000)]

• *Employees of independently owned wholesale petroleum distributors.* The following conditions must be met for the exemption to apply: (1) annual gross volume of sales of the enterprise must be less than $1 million, exclusive of excise taxes; (2) more than 75 percent of the business's annual dollar volume of sales must be within the state in which the enterprise is located; and (3) not more than 25 percent of the annual dollar volume of sales of the enterprise can be to customers who are engaged in the bulk distribution of petroleum products for resale. The employee must be paid at least one and one-half times the minimum wage for hours worked in excess of 40 hours per week and must be paid at least one and one-half times his or her regular rate for hours worked in excess of 12 hours in a workday or in excess of 56 hours in any workweek. [29 U.S.C. § 207(b)(3)]

Q 5:43   What are the specific requirements for application of the 7(k) exemption for fire protection and law enforcement employees?

Under the 7(k) exemption, a work period of not less than 7 and not more than 28 days may be elected rather than the traditional 7-day workweek time frame in which overtime hours and overtime pay are calculated. If a 28-day work period is established, overtime pay is owed after 171 hours for law enforcement officers and after 212 hours for firefighters, according to current Wage and Hour Division enforcement policy. Pro rata hour limits apply to work periods of less than 28 days. There is no requirement that there be any particular relationship between the work period adopted by the employer and the work schedule adopted for the employees. An employer may have one work period applicable to all of its employees or different work periods for different employees or groups of employees. The Wage and Hour Division analysis is that civilian support personnel, including dispatchers, are excluded from the definition of fire protection and law enforcement personnel. [29 C.F.R. §§ 553.224, 553.230] Public agencies that adopt the exemption are subject to special rules for purposes of calculating compensable work time. [29 C.F.R. §§ 553.222, 553.223, 553.225]

The Section 7(k) exemption may be lost by fire protection and law enforcement employees spending more than 20 percent of their working time on nonexempt work (i.e., work that is unrelated and not incident to fire protection or law enforcement activities). However, time spent by fire protection and law enforcement employees at their own option for sporadic and occasional special details for their same employer do not count toward the 20 percent nonexempt work limitation. [29 C.F.R. § 553.212] This 20 percent limitation on nonexempt work also applies to emergency medical service (EMS) employees for whom employers claim the Section 7(k) exemption. [Wage & Hour Opinion Letter, FLSA1999-2118 (Feb. 1999)]

Section 7(k), public sector comp-time plans, and use of a salaried fluctuating workweek (FWW) pay plan (see Qs 10:13–10:28) are deemed to be inconsistent by the DOL. The DOL has informally stated that all three exemptions or plans cannot be combined, but any two can be combined. Further, the DOL's position is that employers that use the FWW method of calculating overtime compensation for salaried employees may not pay the half-time premium in an equivalent amount of comp time. The DOL has cited statutory language in FLSA Section 7(o) that provides that public agency employees must receive comp time "at a rate not less than one and one-half hours for each hour of employment for which overtime compensation is required." [See DOL comments to 29 C.F.R. pt. 553, 52 Fed. Reg. 2012]

Emergency Medical Services (EMS) personnel working for a public employer do not automatically qualify for the partial overtime exemption under FLSA Section 207(k) because they may fail to meet the regulatory requirements. [Roy v. County of Lexington, 141 F.3d 533, 539 (4th Cir. 1998)]. The *Roy* court relied in part on the legislative history and its lack of reference to EMS personnel as engaging in firefighting or law enforcement activities. For EMS personnel working for an agency independent of law enforcement or fire protection to qualify for the exemption, the employer must meet the "substantially related" regulatory test under 29 C.F.R. Section 553.215. In *Lockwood v. Prince George's County* [217 F.3d 839 (4th Cir. 2000)], the court determined that fire investigators who, once a fire is extinguished, determined the origin of the fire and helped track down arsonists were not engaged in the prevention, controlling, or extinguishing of fires, and thus were not exempt as fire protection or law enforcement employees. Although the county employer argued that the investigators were engaged in the prevention of fires, the court explained that an indirect connection between the investigators' duties and fire prevention is not adequate to qualify for the exemption. The court determined that investigation of fires is not analogous to prevention of fires.

Firefighters who are also cross-trained to provide EMS services as part of their job duties may not lose their exempt status when responding to non-fire emergencies if performances of those duties are "incident to or in conjunction with [their] fire protection services." [Adams v. City of Norfolk, 274 F.3d 148 (4th Cir. 2001)] In *Adams,* the court determined that firefighters who were also trained to perform EMS duties did not lose their exempt status when performing EMS duties because when the employees responded to non-fire emergencies, they were still trained firefighters, while responding to a non-fire emergency, they may be called away to fight a fire and the employees were required to have their firefighting tools with them when responding to non-fire emergencies.

Exempt Minors

Q 5:44   What are the FLSA's provisions for exemption of minors?

Farm employment is allowed in nonhazardous occupations outside of school hours with restrictions based on a minor's age. Parental employment of children is allowed outside of school hours other than in manufacturing, mining, or hazardous occupations. Employment of children as actors or performers is allowed, but state law may restrict employment. The 1977 amendments created an exemption allowing the Secretary of Labor to waive child labor restrictions under limited circumstances for employment of children as hand-harvest agricultural laborers paid on a piece-rate basis. [29 U.S.C. § 213(c)] Chapter 9 provides a more thorough discussion of child labor laws.

Recordkeeping for Exempt Employees

Q 5:45 Do recordkeeping requirements differ for exempt employees?

Exemptions from the minimum wage, equal pay, overtime pay, and child labor provisions do not excuse employers that are otherwise subject to the FLSA from the recordkeeping requirements imposed by it. The only exemption from recordkeeping is for employment in a foreign country or within a territory under the jurisdiction of the United States, except in specific areas controlled by the United States (i.e., a state of the United States, the District of Columbia, Puerto Rico, the Virgin Islands, Outer Continental Shelf as defined in the Outer Continental Shelf Lands Act, American Samoa, Guam, Wake Island, Eniwetok Atoll, Kwajalein Atoll, and Johnston Island). [29 U.S.C. § 213(f)]

Chapter 6

Computation of Hours Worked

To maintain compliance with the minimum wage and overtime provisions of the Fair Labor Standards Act (FLSA) and thereby avoid liability, it is essential that employers understand how to compute the hours worked by their nonexempt employees. In most situations, the determination of hours worked will be governed by facts specific to the employment situation, including, but not limited to, the nature of the employee's duties, the requirements of the employer, the restrictions, if any, on the employee's free time, and the employer's adoption and enforcement of rules prohibiting unpaid work time. In addition, the number of hours worked by an employee for FLSA purposes is not confined to the number in the employer's time records, since employers often permit or even require off-the-clock work by their employees that is not reflected in the employer's records. It is not uncommon for employees to continue working voluntarily at the end of a designated shift in order to finish assigned tasks, correct errors, or prepare time or production reports. When off-the-clock work is performed with the acquiescence of the employer, the computation of the number of hours worked is based on actual hours worked rather than on the number on the employer's books. Therefore, as a fundamental precaution, employers should implement rules prohibiting off-the-clock work and such rules should be strictly enforced. By doing so, employers will have a valid defense to overtime claims based on off-the-clock work and can avoid significant liability.

Hours Worked Defined

Q 6:1   What is the definition of *hours worked* for purposes of the Fair Labor Standards Act (FLSA)?

Working hours include:

1. All time during which an employee is actually working, whether or not he or she is required to be working that entire time. [Walling v. Sun Publ'g Co., 84 F. Supp. 180 (W.D. Tenn. 1942)]

2. All time during which an employee is required to be on duty, on the company property or at a particular workplace, whether or not he or she is actually working [Walling v. Sun Publ'g Co., 84 F. Supp. 180 (W.D. Tenn. 1942)]

3. Work not requested, but "suffered or permitted" by an employer. [29 C.F.R. §§ 778.223, 785.11] That is, an employer that knows or has reason to believe that an employee is spending extra time working must compensate the employee for that time, even if the work is performed away from the employer's premises, at home, before or after scheduled hours, or during meal periods. [29 C.F.R. § 778.12; Mumbower v. Callicott, 526 F.2d 1183 (8th Cir. 1975) (employer had to pay switchboard operator when employer knew she regularly performed duties before and after the switchboard was open, as well as during her lunch hour)]

4. Hours spent on work pursued "necessarily and primarily" for the benefit of the employer. This *excludes* activities such as duty fitness training by Special Response Team officers, due to the flexibility of the training and the personal value of such exercise [Dade County v. Alvarez, 124 F.3d 1380, 4 Wage & Hour Cas. 2d (BNA) 225 (11th Cir. 1997)], and voluntary work on stock cars while an employee was supposed to be engaged in welding work. [Roman v. Maietta Constr. Inc., 4 Wage & Hour Cas. 2d (BNA) 1293 (1st Cir. 1998)] However, this *does not exclude* time spent showering or changing clothes if done at the employer's request or if due to the nature of the employee's principal duties (e.g., meat processing). [IBP, Inc. v. Alvarez, 546 U.S. 21 (2005)]

Q 6:2   What is the Portal to Portal Act, and how does it affect pay practices in the workplace?

A *workday* is the period between the time an employee begins and the time an employee ends his or her principal work activities. Under the Portal to Portal Act (Portal Act), a workday corresponds to the "whistle-to-whistle" period that starts when workers begin, and finishes when they stop their principal work activities. Certain idle times, such as rest periods and lunch breaks, are part of the "workday"; accordingly, the FLSA, not the Portal Act, governs whether such times must be treated as hours worked. A workday can last longer than an employee's scheduled hours or shift, and its duration can vary from day to day depending on when workers start or finish their principal activities. Portal Act Section 4 does not affect the computation of hours worked *within the workday proper,* and its provisions have nothing to do with compensability under the FLSA of any activities engaged in by an employee during that time period. Accordingly, to the extent that an employee's activities occur after the employee begins performing the first principal activity on a workday and before he or she stops performing the last principal activity on a workday, the provisions of the Portal Act have no application whatsoever. [29 C.F.R. §§ 785.9(a), 790.6(a)]

The principles for determining hours worked within the workday proper continue to be those established under the FLSA—without reference to the Portal Act. The workday (i.e., the time period between the commencement and completion of an employee's principal activities on a given workday) includes all time within that period, whether or not the employee engages in productive work throughout the entirety of that period. For example, if an employee is required to report to the work site at a specific time, his or her workday begins at the time he or she reports there for work in accordance with the employer's requirement, even though the employee may not be able to begin performing any productive activity until a later time. In such a situation, the time spent waiting for work is part of the workday, and the Portal Act does not affect its inclusion in hours worked for purposes of the FLSA. [29 C.F.R. § 790.6(b)]

However, the Portal Act allows certain "preliminary" and "postliminary" activities performed before or after an employee's regular workday that are not part of the employee's principal work activities to be excluded from hours worked—unless provided otherwise by contract, custom, or practice. [29 U.S.C. §§ 251 *et seq.*]

The term *principal activity* encompasses any work of consequence performed for an employer, no matter when performed. A principal activity need not be the predominant activity of all work the employee performs, and an employee may be engaged in several principal activities during the workday. [29 C.F.R. § 790.8(b) & (c)] For example, the 30 minutes spent each day by security guards traveling to a central location to obtain their weapons and return to the job site was an integral and indispensable part of their principal activities. [Int'l Bus. Inv. Inc. v. United States, 27 Wage & Hour Cas. (BNA) 1704 (Ct. Cl. 1987)] In contrast, police officers were not entitled to compensation for time spent maintaining and keeping police vehicles clean, where the activities were deemed minor and incidental, and the officers were not required to do the activities as part of their job. [Aiken v. City of Memphis, Tenn., 4 Wage & Hour Cas. 2d (BNA) 408 (W.D. Tenn. 1997)]

Typical examples of "preliminary" or "postliminary" activities include:

- Change of clothes
- Wash-up time

- Commuting time
- Waiting time on duty
- Waiting time off duty
- Punching time cards

Incidental Activities

Q 6:3   What are *incidental activities*, and must time spent doing them be counted as hours worked?

Incidental activities are activities that do not constitute the principal duties of the employee. Under the FLSA, time spent in incidental activities that are an integral part of an employee's principal duties generally must be counted as work time. For example, time spent stopping to pick up supplies on the way to the office, depositing the mail, or banking on the employer's behalf after the close of business or on the way home is counted as work time. In addition, under FLSA regulations, time spent changing clothes and showering or washing up is considered work time if that is required by the employer or necessary to the employee's performance of his or her job. [*See* 29 C.F.R. §§ 785.24–785.26] Indeed, incidental activities integral to an employee's principal duties are compensable and time spent doing them must be counted as work time even when they are performed before or after the employee's usual shift. For example, in *IBP, Inc. v. Alvarez* [546 U.S. 21 (2005)], the United States Supreme Court concluded that time spent putting on required protective gear that was "integral and indispensable to the employee's work" and time spent waiting to take off the required protective gear was working time and required to be paid unless the time was "*de minimis*"—less than a total of five minutes.

Another example is *Ladegaard v. Hard Rock Concrete Cutters, Inc.* [2004 U.S. Dist. LEXIS 16288 (N.D. Ill. 2004)] In that case, drivers for a concrete cutting company stopped by the company's yard prior to traveling to the job site—to perform activities such as picking up work orders, filling water tanks and portable gas tanks on work trucks, picking up additional equipment necessary for the day's work, hooking up trailers needed for work, and performing safety and operational checks on the vehicles and trailers. Following the work day, drivers occasionally needed to stop by the yard to drop off vehicles or equipment for repair or to turn in completed work orders. A federal district court determined that "having tools, supplies and equipment available and properly functioning, having water necessary for performing the cutting process, unloading debris, cleaning equipment, and completing paperwork were all activities necessary for the predominant activity of concrete cutting." All of these activities benefited the employer. Thus, on any day that a driver performed some preparation at the company's yard, the time spent performing that activity and the travel time from the yard to the job site was compensable. Similarly, on any day that a driver performed some cleanup in the yard, the time spent performing that activity and the travel time from the last job site to the yard was also compensable.

Q 6:4   Is time spent waiting in line to pick up clothing or equipment, putting on safety equipment, or walking from a locker room to the work area considered work time?

It depends on the type of clothing worn and the amount of time it takes to put the clothing on and take it off.

The United States Supreme Court ruled that unless *de minimis,* the time spent putting on required protective gear that is "integral and indispensable to the employee's work" is compensable time because it is "integral and indispensable" to the employee's "principal activity." The Court also ruled that the time spent walking to the production area after putting on the protective gear, the time spent walking from the production area to the changing room, the time spent taking off the required protective gear, and the time spent waiting to return the protective gear are also compensable because all of the activities were "integral and indispensable" to the employee's principal activities as meat processors. [IBP v. Alvarez, 546 U.S. 21 (2005)]

Because donning and doffing gear that is "integral and indispensable" to employees' work is a "principal activity," the continuous workday rule mandates that the time the workers spend walking to and from the production floor after donning and before doffing gear is not affected by the Portal Act and is compensable time. The same holds true for the time spent waiting to doff the clothing. However, the Portal Act excludes from compensable time the period employees spend waiting to don the first piece of gear that marks the beginning of the continuous workday. According to the Court, "such waiting—which is two steps removed from the productive activity on the assembly line—comfortably qualifies as a 'preliminary' activity." [546 U.S. 21 (2005)]

Many jobs require employees to dress in uniforms. For example, nurses in hospitals and servers in many restaurants generally wear special garb that would not normally be considered street clothing. Is the time these employees spend donning their uniforms compensable work time? This situation is distinguishable from that of employees in *Alvarez,* who were required to wear protective equipment over and above their street clothes. Putting on cumbersome safety equipment involves a fairly significant expenditure of time and effort, but dressing in uniforms does not generally require any more time or exertion than dressing in regular street clothes. Clothing worn as scrubs or uniforms falls under a different exemption—which allows changing time to be noncompensable if it is a matter of practice or part of a union contract. [29 U.S.C. § 207(o)]

Q 6:5   When are rest periods considered compensable hours worked?

Short rest periods of 20 or fewer minutes are customarily paid for as working time and should be counted as hours worked. [29 C.F.R. § 785.18; Wage & Hour Field Operations Handbook § 31a01(a)] Coffee and snack breaks lasting 20 or fewer minutes are considered as rest periods. [29 C.F.R. § 785.19(a)] However, where a rest period of known duration is longer than 20 minutes and the employees are free to use it for their own purposes, such periods are not hours worked. [Wage & Hour Field Operations Handbook § 31a01(b)]

Contrary to popular belief, there is no obligation on the part of an employer under the FLSA to provide 15-minute rest periods. In fact, the FLSA does not require rest periods at all; it merely addresses whether such periods—if provided—must be counted as hours worked. In contrast, state laws may require rest periods—especially in the case of employees under 18.

Q 6:6 When are meal periods considered compensable?

Bona fide meal periods during which an employee is relieved from duty for the purposes of eating do not have to be counted as time worked. The regulations [29 C.F.R. § 785.19] provide that the employee must be completely relieved from duty for the purposes of eating regular meals. Ordinarily, 30 minutes or more is long enough for a bona fide meal period, and the regulations even speak of 20-minute bona fide meal periods. According to the regulations, it is not necessary that an employee be permitted to leave the premises during his or her meal period, but the time will have to be counted as time worked if the employee is required to perform any duties, whether active or inactive, while eating. While it is not necessary that an employee be permitted to leave the premises, the employee must be permitted to leave his or her work station.

The Department of Labor (DOL) addressed the issue of "meal periods" in a November 22, 2004, opinion letter. Corrections officers were provided an unpaid 20-minute meal break. The question presented was whether the employer would incur a liability to pay compensation for an unpaid 20-minute meal break to the corrections officers when during the meal period, the employees would be completely relieved from duty for the purpose of eating a regular meal, and the 20 minutes would be sufficient for employees to eat a meal. Generally, 30 minutes is considered sufficient time for a bona fide meal period; however, the DOL advised that "a shorter period may be long enough." Because the employer, the employees, and the employees' collective bargaining agent agreed that a shorter bona fide meal period was sufficient, and the particular circumstances (e.g., short distance to the break room) demonstrated the shortened period's sufficiency, the DOL opined that 20 minutes constituted a bona fide (noncompensable) meal period. [Wage & Hour Opinion Letter, FLSA2004-22 (Nov. 2004)]

Even meal periods of 30 minutes or longer are likely considered work time if the employee must (1) perform some duties or (2) remain in a particular place on the premises during the meal period—for example, being available to provide security during lunch. [Reich v. New England Telecomms. Corp., 121 F.3d 58 (2d Cir. 1997) (employees working on outdoor sites were required to bring their lunches and eat at the sites for the express purpose of preventing damage to the sites and protecting the public from accidents)] Employees may also be found not to have been "completely relieved of duty" if they are required to remain on the premises *and* carry a pager for calls during lunch, as was the case with respiratory therapists in *Hoffman v. St. Joseph's Hospital, Inc.* [1998 U.S. Dist. LEXIS 7911

(N.D. Ga. 1998), *vacated*, 1999 U.S. Dist. LEXIS 23316 (N.D. Ga. 1999)] However, merely being "on call" or being required to remain in uniform during meal periods is not sufficient to render the meal period compensable. [*See* Roy v. County of Lexington, 141 F.3d 533 (4th Cir. 1998) (mere requirement that emergency services personnel be prepared to respond to an emergency call if called upon was not sufficient to destroy the employee's mealtime exclusion)] Nor is a requirement that the employee remain on the employer's premises—standing alone—sufficient to convert a meal period into working time. [*See* Brown v. Howard Indus., Inc., 116 F. Supp. 2d 764 (S.D. Mass. 2000) (although when employees were required to remain on the employer's premises for the duration of their 30-minute meal period, it did not make that meal period compensable)]

Some courts, however, have rejected the "completely-relieved-from-duty" test in favor of a less stringent standard. Under that standard, an employee must be compensated for meal time if the meal period is spent *predominantly for the benefit of the employer.* [*See* Henson v. Pulaski County Sheriff's Dep't, 6 F.3d 531 (8th Cir. 1993)]

In light of FLSA regulatory provisions and case law interpreting the FLSA, the safest course for an employer that does not wish to have mealtime considered compensable work time is as follows:

1. Designate a meal period of at least 30 minutes for all nonexempt employees.

2. Make it clear that no duties are to be performed during the meal period.

3. Make it clear that employees are free to and should leave their *posts* during the meal period, although it is not necessary that the employees be permitted to leave the *premises* during the meal period.

4. If there is automatic deduction from time cards of time for a meal period, have a method to allow employees to claim time worked if the employee is interrupted during a meal break.

It would be wise for employers to spell out their policies recognizing employee meal periods in an employee handbook or in other written form and to make sure the written policy is adequately disseminated and enforced.

Training Time

Q 6:7 Is time spent by an employee in attending training or educational programs work time that must be counted in the computation of hours worked?

Time spent by employees attending lectures, meetings, and training programs sponsored by the employer need not be counted as hours worked if all the following are met:

1. The meetings are held outside working hours;

2. Attendance by employees is truly voluntary;

3. The course, lecture, or meeting is not directly related to the employee's job;

4. The employee does not perform any productive work during his or her attendance.

[29 C.F.R. § 785.27]

Q 6:8   When is attendance at training considered voluntary?

One of the most difficult aspects of evaluating training time is ascertaining whether the attendance at training is truly voluntary. The meeting time must be counted as hours worked if (1) attendance is required by the employer or (2) the employee is led to believe that his or her *present* working conditions or continued employment would be adversely affected by not attending. [29 C.F.R. § 785.28] Thus, even when satisfactory completion of a prescribed course of study is a prerequisite for promotion within an occupational classification or to a higher classification, attendance at or participation in the course is still voluntary because the employee's *current* classification and working conditions are not adversely affected by a decision not to participate. [Wage & Hour Field Operations Handbook § 31b17; Price v. Tampa Elec. Co., 806 F.2d 1551 (11th Cir. 1987) (employee training course was voluntary even though salary would change upon entry, where to decline to participate would leave employees in current classification with the same responsibilities and benefits)]

> **Example 1.** Assume an employer offers a training session for which attendance is voluntary and during which the employee does no productive work. Assume further that the seminar is not directly related to the employee's job. The time spent at the seminar is still considered work time if the seminar is held *during the employee's regular work hours*.

> **Example 2.** Assume that outside regular work hours, an employee attends a training session that is not directly related to the employee's job and during which the employee does no productive work. If the employee's attendance at the program is mandated by the employer, the time spent in attendance remains compensable work time.

Q 6:9   When is training considered directly related to the employees' job?

Training is considered to be directly related to employees' jobs if it is designed to make employees handle their present jobs more effectively. Training time can be excluded from time worked if it only incidentally improves the employees' skill at their regular work, or if it will teach them to perform a new or different job. [29 C.F.R. § 785.29]

However, there are three significant exceptions to the "directly related" requirement. Time spent outside regular hours voluntarily attending courses established by an employer for the benefit of its employees, that correspond to courses offered by an independent institute of learning, is not compensable, even if the courses are directly related to the employees' jobs or are paid for by the employer. [29 C.F.R. § 785.31] Second, if employees attend courses at an independent school, college, or trade school after hours, and of their own initiative, the time spent is not hours worked even if directly related to their current jobs. [29 C.F.R. § 785.30; Furr's Supermarket, Inc. v. United Food & Commercial Workers Union, 129 F.3d 130 (10th Cir. 1997) (unpublished)] Finally, training is not considered "directly related" if it is for the benefit of employees and corresponds to courses offered at schools—assuming attendance is truly voluntary. [29 C.F.R. § 785.31; Wage & Hour Opinion Letter, FLSA1996 (Sept. 1996)]

Example 1. Outside work hours, an employee voluntarily attends a course offered by an independent institution or an employer-sponsored course similar to courses offered by independent institutions. The time spent in attendance by the employee need not be counted as hours worked even if the course relates to the employee's job or is paid for by the employer.

Example 2. Jason, an employee, decides to attend a company-sponsored lecture and training program designed to enable him to perform his duties as an auto mechanic more efficiently. Jason attends the program voluntarily and the program is outside his regular work hours. Even if Jason does no productive work for his employer during this program, the time Jason spends in attendance at the program would nevertheless be considered compensable work time and would count as hours worked. Although Jason is learning new skills, these new skills would help him perform his present job better. Consequently, the program would most likely be considered directly related to Jason's job and the time spent would be considered hours worked. If, however, the program is not specific to Jason's employer and is offered by an independent source, there is a good chance the training time would not count as compensable work time.

Example 3. Assume the same facts as those in Example 2, except that the lecture and training program is designed to teach Jason skills very distinct from his job as a mechanic, such as accounting or marketing a car repair shop. Since the program is not directly related to Jason's present job, but actually training for a new or additional job, Jason's attendance at the program would not be considered compensable work time under the FLSA.

Example 4. Assume that Jason is an attorney. As an attorney, Jason is required by the Bar to attend yearly continuing education classes. In this case, despite the fact that most, if not all, of the courses Jason attends are directly related to the job that he performs, his time at the classes will not be compensable because the course requirements are not mandated or imposed on him *by the employer*.

Q 6:10   Must training required by the state, not the employer, be counted as compensable hours worked under the FLSA?

No. One of the requirements for training time to be noncompensable is that the employees' attendance at the training be "voluntary." When the state, as opposed to an employer, requires individuals to take training as a condition of employment, then attendance at such training is considered voluntary because the employer is not requiring the attendance. For example, continuing education attendance is considered voluntary so long as the employer does not impose additional requirements on the employee. This is true even if the training may be related to the employee's job and attendance is mandated by the state. However, if the state requires *employers* to provide training *as a condition of employment*, then the time spent in training is considered hours worked. [Wage & Hour Opinion Letter, FLSA1996 (Sept. 9, 1996)]

A DOL comment to 29 C.F.R. Section 553.26 provides some guidance. That comment states that "where the training occurs during the course of regular working hours, the time is always compensable hours worked." [*See also* Wage & Hour Opinion Letter, FLSA1999 (Sept. 30, 1999)] Thus, if an employer becomes aware that its employees are required to attend training sessions mandated by the state and gives an employee the day off to fulfill the requirement, the time will be considered work time by the Wage and Hour Division. If an employer is adverse to compensating employees for the time spent in state-mandated training and does not want the time counted as hours worked, the wisest course would be to have the employee attend on his or her own time, rather than during the employee's regular work hours.

Q 6:11   Is the time spent waiting for a medical examination compensable?

Yes. Time spent by an employee in waiting for and receiving medical attention on the employer's premises or at the direction of the employer during the employee's normal working hours constitutes "hours worked." Also, if the employer requires an employee to obtain and pass a yearly physical examination in order to continue employment, this time must be considered "hours worked." [Wage & Hour Opinion Letter, FLSA1998 (June 1998)] The time spent taking a mandatory drug test is also considered hours worked. [Wage & Hour Opinion Letter, FLSA1997 (Sept. 1997)]

Q 6:12   Must an employee be compensated for time spent in mandatory counseling to minimize workplace stress?

Yes, according to the Northern District of Illinois. In *Sehie v. City of Aurora* [2003 WL 21730120 (N.D. Ill. 2003), *aff'd*, 432 F.3d 749 (7th Cir. 2005)], the plaintiff worked as a telecommunicator, answering phone calls from the public for the city police department. One day, she left work early due to emotional and stress-related reasons. She was required to submit to a fitness-for-duty evaluation before returning to work. The physician who evaluated her said that she was fit to return to work but recommended that she attend weekly psychotherapy sessions for six months as a condition of continuing her employment. The plaintiff attended the required counseling sessions with her employer's chosen therapist during nonworking hours in weeks she worked 40 or more regular hours. She was not compensated for the hour spent at each session or for the two hours traveling to and from each session. She sued the city for unpaid overtime related to the counseling sessions. The city argued that the claim was barred by a U.S. Department of Labor regulation, which states:

> Time spent by an employee in waiting for and receiving medical attention on the premises or at the direction of the employer during the employee's normal working hours on days when he is working constitutes hours worked.

[29 C.F.R. § 785.43]

The employer argued that, because the counseling sessions did not take place during plaintiff's "normal working hours," the time was not compensable. The court disagreed, however, explaining that there is no authority for the suggestion that the regulation is intended to be all encompassing with respect to the compensability of time spent tending to medical problems. Instead, the court focused on the general rule that compensation is required under the FLSA for all time spent in "physical or mental exertion (whether burdensome or not) controlled or required by the employer and pursued necessarily and primarily for the benefit of the employer or his business." [citing 29 C.F.R. § 785.7] The court explained that the counseling sessions attended by the plaintiff fit within this definition as they were required by the city for its own benefit—to ensure that the plaintiff could perform her work duties. The court further concluded that time spent traveling to and from the counseling sessions constituted compensable work time.

Sleeping Time

Q 6:13   Do employers have to pay for employees' sleeping time?

Maybe. Sleeping time, the time allocated by the employer for an employee to sleep while on duty, may or may not be considered compensable work time under the FLSA and the regulations interpreting it, depending on the circumstances.

On duty less than 24 hours.
Generally, employees required to be on duty for less than 24 hours are working even if permitted to sleep, since that time is given to their employer. [29 C.F.R. § 785.21] However, sleeping time has been deducted when the circumstances show that the employees have adequate sleeping facilities and time to sleep. For example, house parents at a residential school who received at least five hours of uninterrupted sleep in adequate facilities per shift did not receive compensation for the time spent sleeping. [Beaston v. Scotland Sch. for Veteran's Children, 693 F. Supp. 234 (M.D. Pa. 1988)]

The Wage and Hour Division's 24-hour rule appears to be arbitrary and is not completely supported by the courts, as evidenced by the case law. Revising its position from earlier opinion letters dated June 25, 1990 and January 6, 2000, the DOL issued an opinion letter on July 27, 2004 that time spent sleeping by group home employees who live on the employer's premises, and who are required to remain on the premises during the time, need not be compensated under the FLSA if there is a reasonable agreement between the parties that takes into account all facts relevant to the employment arrangement. The opinion letter said that employers do not necessarily have to compensate employees who permanently reside at group homes for sleep time if the workers have periods of complete freedom outside of sleep time that is sufficient to engage in normal private pursuits. Pertinent facts include whether the employee has time—other than the sleep time—for normal private pursuits, whether the employee's personal time is limited or restricted by the conditions of employment, and the extent of interruption to eating and sleeping times. The agency decided that any reasonable agreement reached between the employer and employees to exclude sleep time would be excepted by the Division as compliant with the FLSA. [Wage & Hour Opinion Letter, FLSA2004-7 (July 2004)]

On duty 24 hours or more.

When employees are required to be on duty for 24 hours or more, sleeping time will be counted as hours worked, unless there is an express or implied agreement to the contrary. [29 C.F.R. § 785.22(a)] Employees are "on duty for 24 hours or more" when: (1) they have no regular schedule of hours or a schedule in name only, and are required to perform work on a helter-skelter basis at any time during the day or night; or (2) they have a regular schedule of hours, but the periods during which no work is scheduled are so disrupted by frequent calls to work that the time is not the employee's own. [Wage & Hour Field Operations Handbook § 31b02(b)]

If, as a result of interruptions, employees on duty for more than 24 hours do not get at least five hours' sleep during their scheduled sleeping period, the entire time is working time. [29 C.F.R. § 785.22(b); Hultgren v. County of Lancaster, 913 F.2d 498, 506 (8th Cir. 1990);Masters v. Maryland Mgmt. Co., 493 F.2d 1329 (4th Cir. 1974)]

However, regardless of whether employees are on duty for more or less than 24 hours, if an employee is frequently interrupted to perform duties, sleeping time may still be compensable even if it exceeds five hours. [Wage & Hour Field Operations Handbook § 31b12(b)]

Although there is not much guidance on what constitutes an implied agreement to exclude sleeping time, at least one federal court has ruled on what does *not* constitute such an implied agreement. In *International Association of Firefighters, Local 349 v. City of Rome* [682 F. Supp. 522 (N.D. Ga. 1988)], the district court held that continuing to work and accept paychecks after the employer instituted a policy excluding sleeping time from compensable work time did not constitute an implied agreement to exclude such time (at least in regard to employees who made protests to the employer's policy upon learning of it). The court also rejected the employer's claim that it had relied on the oral advice of the Regional Assistant Wage and Hour Administrator that advance notification of its change in policy was sufficient to constitute an implied agreement to exclude sleeping time from work time.

The Wage and Hour Division has indicated that it will accept any "reasonable agreement by the parties" as to intermittent and unpredictable sleeping time—such as an employer's requirement that certain personnel remain on the premises during emergencies, such as natural disasters. Unfortunately, the Wage and Hour Division did little to explain what would be a "reasonable agreement" distinguishing hours worked from sleeping time.Until the Division provides that explanation, employers in those circumstances would be well-advised to pay for the extended hours necessitated by emergency conditions.

The wisest course for an employer that wants to exclude sleeping time from compensable work time is to enter into an express written agreement with its employees or to issue a written notice clearly spelling out the terms and conditions in effect.

Public safety personnel under FLSA Section 7(k) [29 U.S.C. § 207(k)] are subject to special rules requiring shifts to be greater than 24 hours in length in order for up to 8 hours of sleeping time to be excluded from the computation of hours worked. [29 C.F.R. § 553.222]

Calls during sleep time.
If a sleeping period that is otherwise not compensable is interrupted by a call to duty, the interruption must be counted as hours worked. [29 C.F.R. § 785. 22(b)] For example, firefighters were entitled to compensation when their sleep, normally excluded by agreement, was interrupted to respond to alarms, calls for an ambulance, or to inspect equipment. [*See, e.g.,* Eustice v. Federal Cartridge Corp., 66 F. Supp. 55 (D. Minn. 1946)]

Volunteer Work

Q 6:14   Is time spent doing volunteer work compensable?

The time spent working for public or charitable purposes at the employer's request, or under its direction or control, or while the employee is required to be on the premises, is working time. [See Qs 2:17–2:18]

Waiting Time or On-Call Time

Q 6:15   What is *waiting time* ?

Waiting time is time during which an employee must be available for work, although the employee is not actually engaged in his or her duties. Waiting time can also include "on-call" time. Examples include a tow truck driver who is waiting to be dispatched to the next location, a property maintenance employee who is subject to being called for after-hours repairs, and a nurse who must remain ready and available to report and perform duties at the hospital within a short response time (especially if the nurse must remain at the hospital for all practical purposes, although not directly required by the hospital to do so). Waiting time also includes time spent by employees waiting for assignments or tasks to be assigned and other similar unproductive time on the employer's premises. Compensable waiting time can occur on or off the employer's premises and even while an employee is at home.

Q 6:16   What is *on-call* time?

An employee who is required to remain on-call on the employer's premises or so close thereto that he or she cannot use the time effectively for his or her own purposes is working while "on-call." An employee who is not required to remain on the employer's premises but is merely required to leave word at the employee's home or with company officials where he or she may be reached *is not* working while on-call. [29 C.F.R. § 785.17 (citations omitted); *see also* 29 C.F.R. § 553.221(b)–(d) (discussing compensability of on-call time for public sector employees)]

Q 6:17   Must an employee who is restricted when on-call be paid?

An employee who is required to remain on the employer's premises or who is highly restricted in his or her activities while on-call is generally referred to as being on "restricted on-call." An employee who is restricted while on-call is "engaged to wait" and is required to be paid at least the minimum wage because the time spent while on-call is considered hours worked. [*See, e.g.,* 29 C.F.R. § 785.15; Wage & Hour Opinion Letter, FLSA1970-WH-74 (Sept. 1970) (employee on restricted on-call may be compensated at any rate not less than minimum wage)] This is a gray area, and even Wage and Hour Division officials have different interpretations of the rules. For example, some officials believe that if an employee is required to remain at home or at any other single location in an on-call status, that is sufficient to convert the time to work time. This view seems to be based on the fact that the employee's freedom of movement is restricted, and the employee must remain alert and ready to respond. Other officials take the position that if the employee is allowed to remain at home, where he or she can attend to personal pursuits, the time is not work time.

Q 6:18   Does the reasoning change if the employee is unrestricted when on-call?

An employee who is not required to remain on the employer's premises while on-call and who is not unduly restricted in his or her activities while on-call is referred to as being on "off-premises" or "unrestricted on-call." An employee scheduled for unrestricted on-call need not be paid any compensation while on-call because the time is not considered hours worked. Moreover, if the employee is paid compensation, the compensation does not have to be the minimum wage since the work is not covered by the FLSA. In circumstances where an employee is on unrestricted on-call, the employee is deemed to be "waiting to be engaged." [*See, e.g.*, 29 C.F.R. § 785.16 (when an employee is relieved of duties, the employee is waiting to be engaged); 29 C.F.R. § 778.223 (discussing the fact that hours spent by an employee who is paid less than minimum wage while on off-premises/on-call are not considered hours worked)]

One factor is the amount and degree of restriction placed on the employee while the employee is required to remain at home. [*See, e.g.*, Rutlin v. Prime Succession, Inc., 220 F.3d 737 (6th Cir. 2000)] For instance, it may be that in addition to being required to remain home, the employee must also remain clean, sober, and ready to respond within a relatively short time. In this situation, it is likely that the time the employee must remain available would be construed as work time by the DOL. Other factors pertinent to determine whether on-call time spent by employees is compensable work time include the terms of any employment agreement, whether employees can maintain a flexible schedule by switching on-call shifts with other employees, how quickly employees must report back to work after being called (response time), the share of calls employees are required to answer, and the frequency of actual calls to which employees must respond. [*See* Ingram v. County of Bucks, 144 F.3d 265 (3d Cir. 1998); Rousseau v. Teledyne Mobile Offshore, Inc., 805 F.2d 1245 (5th Cir. 1986); Boehm v. Kansas City Power & Light Co., 868 F.2d 1182 (10th Cir. 1989); Renfro v. City of Emporia, 948 F.2d 1529 (10th Cir. 1991)] The Wage and Hour Division has said that—regardless of other restrictions—on-call time during which an employee receives so many calls that he or she cannot effectively use the time for personal pursuits may be entirely compensable. [Wage & Hour Opinion Letter, FLSA1999 (Sept. 1999)]

Employers seeking to have their employees' on-call or waiting time considered noncompensable should bear in mind the general rule that employees should be able to use their nonworking time for personal pursuits. Requiring pagers or mobile phones and permitting "reasonable" response times—often interpreted as no less than 5 minutes and up to 20 minutes—as well as not imposing inflexible scheduling requirements will do much to avoid liability on this question. However, with no clear guidelines on what constitutes compensable waiting time or on-call time, when in doubt an employer might do well to seek advice from counsel on the latest DOL and court pronouncements or obtain an opinion from the Wage and Hour Division regarding whether, and to what extent, the time constitutes compensable work time under the FLSA.

Travel Time

Q 6:19   Is travel time considered hours worked?

Whether travel time constitutes hours worked depends upon the nature of the travel, the nature of the employee's work, and the connection between the two. The Portal Act provides that employers do not have to pay minimum wage to an employee for the following activities:

1. Walking, riding, or traveling to and from the actual place of performance of the principal activity or activities that such employee is expected to perform; and

2. Activities that are preliminary or postliminary to said principal activities that occur either prior to the time on any particular workday at which such employee commences, or subsequent to the time on any particular workday at which he or she ceases, such principal activities or duties.

[29 U.S.C. § 254(a)] The Portal Act provides that its provisions may be altered by custom or contract.

As discussed in Qs 6:2 and 6:4, the term *principal activity* encompasses any work of consequence performed for an employer, no matter when performed. *Principal activity* also includes all activities that are an integral and indispensable part of the employee's principal duties. A principal activity need not be the predominant activity of all work the employee performs, and an employee may be engaged in several principal activities during the workday. [29 C.F.R. § 790.8(b) & (c)] For example, the 30 minutes spent each day by security guards traveling to a central location to obtain their weapons and then returning to the job site was an integral and indispensable part of their principal activities. [Int'l Bus. Inv., Inc. v. United States, 27 Wage & Hour Cas. (BNA) 1704 (Ct. Cl. 1987)] In contrast, police officers were not entitled to compensation for time spent maintaining and keeping police vehicles clean, where the activities were deemed minor and incidental, and the officers were not required to do them as part of their job. [Aiken v. City of Memphis, Tenn., 4 Wage & Hour Cas. 2d (BNA) 408 (W.D. Tenn. 1997)]

Q 6:20   Is time that an employee spends commuting or traveling to a work site compensable work time?

An employee who travels from home before his or her regular workday and returns home at the end of the workday is engaged in ordinary home-to-work travel, which is a normal incident of employment. This is *not work time* even if the employee does not work at a fixed location. [29 C.F.R. § 785.35; *see also* Kavanagh v. Grand Union Co., 192 F.3d 272 (2d Cir. 1999) (mechanic commuting up to eight hours a day not entitled to be compensated for travel time)]

Travel time from a central location (such as an office) to an outlying work site before the beginning of work is not working time. [29 C.F.R. § 790.35] But travel from a central location to another work site may be compensable *if the employee performs work at the central location before traveling to the other work site.* [29 C.F.R. §§ 785.38; 785.41] The reason for the different results, according to the DOL, is as follows: If the employees go to the office to receive work instructions or to pick up parts and equipment needed to perform their jobs, the travel time from the office to the work site is compensable. If the employees merely use the office as a meeting place, where the employees park their personal vehicles, the travel time to the work site would be considered to be part of the home-to-work trip. [Wage & Hour Opinion Letter, FLSA1996 (May 1996); Dole v. Enduro Plumbing, 30 Wage & Hour Cas. (BNA) 196 (C.D. Cal. 1990) (plumbers entitled to travel time for reporting to the shop to receive work instructions)] An employee who is required to drive to work, pick up a company car, and then report to the first work site of the day need not be compensated for the travel time from home to the "operating base" to pick up the company truck. That time is commuting time. The same is true if the employee voluntarily drives company vans to and from the work site. [Wage & Hour Opinion Letter, FLSA1995-(Nov. 1995)] On the other hand, if an employee is required by the employer to report to a particular location before traveling to the actual work site, the time will be compensable. For example, if a painter must first report to the employer's premises before going to another location to paint a house, the time spent traveling from home to the employer's premises is not compensable work time, *but the time spent traveling from the employer's premises to the work site is compensable work time.* Travel time may also be considered work time if the travel time is an indispensable and integral part of the purpose for which the employee was hired. For example, welders hired to perform welding work on oil and gas pipelines, usually at some distance from their homes, who were required to report to the site each day with refueled and restocked welding rigs were likely to be entitled to compensation for the travel time associated with refueling and restocking the welding rigs. [*See* Baker v. Barnard Constr. Co., 146 F.3d 1214 (10th Cir. 1998)]

Q 6:21 Is commuting time compensable if the employee performs employment-related work at home as well as elsewhere?

Possibly. The Portal Act [29 U.S.C. § 254(a)] excludes commuting from compensable work time only if the commuting precedes or follows the start of the workday. However, if the employee performs work at home *before* he or she travels to a work site or performs work *after* he or she arrives home from the work site, the workday may begin or end at home. In that case, the Portal Act would not apply.

Whether the workday starts or ends at home depends on whether the work at home is a "principal activity" that the employee has been employed to perform. In 29 C.F.R. Section 790.8(a), the DOL states that in order for an activity to be a "principal" activity, it need not be predominant over all other activities; instead, an employee may be engaged in several "principal" activities during the workday. The legislative history further indicates that Congress intended the words "principal activities" to be construed liberally to include any work of consequence performed for an employer—no matter when the work is performed. A majority member of the committee that introduced this language explained to the Senate that it was considered "sufficiently broad to embrace within its terms such activities as are indispensable to the performance of productive work."

A recent case on this issue involved employees of an insurance company who worked as auto damage appraisers. Appraisers are required to travel to the location selected by the insured to perform the appraisal. Before traveling to their first appraisal, employees sometimes start their laptop computers; open necessary software; check their voice mail; check their e-mail; respond to messages; set a new voice mail greeting on their phones; review their day's assignments; map out a geographical route for the day; and load their computer, printer, docking station, digital camera, and other supplies into their vehicles. Similarly, appraisers sometimes perform certain work-related tasks at the end of the day in their homes. These tasks include checking their e-mail and voice mail; calling body shops, parts suppliers, insureds, and claimants; completing estimates or appraisals that they were unable to complete in the field; faxing paperwork to the insurance company; electronically sending the day's appraisals to the insurance company; electronically completing a time log for the day; and downloading and reviewing assignments for the following day.

A federal district court ruled that the work the appraisers performed at home constitutes "principal activities." These tasks are part of the regular work of the employees. As a result, the travel time between an employee's home and the first appraisal and the travel time between an employee's last appraisal and home must be counted as hours worked on those days the employee performs those "principal activities" at home. [Dooley v. Liberty Mut. Ins. Co., 307 F. Supp. 2d 234 (D. Mass. 2004)]

In addition to FLSA regulations regarding travel time, the 1996 amendments to the Portal Act [29 U.S.C. § 254(a)] specifically address company vehicles and travel time. The intent behind those amendments was to clarify the definition of hours worked for employees who use their employer's vehicle for travel and to identify activities that are incidental to the use of the employer's vehicle for commuting. Time spent commuting and in incidental activities is not considered hours worked if use of the employer's vehicle for travel is within the normal commuting area for the employer's business or establishment and use of the employer's vehicle is subject to an agreement between the employer and employee (or the employee's representative).

Q 6:22   Is travel at the beginning or end of the day compensable?

Travel at the beginning or end of a workday may constitute hours worked if the travel time benefits an employer. This would include, for example, underground travel in mines [29 C.F.R. § 785.34] or when travel is combined with an indispensable activity such as transporting special equipment [Wage & Hour Field Operations Handbook § 31c05] Such activity must involve more than negligible amounts of time or effort to be compensable. [Reich v. New York City Transit Auth., 45 F.3d 646 (2d Cir. 1995) (time spent by canine unit officers with police dogs was not compensable, even though officers were required to provide their own transportation and had to occasionally care for their dogs during their commute, because the actual time spent doing so was so negligible as to be *de minimis*, and therefore treated as noncompensable commuting time)]

Q 6:23   Is travel during working hours compensable?

Time spent in travel as part of an employee's principal activity, such as travel between job sites, must be counted as hours worked because it is considered "travel all in a day's work." [29 C.F.R. § 785.38; *see* UTU Local 1745 v.

Albuquerque, 5 Wage & Hour Cas. 2d (BNA) 555, 561 (10th Cir. 1999) (travel time for bus drivers between routes is compensable; travel time at the beginning or end of the day is not)]

Q 6:24 Is emergency travel compensable?

In some instances, travel from home to work will be compensable. The regulations give as an example the situation where an employee is called out at night to travel a substantial distance to perform an emergency job for a customer of the employer. This is compensable travel time. [29 C.F.R. § 785.36] However, it will not be considered an emergency call if the employee is given prior notice—such as being told on Friday that he will be required to work at a customer's business on Saturday. [Wage & Hour Field Operations Handbook § 31c06(a)]

Q 6:25 What are the rules for out-of-town travel?

When an employee is required to travel some distance to perform a work assignment in a different location, the travel time is not considered ordinary home-to-work travel. Such travel is ordinarily considered working time because it is performed for the employer's benefit and at the employer's special request. However, only travel in *excess of ordinary home-to-work* travel must be counted. [29 C.F.R. § 785.37] The regulations illustrate this principle in the following example.

> **Example.** An employee who works in Washington, D.C., with regular hours of 9 a.m. to 5 p.m. may be given a special assignment in New York City, with instructions to leave Washington at 8 a.m. He arrives in New York at 12 noon, ready for work. The special assignment is completed at 3 p.m., and the employee arrives back in Washington at 7 p.m. Such travel cannot be regarded as ordinary home-to-work travel occasioned merely by the fact of employment. It was performed for the employer's benefit and at its special request to meet the needs of the particular and unusual assignment. It would thus qualify as an integral part of the "principal" activity that the employee was hired to perform on the workday in question. It is like travel involved in an emergency call, and is travel that is "all in the day's work." All the time involved, however, need not be counted. The travel between the employee's home and the railroad depot may be deducted, it being in the "home-to-work" category. Also, the usual meal time would be deductible. [29 C.F.R. § 785.37]

Q 6:26 How does an employer determine whether travel in one day is a special one-day assignment or local travel?

Unfortunately, the DOL has not provided the clearest guidance. In response to a question about travel within the same state, the DOL responded:

> Merely stating that the employees in question work in the same state where they live does not necessarily mean that all their work is "local."

> [O]ur response to this question might be different for employees who live and work in Texas than for employees who live and work in Rhode Island. In Texas, our answer might flow from § 785.35 [home-to-work; ordinary travel] or § 785.37 [home-to-work on special one-day assignment in another city], depending on the distance involved; in Rhode Island, § 785.35 [ordinary travel] Also, regardless of the distance involved, if the employee is *required* to drive the company van, all the travel time is compensable.

[Wage & Hour Opinion Letter, FLSA1995 (May 1995)]

Based on a DOL opinion letter, the focus of whether travel time on a special one-day assignment is compensable depends on whether the travel time is "ordinary" or "extraordinary." [Wage & Hour Opinion Letter, FLSA1999 (Jan. 1999)] The example given by the DOL is as follows:

> Where a field engineer's commute to the first job site in the morning takes four hours, we would consider the greater portion of travel time compensable under the principles described in 29 C.F.R. § 785.37 [home-to-work on a special one-day assignment in another city] That rule allows a portion of the total commute time to be considered non-compensable home-to-work travel. If the employer treated three of the four hours as compensable travel, we would not question such practice.

Based on that opinion, travel time of greater than one hour would be considered "extraordinary."

The DOL's position appears to be directly contrary to the court's decision in *Kavanagh v. Grand Union Co.* [192 F.3d 269, 272 (2d Cir. 1999)], where the Second Circuit held that a refrigerator and utility mechanic in New York—who traveled up to eight hours a day—was not entitled to be compensated for his travel time because the travel time was part of the "normal" commuting time.

Q 6:27   Is overnight travel away from the employee's home compensable?

Travel that keeps an employee away from home overnight is travel away from home and is work time when it "cuts across the employee's workday," because the employee is substituting travel for other duties. [29 C.F.R. § 785.39]

Thus, travel time is hours worked on regular workdays during normal working hours, as well during the corresponding hours of non-workdays. [29 C.F.R. § 785.39]

Q 6:28   Does the mode of transportation make a difference?

As a matter of enforcement, the Wage and Hour Division does not consider work time to include any time spent outside regular working hours as a passenger on a plane, train, boat, bus, or automobile. [29 C.F.R. § 785.39; *see also* Boll v. Reserve Bank, 21 Wage & Hour Cas. (BNA) 877, 883 (E.D. Mo. 1973), *aff'd*, 21 Wage & Hour Cas. (BNA) 886 (8th Cir. 1974) (bank examiner not entitled to compensation for travel time outside his regular working hours when he was a passenger in a car)]

However, whenever an employee is *required to drive* —even outside regular working hours—the driving time is compensable. [Wage & Hour Opinion Letter, FLSA1996 (May 6, 1996)]

> **Example.** An employee travels by plane to another state. The employee leaves for the airport at 8:00 a.m. on Sunday morning, and arrives at 8:45 a.m. for a 9:30 a.m. flight. The employee travels to another city from 9:30 a.m. to 3:30 p.m., and goes straight from the airport to the hotel, where she immediately goes to the pool and orders a drink. The time from 8:45 a.m. to 3:30 p.m. is compensable travel time because it cuts across the employee's regular work hours. This is true even though the travel took place on a Sunday, because the time corresponds to the employee's regular working hours.

On Friday, the employee leaves the city at 3:30 p.m. and travels until 9:30 p.m. The employee is entitled to 1.5 hours of travel time. The remaining travel time on Friday night is noncompensable under the DOL's "special enforcement" policy that time spent as a passenger outside regular working hours is not compensable. The analysis would be completely different if the employee was required to drive his or her car to the other city. Whenever an employee is required to drive, he or she is entitled to all the travel time.

Q 6:29   Are there any special travel rules?

Working While Traveling. Travel during which work is actually performed is compensable hours worked. [29 C.F.R. § 785.41]

Private Automobile Use. The regulations provide that if an employee is given the opportunity to use public transportation but elects to drive his or her own automobile, an employer may count as hours worked only the time the employer would have had to count had the employee used public transportation instead. [29 C.F.R. § 785.40]

Employer-Provided Transportation. When an employer provides transportation solely for the convenience of the employees, the travel time is not compensable. [Wage & Hour Opinion Letter, FLSA1973 (Jan. 1973)] But the driver of the company-furnished vehicle is entitled to compensation because the driver's principal activity is to drive. [*See also* Vega *ex rel.* Trevino v. Gaspar, 36 F.3d 417 (5th Cir. 1994)]

Travel Time as a Passenger. An employee who is required to ride in a plane, train, or car as a passenger is working while riding [29 C.F.R. § 785.41], although the special enforcement policy regarding travel as a passenger outside regular working hours applies. Practically, this means that an employee who rides with another employee in a car, outside normal working hours, need not be compensated for the travel time, but the driver will be entitled to compensation. [Boll v. Reserve Bank, 21 Wage & Hour Cas. (BNA) 877, 883 (E.D. Mo. 1973), *aff'd*, 21 Wage & Hour Cas. (BNA) 886 (8th Cir. 1974)]

Meal and Sleep Time. Employees who are entitled to compensation for travel time may have bona fide meal periods deducted as well as sleep time if "adequate facilities" are furnished by the employer. [29 C.F.R. § 785.41]

Voluntary Payment. The DOL has stated that an employer may make voluntary payment for travel time hours that are not "hours worked" under the regulations. Such payment will not convert the travel time into compensable hours worked—which is beneficial to employers because it does not affect the employee's entitlement to overtime. [Wage & Hour Opinion Letter, FLSA1996 (May 1996)]

Different Rates of Pay. The DOL will permit an employer that is required to count travel time as hours worked to pay the employee a lower hourly wage for the travel time. [29 C.F.R. §§ 778.415–778.417; Wage & Hour Opinion Letter, FLSA1999 (Jan. 1999)] The employee's regular rate for calculating overtime would be a blended rate, unless the employer/employee agreed to pay the employee an overtime rate based on the rate the employee was earning at the time the overtime was incurred.

Recording Time Worked

Q 6:30   How is working time recorded?

In recording working time under the FLSA, insubstantial or insignificant periods of time beyond the scheduled working hours that cannot, as a practical administrative matter, be precisely recorded for payroll purposes may be disregarded, as courts have held that such trifles are "*de minimis.*" [Anderson v. Mount Clemens Pottery Co., 328 U.S. 680 (1961)] This rule applies only where there are uncertain and indefinite periods of time of no more than a few seconds or minutes in duration, and where the failure to count such time is due to considerations justified by industrial realities.

Q 6:31   Is rounding to the nearest fraction of an hour permitted?

Rounding to the nearest tenth of an hour, quarter-hour, or similar period is permissible provided that doing so *averages out* so that the employees are fully compensated for all the time they actually work. For enforcement purposes, this practice of computing working time will be accepted provided that it is used in such a manner that it will not result, over a period of time, in failure to compensate the employees properly for all the time they have actually worked (e.g., it is permissible to round to the nearest tenth, but not to *round down* to the nearest tenth.). [*Interpretative Bulletin* 785.48(B)]

Q 6:32   Must an employee be paid for the time it takes to punch out?

The question of rounding arises when employees must travel a distance in order to punch out at the conclusion of work. Oftentimes this will result in the employee's punching out anywhere from 5 to 15 minutes after his or her shift has actually ended. Under some systems of rounding, this time might result in the employee being entitled to overtime payments. However, the Portal Act has determined that some activities are deemed "postliminary" and no compensation is required to be paid for this time as it is not considered "hours worked." Thus, time spent by employees traveling to and from time clocks is not considered "hours worked," and no compensation is required. It should be pointed out that travel time of approximately 5 to 15 minutes is reasonable and will not be considered "hours worked" for overtime purposes so long as the employee is not actively pursuing his or her work duties but is on his or her own time. There is no hard-and-fast rule in this area, and each case should be judged on its own facts, but time lags of 30 minutes or longer might be considered suspect.

Q 6:33   Must employees use a time clock to record their hours worked?

There is no requirement that time clocks be utilized. Where they are used, a record of time worked as reflected on the time card is not conclusive, and punching in early or later by an employee may be disregarded if the employee does not engage in any work during these periods. Since the time card is the best record of hours worked, it is obviously difficult to dispute the hours of work reflected on such card. Because of this fact, employers should issue clear instructions regarding punching in and out so that the cards will accurately reflect the exact number of hours worked. When time clocks are not used, it is important that supervisors be careful to inspect time cards of employees arriving late or leaving early in order to determine that the correct times have been filled in. Careful inspection of employees' time cards should also be made where an employee has worked overtime.

Special Public Employee Issues

Q 6:34   Are K-9 unit police officers entitled to compensation for the time they spend caring for and training police dogs and for the time they spend transporting the dogs between their homes and work?

Officers with canines and other police equipment may be entitled to compensation for the time they spend caring for their canines or other equipment if they must spend after-hours time performing that care. However, the commute time of the officers does not become compensable merely because they are transporting their canines or other equipment with them.

Police officers have some unique working time issues because many officers are assigned canines or police vehicles or other equipment (such as firearms) that requires care and maintenance, often outside of regular working hours. The DOL has taken the position, followed by various courts, that time spent by officers caring for the equipment (including canines, motorcycles, horses, and police cars) necessary and integral to the performance of the officers' duties is working time. Thus, if such care and maintenance must be done at home (e.g., grooming, feeding, or training a canine, or cleaning a motorcycle or other police vehicle) because of the nature of the care or maintenance, a lack of facilities on the employer's premises, or a lack of time during the normal workday, such time must be counted as hours worked. [Reich v. New York City Transit Auth., 45 F.3d 646 (2d Cir. 1995) (feeding, training, and washing police canines are work activities that are indispensable to the dogs' well-being and to the employer's use of the dogs in its business, and are thus compensable activities); Holzapfel v. Town of Newburgh, 950 F. Supp. 1267 (S.D.N.Y. 1997) (time spent caring for, grooming, and feeding police dogs is compensable work time), *aff'd in relevant part*, 145 F.3d 516 (2d Cir. 1998); Hellmers v. Town of Vestal, 969 F. Supp. 837 (S.D.N.Y. 1997) (not only would time spent in caring for assigned canines be compensable, but also time spent in cleaning police vehicles and firearms, because all of those duties were an integral and indispensable part of the principal work activity of the officers); Andrews v. DuBois, 888 F. Supp. 213 (D. Mass. 1995) (the time spent by corrections officers in grooming, cleaning, feeding, exercising, and training their dogs was compensable work time); Howard v. City of Springfield, 274 F.3d 1141 (kennel time to care for dogs on officers' vacation, personal, or sick days was compensable under the FLSA)]

The reasoning for this position is based on an analysis of what constitutes an activity that is integral and indispensable to the principal work activity of the employee and, therefore, compensable. According to the Supreme Court, the factors to consider in determining whether an activity is integral and indispensable are:

1. Is the activity necessary because of the nature of the employee's work?
2. Does the activity fulfill employer-employee obligations?
3. Does the activity directly benefit the employer's business?
4. Is the activity so closely related to the other duties performed by the employee that it is an integral part of the job?

Considering these four factors, courts looking at the question of canine care have determined that the nature of a canine officer's work is K-9-assisted patrol and response. Police dogs are indispensable to those duties because they are, in essence, security equipment without which the canine officer cannot perform his or her job. As such, "feeding, grooming, and walking the dogs are therefore indispensable (albeit incidental) parts of maintaining the dogs as law enforcement tools; these are activities closely related to the work of a K-9 officer." Additionally, time spent by officers caring for these dogs is time that these officers do not have for themselves. [Andrews v. DuBois, 888 F. Supp. 213 (D. Mass. 1995)]

Note that, although the time spent in maintaining and caring for police equipment, including canines, is compensable work time, nothing requires that such time be compensated at the officer's regular rate. Thus, employers may set a lower rate for time spent caring for police equipment. (See Chapter 7 for overtime rules relating to use of different rates.)

However, the mere presence of a canine or police-issued firearm in the car, or the mere use of a police vehicle, will not convert noncompensable commuting time into compensable travel time, absent exceptional circumstances. [Reich v. New York City Transit Auth., 45 F.3d 646 (2d Cir. 1995) (commute with canines is not compensable time unless actual work relating to the canines must be performed, and even work in those circumstances is likely to be too minimal to count as working time); Aiken v. City of Memphis, 190 F.3d 753 (6th Cir. 1999) (same)] Furthermore, where an officer "volunteers" his or her own horse, horse trailer, and equipment for use on an assignment with a mounted unit, that commute with the horse will not be converted into compensable travel time merely because the officer is transporting his or her own equipment. [Wage & Hour Opinion Letter, FLSA1985 (Dec. 1985)]

Q 6:35   Can a police department and its K-9 officers make an agreement as to how the officers will be compensated for after-hours care of the dogs at the officers' homes?

Yes. 29 C.F.R. section 785.23 deals with situations where employees work from their homes for extended periods of time, such that it would be difficult to compute the exact number of hours actually worked by the employee. In those circumstances, an employer and an employee are permitted to agree on an alternative means of compensating the employee so long as the agreement is "reasonable" and takes into account "all of the pertinent facts."

The key point here is that the agreement must be *reasonable*. Several courts have examined the reasonableness of agreements in the K-9 context.

In *Holzapfel v. Town of Newburgh* [145 F.3d 516, 526 (2d Cir. 1998)], Holzapfel, a canine officer, claimed that he spent up to 45 off-duty hours per week working with his assigned police dog, "Bandit." The employer instructed the officer to fill out a weekly overtime slip requesting two hours' pay rather than calculate the actual amount of time he spent caring for Bandit. The court held that there was no "agreement" between the employee and the employer because the two-hour overtime limit was imposed on the employee unilaterally. Even if there had been an agreement, the court noted, it would have been unreasonable as a matter of law because the employer knew that the employee worked at least seven off-duty hours per week, but the agreement only provided for two hours of overtime pay.

In *Rudolph v. Metropolitan Airports Commission* [103 F.3d 677 (8th Cir. 1996)], two airport police officers sued their employer for overtime wages for their off-duty work with their police dogs. The officers' contract provided that they would be paid one half-hour of overtime per on-duty day and one hour of overtime per off-duty day as compensation for their overtime work caring for their dogs. The contract specified that the officers were not to spend more time caring for their dogs than they were paid for without seeking prior approval from the employer. The court held that the agreement was reasonable, despite the fact that the employees claimed to have regularly worked in excess of the time for which they were paid, because the employees agreed not to do so and the employer was entitled to rely on the clear terms of the agreement.

In another case, *Leever v. City of Carson* [360 F.3d 1014 (9th Cir. 2004)], a federal court of appeals ruled that an agreement setting out a biweekly salary differential to care for a police dog was not reasonable because the approximate number of off-duty hours a deputy sheriff would spend caring for a police dog was not considered by the employer when negotiating it. While the officer said she spent 28 off-duty hours a week tending to her dog, she was compensated for only one hour per week at her pay level. Thus, the agreement was not reasonable as a matter of law, because the city relied on an unsubstantiated parity study of other law enforcement agencies instead of inquiring into the approximate number of hours canine duty would take.

Q 6:36　If K-9 officers are not required to take their dogs home and the employer provides a kennel where the officers can keep the dogs if they want to, may employers then maintain that time spent caring for the dogs is not work time when officers elect to keep the dogs at their homes?

In some lawsuits against cities for overtime pay, questions have been raised regarding whether taking the dogs home is truly voluntary and regarding ownership of the dogs. The best defense for employers may be that officers are not required to take the dogs home and that the employer provides a kennel where officers can leave the dogs at their option. If this option is given, few canine officers might be expected to leave dogs at the kennel, but the possibility exists. The countervailing considerations that employers should keep in mind are that although they may save in payment of compensation and overtime, they will still have to pay kennel costs. Moreover, there is a belief that kenneled dogs tend to be more vicious; therefore, by decreasing overtime pay liability, an employer may be increasing its potential civil liability.

In any event, the K-9 cases seem to be settling on the basis of 30 to 40 minutes per day of overtime pay for home care of dogs. For example, in *Levering v. District of Columbia* [869 F. Supp. 24 (D.D.C. 1994)], the court ruled that officers were entitled to 30 minutes of overtime pay for home care of their dogs. The court declined to consider the transportation time with the dogs to be compensable time, reasoning that transportation of the dogs was the functional equivalent of transportation of the officers' equipment and did not make the time compensable. Many settlements include a reduced workweek so that the time spent caring for the dog is paid at the straight-time rate and not the overtime rate.

Exercise Time

Q 6:37　Does off-duty time spent by police officers exercising to meet job-required physical fitness standards count as hours worked?

Although later overruled on appeal, a Florida district court in *Alvarez v. Dade County* [No. 94-636-CIV-ATKINS (S.D. Fla. 1995)] ruled that Dade County was required to pay overtime to the members of its elite police unit for off-duty hours spent exercising to meet job-required physical fitness standards. The Dade County department required its elite officers to pass a semiannual test that included being able to run 1.5 miles in 12 minutes or less, bench press their own body weight plus 25 pounds, and complete 50 push-ups. Each month, the officers spent approximately two weeks engaged in special response training, including working out, as part of their paid hours. During each cycle of training, however, the officers served felony arrest warrants and were not allowed to exercise during paid hours. In the suit, the officers successfully argued that ongoing training was necessary to maintain the level of fitness needed to pass the county's test. The jury awarded the officers roughly $2 million in damages.

The county appealed this decision to the Eleventh Circuit Court of Appeals, which reversed the ruling of the district court. Relying on a DOL opinion letter to another employer involving similar facts and on DOL guidelines on training, the court of appeals concluded that the off-duty time spent by the officers to maintain the level of fitness required for their job was not compensable under the FLSA. First, the court determined that the off-duty training at issue was conducted outside regular work hours. Second, the officers did not perform any productive work during their training, such as responding to life-threatening emergencies. Third, the court noted that the off-duty training was voluntary, reasoning that the "officers were free to train at any location, at any time and for any duration." Finally, the court found that the off-duty training was not directly related to the officers' employment because "[t]he county did not require the officers to acquire or develop a skill unique to their employment as SRT officers." [*See* Dade County v. Alvarez, 124 F.3d 1380, 1385 (11th Cir. 1997)]

The Eleventh Circuit's reasoning may be questioned by some because very few jobs require an employee to bench press his or her weight plus 25 pounds, do 50 push-ups, and run 1.5 miles in 12 minutes. These could be viewed by other courts as unique job requirements demanding unique physical skills. Moreover, although the training may have been voluntary on paper, it is doubtful that officers in that elite corps would be able to keep their jobs without the training. Nevertheless, in view of the Eleventh Circuit's decision and DOL guidelines, it appears off-duty training time, even to meet mandated on-duty standards, will not count toward computation of hours worked. It may be a different matter, however, if an employer specifically requires off-duty training, since that would remove any argument that the training is voluntary and not a work requirement.

Chapter 7

Overtime Pay

One of the primary objectives of the Fair Labor Standards Act (FLSA) is to ensure that covered employees are compensated appropriately for each hour worked in excess of 40 hours in any workweek. Generally, overtime pay is calculated as one and one-half times a nonexempt employee's regular rate of pay. The regular rate, an hourly wage rate calculated for each nonexempt employee for each workweek, is determined by dividing the total number of hours worked into the employee's total weekly compensation. This chapter explains in detail how overtime pay is calculated and how differing circumstances and compensation methods affect the calculation of overtime pay under the FLSA.

Regular Rate

Q 7:1   What is an employer's basic overtime obligation under the Fair Labor Standards Act (FLSA)?

The FLSA requires employers to pay covered employees one and one-half times their regular rate for each hour, or fraction of an hour, worked in excess of 40 hours during any workweek. [29 U.S.C. § 207] The FLSA does not require employers to pay overtime for 40 or fewer hours of work per workweek, but employers can contract to do so. The FLSA also does not require employers to pay overtime for extra hours worked in a day or hours worked on weekends or holidays, except to the extent that the employee has already worked 40 hours in the workweek in question. [29 C.F.R. § 778.102] Overtime pay due under the FLSA cannot be waived prospectively by an employee or by an employee's union representative (see Q 7:80).

Employers should pay their employees earned overtime pay on the regular payday for the period in which the overtime is worked. If, because of commissions or quota bonuses, the amount of overtime compensation cannot be determined until some time after the regular payday, the employer must pay the excess overtime compensation due as soon after the regular payday as possible. As a general rule, however, prompt payment of overtime is required. [29 C.F.R. § 778.106; Brooks v. Village of Ridgefield Park, 185 F.3d 130 (3d Cir. 1999) (employer not allowed to accumulate overtime pay for a monthly payment)]

Q 7:2   What is the *regular rate of pay* for overtime calculation purposes?

FLSA Section 207(e) defines an employee's *regular rate of pay* as "all remuneration for employment paid to, or on behalf of, the employee." [29 U.S.C. § 207(e)] The regular rate is frequently not the same as the statutory minimum wage, and employers are not entitled to offset their overtime liability with wages paid in excess of the statutory minimum wage rate. If the employee's regular rate of pay is higher than the minimum wage, the employee's overtime compensation must be computed at a rate not less than one and one-half times that higher rate. In addition, the regular rate is determined before any voluntary deductions from wages, such as payments for voluntary employee stock purchases, are made. [29 C.F.R. § 778.107] However, under limited circumstances bona fide deductions may be made prior to determining the regular rate. (See especially Q 3:31 on the Wage and Hour Division's enforcement policy on deductions for a detailed analysis.)

While employers and employees are free to establish whatever pay arrangement and/or wage level they can both agree to, they cannot evade the FLSA or agree to compute the regular rate in an unrealistic and artificial manner. Therefore, courts evaluating wage claims are obliged to look beyond the terms of the parties' agreement to the reality of what is occurring in the employment relationship. [Herman v. Anderson Floor Co., 11 F. Supp. 2d 1038, 1042–47

(E.D. Wis. 1998) (the court held that premium pay argued to be a discretionary bonus by the employer must be included in the regular rate)]

As a general rule, in order to calculate an employee's regular rate of pay, the total number of hours worked is divided into the employee's total weekly remuneration (including straight-time wages, incentive bonuses, certain types of premium pay, and the reasonable cost of furnishing board, lodging, and other facilities for the employee's benefit). The total hourly rate cannot be less than the minimum wage. An additional half of the regular hourly rate is owed for each hour worked in excess of 40 per workweek unless one of many exemptions applies. [29 C.F.R. §§ 778.107, 778.109]

Q 7:3 Over what period can an employer calculate the regular rate?

Generally, an employer can calculate the regular rate over one workweek only. The regular rate is an hourly figure that must be calculated on a weekly (i.e., workweekly) basis. An employer is not permitted to average hours and/or pay over two weeks (or more) to calculate the regular rate. [29 U.S.C. § 207(a); 29 C.F.R. §§ 778.103, 778.104]

Q 7:4 How is the regular rate affected by different payment methods?

The method by which the regular rate is calculated changes with different compensation methods. Employers can pay nonexempt (i.e., hourly) employees a salary, or an hourly wage plus a bonus, or a salary plus commissions, or according to any other method the employer and employee choose. No matter what the compensation method, however, employers must calculate the employee's regular rate to determine overtime compensation due.

When an employee is compensated solely by an hourly wage, the employee's regular rate is the same as the employee's hourly wage. Therefore, the overtime rate for an employee paid only an hourly wage is one and one-half times that hourly rate. [29 C.F.R. § 778.110]

When a nonexempt employee is paid on anything other than an hourly wage basis, such as by salary, commission, piece rate, or day rate regardless of actual hours worked, the regular rate must still be calculated as an hourly figure. To do this, the employer must take into consideration all compensation paid to the employee for the relevant period and all hours worked by the employee for the relevant period. For most nonhourly compensation methods, the regular rate is determined by dividing the total number of hours worked by the employee in a week into the employee's total regular compensation for that week. [29 C.F.R. § 778.113; Kohlheim v. Glynn County, 915 F.2d 1473 (11th Cir. 1990); DuFrene v. Browning-Ferris, Inc., 207 F.3d 264 (5th Cir. 2000)]

For instance, when an employee is paid a salary or some combination of hourly pay and bonus for a workweek regardless of hours, the regular rate is calculated as described above—by dividing the total compensation paid by the total hours worked. If the employee works overtime hours in one week, the employer is required to pay an additional half of the regular rate for each hour over 40 worked in the workweek. In this type of situation, the additional half of the regular rate that the employer pays for the overtime hours is the overtime pay premium that is required by the FLSA.

Example 1. A nonexempt employee who earns $600 on a commission basis and works a 60-hour week has a regular rate of $10 per hour ($600 ÷ 60 hours = $10). Since the employee has already been paid $10 per hour for all 60 hours worked, the employee is entitled to overtime pay only for twenty hours at half the regular rate, or $5 per hour, which amounts to an additional $100 ($5 × 20 hours = $100).

For employees paid in this manner, a new regular rate must be computed for each week in which the employee works overtime, based on the number of hours worked and total straight-time compensation earned in that week. [29 C.F.R. § 778.114]

In the case of a nonexempt employee who is paid a salary for working a specific or fixed number of hours per week, an additional half of the regular rate must be paid for hours worked in excess of 40 that are part of the employee's regular work-week and an additional one and one-half times the regular rate must be paid for hours worked in excess of the employee's specific or fixed hours.

Example 2. An employee who works a 60-hour workweek for a weekly salary of $480 has a regular rate of $8 per hour ($480 ÷ 60 hours = $8). When the employee works 60 hours in one week, an additional $4 per hour, half the regular rate, is owed for the 20 overtime hours (i.e., those hours over 40 worked during the week).

[29 C.F.R. § 778.113(a)]

Some employers choose to pay their employees a day rate, which is a fixed rate for a day's work, regardless of how many hours are worked that day. Under a day rate pay plan, the employer must pay the full day rate even if the employee only works one (or even less than one) hour in that day. As with other nonhourly pay methods, the regular rate is calculated for a day rate pay plan by dividing the total compensation for the workweek by the total number of hours actually worked in that week.

Example 3. Granite Plus, a company that specializes in granite countertops, pays its employee installers a day rate of $200 per day. The employer expects that the employees will work between 5 and 8 hours per day, 5 days per week, but understands that some employees may work more than 8 hours in a day. If an employee works 30 hours over the course of 5 days, his total compensation is $1,000 ($200 per day × 5 days) and his regular rate is $33.33 per hour ($1,000 ÷ 30). In this example, no overtime would be owed.

Q 7:5   How does an employee's regular rate compare to his or her base hourly wage?

An employee's regular rate is often higher than the employee's base hourly wage unless the employee works for a strictly hourly wage. The first step in determining the regular rate is separating all the compensation that an employee receives into three categories: (1) an employee's regular compensation; (2) amounts that can be excluded from regular compensation but that are not creditable toward overtime pay due; and (3) amounts that are excluded from regular compensation and that can be credited toward required overtime pay. [29 U.S.C. § 207(e)] Regular compensation includes all hourly wages, salary, commissions, shift differentials, standby compensation, the value of employer-provided meals and lodging, and any bonuses that are based on the quantity or quality of an employee's work. Since the regular rate is calculated by dividing regular compensation by hours worked, and since an employee's regular compensation often includes amounts in addition to his or her base hourly wage, such as commissions, bonuses, or premiums, an employee's regular rate is often higher than the employee's base hourly wage. [*See* 29 U.S.C. § 207(e); 29 C.F.R. § 778.108]

> **Example.** Assume a nonexempt employee is paid a salary of $400 per week. If the employee also receives a $50 shift differential and a $50 lead-person premium for the week, the employee will earn $500 in total regular compensation for the week. If the employee works 50 hours in one workweek, the employee's regular rate for that week will be $500 divided by 50 hours, or $10 per hour. The employee's base hourly wage, however, is only $8 per hour ($400 salary per week ÷ 50 hours worked in the week = $8 per hour), because the base hourly wage takes into account only salary or wages, not bonuses or position premiums. The regular rate is greater than the base hourly wage for this employee in this workweek. The employee is due half of the $10 regular rate for each of the 10 hours of overtime worked, for a total of $50 as an overtime premium.

Q 7:6 What should an employer do to comply with the overtime pay requirements of the FLSA?

An employer should pay overtime when due at the rate of one and one-half times the regular rate for each hour worked in excess of 40 hours in a workweek. The regular rate of pay, by its very nature, must reflect all payments that the parties have agreed must be received regularly during the workweek, exclusive of overtime payments. The determination of an employee's regular rate cannot be left to a declaration by the parties as to what is to be treated as a regular rate for the employee. It must be determined from what actually happens in the course of the employment relationship. [Bay Ridge Operating Co. v. Aaron, 334 U.S. 446, 464 (1942)] For an employer to satisfy the overtime pay requirements of the FLSA, it must calculate the regular rate of pay for each employee, calculate each employee's overtime pay on the basis of the employee's regular rate, and keep accurate and complete records of each employee's work time. [29 U.S.C. § 207(a); 29 C.F.R. § 778.108; Hodgson v. Elm Hill Meats of Ky., Inc., 327 F. Supp. 1009, 1014 (E.D. Ky. 1971)]

Q 7:7   How does the Portal to Portal Act affect an employer's overtime pay obligations?

The Portal Act is relevant in determining what work-related activities count as hours worked, which therefore must be compensated. Determining the number of compensable hours worked by an employee during a pay period is an essential part of complying with the FLSA's overtime pay requirements. Employees must be paid overtime wages for hours worked in excess of 40 per week for any time that they are required to be at work or on duty and are subject to their employer's control. [29 U.S.C. § 207(a)]

Usually, there are few problems in determining the number of hours worked by employees who are performing their principal job duties during their normal work schedule. Questions frequently arise, however, about whether time spent on a wide variety of other job-related activities, ranging from travel and on-call time to rest periods and sleeping on the job site, is compensable time. In deciding whether these activities—especially those that occur before or after employees have performed their principal duties—count as hours worked, an employer must comply with both the FLSA and the Portal Act. (See Chapter 12 for a detailed description of the Portal Act and Chapter 6 for a detailed discussion of hours worked.)

The Portal Act excludes the following from the FLSA's minimum wage and overtime pay requirements:

1. Time spent by an employee "walking, riding, or traveling to and from the actual place of performance of the principal activity or activities" unless such walking, riding, or traveling is compensable under the terms of a contract, custom, or practice; and

2. Time spent on any activities that are "preliminary to" (i.e., performed before) or "postliminary to" (i.e., performed after) the worker's principal activities in a workday in the absence of a contract, custom, or practice to the contrary.

[29 U.S.C. § 254] (See Q 12:1.)

The FLSA does not define the term *work*. FLSA Section 3(g), however, defines the term *employ* to mean "to suffer or permit to work." [29 U.S.C. § 203(g)] Thus, an employer must compensate its employees for unauthorized work that, even though prohibited, is performed with the knowledge and acquiescence of management. All time spent performing unrequested work that an employer suffers or permits is considered compensable time. For example, if a worker voluntarily continues a task or assignment beyond the end of a shift, and a supervisor or manager knows or has reason to believe that the work is occurring, the employer is obliged to pay for the extra time in accordance with the FLSA's overtime pay requirements. Thus, even when an employer has a formal policy forbidding unauthorized work, it has to pay workers for time spent on unauthorized work if it suffers or permits the work performance. (See Q 6:1 for a more detailed discussion of unrequested work as compensable time.) [29 C.F.R. §§ 785.7–785.11; *see* Reich v. Dep't of Conservation & Natural Res., 28 F.3d 1076 (11th Cir. 1994)]

Therefore, for purposes of FLSA compensability and overtime, *hours worked* means not only time spent performing job duties within a worker's normal schedule, but also time spent performing other work or duties controlled or requested by the employer, suffered or permitted by the employer, or devoted primarily to the employer's benefit (see Q 6:1).

Basic Rate as an Alternative to Weekly Calculation of the Regular Rate

Q 7:8 What is a *basic rate* of pay and how is it related to an employee's regular rate?

As an alternative to a weekly regular rate, FLSA Section 7(g) permits employers to calculate straight and overtime pay using a *basic rate of pay*, a rate that is substantially equivalent to the employee's regular hourly rate and has been agreed to by both the employer and employee. Establishing a basic rate may occasionally be advisable to simplify overtime calculations when employees receive job or day rates, piece rates, commission payments, incentive bonuses, or employer-provided facilities. A basic rate is authorized only when it meets several general conditions and is derived using one of six approved methods (or has the special approval of the Wage and Hour Administrator). Use of a basic rate is rare in practice. [29 U.S.C. § 207(g)(3); 29 C.F.R. § 548.100]

Q 7:9 What are the general conditions for establishing a basic rate?

The general conditions for establishing a basic rate are the following:

1. The employee and the employer must agree to the establishment of an authorized basic rate for overtime pay purposes, either individually or through a union contract, before the overtime work is performed.

2. The basic rate established must be a specified rate or a rate that can be derived from the application of a specified method of operation.

3. The basic rate must not be less than the applicable minimum wage rate and must be substantially equivalent to the employee's average hourly straight-time earnings for the particular work over a representative period of time.

4. Overtime hours must be compensated at not less than one and one-half times the basic rate so established.

5. The hours for which the employee is paid one and one-half times the basic rate must include hours that qualify for overtime treatment with daily, weekend, and holiday premiums, and any other premiums described in Qs 7:48 and 7:50.

6. Extra overtime compensation must be paid on other additional pay that has not been considered in calculating the basic rate but that must be

included in the regular rate, such as incentive bonus pay or a shift differential.

[29 C.F.R. §§ 548.2, 548.200]

Any basic rate must include all of the additional pay to its employees that would otherwise be included in the regular rate. This would include such payments as bonuses or shift differentials. A "basic rate" which purports to exclude those payments is not a valid basic rate and may not be relied upon by an employer, regardless of whether it is contained in a collective bargaining agreement with the union representing the employees subject to the rate. For example, in *Featsent v. City of Youngstown* [70 F.3d 900 (6th Cir. 1995)], the court held that the employer had violated the FLSA by failing to pay overtime on additional payments made to employees in the form of shift differentials and hazardous duty pay, longevity bonuses, and other bonuses, all of which would have to be included in a regular rate calculation for overtime purposes.

Q 7:10 What are the approved methods for calculating an employee's basic rate of pay?

The Wage and Hour Division has published regulations allowing employers to establish a basic rate under any one of six approved methods without the Division's specific approval. [29 C.F.R. § 548.3] Provided that the general conditions for a basic rate discussed in Q 7:9 are met, the basic hourly rate can be arrived at by any of the following methods:

1. *Averaging salary.* A basic rate can be obtained by dividing a monthly or semimonthly salary by the number of workdays in each monthly or semimonthly period and then dividing the resulting figure by the number of hours in the normal or regular workday. This permits the employer to take into account the variations in the number of regular workdays in each pay period. This method is applicable only when the salary is paid for a specified number of days per week and a specified number of hours per day normally worked by the employee. [29 C.F.R. §§ 548.3(a), 548.301]

2. *Averaging earnings for periods other than a workweek.* The basic rate can also be obtained by averaging the employee's earnings, exclusive of premium payments excludable from the regular rate of pay, for all work performed during the workday or any other longer period not exceeding 16 calendar days. This method allows the employer, instead of averaging hours for the workweek, to average hourly earnings for a day or a specified number of days not to exceed 16, such as a biweekly or semimonthly pay period, or to average hourly earnings for the period required to complete a specified job or jobs. Under this method, although the basic rate can be obtained over a period longer than the workweek, overtime hours must still be determined on a workweek basis. [29 C.F.R. §§ 548.3(b), 548.302]

3. *Averaging earnings for each type of work.* The basic rate can be obtained by averaging the employee's earnings, exclusive of premium payments

excludable from the regular rate of pay, for each type of work performed during the workweek, or any other longer period not exceeding 16 calendar days, for which such average is regularly computed under the wage agreement between the employer and employee. This method allows the employer to compute separate basic rates of pay for each type of work performed. Overtime rates are then computed on the basis of the rate or rates applicable to the type of work performed during the overtime hours. [29 C.F.R. §§ 548.3(c), 548.303]

4. *Regular rate minus certain meals.* An employer can establish, pursuant to the wage agreement, a basic rate consisting of the employee's regular rate minus the cost of meals when the employer customarily furnishes not more than a single meal per day. The policy behind this basic rate method is that the overtime involved when an employer provides one meal per day is trivial and should be excluded. [29 C.F.R. §§ 548.3(d), 548.304]

5. *Regular rate minus incidental payments.* Under this wage agreement, an employer can establish a basic rate based on the employee's regular rate, excluding certain incidental payments in cash or in kind, such as bonuses or prizes, modest housing allowances, and school tuition. These payments must be small, such that if they were included in overtime computations, they would not increase the total overtime pay of the employee by more than 50 cents per week on the average for all overtime weeks in the period for which the additional payments are made. [29 C.F.R. §§ 548.3(e), 548.305]

6. *Average earnings for year or quarter preceding the current quarter.* An employer can establish a basic rate for a particular workweek equal to the employee's average hourly pay during the annual period or the quarterly period immediately preceding the calendar or fiscal quarter in which the workweek ends. This method can be used only when the employer sufficiently documents that the terms, conditions, and circumstances of employment during the prior period are not significantly different from those affecting the employee's regular rate during the current period. Moreover, the employer must follow Wage and Hour Division guidelines in computing average hourly pay in the prior period. [29 C.F.R. §§ 548. 3(f), 548.306]

Example. As a proper application of Section 548.3(b), described in number 2 above, a court approved an employer's and union's agreement to pay meter readers on a pay-per-route basis, which involved paying for a route expected to take eight hours by multiplying the established hourly rate of the collective bargaining agreement by eight hours, regardless of how long it would actually take any given employee to run the route. If an employee took less than eight hours, he or she would still be paid the full per-route sum. If an employee required more than eight hours to run a route, then he or she would be bumped up to one and one-half times the established hourly rate of the agreement for those hours in excess of eight for the day. The court agreed with the employer that this was a proper "basic rate" using an average daily rate. [Firestone v. S. Cal. Gas Co., 219 F.3d 1063 (9th Cir. 2000)]

Q 7:11 What other methods of establishing a basic rate have been approved?

In addition to the approved basic rates listed in Q 7:10, the Wage and Hour Administrator has approved the following basic rate agreement for the operator of a waste treatment facility. Under this agreement, the basic rate is calculated by either of the following methods:

1. Dividing the monthly total of the employee's base salary, shift differential, and cost-of-living allowance by 1/12 of the employee's regular scheduled hours per year; or

2. Dividing the monthly total of the employee's base salary, shift differential, and cost-of-living allowance by 1/12 of 2,080 hours (2,080 hours represents 52 weeks of 40-hour workweeks).

[Wage & Hour Opinion Letter, FLSA1973-1285 (July 1973)]

Q 7:12 Can an employer depart from approved methods of determining a basic rate?

Yes. If an employer wants to use an established basic rate other than one established under one of the approved methods detailed in Q 7:10, or to take advantage of two or more methods of determining a basic rate, the employer must file an application with the Wage and Hour Administrator for authorization. [29 C.F.R. §§ 548.4(a), 548.400] No particular form of application is required, but the employer or counsel should supply the following minimum information:

1. The agreement between the employer and the employee establishing the basic-rate plan, or a summary of the agreement if it is not in writing, including the proposed effective date, the term of the agreement, and a statement of the applicable overtime provisions;

2. A description of the basic rate or of the method or formula used to compute the basic rate for the type of work or position to which the rate is being applied;

3. A statement of the kind of jobs or employees covered by the basic rate; and

4. Facts and reasons relied on to show that the basic rate so established is substantially equivalent to the average hourly earnings of the employee, exclusive of overtime premiums.

[29 C.F.R. § 548.4(b)]

The application can be made by an employer or group of employers. If any of the covered employees is represented by a collective bargaining agent, a joint application of the employer and the bargaining agent should be filed with the Wage and Hour Administrator. [29 C.F.R. § 548.400(a)]

Q 7:13   Does use of a basic rate alter the fundamental obligation to calculate and pay overtime?

No. The use of a basic rate does not change the fact that overtime must be paid, or the methods used to calculate it. The methods of computing overtime pay on the basic rate for pieceworkers, hourly employees, and salaried employees are the same as the methods of computing overtime pay on the regular rate that are discussed throughout this chapter. [29 C.F.R. § 548.500]

Employees Entitled to Overtime

Q 7:14   Which employees are entitled to overtime compensation?

Employees covered by the FLSA or comparable state laws, who are not otherwise exempt from these provisions, are entitled to overtime pay at one and one-half times the regular rate for all hours worked in excess of 40 hours per workweek. A workweek must consist of seven consecutive days, but the workweek is not required to start or to end on any particular day of the calendar week. The beginning day and time of the workweek can be changed if the change is not intended as a method of avoiding payment of overtime compensation. (See Q 7:87 for discussion of changing the workweek.) [29 C.F.R. §§ 778.10, 778.103, 778.105]

Q 7:15   Aside from the exemption for executives, administrators, professionals, and outside sales persons, what are some of the other exemptions from the FLSA's overtime pay requirements?

The FLSA contains numerous total and partial exemptions that were put into the Act because of political and economic pressures. (See Chapters 4 and 5 for a detailed discussion of exemptions.) These include the following:

1. Employees in retail and service establishments whose regular hourly rate is greater than one and one-half times the applicable minimum wage for all hours worked in a workweek in which they work more than 40 hours, and who receive commissions that amount to more than half their total compensation (in a representative period of not less than one month) are exempt from the overtime requirements (see Q 5:35). [29 U.S.C. § 207(i)]

2. Employees in health care institutions need not receive time and one-half for hours worked in excess of 40 in a single workweek if they receive overtime pay for hours worked in excess of eight in a day and in excess of 80 in any 14-day period (see Q 5:42). [29 U.S.C. § 207(j)]

3. Police and firefighters whose tours of duty meet certain requirements are exempt. This exemption can apply to a cycle of employment of not less than 7 and not more than 28 consecutive days. For law enforcement personnel, overtime compensation is due for all hours worked in excess of 171 hours in a 28-day work period at one and one-half times the

employee's regular rate of pay; for firefighters, overtime pay is due after 212 hours (see Q 5:43). [29 U.S.C. § 207(k); 29 C.F.R. §§ 553.224, 553.230]

4. Employers in the tobacco industry can hire workers to assist in auctioning tobacco or providing services necessary and incidental to the sale at auction of tobacco for up to 14 weeks in the aggregate in any calendar year without paying premium pay if the employees receive not less than one and one-half times the applicable minimum wage for each hour worked in excess of 10 hours in any workday or in excess of 48 hours in any workweek. [29 U.S.C. § 207(m)]

5. State and local government agencies (but not private employers) can provide workers with compensatory time off at the rate of one and one-half hours for every hour of overtime worked in lieu of paying premium pay within regulatory limitations (see Qs 7:67–7:76 for further discussion of compensatory time). [29 U.S.C. § 207(o)]

6. An employer is permitted to employ a worker for not more than 10 hours above the normal 40 hours in a workweek without paying overtime compensation for the purpose of providing remedial education designed to provide reading and other basic skills at an eighth-grade level or below if the remedial education is provided to employees who lack a high school diploma or educational attainment at the eighth-grade level and as long as the remedial training is not designed to give the employee the specific training for a particular job (see Q 5:34). [29 U.S.C. § 207(q)]

See Chapters 4 and 5 for a complete discussion of exemptions from the overtime requirements of the FLSA.

Effect of Other Payments on Calculation of the Regular Rate and Overtime

Q 7:16　Which supplemental payments must be included in an employer's overtime pay computation?

Generally, all payments that constitute remuneration for work performed must be included in the regular rate for purposes of computing overtime pay. These payments include the following:

- Awards and prizes won based on the quality, quantity, or efficiency of an employee's performance of his or her normal work activities during regular work hours; [29 C.F.R. §§ 778.330, 778.331]

- Bonuses and incentive payments based on quality, quantity, or efficiency; [See 29 C.F.R. §§ 778.207(b), 778.208, 778.209]

- Commission payments; [29 C.F.R. § 778.117]

- Payments for meals, lodging, and facilities, when regarded as part of wages; [29 C.F.R. § 778.116]

- Shift differentials (i.e., extra wages for working undesirable hours) and dirty-work premiums (i.e., extra pay for work that is hazardous, arduous, or dirty); [29 C.F.R. § 778.207]
- Tip credits taken by an employer to fulfill minimum wage requirements; [29 C.F.R. § 531.60] and
- Other payments for work performed. [29 U.S.C. § 207(e)]

Q 7:17   What awards and prizes to an employee must be included in the regular rate?

The value of prizes won by an employee for quality, quantity, or efficiency in the performance of his or her customary tasks during regular work hours must be included in the calculation of the regular rate. An employer must generally allocate the prize value over the period in which it is earned. If merchandise is awarded, the amount the employer must allocate is the cost of the merchandise. [29 C.F.R. § 778.331]

When a prize is awarded for activities beyond the scope of the employee's customary duties or outside of the employee's customary work hours, whether the prize should be included as part of the regular rate depends on several factors:

- The amount of time, if any, spent by the employee on the contest;
- Whether the contest activities are related to the employee's customary tasks;
- Whether the competition involves work usually performed by other employees for the employer; and
- Whether the employer specifically urges the employee to participate in the contest or leads the employee to believe that he or she will not merit advancement or promotion if he or she does not participate.

[29 C.F.R. § 778.332]

Q 7:18   What bonuses and incentive payments must be included in the regular rate?

Any kind of bonus and incentive payment that depend on the quality, quantity, efficiency of production, or hours worked are considered remuneration to the employee and generally must be included in the regular rate. (See Q 7:39 for examples of bonuses and incentive payments that must be included in the regular rate.) [*See* 29 U.S.C. § 207(e); 29 C.F.R. § 778.208; Wage & Hour Opinion Letter, FLSA2005-4NA (July 2005)]

Q 7:19   What commissions are included in the regular rate?

For commissioned employees, who are not exempt from overtime under Section 207(i), weekly commission payments must be added to all other earnings for the workweek. That total is then divided by the hours worked in the workweek to obtain the employee's regular rate. When commission payments are deferred beyond the week in which they are earned, an employer must apportion the commission over the workweeks during which it was earned. Where appropriate, an employer may accomplish this by allocating an equal portion to each workweek or to each hour worked during the relevant time period in which the commission was earned. [29 C.F.R. §§ 778.117–778.119; Wage & Hour Opinion Letter, FLSA1997-2065 (Dec. 1997)]

Q 7:20   Are meals, lodging, and other facilities furnished by the employer included in the employee's regular rate?

Yes, under most circumstances, the reasonable cost of certain employer-provided lodgings, meals, and other facilities furnished to an employee must be included in the employee's regular rate unless it is specifically excluded under the terms of a bona fide collective bargaining agreement. The lodging, meals, or facilities provided must be "customarily furnished" to be counted as wages. In addition, lodging, meals, and facilities can be counted as wages only when they are for the convenience of the employees and are accepted voluntarily. [29 U.S.C. §§ 203(m), 207(e); 29 C.F.R. § 778.116; Wage & Hour Opinion Letter, FLSA1985-1584 (July 1985)]

Examples of what should be considered "lodging, meals, and facilities" include: meals furnished at company restaurants or cafeterias or by hospitals, hotels, or restaurants to their employees; meals, dormitory rooms, and tuition furnished by colleges to their student-employees; housing furnished for dwelling purposes; general merchandise furnished at company stores (including food, clothing, and household articles); fuel, electricity, water, and gas furnished for the noncommercial use of employees; and transportation to employees between their homes and work (when the travel time does not constitute hours worked under the FLSA and the transportation is not incidental and necessary to the employment). [29 C.F.R. § 531.32]

Yet it is possible for "in-kind" items to be excluded from the regular rate. The DOL has said that the value of an apartment that an apartment complex manager was required to live in as a condition of employment, and which the employer and the employee did not consider to be a means of compensation, need not be included in the employee's regular rate for purposes of calculating overtime. Note that this opinion is highly unusual, hinging on the fact that the employer considered this apartment occupancy to serve a business purpose. The opinion letter points out that where facilities are furnished to employees as payment for services, those facilities must be included in the regular rate. [Wage & Hour Opinion Letter, FLSA1999-2182 (Sept. 1999)]

Q 7:21   Are shift differentials and dirty-work premiums included in the regular rate?

Usually, yes. Some employers pay employees an additional amount for working unusual shifts (shift differentials) or for work that is hazardous, arduous, or dirty (dirty-work premiums). Shift differentials and dirty-work premiums must be included in the regular rate if the employee receiving the differential is regularly scheduled to work the shift that is eligible for the differential. If, however, the differential is at least one and one-half times the employee's regular rate and paid to the employee pursuant to a collective bargaining agreement that specifies regular work hours, the differential can be excluded from the employee's regular rate and credited against overtime under clock-overtime rules (see Qs 7:47, 7:50). [29 U.S.C. § 207(e)(7); 29 C.F.R. § 778.207; Herman v. City of St. Petersburg, 131 F. Supp. 2d 1329 (M.D. Fla. 2001) (city police department violated the FLSA in calculating overtime by failing to include shift differential pay when computing the regular rate, despite term in collective bargaining agreement which purported to permit calculation of overtime without reference to shift differential pay)]

Q 7:22 How is a tip credit included in the regular rate?

Under the FLSA, employers can reduce a tipped employee's pay below the minimum wage provided that the employee is able to earn the difference in tips paid by customers. The amount by which the employee's wage is reduced is referred to as the tip credit. The amount of the tip credit taken by an employer to fulfill minimum wage requirements must be included in a tipped employee's regular rate of pay. Employers are limited to a tip credit of $3.72 ($4.42 effective July 24, 2008) per hour, and employers cannot use a different tip credit during overtime hours than they use during straight-time hours. (See Qs 3:13 and 3:14 for further discussion of the tip credit and its requirements.) [29 U.S.C. § 203(m); 29 C.F.R. §§ 531.52, 531.60; Wage & Hour Opinion Letter, FLSA1976-1439 (July 1976)]

Further, the FLSA requires that the employer give employees notice that it intends to claim a tip credit. The mere fact that employees were willing to work for an amount less than the statutory minimum wage does not, by itself, suggest that the employees knew that a tip credit was being taken. [Martin v. Tango's Rest., Inc., 969 F.2d 1319 (1st Cir. 1992)]

When analyzing tip credits, the label applied to a service charge is not controlling. For example, when a collective bargaining agreement labels a percentage service charge added by a hotel to customers' bills as a "gratuity" for banquet waiters, that charge is regarded as a commission rather than a tip. In one case, the court concluded that since the service charge in question was not discretionary, the entire amount of the charge had to be included in the calculation of the employee's regular rate. [Mechmet v. Four Seasons Hotel, Ltd., 825 F.2d 1173 (7th Cir. 1987); see also Wage & Hour Opinion Letter, FLSA1997-2045 (Aug. 1997)]

Q 7:23 What are some other payments that might be required to be included in the regular rate?

Additional wage payments made to employees because of their completion of educational requirements, training, or a degree program, or for the possession of specialized skills, must be included in the regular rate.

For example, in a recent federal appeals court case, a town made certain annual payments to its police officers for educational attainments (e.g., an officer receiving a bachelor's degree from an accredited institution in a field directly related to the officer's responsibility received an additional $250 per year). The appeals court ruled that such payments must be included in the regular rate of pay. [Wheeler v. Hampton Township, 399 F.3d 238 (3d Cir. 2005); *see also* Wage & Hour Opinion Letter, FLSA1985-1598 (Oct. 1985)] Similarly, a court recently held that an employer that paid employees a lump-sum amount for a sick leave buyback were required to include the amount in the regular rate of pay. [Acton v. City of Columbia, Mo., 436 F.3d 969 (8th Cir. 2006)]

Other payments that should be included in the regular rate are the following:

- Earned work credits under a collective bargaining agreement; [Reich v. Interstate Brands Corp., 57 F.3d 574 (7th Cir. 1995)]
- The monthly fee, if any, paid to canine officers for the care and grooming of police canines; [Theisen v. City of Maple Grove, 41 F. Supp. 2d 932 (D. Minn. 1999)]
- Longevity pay paid pursuant to a collective bargaining agreement or other contract; and [Wage & Hour Opinion Letter, FLSA1985-1604 (Nov. 1985)]
- Supplemental payments made to account for an employee's inability to earn his pre-disability wages. [Local 246 Util. Workers Union of Am. v. S. Cal. Edison Co., 83 F.3d 292 (9th Cir. 1996)]

In 1999, the Wage and Hour Division issued an opinion letter stating that certain stock option plan profits would constitute remuneration that had to be included in the regular rate of participant employees. That opinion letter was limited in a subsequent opinion letter. However, as a result of public outcry and concern about the impossibility of complying with overtime requirements if such a fringe benefit had to be included in the regular rate, the Worker Economic Opportunity Act was signed into law May 2000. That statute excludes from the regular rate the value of income derived from employer-provided grants or rights provided pursuant to a stock option, stock appreciation right, or stock purchase program. (See Q 7:38 for further discussion of this provision.) [Wage & Hour Opinion Letter, FLSA1999-2112 (Feb. 1999), limited by Wage & Hour Opinion Letter, FLSA2000-2167 (Jan. 2000), and overruled by 29 U.S.C. § 207(e), as amended]

Q 7:24   What types of payments are excluded from an employer's calculation of the regular rate?

The FLSA excludes certain payments from the regular rate if they are made for time not worked by the employee or if they are not based on hours worked, quantity produced, quality produced, or efficiency. [29 U.S.C. § 207(e)] Payments to employees that generally fall within these exceptions include the following:

- Gifts and service rewards
- Paid leave from work (e.g., holiday, sick leave, and vacation pay)

- Irregular discretionary bonuses
- Reimbursement of expenses
- Talent fees
- Employee benefit plan contributions
- Employee referral bonuses
- Suggestion plan awards
- Severance pay
- Veterans' subsistence pay
- Certain employee stock options
- Bona fide employee stock purchase programs
- Fringe benefits such as health and retirement which are provided through third parties

[See 29 C.F.R. §§ 778.200, 778.211–778.214, 778.217, 778.218, 778.221, 778. 223, 778.332, 778.333, 778.600]

Certain premium payments, discussed in Qs 7:46 through 7:50, are also excluded from the regular rate.

Q 7:25   Are gifts to employees excluded from the regular rate?

It depends on why the gift was made. Employer gifts or payments in the nature of gifts are excluded from the regular rate as long as the gifts are given or the payments are made as a reward for service, at Christmas time, or on other special occasions and are not measured by or dependent on hours worked, production, or efficiency. [29 U.S.C. § 207(e)(1)] A payment (in cash or otherwise) is not considered a gift if it is:

1. Measured by or dependent on hours worked, production, or efficiency;
2. So substantial that employees consider the gift part of the wages for which they work; or
3. Paid pursuant to a contract.

[29 C.F.R. § 778.212]

Examples of gifts that can be excluded from the regular rate are birthday presents, gifts to longtime employees on the anniversary of their employment, turkeys at Thanksgiving, Christmas bonuses, and longevity pay if not paid pursuant to contract. [See 29 C.F.R. § 778.212]

Q 7:26   Is pay for vacation or leave or sick time excluded from the regular rate?

Yes. Payments for time not worked are excluded from the computation of the regular rate under the FLSA. Many fringe benefits fall into this category, including payments for vacations, holidays not worked, periods of illness, failure of the employer to provide sufficient work after employees have been asked to report, and other payments that are not made as compensation for hours in employment. Further, since such payments are not made as compensation for hours worked, they cannot be credited toward any overtime pay due to employees. Indeed, even an express agreement between the employer and its employee stating that fringe benefits would accrue to employees in lieu of overtime compensation will not be upheld, since waiver of statutory wages is not permitted. [29 U.S.C. § 207(e)(2), (h); 29 C.F.R. § 778.218; Dunlop v. Gray-Goto, Inc., 528 F.2d 792 (10th Cir. 1976); Wage & Hour Opinion Letter, FLSA2006-22NA (Oct. 2006); Wage & Hour Opinion Letter, FLSA1997-2032 (June 1997)]

The Wage and Hour regulations also provide that exclusion for time not worked applies when the employee foregoes a holiday or vacation but still receives the holiday or vacation pay. Thus when an employee who is entitled to a paid holiday or vacation foregoes the holiday or vacation, performs work for the employer, and is paid at the customary rate (or higher) for hours worked on a holiday or vacation day, the additional specified sum received as holiday or vacation pay is to be excluded from the regular rate. [29 C.F.R. § 778.219(a); *see also* Wage & Hour Opinion Letter, FLSA2006-18NA (July 2006)] One caveat, however: many collective bargaining agreements require employees to count compensated hours as hours worked. This is permissible under the FLSA.

Q 7:27   What are the requirements for a discretionary bonus to be excluded from the regular rate?

A bonus that is paid in recognition of services during a given period is excluded from the regular rate for purposes of calculating overtime if:

1. The fact that payment is to be made and the amount of the bonus are both determined by the employer in its sole discretion, at or near the end of the period the bonus covers; and

2. The payment is not made pursuant to any prior contract, agreement, or promise that would lead the employee to expect the payment on a regular basis.

[29 U.S.C. § 207(e)(3); 29 C.F.R. § 778.211] Further discussion of bonuses follows in Qs 7:39 through 7:45.

Q 7:28   Are business-related expenses that are reimbursed by the employer excluded from the regular rate?

Yes. Reimbursement by an employer for the actual expense that an employee incurs on an employer's behalf is not included in the employee's regular rate as long as the reimbursement reasonably approximates the expense incurred. [29 U.S.C. § 207(e)(2)] Such excludable expenses for which employees are commonly reimbursed include the following:

- The purchase of supplies, tools, materials, or equipment used on the job;

- The purchase, laundering, and repair of uniforms or special clothing that the employer requires;
- Certain travel, lodging, and meal expenses incurred when the employee is on the road for the employer's business;
- "Supper money" given to an employee who normally is able to return home for dinner to compensate for the cost of dinner when the employee is required to continue work beyond the normal business day; and
- Relocation expenses or travel expenses for the commute when the employee is on a temporary assignment to a place other than the employee's regular workplace.

[29 C.F.R. § 778.217]

The reimbursement does not have to be accurate down to the penny. The Wage and Hour regulations merely require that "the amount of the reimbursement reasonably approximates the expenses incurred." So, for example, mileage and per diem allowances are excludable as long as they are not excessive. In one recent federal court case, an electrician was hired to work at a jobsite 100 miles away from his home and given a "per diem" of $100 a week. Because all employees received the same per diem—regardless of where they lived—the electrician contended that the per diem policy was simply a way to increase the employees' salaries without raising their FLSA regular rate of pay for overtime purposes. The appeals court said that the FLSA requires each employee's expenses to be examined on a case-by-case basis to see whether the per diem is appropriate and reasonable. In the electrician's particular situation, the per diem was reasonable and was therefore excludable from the regular rate. [Berry v. Excel Group, Inc., 288 F.3d 252 (5th Cir. 2002)]

The expenses for which reimbursement is made must, in order to merit exclusion from the regular rate, be incurred by the employee on the employer's behalf or for its benefit or convenience. If the employer reimburses the employee for expenses normally incurred by the employee for his or her own benefit, the employer is, of course, increasing the employee's regular rate. For example, an employee normally incurs expenses in traveling to and from work, buying lunch, paying rent, and the like. If the employer reimburses the employee for these normal everyday expenses, the payment is not excluded from the regular rate as "reimbursement for expenses." Whether the employer "reimburses" the employee for such expenses or furnishes the facilities (such as free lunches or free housing), the amount paid to the employee (or the reasonable cost to the employer or fair value where facilities are furnished) enters into the regular rate of pay. [29 C.F.R. §§ 778.116, 778.217]

Q 7:29   Are talent fees excluded from the regular rate?

Usually. Talent fees, which are extra payments made to secure the services of a performer, generally can be excluded from the regular rate for overtime purposes. [29 U.S.C. § 207(e)(3)(c)] Talent fees must satisfy the following conditions to be excludable:

1. Payment must be made to an employee having regular duties as a staff performer (including announcers) and must be rendered for services as a performer on a particular program or series of programs, or for special services on a particular program or series of programs.

2. Payment must be pursuant to an employment contract or collective bargaining agreement in a specified amount agreed on in advance.

3. Payment must be in addition to the straight-time and overtime pay that would be due to the performer under the agreement or the law, but must not include any payment that can be offset against any compensation otherwise due to the employee.

4. Payment cannot be made to persons who do not actually appear on the program, such as script writers, engineers, and stage hands.

[29 C.F.R. §§ 550.1, 550.2]

Q 7:30   Are employee benefit plan contributions excluded from an employee's regular rate even though they are paid on behalf of the employee?

The FLSA expressly excludes from the regular rate "contributions irrevocably made by an employer to a trustee or third person pursuant to a bona fide plan for providing old-age, retirement, life, accident, or health insurance or similar benefits for employees." [29 U.S.C. § 207(e)(4); 29 C.F.R. § 778.200(a)]

A bona fide benefit plan is a plan that:

1. Is funded by contributions made pursuant to a specific plan or program adopted by the employer or pursuant to a collective bargaining agreement;

2. Is communicated to the employees;

3. Is primarily for the purpose of providing systematically for the payment of benefits to employees on account of death, disability, retirement, illness, medical expenses, and the like;

4. Provides for a definite formula for determining contributions and benefits;

5. Provides for the irrevocable payment of employer contributions to a trustee or third person pursuant to an insurance agreement, trust, or other funded arrangement;

6. Does not permit employees to assign their benefits; and

7. Does not permit employees to receive any part of the employer's contribution in cash instead of the provided benefits.

[29 C.F.R. § 778.215]

A plan can be either wholly employer-financed or contributory, and it can be financed out of profits or with matching employee contributions. If a plan otherwise qualifies as a bona fide benefit plan, it is not disqualified because it provides, incidentally, for payment to an employee of all or part of the amount credited on behalf of the employee at the time the employee leaves employment, or on termination of the plan, or under certain circumstances during the employee's employment (such as a qualified loan against a retirement account). [29 C.F.R. §§ 778.214, 778.215] The Wage and Hour Division also says that it makes no difference if the required contribution levels differ among employees who participate in the plan. For example, if nonsmoking participants in a health plan have to contribute $100 less per month than participants who smoke, this has no impact on the employees' regular rate of pay. [Wage & Hour Opinion Letter, FLSA2004-2391 (Oct. 2004)]

If a benefit plan does not meet these requirements, it is not bona fide and employer contributions must be treated as part of the employee's regular rate of pay and apportioned over the workweeks for the period during which the benefits accrued.

Employer contributions to an employee's 401(k) plan may also be excluded from the regular rate as long as the plan meets the requirements of a bona fide thrift or savings plan as defined in the regulations. [29 C.F.R. pt. 547] These requirements include that:

1. The plan is a program in writing, adopted by the employer or pursuant to a collective bargaining agreement, for the purpose of encouraging employees to accumulate savings.

2. The plan is communicated or made available to employees.

3. The plan must set forth the categories of employees and eligibility requirements, which may not include hours of work (except for part-time or casual employees), production, or efficiency.

4. The amount an employee may save must be specified in the plan.

5. The employer's contribution to the plan generally may not exceed 15 percent of the participating employee's total annual earnings, nor may it exceed the employee's contribution to the plan.

6. The employer must apportion its contributions to participating employees by an established formula.

Further, an employee's participation must be voluntary and no employee's wage or salary may be dependent on or influenced by the plan. [29 U.S.C. § 207(e)(3)(b); 29 C.F.R. §§ 547.1, 547.2; Wage & Hour Opinion Letter, FLSA999-2135 (Apr. 1999)]

Q 7:31   Are payments made pursuant to an employer's profit-sharing plan excluded from the regular rate?

Yes, if the plan is a bona fide profit-sharing plan as defined in the regulations. [29 C.F.R. pt. 549] These requirements include the following:

1. The plan or arrangement is a program, in writing and communicated or made available to the employees, for the purpose of distributing to employees a share of the profits in addition to their regular wages and salaries;

2. All contributions or allocations by the employer are derived solely from profits and are made periodically;

3. Eligibility extends at least to all nonexempt employees (officers may be excluded) or to a designated classification of employees with the approval of the Wage and Hour Administrator;

4. The amounts paid to employees are determined in accordance with an established formula;

5. An employee's total share may not be diminished because of any other remuneration received; and

6. Provision for payment is made within a reasonable time after the profit distribution is determined.

[29 C.F.R. §§ 549.1, 549.2]

Thus, an employer's semiannual bonus (profit sharing plan) was found to meet the requirements of a bona fide thrift or savings plan excludable from the regular rate. The purpose of the plan was to allow employees to share in the economic reward for the success of the corporation. The profit bonus was based upon the company's semiannual financial performance from operations—the difference between net sales revenue and net expense to produce the revenue, for one half of the corporate fiscal year. A positive difference between net sales and net expenses (profit) would result in a semiannual bonus distribution of 15 percent to eligible employees as a group. To be eligible for the incentive bonus, an employee had to be actively listed on the payroll as of the last day of the six-month period. No employee share may be determined based on attendance, quality or quantity of work, rate of production, or efficiency. Further, the amount to be paid periodically to employees may not be a fixed sum. The employer's payments must not be based on any factors other than profits (such as hours of work, production, sales, or savings costs). [Wage & Hour Opinion Letter, FLSA1999-2143 (Apr. 1999)]

Q 7:32 Are on-call and call-back pay excluded from the regular rate?

Not usually. On-call and call-back pay typically consist of pay for a specified number of hours at straight-time or overtime rates, paid on occasions when, after an employee's scheduled hours of work have ended and without prearrangement, he or she remains available to respond or does respond to a call from the employer to perform some extra or emergency work.

Pay of this type must generally be included in the computation of an employee's regular rate for FLSA overtime-pay purposes. However, in certain circumstances, it may qualify for the exclusion from the regular rate for "payments made for occasional periods when no work is performed due to . . . failure of the employer to provide sufficient work or other similar cause" (see Q 7:63).

Note that while the on-call or call-back pay must usually be included in the regular rate, the on-call or call-back period is not always considered compensable working time under the FLSA. The degree of readiness in which the employees must hold themselves and the degree to which their liberty is restricted seem to be the factors that are most frequently determinative. If the employees are closely confined, either upon the employer's premises or elsewhere, the period is compensable. On the other hand, if employees may come and go as they please, even though they must leave a telephone number where they can be reached, the time is not compensable.

Whether the period qualifies as compensable time does not affect the inclusion of an on-call or call-back payment in the regular rate of pay.

- If the period qualifies as compensable hours worked, the payment is compensation for those hours.

- If the period is not compensable hours worked, the payment is not allocable to any specific working hours but is clearly paid as compensation for performing a duty involved in the employee's job.

Example. Smith is employed under a contract which provides that during specific eight-hour periods when he is away from work and assigned to make calls, he will receive $8 for each period in addition to pay at his regular (or overtime) rate for hours actually spent in making calls. He is not confined to his home during these periods, but may come and go as he pleases so long as he leaves a telephone number where he can be reached. Hours spent by Smith on call, as distinguished from those hours spent making calls, are not hours worked within the meaning of the FLSA, but the $8 received as on-call compensation must be included in the computation of his regular rate.

(See Qs 6:16 through 6:18 for discussion of on-call time.) [29 C.F.R. §§ 778. 221, 778.223, 785.15–785.17]

Q 7:33   If an employer requires any employee who reports that he or she is sick and/or unable to work due to illness or disability to remain in his or her home for the entire 24-hour work day associated with his or her shift, is any of that time counted as work time for purposes of calculating overtime?

No, according to several district court decisions. For example, a city police department mandated that any police officer, detective, sergeant, and/or lieutenant who reported in sick and/or unable to work due to illness or disability was required to remain in his or her home for the entire 24-hour work day associated with his or her shift. Further, any of these same employees who reported sick on a Friday or Saturday were required to remain in their residence throughout the weekend. The employees argued that the time spent at home under this policy was like "on call" time for which employees must be compensated if personal activities are severely restricted. The courts, however, disagreed and noted the reasonableness of requiring an officer taking a sick day to behave in accord with the representation of illness or injury that led the employer to grant the leave in the first place. The court further held that sick and injured officers are not fit to work, are not engaged to wait at home for work, and therefore are not working (unlike employees on call). Additionally, in this particular case, the court noted that the policy only applied to those employees unable to perform even "limited capacity assignments." Therefore, the court believed that the policy made it clear that the only people calling in sick are those too ill or too injured to work in even a limited function. [Monserrate v. City of N.Y., 142 Lab. Cas. (CCH) ¶ 34,171, 2000 U.S. Dist. LEXIS 17013 (S.D.N.Y. Nov. 22, 2000); *see also* Aiken v. City of Memphis, 190 F.3d 753 (6th Cir. 1999); DeBraska v. City of Milwaukee, 189 F.3d 650 (7th Cir. 1999)]

Q 7:34   Is an employee referral bonus excluded from the regular rate?

It depends. Under an older Wage and Hour opinion letter, when a company has a plan under which employees who recruit new workers are paid sums of money after the new employee has remained on the job at least 90 days, such sums need not be included in the employee's regular rate if:

1. Participation in the activity is strictly voluntary;
2. The employee's efforts in connection with the recruiting do not involve significant amounts of time; and
3. The activity is limited to after-hours solicitation as part of the employee's social affairs.

[Wage & Hour Opinion Letter, FLSA1969-941 (Jan. 1969)]

Contrast that with a 1999 opinion letter in which the DOL said on a different set of facts that employee referral bonuses should be *included* in the regular rate.

The 1999 letter involved a company that sold a variety of products and services. The company was implementing a program intended to reward employees who identified the names of potential customers. Employees would be eligible for an award if they forwarded to the sales department the name of a potential new customer and the customer agreed to purchase one or more of the company's products or services. No sales department employees were permitted to participate. The company anticipated that the majority of referrals would come from employees who interact with the public, such as those who make deliveries.

The DOL acknowledged that a referral bonus received by an employee for merely recommending a potential customer is not includible in the regular rate if the employee performs no work in securing the name of the sales prospect and spends no time on the matter. However, that was not the case on the facts of the ruling. The participating employees will engage in an activity for their employer's benefit—filling out a card with the name and location of both the potential new customer and the employee. The fact that the program was expected to last one year or more increased the potential for employees to spend significant amounts of time and effort in such work activities. Therefore, the bonuses cannot be excluded from the regular rate. [Wage & Hour Opinion Letter, FLSA1999-2180 (Aug. 1999)]

Q 7:35   Can employer-paid awards to employees be excluded from the regular rate?

Some employer-paid awards to employees can be excluded from the regular rate. For an award to be excluded from the regular rate, it must be shown either that the award was not paid to the employee for employment or that it is not a thing of value that is part of wages. For example, if an employee is given a prize for recommending a potential customer to whom a sale is later made, the award would not be considered compensation if the winner performed no work in securing the name of the sales prospect and spent no time on the matter for the company in any way. [29 C.F.R. §§ 778.330, 778.332] However, this result is currently in question as the result of a 1999 Wage and Hour Division Opinion Letter. In that letter, the DOL cited the very regulatory sections cited above but held that a proposed prize plan would violate that section, because employees would be engaged in "work" when they filled out a card containing the name and address of a prospective customer. The proposed plan rejected by the DOL involved the following: nonsales employees of a company that sells a variety of products and services would be eligible to receive a prize if a forwarded sales prospect actually bought services or products from the company. The program was set up so that the time required to forward a potential customer's name would be negligible; forwarding potential customer information would not be a normal part of the eligible participants' jobs; the specific activity of forwarding potential customer information is not a job duty normally performed by other employees; and the program would be voluntary. Although this appears to meet each and every one of the requirements set forth in 29 C.F.R. Section 778.332(b), the Wage and Hour Division rejected the plan and indicated that the prize money would have to be included in the regular rate of the prize recipients. The Wage and Hour Division felt that the work involved—obtaining the names of potential customers—was work normally performed by employees of the company—that is, the sales staff. Furthermore, the Wage and Hour Division was impressed with the fact that employees would gather this information during their regular working hours while performing their normal work activities. [Wage & Hour Opinion Letter, FLSA1999-2180 (Aug. 1999)]

Q 7:36   Under what circumstances can suggestion plan awards be excluded from an employee's regular rate?

Awards and prizes paid under a bona fide suggestion system can be excluded from the regular rate if:

1. The amount of the prize has no relation to the employee's earnings, but is based on the value of the suggestion to the company;

2. The prize is the result of additional effort or ingenuity unrelated to and outside the scope of the usual and customary duties of any employee of the class eligible to participate;

3. The prize is not a substitute for wages;

4. No employee is required or specifically urged to participate or led to believe that promotion or advancement depends on submitting suggestions;

5. There is no time limit on the submittal of suggestions;

6. The invitation to submit suggestions is general in nature and no specific assignment is outlined; and

7. The employer has no knowledge or notice, before the submission of the suggestion, that an employee is preparing it under circumstances that would indicate the employer's approval of the particular task or schedule of the employee.

[29 C.F.R. § 778.333]

Q 7:37 Are severance pay and subsistence payments excluded from the regular rate?

Mostly, yes. Severance pay given to an employee at the time of separation from employment has been considered on at least one occasion to be a gratuity and, as such, was not included as part of the regular rate used in computing overtime payments due to the employee. [Tobin v. Memphis Bearing & Supply Co., 11 Wage & Hour Cas. (BNA) 228 (W.D. Tenn. 1952); *see also* Dep't of Labor v. Green Giant Co., 23 Wage & Hour Cas. (BNA) 1207 (Del. 1978) (severance pay not wages for purposes of state wage payment statute)] Although there are no recent decisions on the question, it is reasonable to assume that severance pay that is paid not as a matter of contract is something of a gift or other payment made for hours not worked, and therefore excluded from the calculation of the regular rate. [*See* 29 U.S.C. § 207(e)]

Subsistence payments to veterans employed in on-the-job training programs are not included in the regular rate on which overtime pay is based under the FLSA. These payments are excluded because they are not paid as compensation for services rendered to an employer or intended as subsidy payments for the employer. As such, they do not qualify as wages. [29 C.F.R. § 778.600]

Q 7:38 Are employee stock options, stock appreciation rights, and bona fide employee stock purchase programs excludable from the regular rate?

Yes, as long as certain conditions are met. The Worker Economic Opportunity Act amended FLSA Section 207(e) (and was signed into law on May 18, 2000) to provide a safe harbor to employers to protect them from liability for stock option or similar programs extended to employees in past years. The law was designed to encourage companies to include hourly workers in their stock option programs. Any value or income derived from employer-provided grants or rights provided pursuant to a stock option, stock appreciation right, or a bona fide employee stock purchase program is excludable from an employee's regular rate if: (1) grants are made pursuant to a program, the terms and conditions of which are communicated to participating employees either at the beginning of the employee's participation in the program or at the time of the grant; or (2) in the case of stock options and stock appreciation rights, the grant or right cannot be exercisable for a period of at least six months after the time of grant (except that grants or rights may become exercisable because of an employee's death, disability, retirement, or a change in corporate ownership, or other circumstances permitted by regulation), and the exercise price is at least 85 percent of the fair market value of the stock at the time of grant; and for both grants and rights; (3) exercise of any grant or right is voluntary; and (4) any determinations regarding the award of, and the amount of, employer-provided grants or rights that are based on performance are (a) made based upon meeting previously established performance criteria (which may include hours of work, efficiency, or productivity) of any business unit consisting of at least ten employees or of a facility, except that any determinations may be based on length of service or minimum schedule of hours or days of work; or (b) made based upon the past performance (which may include any criteria) of one or more employees in a given period so long as the determination is in the sole discretion of the employer and not pursuant to any prior contract. [29 U.S.C. § 207(e)(8)]

Effect of Bonuses on the Regular Rate

Q 7:39   What effect do bonuses have on an employer's computation of the regular rate?

Production, incentive, and attendance bonuses generally constitute earnings related to hours worked and must therefore be included in the computation of the regular rate. Specifically, bonuses and incentive payments that depend on the quality, quantity, or efficiency of production or hours worked are includible in the computation of the regular rate. Such bonus payments have the effect of increasing the regular rate, and an increase in the regular rate increases the amount of overtime pay owed. [29 U.S.C. § 207(e); 29 C.F.R. §§ 778.210, 778.211, 778.213]

Examples of types of bonuses that would constitute earnings include the following:

- Lump-sum bonuses paid pursuant to a labor contract or other agreement. [29 C.F.R. § 778.211(c)]
- Production or work incentive bonuses. [29 C.F.R. § 778.211(c); Wage & Hour Opinion Letter, FLSA1995-1821 (Jan. 1995)]
- Bonuses that are based on a percentage of sales. [29 C.F.R. § 778.211(b)]
- Bonuses for exceeding certain goals in the preceding year related to return on assets, return on equity, deposit growth, and efficiency ratio. [Wage & Hour Opinion Letter, FLSA2006-9NA (May 2006)]
- Cost-of-living bonuses or allowances. [Wage & Hour Opinion Letter, FLSA1994-1871 (Feb. 1994)]

- Guaranteed-wage bonuses paid to bring employees up to a specified wage level. [*See* 29 C.F.R. § 778.211(c)]

- Attendance bonuses. [29 C.F.R. § 778.211(c); Wage & Hour Opinion Letter, FLSA1995-1821 (Jan. 1995)]

- Lump-sum payments "buying back" unused sick days. [Acton v. City of Columbia, 436 F.3d 969, 977 (8th Cir. 2006)] The Sixth Circuit reached a different result in *Featsent v. City of Youngstown* [70 F.3d 900, 905 (6th Cir. 1995)], ruling that bonuses for the nonuse of accrued sick leave could be excluded from the regular rate of pay because of their lack of relation to the employees' compensation for services and hours of service.

- Signing bonuses. [Wage & Hour Opinion Letter, FLSA1995-1821 (Jan. 1995); *see* 29 C.F.R. § 778.211(c)]

- Quarterly payments for as long as the employees remain employed with the employer in exchange for the employees' promise not to compete during 30 months after their employment. [Wage & Hour Opinion Letter, FLSA1999-2211 (Nov. 1999)]

There are certainly other categories of reward or compensation created by employers and employees. To the extent those payments are based on an employee's hours, or quality or quantity of production or sales, they must be included in the employee's regular rate for overtime purposes. [29 C.F.R. §§ 778.209, 778.211(a)]

Bonuses includible in the regular rate, even when payment is not actually made for many weeks, must be apportioned over the workweeks in which the bonus amounts were earned, and additional overtime pay must be calculated for those weeks in which more than 40 hours were worked. [29 C.F.R. § 778.209]

Q 7:40   What factors do courts look to in determining whether a bonus payment is discretionary and thus excludable from the regular rate?

When both the fact of and amount of a bonus are solely within the discretion of the employer, and the employee has no contractual right to any specific bonus payment amount, the bonus so paid is considered discretionary and can be excluded from the employee's regular rate (and thus is not counted for purposes of overtime). [29 U.S.C. § 207(e)(3)(a); 29 C.F.R. § 778.211] For a bonus to be discretionary and therefore excludable from the regular rate, both the fact that the payment is to be made and the amount of the payment must be determined at the sole discretion of the employer, at or near the end of a given bonus period and not pursuant to any prior contract or agreement. Therefore, any bonus that is the result of a collective bargaining agreement, or that is promised to the employee, would be regarded as remuneration for employment and included in the regular rate. This has the effect of increasing overtime pay calculated under the FLSA. Similarly, a bonus payment conditioned on active employment at the time of the payment is viewed as an inducement for an employee to continue in employment until the payment is made and must be included in the regular rate. [29 C.F.R. § 778.211; Wage & Hour Opinion Letter, FLSA1986-1581 (Apr. 1986)]

An incentive pay plan that was labeled by the employer as a "discretionary bonus" was actually a bonus that had to be included in the employees' regular rate of pay in *Herman v. Anderson Floor Co.* [11 F. Supp. 2d 1038 (E.D. Wis. 1998)] The employer had devised a system to pay to the employees those labor costs not used by the crew in the following fashion: for each job a job labor figure would be determined and the crew leader would be paid that figure as a minimum for the job; if the crew leader could keep the labor costs below that job labor figure, the extra money could be paid to the crew members as decided by the crew leader. The employer argued that this was a discretionary bonus, because it was up to the crew leader to decide how much, if any, of the extra went to each crew member. The court, however, held that this "premium pay" was really incentive pay. It was not a discretionary bonus, because the employer was committed to pay the premium, albeit in varying amounts based on the job, and thus the premiums were an expected part of the employees' wages. [*Id.* at 1045–46]

Q 7:41 Are vendor bonuses considered discretionary and thus excludable from the regular rate?

It depends. A vendor bonus is a payment from a manufacturer or distributor to the sales employees of another employer (e.g., a retailer). The payment is made an incentive or a reward for selling the product or service of the manufacturer/distributor.

According to the Wage and Hour Division's Field Operations Handbook extra payments from manufacturers or distributors to the sales employees of a retail establishment for selling certain items or brands are wages that must be included in the regular rate. [Wage and Hour Division's Field Operations Handbook § 32b07]. But a recent Wage and Hour Opinion Letter [FLSA2005-2424 (July 2005)] indicates that this blanket statement is not precisely true. Whether or not a vendor bonus is included in the regular rate depends on whether or not it is considered discretionary. And the same discretionary versus nondiscretionary analysis that applies to bonus payments from employers applies to vendor bonuses. In other words, the vendor steps into the shoes of the employer for purposes of determining whether or not the bonus must be included in the regular rate.

The opinion letter involved an employer whose employees sell products from several vendors. Occasionally a vendor sponsors a bonus program relating to its products. The vendor then pays to the employer the bonus earned by each employee based on the vendor's established formula. The employer, in turn, pays the employees the vendor's bonus. The vendor decides if and when to provide these bonuses and how to calculate the amount each employee will receive. The vendor announces the bonus to employees prior to the employees' selling the vendor's product.

The DOL pointed out that FLSA Section 7(e)(3)(a) excludes bonuses from the regular rate of pay if "both the fact that payment is to be made and the amount of the payment are determined at the sole discretion of the employer at or near the end of the period and not pursuant to any prior contract, agreement, or promise causing the employee to expect such payments regularly." Since the vendor informs the employees of the requirements for the bonus prior to the work being performed, these bonuses are promised to the employees who meet the vendor's requirements, rather than being paid at the discretion of the employer.

Additionally, Wage and Hour regulations [29 C.F.R. § 778.211(c)] provide that "[b]onuses which are announced to employees to induce them to work more steadily or more rapidly or more efficiently or to remain with the firm are regarded as part of the regular rate of pay." Consequently, the vendor bonus should be included in the regular rate of pay for overtime purposes.

Q 7:42   Can the percentage of total earnings method be used when a bonus paid in one year is based on the previous year's earnings and is not included in the calculation of the current bonus?

Yes. In a Wage and Hour Opinion Letter [No. FLSA2005-22 (Aug. 2005)], the Department of Labor examined a situation where an employer that used the percentage of total earnings method to calculate bonuses paid an incentive bonus to nonexempt employees in February of each year based on the company's performance during the previous year. Because the bonus was considered nondiscretionary, it had to be includible in the regular rate for computing overtime. When calculating the amount of the bonus for the current year, the employer did not include the February bonus that was based on the previous year's earnings.

According to the Department of Labor, in this situation, the employer could still use the percentage of total earnings method when it did not include the bonus paid for the preceding year to compute the bonus amount due for the current year even if the bonus paid for the preceding year was actually paid in the current year. Proper recordkeeping had to substantiate that an incentive bonus payment made in a particular year was given based on total compensation earned in the preceding calendar year.

Q 7:43   Apart from the discretionary bonus, what other types of bonus payments are properly excluded from the computation of the regular rate?

Bonuses that are based on a percentage of the employee's total earnings (both straight-time and overtime pay) or are paid under a formal approved profit sharing or benefit plan can be excluded from the calculation of the regular rate. [29 C.F.R. §§ 778.210, 778.213, 778.214]

A bonus that is paid on total compensation (straight-time and overtime pay) can be excluded from the regular rate on the grounds that the overtime that would otherwise be due on the bonus is effectively being paid by calculating the bonus on total earnings (including overtime). [29 C.F.R. § 778.210; Wage &

Hour Opinion Letter, FLSA2005-22 (Aug. 2005); Wage & Hour Opinion Letter, FLSA1997 (Jan. 1997)]

FLSA Section 207(e)(3)(b) provides that it is not necessary to include in the regular rate sums paid to or on behalf of an employee pursuant to a bona fide profit sharing plan or trust. [29 C.F.R. § 549.0] A bona fide profit-sharing plan or trust is a plan or trust that meets the following requirements:

1. It is a definite program or arrangement, in writing and communicated to the employees, established and maintained for the purpose of distributing a share of profits to the employees.

2. All contributions or allocations by the employer are made periodically and derived solely from the profits of the employer.

3. Eligibility to share in profits extends to all nonexempt employees (subject to length of service and other eligibility requirements) or to a designated group of employees with the approval of the Wage and Hour Administrator.

4. The amounts paid to employees are determined in accordance with a definite formula.

5. No employee's profit share can be diminished because of other remuneration received by the employee.

6. Provision is made for payment within a reasonable period after the profit distribution is determined.

[29 C.F.R. § 549.1]

A profit-sharing plan or trust is not considered bona fide when:

1. The profit share for any employee is determined on the basis of attendance, quantity or quality of work, rate of production, or efficiency;

2. The periodic amount to be paid is a fixed sum;

3. Periodic payments of minimum amounts are guaranteed by the employer;

4. Any employee's share is set at a predetermined fixed sum; and

5. The employer's contributions to the plan or trust are based on factors other than profit.

[29 C.F.R. § 549.2]

If a contribution is made to a profit-sharing plan or trust that is found to be unqualified because it does not meet the above requirements, or because of some disqualifying feature, that contribution is treated as a bonus payment and must be included in the regular rate. [29 C.F.R. § 778.214(c)]

There are other circumstances under which a profit share may have to be included in the regular rate. Consider a situation where a profit share is distributed before the end of the fiscal year, based on projected profits to the end of the fiscal year (June 30). If, in such case, the employer experiences an unanticipated business downturn between the time of the distribution and the end of the fiscal year, such that a loss is sustained for the fiscal year, the so-called profit share would have to be included in the regular rate of pay, since it is not actually derived from profits. [Wage & Hour Opinion Letter, FLSA1488 (Oct. 1977)]

Normally, payments made in the nature of gifts at Christmas time or on other special occasions, which may be called "bonuses," can be excluded from the employee's regular rate of pay pursuant to the FLSA (see Q 7:25). [29 C.F.R. § 778.212] Also, a one-time quarterly increase in the hourly rate of pay based on performance in previous quarters is included in the regular rate earned and is not considered a bonus under the FLSA. [Wage & Hour Opinion Letter, FLSA2006-16NA (June 2006)]

Q 7:44 Is bonus pay given to an employee for taking the minimal amount of sick leave available included in calculating the regular rate?

Yes. When bonus pay is offered to an employee as an incentive to avoid using available sick leave, the bonus pay must be included in the employee's regular rate because, like an attendance bonus, such payment constitutes remuneration for services rendered. Similarly, extra pay offered to employees to induce them to forego vacation time or holidays must also be included in the regular rate. [29 C.F.R. § 778.219] Although a day's pay as a bonus would be included in the regular rate as akin to an attendance bonus, one bonus day of leave with pay, offered as an alternative option to an employee, need not be included in the regular rate of pay because such payment is not compensation for services rendered. [Wage & Hour Opinion Letter, FLSA1986-1627 (Feb. 1986)]

Q 7:45 How is the regular rate for a workweek calculated when a bonus must be included in the regular rate of pay?

Where a bonus payment is considered as a part of the regular rate at which an employee is employed, it must be included in computing his regular hourly rate of pay and overtime compensation. No difficulty arises in computing overtime compensation if the bonus covers only one weekly pay period. The amount of the bonus is merely added to the other earnings of the employee (except statutory exclusions) and the total divided by total hours worked. Under many bonus plans, however, calculation of the bonus may necessarily be deferred over a period of time longer than a workweek. In such a case the employer may disregard the bonus in computing the regular hourly rate until such time as the amount of the bonus can be ascertained. Until that is done, the employer may pay compensation for overtime at one and one-half times the hourly rate paid the employee, exclusive of the bonus. When the amount of the bonus can be ascertained, it must be apportioned back over the workweeks of the period during which it may be said to have been earned. The employee must then receive an additional amount of compensation for each workweek that he or she worked overtime during the period equal to one-half of the hourly rate of pay allocable to the bonus for that week multiplied by the number of statutory overtime hours worked during the week. [29 C.F.R. § 778.209(a)]

If it is impossible to allocate the bonus among the workweeks of the period in proportion to the amount of the bonus actually earned each week, the DOL says some other "reasonable and equitable" method of allocation must be adopted. For example, it may be appropriate to assume that the employee earned an equal amount of bonus each week of the period to which the bonus relates. If so, additional compensation for each overtime week of the period may be computed and paid in an amount equal to one-half of the average hourly increase in pay resulting from bonus allocated to the week, multiplied by the number of statutory overtime hours worked in that week. On the other hand, if there are facts that make it inappropriate to assume equal bonus earnings for each workweek, it may be "reasonable and equitable" to assume that the employee earned an equal amount of bonus each hour of the pay period. The resulting increase in the hourly rate is determined by dividing the total bonus by the number of hours worked by the employee during the period for which it is paid. The additional compensation due for the overtime workweek in the period is then computed by multiplying the total number of statutory overtime hours worked in each such workweek during the period by one-half this hourly increase. [29 C.F.R. § 778.209(b)]

> **Example.** XYZ Inc. is unable to determine a job production bonus for Bill Smith until four workweeks have elapsed. XYZ then determines that Smith has earned a bonus of $105.60 for the four weeks, but because of the nature of the job performed, XYZ is unable to allocate a particular portion of the bonus to each of the four weeks. In such a case, XYZ may assume that Smith earned the same amount of bonus each hour he worked during the period. Smith's statutory straight-time workweek is 40 hours. He worked 44 hours the first week, 42 hours the second week, 41 hours the third week, and 49 hours the fourth week, making a total of 176 hours for the period covered by the bonus, composed of 160 straight-time hours and 16 overtime hours. $105.60 ÷ 176 results in a 60-cent-an-hour bonus. Smith's hourly rate aside from the bonus is $8.00. The total number of overtime hours multiplied by one-half the hourly rate of pay is 16 hours × [1/2 of ($8.00 + 60¢)], which equals $68.80, the total overtime compensation due the employee after determination of the bonus.

Effect of Premium Pay on the Regular Rate

Q 7:46   What is *premium pay* and how does it affect the calculation of overtime pay?

Certain payments in the form of an increased hourly wage made by employers for work performed in excess of or outside of specified daily or weekly standard work periods or on certain special days are regarded as *premium pay*. If it qualifies, the extra compensation provided by premium pay need not be included in the employee's regular rate of pay for the purpose of computing overtime compensation due under the FLSA. Moreover, this extra compensation can be credited toward any overtime payments required by the FLSA. [29 U.S.C.

§ 207(e)(5)–(7), (h); 29 C.F.R. §§ 778.200, 778.201; Wage & Hour Opinion Letter, FLSA1997-2032 (June 1997)]

Q 7:47   Under what circumstances can voluntary premium pay be excluded from the calculation of the regular rate and offset against overtime pay?

In the following situations, premium pay can be excluded from the regular rate and credited against any overtime due:

1. An employee receives premium pay of any amount for hours worked in excess of eight per day or 40 per week. For example, when an employee receives a wage of $8 per hour and an additional $1 per hour for any hours worked in excess of eight per day, the premium of $1 per hour is excludable from the calculation of the regular rate and creditable against any overtime pay for working more than 40 hours during that workweek. [29 U.S.C. § 207(a)(5); 29 C.F.R. § 778.202]

2. An employee receives premium pay of any amount for hours worked in excess of daily or weekly normal or regular work hours. For example, an employee who works a seven-hour standard workday may receive premium pay for time worked between the seventh and eighth hours. [29 U.S.C. § 207(e)(5); 28 C.F.R. § 778.202]

3. An employee receives premium pay of at least one and one-half times the regular rate paid for actual hours worked on Saturday, Sunday, holidays, a day of rest, or the sixth or seventh day of work. Payment of less than time and one-half is not sufficient. For example, 115 percent of the regular wage rate would not be sufficient and the 15 percent premium would be includible in the calculation of the regular rate. [29 U.S.C. § 207(e)(6); 29 C.F.R. § 778.203]

4. An employee receives clock-time premiums of at least one and one-half times the regular rate paid for work outside of a contractual daily time period not exceeding eight hours, or outside a contractual weekly time period not exceeding 40 hours. [29 U.S.C. § 207(e)(7); 29 C.F.R. § 778. 204]

One Wage and Hour opinion letter examined these premium pay exclusion requirements in the context of fire protection employees. Under a special rule, fire protection employees must be paid overtime after 106 hours in a 14-day work period (see Q 7:81). The employer in question paid its firefighters the same amount every two weeks and that amount was determined by dividing an annual salary by 26. Included in that amount pursuant to a collective bargaining agreement was a premium equal to 125 percent of the regular hourly rate of pay for all hours worked in excess of 80 but less than 106 during the 14-day work period.

The employer asked if the 125 percent premium could be excluded from the total compensation when computing the firefighters' regular rate under (2), (3), or (4) above. The DOL said the premium could not be excluded. Exclusions (3) and (4) are limited to payments that are at least 150 percent of the regular rate of pay and thus are not applicable. And exclusion (2) is limited to compensation for hours "*in excess of* the employee's normal working hours or regular working hours." Since the premium payments to the firefighters apply to time worked *during* the employees' normal working hours or regular working hours (between 80 and 106), this exclusion is also not applicable.

According to the DOL, since the 125 percent payment must be included in the employees' regular rate of pay, the employer may not "blend" this amount into the regular rate by dividing the biweekly payment received by the employees by 112.5 to determine the employees' regular rate of pay. The compensation received by the employees must be divided by the 106 scheduled hours to determine their regular rate of pay for overtime purposes, pursuant to the standard method for the computation of overtime [Wage & Hour Opinion Letter, FLSA1999-2004 (Oct. 1999)].

Q 7:48   Can a lump-sum premium, which is unrelated to the actual number of hours worked in excess of 40, be excluded from the computation of the regular rate?

No. A premium in the form of a lump sum, which is paid for work performed for overtime hours and without regard to the number of overtime hours worked, does not qualify as an overtime premium, even though the amount of money may equal or exceed the sum owed on a per-hour basis. Therefore, the premium cannot be excluded from the regular rate and does not offset the employer's overtime pay obligation. [29 C.F.R. § 778.310; Wage & Hour Opinion Letter, FLSA1999-2181 (Aug. 1999)]

Q 7:49   Is an employer limited to using premium payments during a particular workweek to offset overtime pay deficiencies only during that same workweek?

Maybe. The Eleventh Circuit Court of Appeals held in *Kohlheim v. Glynn County* [915 F.2d 1473, 1481 (11th Cir. 1990)] that the county employer could set off all previously paid overtime premiums against overtime found to be due at trial. Thus, the employer was not limited to using such credit only in the same work period in which it incurred an overtime deficiency. [*See* Singer v. City of Waco, 324 F.3d 813 (5th Cir. 2003) (holding that overpayments could be offset against overtime shortfalls in other periods, finding it more appropriate to view the overpayments as prepayments on the subsequent shortfalls)]

However, the Sixth Circuit Court of Appeals has held that an employer could use its contract premiums to offset overtime owed to employees only within the same workweek as the missed overtime, and not against the total amount of overtime owed. [Herman v. Fabri-Centers of Am., Inc., 308 F.3d 580 (6th Cir. 2002); *see* Howard v. City of Springfield, 274 F.3d 1141, 1149 (7th Cir. 2001) (holding that the employer could apply credits against overtime owed on a pay-period-by-pay-period basis, but not to all overtime liability)]

Q 7:50   Does the clock-time premium exception apply when some, but not all nonstraight-time hours are compensated at a premium rate?

No. As described in Q 7:47, a clock-time premium is extra compensation paid for hours worked outside of the contractually established basic, normal, or regular workday or workweek. The clock-pattern exception applies only when all, not just some, of the hours worked outside of the established workday or workweek are compensated, and at a rate not less than one and one-half times the straight hourly rate. [29 C.F.R. § 778.204]

A higher wage rate paid merely as a job or shift differential does not qualify as an overtime premium that is excludable from the calculation of the regular rate. [29 C.F.R. §§ 778.204(b), 778.207]

Effect of Job Rate, Day Rate, Piece Rate, Commissions, or Fluctuating Workweek Salary on the Regular Rate

Q 7:51   How is an employee's regular rate determined when he or she is paid on a job rate, day rate, piece rate, or commission basis?

Generally, for employees paid on the basis of a job rate, a day rate, a piece rate, or commissions, total compensation earned during a workweek should be divided by total number of hours worked to determine the regular rate. Half of the resulting hourly rate (i.e., the regular rate) is the overtime premium owed for each hour in excess of 40 hours worked during the workweek. [29 C.F.R. § 778.109]

Q 7:52   How should an employer calculate overtime pay for an employee who is paid on the basis of a day rate or a job rate?

When a worker is paid a flat sum for a day's work or for completing a particular job, without regard to the number of hours worked, the worker's regular rate is determined by totaling all sums received at day or job rates during the week-plus any includible bonuses or supplements—and dividing such amount by the total number of hours actually worked. Half of the worker's regular rate is due for all hours worked in excess of 40 hours during a workweek. [29 C.F.R. § 778.112]

> **Example.** An employer pays its mechanics $200 per day, regardless of the number of hours worked each day. An employee works the following hours in one workweek for a total of 45 hours: 10 hours on day 1, 8 hours on day 2, 12 hours on day 3, 0 hours on day 4, 8 hours on day 5, 7 hours on day 6, and 0 hours on day 7. Because the employee worked five days, his total straight-time compensation for the week is $1,000 ($200 per day × 5 days), for a regular rate of $22.22 per hour ($1,000 divided by 45 hours).

This employee is also entitled to an additional $55.55 for his 5 hours of overtime (5 hours × ½ × $22.22 per hour). The total straight and overtime compensation for this employee for the week is $1,055.55.

Q 7:53   How is overtime pay calculated for piece rate employees?

Some employees may be paid on the basis of the number of units they produce. These employees are commonly called piece rate workers or pieceworkers. The general method for calculating a pieceworker's regular rate is to average his or her total earnings over the hours worked in a particular workweek. Overtime pay is then computed at half the regular rate for hours worked in excess of 40 hours.

> **Example.** A pieceworker who is paid $1 per unit of production and completes 500 units in 50 hours in one workweek earns $500. The $500 is divided by the hours worked, 50, to calculate the regular rate of $10 per hour. The pieceworker is entitled to an additional $5 per hour for each of the 10 overtime hours worked, for total weekly pay of $550 ($500 in piece-rate earnings + $50 overtime).

[29 C.F.R. § 778.111]

In some cases an employee may be hired on a piece rate basis coupled with a minimum hourly guarantee. If so, the employee's regular rate can be calculated by adding the total hourly earnings and the total piece-rate earnings, and then dividing that sum by the number of hours worked during the workweek in question. Employers must pay employees half of the resultant regular rate for all hours worked in excess of 40 during that workweek. If the employee's total piece rate earnings for the workweek fall short of the amount that would be earned at the guaranteed hourly rate, the employer must pay the difference up to the guaranteed hourly wage. In such weeks, the guaranteed hourly rate, which must be at least equal to the minimum wage, becomes the regular rate. [29 C.F.R. § 778.111]

As an alternative to the weekly calculation of an hourly regular rate, an employer and pieceworker can agree in advance of the performance of the work that the pieceworker will be paid at a rate of at least one and one-half times the piece rate for each piece produced during the overtime hours. No additional overtime is due as long as the piece rate is a bona fide rate and the compensation is at least equal to one and one-half times the minimum wage. [29 C.F.R. § 778.418]

When it is not possible to allocate piecework earnings between workweeks worked in one pay period, either because an employer fails to keep accurate records or because of some other reason, the employee's regular rate can be calculated by dividing the employee's total piecework earnings for the pay period by the employee's total hours worked during the pay period. [Martin v. Liu, 30 Wage & Hour Cas. (BNA) 1332 (C.D. Cal. 1992)]

Q 7:54   How is overtime pay calculated for commissioned employees?

Computing regular rates and overtime for commissioned employees is relatively simple when employees are paid a weekly commission. If the employee is not exempt from overtime as an outside salesperson (see Qs 4:47–4:50), the weekly commission payment is added to all other earnings for the week and that total is divided by the hours worked in the workweek to calculate the employee's regular rate. Half of the regular rate is owed for all hours worked in excess of 40 hours during the workweek in question. [29 C.F.R. § 778.118] Of course, if that regular rate is less than the applicable minimum wage, the employer must supplement the employee's pay up to the minimum wage level.

When commission payments are deferred beyond the week in which they are earned, an employer must apportion the commission over the workweeks during which it was earned. Where appropriate, an employer can accomplish this by allocating an equal portion to each workweek or to each hour worked during the period in which the commission was earned. Once the amount of commission allocable to a workweek has been ascertained for each week in which overtime was worked, the commission for that week is divided by the total number of hours worked in that week to get the increase in the hourly rate. That new hourly rate can then be used to determine what the overtime rate should have been; the employer must pay the difference between what was paid for overtime and what would have been due for overtime had the commission been included. [29 C.F.R. § 778.120]

Q 7:55   How is overtime pay computed for salaried employees on a fixed or fluctuating workweek?

Nonexempt employees may be paid a salary. If a nonexempt employee is paid a salary, the regular rate must still be calculated as an hourly figure. If the employee is not paid on a weekly basis, the employee's salary must be converted to a weekly salary before it is converted to an hourly rate. For example, a monthly salary is reduced to a weekly wage by multiplying the monthly salary by 12 (the number of months in a year) and dividing the product by 52 (the number of weeks in a year). [29 C.F.R. §§ 778.109, 778.113] When converting salaries to an hourly figure, an employer must first determine if the employee is paid a salary for a fixed workweek or a fluctuating workweek.

When an employee is paid for a fixed workweek, the employer pays a salary that is intended to cover a specified number of hours per workweek, for example, 40 hours. In contrast, under a fluctuating workweek pay plan, the salary paid by the employer is intended to compensate the employee on a straight-time basis for all hours worked during the workweek, regardless of how many or how few. [29 C.F.R. § 778.114]

A salaried employee on a fluctuating workweek ordinarily is entitled to a lower overtime rate than a salaried employee on a fixed workweek when both employees are paid the same salary and work the same number of hours over 40.

This is because the regular hourly rate for an employee working a fluctuating workweek is calculated by dividing the salary by the total number of hours actually worked in the week. As the number of hours worked increases, the regular rate decreases. The regular rate for a fixed-workweek employee does not vary from week to week because it is calculated by dividing the weekly salary by the number of hours at which the workweek is fixed, even though the employee may work longer hours in a particular week. [29 C.F.R. § 778.114; Highlander v. KFC Nat'l Mgmt. Co., 805 F.2d 644 (6th Cir. 1986)]

Q 7:56   What are the requirements for use of a fluctuating workweek pay plan?

First, a fluctuating workweek pay plan can be used only when there is a clear mutual understanding between the parties that the salary is intended to compensate the employee for all of the hours worked in each workweek, whatever their number, rather than for a fixed weekly period, such as 40 hours. [29 C.F.R. § 778.114]

A clear mutual understanding that a salary is intended to compensate for all hours worked does not necessarily require that the employer get a written agreement from its employees. Indeed, the necessary mutual understanding may be implied from the parties' conduct in the employment relationship. For example, in one case an employee was improperly treated as exempt for several years. During that time, he was paid a salary, and his paychecks were the same each pay period regardless of the hours that he worked during that period. Later, the parties realized their mistake and reclassified the employee as nonexempt, and the employer began to pay him overtime on a half-rate basis for all hours worked over 40. The employee sued, arguing that his overtime rate should be one and one-half times the hourly rate that resulted when his weekly salary was divided by 40 hours (i.e., essentially arguing that his salary was a salary for a fixed workweek rather than a salary for a fluctuating workweek). The court rejected the employee's argument, holding that because he accepted a fixed salary for fluctuating hours without comment or protest for over two years, it was implied that the parties had agreed that he was to be paid a fixed salary for a fluctuating workweek. As a result, his overtime pay would be calculated at half of the regular rate for each hour worked over 40. [Zoltek v. Safelite Glass Corp., 884 F. Supp. 283 (N.D. Ill. 1995)]

In another case, county deputy sheriffs who were paid pursuant to a fluctuating pay plan were held to understand clearly that their salaries were intended to cover all hours of work, whether many or few, even though they might not have clearly understood how their overtime pay was calculated. According to the court, although the deputies argued otherwise, the county was not required to prove that the deputies knew that the more overtime they worked, the less they would be paid for each overtime hour. Although the employer and employee must reach a clear understanding that the fixed salary is compensation for all hours worked each workweek (excluding the overtime premium), there is no requirement that the employee understand how overtime is being paid or that the employer get the employee's written acknowledgment of the pay plan. [Bailey v. County of Georgetown, 94 F.3d 152 (4th Cir. 1996); *see also* Valerio v. Putnam Assocs. Inc., 173 F.3d 35 (1st Cir. 1999)]

The clear mutual understanding requirement does not require that the employees know the hours expected to be worked or that the salary will not be paid if the employees work no hours in a workweek. It is enough that the employees know that they will receive a salary designed to cover all hours worked in one workweek. [Samson v. Apollo Res. Inc., 2001 U.S. App. LEXIS 2417 (5th Cir. 2001)]

In addition to requiring a clear mutual understanding, the fluctuating work-week pay plan also requires employers to pay the overtime premium at one-half the regular rate for each overtime hour worked, even though the salary itself compensates for the straight time for all hours worked. The fluctuating work-week pay plan does not contemplate some maximum number of hours per week that employees may work without an adjustment to the salary or an additional premium. In *Samson v. Apollo Resources Inc.* [2001 U.S. App. LEXIS 2417 (5th Cir. 2001)], plaintiffs argued that their overtime premium would have to be greater than one-half times the regular rate where they worked more than 60 hours in one workweek. This is because at 60 hours, the fluctuating workweek results in the payment of an overtime premium that only brings the hourly rate to what it would have been had the employee worked just 40 hours. To illustrate, an employee paid $500 per week effectively makes $12.50 per hour if he or she works only 40 hours. If, however, the employee works 60 hours, the overtime rate for the 20 overtime hours is only $12.50 ($8.33 regular rate plus one-half of $8.33 as the overtime premium). "After 60 hours, unless an overtime premium of greater than one-half the regular rate is paid, the rate of pay for overtime hours is [less than] the rate of pay . . . if he or she only worked 40 hours." [*Id.* at *10] Yet, this is exactly what the regulations permit, according to the court, and therefore the plaintiffs' claims for additional overtime failed. Under a fluctuating workweek pay plan, the only additional pay an employer must pay beyond the fixed salary and the overtime premium is an amount to bring the regular rate back up to the minimum wage if the employee works so many hours that the regular rate falls below the minimum wage. [*Id.* at *13–*14]

One thing that the fluctuating workweek pay plan does not require is that the working hours of the employee fluctuate above and below the 40-hour mark or that the workers not be assigned to a fixed work schedule. The language of Section 778.114 suggests that the workweek must "fluctuate." But this does not mean that employees on a fluctuating workweek pay plan cannot be assigned to a fixed, regular, or repeating schedule. It is not necessary that the regular hours be sporadic for the regulation to apply as long as there is some fluctuation in hours over the weeks (even if that fluctuation is regular, such as with rotating shifts). [Flood v. New Hanover County, 125 F.3d 249, 253 (4th Cir. 1997)]

The fixed-pay method of paying overtime requires the payment of the salary regardless of the number of hours worked in a week—even if there is lack of work. The fixed-pay method does not follow the salary basis test outlined in Q 4:6, with one exception: an employer may withhold the salary only if the employee takes the entire week off. The employer may not make deductions for daily absences, even if the employee requests a full-day deduction.

Use of Two or More Wage Rates

Q 7:57   Can different wage rates be adopted to compensate employees for different job duties?

Yes. Different wage rates can be adopted for different job duties even if the different jobs are performed for the same employer during the same workweek, provided that the different rates are bona fide rates and the agreement to pay different rates is reached before the work is performed. Likewise, different or lower wage rates can be adopted to compensate workers for nonproductive time counted as hours of work, such as travel time, waiting time, or sleeping time. [29 U.S.C. § 207(g)(2); 29 C.F.R. §§ 778.115, 778.318(b)]

Q 7:58   If an employee works two different jobs at the same company, and his or her workweek totals more than 40 hours for the two jobs, must the employee be paid overtime?

Generally, an employee who works two different jobs for the same employer at different rates of pay (or at the same rate) must be paid time and one-half for all hours worked in excess of 40. If the employee is paid at two (or more) different rates during one workweek, the two (or more) different wage rates must be averaged to determine the weighted regular rate for the week. This is typically calculated by taking the total compensation from both jobs, less any exclusions from the regular rate, and dividing by the number of hours worked at both jobs. The resulting number—the regular rate—reflects a blending of the rates from both jobs. For any overtime hours, the employer must pay one-half the weighted average regular rate for each overtime hour. [29 C.F.R. §§ 778.115; Wage & Hour Opinion Letter, FLSA1998-1928 (Apr. 1998)]

Alternatively, the employer and the employee can agree, before the work is performed, to have overtime paid on the basis of the specific rate in effect during the overtime hours (i.e., one and one-half times the hourly rate assigned to the work being performed during overtime hours) as long as that rate is not less than the minimum wage. This requires the employer to keep track of precisely what work is performed during the overtime hours and pay the employee in question one and one-half times the regular rate for that work. [29 U.S.C. § 207(g)(2); 29 C.F.R. § 778.419] If the secondary work usually occurs all at one time in the workweek, it might be worth considering a permanent change in the workweek to accommodate a lower rate for that work.

Example. The employer employs a secretary who performs cleaning work every Sunday afternoon, but the workweek runs on a calendar week (Sunday through Saturday). In this case, it might be worth changing the secretary's workweek to run from 12:01 a.m. Monday morning to midnight Sunday instead of a standard calendar week of 12:01 a.m. Sunday to midnight Saturday. The secondary work takes place on Sunday afternoon. Under the calendar week default, those are the first hours of work for the week. The employee then gets overtime for her primary work performed at the end of the week (Friday) at the higher primary work rate. If the employer alters the workweek so that Sunday is the end of the workweek, the employee's overtime hours on Sunday afternoon will be paid at the lower rate established for the secondary work. Of course, this change must be intended to be permanent. [29 C.F.R. § 778.105]

Q 7:59   How does the alternative method of paying different hourly rates work in practice?

Recent opinions and case law have shown that the alternative method of paying different hourly rates discussed in Q 7:58 has more flexibility than indicated by the regulations. The regulation requires that to pay different hourly rates for two or more jobs, the hourly rates must be bona fide; the overtime for which the lower rate is paid at time and one-half must qualify as overtime hours; and the number of overtime hours for which the overtime rate is paid must equal the number of actual hours worked over 40. [29 C.F.R. § 778.419] Taken literally, this regulation would prevent employers from assigning a lower rate to nonproductive time, such as waiting time or on-call time, and would require employers to pay overtime at a weighted average for those hours. It has been held on several occasions, however, that a lower hourly rate can be established for secondary duties or nonproductive time.

For example, a hospital did not violate the FLSA when it paid its operating room technicians and nurses for on-premises waiting time during an overtime shift at a rate of one and one-half times the minimum wage, rather than one and one-half times their regular rate. In this case, each employee had agreed as a condition of employment to accept the minimum wage rate as a basis for the overtime calculation for the waiting time. [Townsend v. Mercy Hosp. of Pittsburgh, 862 F.2d 1009 (3d Cir. 1988)] The waiting time involved was nonproductive but compensable work time and therefore could be paid for at a rate lower than the employees' tendered wage rate (i.e., paid for as a secondary duty). Employers are permitted to seek agreements with employees to pay different wage rates for different kinds of work. [29 U.S.C. § 207(g)(2); 29 C.F.R. § 778.318(b)]

In another case, pursuant to a policy that was made known to them, firefighters were paid a lower rate of pay for performing fire inspector duties occasionally. The firefighters sued, arguing that they should be paid their higher firefighter rate for all hours worked. They argued that the hourly rates established were not bona fide, because the challenged (lower) rate applied only to overtime hours, even though the work might be performed technically in nonovertime hours. The court rejected this argument and explained that a bona fide rate can exist in this context even if the second job or job duty is performed only during overtime hours. As long as the employer sets an hourly rate for the secondary job or duty and strictly adheres to that rate when secondary work is performed, and pays one and one-half times that rate for work on that secondary job or duty performed during overtime hours, the rate is bona fide. [Mathias v. Addison Fire Prot. Dist. No. 1, 43 F. Supp. 2d 916 (N.D. Ill. 1999)]

Q 7:60 When an employer pays overtime at the rate established for a worker's secondary job for all hours over 40 worked in a workweek, regardless of when in a workweek the secondary work is performed, is the employer in compliance with the FLSA?

Probably not. Consider the case of an employee who works seven hours per day, Monday through Friday, on her regular job. In addition, this employee works additional hours during the week or on the weekend on a secondary job, which is distinctly different from her regular job, and for which a different rate of pay is established. In this case, if the employee worked 35 hours at her regular job and two seven-hour shifts at her secondary job, overtime pay would be due for nine hours ($35 + 7 + 7 = 49; 49 - 40 = 9$). Under the described pay plan, the employer would pay that overtime at one and one-half times the rate paid for the secondary job, regardless of whether the work was performed early in the week or later (i.e., even if the work performed during hours 41 through 49 was not performed on the secondary job but on the primary job).

The employer would not be in compliance with the FLSA's overtime pay provisions, because it is not paying premium pay for overtime hours on the basis of other than a 40-hour workweek and the hours on the secondary job are not necessarily overtime hours. Since some of the hours worked by the employee on her regular job could occur beyond the 40th work hour of the week, the employer would have to pay for overtime hours either at one and one-half times a weighted average rate or at the rate, regular or secondary, at which the employee actually works during each hour over 40 during the workweek in question. [See 29 C.F.R. § 778.419; Wage & Hour Opinion Letter, FLSA1997-2048 (Sept. 1997)]

Q 7:61 When two or more compensation methods are used, do the same overtime pay standards apply to employers in both the public and private sectors?

No. The FLSA was amended in 1985 by a set of amendments that related only to state and local governments. The FLSA now provides that different results can occur in the public and private sectors when an employee performs different duties at two or more different rates of pay. This is because a public employee has the option of working a second job, even for the same public employer, without the hours of work in the second job being added to the hours of regular employment for overtime pay calculation purposes. The amendments require that the secondary work must be (1) "occasional or sporadic" and (2) solely at the employee's option. In addition, the work in question must be different from the work normally performed by the employee in his or her primary employment with the public employer. [29 U.S.C. § 207(p); 29 C.F.R. § 553.30]

For example, a school custodian may volunteer for or occasionally assist in the coaching of the school's baseball team without the hours being combined. If the school custodian is hired to work as the assistant baseball coach for the same school at which he or she cleans, however, his or her hours in both jobs must be combined for payment purposes. This is because in the second case, the school custodian's service as the baseball coach is not occasional or sporadic, but rather regular and recurring. [29 C.F.R. § 553.30; Wage & Hour Opinion Letter, FLSA1986-1656 (May 1986)] Department of Labor (DOL) regulations that went into effect in 1987 (after the cited opinion letter) indicate, however, that part-time work for a seasonal program of scheduled sporting events can still be considered occasional even though it is recurring. [29 C.F.R. § 553.30(b)(3)] Although the regulation may seem inconsistent with the opinion letter cited above, they can be harmonized as follows: The school custodian who assists the baseball coach at the school is engaged in sporadic and occasional (albeit recurring) activity; however, the school custodian who is also hired to be the baseball coach is working a second job (and not performing sporadic and occasional secondary duties) and those hours must be counted.

There are two prominent exceptions to the above:

1. Public safety employees taking on security or safety functions on an occasional or sporadic basis for their public sector employer are never considered employed in a different capacity.

2. Any activity traditionally associated with teaching, such as coaching, career counseling, and so forth, is not considered employment in a different capacity when it is performed by one who is already a teacher.

[29 C.F.R. § 553.30(c); Wage & Hour Opinion Letter, FLSA1997-2056 (Sept. 1997)]

Trading Hours of Work

Q 7:62 Can public sector employers permit employees to trade hours of work without incurring overtime pay liability?

Yes. The FLSA provides:

> If an individual who is employed in any capacity by a public agency which is a State, political subdivision of a State, or an interstate governmental agency, agrees, with the approval of the public agency and solely at the option of such individual, to substitute during scheduled work hours for another individual who is employed by such agency in the same capacity, the hours such employee worked as a substitute shall be excluded by the public agency in the calculation of the hours for which the employee is entitled overtime compensation under [the FLSA].

[29 U.S.C. § 207(p)(3)]

Thus, under certain circumstances (as described in the statutory section quoted above), public employees can voluntarily trade hours of work without creating overtime pay liability for the employer to the employee who is performing the substitute work. [29 C.F.R. § 553.31]

Q 7:63   In the substitute work scenario in Q 7:62, who receives credit for the hours worked?

The employee who is scheduled for the time, but who does not work, receives credit for the hours worked. The employee scheduled to work receives credit and compensation as if he or she had worked; the employee actually working (substituting) receives no credit or compensation from the employer for the hours worked. [29 C.F.R. § 553.31(a)]

Q 7:64   Are employers in the private sector exposed to overtime pay liability when employees trade hours of work?

Yes. The FLSA's statutory exemption for substitute work is exclusive to public sector employees. Therefore, the substitute employee in the private sector is entitled to have his or her substitute hours of work included for purposes of overtime pay calculation. Private sector employers need to be aware that permitted work substitution can result in unexpected liability.

Effect of Paid Leave Time and Meal Periods on Calculating Overtime

Q 7:65   Is an employer required to count paid leave time as hours worked for purposes of computing overtime pay?

No. Hours of work for overtime purposes does not include paid absences. As discussed in Q 6:6, qualified meal periods need not be counted as hours worked or compensated. In both the public and private sectors, paid meal periods (if the employee is relieved of duty), like paid sick leave, paid holidays, or paid vacation, need not be counted as actual hours worked unless the employer so desires. If the employer elects to make payments for such nonwork time, those payments can properly be excluded from the calculation of the regular rate. [29 C.F.R. §§ 778.216–778.218, 778.320; Abbott v. United States, 204 F.3d 1099 (Fed. Cir. 2000)]

Indeed, the FLSA specifically states that the regular rate does not include:

> payments made for occasional periods when no work is performed due to vacation, holiday, illness, failure of the employer to provide sufficient work, or other similar cause; reasonable payments for traveling expenses, or other expenses, incurred by an employee in the furtherance of his employer's interests and properly reimbursable by the employer;

and other similar payments to an employee which are not made as compensation for his hours of employment.

[29 U.S.C. § 207(e)(2)]

Q 7:66   Is the noncompensable status of a meal period affected when employees are not relieved of all duties during the meal period?

Yes. Employees are entitled to compensation for their meal periods when they remain on call or continue to perform any work during the meal periods. If employees are required to continue with any duties related to work during their meal periods, the employer cannot make deductions from employees' wages during these breaks. [29 C.F.R. § 785.19; Brennan v. Elmer's Disposal Serv., Inc., 510 F.2d 84 (9th Cir. 1975)] A 30-minute meal period during which employees are relieved of duties does not constitute regular hours worked for purposes of computing overtime due under the FLSA. (See Q 6:6 for further discussion of the compensability of meal periods.) [29 C.F.R. § 785.19]

Compensatory Time Off

Q 7:67   How are the terms *compensatory time* and *compensatory time off* defined for purposes of the FLSA?

The terms *compensatory time* and *compensatory time off* are interchangeable terms meaning "paid time off the job which is earned and accrued by an employee in lieu of immediate cash payment for employment in excess of the statutory hours for which overtime compensation is required by section 7 of the FLSA." The compensatory time must be earned at a rate not less than one and one-half hours for each hour of employment for which overtime compensation would ordinarily be due. [29 U.S.C. § 207(o)(7)(B); 29 C.F.R. § 553.22]

Q 7:68   Under what circumstances can employers satisfy their overtime pay obligations by providing employees with compensatory time off?

Employees of public agencies can receive, in lieu of overtime compensation, compensatory time off at a rate of not less than one and one-half hours for each hour of employment for which overtime compensation is required under the FLSA. [29 U.S.C. § 207(o)(1)]

A public agency can provide compensatory time off only pursuant to:

1. A collective bargaining agreement, memorandum of understanding, or other agreement between the public agency and representatives of its employees; or

2. An agreement or understanding arrived at between the employer and the employee before the performance of the work in question.

[29 U.S.C. § 207(o)(2)]

In either event, compensatory time can be used only for employees who have not accrued compensatory time in excess of the limits established by the statute (see Q 7:69). [29 U.S.C. § 207(o)(2)]

A compensatory-time plan requires an agreement or understanding between the public sector employer and each employee or his or her agent (such as a union). If the agreement or understanding is with the employees' representative, it must be through a collective bargaining agreement, a memorandum of understanding, or some other oral or written agreement. The representative need not be a formal bargaining agent, as long as the representative is designated by the employees. If the agreement or understanding is with the employees individually, the agreement must be reached before the performance of the work. Although the agreement need not be in writing, a record of its existence must be kept. [29 C.F.R. § 553.23(b), (c)]

Q 7:69   What limits on the accumulation of compensatory time off are established under the FLSA?

When the work of an employee for whom compensatory time can be provided includes working in a public safety activity, an emergency response activity, or a seasonal activity, the employee engaged in the work can accrue not more than 480 hours of compensatory time for overtime hours worked. If the overtime work is for any other type of work, the employee can accrue not more than 240 hours of compensatory time for the overtime hours worked. Once an employee has accrued either 480 or 240 hours of compensatory time off, as the case may be, he or she must be paid at overtime rates for any additional overtime hours of work. [29 U.S.C. § 207(o)(3)(A)]

Q 7:70   Does the employer have the option to pay overtime rather than permit compensatory time to accrue, or to cash out accrued compensatory time off?

Yes. The employer always has the option of actually paying for overtime compensation in lieu of allowing further compensatory time off to accrue, without affecting the parties' ability to use or accrue compensatory time in the future. Further, an employer can, at its option, pay cash for the accrued compensatory time of its employees. If compensation is paid to an employee for accrued compensatory time off, that compensation must be paid at the regular rate earned by the employee at the time that the employee receives the payment. [29 U.S.C. § 207(o)(3)(B); 29 C.F.R. §§ 553.26, 553.27(a)]

Q 7:71   What happens to compensatory time off on termination of employment?

An employer must pay for it. On termination of employment of a public sector employee who has an accrued balance of compensatory time, the public employer must pay for that time. When paying at the time of termination, the employer must pay for accrued compensatory time off at a rate of compensation that is not less than (1) the average regular rate received by the employee during the last three years of the employee's employment, or (2) the final regular rate received by the employee, whichever is higher. [29 U.S.C. § 207(o)(4); 29 C.F.R. § 553.27(b)]

Q 7:72   Can an employer unilaterally control when an employee can make use of compensatory time off?

Yes and no. A public employee who has accrued compensatory time off and has requested the use of the compensatory time off must be permitted by the employer to use the time, within a reasonable period after making the request, if the use of the compensatory time off does not unduly disrupt the operations of the public agency in question. [29 U.S.C. § 207(o)(5); 29 C.F.R. § 553.25] But an employer can force an employee to use his or her compensatory time or require the employee to use the time only on days or at times selected by the employer.

For example, a county became concerned that it lacked the resources to pay monetary compensation to employees who worked overtime after reaching the statutory cap on compensatory time accrual and to employees who left their jobs with sizable reserves of accrued time. As a way to reduce accumulated compensatory time, the county implemented a policy under which the employees' supervisor set a maximum number of compensatory hours that could be accumulated. When an employee's hours approached that maximum, the employee was advised of the maximum and was asked to take steps to reduce accumulated compensatory time. If the employee did not do so voluntarily, a supervisor was able to order the employee to use his or her compensatory time at specified times. The U.S. Supreme Court resolved a split in the Circuit Courts of Appeals and ruled that despite the lack of a prior agreement between the employer and the employees to compel use of compensatory time off, the employer could do this because the FLSA does not prohibit employers from forcing employees to use compensatory time. The Court rejected the DOL's position that, absent an agreement between the parties, the statute and regulations did not permit an employer to compel the use of accrued compensatory time, effectively overruling a 1992 opinion letter to that effect. [Christensen v. Harris County, 529 U.S. 576 (2000)]

This decision calls into question the DOL's stated position that the parties cannot voluntarily, by agreement, place controls (other than the control of undue disruption) on when compensatory time can be taken. The Wage and Hour Administrator has declared that an agreement between a police union and a city limiting the taking of compensatory time to one employee per watch, subject to city approval, was invalid. [Wage & Hour Opinion Letter, FLSA1994-1736 (Aug. 1994)] On the other hand, the terms of an agreement between the parties can govern what is the reasonable period within which a request for compensatory time off should be granted. [29 C.F.R. § 553.25(c)(2); *see also* Aiken v. City of Memphis, 985 F. Supp. 740 (W.D. Tenn. 1997) (parties' agreement to logbook method for determining reasonable period for use of compensatory time by officers was acceptable limitation on compensatory time arrangement), *aff'd in relevant part*, 190 F.3d 753 (6th Cir. 1999)]

The DOL has stated that situations may, in fact, arise in which overtime can be required of one employee to permit another employee to use his or her compensatory time off. The DOL has stated that such a situation, in and of itself, would not be sufficient for an employer to claim that the practice is unduly disruptive. [29 C.F.R. § 553.25(d); Wage & Hour Opinion Letter, FLSA1994-1736 (Aug. 1994); Canney v. Town of Brookline, 142 Lab. Cases (CCH) ¶ 34,169, 2000 U.S. Dist. LEXIS 16279 (D. Mass. 2000)]

The Ninth Circuit ruled, however, that it need not defer to 29 C.F.R. section 553.25 or the 1994 opinion letter on this issue, as 29 U.S.C. section 207(o)(5) is unambiguous with respect to the use of compensatory time. [Mortensen v. County of Sacramento, 368 F.3d 1082 (9th Cir. 2004)] In *Mortensen*, the plaintiff submitted a request to use 12 hours of accumulated compensation time on a specific date. The employer denied the request because it had already granted the maximum number of leave requests for the day in question, consistent with minimum staffing requirements, and granting the request would have resulted in another employee's working overtime. The employee sued, claiming the employer violated the FLSA by failing to establish that allowing the employee to use his comp time on the day he requested would have been unduly disruptive. The court ruled in favor of the employer, holding that an employee does not have the right to request a specific day off for comp time. Instead, pursuant to the unambiguous language of 29 U.S.C. section 207(o)(5), the employer has a reasonable amount of time to grant the request for leave once the request is made. In this case, the employer and the employees' representative had entered into an agreement under which the employer had one year to grant a request for use of compensatory time once the request was made. The court ruled that this agreement was reasonable. [*See also* Houston Police Officers' Union v. City of Houston, 330 F.3d 298 (5th Cir. 2003) (holding that a public employer must permit an employee to use compensatory leave time within a reasonable period after the employee requests its use, but not as specifically requested by the employee)]

On a somewhat different set of facts, the Sixth Circuit Court of Appeals recently ruled that Cleveland, Ohio, could not deny police officers' timely requests for compensatory leave solely because it would have resulted in the payment of overtime to substitute officers. [Beck v. City of Cleveland, Ohio, 390 F.3d 912 (6th Cir. 2004)] As a matter of policy, Cleveland did not allow a substitute officer to earn overtime compensation to work in the place of the officer who requests compensatory leave. The Sixth Circuit found that the Wage and Hour Administrator's 1994 opinion letter was consistent with the legislative history of the compensatory time provision—that compensatory time should not be used to avoid overtime pay and that "unduly disrupt" applies to governmental operations, not finances.

The Sixth Circuit disagreed with the *Mortensen* ruling because to grant a government the unlimited discretion to deny compensatory leave requests relieves the government of establishing the "undue disruption" requirement imposed by Congress. To comply with the FLSA, a government must be required to make a factual showing of undue disruption, financial or otherwise. The court declined "to adopt a wholesale deference rule that would allow the City to adopt a compensatory leave policy that deprives the officers of the enjoyment of their accrued leave that Congress awarded and intended public employees to enjoy."

Q 7:73   Can a public sector employer's compensatory-time plan adversely affect its use of a fluctuating workweek salary plan?

Yes. Public sector compensatory time plans and salaried fluctuating work-week plans may very well be inconsistent. The DOL has taken the position that employers that use the fluctuating workweek method of calculating overtime compensation for salaried employees cannot pay the half-time premium in an equivalent amount of compensatory time. In support of its position, the DOL has cited to statutory language providing that public agency employees must receive compensatory time "at a rate not less than one and one-half hours for each hour of employment for which overtime compensation is required." [Wage and Hour Opinion Letter, FLSA1991 (Feb. 1991)]

Q 7:74   Are compensatory-time plans available to private sector employees?

No. There is no true compensatory-time plan that can be used for nonexempt employees of a private sector employer whereby overtime hours worked in one workweek are compensated in a subsequent workweek by paid time off. The only exception is the very difficult to administer time-off plan. A time-off plan allows an employer to comply with the FLSA by giving an employee time off in a certain week of pay so that the desired salary for the entire period matches the entire amount of compensation owed to the employee, including overtime. [Wage & Hour Opinion Letter, FLSA1950]

Example. An employee earns $800 for a two-week period ($400 a week) consisting of 80 hours of work ($10 an hour). During the first week the employee worked 42 hours. Thus, the employer owes the employee $400 for the first 40 hours and $30.00 for the overtime hours ($10.00 at time and one-half equals $15.00 an hour). Instead of allowing the employee to work 40 hours in the second week and paying the $30.00 in overtime, the employee is instead given three hours off in the next week (3 hours times $10.00 an hour equals $30.00). Thus the employee would work only 37 hours in the second week and still bring home the standard $800 paycheck.

Time-off plans are allowed under the FLSA as long as the employee receives all the compensation he or she is owed for regular hours and overtime. Employers do not typically make use of time-off plans, because it is difficult for the employer to determine how much work it will need a specific employee to complete for any given week.

Q 7:75   Are there certain employees for which time-off plans are not applicable?

Since the main goal of a time-off plan is to control an employee's hours during specific weeks so that earnings can be maintained on a constant level, an employer will not be able to implement such a plan on certain classifications of employees such as the following.

- Time-off plans do not work for employees who are paid weekly, because there is not an extra week to provide time off to the employee.
- Time-off plans cannot be used for employees paid on the fluctuating workweek basis because the employee has agreed to work as many hours as are necessary to complete his or her assignment. Thus, the employee's hours cannot be controlled.

Q 7:76   Is there a restriction as to when hours earned under a time-off plan must be used?

An employee cannot be forced or allowed to use time off in another pay period. Thus, if an employee earns six hours off during the first week of a two-week pay period, the employer must guarantee that the employee will have nine hours off during the second week. Otherwise, the plan is invalidated by the FLSA.

Compensatory-time plans of any nature can be voluntarily adopted for use with exempt employees either in the private sector or the public sector. In that context, the employer is merely providing an additional (and nonmandatory) benefit to its exempt employees. The use of compensatory time off for nonexempt employees, however, is forbidden in the private sector. [Wage & Hour Opinion Letter, FLSA1990-1715 (June 1990)]

Alternative Wage Payment Plans and Alternative Work Periods

Q 7:77   What is a *Belo contract*?

A *Belo contract*—so named after the Supreme Court case that approved its use—is an agreement that provides a means whereby the employer of an employee whose duties necessitate irregular hours of work, and whose wages would vary widely from week to week if they were hourly wages, can guarantee a fixed weekly payment based on the employee's regular rate. [29 C.F.R. § 778.404; Walling v. A.H. Belo Corp., 316 U.S. 624 (1942)]

The use of a Belo contract permits the employer to pay what appears to be a fixed weekly salary except in weeks in which an exceptionally large number of hours are worked. A Belo plan is essentially a guaranteed wage plan that benefits both the employee and the employer: The employee gains the security of a regular weekly income, and the employer is able to anticipate, control, and limit overtime compensation costs. Under a Belo contract, the employer and the employee must agree on an hourly rate of pay to cover a predetermined number of hours that should not be more than the average number of hours worked in an ordinary week. The employee is promised this hourly rate for the first 40 hours each week and one and one-half times the rate for overtime hours. Employees are paid the guaranteed weekly wage regardless of the number of hours they actually work. [29 C.F.R. §§ 778.404, 778.408]

The following restrictions apply to Belo contracts:

1. The employee must work fluctuating hours that are not controllable by either the employee or the employer.

2. The regular rate of pay must not be less than the statutory minimum wage.

3. The guaranteed wage must be set pursuant to an employment contract (either written or oral) or collective bargaining agreement.

4. The number of hours for which pay is guaranteed must be reasonably related to the number of hours the employee may be expected to work.

5. The guaranteed wage must be weekly, not semimonthly or monthly.

6. The guarantee must not cover more than 60 hours per week based on the specified rate.

7. The plan must provide compensation of at least one and one-half times the regular rate for all hours worked in excess of the statutory maximum.

[29 C.F.R. §§ 778.405–778.414]

This method of payment can be implemented only for employees whose duties require irregular hours of work that the employer cannot reasonably control or anticipate. The irregularity of hours worked must result in significant variations below as well as above the standard 40-hour workweek. When the variation in hours occurs only in the hours over 40, there would not be sufficient irregularity of hours and a Belo contract would not be authorized. There must also be irregularity in the hours worked under 40. [Donovan v. Tierra Vista, Inc., 796 F.2d 1259 (10th Cir. 1986)] In addition, irregularity caused by absences for personal reasons, illness, vacations, holidays, or scheduled days off does not meet the requirements of FLSA Section 7(f), because the irregularity must be due to the specific duties of the employee. [See 29 C.F.R. § 778.405]

An employer's employees must agree to any pay plan that is established as a Belo contract. A valid Belo contract requires either an individual agreement with the affected employee or a contract with the union representing the affected employee. [Wirtz v. Harper Buffing Mach. Co., 280 F. Supp. 376 (D. Conn. 1968)] In addition, the FLSA requires employers to maintain a copy of any written agreement concerning the implementation of a Belo plan, or in the case of a verbal understanding, a written memorandum summarizing the terms of the understanding. (See Q 8:19 on recordkeeping requirements.) [29 C.F.R. §§ 516. 24, 778.407]

In practice, Belo contracts are not common; however, they are used on occasion. For example, a home health agency's proposed guaranteed wage agreement (Belo plan) for its licensed vocational nurses met all of the above-described requirements when the nurses' workloads fluctuated from week to week based on patient caseload and conditions; the nurses' hours varied from 32 to 64 each workweek; the agency would pay the nurses a guaranteed weekly salary for 60 hours; of the 60 hours, 20 would be paid at one and one-half times the nurses' regular rates; and the nurses would be paid one and one-half times their regular rates for all hours worked in excess of 60 hours in a workweek. [Wage & Hour Opinion Letter, FLSA1997-2055 (Sept. 1997)]

Q 7:78 Does a wage plan that refuses to pay overtime but allows employees to schedule their work hours provided that total hours do not exceed 75 in a two-week period violate the FLSA?

Yes. The FLSA is explicit that overtime must be paid for hours over 40 "in any workweek" and an employee cannot waive his or her statutory right to be paid overtime compensation. The hypothetical wage plan would violate the FLSA because an employee could work 50 hours in the first week and 25 in the second week without receiving any overtime compensation. In addressing overtime, employers cannot combine workweeks and average the time worked. An employee working 50 hours in one week and 25 in the second week is entitled to ten hours of overtime pay for the first week. [29 C.F.R. §§ 778.100, 778.103, 778.104; *see also* Wage & Hour Opinion Letter, FLSA1990-1719 (May 1990)]

Q 7:79 Is there an exception to the standard seven-day workweek for hospitals or establishments that are engaged in the care of the sick, aged, or mentally ill?

Yes. A limited exception to the workweek standard is made for hospitals and residential care establishments under FLSA Section 7(j). These institutions can compute overtime using a designated work period of 14 consecutive days in lieu of the general seven-day workweek, provided that there is an agreement to that effect in advance with the employees. [29 U.S.C. § 207(j); 29 C.F.R. § 778.601; Hodgson v. Washington Hosp., 19 Wage & Hour Cas. (BNA) 1101 (W.D. Pa. 1971) (hospital violated overtime provisions when it did not have an agreement with workers before performance of the work)]

Under FLSA Section 7(j), overtime pay of at least one and one-half times the employee's regular rate is due after eight hours in a workday or after 80 hours in a work period of 14 consecutive days. The extra compensation provided by the premium rate paid after eight hours in a day can be credited toward any overtime compensation due for hours worked in excess of 80 in the 14-day work period. When the 14-day work period is elected, the 14-day period is used in lieu of the workweek for the calculation of the regular rate. [29 U.S.C. § 207(e)(5), (j); 29 C.F.R. § 778.601]

Although the Section 7(j) limited exemption from overtime is linked to a 14-day work period, nothing in the regulations governing this exemption prevents an employer from making weekly wage payments to its employees. Nor would weekly payments under a 14-day work period violate any requirements with respect to the timely payment of overtime. As long as the other provisions of Section 7(j) are complied with, the employer could pay on a weekly basis. [Wage & Hour Opinion Letter, FLSA1999-2165 (June 1999)]

Q 7:80 What are annual and semiannual wage contracts and how do they affect an employer's overtime pay obligations?

Under FLSA Section 7(b), there is an overtime pay exemption in the case of 1,040-hour and 2,080-hour contracts. This exemption applies to collective bargaining agreements under which either: (1) the employees are limited to a maximum of 1,040 hours of work in a period of 26 consecutive weeks; or (2) the employees are limited to a maximum of 2,280 hours of work in a period of 52 consecutive weeks but are guaranteed between 1,040 and 2,080 hours of regular employment during the year. A 1,040 or 2,080 clause permits employers not to pay overtime until the employees work more than 12 hours per day or 56 hours per week. Either type of agreement requires that the employer make the contract with a representative of the company's employees who has been certified by the National Labor Relations Board (NLRB) (i.e., a union). [29 U.S.C. § 207(b); 29 C.F.R. § 778.602]

Q 7:81 Are there any special FLSA provisions that apply to firefighters or police officers?

Yes. Under FLSA Section 7(k), a public employer can establish a work period of not less than seven and no more than 28 days for the purpose of a partial overtime exemption for employees who are employed in fire protection or law enforcement activities (including employees of correctional facilities). The maximum hours standard for fire protection personnel ranges from 53 hours worked in a seven-day work period to 212 hours worked in a 28-day work period. The maximum hours standard for law enforcement personnel ranges from 43 hours worked in a seven-day work period to 171 hours worked in a 28-day work period. For a 14-day work period, fire protection employees must be paid overtime after 106 hours, and law enforcement personnel must be paid overtime after 86 hours. [29 U.S.C. § 207(k); 29 C.F.R. §§ 553.201, 553.230]

Example. A fire department has established a 14-day work period for its firefighters (for which the maximum hours standard is 106 hours). In a 14-day work period in which firefighters are scheduled to work 96 hours, no FLSA overtime premium compensation is due, since the 106-hour maximum standard has not been exceeded. If the firefighters work an additional 24 un-scheduled hours during this same work period for a total of 120 hours, they must receive overtime pay at one and one-half times their regular rate of pay for the 14 hours performed in excess of the 106 maximum hours standard. They must also receive straight-time pay for the 10 hours between the 106-hour maximum and the 96-hour schedule. The FLSA does not require over-time compensation at one and one-half times the regular rate between hours 96 and 106. [Wage & Hour Opinion Letter, FLSA1998-1799 (Sept. 1988)]

The adoption of a 14-day (or other length) work period for firefighters or law enforcement officers for purposes of the Section 7(k) exemption need not be formalized with an official resolution. Nor must the employer do the bare minimum in terms of pay and benefits for fear of waiving the exemption if employees are given any additional pay or benefit. For example, a federal court of appeals held that a state's practice of averaging its officers' hours over a two-week period was sufficient to reflect the state's adoption of a 14-day work period for these law enforcement officers. In addition, the state's practice of paying overtime for hours exceeding 80 hours in a two-week period, even though under Section 7(k) this would not require overtime until after the 86th hour, did not constitute a waiver of the Section 7(k) exemption. [AFSCME Local 889 v. Louisiana, 145 F.3d 280 (5th Cir. 1998)]

Q 7:82 Can emergency medical service (EMS) employees be paid for overtime in the same manner as firefighters and/or police officers?

Sometimes. EMS employees who are employed by a public fire protection or law enforcement agency may qualify for the partial overtime exemption found in FLSA Section 7(k) if their services are substantially related to firefighting or law enforcement activities and are an integral part of that agency's fire protec-tion or law enforcement. Even EMS employees who are not employed by a fire protection or law enforcement agency, but are stationed at a fire station or police station to respond to calls, can be paid in accordance with this exemption when they are an integral part of fire protection or law enforcement activities. Further, EMS employees of a public agency other than a fire protection or law enforce-ment agency (a "third service" agency) can be treated as employees engaged in fire protection or law enforcement activities if their services are substantially related to fire protection or law enforcement. The provisions of FLSA Section 7(k) do not, however, apply to: (1) EMS employees of a public agency, such as a hospital, that was subject to the FLSA before the 1974 amendments; or (2) personnel employed by private EMS organizations, even if their activities are substantially related to the fire protection and law enforcement activities of a public agency or their employer is under contract to provide such services to a public agency. [29 U.S.C. § 207(k); 29 C.F.R. §§ 553.3(a), 553.215, 553.24(d); Wage & Hour Opinion Letter, FLSA1995-1823 (Feb. 1995)]

On December 9, 1999, the definition of a firefighter was amended to resolve various court disputes and broaden the application of the Section 7(k) exemption to paramedics and emergency medical technicians who work for public fire departments if the employee is also trained in and responsible for fire suppression.

Miscellaneous

Q 7:83 Can a worker's right to overtime pay be waived through the collective bargaining process?

No. Neither an employer nor a labor organization can waive the rights of employees to overtime. The minimum wage and overtime provisions of the FLSA are guarantees to individual workers that cannot be waived through collective bargaining. Agreements to waive the minimum wage and overtime provisions of the FLSA are considered to be against public policy and therefore unenforceable. [Featsent v. City of Youngstown, 70 F.3d 900 (6th Cir. 1995); Herman v. City of St. Petersburg, 131 F. Supp. 2d 1329 (M.D. Fla. 2001) ("the FLSA forbids pay plans that have the effect of reducing the pay for overtime . . . even though the plans may be acceptable to the employees involved"); *see also* Barrentine v. Arkansas-Best Freight Sys., 450 U.S. 728 (1981)]

Q 7:84 Can an employer's rights under the overtime rules be waived through the collective bargaining process?

Yes. For example, an employer may have the right not to include certain items in the regular rate for purposes of computing overtime. However, it can bargain away that right in union negotiations.

A recent federal appeals court decision illustrates this very point. In a collective bargaining agreement with its police officers' union, a town agreed to pay the officers for a set number of vacation, sick, and personal days each year. Subsequently, the police officers sued the town for not including certain incentive pay in the regular rate for overtime purposes. The town sought to claim an offsetting credit for the vacation and other paid nonworking days. The court ruled that no credit was allowed.

Section 207(e) of the FLSA provides that the regular rate of pay "shall not be deemed to include . . . payments made for occasional periods when no work is performed . . . and other similar payments." And the federal appeals court agreed that under Section 207(e), the town was not required to sign a collective bargaining agreement that included nonwork pay in its regular rate. However, the court said that once nonwork pay is included in the collective bargaining agreement, it must also be included in the regular rate. Section 207(e) does not suggest that a court should relieve the town of its obligation. According to the appeals court, "Section 207(e) does not say 'shall be *deemed not* to include,' but '*shall not be* deemed to include.' The difference in meaning between those two statements is immense. The former requires court intervention in the face of a labor agreement already containing nonwork pay augments to the regular rate. The latter signals court passivity in the face of such an agreement." [Wheeler v. Hampton Township, 399 F.3d 238, 244 (3d Cir. 2005)]

Q 7:85   Is there a "minimal threshold" rule that applies to an employer's overtime pay obligations?

Maybe. For federal employees, the Office of Personnel Management (OPM) has established a *de minimis* rule that time spent on preliminary activities is compensable only if total time spent on preliminary activities exceeds ten minutes. In one case, the Federal Aviation Administration lawfully denied five minutes per week of overtime to an air traffic controller, pursuant to its policy of paying for overtime in six-minute segments and eliminating overtime pay for periods of less than six minutes. In that case, overtime in the amount of five minutes or less accrued over the course of each week. Because these few minutes did not constitute a substantial measure of the employee's time and effort, the court found that the time was too *de minimis* to be compensable. [Brandon v. United States, 652 F.2d 69 (Ct. Cl. 1981)] (See Q 12:8.)

Various courts have held that matters of minutes or seconds of work beyond the 40th hour can be disregarded, even in the private sector. [*See* Anderson v. Mt. Clemens Pottery Co., 328 U.S. 688, 692 (1946) (stating premise, but holding that the few minutes spent walking from the time clock to a workbench and back should be compensated as work time. The Court stated, "It is only when an employee is required to give up a substantial measure of his time and effort that compensable working time is involved."); *see also* IBP v. Alvarez, 546 U.S. 21 (2005) (finding that any activity that occurs after a "principal activity" is covered time under the FLSA.)]

If unpaid minutes are routinely or often worked, the *de minimis* rule does not apply. For example, 5 minutes of unpaid work time per day would be 25 minutes per week, or about 21 hours per year. If these were overtime hours and the employee made $10 per hour, the result would be liability of $315 per year per employee. Waits of less than 15 minutes at the beginning of an assembly-line worker's work shift have been held not to fall within the *de minimis* rule (and, therefore, were compensable) when such waits occurred after workers were required to be at work and after they signed in, although workers were not clocked in on the master time card controlled by the employer. These periods were neither insignificant nor administratively impractical to capture. [Mireles v. Frio Foods, Inc., 899 F.2d 1407 (5th Cir. 1990)]

The factors that trial courts should examine when assessing whether the work underlying a compensation claim is *de minimis* are (1) the practical administrative difficulty of recording the additional time, (2) the aggregate amount of compensable time in question, and (3) the regularity of the additional work. [Bobo v. United States, 136 F.3d 1465, 1468 (1st Cir. 1998) (citing Lindow v. United States, 738 F.2d 1057, 1063 (9th Cir. 1984))]

Q 7:86   By what method of payment can employers satisfy their overtime pay obligations?

Employees must be paid statutory wages in cash or its equivalent. Scrip, tokens, or credits of any kind are not proper as payment under the FLSA. Further, payment must be made free and clear without kickbacks or payments to the employer or a third party (except for authorized and mandated deductions for such things as taxes or loans). An employer's intent to pay overtime compensation at a later date does not excuse its present violation of the FLSA. Thus, unless proper overtime compensation cannot be determined at the time of the regular payday (because of commissions, for example), the employer must pay overtime for the pay period on the regular payday for that period. [29 C.F.R. §§ 531.27, 531.34, 531.35, 778.106]

Q 7:87   Can an employer change the official workweek without violating the FLSA?

Yes. A workweek is any fixed and regularly recurring period of seven consecutive days, which can begin on any day and at any hour. The beginning of the workweek can be changed if the change is intended to be permanent and is not adopted to evade the overtime pay requirements of the FLSA. [29 C.F.R. § 778.105]

If an employee's workweek is changed from one period of seven consecutive days to another period of seven consecutive days, part of the employee's time will come in both workweeks. [29 C.F.R. § 778.301] In such a case, the employee's pay for the overlap will have to be calculated twice: once with the overlap hours included in the old workweek and once with the overlap hours included in the new workweek. The employee should then be paid the greater of the two amounts. Of course, if the employee does not work during the overlap period, both calculations will yield the same amount, and there will be no need to use a different method to calculate the overtime. [29 C.F.R. §§ 778.301, 778.302]

Q 7:88   Can an employer change the work schedule for employees and lower those employees' hourly rates?

Probably, yes. Employers are free to change the regular schedule for employees and to lower pay rates, as long as such changes are not designed to evade the requirements of the FLSA. Therefore, an employer could lower pay rates while maintaining the same schedule or could change schedules while lowering some pay rates but not others. As long as none of these changes are designed to evade the requirements of the FLSA, then they are a matter of contract and not a violation of the FLSA. Thus, the Wage and Hour Division approved a plan in which an employer had its employees choose between a rotating 12-hour shift and continuing on regular 8-hour shifts 5 days per week. As part of this selection, employees who selected the rotating 12-hour shift schedule would also receive a slightly lower hourly rate than the employees continuing on the regular schedule. This was done to account for the overtime hours that would result in one of the rotating workweeks under the 12-hour shift schedule but that would not regularly result under the regular 8-hour shifts. [Wage & Hour Opinion Letter, FLSA1999-2157 (May 1999)]

Q 7:89   How is *work* defined for purposes of the FLSA?

As noted previously, the FLSA does not define the term *work*. FLSA Section 203(g), however, defines the term *employ* to mean "to suffer or permit to work."

From that definition of *employ*, courts have created a definition of *work* for purposes of applying the provisions of the FLSA. In Tennessee Coal, Iron & R. Co. v. Muscoda Local No. 123 [321 U.S. 590, 598 (1944)], the Supreme Court defined work as "physical or mental exertion (whether burdensome or not) controlled or required by the employer and pursued necessarily and primarily for the benefit of the employer and its business." [29 U.S.C. § 203(g)] However, in *Armour & Co. v. Wantock* [323 U.S. 126 (1944)], the Court held that "exertion" was not necessary for an activity to constitute work. Two years later, in *Anderson v. Mt. Clemens Pottery Co.*, 328 U.S. 680 (1946), the Court noted that it defined "the statutory workweek" to "include all time during which an employee is necessarily required to be on the employer's premises, on duty or at a prescribed workplace." Those hours that are considered to be "hours worked" are discussed in Chapter 6.

State Law

Q 7:90 Can a state legislate overtime provisions that differ from the FLSA provision?

Yes, each state may have its own labor laws, which set the minimum wage and overtime provisions that apply to employees covered by the state law. When an employee is covered by both the federal and the state laws, the employee must be paid under whichever law would provide the higher wages. See Table 7-1 below for the general requirements as to when overtime at a rate of time-and-one-half must be paid. Note that the states may have different provisions for specific industries. See the end of appendix A for state agencies responsible for wage and hour or labor matters.

Table 7-1. State Overtime Provisions

Alabama	No provision
Alaska	Over 40 hours a week or 8 hours a day (unless four 10-hour days as approved by the Alaska Department of Labor); not applicable to employers of fewer than four employees
Arizona	No provision
Arkansas	Over 40 hours a week
California	Over 40 hours a week, 8 hours a day, or on the 7th day of work in a workweek; double-time for more than 12 hours in a day and more than 8 hours on the 7th day of work in a workweek; by wage and hour order, 7th-day premium pay not required when total weekly work hours do not exceed 30 and total hours in any one workday thereof do not exceed 6
Colorado	Set by wage order; over 40 hours a week, 12 hours a workday, or 12 consecutive hours, whichever calculation results in greater payment of wages

Table 7-1. (cont'd)

Connecticut	Over 40 hours a week, and for 7th consecutive day of work for restaurant and hotel restaurant employees
Delaware	No provision
District of Columbia	Over 40 hours a week
Florida	No provision
Georgia	No provision
Hawaii	Over 40 hours a week
Idaho	No provision
Illinois	Over 40 hours a week
Indiana	Over 40 hours a week
Iowa	No provision
Kansas	Over 46 hours a week
Kentucky	Over 40 hours a week or 7th day in a workweek
Louisiana	No provision
Maine	Over 40 hours a week
Maryland	Over 40 hours a week
Massachusetts	Over 40 hours a week
Michigan	Over 40 hours a week
Minnesota	Over 48 hours a week
Mississippi	No provision
Missouri	Over 40 hours a week; over 52 hours for seasonal amusement or recreational employees
Montana	Over 40 hours a week
Nebraska	No provision
Nevada	Over 40 hours a week or 8 hours a day (unless four 10-hour days by mutual employee/employer agreement); not applicable to employees who are compensated at not less than one and one-half times the minimum rate or to employees of enterprises having a gross annual sales volume of less than $250,000
New Hampshire	Over 40 hours a week
New Jersey	Over 40 hours a week
New Mexico	Over 40 hours a week
New York	Over 40 hours a week
North Carolina	Over 40 hours a week; over 45 hours for seasonal amusement or recreational employees
North Dakota	Over 40 hours a week
Ohio	Over 40 hours a week

Table 7-1. (cont'd)

Oklahoma	No provision
Oregon	Over 40 hours a week, and after 10 hours a day for employees of nonfarm canneries, driers, packing plants, mills, factories, or manufacturing establishments (excluding sawmills and certain related employers)
Pennsylvania	Over 40 hours a week
Rhode Island	Over 40 hours a week, and on Sundays or holidays in retail and certain other businesses
South Carolina	No provision
South Dakota	No provision
Tennessee	No provision
Texas	No provision
Utah	No provision
Vermont	Over 40 hours a week
Virginia	No provision
Washington	Over 40 hours a week
West Virginia	Over 40 hours a week
Wisconsin	Over 40 hours a week
Wyoming	No general provision

Chapter 8

Employer's Recordkeeping Obligations

The Fair Labor Standards Act (FLSA) contains explicit record-keeping requirements. Before an employer can begin to digest the material in this chapter, it must take stock of the type of employees it employs and read the chapters discussing coverage under the FLSA, its amendments, and the various other federal wage and hour statutes (Chapters 2, 11, and 12), and the chapters on exemptions and special wage and hour practices (Chapters 4, 5, and 10). Only then will the need for these detailed recordkeeping requirements make sense.

This chapter discusses the records that employers are generally required to keep, how these records are to be stored, in what form they may be kept, and how long they must be kept, among other miscellaneous requirements. Also discussed are the records that must be kept for employees covered solely by the minimum wage provisions or covered by both the minimum wage and overtime provisions, and records that must be kept by employers covered by the Equal Pay Act. Because some of these general requirements may apply to all employees, notwithstanding a total or partial exemption, all employers should review the general requirements. Employers that employ employees under a government contract are also advised to review Chapter 11, which contains a section on recordkeeping requirements for government contractors. In addition, employers must keep payroll and other records to comply with the Family and Medical Leave Act of 1993 and its regulatory requirements, which are set forth at 29 C.F.R. section 825.500.

This chapter also covers specific recordkeeping requirements for employees exempt from the overtime provisions, exempt from the minimum wage *and* overtime pay provisions, or from the child labor provisions. Employers that pay employees according to special pay practices provided for under the FLSA must be able to document these pay practices, and therefore, must maintain records with that end in mind. These recordkeeping requirements are covered in this chapter.

The chapter closes with a discussion of the retention periods applicable to various categories of documents, as well as practical issues involving the use of time clocks and rounding. Employers should be aware that these requirements are imposed by law and regulation *on the employer*, and they generally cannot be delegated to the employees.

General Information Required

Type of Records Required

Q 8:1   What are the basic recordkeeping requirements for employers of employees subject to the minimum wage or minimum wage and overtime provisions of the Fair Labor Standards Act?

The recordkeeping regulations provide that all employers must keep records for all covered employees, i.e., for all employees to whom the FLSA applies (see Qs 2:1–2:11). Under the FLSA, employers include public employers. [29 U.S.C. § 203(d), (x)] Records do not need to be kept for employees excluded from the definition of employee under FLSA Section 203(e) (see Qs 2:12–2:18). State, local, and interstate government agencies must keep the records for compensatory time. [29 C.F.R. § 553.50] (see Q 8:15). An employer's records must include the following information for each covered employee:

1. *Name in full* including, on the same record, any identifying symbol or number used in place of the employee's name on any time, work, or payroll record.

2. *Home address*, including ZIP code.

3. *Date of birth*, if the employee is under age 19.

4. *Sex and occupation* in which the employee is employed.

5. *Workweek.* The time of day and the day of the week when the employee's workweek begins.

6. *Regular rate and basis of pay.* An employee's regular rate of pay must be shown for any workweek in which overtime is worked and overtime compensation is due. These records must also show the amount and nature of any payment that is excluded from the regular rate. An explanation of the basis for an employee's pay must be shown—indicated by the monetary amount paid for each pay period on a per-hour, per-day, per-week, per-piece, commission, or other specified basis.

7. *Hours worked.* The total number of hours worked each workday and each workweek. A *workday* is any fixed period of 24 consecutive hours. A *workweek* is any fixed and regularly recurring period of seven consecutive workdays. For employees on a fixed schedule, the employer may simply record the schedule of daily and weekly hours the employee normally works, indicating deviations from this schedule by recording the actual number of hours worked for each workday and each workweek.

8. *Straight-time.* The total daily or weekly straight-time earnings or wages. This includes all earnings or wages received on an hourly, piece rate, commission, or salary basis—but it excludes overtime pay.

9. *Overtime pay.* The total premium pay for overtime hours, excluding straight-time earnings or wages.

10. *Wage deductions or additions.* The total deductions from or additions to each employee's wages for each pay period, including employee purchase orders or wage assignments. These individual records must show the dates of the additions or deductions and the types of items added or deducted, and must separate each specific credited or debited amount.

11. *Total wages.* The total wages paid each pay period, including straight-time pay, total weekly overtime pay, and additions to or deductions from wages.

12. *Pay period.* The date each employee was paid wages and the pay period covered by the payment.

13. *Retroactive pay.* If Wage and Hour Division officials are supervising an employer's payment of back wages to an employee, these retroactive payments must be recorded in the employer's records as follows: the employee receiving payment; the amount of payment; the date of, and period covered by, the payment; and receipt of the payment. Reports of retroactive payments must be made on authorized receipt forms, with the original filed with the Wage and Hour Division within 10 days after payment is made, one copy delivered to the employee, and one copy preserved in the employer's records.

14. *Employees working on fixed schedules.* For employees working on a fixed schedule, an employer may maintain records showing the schedule of daily and weekly hours such employees normally work rather than the

hours worked each day and each workweek. In weeks in which an employee working on a fixed schedule adheres to the schedule, the employer should indicate by checkmark or other method that such hours were in fact worked by such employee, and in weeks in which more or less than the scheduled hours are worked, the employer should record the exact number of hours worked each day and each week.

[29 C.F.R. § 516.2(a), (b), (c)]

Q 8:2   What are the recordkeeping requirements under the Equal Pay Act?

The Equal Pay Act prohibits discrimination on the basis of sex in the payment of wages. The Equal Pay Act is part of the FLSA and applies to employers that are covered under the FLSA. Covered employers must keep records *not only* for nonexempt employees, *but also for* exempt employees and employees covered by special wage and hour practices set forth in this chapter. Employers must keep the following records:

- *Pay-related records*. Records made in the regular course of business that relate to the payment of wages, wage rates, job evaluations, job descriptions, merit systems, seniority systems, and collective bargaining agreements.
- *Explanation of pay practices*. Descriptions of pay practices that explain the basis for any wage differentials among employees of the opposite sex in the same establishment that may be pertinent to determining whether the differential is based on sex or on other factors. These records must be preserved for two years.

[29 U.S.C. § 206(d); 29 C.F.R. § 1620.32]

Storage and Form of Records

Q 8:3   Where must records be kept?

Records must be kept where the employees work or at one or more established central recordkeeping offices where such records are typically kept. The Department of Labor's (DOL's) interest is in safe storage and ready accessibility. Therefore, if records are kept at a central recordkeeping office that is not also the employees' place of employment, the records must be available for inspection and copying within 72 hours of notice from the Wage and Hour Administrator or an authorized representative. [29 C.F.R. § 516.7]

Q 8:4   In what form must records be kept?

Records need not be kept in any specific form. They may be maintained on microfilm or in automatic word or data processing memory. Adequate projection or viewing equipment must be available, and the reproductions must be clear and identifiable by the date or pay period. Extensions or transcriptions of this information must also be made available on request. [29 C.F.R. § 516.1]

Q 8:5   How can an employer be relieved from certain recordkeeping duties?

An employer may petition for an exception to the requirements for which records must be kept or the requirements for how long certain documents must be preserved. To obtain an exception, the employer must submit a written petition to the Wage and Hour Administrator setting forth the peculiar operating conditions that warrant an authorized waiver of the requirements. The Wage and Hour Administrator will review the petition to determine whether the requested exception will hinder enforcement of the FLSA, and he or she may revoke the exception if the employer fails to comply with the conditions specified in the exception. The employer must continue to comply with all recordkeeping requirements while the Wage and Hour Administrator reviews its petition. [29 C.F.R. § 516.9]

Posting Requirements

Q 8:6   Do all employers have to hang notice posters informing employees of their rights under the FLSA?

No; only employers whose employees are subject to the minimum wage requirements must maintain notice posters in a conspicuous place. An employer of employees to whom the overtime requirements do not apply because of a broad exemption may modify the poster with a legible notation to show that the overtime provisions do not apply, for example: "Overtime Provisions Not Applicable to Taxicab Drivers (Section 13(b)(17))." Posters and brochures may be obtained from regional offices of the Wage and Hour Division or downloaded from the DOL's Web site at http://www.dol.gov/elaws/posters.htm. Employers that pay employees a training wage must post the notice set forth at 29 C.F.R. pt. 517, appendix A, which is also available from the regional offices of the Wage and Hour Division. [29 C.F.R. § 516.4; 29 C.F.R. pt. 517, App. A]

Penalties for Noncompliance

Q 8:7   What penalties does an employer face if it fails to comply with the FLSA's recordkeeping requirements?

Employers that willfully fail to comply with the FLSA's recordkeeping requirements or willfully and knowingly keep records that contain materially false statements may, on conviction, be fined up to $10,000. Employers may also face up to six months in prison if this is their second or subsequent violation. [29 U.S.C. §§ 211(c), 215(a)(5), 216(a)]

Specific Information Required

Exempt Employees

Although an employer is not subject to the same recordkeeping requirements for employees who are exempt or partially exempt from the FLSA's minimum wage, overtime, or child labor provisions, the employer may still need employees' records to prove that the exemptions apply. The technical recordkeeping requirements for these exempt categories of employees are too extensive to summarize. Therefore, this chapter covers only the recordkeeping requirements for exempt employees likely to be relevant to a broad spectrum of employers. They are as follows: white-collar exempt employees; full-time employees; disabled employees; domestic employees; salespersons; parts and service employees; seamen; employees of hospital and resident care facilities; and firefighters and law enforcement employees. Employers should first read Chapters 4 and 5 to determine whether the particular exemption applies.

For information on the recordkeeping requirements for employers of exempt employees in specific industries or occupations not covered above, employers should consult the following statutory provisions and regulations:

Exempt Employee Occupation, Industry, or Establishment	*FLSA Provision(s)*	*Regulation(s)*
Agricultural establishments	29 U.S.C. § 213(a)(6), (b)(12)	29 C.F.R. §§ 516.33, 575.8
Air carrier operations	29 U.S.C. § 213(b)(3)	29 C.F.R. § 516.12
Charter carrier industry	29 U.S.C. § 207(n)	29 C.F.R. § 516.22
Cotton ginning establishment	29 U.S.C. § 213(h), (i)	29 C.F.R. § 516.18
Country elevator establishment	29 U.S.C. § 213(b)(14)	29 C.F.R. § 516.14
Drivers and helpers, local deliveries	29 U.S.C. § 213(b)(11)	29 C.F.R. § 516.15
Employees receiving remedial education	29 U.S.C. § 207(q)	29 C.F.R. § 516.34
Forestry or lumbering operations	29 U.S.C. § 213(b)(28)	29 C.F.R. § 516.12
Fruit and vegetable operations	29 U.S.C. § 213(b)(16)	29 C.F.R. § 516.12
Learners, apprentices, messengers	29 U.S.C. § 214(a)	29 C.F.R. §§ 516.30, 520.203, 520.412
Livestock auction operations	29 U.S.C. § 213(b)(13)	29 C.F.R. § 516.13
Maple sap processing	29 U.S.C. § 213(b)(15)	29 C.F.R. § 516.12

Exempt Employee Occupation, Industry, or Establishment	FLSA Provision(s)	Regulation(s)
Marine product operations	29 U.S.C. § 213(a)(5)	29 C.F.R. § 516.11
Married couples employed at a nonprofit group home	29 U.S.C. § 213(b)(24)	29 C.F.R. § 516.12
Movie theater establishments	29 U.S.C. § 213(b)(27)	29 C.F.R. § 516.12
Newspaper circulation	29 U.S.C. § 213(a)(8)	29 C.F.R. § 516.11
Other amusement or recreational establishments	29 U.S.C. § 213(a)(3)	29 C.F.R. § 516.11
Outside dairy or poultry buyer	29 U.S.C. § 213(b)(5)	29 C.F.R. § 516.12
Private amusement or recreational establishment in a national park	29 U.S.C. § 213(b)(29)	29 C.F.R. § 516.29
Radio and TV industry, select employees	29 U.S.C. § 213(b)(9)	29 C.F.R. § 516.12
Rail carrier operations	29 U.S.C. § 213(b)(2)	29 C.F.R. § 516.12
Sugar beet or sugar cane processing	29 U.S.C. § 213(j)	29 C.F.R. § 516.18
Switchboard operator	29 U.S.C. § 213(a)(10)	29 C.F.R. § 516.11
Taxicab driver	29 U.S.C. § 213(b)(17)	29 C.F.R. § 516.12
Tobacco industry	29 U.S.C. § 207(m)	29 C.F.R. § 516.18
Transportation employees regulated under 49 U.S.C. § 31502	29 U.S.C. § 213(b)(1)	29 C.F.R. § 516.12
Wholesale or bulk petroleum product distribution	29 U.S.C. § 207(b)(3)	29 C.F.R. § 516.21

Q 8:8   What records is an employer required to keep for employees who are subject to the white-collar exemptions?

For executive, administrative, professional, and outside sales employees who are exempt from the FLSA's overtime and minimum wage requirements, the employer must keep records of the following:

- *Name in full*, including, on the same record, any identifying symbol or number used for that employee on any time, work, or payroll record.
- *Home address*, including ZIP code.
- *Date of birth*, if the employee is under age 19.

- *Sex, and occupation* in which the employee is employed.
- *Workweek.* The day of the week on which the employee's workweek begins.
- *Basis of pay, plus fringe benefits.* For example, $500 per week, plus hospitalization and insurance plan A; or $800 per month, plus 3 percent commission, plus two weeks paid vacation.
- *Total pay per pay period.* The date each employee was paid, the pay period covered by the payment, and the total payment.

[29 C.F.R. § 516.3]

Q 8:9   What records must be kept for employees who are full-time students?

The regulations contain specific recordkeeping requirements for institutions of higher education and operators of farm, retail, or service establishments that employ full-time students. Generally, employers of full-time students employed outside of school hours must maintain and preserve the same records required of other employees in the same occupation. However, pay records for full-time students must be segregated from other employees' records and must identify the employees as students—using a letter or symbol. Furthermore, employers must keep the following records for three years:

- *Certificate.* The certificate described in FLSA Section 214(b), which is obtained from the Secretary of Labor and permits the employer to employ a full-time student at subminimum wages. The certificate must be preserved for at least three years after the certificate's expiration date.
- *Full-time status.* Documentation that the student receives daytime instruction and the location of his or her school.
- *Enrollment status.* Documentation that the student is classified by the school as a full-time student. For students who are not legally required to return to school after a vacation, employers can document the employee's status as a full-time student with a statement of the employee's express intent to return to school, with enrollment papers for the semester or session immediately following the vacation, or with a certificate from the school to be attended next.

Finally, institutions of higher education must keep a record of the total number of full-time students employed at subminimum wages and the total number of employees to whom the minimum wage provisions of the FLSA apply. Operators of any farm, retail or service establishment must maintain records of the monthly hours of full-time students employed at subminimum wages and the total hours of employment during that month for all employees—except agricultural employees who are exempt from the minimum wage requirements. [29 U.S.C. § 214(b); 29 C.F.R. §§ 516.30, 519.7, 519.17]

Q 8:10   What are the recordkeeping requirements for disabled employees?

Employers of disabled employees must maintain and preserve the same records required of other employees in the same occupation. However, pay records for disabled employees must be segregated from other employees' records and must identify the disabled employees with a letter or symbol. Moreover, employers must keep the following records:

- *Certificate.* The certificate described in FLSA Section 214(c), which is obtained from the Secretary of Labor and permits the employment of a disabled employee at subminimum wages.

- *Disability.* Records verifying the employee's disability.

- *Productivity.* Documentation of the productivity level of the disabled employee, gathered on a continuous basis or at intervals not to exceed six months for employees paid hourly wage rates.

- *Prevailing wage and productivity standards.* Records of the prevailing wage and productivity standards for nondisabled employees performing the same job.

[29 U.S.C. § 214(c); 29 C.F.R. §§ 516.30, 525.16]

Q 8:11   What are the recordkeeping requirements for domestic service employees?

For domestic services employees who are exempt from the FLSA's overtime provisions, employers must keep the records set forth in Q 8:1, items 1 through 5, 7, 8, and 10 through 12. There are no recordkeeping requirements for casual babysitters. For "basis-of-pay" records, employers must keep information and data regarding the basis of pay—expressed as earnings per hour, per day, or per pay period. The following recordkeeping deviations are permitted:

- *Fixed schedule.* For domestic service employees who work on a fixed schedule, the regulations simplify the requirements. The employer may use a schedule of daily or weekly hours that the employee normally works and either the employee or the employer may indicate, by check mark, if those hours were worked. Otherwise, the exact number of hours worked must be shown.

- *Employee to keep records of hours.* The regulations provide an exception to the general rule that *employers* must keep all records of hours worked. A domestic service employer may require that the *employee* keep his or her records and submit them to the employer.

- *Agreements.* With respect to live-in domestic service employees, employers may enter into an agreement that meal and sleeping times and other periods when the employee is relieved of duties are excluded from the wage rate, or that sets forth the hours to be worked. As long as the agreement does not substantially deviate from the hours actually worked, it can be used in lieu of maintaining precise records; otherwise, separate records must be kept. This limited recordkeeping requirement does not apply to third-party employers.

- *Board, lodging, and other facilities.* Employers that take credits for board, lodging, and other facilities pursuant to the limitations set forth in 29 C.F.R. section 552.100 but want to apply the credits based on the reasonable cost or fair value of such items—rather than the amounts enumerated in the regulation—must keep records that justify the different cost figures. These records must be kept for three years.

[29 U.S.C. § 213(b)(21); 29 C.F.R. §§ 516.12, 552.100, 552.102, 552.110]

Q 8:12   What are the recordkeeping requirements for conveyance sales and service employees?

For overtime-exempt sales, parts, or mechanical employees who sell or service the conveyances described in FLSA Section 213(b)(10)(A) and (B), employers must keep the records set forth in Q 8:1, items 1 through 5, 7, 8, and 10 through 12. (See appendix B) In addition, employers must keep information and data regarding the basis of pay—expressed as earnings per hour, per day, or per pay period. [29 U.S.C. § 213(b)(10); 29 C.F.R. § 516.12]

Q 8:13   What are the recordkeeping requirements for seafarers?

There are separate recordkeeping requirements for seafarers, depending on whether the work is performed on an American vessel. Employees employed as seafarers on other than an American vessel are exempt from both the minimum wage and overtime pay requirements; but the recordkeeping requirements set forth in Q 8:1, items 1 through 4, apply to those employees. [29 U.S.C. § 213(a)(12); 29 C.F.R. § 516.11]

Employees employed as seafarers on an American vessel are exempt from the overtime requirements. For these employees, an employer must keep the records described in Q 8:1, items 1 through 4 and 10 through 12. Such employers must keep the following records:

- *Basis of pay.* The basis on which wages are paid. For example, the dollar amount paid per hour, per day, or per other pay period.
- *Hours worked.* The total hours worked for each workday and for each pay period, as defined in FLSA Section 206(a)(4).
- *Total straight-time pay.* Total straight-time earnings or wages for each pay period.
- *Vessel(s).* The vessel's name, type, and documentation, registry number, or other identification.

[29 U.S.C. § 213(b)(6); 29 C.F.R. § 516.17]

Q 8:14 What are the recordkeeping requirements for hospital and resident care facilities employees?

The following records must be kept for employees at hospitals and institutions primarily engaged in the care of the sick, aged, mentally ill, or disabled who reside on the premises and who—pursuant to an agreement—are compensated for overtime on the basis of a 14-consecutive-day work period:

- *General requirements.* The records set forth in Q 8:1, items 1 through 4, 6, and 10 through 14.
- *Beginning of work period.* The time and day of the week on which the 14-day work period begins.
- *Hours.* Hours worked each workday and total hours worked each 14-day work period.
- *Straight time.* Total straight-time wages paid during the 14-day period.
- *Overtime.* Total overtime paid for hours worked in excess of eight hours per workday or 80 hours per 14-day period.
- *Agreement.* A copy of the agreement or understanding—or a memorandum summarizing the terms of an oral agreement—that establishes a 14-day work period for overtime purposes and that sets forth the date it was entered into and its duration.

[29 U.S.C. § 207(j); 29 C.F.R. § 516.23]

Q 8:15 What are the recordkeeping requirements for firefighters and law enforcement employees?

For overtime-exempt firefighters and law enforcement employees, public employers must keep the records set forth in Q 8:1, items 1 through 5, 7, 8, and 10 through 12. For the workweek recordkeeping requirements set forth in Q 8:1, item 5, the work period, the starting time, and the length of each employee's workweek must be recorded. These requirements can be satisfied on a collective basis if a group of employees has the same starting time and work period. In addition, public employers must keep the following records:

- *Basis of pay.* Information and data regarding the basis of pay, expressed as earnings per hour, per day, or per pay period.
- *Compensatory-time ("comp-time") hours and agreements.* For employees subject to the comp-time provisions in FLSA Section 207(o), the following records of hours for each workweek or pay period must be kept for each employee: (1) the number of comp-time hours earned at the rate of one and one-half hours for each overtime hour; (2) the number of comp-time hours used; and (3) the number of comp-time hours paid in cash, the total amount paid, and the date of payment. In addition, any collective bargaining agreement or memorandum of understanding that pertains to comp time must be kept. State, local, and interstate government agencies of employees subject to the comp-time and time-off provisions of FLSA Section 207(o) must also keep these records.

[29 U.S.C. §§ 213(b)(20), 207(o); 29 C.F.R. §§ 516.12, 516.2(a)(5), 553.50, 553.51]

Special Wage and Hour Practices

Several alternative pay practices for determining overtime or minimum wages are provided for under the FLSA. These include crediting tips as part of the minimum wage; paying commissions as part of wages; paying employees pursuant to certain collective bargaining agreements; using Belo plans or guaranteed weekly pay; paying employees according to a piece-rate schedule, including employees who work at home; and deducting from or including in wages the cost of board, lodging, or other facilities customarily provided. All of these pay practices are described in detail in Chapters 3, 7, and 10. The FLSA has rigid requirements for these special wage and hour practices. The recordkeeping rules associated with these pay practices essentially serve the purpose of documenting an employer's compliance with the FLSA's requirements.

Q 8:16   What records must an employer keep for employees who receive tips as part of their wages?

A tipped employee is an employee engaged in an occupation in which he or she regularly or customarily receives more than $30 per month in tips. The general recordkeeping requirements set forth in Q 8:1, items 1 through 13, apply to tipped employees. These records must identify the employees as tipped with a letter or symbol. In addition, the following records must be kept for each employee:

- *Amount of tips.* The weekly or monthly amount of tips reported by the employee. This can consist of reports made *by the employees* on IRS Form 4070.
- *Tips credited.* Amount of tips credited toward each tipped employee's wages. If the amount per hour that the employer takes as a tip credit changes from the amount taken in the preceding period, the employer must report this to the employee in writing.
- *Tipped and nontipped work.* Hours worked each workday in an occupation in which the employee does not receive tips, and total daily or weekly straight-time paid for those hours. The same records must be kept for each employee for daily hours worked in a tipped occupation, including the total daily or weekly straight-time paid for those hours.

[29 C.F.R. § 516.28]

Q 8:17   What are the recordkeeping requirements for employees who work at a retail or service establishment on commission?

Employees who work at a retail or service establishment and earn more than half of their compensation over a period of one month or longer from commissions are paid overtime on a basis different from that prescribed in FLSA Section

207(a). For these employees, an employer must keep the records described in Q 8:1, items 1through 5, 7, 10, and 12. The payroll records must identify those employees as being paid on commission with a letter or symbol. In addition, the employer must keep the following records:

- *Terms of agreement.* A copy of the written agreement or memorandum of understanding describing the commission rate and the terms of payment, the pay period, the date the agreement was entered into, and how long it remains in effect. These agreements or understandings may be entered into individually or collectively.

- *Total compensation.* The total compensation paid to each employee per pay period, separately showing the total amount of commissions paid and the total straight-time earnings.

[29 U.S.C. § 207(i); 29 C.F.R. § 516.16]

Q 8:18   What are the recordkeeping requirements for employers of employees who work under certain collective bargaining agreements?

Employers whose employees are organized under the National Labor Relations Act must keep specific records relating to wages paid under the collective bargaining agreement. For employees employed under a collective bargaining agreement described in FLSA Section 207(b)(1) and (2), all of the requirements set forth in Qs 8:1 and 8:2 apply. In addition, the employer must keep records of the following:

- *Agreement.* Copies of the collective bargaining agreement and any amendments.

- *Certification.* Proof that the union has been certified by the National Labor Relations Board to represent the employees covered by the collective bargaining agreement.

- *Bargaining unit employees.* Either separately or as part of the payroll records, a list of each employee covered under the collective bargaining agreement.

- *Period of employment.* Either separately or as part of the payroll records, the period or periods each employee has been employed pursuant to the collective bargaining agreement.

- *Total hours worked.* For agreements described in FLSA Section 207(b)(1), the total hours each employee worked for 26 consecutive weeks. For agreements described in FLSA Section 207(b)(2), the total hours each employee worked for 52 consecutive weeks.

- *Overtime.* Daily and weekly overtime compensation for each employee.

[29 U.S.C. § 207(b)(1), (2); 29 C.F.R. § 516.20]

Q 8:19 If an employer pays wages pursuant to a Belo contract, what records must it keep?

A *Belo contract* is a wage contract entered into between an employer and an employee or group of employees when neither party can anticipate the number of hours to be worked from one week to the next and when the employee's workweek fluctuates both above and below the 40-hour workweek (see Q 7:77). FLSA Section 207(f) sets forth the specific requirements for those agreements. Employers that are party to a Belo contract must keep the records set forth in Q 8:1, items 1 through 7 and 10 through 12, plus the following records:

- Total weekly guaranteed earnings.
- Total weekly compensation in excess of the weekly guarantee.
- A copy of the bona fide individual contract, collective bargaining agreement, or written memorandum summarizing the terms of the Belo contract.

[29 U.S.C. § 207(f); 29 C.F.R. § 516.24]

Q 8:20 What records must an employer keep for employees who are paid according to a piece rate?

Employers that, pursuant to an agreement or understanding, pay nonexempt employees on a piece rate basis described in FLSA Section 207(g)(1) or (2) must keep the records set forth in Q 8:1, items 1 through 5, 7, 8, and 10 through 12, plus the following records:

- *Payroll data.* The hourly or piece rate for each employee; the basis on which wages are paid; and the amount and nature of each payment that is excluded from the regular rate under FLSA Section 207(e).
- *Overtime records.* For each workweek, the number of overtime hours worked, or the number of units completed at each applicable piece rate during overtime hours; and total weekly overtime compensation in excess of all straight-time earnings or wages during overtime hours.
- *Date of agreement.* The date the agreement or understanding for the piece-rate method of compensation was entered into.

For employers that pay piece rate employees a basic rate authorized by regulation as representative of the rate for employees in a particular type of work over a representative period of time—as described in FLSA Section 207(g)(3)—the records set forth in Q 8:1, items 1 through 5 and 7 through 14, must be kept for each employee, in addition to the following records:

- *Payroll data.* The hourly rates, piece rates, or commission rates applicable to each type of work performed by the employee; the computation that establishes the basic rate for overtime hours; and the amount and nature of each payment that is excluded from the regular rate under FLSA Section 207(e).

- *Representative basic-rate data.* (1) The representative period for computing the basic rate; (2) the period during which the established basic rate is to be used for computing overtime compensation; and (3) the information establishing that there is no significant difference between the terms, conditions, and circumstances of employment in the period selected under item (2), above, and the representative period that could affect the character of the representative period in item (1), above.

- *Agreement.* A copy of the written agreement or memorandum summarizing the terms of an oral agreement, showing the method for computing the piece-rate and the date and period covered by the agreement.

[29 U.S.C. § 207(g); 29 C.F.R. §§ 516.25, 516.26]

Q 8:21   If an employer deducts board, lodging, and other facilities from wages or provides them as an addition to wages, what records must it keep?

Employers that deduct from, or provide as an addition to, wages any noncash items such as board, lodging, and other facilities described in FLSA Section 203(m) must maintain the following records, in addition to the records set forth in Q 8:1:

- *Class-of-facility records.* Any records that substantiate the reasonable cost of furnishing the class of facility. Records do not need to be kept for the cost of furnishing each individual item if the items can be classed together—either because groups of facilities were acquired at the same time or because the facilities are similar or closely related and not easily separable. The records that must be kept include, but are not limited to: detailed records necessary for determining the depreciation value of the facility or assets allocable to the facility; records establishing the nature and amount of expenses that are figured into the cost; records that document the employer's average net investment in inventory, if those assets include merchandise sold to employees; and records showing the gross income derived from each class of facility.

- *Individual records.* An employer must keep individual records on a workweek basis of additions or deductions if: (1) the additions or deductions in any workweek bring the employee's wage below minimum wage; or (2) the employee works in excess of the applicable maximum hours standard and any additions made are part of the wage, or any deductions are allowable under FLSA Section 203(m).

[29 U.S.C. § 203(m); 29 C.F.R. § 516.27]

These requirements do not apply to an employee in any workweek in which the employee is not subject to overtime and receives at least minimum wage *in cash* for all hours worked during that workweek.

Q 8:22 What does the dual recordkeeping system for homeworkers entail?

Employees who work in a home, apartment, tenement, or room in a residential establishment to produce goods for an employer are considered homeworkers. Dual records must be kept for these employees, as follows:

- The payroll records must be maintained by the employer.
- Records of hours worked must be kept by each employee in a special handbook that employers can obtain from the Wage and Hour Division.

Both employers and employees must retain the certificate required to employ homeworkers in industries where employment of homeworkers is otherwise prohibited. Employers of workers with disabilities who are employed by a recognized nonprofit rehabilitation facility and work in or about a home, apartment, tenement, or room in a residential establishment are not required to keep the records specified in Qs 8:1 and 8:20. A homeworker handbook must be kept, in addition to the records that must be kept for disabled employees (see Q 8:10). [29 C.F.R. §§ 525.16(e), 516.31; for further information on homeworker certificates, *see* 29 C.F.R. §§ 530.3, 530.4, 530.6, 530.7]

Q 8:23 Other than dual records, what are the recordkeeping requirements for homeworkers?

In addition to the requirements specified in Qs 8:1 and 8:2, employers of homeworkers must maintain the following records:

- *Assignment of work.* For each lot of work, the date on which the work was given out or begun by the employee, and amount of work given out or begun.
- *Completion of work.* The date the work was turned in by the worker and the amount of such work.
- *Type of work.* Kind of articles worked on and operations performed.
- *Piece rates paid.*
- *Hours worked on each lot turned in.*
- *Wages paid for each lot turned in.*
- *Agent, distributor, or contractor information.* If homework is distributed through an agent of the employer or through a distributor or contractor, employers must keep a record of his or her name and address, and the name and address of the homeworker to whom the homework was distributed or from whom it was collected.

[29 C.F.R. § 516.31]

Employers of the following homeworkers are excluded from these requirements: homeworkers covered under FLSA Section 213(d); homeworkers in Puerto Rico—to whom 29 C.F.R. Part 545 applies; and homeworkers in the Virgin Islands—to whom 29 C.F.R. Part 695 applies.

Time for Maintaining Records

Q 8:24 What records are subject to the three-year retention requirement?

Except for lesser requirements described above for specific categories of employees, the following records must be kept for at least three years:

1. *Payroll records.* Records containing information required by the record-keeping requirements set forth in Qs 8:1 and 8:2.

2. *Certificates and notices.* From their last effective date, certificates and notices mentioned in the recordkeeping regulations as described in this chapter—including certificates authorizing the employment of learners, apprentices, handicapped workers, full-time students, homeworkers, and child laborers.

3. *Agreements.* From their last effective date, the following agreements:

   a. Collective bargaining agreements that set the terms under which board, lodging, or other facilities are provided to employees (see Q 3:17); [29 U.S.C. § 203(m)]

   b. Collective bargaining agreements described under FLSA Section 207(b)(1) or (2), including amendments and additions to the agreements;

   c. Written individual employment contracts or memoranda describing the terms of any oral agreement, providing for employment of an employee whose duties require irregular hours of work, as set forth in FLSA Section 207(f) (see Qs 7:77, 10:34);

   d. Written agreements or memoranda summarizing the terms of oral agreements or understandings for employees paid overtime on a piecework basis (see Q 7:51); [29 U.S.C. § 207(g)]

   e. Written agreements or memoranda summarizing the terms of oral agreements or understandings for employees of hospitals or institutions engaged primarily in the care of the sick, aged, or mentally ill and who are paid overtime pursuant to the requirements in FLSA Section 207(j) (see Chapter 7); and

   f. Plans, trusts, employment contracts, and collective bargaining agreements that involve exclusions from the regular rate as described in FLSA Section 207(e) (see Qs 7:24–7:38).

4. *Sales and purchase records* necessary to determine whether the employer meets the enterprise business volume test (see Chapter 2). These records must be in the same form in which the employer maintains records in the ordinary course of business.

[29 C.F.R. §§ 516.5, 519.7, 520.203, 530.8]

Q 8:25   What records are subject to the two-year retention requirement?

The following records must be kept for at least two years:

- *Basic employment and earnings records.* From the last date of entry, all time cards or earnings cards for individual employees (or for separate workforces) showing the daily starting and stopping times, records documenting the amounts of work completed by an employee on a daily, weekly, or pay-period basis when pay is based on those amounts, or work-time schedules of separate workforces.

- *Wage-rate tables.* From their last effective date, piece-rate schedules or wage-rate tables on an hourly, daily, weekly, or pay-period basis.

- *Order, shipping, and billing records.* From the last date of entry, all orders or invoices, incoming or outgoing shipping or delivery records, bills of lading, and noncash billings to customers as are kept or made in the usual course of business. Originals or copies are sufficient.

- *Records of additions or deductions.* The total deductions from (or additions to) each employee's wages for each pay period, including employee purchase orders or wage assignments. These individual records must show the dates of the additions or deductions and the types of items added or deducted—separating the credited or debited amounts. If an employer figures into these additions or deductions the original cost, operating costs, and maintenance costs, all records used by the employer to determine those costs must also be kept for two years. For domestic service employees, records documenting credits taken for meals or lodging must be kept for three years.

- *Equal Pay Act records.* Descriptions of pay practices that explain the basis for any wage differentials among employees of the opposite sex in the same establishment that may be pertinent to determining whether the differential is based on sex or on factors other than sex.

[29 C.F.R. §§ 516.6, 552.100(2)(c), (d), 1620.32]

Chapter 9

Child Labor Restrictions Under the FLSA

This chapter addresses child labor restrictions, which limit the tasks minors (persons under the age of 18) can perform and the hours they can work. Occupational limits placed on minors are different for farm and nonfarm occupations. An exception applies to apprentices and student-learners, who may work in jobs the Department of Labor (DOL) has deemed hazardous as long as certain conditions for bona fide cooperative programs have been met. This chapter also addresses maintenance of age certificates and penalties for child labor violations.

Overview

Q 9:1 What does the Fair Labor Standards Act (FLSA) regulate with regard to child labor?

The FLSA regulates the employment of minors (persons under 18 years of age) and applies to both private employers subject to the FLSA and to public employers (see Qs 9:5–9:8). The Walsh-Healey Public Contracts Act (Walsh-Healey Act) also prescribes child labor standards for government contractors (see Q 9:36).

The focus of federal child labor laws is prevention of "oppressive child labor" in businesses engaged in commerce or in the production of goods for commerce. This is accomplished by regulating minimum ages for employment, limiting the number of hours minors can work, and prohibiting or restricting employment in "hazardous occupations" for those under 18 years of age. [29 U.S.C. §§ 203(l), 213(c)]

Employers face possible criminal penalties for violating the federal child labor laws (see Q 9:38), and the Department of Labor (DOL) has the power to investigate and inspect employers suspected of violating child labor laws (see Chapter 13). The Secretary of Labor can seek injunctions against employers that violate the law (see Chapter 14).

Q 9:2   What is oppressive child labor?

The FLSA defines *oppressive child labor* to mean any employment situation in which a minor under 16 years of age is employed by an employer (other than a parent or guardian) in any occupation, or employment of children ages 16 and 17 in an occupation found to be "particularly hazardous" by the DOL. Notwithstanding the definition of oppressive child labor, the FLSA provides that minors under age 16 can be employed in certain occupations in retail, food service, or gasoline service establishments, with restrictions placed on the hours they can work. [29 U.S.C. § 203(l); 29 C.F.R. § 570.34]

This policy of protecting children against harmful employment is so strong that at least one court has rejected an employer's argument that the Free Exercise of Religion Clause of the First Amendment permitted employment of children. [Brock v. Wendell's Woodwork, Inc., 867 F.2d 196, 199 (4th Cir. 1989)] The religious sect involved in *Brock* claimed that employing children in vocational apprenticeships was a spiritual benefit and taught the children principles of industry and hard work. The court found that protecting children from the hazards of working at power-saw tables and on scaffolding outweighed the employer's religious beliefs. The court also noted that unlike the Amish, who prepare their children for life in a separatist agrarian society, this religious sect used its apprenticeship program for a commercial purpose. [*Id.* at 197–99]

Q 9:3   What distinctions does the FLSA make with respect to child labor in various occupations?

The FLSA and federal regulations pertaining to oppressive child labor distinguish between agricultural and nonagricultural employment and younger and older minors in determining what is a hazardous occupation and what is not. What is acceptable in agricultural employment, based on agrarian tradition, may not be acceptable in manufacturing or other industrial operations. What is hazardous for one age group may not be hazardous for an older age group. [*See* 29 C.F.R. § 570.2; *compare* 29 C.F.R. pt. 570, subpt. C, *with* 29 C.F.R. pt. 570, subpt. E] Employers must abide by regulations prohibiting employees from performing jobs labeled as hazardous for employees of certain ages. In no case, however, is it enough for an employer to provide safety measures for operating hazardous machinery. [*See, e.g.*, Marshall v. Emes Provisions Co., 23 Wage & Hour Cas. (BNA) 63, 67 (DOL Feb. 3, 1977) (providing safety device on a machine that minors are prohibited from operating does not relieve an employer of its violation of the child labor restrictions)]. Specific provisions regarding what work can or cannot be performed by minors based on their age are discussed in more detail in Qs 9:9 through 9:29.

Q 9:4   How do state laws affect federal child labor laws?

As is true of most other areas covered by the FLSA, states can enact laws regulating child labor. To the extent state law provides greater protection to minors, that law applies as long as the state law does not conflict with the FLSA.

State laws also can address child labor concerns not covered at all by the FLSA. An example is California's extensive regulation of the employment of child actors and performers. Federal law provides only that the FLSA exempts from its coverage any child employed as an actor or performer in movies or theatrical productions or on radio or television productions. California law, on the other hand, is far more stringent. California employers must obtain written consent from the state labor commissioner before any minor under age 16 can be employed, for example, as an actor in plays or on radio or television, as a performer in concerts, at any noncommercial appearance, as an advertising or photographic model, or as a recording artist. California law also restricts the hours that minors from the age of eight to the age of 18 can work, requiring permission from the state labor commissioner before a minor can work from 10 p.m. through midnight. [29 C.F.R. § 570.125; Cal. Lab. Code § 1308.5(a)]

Employers Subject to Federal Child Labor Laws

Q 9:5   Which employers are required to comply with federal child labor laws?

Any employer that is considered a qualified enterprise for purposes of the FLSA, because its business relates to interstate commerce, is subject to the federal child labor provisions.

An employer that is not covered by the FLSA because it does not operate an enterprise engaged in interstate commerce still must comply with federal regulations with respect to individual employees who fall within the purview of the FLSA. This situation can arise when individually the employee's position relates to interstate or foreign commerce or involves producing goods for transportation in interstate or foreign commerce even though the employer's business functions as an intrastate enterprise.

An example of such an employer is a group home for mentally handicapped persons. Although the business may not relate to interstate commerce in a way that would place the home under the coverage of the FLSA, if the home's employees purchase goods from outside the state or communicate with persons in other states as part of their duties, the individual employees fall within the scope of the FLSA, and they would be subject to child labor laws.

Child labor laws apply to employers in two ways:

1. The FLSA forbids any "producer, manufacturer, or dealer" from shipping or delivering for shipment into commerce any goods produced in the United States that were the result of oppressive child labor within 30 days before their shipment, also known as "hot goods."

2. The FLSA prohibits use of oppressive child labor in the production of goods for commerce or in any enterprise engaged in commerce or in the production of goods for commerce.

[29 U.S.C. § 212(a), (c)]

The law requires the existence of an employment relationship between the minor and the employer before the employer can be held liable for oppressive child labor in commerce or in the production of goods for commerce. An employment relationship can be found to exist even when the employer has not actually hired the minor. For instance, the employer may know that a minor whom the employer did not hire is assisting an employee in operating a piece of machinery prohibited by the DOL regulations. If the employer permits this to continue, the employer is liable regardless of whether the employer actually hired the minor as an employee. This principle is similar to an employer's obligation to pay overtime when it is aware that employees are working beyond the 40-hour workweek set by the FLSA or the hours prescribed by state law. (Overtime provisions under the FLSA are discussed more fully in Chapter 7.) [29 C.F.R. § 570.113(a)]

Q 9:6   What is a *producer?*

For purposes of determining whether an employer falls within the scope of the FLSA, the DOL has interpreted *producer* to mean "one who engages in producing, manufacturing, handling, or in any other matter working on goods in any State." [29 C.F.R. § 570.105]

Goods are *produced* within the meaning of the FLSA when they are produced, manufactured, mined, handled, or worked on in any state. *Handling* or *working on* means preparing goods for entry into the stream of commerce, such as sorting, grading, storing, packing, or labeling. This is not a strict definition of producing but rather encompasses businesses such as warehouses, distribution yards, and fruit and vegetable packing sheds. Employees of the carriers that transport the goods are not involved in producing. [29 U.S.C. § 203(j); 29 C.F.R. § 570.108(b)]

Q 9:7   What is a *manufacturer?*

A *manufacturer* is one who engages in manufacturing, which is interpreted more narrowly than producing. *Manufacturing* has been defined as "the transformation of raw materials or semifinished goods into new or different articles," even if the work was done by hand in the employee's home. An employer does not have to be engaged solely in manufacturing to be considered a manufacturer by the DOL. [29 C.F.R. § 570.105]

Q 9:8   What is a *dealer?*

A *dealer* is one who deals in goods, by buying, selling, trading, distributing, or delivering goods. This includes middlemen, factors, brokers, commission merchants, wholesalers, and retailers. [29 C.F.R. § 570.105]

Minimum Ages for Employment and Restrictions on Hours of Work

Q 9:9   What are the ages at which minors can be employed?

In general, the ages for employment of minors are as follows:

1. Minors under age 14 cannot be employed in any occupation, unless they are employed by a parent who is the sole proprietor of a business. There are exceptions for minors who work as actors or deliver newspapers. There are also exceptions for minors employed in agriculture and wreath-making. [29 U.S.C. §§ 203(l), 213(c), (d)]

2. Minors ages 14 and 15 can be employed only in nonhazardous jobs and are limited in the hours they can work. While school is in session, minors can work up to 3 hours per day or 18 hours per week. During holidays and school vacations, 14- and 15-year-olds can work up to 8 hours per day or 40 hours per week. An added restriction is that they can work only between 7 a.m. and 7 p.m. during these breaks (until 9 p.m. while on vacation between June 1 and Labor Day). [29 U.S.C. §§ 203(l), 212(c); 29 C.F.R. §§ 570.35, 570.119(f)]

3. Minors ages 16 and 17 face no federal restrictions on the number of hours they can work per day or per week, but limits are placed on the types of occupations in which they can be employed. There are exceptions to these restrictions for those employed as student-learners and apprentices. Minors 16 and 17 years old can work in any nonfarm occupation—other than the particularly hazardous positions discussed in Q 9:16, which are restricted to those age 18 or above. [29 U.S.C. § 203(l); 29 C.F.R. pt. 570, subpt. E]

Q 9:10   What jobs and hours of work are permissible for minors performing nonfarm work under the FLSA?

- Minors 18 years or older may perform any job for unlimited hours.
- Minors age 16–17 may perform any job not declared hazardous for unlimited hours.
- Minors age 14–15 may work outside of school hours in various nonmanufacturing, nonmining, nonhazardous occupations with limitations on their hours of work.

Note. Minors enrolled in the work experience and career exploration program are provided an exception to hours worked limitations (see Q 9:11). Always check state law to see if child labor laws impose greater restrictions.

Q 9:11   What is a *career exploration program*?

Under the FLSA, a *career exploration program* is a school-supervised or school-administered program under which 14- and 15-year-olds can work up to 3 hours per school day and 23 hours in any school week. To be considered a valid career exploration program under FLSA, the program must meet state educational agency standards, which must provide the following:

1. Any student who is 14 or 15 years old and is deemed by local school officials to be someone who would benefit from the program is eligible to participate.
2. The student must receive school credit for participation.
3. Each program unit must be a reasonable size, such as 12 to 25 students per teacher/coordinator.
4. Students must receive classroom instruction in subjects the state requires for graduation as well as instruction in job-related skills.
5. There must be a teacher-coordinator appointed by the school.
6. There must be a written agreement signed by the teacher-coordinator, the employer, the student, and the student's parent or guardian.

[29 C.F.R. § 570.35a(b)(3), (d)]

Fourteen and 15-year-olds enrolled in a career exploration program cannot be employed in the following jobs:

* Manufacturing and mining jobs;
* Occupations the DOL has deemed hazardous for persons ages 16 and 17;
* Agricultural occupations deemed as hazardous for minors under the age of 16;
* Occupations prohibited for 14- and 15-year-olds; and
* Occupations in retail, food service, and gasoline service establishments not permitted by the DOL for minors ages 14 and 15.

Applications for special variations are determined by the Wage and Hour Division on a case-by-case basis. [29 C.F.R. § 570.35a(c)]

Career exploration programs are further restricted in that students may not displace existing workers of the employer. [29 C.F.R. § 570.35a(e)]

Q 9:12   Are there any occupations in which minors can be employed without being subject to the FLSA?

Yes. In addition to employment not governed by the FLSA because of its purely intrastate nature, the DOL has singled out certain occupations for exemption from its child labor provisions. The following occupations have been exempted from the FLSA's child labor provisions:

- Jobs in agriculture outside of school hours for the school district where the minor-employees live while they are working;
- Jobs as newspaper delivery persons;
- Jobs as child actors or performers in motion pictures or in theatrical, radio, or television productions;
- Jobs for which the employee works for a parent or person standing in the place of a parent (applicable to children under 16 years of age in any occupation, except manufacturing, mining, or an occupation deemed particularly hazardous for the employment of children ages 16 and 17 or detrimental to their health and well-being);
- Jobs related to wreath-making; and
- Employment where services during the workweek are performed outside the jurisdiction of the United States, such as in a foreign country.

[29 U.S.C. § 213(c), (d), (f); 29 C.F.R. § 570.122]

Additionally, children ages 14 and 15 can work as sports attendants but must be employed outside school hours. These employees are not subject to the limitations placed on other 14- and 15-year-olds regarding maximum hours per week and hours per day that they can be employed. The DOL has delineated acceptable and unacceptable duties minors can perform as sports attendants. Acceptable duties are the following:

- Pre- and post-game or practice setup of balls, items, and equipment;
- Supplying and retrieving balls, items, and equipment during a sporting event;
- Clearing the field or court of debris or moisture during play;
- Providing the players with ice, drinks, and towels during a game;
- Running errands for trainers, managers, coaches, and players before, during, and after a sporting event; and
- Returning or storing equipment in a clubhouse or locker room after a game.

[29 C.F.R. § 570.35(b)]

Impermissible duties include the following:

- Grounds or field maintenance;
- Cleaning or repairing equipment;
- Cleaning locker rooms, showers, restrooms, vehicles, clubhouses, dug-outs, etc.;
- Loading and unloading balls, items, and equipment from team vehicles before and after a sporting event;

- Doing laundry; and
- Working in concession stand or other selling activities.

[29 C.F.R. § 570.35(b)]

Hazardous Duties Outside of Agriculture

Q 9:13   Which occupations are hazardous for 14- and 15-year-olds?

The following jobs in retail, food service, or gasoline service are hazardous, and therefore prohibited, to minors ages 14 and 15:

- Work performed in or about boiler or engine rooms;
- Work in connection with maintenance or repair of the establishment, machines, or equipment;
- Outside window washing that involves working from window sills, and all work requiring the use of ladders, scaffolds, or their substitutes;
- Baking and cooking (except with electric or gas grills that do not involve cooking over an open flame and with deep fat fryers that are equipped with and utilize devices that automatically lower and raise the baskets into and out of the oil or grease);
- Occupations that involve operating, setting up, adjusting, cleaning, oiling, or repairing power-driven food slicers and grinders, food choppers, and cutters, and bakery-type mixers;
- Work in freezers and meat coolers and all work in the preparation of meats for sale (except wrapping, sealing, labeling, weighing, pricing, and stocking when performed in other areas);
- Jobs requiring loading and unloading goods to and from trucks, railroad cars, or conveyors; and
- All occupations in warehouses except office or clerical work.

[29 C.F.R. § 570.34(b)]

Work in the following is hazardous, and therefore prohibited, to minors ages 14 and 15:

- Manufacturing, mining, or processing occupations;
- Occupations that involve the operation or tending of any hoisting apparatus or power-driven machinery (including lawn mowers, trimmers, and "weed whackers") other than office machines;
- Operation of or assistance with motor vehicles;
- Public messenger service;
- Particularly hazardous occupations (see Q 9:16); and
- Occupations (except office or sales work) in connection with transportation, warehousing, storage, communications, public utilities, and construction.

[29 C.F.R. § 570.33]

Q 9:14   Which occupations are not hazardous for 14- and 15-year-olds?

The following positions in retail, food service, or gasoline establishments are not hazardous, and are therefore acceptable, for 14- and 15-year-olds:

- Office and clerical work, including operating office machines;
- Cashiering, selling, modeling, art work, work in advertising departments, window trimming, and comparative shopping;
- Price marking and tagging by hand or by machine, assembling orders, packing, and shelving;
- Bagging and carrying customers' orders;
- Errand and delivery work by foot, bicycle, and public transportation;
- Cleanup work, including the use of vacuum cleaners and floor waxers;
- Cleaning of kitchen equipment, including the filtering, transporting, and disposal of oil and grease, as long as the temperatures of surfaces and the oil and grease do not exceed 100°F;
- Maintenance of grounds, but not including the use of power-driven mowers or cutters;
- Kitchen work and other work involved in preparing and serving food and beverages, including the operation of machines and devices used in the performance of such work, such as, but not limited to, dishwashers, toasters, dumbwaiters, popcorn poppers, milkshake blenders, coffee grinders, and microwave ovens that do not have the capacity to warm above 140°F;
- Work in connection with cars and trucks if confined to dispensing gasoline and oil; courtesy service; car cleaning, washing, and polishing; and other occupations permitted by 29 C.F.R. Section 570.34, but not including work involving the use of pits, racks, or lifting apparatus, or involving the inflation of any tire mounted on a rim equipped with a removable retaining ring; and
- Cleaning fruits and vegetables and wrapping, sealing, labeling, weighing, pricing, and stocking goods, when performed in physically separate areas from other hazardous kitchen work.

[29 C.F.R. § 570.34(a)]

Q 9:15   What types of cooking and other restaurant duties can 14- and 15-year-old employees perform?

The Department of Labor has significantly revised and modernized the restrictions on cooking by 14- and 15-year-old minors.

In the past, Department of Labor regulations expressly prohibited these minors from "cooking (except at soda fountains, lunch counters, snack bars, or cafeteria serving counters)." Over the years, that regulation evolved into an "in plain view" rule. That is, cooking performed "in plain view" of customers was permissible even if the minor was not working at a traditional soda fountain or snack bar, and cooking performed out of plain view (i.e., in the kitchen or behind a partition) was not permissible.

Acknowledging that times have changed since the original regulation was developed in 1961—and that the traditional soda fountains and snack bars on which the regulations were based have been supplanted by fast food chains with new types of cooking equipment—the department has issued new regulations that focus on the type of cooking involved, not where the cooking takes place. The "in plain view rule" no longer applies. The new regulations became effective February 14, 2005. [29 C.F.R. § 570.34]

Under the new regulations, a 14- or 15-year-old minor MAY:

• Perform cashiering, table service and "busing," and clean up work, including the use of vacuum cleaners and floor waxers;

• Perform kitchen work and other work involved in preparing food and beverages, including the operation of devices used in such work, such as dishwashers, toasters, milk shake blenders, warming lamps, and coffee grinders;

• Do limited cooking duties involving electric or gas grills that do not entail cooking over an open flame;

• Cook with deep fat fryers that are equipped with and utilize devices that automatically raise and lower the "baskets" into and out of the hot grease or oil;

• Dispense food from cafeteria lines and steam tables and heat food in microwave ovens that do not have the capacity to heat food over 140°F; and

• Clean kitchen surfaces and nonpower-driven equipment, and filter, transport and, dispose of cooking oil, but only when the temperature of the surface and oils do not exceed 100°F.

However, a 14- or 15-year-old minor MAY NOT:

• Operate "Neico broilers," rotisseries, pressure cookers, fryolators, and other cooking devices that operate at extremely high temperatures;

• Perform any baking activities;

• Operate, clean, set up, adjust, repair, or oil power-driven machines, including food slicers, processors, or mixers;

• Operate power-driven lawn mowers or cutters, work in freezers or meat coolers, or load or unload goods to or from trucks or conveyors; and

• Perform work in any hazardous occupations (see Q 9:16).

Q 9:16   Which occupations are particularly hazardous for minors?

A number of occupations are considered particularly hazardous for minors and are therefore unlawful for anyone under age 18. There are 17 specific Hazardous Occupations Orders (HOs) for nonagricultural employment.

HO 1—Manufacturing or Storage Occupations Involving Explosives. This rule prohibits minors from holding jobs in plants that handle or store explosives or any goods containing explosives, including all jobs in any plant or establishment that manufactures or stores explosive material, unless the minor will be performing a job in a nonexplosive area. This means that none of the work in the area involves handling or use of explosives, the area in which the minor works is separated from the explosive area by at least the distance set out in the American table of distances for protection of inhabited buildings from explosives, the explosive area is separated by a fence, and the employer has put in place safeguards to prevent persons under age 18 from entering the explosive area of the plant.

The prohibition on employment in plants manufacturing explosives applies to minors in plants that manufacture small-arms ammunition. It does not, however, prohibit employment of minors in retail establishments that may sell the end product produced by such manufacturers.

The Department of Labor recently revised the regulations governing the ban on youth employment in jobs involving explosives to update the definition of explosives. The definition in prior regulations, issued in 1939, which included "ammunition, black powder, blasting caps, fireworks, high explosives, primers, smokeless powder, and all goods classified and defined as explosives by the Interstate Commerce Commission" had become obsolete in part because of the development of new-fangled high-tech explosives and in part because Congress abolished the ICC in 1995. The new regulations expand the definition of explosives to include "any chemical compound, mixture, or device, the primary or common purpose of which is to function by explosion, as well as all goods identified in the most recent list of explosive materials published by the Bureau of Alcohol, Tobacco, Firearms, and Explosives." [29 C.F.R. § 570.51]

HO 2—Motor Vehicle Operations. HO 2 prohibits minors from performing jobs as motor vehicle drivers and outside helpers on any public road, on any highway, in or about any mine, in or about any place where logging or sawmill operations are in progress, or in most excavation operations. [29 C.F.R. § 570.52]

Under a limited exception, enacted on October 30, 1998, 17-year-olds may drive automobiles and trucks as part of their employment on an occasional and incidental basis if all the following requirements are met:

1. The automobile or truck does not exceed 6,000 pounds gross vehicle weight.

2. The driving is limited to daylight hours.

3. The 17-year-old holds a state license that is valid for the driving involved.

4. The 17-year-old has successfully completed a state-approved driver education course and has no record of any moving violations at the time of hire.

5. The driving takes place within a 30-mile radius of the minor's place of employment,

6. The automobile or truck is equipped with a seat belt for the driver and any passengers, and the employer has instructed the minor that seat belts must be used when driving the vehicle.

7. The driving does not involve:

   • Towing vehicles

   • Route deliveries or route sales

   • Transportation for hire

   • Urgent, time-sensitive deliveries

   • Transporting more than three passengers, including other employees

   • More than two trips away from the primary place of employment in a single day to deliver goods to customers (other than urgent, time-sensitive deliveries, which are prohibited)

   • More than two trips away from the primary place of employment in a single day to transport passengers, other than employees of the employer

[Pub. L. No. 105-334 (amending 29 U.S.C. § 213(c)(6))]

HO 3—Coal Mining Occupations. All occupations in or about a coal mine are prohibited except "the occupation of slate or other refuse picking at a picking table or picking chute in a tipple or breaker" or jobs in offices or repair shops above the surface of the coal mine. [29 C.F.R. § 570.53]

HO 4—Logging and Sawmilling Occupations. Minors under 18 may not hold jobs in logging operations, including sawmills, lathe mills, shingle mills, and cooperage stock mills. There are exceptions to this broad prohibition. In logging operations, minors can work in offices or repair and maintenance shops. They can be employed in positions relating to the repair, construction, operations, or maintenance of living quarters or the administrative portion of the logging business.

Minors are allowed to take part in surveying or engineering parties; repairing roads, railroads, or flumes; preventing fire by clearing fire trails and roads; maintaining fire equipment; or acting as a fire lookout, as long as the job is away from the actual logging operations.

With respect to the sawmill itself, minors, in general, can perform office or clerical, cleanup, or stacking and sorting work, as long as the sorting or cleanup is not actually performed in the mill building. If an employer wants to hire a minor to load bundles of shingles or shakes onto trucks or railroad cars, the employer must obtain a statement from a doctor stating that the employee is capable of performing this job without injury. [29 C.F.R. § 570.54]

HO 5—Power-Driven Woodworking Occupations. Jobs involving power-driven woodworking machines are generally barred for minors under 18. However, this prohibition does not apply to apprentices or student-learners, which are discussed in Q 9:20. [29 C.F.R. § 570.55]

HO 6—Occupations Involving Exposure to Radioactive Substances and to Ionizing Radiation. This rule prohibits minors from holding jobs involving exposure to radioactive materials. The federal regulations prohibit employment in the workroom where radioactive substances are made, processed, packaged, stored, or in use, or in work that involves exposure to ionizing radiations in excess of 0.5 rem per year. [29 C.F.R. § 570.57]

HO 7—Power-Driven Hoisting Apparatus Occupations. This HO bans jobs operating elevators and other power-driven hoisting apparatus. This prohibition extends to work that involves riding on a man-lift or on a freight elevator, unless the freight elevator is operated by an assigned operator. The provision does not prohibit minors from operating unattended automatic passenger elevators or electric or air-operated hoists with a capacity of one ton or less. [29 C.F.R. § 570.58]

HO 8—Power-Driven Metal Forming, Punching, and Shearing Machine Occupations. Jobs involving power-driven metal forming, punching, and shearing machines cannot be performed by minors under age 18. Minors can, however, be employed in positions operating pressing or punching machines as long as the machines are equipped with "full automatic feed and ejection and with a fixed barrier guard to prevent the hands or fingers of the operator from entering the area between the dies." This prohibition does not apply to apprentices or student-learners. [29 C.F.R. § 507.59]

HO 9—Occupations in Connection with Mining, Other than Coal. Prohibited jobs in mining operations, other than coal mining, include work in quarries, clay pits, sand and gravel operations, dredging operations, and operations involved in washing, grinding, or extracting minerals. This regulation does not prohibit work in manufacturing or processing of the post-mining product; petroleum or natural gas production; or dredging operations that are not connected with mining, such as for construction or navigation purposes. As with other hazardous occupations, minors can lawfully work in the offices, warehouse or supply house, change house, laboratory, or repair shop of a mine, but not underground. Additionally, minors can work in operation or maintenance of living quarters, positions surveying and repairing roads, and general cleaning up of mine property by clearing brush or digging drainage ditches. Minors can also work on building or maintaining railroad track located in areas of open cut metal mines, provided there is no mining activity being conducted at the time and location of the maintenance work. [29 C.F.R. § 570.60]

HO 10—Occupations Involving the Operation of Power-Driven Meat-Processing Machines and Occupations Involving Slaughtering, Meatpacking, Processing, or Rendering. Jobs involving power-driven meat processing machines and those involving slaughtering, rendering, recovery of oils and lard, boning, and meat packing are banned for minors under age 18. This regulation does not bar employment of minors in such positions as messengers, runners, or handtruckers if they are required to enter the workroom only occasionally and for a short duration. The regulation does not limit the killing and processing of poultry, rabbits, or small game away from the killing floor or apply to apprentices or student-learners. [29 C.F.R. § 570.61]

The prohibition against working in meat packaging or processing occupations has been extended to restaurants, where minors cannot operate meat slicers. [Dole v. Stanek, 29 Wage & Hour Cas. (BNA) 1422 (N.D. Iowa 1990)]

HO 11—Power-Driven Bakery Machine Occupations. This order bans occupations relating to bakery machines. This prohibition includes assisting another person in the operation of or setting up, repairing, or cleaning of any dough or batter mixer; bread dividing, rounding, or molding machine; or bread slicer; and setting up or adjusting a cookie or cracker machine. [29 C.F.R. § 570.62]

HO 12—Power-Driven Paper-Products Machine Operations Including Scrap Paper Balers and Paper Box Compactors. This order prohibits minors from performing jobs involving operation, setting up, adjusting, repairing, oiling, or cleaning of paper-products machines, such as stitchers, staplers, circular or band saws, paper or envelope cutters, and press machines, including those machines that do not require hand feeding. Apprentices and student-learners employed under 29 C.F.R. § 570.50(b) or (c) are not subject to this regulation. [29 C.F.R. § 570.63]

A limited exemption permits 16- and 17-year-old employees to load, but not operate or unload, certain scrap paper balers and box compactors if all the following safety requirements are met:

- The scrap paper balers and box compactors meet applicable standards set by the American National Standard Institute (ANSI).
- The balers and compactors cannot be operated while being loaded.
- The balers and compactors include an on-off switch incorporating a key-lock or other system and the control of the system is maintained in the custody of employees who are 18 years of age or older.
- The on-off switch is maintained in the off position when the equipment is not in operation.
- The employer posts a notice on each machine stating that the equipment meets ANSI standards, that 16- and 17-year-olds may only load the baler or compactor, and that any employee under 18 may not operate or unload the baler or compactor.

Additionally, employers must submit to the Secretary of Labor reports regarding any injury requiring medical treatment, other than first aid, or fatality that results from contact with a scrap paper baler or paper box compactor. The report must provide the name, address, and telephone number of the employer and place where the injury occurred; the name, address, and telephone number of the minor who suffered the injury; the date of the incident; and the manufacturer and model number of the machine involved in the incident. [29 U.S.C. § 213(c)(5)]

HO 13—Occupations Involved in the Manufacture of Brick, Tile, and Kindred Products. Jobs involving manufacturing brick, tile, or other clay construction products are prohibited for minors under 18. The exceptions to this regulation are that minors can be employed in storage or shipping, offices, laboratories, or storerooms, or in drying departments of sewer pipe manufacturers. [29 C.F.R. § 570.64]

HO 14—Occupations Involved in the Operation of Power-Driven Circular Saws, Bandsaws, and Guillotine Shears. This order bars minors from performing jobs requiring operation, cleaning, or setting up of circular saws, band saws, or guillotine shears, except those machines with full automatic feed and ejection, which are machines equipped with a fixed barrier guard that prevents the operator from placing any body part in the point-of-operation area. This prohibition does not apply to apprentices or student-learners. [29 C.F.R. § 570.65]

HO 15—Occupations Involved in Wrecking, Demolition, and Shipbreaking Operations. Occupations involving wrecking, demolition, and shipbreaking, including cleanup and salvage work, are prohibited for minors under age 18. [29 C.F.R. § 570.66]

HO 16—Occupation in Roofing Operations and All Work on or about a Roof. In the past, this hazardous occupations order prohibited minors under age 18 from performing all roofing operations whether performed at elevations or at ground level. However it did not prohibit other jobs performed on or near roofs such as the installation, repair, and maintenance of television and microwave antennas, air conditioning equipment, and gutters and downspouts. However, the Department of Labor has issued new regulations, which took effect on February 14, 2005, banning minors from performing all work on or about a roof.

The term *on or about a roof* includes all work performed on or in close proximity to a roof. Moreover, this prohibition is not limited to circumstances where the minor employee is standing or working on the roof itself but extends to standing or working on a ladder or scaffold at or near the roof, as well as working from or being transported to or from the roof in mechanical devices such as hoists.

Apprentices and student-learners do not fall within the scope of this provision. [29 C.F.R. § 570.67]

HO 17—Occupations in Excavation Operations. Excavation work is not considered particularly hazardous when it involves excavating, backfilling, or working in trenches that are no deeper than four feet. Excavating for buildings or other structures is not hazardous if the work is being performed manually and will not exceed four feet in depth. Minors can work in an excavation no deeper than four feet or one in which the side walls have been shored up to their permanent position. Minors cannot work within tunnels before all driving and shoring operations are complete and cannot work within shafts before all sinking and shoring operations are complete. Apprentices and student-learners are not subject to this provision. [29 C.F.R. § 570.68]

Employers should know that not only are they prohibited from employing and utilizing minors directly in the hazardous occupations outlined above, but they are also prohibited from allowing minors to work in otherwise nonhazardous occupations with equipment where it would be possible for the minor to use that equipment in a hazardous fashion. For example, in a recent administrative decision of the DOL, an employer involved in the interstate transport of livestock was liable for civil money penalties for child labor violations arising out of minor employees' use of a skid loader, which is an industrial type high-lift truck. The skid loader has a lifting capacity of up to 12.5 feet, but can also be used in a lowered position as a shovel type of device. The skid loader in question was used by the minor employees to pull or push manure and other materials around while cleaning. The minors never actually used the skid loader in its fully extended position, but could have at any time during its operation. The Secretary of Labor has determined that it is particularly hazardous for minors to be engaged in an occupation involving the operation of an elevator, crane, derrick, hoist, or high-lift truck. [29 C.F.R. § 570.58(a)] Because the skid loader could have been used like a high-lift truck, having minors operate it, even for permissible uses such as shoveling, was impermissible. [USDOL v. Lynnville Transp., Inc., 1999-CLA-18 (Dep't of Labor Aug. 29, 2000)]

Q 9:17   What special restrictions apply to teen driving?

Minors under age 17 are strictly prohibited from driving in the course of their employment.

Under the Drive for Teen Employment Act, 17-year-olds may drive automobiles and trucks on public roads as part of their employment on an *occasional and incidental* basis if all the following requirements are met:

1. The automobile or truck does not exceed 6,000 pounds gross vehicle weight.

2. The driving is limited to daylight hours.

3. The 17-year-old holds a state license that is valid for the driving involved.

4. The 17-year-old has successfully completed a state-approved driver education course and has no record of any moving violations at the time of hire.

5. The driving takes place within a 30 mile radius of the minor's place of employment.

6. The automobile or truck is equipped with a seat belt for the driver and any passengers, and the employer has instructed the minor that seat belts must be used when driving the vehicle.

7. The driving does not involve:
   - Towing vehicles
   - Route deliveries or route sales
   - Transportation for hire
   - Urgent, time-sensitive deliveries
   - Transporting more than three passengers, including other employees
   - More than two trips away from the primary place of employment in a single day to deliver goods to customers (other than urgent, time-sensitive deliveries, which are prohibited)

- More than two trips away from the primary place of employment in a single day to transport passengers, other than employees of the employer.

[Pub. L. No. 105-334 (amending 29 U.S.C. § 213(c)(6))]

Department of Labor regulations, effective February 15, 2005, spell out the circumstances in which teens can—and cannot—drive on the job.

According to the regulations, driving will be considered occasional and incidental only if it involves no more than one-third of an employee's worktime in any workday and no more than 20 percent of an employee's worktime in any workweek.

Urgent, time-sensitive deliveries—which are strictly prohibited for minor drivers—are trips that a driver might be impelled to hurry to complete because of such factors as:

- Customer satisfaction
- The rapid deterioration of the quality or change in temperature of a product
- Economic incentives
- Time-lines
- Schedules
- Turn-around times

According to the regulations, prohibited trips include, but are not limited to:

- Delivery of pizzas and prepared foods to customers;
- The delivery of materials under a deadline (such as deposits to a bank at closing); and
- The shuttling of passengers to and from transportation depots to meet transport schedules.

Urgent, time-sensitive deliveries do not depend on the delivery's points of origin and termination. So they may include the delivery of people and things to the employer's place of business as well as from that business to some other location. [29 C.F.R. § 570.52]

Q 9:18   Under what circumstances can minors under age 18 work on or about a roof?

Under new Department of Labor regulations, effective February 14, 2005, all occupations in roofing and all work on or about a roof are prohibited for employees under age 18.

Prior regulations banned minors from all roofing operations and related occupations whether performed at elevations or at ground level. However, other tasks performed on or near roofs such as the installation, repair, and maintenance of roofing sheathing, television and microwave antennas, air conditioning equipment, and gutters and downspouts were not prohibited.

Under the new regulations, prohibited work on or about a roof includes all work performed on or in close proximity to a roof. Examples of such work are:

- Carpentry and metal work, alterations, additions, maintenance and repair, including painting and coating of existing roofs;
- The construction of the sheathing or base of roofs (wood or metal), including roof trusses or joists;
- Gutter and downspout work;
- The installation and servicing of television and communication equipment such as cable and satellite dishes;
- The installation and servicing of heating, ventilation, and air conditioning equipment or similar appliances attached to roofs; and
- Any similar work that is required to be performed on or about roofs

Roofing operations means all work performed in connection with the installation of roofs. The term also includes all jobs on the ground related to roofing operations such as roofing laborer, roofing helper, materials handler, and tending a tar heater. [29 C.F.R. § 570.67]

Q 9:19   Under what circumstances can a minor under age 18 operate a scrap paper baler or box compactor?

The Compactor and Baler Act [Pub. L. No. 104-174 (amending 29 U.S.C. § 213(c)(5))] sets conditions that permit 16- and 17-year-old workers to load—but not operate or unload—certain scrap paper balers and paper box compactors.

Department of Labor regulations, effective February 14, 2005, implement the provisions of the Compactor and Baler Act.

Under those regulations, a 16- or 17-year-old employee may load a scrap paper baler or paper box compactor only if all the following conditions are met:

1. The scrap paper baler or paper box compactor meets the applicable standard of the American National Standard Institute (ANSI Z245.5-1990 or ANSI Z245.5-1997 for scrap paper balers and ANSI Z245.2-1992 or ANSI Z245.2-1997 for paper box compactors).

2. The scrap paper baler or paper box compactor cannot be operated while being loaded.

3. The scrap paper baler or paper box compactor includes an on-off switch incorporating a key-lock or other system, and the control of the system is maintained in the custody of employees who are 18 years of age or older.

4. The on-off switch of the scrap paper baler or paper box compactor is maintained in an off position when the equipment is not in operation.

5. The employer provides notice and posts notice on each scrap paper baler and each paper box compactor that 16- and 17-year-olds will be loading that states that:

   • The equipment meets the appropriate ANSI Standard (or a more recent applicable ANSI Standard that the Secretary of Labor has certified as being as protective of minors); and

   • 16- and 17-year-old employees may only load the scrap paper baler or paper box compactor, and any employee under the age of 18 may not operate or unload the scrap paper baler or paper box compactor.

There is no prescribed format for the notice, but it must contain all the required information, including identification of the specific ANSI standard that applies to the baler or compactor. [29 C.F.R. § 570.63]

Q 9:20   What does the FLSA provide regarding apprentices and student-learners?

Employers that want to categorize their minor-employees as apprentices in order for them to work in occupations deemed particularly hazardous must satisfy the following conditions:

   • The apprentice must be employed in a craft recognized as an apprentice-able trade.

   • The work in areas deemed particularly hazardous must be incidental to the apprentice's training.

   • The hazardous work must be intermittent and only for brief periods of time, closely supervised by a journeyman, and necessary to the apprentice's training.

   • The apprentice must register with the Bureau of Apprenticeship and Training of the DOL or with an accepted state agency that abides by federal standards or must work under a written apprenticeship agreement that satisfies federal or state standards.

[29 C.F.R. § 570.50(b)]

Student-learners can work in particularly hazardous occupations subject to the following conditions:

   • The student-learner must be enrolled in a cooperative vocational program through a state or local educational authority or in a similar program through a private school.

   • The student-learner must work under a written agreement that states that the hazardous work is incidental to the student's training; the hazardous work will be intermittent, for short periods of time, and supervised by a "qualified and experienced person"; safety instructions will be given by the school and incorporated into the training; and the employer will prepare a schedule of organized and progressive tasks for the employee to perform.

- The written agreement must be signed by the employer and the school coordinator or principal and must contain the name of the student-learner. The agreement must be kept on file with both the school and the employer.

[29 C.F.R. § 570.50(c)]

Any person who is not yet 18 years old but who has graduated from high school and has completed training through a student-learner program is not subject to the regulations prohibiting work in the hazardous occupations listed in Q 9:16. [29 C.F.R. § 570.50(c)]

Hazardous Duties in Agriculture

Q 9:21   How does the FLSA limit occupations minors can hold in agriculture?

There are two things to keep in mind with respect to employment of minors in agricultural positions:

- Children age 15 and under cannot work in agricultural occupations that have been declared hazardous by the DOL; however, the limitation does not apply as long as the minor is employed by a parent or guardian on a farm owned or operated by the parent or guardian. The minor cannot work in a manufacturing or mining position, or any other position deemed particularly hazardous, even if employed by his or her parents on a farm (see Q 9:16). [29 U.S.C. § 213(c)(2); 29 C.F.R. §§ 570.122(d), 570.123(c)]
- Except for restrictions on hazardous occupations for minors under age 16, there are no restrictions on minors employed in agriculture outside of school hours (with school hours being determined by the school district in which the minor lives) if the minor is:
  a. Age 11 or younger, and employed by a parent or guardian on a farm owned or operated by the parent or guardian or employed with the consent of a parent or guardian on a farm that qualifies for the man-days exemption from the FLSA's minimum wage, equal pay, and overtime rule;
  b. Age 12 or 13, and employed with a parent's or guardian's consent or employed on the same farm as the farm on which the parent or guardian is employed.
  c. Age 14 or over.

[29 U.S.C. § 213(c)(1)]

The *man-days exemption* is an exemption from the FLSA for employers that did not employ more than 500 man-days of agricultural labor during any calendar quarter of the preceding calendar year. A *man-day* is any day during which an employee performs agricultural labor for at least one hour. An employer can also seek a waiver for children ages 10 and 11 to work as hand-harvest laborers for up to eight weeks in a calendar year. [29 U.S.C. §§ 213(a)(6), 213(c)(4); 29 C.F.R. § 500.30(b)]

None of the provisions restrict the agricultural employment of a minor who has graduated from high school. [29 C.F.R. § 570.123(b)]

Q 9:22   What does *outside of school hours* mean?

The federal regulations define *outside of school hours* to mean before or after school hours, holidays, summer vacation, Sundays, or any other day on which classes in the school district are not held. The regulations refer to the school district, not the student; this means that if the student receives an excused absence from school but school is still in session, the exemption is inapplicable. [29 C.F.R. § 570.123(b)]

Because the law specifies that a child can be employed outside school hours in the school district where the child is living while he or she is employed, federal regulations provide and several courts have found that minors cannot work while school is in session in the district in which they live while they are working regardless of the fact that their permanent home may be in a school district where school is not in session. [Wirtz v. Fettig Canning Corp., 15 Wage & Hour Cas. (BNA) 818 (S.D. Ind. 1963); Mitchell v. Carmichael, 14 Wage & Hour Cas. (BNA) 91 (N.D. Ill. 1958)]

Q 9:23   What if school is not in session?

Federal regulations state that a minor moving into a new school district can be lawfully employed if the school district the minor last attended has completed the school year and is closed for the summer. The regulations caution employers that they should not put a minor to work before May 15, and even after that date, a minor should provide a written statement signed by a school official indicating that the school he or she attended is closed for the summer and the date on which it closed, along with the minor's name, the school's name and address, the date the statement was signed, and the title of the signor. [29 C.F.R. § 570.123(b)]

The DOL has determined that school is not in session for 14- or 15-year-olds who have been expelled from school or are prohibited from attending because of a juvenile court order. Such minors can work up to eight hours per day and up to 40 hours per week. [Wage and Hour Field Operations Handbook § 33b10]

Q 9:24   Are restrictions placed on the occupations in agriculture that a minor child can perform?

Yes. The law forbids performance of the following agricultural occupations by children under age 16.

- Operating a tractor with more than 20 horsepower, or connecting or disconnecting an implement or any of its parts to or from such a tractor, unless the minor is at least 14 years old and participating in the 4-H tractor operation program.

- Operating or assisting another in the operation of a corn picker, cotton picker, grain combine, hay mower, forage harvester, hay bailer, potato digger or mobile pea viner, feed grinder, crop dryer, forage blower, auger conveyor, power post-hole digger, power post driver, nonwalking-type rotary filler, or the unloading mechanism of a nongravity self-unloading wagon or trailer, unless the minor satisfies the requirements of the 4-H machine operation program.

- Operating or assisting another in operating a trench or earth-moving equipment; fork lift; potato combine; or power-driven circular, band, or chain saw.

- Working on a farm or in a yard, pen, or stall containing a bull, boar, or stud horse kept for breeding purposes, or working around a sow with suckling pigs or cow with a newborn calf that still has its umbilical cord.

- Felling, bucking, skidding, loading, or unloading timber with a butt diameter greater than six inches.

- Working from a ladder or scaffold from a height of more than 20 feet, including painting, repairing, or building structures; pruning trees; and picking fruit.

- Driving a bus, truck, or car when transporting others, or riding on a tractor as a passenger or helper.

- Working inside a fruit, forage, or grain storage facility designed to retain an oxygen-deficient or toxic atmosphere; in an upright silo within two weeks after silage has been added or when a top unloading device is in operating position; in a manure pit; or in a horizontal silo while driving a tractor for packing purposes.

- Handling or applying agricultural chemicals classified under the Federal Insecticide, Fungicide and Rodenticide Act as toxicity category I or II and labeled "poison" or "warning".

- Handling or using a blasting agent, including dynamite, black powder, sensitized ammonium nitrate, blasting caps, and primer cord.

- Transporting, transferring, or applying anhydrous ammonia.

[29 C.F.R. §§ 570.71, 570.72]

Q 9:25   Which occupations in agriculture can minors lawfully perform?

The DOL has found the following agricultural occupations not to be hazardous, and thus lawful for minors to perform:

- Driving a truck, bus, or automobile on the farm itself, or serving as a helper on a truck, bus, or automobile driven on the farm;

- Handling certain chemical pesticides and fertilizers;

- Loading and unloading trucks;

- Operating garden tractors;

- Picking vegetables and berries and putting them in containers or on conveyor belts;
- Clearing brush and harvesting trees up to six inches in butt diameter;
- Working from ladders at heights of less than 20 feet, such as picking fruit;
- Working with farm animals (except for work with certain breeding stock in confined areas), including showing animals at livestock shows, fairs, or exhibits, and similar activities when the activities are not on a farm;
- Hand planting and cultivation;
- Raising and caring for poultry;
- Milking cows;
- Processing and storing milk and dairy products;
- Cleaning barns, equipment storage buildings, chicken coops, and other farm structures;
- Mowing lawns;
- Riding, driving, or exercising horses;
- Picking cotton;
- Handling irrigation pipes;
- Harvesting and storing tobacco; and
- Riding on transplanters.

[Wage and Hour Field Operations Handbook § 33d03(h)]

Q 9:26   Are there any exceptions for student-learners in agricultural occupations?

Yes. Exceptions to the regulations governing hazardous agricultural occupations are allowed for student-learners when each of the following conditions has been satisfied:

1. The student-learner is enrolled in a vocational education training program through a state or local educational institution or private school.

2. By written agreement, the student-learner will perform hazardous work that is incidental to his or her training; the work will be intermittent, for short periods of time, and under the direct and close supervision of a qualified and experienced person; safety instructions will be given by the school and reinforced by the employer through on-the-job training; and a schedule of organized and progressive work processes to be performed on the job have been prepared.

3. The written agreement contains the name of the student-learner and is signed by the employer and an authorized school representative.

4. Copies of each agreement are kept on file by the educational authority or school and by the employer.

[29 C.F.R. § 570.72(a)]

Q 9:27　When can an employer seek and the DOL grant a waiver of federal regulations on child labor?

Employers can seek a waiver under FLSA Section 213(c)(4), which permits employment of 10- and 11-year-olds as hand-harvest laborers. There are no other waivers available with respect to child labor requirements except when working for a parent or a guardian as hand-harvest laborers (see Q 9:21).

The regulations, specifically 29 C.F.R. § 575.1, provide that the DOL can grant employers such a waiver if the employer proves the following:

- The crop being harvested is one with not more than an eight-week season and restricting employment of 10- and 11-year-olds would cause "severe economic disruption in the industry of the employer or group of employers applying for the waiver."
- The employment of 10- and 11-year-olds would not be harmful to the children's health or well-being.
- The level and type of pesticides and other chemicals used on the crops would not be harmful to the children's health or well-being.
- The employer cannot obtain services of workers age 12 and above for this task.
- This employer's industry or a group of employers traditionally has employed 10- and 11-year-olds for this type of work without displacing workers over 16 years of age.

[29 C.F.R. § 575.1(a)(A)(i)–(v)]

Any waiver granted requires the following:

1. The minors under age 12 must be employed outside school hours for the school district in which they live while they are employed in this occupation.
2. The workers must commute daily from their homes to the farm on which they are working.
3. The workers must be employed for not more than eight weeks between June 1 and October 15 of any calendar year.

[29 C.F.R. § 575.1(a)(B)(i)–(iii)]

Courts closely examine the public interest in protecting 10- and 11-year-old children from harm resulting from harvesting. For example, the District of Columbia Circuit balanced the prospect of lower food prices with the health risks from pesticide exposure and concluded no waiver of the FLSA should be permitted because any short-term reduction in food prices "would never approach the value of the children's health to the nation." [National Ass'n of Farmworkers Orgs. v. Marshall, 628 F.2d 604, 616 (D.C. Cir. 1980); *see also* Wash. State Farm Bureau v. Marshall, 625 F.2d 296, 301–06 (9th Cir. 1980) (denial of waivers upheld for strawberry growers using two pesticides that the Environmental Protection Agency determined may cause birth defects in children of those exposed to the pesticides)]

Q 9:28   How can an employer seek a waiver?

The application for any waiver under 29 C.F.R. part 575 must be filed with the Wage and Hour Division, Employment Standards Administration, in Washington, D.C. The following information is required for the waiver:

- Name, address, and ZIP code of the employer or group of employers and the name of an authorized representative of the employer or group of employers;
- Telephone number and area code for the employer or authorized representative, in case additional information is needed;
- Address or state, county, or other location information identifying the farm and/or field on which the 10- and 11-year-old harvesters will be employed;
- Specific crops to be hand harvested at each farm or field;
- "Substantiation of the claim that such agricultural operation is customarily and generally recognized as being paid on a piece rate basis in the region in which such individuals would be employed" (The Wage and Hour Administrator will accept signed statements to that effect from farmers and farm agents in the area who are familiar with the farming practices in the area.);
- Dates of not more than eight weeks in a calendar year between June 1 and October 15 during which it is anticipated the 10- and 11-year-olds will be employed in hand harvesting; and
- A statement that the 10- and 11-year-olds will be employed outside of school hours.

[29 C.F.R. §§ 575.3, 575.4]

Q 9:29   What additional restrictions are placed on an employer granted a waiver?

If the DOL grants an employer a waiver and permits employment of 10- and 11-year-olds as hand harvesters, the employer must abide by the following conditions:

1. The employer must keep a signed statement of the parent or guardian of the child consenting to the employment of the child.
2. The employer must abide by both state and federal laws and regulations on child labor.
3. The employer must not allow the 10- or 11-year-old to work for more than five hours in one day or more than 30 hours in any week. The child must be given a minimum 30-minute meal break and at least two 15-minute breaks each day.
4. The employer must provide adjacent to the field being harvested adequate toilet facilities, drinking water, and an adult capable of rendering first-aid treatment.

5. The employer must provide emergency transportation to the minor's permanent home or the nearest hospital if the 10- or 11-year-old becomes ill or injured during normal hours of employment.

6. The employer must not allow the 10- or 11-year-old to ride on or work in close proximity to any power-driven machinery or equipment. The federal regulations indicate that 50 or more feet from the child generally is a safe distance.

7. The employer is responsible for ensuring that every vehicle used for transportation of such minor complies with federal and state health and safety standards and with all Federal Highway Administration regulations, is operated by a licensed driver, and is insured in an amount that meets the levels set by the Interstate Commerce Act.

8. Presently, insurance requirements are $100,000 in coverage for bodily injuries to or death of one person; $300,000 in coverage for bodily injuries to or death of all persons injured or killed in one accident (subject to the limit of $100,000 for bodily injuries to or death of one person); and $50,000 in coverage for property damage or loss in any one accident.

9. The employer must post a copy of the waiver at the site of the minor's employment during the entire period of the minor's employment.

10. The employer must maintain a record of the minor's name, address, occupation, and date of birth; name and address of the school at which the minor is enrolled; and number of hours worked by the minor each day and each week. This record must be kept for at least two years.

11. The waiver is effective only for the period permitted by the DOL and is not subject to amendment.

[29 C.F.R. § 575.8]

Age Certificates

Q 9:30   What records are employers required to keep on minors they employ?

Employers must maintain records of their date of birth, starting and quitting times, daily and weekly hours worked, and their occupation. Additionally, employers may protect themselves from unintentional violation of the child labor provisions by maintaining an employment or age certificate indicating an acceptable age for the occupation and hours worked. Certificates issued under most state laws are acceptable (see Q 9:31).

Q 9:31   How is an age certificate obtained?

Either the minor or the prospective employer can request an age certificate from the state or the Wage and Hour Division. The age certificate for a prospective employee under the age of 18 is sent by the person issuing the age certificate to the prospective employer. An age certificate issued for an 18- or

19-year-old can be given directly to the individual, who must give it to the employer on beginning employment. The certificate must be kept on file for the duration of the minor's employment. [29 C.F.R. § 570.6(b)]

Over 40 states, plus the District of Columbia and Puerto Rico have been designated as states that have age certificates that can be used as proof of age for purposes of federal regulations. (Exceptions are Arizona, Idaho, Kansas, Mississippi, South Carolina, Texas, Utah, and Washington.) In Idaho, Mississippi, South Carolina, and Texas, employee age certificates can be obtained through Wage and Hour Division offices. (See appendix A for the nearest Wage and Hour Division office in those states.) [29 C.F.R. §§ 570.8, 570.9]

Q 9:32   What information must an age certificate contain?

An age certificate must contain the following information under federal law:

- Name and address of the minor-employee
- Minor's date and place of birth
- Minor's sex
- Minor's signature
- Name and address of the minor's parent or guardian
- Name and address of the employer, and industry and occupation of the prospective employee if he or she is under age 18
- Signature of the issuing officer
- Date and place of issuance

[29 C.F.R. § 570.6(a)]

Q 9:33   What is an employer required to do with an age certificate when a minor employee terminates employment?

Under longstanding Department of Labor regulations, an employer generally was required to return a certificate of age to the issuing agency when the employee left employment. There were, however, two exceptions: a certificate issued for employment in agriculture could be given to the named minor at termination of employment, and a certificate issued to an 18- or 19-year-old was required to be given to the named worker at termination of employment.

The Department of Labor has revised the regulations, effective February 14, 2005, to direct the employer to give all certificates to employees when their employment ends. The minor may then present the previously issued certificate to future employers as proof of age. [29 C.F.R. § 570.6(b)]

Q 9:34   What documents are acceptable for proof of age?

The DOL considers the following documents acceptable for proof of age:

- A birth certificate or an attested statement of the recorded date and place of birth, issued by a registrar of vital statistics or any other officer responsible for recording births.

- A record of baptism showing the date and place of birth and date and place of baptism, or a contemporaneously recorded record of birth kept in a Bible that records births in the family.

- Other documentary evidence that is deemed satisfactory by the Wage and Hour Administrator, such as a passport showing the minor's age, an Immigration and Naturalization Service document showing the minor's age, or a life insurance policy, provided that such documentary evidence existed for at least one year before it was offered as evidence.

- A school record or school census record of the minor's age, plus a sworn statement of a parent or guardian as to the child's age and a signed certificate by a doctor including the doctor's estimate of the child's age and indicating the minor's height and weight and other facts regarding the minor's physical development based on a personal evaluation. (If the school record is not available, a sworn statement by the parent or guardian plus the physician's statement may suffice.).

[29 C.F.R. § 570.7(a)]

The DOL prefers that age certificates be issued based on a birth certificate or statement of a registrar of births. The other documentary evidence is permissible only when "reasonable efforts have been made to obtain the preferred evidence." [29 C.F.R. § 570.7(b)]

Q 9:35   What if an employee lies about his or her age?

Federal regulations recommend that employers seek age certificates whenever there is reason to believe the prospective employee's age is below the permissible age for the position for which he or she is applying, particularly if the applicant is claiming to be one or two years above the minimum age or if he or she is claiming to be more than two years above the minimum age for the job for which he or she is applying but appears younger than that age. An unexpired age certificate on file shields an employer from liability for unintentional violations. [29 C.F.R. § 570.5(a), (c)]

An employee's misrepresentation of age affords no defense to an employer that does not require employees to furnish reliable proof of age. [Marshall v. General Motors Corp., Frigidaire Div., 23 Wage & Hour Cas. (BNA) 1133 (Dep't of Labor Aug. 23, 1978) (although minor falsified her birth date, employer still violated child labor provisions because employer took no action to verify employee's age)]

Child Regulations Relating to Public Contractors

Q 9:36   How are federal contractors regulated with respect to child labor?

The Walsh-Healey Act [41 U.S.C. §§ 35–45] governs child labor for federal contractors. It provides that public contracts for more than $10,000 for which bids are made by a "manufacturer" or "regular dealer" must include language providing that no male under 16 and no female under 18 will be employed by the contractor. An employer has a defense against child labor violations when the employer has unexpired age certificates on file showing that the minor is at least age 16. [41 U.S.C. § 35(c); 41 C.F.R. § 50-201.104]

A contractor is in violation of the Walsh-Healey Act if it knowingly employs an underage child. The term *knowingly* does not require a contractor to violate the Act intentionally. A contractor may also be liable when it fails to make an effort to obtain age certification from its employees when it reasonably should have. [United States v. Sweet Briar, Inc., 92 F. Supp. 777, 781 (W.D.S.C. 1950)] The minors at issue in *Sweet Briar* represented themselves as being 16 years old. Although they were not 16 years old, the mere fact that they were supposed to be under the age of 18 was sufficient to impose on the employer a duty to obtain an age certification for each in light of the terms of the exemption granted to the contractor. [41 U.S.C. § 35(c); 4 C.F.R. § 50-201.104]

In another case, the Seventh Circuit held an employer liable for the "knowing" employment of children when the employer's records showed, and the manager knew, the children's ages and that the children were employed for more than eight hours per day. [United States v. Smoler Bros., Inc., 187 F.2d 29, 31 (7th Cir. 1951)] The court rejected the employer's argument that since officials at corporate headquarters in Chicago did not know about the minors' ages at its plant in South Bend, Indiana, the company should not be held liable. Because the plant manager knew information sufficient to reveal the violations, the company was charged with knowledge. [*Id.*]

Q 9:37   How can a contractor avoid liability for child labor violations?

The law provides three avenues for a contractor to avoid liability for child labor violations:

1. The employer can seek a written stipulation from the federal agency employing the contractor that the requirements (including those precluding child labor) normally imposed on government contractors would impair the conduct of government business. [41 U.S.C. § 40]

2. The contractor will not be held liable for a knowing violation of the Walsh-Healey Act if the employer has on file an unexpired child labor certificate issued in accordance with DOL regulations, showing the child is 16 years old or older. [29 C.F.R. § 570.5(a); 41 C.F.R. § 50 201.104]

3. At least one court has held that the contractor will not be liable for making a reasonable effort to determine whether applicants and employees were underage and terminating the employment of any person it found to be underage. [United States v. Craddock-Terry Shoe Corp., 178 F.2d 760, 762 (4th Cir. 1949)] Employers probably should not, however, expect protection on this basis. The court, in part, based its decision on the fact that the violations occurred during World War II and stated that a "more diligent

and extended investigation as to the age of the applicants for employment . . . might seem proper under more normal circumstances." [*Id.*]

Penalties

Q 9:38   What punishment is provided for employers that commit child labor violations?

The FLSA provides penalties for violation of child labor statutes. The general provision for willful violations of any portion of the FLSA is not more than $11,000 for each employee who was the subject of the employer's violation or imprisonment for not more than six months, or both. Imprisonment is a possibility only when the offender has previously committed a willful violation of the FLSA. Additionally, the DOL often goes to court to get an injunction to force an employer to cease ongoing or potential child labor violations. The amount of a civil money penalty depends on consideration of various factors, including the size of the business, the gravity of the violation, the investigation history of the person charged, and whether the violation is de minimis and the person charged has given credible assurance of future compliance. [29 U.S.C. § 216(a); 29 C.F.R. §§ 579.1, 579.5]

Federal regulations define the following as violations subjecting employers to monetary penalties:

- Each shipment or delivery for shipment in commerce by a producer, manufacturer, or dealer of any goods produced in an establishment situated in the United States in which within 30 days before the removal of the goods from the facility a minor was unlawfully employed.
- Each unlawful employment of a minor for any period in commerce or in the production of goods for commerce or in any enterprise engaged in commerce or in the production of goods for commerce.
- Failure of the employer to maintain or preserve records as required by statute and regulation or records regarding the minor's birth and proof of age.
- Failure by the employer to take necessary action to comply with all regulations.

[29 C.F.R. § 579.3(a)]

Employers have certain limited defenses to violations of the FLSA and federal regulations regarding child labor. For instance, an employer can rely on a good-faith defense when the employer received written assurance from the producer, manufacturer, or dealer that the goods received by the employer complied with the FLSA and the employer paid for such goods without any notice of the violation. Additionally, employers can rely on the exceptions described in this chapter, such as those permitting employment of children by their parents in certain occupations not permissible for nonparental employers (see Qs 9:9, 9:12, 9:21), agricultural exemptions (see Qs 9:25, 9:26), or approved employment as apprentices or student-learners (see Qs 9:20, 9:26). [29 C.F.R. § 579.3(c)] For further discussion of penalties imposed for FLSA violations, including child labor violations, see Chapter 14.

Chapter 10

Alternatives for FLSA Compliance

This chapter discusses alternative measures or policies that employers may implement to comply with the Fair Labor Standards Act (FLSA). Complying with the FLSA does not necessarily mean the employer must pay more money to employees. For compliance purposes, the method of payment is more important (other than minimum wage compliance) than the amount of money paid to an employee under federal law. The Department of Labor (DOL) allows employers to use creative pay systems, provided the pay system is properly set up in advance to comply with the form of payment required by the FLSA.

This chapter discusses the benefits and pitfalls of several options available to employers. It is best to review any payment plan carefully and have it reviewed by appropriate legal and/or human resources professionals, prior to implementation. A little preparation up front can save an employer significant amounts of money in the long run.

Q 10:1 Does an employer have to pay its employees more money just to comply with the Fair Labor Standards Act (FLSA)?

No. As long as there are no minimum wage issues involved, FLSA compliance does not necessarily mean that an employer has to pay its employees more money in order to comply with the law. The FLSA is known as a "form over substance" statute. It is more concerned with the manner or method of payment than with the total amount paid to a particular employee. Many employers find that there are alternative methods of paying employees that bring the employer into compliance with the law and result in almost the same amount of money to the employee (and, therefore, the same payroll expense). This chapter focuses on these alternatives.

White-Collar Exemptions

Q 10:2   Must an employer classify employees as either exempt or nonexempt?

Yes. Employers should review the job duties of all employees and appropriately designate specific individuals as exempt or nonexempt. Employers should not take chances and designate as exempt those personnel whose duties are of a questionable, nonexempt nature. Job titles and written job descriptions may be used for assistance in classification, but an individual's actual duties and salary control whether an exemption applies. A properly conducted audit can help in avoiding liquidated (double) damages, should a dispute arise concerning employees' status.

Q 10:3   Once an employer has determined which of its employees are exempt and which are nonexempt, what else can it do to verify FLSA compliance?

The employer can examine payroll and personnel records to verify that the records clearly reflect the salaried status of exempt, white-collar employees. The employer must make sure that impermissible deductions are not taken from such salaries. (See Chapters 4 and 5 for a discussion of exemptions and permissible deductions from salary.)

Q 10:4   If an employee is properly considered nonexempt and entitled to overtime compensation, can the employer restructure the situation to pay the employee a set salary for all hours worked and comply with the FLSA?

Possibly. One of the benefits of being the employer is that the employer has a lot of control over the manner in which jobs are performed and who performs them. If the employer wants a job to be considered a white-collar, salaried exempt position, it can structure the duties and pay of the position to that end. If an employee does not fulfill the exempt duties test because of excessive hands-on or rank-and-file work, the employer may consider restructuring the job and assigning the nonexempt duties to lower grade classifications. If an employer chooses this method of establishing the exempt status of a position, it is a good idea for the employer to reassess the job after several months to ensure that the changes in duties have achieved the desired result.

Reduced Hourly Wage Rate

Q 10:5   If an employer wants to pay its employees an hourly rate, how can the employer comply with the FLSA and still not significantly increase payroll costs?

An employer that has misclassified an employee as salaried, overtime-exempt may have considered the salary to include compensation for all of the employee's hours of work. When re-classifying the employee as nonexempt, the employer may not be in a position to absorb the cost of overtime premiums. Other than the minimum wage, the FLSA does not mandate what that hourly wage rate or regular rate of a nonexempt employee must be. Therefore, with the exception of public sector employers (see Q 10:7), an employer that wishes to commence paying overtime without incurring additional costs can "back into" a wage rate that results in the payment of overtime without an increase in cost to the employer or a loss of income to the employee. [Wage & Hour Opinion Letter, FLSA1961-29 (Sept. 1961); 29 C.F.R. § 778.408(b); Dolan v. Day & Zimmerman, 65 F. Supp. 923 (D. Mass. 1946); White v. Witwer Grocer Co., 132 F.2d 108 (8th Cir. 1942); Walling v. A.H. Belo Corp., 316 U.S. 624 (1942)]

> **Example.** Assume that an employee's compensation was $450 per week for approximately 45 hours of work per week, and the employer wishes to commence paying the employee overtime. If the employee's hourly rate is calculated by dividing the salary by the maximum number of straight-time hours in a week, the employee's hourly rate will be $11.25. The employee's total compensation for a week in which the employee works 45 hours would be $534.38 (($11.25 × 45) + ($11.25 ÷ 2 × 5). The employee would earn $84.38 more in a week than the previous $450 per week salary. If the employee's hourly rate is calculated by dividing the salary by the 45 hours worked in a typical week, the employee's hourly rate would be $10. The employee's total compensation for a week in which the employee works 45 hours would be $475 (($10 × 45) + ($10 ÷ 2 × 5)). If the employee's hourly rate is established by dividing the salary by the total number of hours worked *and* one half of the number of overtime hours ($450 ÷ (45 + (5 ÷ 2))) the employee's hourly rate will be $9.47. The employee's total compensation of $449.83 for a week in which the employee works 45 hours will be essentially the same as the employee's previous salary, and the employer will have achieved compliance with no increase in cost.

Q 10:6   Must employees agree in writing to the reduced wage rate?

There is no federal requirement that a wage rate which is to apply in the future be documented in writing, although individual state laws may require written notice of an employee's wage rate and may require advance notice of a change in wage rate. As a practical matter, however, the employer is usually best served documenting what the new wage rate is so that there is no dispute as to how the employee will be paid in the future.

An employee who is employed at will generally does not have to agree in writing to a new pay plan. If an at-will employee is informed of a new pay plan and continues to work, even under protest, he or she is generally considered to have accepted the new pay plan. [*See* Weir v. Hudson Coal Co., 99 F. Supp. 423 (M.D. Pa. 1951)]

Q 10:7 Is there a different policy for public sector employers?

Probably not now. Prior to the FLSA amendments of 1985 in response to *Garcia v. San Antonio Metropolitan Transit Authority* [469 U.S. 528 (1985)], state and local government employers that did not have a collective bargaining obligation or individual employee contracts could unilaterally set or adjust hourly wage rates at lower levels in order to partially or totally take into account mandatory overtime pay under the FLSA. For nonexempt public employees, overall compensation could be adjusted to be in compliance with the FLSA and yet be very close to that paid prior to *Garcia*.

The FLSA amendments of 1985 contained a nonretaliation provision that stated that public employers are not allowed to retaliate against employees who have raised wage and hour claims, even though all wage and hour claims for employees performing traditional governmental functions were erased until April 15, 1986. [Pub. L. No. 99-150, §§ 8, 2(c)] This provision was troubling to public employers in that the conference committee report stated rather clearly that the provision was intended to prohibit an employer from reducing wage or other monetary benefits for an entire unit of employees when FLSA coverage was asserted. [H.R. Conf. Rep. No. 99-357, at 8–9 (1985)]

The 1985 amendments applied only to state and local governments. In addition, actions taken now by a public employer in response to financial burdens should not be subject to attack under the nonretaliation provisions, which had a limited life, especially if the public employer has been in compliance with the FLSA subsequent to the 1985 amendments. After pay plan changes are made, slight variations from prior total compensation may exist as a result of the necessity of computing wages on the basis of hours worked by nonexempt employees rather than using a set salary or paying only straight-time rates to nonexempt employees for overtime hours.

Q 10:8 Can an employer pay employees different wage rates depending on the time of year or type of work the employees are engaged in?

Yes. Nothing in the FLSA prohibits an employer from paying employees a rate of pay during the busy season different from the rate paid during the nonbusy season. The various pay rates must, however, be agreed upon and specified in advance, be in effect for a substantial period of time, and be bona fide rates (the actual basis of regular and overtime pay). [*See* Wage & Hour Opinion Letter, FLSA1967-664 (Aug. 1967)] An employer cannot decrease wage rates to offset the cost of overtime on a week-by-week basis or over brief periods of time.

In addition, nothing in the FLSA prohibits an employer from establishing different wage rates for different types of work, including waiting time, travel time, training time, and on-call time. An employer that has a different wage rate for a particular type of work must apply that wage rate to all work of that type, regardless of whether the work occurs during straight-time or overtime hours. If an employer uses different wage rates for different types of work, the employer must pay overtime when overtime is worked (see Q 10:9).

Q 10:9   If an employee is paid at different wage rates during the same workweek, how is overtime compensation calculated?

Overtime compensation can be calculated either:

1. On the basis of the hourly rate in effect during the overtime hours, or
2. On the basis of a weighted average rate for the week (see Q 10:10).

Q 10:10   How is the weighted average rate for the week calculated?

Generally, when an employee is paid at different pay rates during one workweek, the weighted average rate is obtained by totaling the employee's straight-time pay, including all compensation earned, for the week and dividing by the total of hours worked that week.

Example. An employee is paid two rates, $7 and $10 per hour, depending on the type of work she is performing. In one workweek, the employee works 25 hours at the $10-per-hour job and 35 hours at the $7-per-hour job. The weighted average hourly rate for this week is calculated as follows:

$7 × 35 hours   = $245
$10 × 25 hours = $250
Total $495

$495 ÷ 60 hours (25 + 35) = $8.25 per hour

The employee is entitled to $82.50 in overtime (OT) compensation (20 OT hours × 0.5 × $8.25) or total compensation for the workweek of $577.50 ($82.50 + $495.00).

Q 10:11   If an employer adjusts wage rates in response to an investigation, will the DOL claim that the employer retaliated against employees because of the investigation?

If an employer waited until an investigation or lawsuit occurred to reduce wage levels generally in order to take overtime pay into account, it is conceivable but unlikely that the DOL would claim retaliation. If it appeared that certain employees were singled out for a reduction in wage levels because of their participation in a Wage and Hour Division audit or legal proceeding, a retaliation claim would be much more likely.

Q 10:12   Are there any restrictions on reducing the wage rates of employees to comply with the FLSA under federal law?

Yes. An employer must still pay the minimum wage to employees; therefore, any wage reduction cannot go below the minimum wage. In addition, employers with collective bargaining obligations need to engage in timely, good-faith negotiations regarding changes in the regular wage rate before a reduction can be implemented. In the private sector, concession bargaining during which hourly wage rates, and therefore the regular rate, are adjusted downward has become commonplace. Moreover, state laws may also place restrictions on an employer's ability to restructure wage rates.

Fluctuating Workweek Salaried Pay Plan

Q 10:13   Can an employer pay a nonexempt employee a salary for all hours worked and comply with the FLSA?

For employees who are salaried but who fall into a gray area in terms of whether they qualify under an overtime exemption, one alternative method of compliance is to adopt a fluctuating workweek (FWW) pay plan. [29 C.F.R. § 778.114] An FWW pay plan involves payment of a base salary that provides compensation for all of an employee's hours of work in a week, whether many or few, with the exception of overtime premiums. Overtime premiums are calculated on the basis of a relatively inexpensive reducing half-time rate, as hours of work increase.

Q 10:14   Must an employer inform an employee of its FWW plan?

Yes. An employee must have a "clear understanding" that he or she is being compensated by a FWW plan. [29 C.F.R. § 778.114] The employee must clearly understand that the salary covers whatever hours the job may demand in a particular workweek, whether many or few, and the employer must pay the salary even though the workweek is one in which a full schedule of hours is not worked.

For example, a court found that there was some question as to whether an employee had a clear understanding that the fluctuating workweek method would be used when an employer's explanatory form, which was required to be signed by the employee, incorrectly stated that pay deductions could be made for full day absences. The fact that the employer correctly explained the method in verbal instructions and written examples and consistently applied the method did not negate those questions. [Garcia v. Allsup's Convenience Stores, Inc., 167 F. Supp. 2d 1308 (D.N.M. 2001)]

Q 10:15   When is the clear understanding requirement met?

The "clear understanding" requirement is met when "[t]here is a clear and mutual understanding of the parties that the fixed salary is compensation (apart from overtime premiums) for the hours worked each workweek, whatever their number, rather than for working 40 hours or some other fixed weekly period." [29 C.F.R. § 778.114]

According to one court, a "clear understanding" does not require that the employee understand or give actual consent to the employer's method of calculating overtime. However, the court found there was not clear mutual understanding when the employer's method of calculating overtime was premised on assumptions that were inconsistent with the fluctuating workweek method. [O'Brien v. Town of Agawam, 350 F.3d 279 (1st Cir. 2003)]

Q 10:16   Are employees required to know the hours expected to be worked under an FWW pay plan?

No. The clear understanding requirement does not require an employer to inform an employee regarding how many hours the employer expects the employee to work. Further, an employer is not required to inform an employee that the fixed salary is not paid in weeks in which the employee performs no work or of the details of how the FWW is administered. [Samson v. Apollo Res., Inc., 242 F.3d 629 (5th Cir. 2001)] However, it is advisable to have a written, signed document which sets forth the pay and an example of how it works.

Q 10:17   Under an FWW pay plan, how is overtime calculated?

The overtime premium due under an FWW pay plan is calculated by dividing the salary for the week by the hours worked in the week and dividing the result by one half. The resulting half-time rate is multiplied by the number of overtime hours worked in the week. The result is that the more hours an employee works, the lower the half-time rate is for overtime compensation. However, an employee's total compensation will still increase as the employee works more hours.

Example. An employee receives a salary of $300 per week under an FWW plan. He works 40 hours in week 1, 50 hours in week 2, 60 hours in week 3, and 30 hours in week 4. His lawful compensation would be:

Week 1 = $300 ($300 ÷ 40 hours = regular rate of $7.50 but no OT).

Week 2 = $330 ($300 ÷ 50 hours = $6 regular rate; 0.5 × $6 × 10 OT hours = $30 OT; $300 + $30 = $330). Note that these amounts will increase when the minimum wage increases to $6.55 an hour.

Week 3 = $360.50 ($300 ÷ 60 hours = $5 (but at least the minimum wage must be paid; therefore, 60 × $5.85 = $351); $5.85 × 0.5 × 20 = $58.50; $351 + $58.50 = $409.50). Note that these amounts will increase when the minimum wage increases to $6.55 an hour.

Week 4 = $300 ($300 ÷ 30 hours = regular rate of $10, no OT, but paid full salary).

Since an FWW pay plan involves payment of a guaranteed salary, it may be used not only to comply with the FLSA but also to differentiate certain low-level administrative, quasi-supervisory, or paraprofessional employees from rank-and-file nonexempt hourly workers.

Q 10:18   Instead of dividing an employee's salary by the actual number of hours worked each week, can an employer always divide the salary by 40 and pay one-half of the resulting amount for all overtime hours worked in every workweek?

Yes. The DOL has specifically approved this calculation, provided there is a clear mutual understanding that employees are being paid a fixed salary for fluctuating hours. [Wage & Hour Opinion Letter, FLSA2002-2336 (Oct. 2002)]

The DOL noted that dividing the salary by 40 will always result in a higher regular rate than dividing the salary by the actual number of hours worked in overtime weeks because the actual number of hours worked will always be greater than 40. Thus, paying one-half of the regular rate achieved by dividing the salary by 40 causes the employees to receive *more* compensation than if the regular rate were computed by dividing the salary by the actual number of hours worked. Where employees are compensated pursuant to a fixed salary for fluctuating hours, the FLSA does not prohibit an employer from paying more than is required. [29 C.F.R. § 778.114(c)] An employer should carefully document in writing its use of such a variation on an FWW pay plan.

Q 10:19   Are there any limits on use of the fluctuating workweek method?

Yes. The fluctuating workweek computation cannot result in a regular rate of pay below the minimum wage. If, in any given week, the employee's regular hourly rate, as computed under the fluctuating workweek method, is less than the statutory minimum, the minimum becomes the base for both regular and overtime compensation.

A salary should be set high enough so that, when the salary is divided by the total hours worked, the result falls below the minimum wage only on rare occasions. Again, any shortfall in compensation as compared to the minimum wage must be made up and overtime paid on a regular rate that is not less than one and one half times the minimum wage. [Wage & Hour Opinion Letter, FLSA1968-896 (Dec. 1968); Wage & Hour Opinion Letter, FLSA1969-945 (Feb. 1969)]

In a recent case, a group of employees argued that the fluctuating workweek method could not be used if an employee worked more than 60 hours in a given week. The employees based their contention on an FLSA provision that states: "[W]here all the facts indicate that an employee is being paid for his overtime hours at a rate no greater than that which he receives for nonovertime hours, compliance with the Act cannot rely on any application of the fluctuating workweek method." [29 C.F.R. § 778.114(c)] According to the employees, if an employee works more than 60 hours in a workweek, the rate of pay for each overtime hour is less than the rate of pay for nonovertime hours, unless the employer pays an overtime premium of more than the one-half the regular rate of pay minimally required under the fluctuating workweek method.

However, an appeals court said the employees' contention was based on a misinterpretation of what constitutes the regular rate of pay for nonovertime hours. The employees calculated the regular rate by dividing the fixed weekly salary by 40 hours. Thus, after 60 hours, the rate of pay for each overtime hour is less than the rate of pay for each hour that the employee would have received if he had worked only 40 hours. The court pointed out that the rate of pay for nonovertime hours in the employees' calculations erroneously includes over-time wages already built into the fixed salary. The fixed salary under the fluctuating workweek method is not intended as compensation only for the 40 hours traditionally recognized as nonovertime hours but for all hours worked each workweek. [29 C.F.R. § 778.114(a)] Thus, based on that calculation, as long as the employer pays an overtime premium as required under the fluctuating workweek method, the rate of pay for overtime hours will always be higher than the rate for nonovertime hours. Therefore, the court concluded that the FLSA does not prevent an employer from using the fluctuating workweek method where the employee works over 60 hours as long as the overtime premium paid is at least 50 percent of the employee's regular rate. [Samson v. Apollo Res., Inc., 242 F.3d 629 (5th Cir. 2001)]

Q 10:20   Is there a limitation on what types of employees may be paid by FWW plans?

No. Any type of employee may lawfully be placed on an FWW pay plan, although from a practical standpoint its use should be carefully considered, since it may not be advisable for use with employees who need close supervision or have high absence rates. Unlike Belo pay plans (discussed elsewhere in this chapter), the actual hours of work do not have to fluctuate above and below 40 in order for the pay plan to be used.

Q 10:21   Can an employer use an FWW pay plan if there are variations in an employee's compensation from week to week?

No. One requirement for use of a fluctuating workweek pay plan is that an employee receives a fixed salary that does not vary with the number of hours worked during the week. [29 C.F.R. § 778.114]

A variation in the salary paid from week to week or payment of amounts in addition to the salary may invalidate an FWW pay plan. For example, a court found that a city impermissibly used the fluctuating workweek method to compensate police officers who received shift differentials for nighttime shifts and extra pay for hours over eight in a day or hours worked on otherwise off-duty time (which were contractually deemed to be overtime hours, although they were not technically overtime under the FLSA). Thus, the court concluded that the officers did not receive a fixed amount as straight-time pay for whatever hours they were called upon to work in a workweek, as required under the fluctuating workweek method. On the contrary, the officers receive more or less straight-time pay depending on how many contractual overtime hours they work each week. [O'Brien v. Town of Agawam, 350 F.3d 279, 288–89 (1st Cir. 2003)]

Q 10:22   Why is this type of plan called a fluctuating workweek pay plan?

The title of the plan comes from the fact that the regular hourly rate fluctuates from week to week. [Wage & Hour Opinion Letter, FLSA1967-693 (Oct. 1967)]

Q 10:23   Is an FWW pay plan similar to "Chinese" overtime?

"Chinese" overtime was once another name for an FWW pay plan. Because the term rightly may be considered an outdated, derogatory, or an inflammatory reference, employers are advised to refer to the pay plan as a fluctuating workweek pay plan.

Q 10:24   Is there a downside to using an FWW pay plan?

Yes. A primary distinction between an FWW pay plan and other pay plans is that traditional sick-leave policies cannot be used with an FWW pay plan. If an employee who is paid by an FWW pay plan works any time at all during a workweek, the entire salary for the week must be paid. [Wage & Hour Opinion Letter, FLSA1966-479 (May 1966)] Therefore, employee absences can cause concerns for employers that use an FWW plan, since there is less financial incentive for attendance. Reasonable controls could be adopted, however, such as requiring a doctor's certificate for absences of two days or more or after the sixth day of absence in a year, or allowing discipline for excessive absenteeism.

Another downside is the effect an FWW pay plan has on employee morale when employees are regularly asked to work large amounts of overtime. Because an employee's regular rate decreases the more hours he or she works, many employees do not want to work more than a few hours of overtime. This can create staffing and morale problems in the workplace. Additionally, states can prohibit the use of an FWW pay plan, like Alaska, California, and Montana, which do not allow the use of FWW pay plans. Also, being competitive in wages and benefits with other employers in the geographic area of the industry should always be considered.

Q 10:25   Large employers are required to grant employees unpaid leave under the Family and Medical Leave Act of 1993 (FMLA). How can the right of an employee to make deductions for intermittent FMLA leave be reconciled with the payment of a salary under an FWW pay plan?

The FMLA allows certain eligible employees to take up to 12 weeks of unpaid leave for certain family and medical situations (e.g., the birth of a child, the employee's serious health condition or that of a child, parent, or spouse). Leave can be taken all at once or intermittently.

For intermittent or reduced schedule leaves of absence that qualify as leave under the FMLA, the employer may compensate an employee on an hourly basis even though the employee is normally compensated by an FWW pay plan. During periods of time that intermittent or reduced schedule FMLA leave is taken, the employee need only be paid for the hours the employee works, including one and one-half times the employee's regular rate for overtime hours. The change to payment on an hourly basis would include the entire period during which the employee is taking FMLA intermittent leave, including weeks in which no leave is taken.

Example. If an employee needs to go to chemotherapy for a four-hour session once every two weeks over a six-month period, the employee can be compensated on an hourly basis throughout the six-month period until the employee finishes chemotherapy. The employee would have to be paid an hourly rate and overtime in all weeks, even those in which he or she does not go for a therapy session. The hourly rate will be determined by dividing the employee's weekly salary by the employee's normal or average scheduled hours worked during normal weeks before the start of FMLA leave. If an employer chooses to follow this exception to the FWW pay plan, it is recommended that it be placed in the FMLA policy and the FWW written contract.

An employer must uniformly apply its FMLA leave provisions to all employees on the FWW pay plan. Therefore, if the employer chooses to convert employees to an hourly rate, it cannot pick and choose which employees to convert. In other words, all FWW-paid employees on FMLA leave must be converted to an hourly rate. If the hourly conversion option is used, an employee could take one hour of FMLA leave per week and be entitled to overtime for the whole year.

Once the need for FMLA leave is over, the employee may be restored to payment on the FWW pay plan. This special exemption to the salary basis requirements of the FWW pay plan applies only to FMLA-eligible employees of covered employers for one of the four types of leave specified under the FMLA. When an FMLA leave is not involved, the standard rules against salary deductions apply. Therefore, treating an employee as paid on an hourly basis when the leave is not FMLA-qualifying prevents the employer from using the FWW method for that employee and perhaps for all other employees in similar classifications. [*See* 29 C.F.R. § 825.206]

If an employer chooses not to convert the employee's compensation to hourly pay, no deduction from base salary may be taken for FMLA leaves of absence in which the employee works at all during the workweek.

Q 10:26 What methods can an employer use to reduce the poor morale and stigma that attaches to overtime work under an FWW pay plan?

A variety of bonus payments for working overtime hours may be added to the FWW formula to provide additional pay or incentive for working long hours. Each employer needs to decide at what point in time and to what extent an additional incentive for working longer hours is to be provided. In one bonus plan approved by the Wage and Hour Division, an amount closely approximating straight-time wages is paid for hours worked in excess of 40. Any bonus paid must be added to the base salary before computing the regular rate. Employers should exercise care when paying bonuses to FWW pay plans as the plan might become invalid. Likewise, a written FWW contract is not required but is highly recommended.

Q 10:27 Can an employer make disciplinary deductions from the salary of an employee who is paid on an FWW pay plan?

Yes. Disciplinary deductions may be made from the base salary, after computation of the regular rate, for willful absences or tardiness, but deductions should be limited so it does not appear that an hourly or day rate is in effect. [29 C.F.R. § 778.307] Again, excessive or improper deductions may invalidate an FWW pay plan.

Q 10:28 How does use of an FWW pay plan interact with the public sector employer's ability to grant compensatory time ("comp time") in lieu of monetary overtime compensation?

A public sector comp-time plan cannot be used consistently with an FWW pay plan. The DOL's position is that employers that use the FWW method of calculating overtime compensation for salaried employees may not pay the half-time premium in an equivalent amount of comp time. The DOL has cited to statutory language in FLSA Section 7(o) that provides that public agency employees must receive comp time "at a rate not less than one and one-half hours for each hour of employment for which overtime compensation is required." [*See* DOL comments on 29 C.F.R. § 553.233]

Fluctuating Day Rate Plan

Q 10:29 Are there other pay plans that are similar to FWW pay plans but do not have as much risk that the employer will have to pay an employee who works only a minimal amount of time during a week a full week's salary?

Yes. One such method is the fluctuating day rate (FDR) plan. An FDR plan can be used when an employer anticipates that, on a regular basis, hours of work will fluctuate above and below 8 hours per day and above and below 40 hours per week, although fluctuation in hours is not a legal requirement for use of the plan. Under an FDR pay plan, a set amount of wages may be paid for each day worked regardless of the number of hours worked in the day. [29 C.F.R. § 778.112] An FDR plan has most of the practical advantages of an FWW pay plan, but does not contain the risk that an employee may work only one day in a week and then be entitled to receive an entire week's pay as under an FWW plan. However, if an employee works six or seven days in a week, the employee may earn more under an FDR plan than the employee would earn under an FWW pay plan.

Q 10:30   Must an employee have a clear understanding that he or she is being compensated under an FDR pay plan?

No. Unlike a fluctuating workweek pay plan, which requires that there be a "clear mutual understanding" that the employee's fixed salary is compensation for all hours worked each workweek [29 C.F.R. § 778.114; see Qs 10:14, 10:15], there is no similar requirement for a fluctuating day rate plan. In order to avoid potential disputes, an employer is well advised to document in writing its use of an FDR plan.

The FLSA rules governing the fluctuating day rate method do not require that employees consent to its application. The triggering requirement is solely that employees are paid a day or job rate. [29 C.F.R. § 778.112; see Dufrene v. Browning-Ferris, Inc., 207 F.3d 264 (5th Cir. 2000)]

Q 10:31   How are wages calculated under an FDR pay plan?

Under an FDR plan, an employee receives his or her day rate for any day on which he or she works, regardless of how many or few hours are worked. If an employee works more than 40 hours in any workweek, the employee must receive an additional half of the regular hourly rate for each hour of overtime worked, as illustrated below.

> **Example.** Assume that an employee receives a day rate of $80 and that her hours of work Monday through Friday fluctuate between 6 and 10 hours—10 on Monday, 9 on Tuesday, 6 on Wednesday, 7 on Thursday, and 10 on Friday—for a total of 42 hours. The employee also works 7 hours on Saturday due to heavy business. Thus, the employee works 49 hours that week, but the employee's compensation is calculated by the day, not by the hour: 6 days × $80 = $480 for the week. Under the FLSA, however, there are 9 overtime hours for which the employee must be compensated. The regular rate is calculated by dividing the total straight-time pay of $480 by total hours worked of 49 hours, for a rate of $9.80 per hour. Total overtime pay for the week is calculated as follows: $9.80 ÷ 2 × 9 overtime hours = $44.10.

Q 10:32   Are there particular types of employees for which an FDR plan works best?

Yes. Because there is an incentive for the employee to complete his or her work quickly each day, an FDR plan is especially useful for employees whose work completion can be controlled to a significant extent by the employees. It follows that an FDR plan may also be useful for employees who are away from central employer locations and without supervision during large portions of a workday. Customization of an FDR pay plan may also be accomplished through use of premium pay rates for weekend work and half-day pay rates for other days of work, depending on the circumstances.

Belo Contracts

Q 10:33   Is there another way an employer can pay nonexempt employees a salary that includes overtime compensation?

Yes. A Belo compensation plan is the only "salary-like" payment method for nonexempt employees in which the set payment lawfully includes overtime compensation. [29 U.S.C. § 207(f); 29 C.F.R. §§ 778.402–778.414] Normally, nonexempt employees are entitled to additional compensation when they work more than 40 hours per week. Under a Belo payment plan, however, the employer has "raised the bar" at which additional compensation is paid to a nonexempt employee. A Belo pay plan guarantees an employee compensation that includes overtime for a predetermined number of overtime hours of work. Once the employee exceeds the predetermined number of overtime hours, additional compensation is paid at one and one half times the base hourly wage rate set out in the Belo plan.

Q 10:34   What must an employer do to use a Belo pay plan?

There are basically three requirements for use of a Belo pay plan:

1. A bona fide individual contract or collective bargaining agreement is required. Although the contract may be oral or in writing, it is recommended that any agreement be in writing and signed by the employee to avoid disputes over the agreement's existence at a later date. The contract must specify a regular rate of pay at least equal to the minimum wage and must specify that at least one and one-half times the regular rate will be paid for hours worked in excess of 40.

2. The contract must guarantee a weekly amount of pay for a set amount of work, but it cannot cover more than 60 hours. This guarantee is paid to the employee regardless of the amount of work performed by the employee. For example, if the contract calls for 55 hours of work, but the employee works only 36 hours, the employee still gets the full payment as guaranteed by the contract. The weekly guaranteed amount must be paid for any workweek in which an employee performs any duties. There must be a reasonable relationship between the number of hours covered by the weekly guarantee and the number of hours expected to be worked by the employee on average, such that additional overtime wages above and beyond the weekly guaranteed amount will be due in a significant number of workweeks.

3. The employee's duties must necessitate irregular hours of work that fluctuate above and below 40 hours per week. The nature of the job itself, as opposed to either the employer's or the employee's discretion, must cause the irregular hours of work.

[*See* 29 U.S.C. § 207(f)]

Example. A clerical employee who regularly works 48 hours per week signs a written Belo contract that provides an hourly wage rate of $8 per hour and time and one half for hours of work over 40. The contract covers 60 hours per week for a total guaranteed weekly payment of $560: ($8 × 60) + ($8 × 0.5 × 20) = $560. He also regularly receives a quarterly attendance bonus of $125. This arrangement does not qualify as a Belo pay plan because the hours of work do not fluctuate, the contract covers more hours than are usually worked, and a regular and recurring quarterly attendance bonus is includible in the regular rate. (See Q 10:35.)

Q 10:35   Can an employer pay bonuses to an employee who is compensated under a Belo contract?

Payment of bonuses that would normally be includible in the regular rate could jeopardize use of a Belo pay plan. However, payment of premiums for work on holidays or for extraordinary excess work, year-end bonuses, and similar payments, which are not regularly paid as part of the employee's usual wages, will not invalidate a Belo contract.

Q 10:36   What types of employee positions may qualify for a Belo pay plan?

Jobs that may qualify for a Belo contract, depending on the circumstances, include certain newspaper reporters, executive secretaries, crime scene law enforcement personnel, vice and narcotics investigators or undercover detectives, outside buyers, on-call service persons, and insurance adjusters. [29 C.F.R. § 778.405] Employers should be aware, however, that Belo plans require ongoing review to ensure continuing compliance with all the requirements of such plans.

Time-Off and Prepayment Plans

Q 10:37   Can a private sector employer pay employee comp-time in lieu of monetary overtime compensation?

Maybe. A private sector employer may agree to a comp-time arrangement with an overtime-exempt employee without running afoul of the FLSA. A private sector employer cannot, however, use comp-time for its nonexempt employees, with one limited exception.

Under time-off and prepayment plans, a constant average weekly wage, more or less, can be paid under appropriate circumstances. An employer can balance overtime work in one week against short hours in another week if both weeks are in the same pay period. This is not an averaging of overtime hours, but is in essence allowing an employee to use what looks like a salary plan or a traditional comp-time plan (which cannot be used with nonexempt employees except in the public sector) but is neither. The differences between time-off and prepayment plans are explained below.

Q 10:38   What is required for a valid time-off pay plan?

There are five basic requirements for a valid time-off plan:

1. The pay period must be two weeks or longer.
2. The employee must be compensated under an hourly wage rate.
3. For each overtime hour worked in one of the workweeks within the pay period (usually the first week in the pay period), the employee must be "laid off" one and one-half hours in another workweek within the same pay period, either before or after the overtime week, with no reduction in wages.
4. The employee must be paid straight-time and overtime compensation computed for the hours actually worked for each workweek in the pay period.
5. An accurate record of the employee's hours worked, hours taken off, and hours paid must be maintained.

[Wage & Hour Opinion Letter, FLSA1965-389 (Sept. 1965)]

Q 10:39   How does a time-off plan work?

Under a time-off plan, an employee receives the same compensation in each workweek by providing the employee with one and one half hours off with pay for each overtime hour worked.

Example. An employee with a biweekly pay period receives $8 per hour in wages and normally works a 40-hour week. This yields gross pay of $640 ($8 × 40 × 2) for the pay period. If the employee works 45 hours in week 1, in order to hold wages at the level of $640 the employee must be "laid off" 7.5 hours in week 2.

Week 1:	45 hours × $8	= $360
	$8 × 0.5 × 5 OT hours	= $20
	$360 + $20	= $380
Week 2:	32.5 hours × $8	= $260
	$380 + $260	= $640

Total hours worked = 77.5 hours for the biweekly pay period

If the employee works 45 hours in week 2, rather than week 1, it would be necessary to anticipate the overtime in order to allow 7.5 hours off in week 1 to hold average compensation for the pay period to $320 per week. If the overtime work is not accurately anticipated, overtime wages would be due for 5 hours of overtime in week 2.

Week 1:	=	$320
Week 2:	=	$380
Total	=	$700

If an employee works more overtime hours than the employee can offset, in the appropriate ratio, by taking time off in another week in the pay period, the employee must be paid for the additional overtime worked. Similarly, if an employee takes off more hours than the employee worked in the appropriate ratio, the employee's compensation must be reduced accordingly.

Q 10:40   What is a prepayment plan?

A *prepayment plan* is similar to a time-off plan but is more flexible, especially if a pay period longer than one week is used. A prepayment plan maintains a constant average weekly wage by paying overtime to an employee in advance of the time that he or she earns it.

Section 32:16c of the DOL Wage and Hour Division Field Operations Handbook provides:

> This is the basic principal of the prepayment plan. Thus some employers, in an attempt to keep the wage or salary constant from pay period to pay period, have resorted to paying their employees a sum in excess of what they earn or are entitled to in a particular week or weeks, which sum is considered to be a prepayment or advance payment of compensation for OT [overtime] to be subsequently worked. In other words, the employer and the employee agree that in any week in which the employee works less than the applicable statutory maximum [workweek] [40 hour workweek usually] the employer will advance to the employee the difference between the amount equal to his regular rate of pay for the applicable statutory maximum [workweek] and the amount he would have received if he had been paid only for the number of hours he worked. Bona fide plans of this type require the use of a record system whereby the employer can maintain a running account.

Example. An employee may be paid straight-time and overtime wages based on $8 per hour covering 45 hours even though only 42 hours are worked.

$8 × 45 hours paid	=	$360 straight-time wages
$8 × 0.5 × 5	=	$20 overtime pay
$360 + $20	=	$380 total pay
$8 × 42 hours worked	=	$336
$8 × 0.5 × 2 OT hours	=	$8

$336 + $8   = $344 total earned

Employer credit   = $380 − $344 = $36

The difference between the amount paid and the actual earnings is an advance or loan against overtime to be worked by the employee in a subsequent week or pay period. An employer's credit (overpayment), but not an employee's credit (underpayment), can be carried forward from one pay period to another indefinitely. [Wage & Hour Opinion Letter, FLSA1964-282 (July 1964)]

The result of the prepayment plan is that the employee is actually paid time and one-half for hours worked over 40 in any week, but by controlling the number of hours the employee works, the employer is able to pay a constant average weekly wage for the pay period as a whole.

The employee must remain absolutely liable for repaying the loan or advance even if employment is terminated without an employee's having "worked off" the excess payments. Recordkeeping is very important for the maintenance of a running account showing the employer's credit. [Wage & Hour Opinion Letter, FLSA1965-374 (June 1965)]

The DOL has emphasized that plans of this type require the use of a system whereby the employer can maintain a running account for each employee of the amount to the employer's credit. At no time may the employer owe the employee overtime compensation. In any workweek in which the prepayment credits are not sufficient to equal the additional overtime compensation due the employee, the difference must be paid on the next payday.

Moreover a prepayment plan cannot be applied to an employee who is paid a salary under an agreement that the employee will receive the salary even when he or she works fewer than the regular number of hours in some weeks. Also, it cannot be applied to an employee paid a salary for a fluctuating number of hours worked from week to week. Since the nature of such employees' employment is that they will receive the fixed basic salary regardless of the number of hours worked, it cannot be said that they are paid in excess of what they earn in any week in which they receive the fixed salary, even though such weeks may have been short workweeks. [Wage & Hour Opinion Letter, FLSA2005-2404 (Jan. 2005)]

Prepayment plans are made even more complex by state law limitations on making deductions from pay, the obligation to provide accurate pay check stubs, and the like. Given all of the requirements of prepayment plans, employers must use great care in the use of such plans, documenting the terms of such plans and keeping accurate records regarding the use of such plans.

Q 10:41   Can an employer prepay employees for shifts that overlap two different workweeks?

Yes. Although compensation due an employee must normally be paid at the time of the employee's regular payday, an opinion letter from the Department of Labor's Wage and Hour Division says the DOL has no objection if an employer pays in advance the compensation that the employee will be due in a subsequent pay period by including all hours worked in a single shift in the workweek in which that shift began. However, employees must always be paid time and one-half their regular rate of pay for each hour actually worked over 40 hours in the workweek, and the employer must not manipulate the schedule in order to avoid the overtime pay requirement of the FLSA. [Wage & Hour Opinion Letter, FLSA2005-2420 (May 2005)]

Reduction in Number of Hours of Work

Q 10:42   What can an employer do if it is unable or unwilling to reduce the regular rate paid to employees and the funds are not available to pay employees overtime compensation?

If the regular rate for employees is not reduced and the funds are not available to pay the required overtime wages, the alternative is reduced staffing, which may mean reduced service levels. The level of service provided and coverage of the work load must be considered if hours of work are reduced. Rotating schedules, reduced service levels, and increased use of part-time employees at nonovertime rates may all be considered. If hourly wage rates are not reduced but hours are cut back, the employer should consider the impact of this reduction in total compensation and its carryover to morale and productivity.

If the hours of work of regular employees are cut back but total compensation is not reduced, and additional employees, either part time or full time, are brought in to maintain the same service levels, there will still be an additional financial burden to the employer to be considered, such as increased benefits, training costs, and related expenses. In addition, increases in the size of the workforce may place the employer within the coverage of additional employment-related laws, such as the FMLA, COBRA health insurance continuation, Title VII discrimination law, and WARN (the plant closing/mass layoff law).

Chapter 11

Government Contracts

This chapter examines in detail the wage and fringe benefit obligations of contractors and subcontractors that do business with the federal government via contracts covered under the McNamara-O'Hara Service Contract Act (Service Contract Act), which covers government services contracts; the Walsh-Healey Public Contracts Act (Public Contracts Act), which covers contracts for the manufacture or furnishing of goods, materials, and equipment; the Davis-Bacon Act, which covers contracts for the construction, alteration, or repair of public buildings or public works; or the Contract Work Hours and Safety Standards Act, which covers contracts involving the employment of laborers and mechanics on public works. Although some of these statutes contain workplace health, safety, and other requirements, this chapter focuses primarily on the minimum wages, fringe benefits, or overtime compensation that must be paid by covered contractors, and sets forth the recordkeeping requirements specific to each act.

All of these statutes and accompanying regulations expressly set forth stipulations that must appear in every covered contract. These stipulations are itemized in the Code of Federal Regulations (C.F.R.). Many of the stipulations are generally discussed in this chapter as contract requirements; some stipulations are highlighted. Employers covered under the statutes discussed in this chapter must display a poster that sets forth the applicable statutory labor standards. Posters for any of the acts may be requested from the Department of Labor (DOL) or downloaded from the DOL's Web site, http://www.dol.gov/osbp/sbrefa/poster/main.htm.

Employers that intend to bid on a federal contract covered by these laws or that currently perform covered contract work must have an understanding of the various requirements under all of these federal statutes, because they interact and may affect an employer's decision to dispute whether the contract is covered under one or another of the statutes. The labor standards established under these statutes differ from the standards of the Fair Labor Standards Act (FLSA) in several respects. They differ most importantly, however, in that they prescribe prevailing wages and benefits rather than a fixed minimum wage. For instance, the Davis-Bacon Act and the Service Contract Act require contractors and subcontractors to pay employees performing contract work wages and fringe benefits prevailing in the locality as determined by the Secretary of Labor. The Public Contracts Act provides only for a prevailing minimum wage and for overtime requirements, making no provision for fringe benefits. The Contract Work Hours and Safety Standards Act provides for the payment of overtime, whereas the Davis-Bacon Act and the Service Contract Act have no overtime requirement, unless contracts covered under those acts are also covered under the Contract Work Hours and Safety Standards Act or the FLSA.

From this patchwork of provisions, it may be more cost-effective for a contractor to argue that a contract at issue is covered under one statute and not another. In fact, litigation in this area often develops over what work constitutes manufacturing covered under the Public Contracts Act, which applies to contracts for the manufacturing of goods, versus what work constitutes extensive repair covered under the Service Contract Act, which statute applies to service contracts. In addition, if tangible items are supplied in connection with the performance of a service, there is a question as to whether the contract is primarily a service contract covered under the Service Contract Act and therefore not covered under the Public Contracts Act. Litigation has also arisen over whether work is performed directly on the site of work, as required for coverage under the Davis-Bacon Act.

There are a few other statutes that affect contractor-employers. The Portal Act [29 U.S.C. §§ 251–262], which applies to the FLSA as well as to the Davis-Bacon Act and Public Contracts Act, defines compensable time, limits the time for actions for underpayment of wages and liquidated damages, and provides for an affirmative defense to underpayment violations for contractors or subcontractors based on good-faith reliance on administrative rulings. The provisions of the Portal Act are discussed more fully in Chapter 12 but are also referenced in this chapter in the discussion of the Public Contracts Act and the Davis-Bacon Act. Another statute that figures in the discussion of the Davis-Bacon Act, as well as in the discussion of the Contract Work Hours and Safety Standards Act, is the Copeland Anti-Kickback Act, which prohibits employers from making unauthorized or impermissible deductions, or receiving kickbacks, from wages.

Walsh-Healey Public Contracts Act

Q 11:1   Why is it important for contractors to understand the Walsh-Healy Public Contracts Act (Public Contracts Act)?

Because work to be performed under the Public Contracts Act is not covered under the McNamara-O'Hara Service Contract Act (Service Contract Act), a frequent point of contention between the Department of Labor (DOL) and contractors involves line-drawing between these two statutes, with the stakes for the contractor being more extensive prevailing wage requirements under the Service Contract Act. Before employers can even hope to understand these fine distinctions, they must first have a basic understanding of the provisions of each Act.

Contracts Covered

Q 11:2   What contracts are covered under the Public Contracts Act?

Contracts in excess of $10,000 between the federal government (including executive departments, independent establishments, agencies, or instrumentalities) and contractors for the manufacture or furnishing of materials, supplies, articles, and equipment are covered under the Public Contracts Act. Also covered under the Public Contracts Act are contracts entered into by a corporation beneficially owned by the United States or by the District of Columbia. [41 U.S.C. § 35]

Q 11:3   What contracts are exempt from the Public Contracts Act?

The Public Contracts Act does not apply to contracts for the construction of public works, which are governed by the Davis-Bacon Act and the Contract Work Hours and Safety Standards Act. For example, a contract to manufacture and install an elevator that requires substantial infrastructure could be considered a contract for the construction of a public work that would not be covered under the Public Contracts Act, even though it also requires the fabrication of an elevator. In addition, the following contracts are exempt from the Public Contracts Act:

- Contracts for public utility services, including electric light and power, water, steam, and gas;

- Contracts for materials, supplies, articles, or equipment no part of which will be manufactured or furnished within the states of the United States, in Puerto Rico, in the Virgin Islands, or in the District of Columbia (If part of the work is performed outside these geographical limits and part within these geographical limits, the Public Contracts Act applies only to the work performed within the geographical limits.);

- Contracts covering purchases against the account of a defaulting contractor when the stipulations required under the Public Contracts Act were not included in the defaulted contract;

- Contracts awarded to sales agents or publisher representatives for the delivery of newspapers, magazines, or periodicals by the publishers;

- Contracts entered into by a contracting officer of an agency authorized by statute to purchase "in the open market," such as when a purchase of articles, supplies, materials, or equipment is made without advertising for bids under circumstances bringing the purchase within the public exigency exception requiring immediate delivery;

- Contracts for perishables, including dairy, livestock, and nursery products (Perishables include products that may decay or spoil, and exclude canned, salted, smoked, or otherwise preserved products.);

- Contracts for agricultural or farm products processed for first sale by the original producers;

- Contracts entered into by the Secretary of Agriculture for the purchase of agricultural commodities or the products of agricultural commodities;

- Contracts with a common carrier for carriage of freight or personnel by vessel, airplane, bus, truck, express, or railway line when published tariff rates are in effect; and

- Contracts for the furnishing of services by radio, telephone, telegraph, or cable companies subject to the Federal Communications Act of 1934.

[41 U.S.C. § 43; 41 C.F.R. §§ 50-201.4, 50-201.603]

Contractors Covered

Q 11:4   What contractors are eligible to bid on a Public Contracts Act contract?

Not only do the contracts have to be those that would otherwise be covered under the Public Contracts Act, but the contractors themselves must be eligible to bid on the contract. Under the Public Contracts Act, eligible bidders include manufacturers, regular dealers, suppliers, or distributors of the materials, articles, or equipment to be manufactured or supplied under the contract. Before amendments to the Public Contracts Act in 1994 and removal of other applicable regulations in 1996, eligible bidders included only manufacturers or regular dealers. [41 U.S.C. § 43b; 61 Fed. Reg. 40714 (Aug. 5, 1996)]

Q 11:5   Are subcontractors covered under the Public Contracts Act?

In most cases, the answer is no. The Public Contracts Act expressly imposes its prevailing wage and other standards on primary contractors. It is not intended to apply to subcontractors. [41 C.F.R. § 50-201.103] A subcontractor that produces goods for a dealer that is a party to a Public Contracts Act contract and then delivers them to the contracting agency may, however, be deemed to have agreed to the stipulations contained in the dealer's contract with the agency. In addition, other courts have found subcontractors jointly liable with primary contractors for violations under the Public Contracts Act. [*See* United States v. Davison Fuel & Dock Co., 371 F.2d 705 (4th Cir. 1967) (subcontractor liable as "substituted manufacturer"); *In re* GW Lisk Co., 17 Wage & Hour Cas. (BNA) 184 (DOL Pub. Contracts Div. 1965) (subcontractor liable as a joint enterprise of the primary contractor, which was owned by substantially the same person, along with other integrated operations)]

Employees Covered

Q 11:6   What employees are covered under the Public Contracts Act?

A government contract generally involves the hiring of many different types of employees, but not all of them are to be paid the wages required under the Public Contracts Act. Employees who are engaged in or connected with the manufacture, fabrication, assembling, handling, supervision, or shipment of materials, supplies, equipment, or articles required under the contract are covered under the Public Contracts Act. The Public Contracts Act does not apply to clerical or custodial employees, or to bona fide executive, administrative or professional employees, or to outside salespersons as defined under the Fair

Labor Standards Act (FLSA). (See Chapters 4 and 5 for discussion of exemptions under the FLSA.) [41 C.F.R. § 50-201.101]

Requirements

Q 11:7   What are the minimum wage requirements under the Public Contracts Act?

The Public Contracts Act requires payment of the "prevailing minimum wages" to all covered employees. These wages are administratively set by the Secretary of Labor for persons employed in similar work in the particular or similar industry or group of industries currently operating in the locality in which the manufacturing or furnishing will occur. The Secretary's decision is called a *wage determination.* The prevailing wage may not be reduced by a wage deduction or rebate. Because the Public Contracts Act is covered under the Portal Act, the provisions on compensable work time covered in Chapter 6 apply to the Public Contracts Act. Apprentices, student-learners, and disabled workers may be paid less than the prevailing wage, pursuant to the same standards and procedures for such employees covered under the FLSA (see Qs 5:13 through 5:15). [29 U.S.C. § 254; 41 U.S.C. § 35(a); 41 C.F.R. §§ 50-201.105, 50-201.1102]

Q 11:8   What are the overtime requirements under the Public Contracts Act?

The Public Contracts Act dictates that covered employees in any one workweek, or part of a workweek, must be paid overtime for hours worked in excess of 40 hours in a workweek. Overtime pay is computed on a weekly basis at one and one-half times the basic rate of pay, which the DOL interprets to be the regular rate as defined under the FLSA, as long as the rate is not less than the applicable minimum wage. This requirement does not apply to employers that have entered into a collective bargaining agreement described under the provisions of FLSA Section 207(b)(1) and (2) (see Q 7:80). The Secretary of Labor is authorized to increase the maximum number of hours of work that may be performed under a contract, as long as the employees are paid one and one-half times the basic rate of pay. [41 U.S.C. §§ 35(b), 40; 41 C.F.R.§ 50-201.102]

Q 11:9   Are there any fringe benefits or other requirements under the Public Contracts Act?

Unlike contractors covered under the Service Contract Act and the Davis-Bacon Act, contractors covered under the Public Contracts Act do not have to provide their employees with fringe benefits. Like the FLSA, however, the Public Contracts Act contains limitations on the age of employees who may perform contract work—males under age 16 and females under age 18 may not perform contract work. The Public Contracts Act also prohibits the employment of convicts and requires that contractors provide a healthy, safe, and sanitary work environment. An employer that complies with state health and safety laws is deemed to be in compliance with the Public Contract Act. Finally, covered contracts must contain the several and various stipulations that incorporate the requirements under the Public Contracts Act, many of which are discussed in this chapter. The required stipulations are set forth in 41 C.F.R. Section 50-201.3. [41 U.S.C. § 35; 41 C.F.R. § 50-201.3]

Q 11:10   What are the recordkeeping requirements under the Public Contracts Act?

There are specific records that must be kept under the Public Contracts Act. These recordkeeping requirements begin on the date that a covered contract is awarded to a bidder. Covered contractors must keep the following records for three years:

- *Basic information.* Name, address, sex, and occupation of each employee.
- *Minors.* Date of birth of each employee under 19 years of age, and if the employer has obtained a certificate of age as provided under the regulations, the title and address of the office issuing the certificate, the number of the certificate, if any, the date of its issuance, and the name, address, and date of birth of the minor as it appears on the certificate.
- *Payroll records.* Wage and hour records for each employee, including the rate of pay, amount paid each pay period, hours worked each day and each week, the period during which each employee was engaged on a government contract, and the number of the government contract.
- *Record of injuries.* Contractors that are parties to a Public Contracts Act contract and subcontractors performing under such a contract must comply with the recordkeeping requirements of the Occupational Safety and Health Act of 1970 under 29 C.F.R. Part 1904.

[41 C.F.R. §§ 50-201.501, 50-201.502]

As discussed previously (see Q 11:7), some employees need not be paid the prevailing wage under the Public Contracts Act. Separate payroll records must be kept for these employees generally under the requirements of the FLSA (see Chapter 8). If a contractor does not keep separate payroll records for employees performing and not performing contract work, it is presumed that all employees were engaged in contract work, absent proof to the contrary. [41 C.F.R. § 50-201.501(c)]

Under the Public Contracts Act, the following records must be kept for two years:

- *Basic employment and earnings records.* Time and earning cards or sheets that record the daily starting and stopping time of individual employees or of separate workforces; or, if earnings or wages are determined by an individual employee's daily, weekly, or other pay period, or amounts of work accomplished (for example, units produced), those records may be kept.
- *Wage-rate tables.* Tables or schedules that provide the piece rates or other rates used in computing straight-time earnings, wages or salary, or overtime compensation.

- *Work time schedules.* Schedules or tables that establish the hours and days of employment of individual employees or of separate workforces.

[41 C.F.R. § 50-201.501]

Enforcement and Penalties

Q 11:11   How is the Public Contracts Act enforced?

The Secretary of Labor enforces the Public Contracts Act by investigating and prosecuting violations, adopting rules and regulations necessary for the enforcement of the act, issuing wage determinations, and granting contractors exceptions to the requirements of the act on a case-by-case basis. Wage determinations may be reviewed by appealing to the DOL Administrative Review Board, with final review by a court. Parties are also entitled to court review of legal questions, including those involving interpretations of the terms *locality* (relevant to wage determinations) and *open market* (relevant to contract exemption). If both parties to a contract recommend a change to the minimum wage and maximum work hour provisions of a contract, the Secretary may make the change as long as the employees are paid not less than one and one-half times the basic hourly rate for overtime hours. A person who is alleging a contract breach or violation, or who is affected by an agency ruling on a proposal or contract that involves any provision of the Public Contracts Act, may request an impartial hearing from the DOL. The health and safety requirements of the Public Contracts Act are enforced by the Occupational Safety and Health Administration (OSHA) or the Mine Safety and Health Administration of the federal government. [41 U.S.C. §§ 38, 39, 40, 43a, 43b]

Q 11:12   What are the penalties for failure to comply with the Public Contracts Act?

A contractor that violates the Public Contracts Act is personally liable for liquidated damages and any other damages resulting from a breach. The Public Contracts Act has been construed by the courts to impose personal liability on covered contractors that controlled or managed the company at the time of the violation. A contractor that knowingly employs minors or convicts in violation of the Public Contracts Act is liable for liquidated damages in the amount of $10 per day for each employee, which may be withheld from payments due the contractor in addition to amounts due for improper wage deductions or underpayment. Actions brought by a contracting agency for unpaid minimum wages or overtime pay, or liquidated damages, must be brought two years from the date the action accrued, or three years if the violation was willful. Employees have one year from the date the contractor is notified of the withholding of payments by the Secretary of Labor to make a claim. Administrative rulings under the Public Contracts Act are authoritative and may, if relied on in good faith, provide an affirmative defense to alleged violations of the act. [29 U.S.C. §§ 255, 259; 41 U.S.C. § 36]

The contracting agency may also cancel the contract, make curative purchases in the open market, and hold the contractor liable for additional costs incurred. In addition, persons or firms that willfully violate the provisions of the Public Contracts Act, including firms, corporations, partnerships, or associations in which such a person or firm has a controlling interest, may be blacklisted (debarred) for a period of three years, unless the Secretary of Labor recommends otherwise. [41 U.S.C. §§ 36, 37]

McNamara-O'Hara Service Contract Act

Q 11:13   What contracts did Congress intend to include under the Service Contract Act, and what distinguishes it from the other acts discussed in this chapter?

In enacting the Service Contract Act, Congress intended to include only contracts the principal purpose of which is to furnish services in the United States through the use of service employees. The Service Contract Act was not intended to cover construction contracts, which may be covered under the Davis-Bacon Act, or contracts for the manufacture or furnishing of materials, supplies, or equipment, which may be covered under the Public Contracts Act. If, however, a service contract also involves the procurement of supplies as an incidental part of what is primarily a security service contract, this does not necessarily remove the contract from coverage under the Service Contract Act. A distinguishing feature of the Service Contract Act is that it does not contain any overtime requirements; however, contractors covered under the Service Contract Act may be required to pay overtime under the FLSA and the Contract Work Hours and Safety Standards Act. [41 U.S.C. § 351; 29 C.F.R. § 4.111]

Contracts Covered

Q 11:14   What contracts are covered under the Service Contract Act?

Any government services contract or subcontract entered into by the United States or the District of Columbia in excess of $2,500 that is not exempt under the Service Contract Act is covered by the Act. [41 U.S.C. § 351(a)] The United States includes only states of the United States, the District of Columbia, Puerto Rico, the Virgin Islands, Outer Continental Shelf lands as defined under the Outer Continental Shelf Lands Act, American Samoa, Guam, Wake Island, Eniwetok Atoll, Kwajalein Atoll, Johnston Island, and Canton Island. [41 U.S.C. § 357(d)] In addition, the principal purpose of the contract must be to provide services, even though an important element of the contract is also the use or furnishing of nonlabor items. For instance, a contract for the repair of typewriters would be covered even though typewriter parts will be provided incidental to the services. The rental of equipment with operators for the performance of a service would also be covered because the work will be performed by service employees. Such contracts are not considered contracts for the furnishing of equipment within the meaning of the Public Contracts Act. [29 C.F.R. §§ 4.110, 4.131] Examples of contracts covered under the Service Contracts Act include the following, other than when the service is provided as part of construction:

- Aerial spraying; aerial reconnaissance for fire detection
- Ambulance service
- Barber and beauty shop services
- Cafeteria and food services
- Carpet laying and cleaning
- Cataloging services
- Chemical testing and analysis
- Computer services
- Concessionaire services
- Data collection, processing, and/or analysis services
- Drafting and illustrating; visual and graphic arts
- Electronic equipment maintenance and operation and engineering support services
- Exploratory drilling
- Film processing
- Firefighting and fire protection; guard and watchperson security service
- Furniture repair and rehabilitation
- Geological field surveys and testing
- Grounds maintenance; snow removal; trash and garbage removal; custodial, janitorial, and housekeeping services (but not when these services are performed as an incident to a lease of building space by the government [29 C.F.R. § 4.134(b)])
- Inventory services
- Keypunching and keyverifying contracts
- Laboratory analysis services
- Landscaping; tree planting and thinning; clearing timber or brush, and so forth (Timber sales contracts that incidentally involve the clearing of timber, the principal purpose of which is a sale, are not covered under the Service Contract Act, and if the clearing of brush or timber is followed by construction of a public work, the contract may be covered under the Davis-Bacon Act. [29 C.F.R. §§ 4.116(b), 4.131(f)])
- Laundry and dry cleaning; linen supply services; clothing alteration and repair
- Lodging and/or meals; mess attendant services; cafeteria and food service
- Mail hauling; mailing and addressing services; packing and crating
- Maintenance and repair of all types of equipment (e.g., aircraft, engines, electrical motors, vehicles, and electronic, telecommunications, office and related business, and construction equipment) [See 29 C.F.R. § 4.123(e)]

- Mortuary services
- Motor pool operation; taxicab services; fueling services; tire and tube repairs; parking services
- Nursing home services
- Operation, maintenance, or logistic support of a federal facility; support services at military installations
- Pest control
- Property management
- Stenographic reporting
- Surveying and mapping services
- Telephone and field interview services
- Transporting property or personnel
- Vending machine services
- Warehousing or storage.

[29 C.F.R. § 4.130]

When the services listed above are provided incident to a lease or license to use real property, the principal purpose of the contract would not be for the provision of services; however, contracts involving a lease of equipment to the government for the performance of a service would be covered under the Service Contract Act, unless that service is ancillary to the construction of a public work or building, in which case the contract may be covered under the Davis-Bacon Act (see Q 11:36). One court has held that contracts between the federal government and travel agencies (travel management contracts), whereby the travel agencies pay the government to provide travel arrangements and ticketing for its employees, are covered under the Service Contact Act. [Ober United Travel Agency, Inc. v. United States, 135 F.3d 822 (D.C. Cir. 1998)]

The $2,500 minimum for a contract to qualify is measured by dollar amount or another item of value given in exchange for the services performed; contracts to provide a concession service are measured by the amount of gross receipts. If a continuing service is provided, the amount is measured in the aggregate for a duration that depends on whether the procurement was formally advertised. For bids, portions of services provided by different bidders may be separable. Contractors should consult 29 C.F.R. Section 4.141. Contracts for an indefinite amount or that provide for service orders that have yet to be placed may also be covered under the Service Contract Act. The dollar amount limitation may vary in amount or duration with any contract changes made to labor requirements or other modifications, or with contracts that are subject to an appropriation. [29 C.F.R. §§ 4.141–4.145]

Generally, a contract otherwise covered under the Service Contract Act remains covered without regard to where in the United States the work is performed, who pays for the services, or who will benefit from the services. Contracts entered into by a state or local government entity with purveyors of services and paid for with federal funds or awarded pursuant to federal law are not covered under the Service Contract Act; however, contracts between a federal agency and a state or local government entity are covered. [29 C.F.R. §§ 4.107, 4.133]

Q 11:15 What contracts are exempt under the Service Contract Act?

To avoid any overlap between the federal government contractor statutes, Congress has made it clear that the Service Contract Act does not apply to any *work* that is covered under the Public Contracts Act. (The Public Contracts Act applies to contracts in excess of $10,000 for the manufacture or furnishing of supplies, materials, articles, or equipment.) The exemption specifically applies to "work to be done" rather than to contracts, to eliminate possible overlap between the Service Contract Act and Public Contracts Act when a hybrid contract has no principal purpose that would place it under the Service Contract Act or Public Contracts Act. [41 U.S.C. § 356(2); 29 C.F.R. § 4.117] Employees under a service contract not performing work under the Public Contracts Act would be paid in accordance with the Service Contract Act—for example, employees providing security or custodial services. The regulations draw a distinction between extensive remanufacture of equipment or articles, which comes under the Public Contracts Act, and basic repair of equipment or articles, which is covered by the Service Contract Act. (The regulations provide very specific circumstances in which remanufacture is deemed to be manufacture and therefore covered under the Public Contracts Act. [29 C.F.R. § 4.117] Employers should contact the Wage and Hour Administrator for a determination on whether the Public Contracts Act or Service Contract Act applies.) In addition, the Service Contract Act is not intended to cover those contracts covered under the Davis-Bacon Act. [41 U.S.C. § 356(1); 29 C.F.R. § 4.116] Therefore, hybrid contracts that require "substantial amounts" of construction that is physically or functionally separate from the service work to be performed under the contract are exempt from the Service Contract Act and covered under the Davis-Bacon Act. [41 U.S.C. § 356; 29 C.F.R. §§ 4.116, 4.117; Wage and Hour Field Operations Handbook § 14c00(a)]

In addition to these distinctions, there are *contracts* for specific types of services that are statutorily exempted from the Service Contract Act, as follows:

- Contracts for the carriage of freight or personnel by vessel, airplane, bus, truck, express railway line, or oil or gas pipeline when published tariff rates are in effect. Carriage under this exemption is by common carrier; therefore, taxicab and ambulance services are not within the exemption. In addition, carriage of anything other than freight, or only incidental carriage of freight, does not fall within this exemption. [29 C.F.R. § 4.118]

- Contracts for public utility services, including electric light and power, water, steam, and gas. "This exemption is applicable to contracts for such services with companies whose rates [] are regulated under state, local, or federal law governing operations of public utility enterprises. Contracts entered into with public utility companies to furnish services through the use of service employees, other than those subject to such rate regulation, are not exempt from the Act." [29 C.F.R. § 4.120]

- Contracts for the furnishing of services by radio, telephone, telegraph, or cable companies provided pursuant to the Federal Communications Act of 1934. [29 C.F.R. § 4.119]
- Services provided directly to a federal agency pursuant to an employment contract. This exemption clarifies that the Service Contract Act is intended to extend only to service contracts entered into with independent contractors. [29 C.F.R. § 4.121]
- Operation of postal contract stations pursuant to a contract with the U.S. Postal Service. Contracts for the delivery of mail are excluded from this exemption. [29 C.F.R. § 4.122]

[41 U.S.C. § 356; 29 C.F.R. § 4.115]

In addition to the statutory exemptions listed above, other types of contracts have been exempted from the Service Contract Act by the Secretary of Labor, because it is in the public interest or to avoid serious impairment of the conduct of governmental business. These exemptions include the following:

- Contracts between the United States and common carriers for the carriage of mail by rail, air (except air star routes), bus, and ocean vessel, when the carriage is performed on regularly scheduled runs of the trains, airplanes, buses, and vessels over regularly established routes and accounts for an insubstantial portion of the revenue from those routes and accounts.
- Any contract entered into by the U.S. Postal Service with an individual owner-operator for mail service when it is not contemplated at the time the contract is made that the owner-operator will hire any service employee to perform the services under the contract except for short periods of vacation time or for unexpected contingencies or emergency situations such as illness or accident.
- Contracts for the carriage of freight or personnel subject to rates covered by Section 10721 of the Interstate Commerce Act.
- Concession contracts principally for the furnishing of food, lodging, automobile fuel, souvenirs, newspaper stands, and recreational equipment to the general public, as distinguished from the U.S. government or its personnel, for example, contracts entered into by the National Park Service (When concession contracts, however, include substantial requirements for other services, those services are not exempt.).

[29 C.F.R. §§ 4.123, 4.133]

Other exemptions are enumerated in detailed regulations and pertain to contracts principally for the maintenance, calibration, or repair of described computer equipment, scientific and medical apparatus or equipment, and some office or business machines. [*See* 29 C.F.R. § 4.123(e)] Although not specifically exempt, another type of contract not covered under the Service Contract Act includes contracts with hospitals for patient care. [Wage and Hour Field Operations Handbook § 14c00(a)] An exemption under the Service Contract Act does not affect the contractor's obligation to comply with the other statutes discussed in this chapter under which the contractor may be covered.

Finally, service contracts involving five or fewer employees are not subject to the Service Contract Act, except: (1) with respect to undetermined wages or benefits in contracts for which one or more, but not all, classes of service employees are the subject of an applicable wage determination; or (2) with respect to successor employers described in Q 11:32. [29 C.F.R. § 4.5(b)]

Employees Covered

Q 11:16   Who is a *service employee*?

A *service employee* is an employee working under a contract or subcontract covered by the Service Contract Act, except executive, administrative, or professional employees who are exempt under the FLSA. (See Chapters 4 and 5 on FLSA exemptions.) The Service Contract Act applies to all service employees performing service work under a covered contract. A service employee may include pilots while they are serving in that capacity, but exclude them if they are employed as flight instructors and therefore fall within the FLSA professional employee exemption for teachers. The fact that a contract is performed by service employees under the supervision of an exempt professional does not take them outside the requirements of the Service Contract Act. Employees necessary to the performance of the contract—for instance, those performing billing services—but who are not performing the specified contract services are also covered under the Service Contract Act. [41 U.S.C. § 357(b); 29 C.F.R. §§ 4.113, 4.153, 4.156]

Employee coverage under the Service Contract Act does not depend on the employee's status as an independent contractor or owner-operator. In addition, the wage and benefit requirements apply equally to part-time, temporary, or full-time employees, although the benefits are provided in proportion to the number of hours worked. [41 U.S.C. § 357(b); 29 C.F.R. §§ 4.155, 4.165(a)(2)]

Requirements

Q 11:17   What are the minimum wage requirements for contracts covered under the Service Contract Act?

Service employees who perform work under a covered contract or subcontract during any workweek must be paid, at a minimum: (1) the prevailing wage in the employees' locality, as set by the Secretary of Labor; or (2) the wage set by a predecessor collective bargaining agreement covering service employees, as long as the collective bargaining agreement is a product of arm's-length negotiations and the rate of pay provided for under the collective bargaining agreement is equivalent to or greater than the minimum wage for nonexempt employees under FLSA Section 206(a)(1). (See Chapter 3 on the minimum wage.) [41 U.S.C. §§ 351(a)(1), 353(c); 29 C.F.R. §§ 4.3(b), 4.163]

The relevant *locality* for purposes of determining the prevailing wage is determined by the Wage and Hour Administrator on a case-by-case basis, but has generally been held to be the area where the services are actually performed. Prevailing rate determinations generally are not made for contracts under which five or fewer employees for whom a prevailing rate determination has not previously been made are to be employed. *Arm's-length negotiations* means negotiations not undertaken with an intent to take advantage of the wage determination requirement under the Service Contract Act. [29 C.F.R. §§ 4.5(b)(1), 4.11(a), 4.54, 4.163(d)]

For contracts equal to or less than $2,500, which are not covered under the Service Contract Act, contractors must pay their employees at least the minimum wage under the FLSA. However, an employer required by law or some other obligation to pay employees more than the federal minimum wage may not avoid doing so because a contract is not covered by the Service Contract Act. Nothing in the Service Contract Act relieves an employer of other obligation(s) to pay more than minimum wage. In addition, employers may employ apprentices, student-learners, disabled employees, and tipped employees pursuant to the lower minimum wage prescribed under the FLSA without violating the Service Contract Act. For a successor employer to apply a tip credit, however, the tip credit must have been permitted under the predecessor collective bargaining agreement. (For discussion of the tip credit, see Chapter 3) [29 C.F.R. §§ 4.6(d)(1), (o), (p), (q)]

If the Secretary of Labor sets a prevailing wage for a specific class of service employees, all employees in that class must be paid the prevailing wage, even if it is higher than the wage specified in an existing collective bargaining agreement. The same is true of fringe benefit determinations. If not all service employees have been classified or if the work performed is not within the scope of any classification, the contractor must initiate proceedings to have the unlisted employees or work classified and a wage and benefit determination made under the procedures described in 29 C.F.R. Section 4.6(b). With the exception of employers providing linen supply services, employees of service contractors whose rate of pay is not governed by the Service Contract Act may not be paid less than the minimum wage under the FLSA. [29 U.S.C. § 206(e), 41 U.S.C. § 351(b); 29 C.F.R. §§ 4.6(b), 4.165(c)]

For employees who work in different capacities under the contract, to which different wage rates are applicable, all work performed by the employee must be compensated at the higher rate, unless the employer properly segregates the work time spent and can affirmatively prove that the time should be differently and separately compensated. The same rule applies if the employee performs contract work and noncontract work at different rates. [29 C.F.R. § 4.169]

Q 11:18   What is the applicable unit of payment and pay period for service employees?

Employees may be paid on a piece-rate, daily, weekly, or other basis, as long as the hourly rate complies with the Service Contract Act. The pay period for wages and hours worked is a fixed and regularly recurring workweek of seven consecutive 24-hour workdays. A biweekly pay period or, at the most, a semimonthly pay period may be used only on advance notice to the affected employees. [29 C.F.R. §§ 4.165(b), 4.166]

Q 11:19   How are hours worked determined under the Service Contract Act?

Hours worked are determined in the same manner as under the FLSA. [29 C.F.R. § 4.178] Chapter 6 explains this computation in detail.

Q 11:20   What are the overtime requirements under the Service Contract Act?

The Service Contract Act does not contain an overtime pay requirement. Employers may, however, be required to pay their employees overtime pursuant to the Contract Work Hours and Safety Standards Act or the FLSA if the interstate commerce and other requirements are met (see Chapters 2 and 8). The regular rate under the Service Contract Act is computed on the same basis as it is under the FLSA (see Chapter 7). In determining the regular rate under the Service Contract Act, unlike the Davis-Bacon Act, fringe benefits or their cash or benefit equivalent may be excluded from the regular rate to the same extent that they would be excluded under the FLSA (see Chapter 7). [41 U.S.C. § 355; 29 C.F.R. §§ 4.177, 4.180–4.182, 778.7; 29 C.F.R. pt. 778]

Q 11:21   How are tip credits, uniforms, and deductions for board, lodging, and other facilities treated under the Service Contract Act?

Generally, all of the rules and laws regarding tip credits, uniforms, and deductions for board, lodging, and other facilities that are applicable to employers covered under the FLSA also apply to employers covered under the Service Contract Act. These issues are covered in Chapter 3. To the extent that deductions for other than board, lodging, or other facilities reduce a service employee's wages below the levels required under the Service Contract Act, they are illegal. In addition, stipends paid to an employee by a party other than the employer may not be treated as part of the employee's wages. [29 C.F.R. §§ 4.167, 4.168]

Q 11:22   Are there any fringe benefit requirements under the Service Contract Act?

Yes. The minimum benefits to be provided are the prevailing benefits in the locality, the levels of which are set by the Secretary of Labor. The benefits contemplated by the Service Contract Act include medical or hospital care, pensions, compensation for occupational illness or injury, accident insurance, life insurance, disability or sick insurance, vacation and holiday pay, and the costs of apprenticeships or like programs, as well as any other bona fide fringe benefits (see Q 11:26) not required by federal, state, or local law, or the cash equivalent of such benefits. Benefits are capped at the hourly amount set in a fringe benefit determination, up to a maximum of 40 hours in a workweek. [41 U.S.C. § 351(a)(2); 29 C.F.R. §§ 4.162, 4.172]

The fringe benefit requirements of the Service Contract Act can be satisfied through various combinations of benefits, or by making a cash payment to the employees of an equivalent value. This cash payment is in addition to the minimum wage requirements. To the extent an employee contributes toward the cost of health care premiums, however, these contributions cannot be used to reduce the amount of fringe benefits that must be paid by the contractor. [29 C.F.R. §§ 4.170, 4.171, 4.177]

Although the Service Contract Act permits apprentices, student-learners, and disabled employees to be employed at subminimum wages, these employees must receive all fringe benefits listed in the wage determination, with the exception that vacation and holiday pay may be prorated on the basis of hours worked and computed based on the wage-rate paid. [29 C.F.R. § 4.6(o), (p)]

Q 11:23   What general rules has the DOL promulgated for vacation benefits?

When the vacation fringe benefit is one for which an employee does not become eligible for a stated period (i.e., an initial probationary period), the DOL has determined the following:

1. Time spent by an employee working for a predecessor contractor on similar contract functions at the same federal facility must be applied to the stated period under a successor contract, unless a fringe benefit determination provides otherwise; and

2. Time spent by an employee working continuously for any successor contractor in any capacity, including performing regular commercial work and contract work, must apply to the stated period.

(See Q 11:32 on successor and predecessor contractors. For other issues involved in the payment of vacation benefits, *see* 29 C.F.R. Section 4.173.) The contractor for whom the employee works at the time the benefit vests is responsible for the full amount of the vacation fringe benefit. [29 C.F.R. § 4.173]

Q 11:24   What general rules has the DOL promulgated for holiday pay?

Unless otherwise provided in a benefit determination, an employee perform-ing covered work is entitled to holiday pay for a full day's pay up to eight hours, in addition to the pay due an employee who works on the holiday. This obligation exists: (1) even if the employee did not actually work on the holiday or the day preceding or following it, as long as the employee performed work during the workweek in which the holiday occurred; (2) even if the holiday falls on a weekend day; and (3) even if the employee is absent during the holiday workweek because the employee is on vacation or sick leave or is laid off in a bad-faith effort to avoid holiday pay. The fact that an employee worked 32 hours in a workweek but received eight hours in holiday pay does not proportionately reduce other benefit levels. [29 C.F.R. § 4.174]

Q 11:25 What general rules has the DOL promulgated for health, welfare, and pension benefits?

Health, welfare, and pension payments made by an employer to an insurance plan or trust must be made not less often than quarterly. Unless a benefit determination provides otherwise, an employer must provide benefits or cash (payable on the next payday) to an employee up to the amount set in the benefit determination if an employer can obtain a health benefit for an employee at a rate less than the rate set in the benefit determination or if a health or welfare benefit plan contains exclusions for part-time employees or employees with spousal coverage. An employee who is off for two weeks' vacation is entitled to the full amount due in health and welfare benefits for the 80 hours of vacation pay the employee receives, not to exceed the 40-hour workweek maximum for a 52-week period. [29 C.F.R. § 4.175]

Q 11:26 What are other bona fide fringe benefits?

The DOL has interpreted *other bona fide fringe benefits* to include any plan, fund, or program that meets all of the following requirements:

1. The plan is a legally enforceable obligation.
2. The plan is in writing and communicated to the employees in writing.
3. Any contributions made by an employee are voluntary and are not used to offset the employer's fringe benefit obligations.
4. The primary purpose of the plan is to provide for the payment of benefits to employees for death, disability, advanced age, retirement, illness, medical expenses, hospitalization, supplemental unemployment benefits, and the like.
5. The plan contains a definite formula for determining the amount to be contributed by the contractor and a definite formula for determining the benefits for each of the employees participating in the plan.
6. The contractor's contributions are paid irrevocably to a trustee or third person pursuant to an insurance agreement, trust, or other funded arrangement. (Unfunded self-insured fringe benefit plans do not satisfy the requirements of the Service Contract Act unless approved by the Wage and Hour Administrator.)
7. The plan complies with the Employee Retirement Income Security Act of 1974 (ERISA) and the Internal Revenue Code (Code).
8. The benefits offered under the plan are not required by law, such as unemployment compensation or Social Security.
9. The benefits offered are not primarily for the benefit of the employer or are not board, lodging, or other facilities (see Chapter 3). Examples of

benefits that are primarily for the benefit of the employer are relocation expenses and uniform expenses.

The following items are not bona fide fringe benefits:

- Contributions by contractors for social functions or parties for employees
- Flowers, cards, or gifts on employee birthdays or anniversaries
- Employee rest or recreation rooms
- Paid coffee breaks
- Magazine subscriptions
- Professional association or club dues
- Automobile allowance

The administrative costs incurred in providing a fringe benefit are a business expense of the employer that cannot be deducted from the benefits paid or given to a service employee. [29 C.F.R. § 4.172]

Q 11:27   May an employer pay a covered employee the cash equivalent of the fringe benefit level specified in a determination?

Yes, as long as the compensation is in addition to the minimum wage due an employee and is paid to the employee on his or her regular payday. If the benefit level is not specified as an hourly rate, the employer must compute the benefit level based on the actual rate of pay and hours worked during the specified period (or based on an eight-hour day for a 40-hour workweek if no period is specified), even if the employee's rate of pay is in excess of the minimum wage.

Example 1. *Vacation pay.* If a fringe benefit determination lists "one week's vacation," the employee's hourly rate is multiplied by 40 (the standard number of nonovertime work hours in a week, unless weekly hours are specified) and that amount is then divided by 2,080 (40-hour workweeks for 52 weeks) to obtain the hourly cash equivalent. If an employee has earned one week's vacation but leaves before the hourly cash equivalent has been paid over the course of the year, the employee must receive the full amount on leaving. Unless the benefit determination specifies otherwise, the hourly rate applicable to the computation of fringe benefit payments is the actual rate in effect in the workweek in which the actual vacation is paid.

Example 2. *Holiday pay.* If a fringe benefit determination lists "nine holidays per year" and the employee's hourly rate of pay is $7.50, then $7.50 is multiplied by 72 (nine days of eight hours each) and the result, $540, is divided by 2,080 (40-hour workweeks for 52 weeks) to arrive at the hourly cash equivalent, $0.2596 per hour.

Example 3. *Health, welfare, and pension benefits.* If the determination lists a fringe benefit in terms of an amount per week, the hourly cash equivalent is determined by dividing the amount stated by the number of work hours to which the amount is attributable. Thus, if a determination lists a fringe benefit as "pension, $8 per week," the hourly cash equivalent is $0.20 per hour ($8 divided by 40 hours, the standard number of nonovertime work hours in a week, unless weekly hours are specified).

[41 U.S.C. § 351(a)(2); 29 C.F.R. § 4.177]

Q 11:28   How frequently must the wage and fringe benefit levels be adjusted?

Wage and fringe benefit levels must be adjusted after the first year and not less often than once every two years, pursuant to the applicable wage determination issued by the Wage and Hour Division. A government services contract may, with the authorization of the Secretary of Labor, have a duration of more than one year with a maximum duration of five years, although adjustments of wages and benefits to levels that comply with the Service Contract Act must be made at least every two years. [41 U.S.C. § 353(d); 29 C.F.R. §§ 4.6(b)(3), 4.145]

Q 11:29   Are there any other contract requirements?

Yes. The Service Contract Act also requires contractors and subcontractors to distribute a form to each employee or to post a notice in a prominent place at the work site informing service employees of the minimum wage and fringe benefit requirements. (This form or notice is available from the DOL.) The form or notice must be distributed or posted on the first day of work on the contract. The government service contract must contain a provision identifying these notice requirements. [41 U.S.C. § 351(a)(4); 29 C.F.R. §§ 4.183, 4.184]

The contract must also state that no work performed under the contract or subcontract will be performed under conditions that are unsanitary, hazardous, or dangerous to the health and safety of service employees. [41 U.S.C. § 351(a)(3)] The specific contract provisions that must appear in a contract or subcontract covered under the Service Contract Act are enumerated in 29 C.F.R. Section 4.6. [29 C.F.R. § 4.6]

Q 11:30   When do the contract obligations begin?

Generally, the contractor's or subcontractor's obligations under the Service Contract Act begin from the date the contractor or subcontractor is notified of the award. The wage and benefit requirements begin from the first date of employment, including any training or phase-in period. [29 C.F.R. § 4.146]

Q 11:31   What are the recordkeeping requirements for employers covered under the Service Contract Act?

An employer covered under the Service Contract Act must keep the following records for three years:

- *General information.* Name, address and Social Security number of each employee.

- *Classification and pay information.* The correct work classification or classifications, rate or rates of monetary wages paid and fringe benefits provided, rate or rates of cash payments in lieu of fringe benefits, and total daily and weekly compensation of each employee. An employer that pays employees a cash equivalent for the fringe benefits required under the Service Contract Act must keep records separately showing the amount paid for wages and the amount paid for fringe benefits.

- *Hours.* The number of daily and weekly hours worked by each employee performing contract work. If an employee performs contract and noncontract work, this work time must be segregated or an employer may be required to compensate all hours under the Service Contract Act.

- *Deductions.* Any deductions, rebates, or refunds from the total daily or weekly compensation of each employee.

- *Subsequent wage and fringe benefit determinations.* A list of monetary wages and fringe benefits for the classes of service employees not included in any initial wage determination attached to the contract but for which wage rates or fringe benefits have been subsequently determined by request of the Wage and Hour Administrator. A copy of the report prepared in connection with the making of such a request will suffice.

- *List of predecessor employees.* Any list of the predecessor contractor's employees and their anniversary dates of employment.

- *Contract.* A copy of the government services contract.

[29 C.F.R. §§ 4.6(g), 4.185]

If an employer does not segregate the records for employees who are and who are not performing contract work, it is presumed that all employees are engaged in covered work. Furthermore, the employer must keep records separately showing amounts paid for wages and amounts paid for fringe benefits. [29 C.F.R. §§ 4.170(a), 4.179]

Successor Contractors and Subcontractors

Q 11:32   Do the Service Contract Act requirements apply to successor contractors or subcontractors?

Yes, as long as the successor contract is in excess of $2,500. In this context, a contract is a collective bargaining agreement. A successor contractor covered under the Service Contract Act cannot pay service employees less than the wage and fringe benefit rates set under the predecessor contract, including any accrued wages or benefits or prospective increases, unless: (1) the predecessor contract was not entered into as a result of arm's-length negotiations; or (2) the successor requests a hearing before the Secretary of Labor for a determination that the wages and benefits set under the predecessor contract substantially vary from the prevailing levels for comparable services in a similar locality. The requirement to provide at least the same wage and fringe benefits as the predecessor does not extend to other provisions relating to seniority, grievance procedures, work rules, overtime, etc. [41 U.S.C. § 353(c); 29 C.F.R. §§ 4.10(a), 4.1b, 4.163]

The prerequisites for initiating a hearing to determine whether the negotiations were proper are set forth in 29 C.F.R. Section 4.11. (The procedures for requesting a hearing from and conducting a hearing before the Wage and Hour Administrator are set forth in 29 C.F.R. Section 4.10 and 29 C.F.R. Parts 6 and 8, and are beyond the scope of this chapter.) Until a new determination is made, however, the predecessor contract terms apply. In addition, variance decisions do not apply retroactively. The purpose of this provision is to prevent cutthroat bidding by nonincumbent bidders that lower wages to ensure that they will be awarded the contract as the lowest bidder, at the expense of bargained-for wages and benefits. [29 C.F.R. §§ 4.10, 4.11; *see* Fort Hood Barbers Ass'n v. Herman, 137 F.3d 302, 310 (5th Cir. 1998)]

There is a caveat to the general rule that the wage and benefit levels of the predecessor contract apply to a successor contract. If the services to be provided by the successor are not substantially the same as those previously performed by the predecessor, a new wage determination must be issued by the Secretary of Labor. A change in the contracting agency or in the place of contract performance, a suspension of contract services, or negotiation of a temporary interim contract does not affect the operation of these requirements. [29 C.F.R. §§ 4.1b, 4.163]

In addition, there are two circumstances in which new or changed terms in a predecessor collective bargaining agreement render the wage and benefit terms previously set under the predecessor collective bargaining agreement ineffective. First, if bids have been invited on a successor contract by formal advertising and the contracting agency receives notice of the new or changed collective bargaining agreement less than ten days before the day set for the opening of bids and there is no reasonable time for the agency to notify the bidders of the new terms, the new or changed terms apply. Second, if the agency receives notice of the new or changed terms after award of the successor contract, and these changes are the result of negotiations, exercise of a renewal option, or extension of a contract term, the new or changed terms are effective provided that: (1) performance of the contract begins within 30 days from the award, renewal option, or extension; or (2) notice of the changed terms is received by the agency not less than ten days before commencement of the contract. These are the two general exceptions to the general rule that the predecessor agreement's wage and benefit levels govern a successor contract only when the contracting officer gives the predecessor contractor and its employees' collective bargaining representative 30 days' notice in advance of any estimated procurement date or of the commencement of the contract resulting from negotiations, exercise of a renewal option, or extension of a contract term. [29 C.F.R. § 4.1b, 4.6(d)(2)]

Finally, when dealing with a successor contractor situation, the predecessor contractor is required to provide a list of covered employees to the successor. [29 C.F.R. § 4.6(l)(2)]

Enforcement and Penalties

Q 11:33   How is the Service Contract Act enforced?

The DOL is generally charged with enforcement of the Service Contract Act, which includes investigating and prosecuting violations, adopting rules and regulations necessary for the enforcement of the act, issuing wage and benefit determinations, and making exceptions to the requirements of the Act on a case-by-case basis. Decisions of the DOL may be appealed to the Administrative Review Board and reviewed by the courts. The health and safety provisions of the Service Contract Act are enforced by OSHA. [41 U.S.C. §§ 352–354; 29 U.S.C. § 4.102] Courts have held under various circumstances that there is no private right of action to enforce violations of the Service Contract Act. [*See, e.g.,* District Lodge No. 166, Int'l Ass'n of Machinists & Aerospace Workers v. TWA Servs., Inc., 731 F.2d 711 (11th Cir. 1984) (holding that if the Secretary of Labor issues a wage determination after the contract has begun, employees cannot bring suit against the contractor to recover the difference between wages actually paid and those that would have been due in the interim had the agency issued the wage determination earlier), *cert. denied,* 469 U.S. 1209 (1985)]

Q 11:34   What are the penalties for noncompliance with the Service Contract Act?

Failure to comply with the minimum wage and fringe benefit requirements of the Service Contract Act may result in cancellation of the contract. The United States may then enter into a contract for the completion of the work, with any additional expenses being charged to the prior contractor. [41 U.S.C. § 352; 29 C.F.R. §§ 4.187, 4.190]

A contractor or subcontractor that violates any provision of the Service Contract Act may also be blacklisted (debarred) by being placed on a list of ineligible contractors. Absent "unusual circumstances," no government service contracts may be awarded to the persons or firms appearing on such a list or to any firm, corporation, partnership, or association in which such persons or firms have a substantial interest for a period of three years. In unusual circumstances, which are determined on a case-by-case basis, the Secretary of Labor may recommend that the contractor not be blacklisted. If a blacklisted party or those with a substantial interest in a blacklisted party enter into a government service contract, the contract is subject to immediate cancellation on written notice and any profits derived from that contract may be forfeited. [41 U.S.C. § 354; 29 C.F.R. § 4.188]

Further, the regulations do not permit relief from debarment simply because the violator pays what should have been paid previously [*see* 29 C.F.R. § 4.188(b)(2)]; such leniency would provide no incentive for contractors to seek out and conform to the regulations governing their conduct. [Dantran, Inc. v. United States Dep't of Labor, 246 F.3d 36 (1st Cir. 2001)]

In addition, the Secretary of Labor may recover underpayment of compensation due an employee for minimum wage and fringe benefit violations by withholding accrued payments from the contractor. To the extent that the accrued payments are insufficient, there is a six-year statute of limitations for recouping underpayment. An officer of a corporation who actively directs and supervises the performance of the contract may be personally liable for underpayment. (The prerequisites for initiating a hearing to determine whether a party has a substantial interest and for disputing a DOL agency finding of liability are set forth in 29 C.F.R. § 4.12 and 29 C.F.R. pts. 6 and 8.) Moreover, a prime contractor is jointly and severally liable for any underpayment by a subcontractor that would violate the prime contract. [41 U.S.C. § 352; 29 C.F.R. §§ 4.187, 4.12]

Failing to keep the records required under the Service Contract Act is a violation of that Act; failure to provide records to the Wage and Hour Administrator on request may result in the suspension of payments or advancements of funds until the violation ceases. [29 C.F.R. § 4.6(g)(3)]

Davis-Bacon Act

Contracts Covered

Q 11:35 What government contracts are covered by the Davis-Bacon Act?

The Davis-Bacon Act covers government contracts between the United States or the District of Columbia and a contractor for laborers and mechanics on federal public buildings or federally financed construction public projects for which the advertised specifications are for an amount in excess of $2,000. The contract must be for the construction, alteration, or repair of public buildings or public works, and the work must be performed by mechanics or laborers. The prevailing wage standards of the Davis-Bacon Act also apply to subcontracts that meet these requirements. [40 U.S.C. § 3142; 29 C.F.R. § 5.2(h)]

The public buildings or public works covered under the Davis-Bacon Act must be those owned by the United States or the District of Columbia and located within their geographical limits, or those constructed, completed, or repaired by a federal agency or with federal funds regardless of whether the agency has title to them. In addition, the terms *public buildings* and *public works* include "buildings, structures, and improvements of all types, such as bridges, dams, plants, highways, parkways, streets, subways, tunnels, sewers, mains, power lines, pumping stations, heavy generators, railways, airports, terminals, docks, piers, wharves, ways, lighthouses, buoys, jetties, breakwaters, levees, canals, dredging, shoring, rehabilitation and reactivation of plants, scaffolding, drilling, blasting, excavating, clearing, and landscaping." Manufactured or furnished materials, articles, supplies, and equipment (whether or not a government agency acquires title to the items or owns the materials from which they are manufactured or furnished) are not buildings or works, unless the manufacturing or furnishing is conducted in connection with and at the site of a public building or public work, or under specified Davis-Bacon-related acts. [29 C.F.R. § 5.2(i)–(k)]

According to the DOL, covered contract work, which is generally referred to as *construction, alteration, or repair,* includes the following:

- Painting and decorating;
- Altering, remodeling, or installation on the site of the work of items fabricated off site;
- Manufacturing or furnishing of materials, articles, supplies, or equipment on the site of the public building or work; and
- Transportation between the actual construction location and a facility that is dedicated to the construction and deemed a part of the site of the work (otherwise, the transportation of materials or supplies to or from the public building or work by employees of the construction contractor or a construction subcontractor is not construction).

Examples of the type of work that constitutes construction, alteration, or repair include:

- Laying carpet and installing draperies during reconstruction of a public building;
- Preparatory clean-up work like window washing or paint scraping, as long as it is performed before the contractors have finished the construction work;
- Demolition work in preparation for further construction activity (but not demolition work not followed by construction activity); and
- Landscaping performed in connection with construction (but not landscaping work alone, i.e., landscaping work not incidental to any construction work, which would be covered under the Service Contract Act, not the Davis-Bacon Act).

(Compare the site-of-work requirements discussed in Q 11:38.)

[29 C.F.R. § 5.2(i), (j), (l); Wage and Hour Field Operations Handbook Pt. 15d]

Q 11:36   What distinguishes the Davis-Bacon Act from the Public Contracts Act and the Service Contract Act?

The Davis-Bacon Act differs from the Public Contracts Act and the Service Contract Act in that it contains no health and safety requirements. Like the Service Contract Act, however, the Davis-Bacon Act includes a fringe benefit requirement. Another distinguishing feature of the Davis-Bacon Act is that several other statutes that authorize federal assistance on construction projects incorporate by reference the prevailing wage provisions of the Davis-Bacon Act. Referred to as Davis-Bacon and Related Acts, these acts involve construction in areas like transportation, housing, air and water pollution reduction, and health. The "Related Acts" are listed in 29 C.F.R. Section 5.1. The Davis-Bacon Act, together with the Contract Work Hours and Safety Standards Act and the

Copeland Anti-Kickback Act, prescribes the labor standards for laborers and mechanics performing work on public construction projects pursuant to a federal contract.

Contractors Covered

Q 11:37 What contractors are covered under the Davis-Bacon Act?

The Davis-Bacon Act applies to contractors and subcontractors performing work under a covered contract. For purposes of the Davis-Bacon Act or Contract Work Hours and Safety Standards Act, state and local governments are not contractors under statutes providing federal loans, grants, or other assistance if the construction is actually performed by the governmental entity's own employees (which is known as a "force account"); however, state and local recipients of federal aid must pay laborers and mechanics pursuant to the Davis-Bacon labor standards if the applicable statute so provides. [29 C.F.R. § 5.2]

Employees Covered

Q 11:38 What employees are covered under the Davis-Bacon Act?

Under the Davis-Bacon Act and the Contract Work Hours and Safety Standards Act, *laborers* and *mechanics* include workers who perform manual or physical labor, and exclude workers whose duties are primarily administrative, executive, or clerical. Under the Davis-Bacon Act, the terms *laborers* and *mechanics* include apprentices and trainees working pursuant to a certified program, and helpers, except apprentices and trainees employed on federal-aid highway projects subject to 23 U.S.C. Section 113. Any employee performing the duties of a laborer or mechanic covered under the Davis-Bacon Act or Contract Work Hours and Safety Standards Act is an employee regardless of any contractual relationship alleged to exist. [40 U.S.C. §§ 3142, 3701; 29 C.F.R. §§ 5.2(m), (o), 5.5(a), 5.16, 5.17]

A distinct classification of *helper* will be issued in Davis-Bacon wage determinations only where the duties of the helper are clearly defined and distinct from any other classification in the wage determination, the use of such helpers is an established prevailing practice in the area, and the helper is not employed as a trainee in an informal training program. [29 C.F.R. § 5.2(n)(4)]

A further limitation of the Davis-Bacon Act is that it applies only to mechanics and laborers who perform construction directly on the site of work. The DOL applies an expansive definition of the term "site of work" for purposes of coverage under the Davis-Bacon Act. *Site of work* is generally defined by the DOL as "the physical place or places where the building or work called for in the contract will remain"; and any other site where a significant portion of the building or work is constructed, provided that such site is established specifically for the performance of the contract or project. The site of work includes nearby fabrication plants, mobile factories, batch plants, borrow pits, job headquarters, tool yards, and other similar facilities, that are exclusively or nearly so dedicated to performance of the contract; however, it excludes such facilities to the extent they belong to a commercial supplier or materialman located off the project site and are established by a supplier of materials for the project before the opening of bids, even though they may be exclusively dedicated to the performance of a contract. [40 U.S.C. § 3142; 29 C.F.R. § 5.2(l)]

Some courts take issue with these expansive site-of-work regulations and reject the DOL's interpretation, maintaining that the statutory language clearly states that the labor standards apply only to "mechanics and laborers employed *directly* on the site of the work." [*See* 40 U.S.C. § 3142 (emphasis added); *see also* LP Cavett Co. v United States Dep't of Labor, 101 F.3d 1111 (6th Cir. 1996) (following decisions from the District of Columbia Circuit, the Sixth Circuit held that truck drivers hauling asphalt from a temporary batch point to a federally assisted highway construction project three miles away from the site of work were not performing directly on the site of work and therefore were not covered by the prevailing wage standards of the Davis-Bacon Act); Building & Constr. Trades Dep't v. United States Dep't of Labor Wage Appeals Bd., 932 F.2d 985 (D.C. Cir. 1991) (holding that truck drivers who deliver materials to a federally funded construction project are akin to materialmen or commercial suppliers and are therefore excluded from the requirements of the Davis-Bacon Act)]

Requirements

Q 11:39   What are the minimum wage requirements under the Davis-Bacon Act?

Covered employees must be paid the prevailing wage determined by the Secretary of Labor. The *prevailing wage* is based on the wages and benefits paid to corresponding classes of laborers and mechanics performing work on a particular project similar to work performed in the city, town, village, or other civil subdivision of the State in which the work is to be performed. This is in contrast to the Public Contracts Act, which calls for industry-wide wage determinations (see Q 11:7). If a laborer or mechanic performs work in more than one classification, the employee may be paid the prevailing wage rate specified for each classification if the employer's payroll records separate the time spent in each classification. Apprentices and trainees performing contract work pursuant to a registered program may be paid at a wage specified in the program; however, apprentices and trainees must be paid the prevailing wage rate if they are not properly registered in a program or they are employed in excess of the ratio permitted by the program. [40 U.S.C. § 3142; 29 C.F.R. § 5.5(a)]

Q 11:40   How are hours worked determined under the Davis-Bacon Act?

Because the Davis-Bacon Act is covered under the Portal Act, hours worked are determined under the Davis-Bacon Act in the same manner as under the

FLSA. [29 U.S.C. § 251] The FLSA's provisions on compensable work time are explained in detail in Chapter 6.

Q 11:41 What contract provisions are required under the Davis-Bacon Act?

Covered contracts must contain the several and various stipulations that incorporate the requirements under the Davis-Bacon Act. The required stipulations are set forth in 29 C.F.R. Section 5.5 and include the following:

1. Wages shall be paid without condition, deduction, or rebate and regardless of any contractual relationship said to exist between the contractors, subcontractors, or covered employees.

2. Wages shall be paid not less often than once a week.

3. The scale of wages to be paid shall be posted by the contractor in a prominent and easily accessible place at the work site.

Failure to include the required stipulations in a covered contract results in denial of approval of the contract, or of payments (unless the contractor has a certification on file) by the contracting federal agency. [40 U.S.C. §§ 3142(c), 3143(a); 29 C.F.R. §§ 5.5, 5.6]

Q 11:42 Are there any fringe benefit requirements under the Davis-Bacon Act?

Yes. Like employees covered under the Service Contract Act, employees covered under the Davis-Bacon Act must be provided the prevailing benefits in the locality, the levels of which are set by the Secretary of Labor. The benefits contemplated by the Davis-Bacon Act are the same as those under the Service Contract Act. They include medical or hospital care, pensions, unemployment compensation, life insurance, disability or sick pay, accident insurance, vacation and holiday pay, and the costs of apprenticeships or like programs, as well as any other bona fide fringe benefits not required by federal, state, or local law (such as Social Security and Medicare contributions or workers' compensation insurance premiums), or the cash equivalent. The Secretary of Labor must make a separate determination of the rate of contribution or cost for fringe benefits, which is ordinarily set at an hourly rate. Bona fide fringe benefits are those "common in the construction industry and which are established under a usual fund, plan, or program." Unconventional fringe benefits must be approved specifically by the Secretary of Labor under 29 C.F.R. Section 5.5(a)(1)(iv). [40 U.S.C. § 3142; 29 C.F.R. §§ 5.5(a), 5.25, 5.29, 5.30]

Under the Davis-Bacon Act, unlike the Service Contract Act, payments made by a covered employer for fringe benefits are considered part of the prevailing wage and must be paid for all hours worked, including both straight-time and overtime hours. The benefits may be paid pursuant to the following methods of contribution:

1. By payments or contributions irrevocably made to a trust or to a third person pursuant to a fund, plan, or program (funded plans);

2. By setting aside or allocating the costs the contractor reasonably anticipates it will incur in providing fringe benefits to employees pursuant to an enforceable, financially sound plan communicated in writing to the employees (unfunded plans); or

3. By making cash payments directly to the employees.

Cash payments may be made in combination with the other two methods of contribution so long as the contractor does not pay or provide less than the prevailing wage obligations.

The regulations require that contributions to fringe benefit plans made by a contractor or subcontractor be made on a regular basis (i.e., not less often than quarterly). [29 C.F.R. §§ 5.5(a)(1)(i)]

Apprentices and trainees performing contract work pursuant to a registered program must be paid fringe benefits as specified in a registered apprentice or trainee program. If these benefits are not specified, the apprentices and trainees generally must be paid the fringe benefits listed in the wage determination, unless the Wage and Hour Administrator determines that a different practice prevails in the locality of the construction project for that particular apprentice or trainee classification. [Wage and Hour Field Operations Handbook §§ 15e01(g), 15e02]

Q 11:43   What are the overtime requirements under the Davis-Bacon Act?

The Davis-Bacon Act does not have its own overtime provision. It provides, however, that for employees who are entitled to be paid overtime under other federal laws, the basic rate of pay under the applicable wage determination serves as the regular rate for purposes of computing overtime. [40 U.S.C. § 3142(e); 29 C.F.R. § 5.32]

There is an issue whether fringe benefits should be included in the regular rate when calculating overtime due an employee. The DOL regulations state that when the overtime provisions of the FLSA, the Contract Work Hours and Safety Standards Act, or the Public Contracts Act apply concurrently with the Davis-Bacon Act and Related Acts, amounts paid by a contractor or subcontractor for fringe benefits are excluded from the regular rate for purposes of calculating overtime pay to the extent provided under the applicable statute. [29 C.F.R. §§ 5.32, 778.6] Because the prevailing wage under the Davis-Bacon Act includes the basic hourly rate of pay and the cash fringe benefit payments; however, at least two courts have affirmed the interpretation of the Wage Appeals Board, and required employers to include cash payments for fringe benefits as part of the regular rate. [Holloway Constr. v. Wage Appeals Bd., 825 F.2d 1072 (6th Cir. 1987); G & C Enters., Inc. v. Wage Appeals Bd., 619 F. Supp. 1430 (D.N.J. 1985)] An employee's contributions for fringe benefits must be included in the basic or regular rate. [40 U.S.C. § 3142(e)]

Q 11:44   What are the recordkeeping requirements under the Davis-Bacon Act?

The following records must be retained by the contractor for the duration of the contract and for a period of three years thereafter:

1. *Payroll and basic information.* The records must contain the name, address, Social Security number, classification, hourly rates of wages paid (including rates of contributions or costs anticipated for bona fide fringe benefits or cash equivalents), daily and weekly number of hours worked, deductions made, and actual wages paid.

2. *Unfunded plan contributions.* If a contractor makes contributions to an unfunded plan as part of the prevailing wage rate, it must keep records that show the commitment to provide such benefits is enforceable and that the plan or program is financially responsible and has been communicated in writing to the laborers or mechanics affected, and records that show the costs anticipated or the actual cost incurred in providing such benefits.

3. *Apprentices and trainees.* Contractors employing apprentices or trainees under approved programs must maintain written evidence of the registration of apprenticeship programs and certification of trainee programs, the registration of the apprentices and trainees, and the ratios and wage rates prescribed in the programs.

[29 C.F.R. § 5.5(a)(3)(i)]

There are also weekly payroll reporting requirements that accompany the prevailing wage requirements of the Davis-Bacon Act. [29 C.F.R. § 5.5(a)(3)(ii)] Required records must be available for inspection by DOL representatives. Failure to maintain or produce the required records may result in the contracting federal agency, after notice to the contractor, suspending further payment on the contract. Such a failure may also be grounds for debarment. [29 C.F.R. § 5.5(a)(3)(iii)]

Enforcement and Penalties

Q 11:45   How is the Davis-Bacon Act enforced?

The DOL is generally charged with enforcement of the Davis-Bacon Act, which includes investigating and prosecuting violations, adopting rules and regulations necessary for the enforcement of the Act, and issuing wage determinations. The Comptroller General of the United States is authorized to make direct wage payments to laborers and mechanics from any withheld payments under the contract. [40 U.S.C. §§ 3142, 3144, 3145; 29 C.F.R. § 5.6]

Actions for unpaid minimum wages, overtime pay, and liquidated damages must be brought no later than two years from the date the action accrued, or no later than three years from the date the action accrued, if the violation was willful. Under the Davis-Bacon Act, covered employees have a right of action or intervention against the contractor or its surety for wages, to the extent the payments withheld are insufficient. However, the Davis-Bacon Act does not expressly provide employees a private right of action to enforce the statute, although in some circumstances courts may find an implied right of action. [29 U.S.C. § 255; 40 U.S.C. § 3144(a)] Although there is a split of authority, most federal appellate courts have concluded that there is no private right of action available to individuals to recover unpaid prevailing wages under the Davis-Bacon Act in a civil suit. [*See, e.g.,* Operating Engineers Health & Welfare Fund v. JWJ Constr. Co., 135 F.3d 671 (9th Cir. 1998); Weber v. Heat Control Co., 728 F.2d 599 (3d Cir. 1984); United States v. Capeletti Bros, Inc., 621 F.2d 1309 (5th Cir. 1980). *Cf.* McDaniel v. University of Chicago, 512 F.2d 583 (7th Cir. 1975), *vacated* 423 U.S. 809 (1975)]

Q 11:46   What are the penalties for failure to comply with the Davis-Bacon Act?

In the event of a violation of the Davis-Bacon Act, the contracting agency may withhold payments or advances under the contract to pay laborers or mechanics. The government may also terminate the contractor's or subcontractor's right to proceed with work and hold it liable for excess costs incurred in completing the contract work in the event of underpayment. It is an affirmative defense to alleged violations if an employer relied in good faith on administrative rulings under the Davis-Bacon Act. Absent such a defense, payments may be withheld from the contractor to cover the underpayment due covered employees, among other penalties available to the contracting agency. [29 U.S.C. § 260; 40 U.S.C. §§ 3142, 3143; 29 C.F.R. §§ 5.8, 5.9, 5.13]

The Davis-Bacon Act contains a blacklisting provision similar to that of the Service Contract Act for contractors that have acted with the intent to "disregard their obligations" under the act. In addition to being blacklisted, if a contractor fails to produce the records required to be kept under the Davis-Bacon Act to the DOL on request, the contracting federal agency may suspend any further payment, advance, or guarantee of funds. [40 U.S.C. § 3144(b); 29 C.F.R. § 5.5(a)(3)(iii)] The procedures for resolving disputes under Davis-Bacon and Related Acts are covered in 29 C.F.R. Section 5.11 and are beyond the scope of this chapter. The procedures and requirements for debarment proceedings are covered in 29 C.F.R. Section 5.12.

Contract Work Hours and Safety Standards Act

Q 11:47   What does the Contract Work Hours and Safety Standards Act regulate, and how does it relate to the other Acts discussed in this chapter?

The Contract Work Hours and Safety Standards Act regulates only the payment of overtime to mechanics and laborers performing on public works under contracts covered by the Act's provisions. Although it expressly excludes from its coverage contracts covered by the Public Contracts Act (covering specified contracts exceeding $10,000), contracts covered under the Contract

Work Hours and Safety Standards Act may also be covered under the Davis-Bacon Act or the Service Contract Act. Because both the Contract Work Hours and Safety Standards Act and the Davis-Bacon Act cover public works contracts, both statutes are covered under some of the same regulatory provisions.

Contracts Covered

Q 11:48   What government contracts are covered under the Contract Work Hours and Safety Standards Act?

The Contract Work Hours and Safety Standards Act applies to any contract or subcontract in excess of $100,000 that may require or involve the employment of laborers or mechanics on the following:

1. A public work of the United States, or any territory of the United States, or of the District of Columbia;

2. A contract to which the United States or any agency, instrumentality or territory thereof, or the District of Columbia, is a party;

3. A contract made for or on behalf of the United States or any agency, instrumentality or territory thereof, or the District of Columbia; or

4. A contract for work financed in whole or in part from loans or grants from, or loans guaranteed or insured by, the United States or any agency or instrumentality thereof pursuant to a federal law providing wage standards for such work.

The fourth category of contracts, however, does not include contracts for which the assistance provided by the United States, agency, or instrumentality is only in the form of a loan guarantee or insurance. The definition of public works is the same as that under the Davis-Bacon Act (see Q 11:35). [40 U.S.C. § 3701(b); 29 C.F.R. § 5.2(k)]

Examples of covered contracts include the following:

- Food services contracts to provide food services to employees in government buildings, where the cooks, food servers, and buspersons are considered laborers and mechanics

- Janitorial services contracts

- Contracts to repair and service vehicles

- Contracts for the packing, loading, and moving of goods from military installations, since the primary purpose of the contracts would not be transportation (which is exempt)

[Wage and Hour Field Operations Handbook pt. 15h]

The Contract Work Hours and Safety Standards Act does not apply to contracts for transportation by land, air, or water; contracts for transmission of intelligence; or contracts for the purchase of supplies, materials, or articles ordinarily available on the open market. It also does not apply to contracts covered under the Public Contracts Act. [40 U.S.C. §§ 3701(b)(3)] In addition, the following contracts have been exempted by administrative rule:

- Contract work performed in a workplace in a foreign country or in a territory under the jurisdiction of the United States other than a state of the United States, the District of Columbia, Puerto Rico, the Virgin Islands, Outer Continental Shelf lands as defined in the Outer Continental Shelf Lands Act, American Samoa, Guam, Wake Island, Eniwetok Atoll, Kwajalein Atoll, and Johnston Island.

- Contracts entered into by or on behalf of the Commodity Credit Corporation providing for the storing in or handling by commercial warehouses of wheat, corn, oats, barley, rye, grain sorghums, soybeans, flaxseed, rice, naval stores, tobacco, peanuts, dry beans, seeds, cotton, and wool.

- Sales of surplus power by the Tennessee Valley Authority to states, counties, municipalities, cooperative organizations of citizens or farmers, corporations, and other individuals pursuant to the Tennessee Valley Authority Act of 1933. [16 U.S.C. § 8311]

[29 C.F.R. § 29.5(15)]

Under the Contract Work Hours and Safety Standards Act, like the Davis-Bacon Act, state and local governments are not contractors under statutes providing loans, grants, or other federal assistance if the construction is performed by the governmental entity's own employees (e.g., "force account"). [Wage and Hour Field Operations Handbook § 15h01]

Employees Covered

Q 11:49   What employees are covered under the Contract Work Hours and Safety Standards Act?

The Contract Work Hours and Safety Standards Act applies to all laborers or mechanics employed by a contractor for work under a covered contract. Laborers and mechanics are defined in the Davis-Bacon Act (see Q 11:38). The Contract Work Hours and Safety Standards Act adds that laborers and mechanics include watchpersons, guards, and persons performing services in connection with dredging or rock excavation in any river or harbor of the United States, or a territory of the United States, or the District of Columbia, except as otherwise provided by law. The Contract Work Hours and Safety Standards Act expressly excludes seamen. [40 U.S.C. § 3701(b)]

Because the Contract Work Hours and Safety Standards Act provides for overtime pay only for employees who work more than 40 hours in a workweek [see 40 U.S.C. § 3702], the Act does not apply to employees who work on a covered contract for less than 40 hours in a workweek.

Requirements

Q 11:50   What are the overtime requirements under the Contract Work Hours and Safety Standards Act?

Unlike the Service Contract Act, the Contract Work Hours and Safety Standards Act expressly provides for overtime pay at a rate of one and one-half times the basic rate of pay for work hours in excess of 40 hours per week. The *basic rate of pay* under the Contract Work Hours and Safety Standards Act means the straight-time hourly rate, excluding fringe benefit payments (or their cash equivalent). The methods for computing the regular rate for overtime purposes are the same as the methods under the FLSA, although the regulations also provide that time spent in specified trainee or apprentice programs may be excluded from work time (see Chapter 7). The overtime requirements are a condition of every contract or of any obligation of the United States or territory of the United States or the District of Columbia covered under the Contract Work Hours and Safety Standards Act. Contracts for veteran nursing home care or fire suppression services otherwise covered under the Contract Work Hours and Safety Standards Act may provide for a modified payment of overtime, as specified in the regulatory provisions at 29 C.F.R. Section 5.15(d). [40 U.S.C. § 3702; 29 C.F.R. § 5.15(c), (d); Wage and Hour Field Operations Handbook § 15k01]

Q 11:51   Are there any other requirements under the Contract Work Hours and Safety Standards Act?

Like the Service Contract Act and the Public Contracts Act, the Contract Work Hours and Safety Standards Act provides that a healthy and safe work environment is a condition of every covered contract. (The enforcement provisions and penalties for noncompliance with the safety standards are beyond the scope of this chapter.) The regulations for the Contract Work Hours and Safety Standards Act also require that covered contracts contain various and lengthy stipulations, in addition to those required under the Service Contract Act, set forth in 29 C.F.R. Section 4.6, or those required under the Davis-Bacon Act at 29 C.F.R. Section 5.5(a). [40 U.S.C. § 3704; 29 C.F.R. §§ 4.6, 5.5]

Q 11:52   What are the recordkeeping requirements under the Contract Work Hours and Safety Standards Act?

In a contract covered under the Contract Work Hours and Safety Standards Act, but not any of the Davis-Bacon and Related Acts or other federal statutes, the contractor or subcontractor is required to keep basic payroll records for three years, including each employee's name, address, Social Security number, classification, hourly rates of wages paid, daily and weekly number of hours worked, deductions made, and actual wages paid. If a contract is covered under another federal statute in addition to being covered under the Contract Work Hours and Safety Standards Act, the record-keeping requirements of the other federal statute must also be followed. [29 C.F.R. § 5.5(c)]

Enforcement and Penalties

Q 11:53   How is the Contract Work Hours and Safety Standards Act enforced?

The DOL is generally charged with enforcement of the Contract Work Hours and Safety Standards Act, which includes investigating and prosecuting violations, and withholding payments due contractors to cover unpaid overtime and liquidated damages. Contractors may appeal a DOL decision to the Administrative Review Board. Assessments are appealed to the head of the contracting agency or to the mayor of the District of Columbia, and then to the courts. The health and safety requirements of the Contract Work Hours and Safety Standards Act are enforced by OSHA. [40 U.S.C. §§ 3702, 3703, 3706]

Q 11:54 What are the penalties for failure to comply with the Contract Work Hours and Safety Standards Act?

Contractors or subcontractors that fail to comply with the overtime requirements of the Contract Work Hours and Safety Standards Act are liable to any employee for unpaid wages. They are also liable to the United States, or any territory of the United States or the District of Columbia for liquidated damages in the amount of $10 for each calendar day the employee was required to work over 40 hours in a workweek without overtime pay. The agency for which contract work is being done, or that is providing financial assistance for the work, is authorized to withhold from the contractor accrued payments in the amount of the overtime pay and liquidated damages due. When the agency finds that an administratively determined assessment of liquidated damages in excess of $500 is incorrect or that the contractor violation was inadvertent, the agency may recommend an adjustment, with review by the Secretary of Labor. Assessments of $500 or less may be adjusted directly by the agency. Contractors may appeal this determination to the head of the agency or territory for which the work is being done, or to the mayor of the District of Columbia, with final review by the Secretary of Labor, and thereafter by the U.S. Court of Federal Claims. (The procedures for resolving disputes under Davis-Bacon-related acts, including the Contract Work Hours and Safety Standards Act, are covered in 29 C.F.R. Section 5.11 and are beyond the scope of this chapter. Debarment proceedings are covered in 29 C.F.R. Section 5.12.) The statute of limitations for an agency to bring an action for money damages for Contract Work Hours and Safety Standards Act violations is six years. [28 U.S.C. § 2415; 40 U.S.C. §§ 3702, 3703; 29 C.F.R. §§ 5.8, 5.11, 5.12]

If withheld payments fall short of fully reimbursing employees for unpaid overtime, workers covered under the Contract Work Hours and Safety Standards Act may bring a cause of action against the contractor and its sureties for underpayment of wages, or may intervene in a proceeding brought by a department or agency of the federal government. In such proceedings, it is no defense that the employee agreed to accept lower wages or voluntarily made refunds to the contractor. [40 U.S.C. § 3703(c)]

A contractor may also be blacklisted for up to three years under the Contract Work Hours and Safety Standards Act when the Secretary of Labor finds that the contractor or subcontractor has had repeated willful or grossly negligent violations of the health and safety standards of the Act. Intentional violation of the Contract Work Hours and Safety Standards Act by contractors or subcontractors whose duty it is to employ, direct, or control any covered worker in the performance of contract work is a misdemeanor punishable by imprisonment of up to six months or a fine not to exceed $1,000 for each violation, or both. [40 U.S.C. §§ 3704(c), 3708]

Copeland Anti-Kickback Act

Q 11:55   What does the Copeland Anti-Kickback Act prohibit, and how does it relate to the other acts discussed in this chapter?

The Copeland Anti-Kickback Act prohibits contractors from making certain deductions from wages or from requiring an employee to give back some of his or her wages. Contractors or subcontractors covered under the Davis-Bacon Act (pertaining to the construction of public works) or Contract Work Hours and Safety Standards Act (pertaining to the employment of laborers and mechanics on public works) are also subject to the Copeland Anti-Kickback Act. In fact, the coverage of the Copeland Anti-Kickback Act is broader than the coverage of those statutes, since it covers all employees who perform "construction, prosecution, completion, or repair" on a public building, public work, or other work at least partially funded by the federal government, not just mechanics and laborers. It also covers all federally funded contracts—not just those in excess of $2,000, even when the financial assistance is in the form of loan guarantees or insurance. [18 U.S.C. § 874; 40 U.S.C. § 3145; 29 C.F.R. §§ 3.1, 3.2]

Q 11:56   What is the purpose of the Copeland Anti-Kickback Act?

The purpose of the Copeland Anti-Kickback Act is to penalize employers that attempt to avoid the requirements of the Davis-Bacon Act or Contract Work Hours and Safety Standards Act by making impermissible wage deductions. The Copeland Anti-Kickback Act describes deductions that are permitted, some of which require approval by the Secretary of Labor before they may be made. [29 C.F.R. §§ 3.1, 3.5, 3.6, 3.9]

Q 11:57   What deductions are permissible under the Copeland Anti-Kickback Act?

Deductions for the "reasonable cost" of board, lodging or other facilities or deductions required by federal, state, or local law as permitted under the FLSA (see Chapter 3) are permitted. In addition, the following deductions listed in the regulations are permissible without advance approval from the Secretary of Labor:

1. Deductions made in compliance with federal, state, or local law, such as withholding income taxes.

2. Deductions for sums previously paid to the employee as a bona fide prepayment of wages when such prepayment is made without discount or interest and is made in cash or its equivalent.

3. Deductions of amounts required by court order to be paid to another, unless the deduction is in favor of the contractor, subcontractor, or any affiliated person, or when collusion or collaboration exists.

4. Deductions for employee contributions to funds established by the employer or representatives of employees, or both, for the purpose of providing fringe benefits, provided, however, that all of the following standards are met:

   a. The deduction is not prohibited by law.

   b. The deduction is voluntarily and unconditionally consented to by the employee in writing and in advance of the period in which the work is to be done, or is provided for in a bona fide collective bargaining agreement between the contractor or subcontractor and representatives of its employees.

   c. No profit or other benefit is otherwise obtained, directly or indirectly, by the contractor or subcontractor or any affiliated person in the form of a commission, dividend, or otherwise.

   d. The deduction serves the convenience and interest of the employee.

5. Employee-authorized, voluntary contributions toward the purchase of U.S. Defense Stamps and Bonds.

6. Employee-requested deductions for the repayment of loans to, or to purchase shares in, credit unions organized and operated in accordance with federal and state credit union statutes.

7. Employee-authorized, voluntary contributions to governmental or quasi-governmental agencies, such as the American Red Cross, or to charitable organizations.

8. Lawful deductions for union initiation fees and membership dues pursuant to a collective bargaining agreement between the contractor or subcontractor and representatives of its employees.

9. Deductions for the actual cost of safety equipment of nominal value purchased by the employee as his or her own property for personal protection, such as safety shoes, safety glasses, safety gloves, and hard hats, if such equipment is not required by law to be furnished by the employer and is not prohibited by the FLSA or other law. In addition, the deduction must either be voluntarily and unconditionally consented to by the employee in writing and in advance of the period in which the work is to be done or provided for in a collective bargaining agreement between the contractor or subcontractor and representatives of its employees.

[29 C.F.R. § 3.5]

Any other deduction is permissible only after written application to and approval by the Secretary of Labor, and only when all of the following requirements are met:

1. The contractor, subcontractor, or any affiliated person does not make a profit or benefit directly or indirectly from the deduction in the form of a commission, dividend, or otherwise.

2. The deduction is not otherwise prohibited by law.

3. The deduction is either voluntarily and unconditionally consented to by the employee in writing and in advance of the period in which the work is to be done, or provided for in a bona fide collective bargaining agreement between the contractor or subcontractor and representatives of its employees.

4. The deduction serves the convenience and interest of the employee.

[29 C.F.R. §§ 3.6, 3.9]

The Secretary of Labor approval of these deductions is good for one year on present and future contracts, and may be renewed on further application and approval. [29 C.F.R. § 3.7]

Q 11:58 What are the requirements of the Copeland Anti-Kickback Act?

The Copeland Anti-Kickback Act requires contractors and subcontractors to furnish a weekly statement of wages paid (Form WH 347 or WH 348, available from the Government Printing Office) except on contracts of $2,000 or less. The statement must be sent within seven days of the regular payment date of the payroll period to the state or federal representative for the project or the contracting agency. As with the other Acts discussed in this chapter, payroll records and weekly payroll reports must be preserved for three years from the date of completion of the contract. [40 U.S.C. § 3145; 29 C.F.R. §§ 3.3, 3.4]

Q 11:59 What are the penalties for failure to comply with the Copeland Anti-Kickback Act?

Contractors or subcontractors that violate the Copeland Anti-Kickback Act by requiring a person performing covered contract work to agree to an impermissible deduction may be fined or imprisoned for not more than five years, or both. [18 U.S.C. § 874]

Chapter 12

Litigation and Defense Issues: Portal to Portal Act

The Portal to Portal Act (Portal Act) was enacted May 4, 1947. It contains provisions that, in certain circumstances, affect the rights and liabilities of employees and employers with regard to alleged underpayments of minimum or overtime wages under the Fair Labor Standards Act (FLSA), the Walsh-Healey Public Contracts Act (Public Contracts Act), and the Davis-Bacon Act. The Portal Act relieves employers, in certain circumstances, from liabilities or punishments to which they might otherwise be subject under the FLSA. The Portal Act does not repeal the FLSA's minimum wage and overtime compensation requirements.

The Portal Act also establishes time limitations for the bringing of lawsuits under the FLSA, the Public Contracts Act, and the Davis-Bacon Act; limits the jurisdiction of the courts with respect to certain claims; and, in other respects, affects an employee's ability to sue under these Acts. This chapter explains how the Portal Act's provisions affect the application of the FLSA to employers and employees. It also explains the Portal Act's provisions regarding its general application, statute of limitations, employer defenses, and liquidated damages. (See Chapter 14 for procedural points and other litigation issues outside of the Portal Act's context.)

General Application

Q 12:1 How does the Portal Act affect pay practices in the workplace?

The Portal Act excludes from the FLSA's minimum wage and overtime pay requirements:

1. Time spent by an employee "walking, riding, or traveling to and from the actual place of performance of his or her principal activity or activities which such employee is employed to perform," and

2. Time spent on any activities that are "preliminary to" (i.e., performed before) or "postliminary to" (i.e., performed after) the employee's principal activities in a workday.

unless such activities are compensated pursuant to the terms of a contract, custom, or practice "between such employee, his agent, or collective bargaining representative and his employer." [29 U.S.C. § 254]

The Portal Act excludes periods of time just before and just after the employee's workday from FLSA coverage, limiting the FLSA's coverage to the period of time during the employee's workday. Thus, work activities that precede or follow an employee's principal duties—and that are not subject to compensation by the terms of an express contract, custom, or practice—need not be counted as work time. However, the general rule remains that activities that are a part of or substantially related to the employee's principal duties are compensable. [29 U.S.C. § 254(a), (b); 29 C.F.R. § 785.9(a)]

Q 12:2 What activities constitute *preliminary and postliminary activities*?

Preliminary and postliminary activities are tasks or actions performed before or after the workday that are not indispensable to performance of a job and are not regarded as part of an employee's principal activities. The Portal Act provides that an employer may exclude these activities from compensable work time unless payment is required by a written or unwritten contract or by a workplace custom or practice. No categorical list of preliminary and postliminary activities (except those named in the Portal Act) can be made, since activities that constitute preliminary or postliminary activities in one situation may be principal activities under other conditions. The following preliminary or postliminary activities are expressly mentioned in the Portal Act: "walking, riding, or traveling to or from the actual place of performance of the principal activity or activities which the employee is employed to perform." Thus, walking, riding, or traveling to or from work are the activities specifically excluded from work time by the Portal Act, in the absence of a contrary contractual provision, custom, or practice. The types of walking, riding, and traveling excluded by the Portal Act are those that occur in the course of an employee's ordinary daily trips between the employee's home or lodging and the actual place where the employee does what he or she is employed to do.

Further, these types of travel are excluded whether they occur on or off the employer's premises. Accordingly, an employer may exclude from hours worked the time that workers spend getting to their job site on the employer's premises (e.g., time spent walking from a plant's entrance to the actual work site). [29 U.S.C. § 254; 29 C.F.R. §§ 790.6(c), 790.7]

Q 12:3   Can a change in workplace conditions transform a noncompensable preliminary or postliminary activity into a compensable principal activity?

Yes. An activity that is preliminary or postliminary under one set of circumstances may be a principal activity under other conditions. Further, if an activity is required by the employer or by the nature of the employees' duties, the time employees spend engaged in the activity is usually compensable. For example, employees who wait for work to begin after voluntarily arriving on the job early are involved in a noncompensable preliminary activity, whereas employees who wait for assignments after reporting in at their scheduled time, as required by the employer, are in a compensable "engaged to wait" status. The difference between the two situations is that in the second the employee is engaged by the employer to wait, but in the first the employee is waiting to be engaged by the employer. [See Skidmore v. Swift & Co., 323 U.S. 134 (1944)]

To determine whether an employee's activity constitutes a principal activity, the courts conduct a fact-specific analysis. Factors considered are whether the activity undertaken is for the benefit of the employee or the employer, the level of discretion the employee can exercise in whether or not to do the task, and how integral the task is to the primary goal of the employee's work. [See Adams v. United States, 471 F.3d 1321 (Fed. Cir. 2006)]

Q 12:4   What are an employer's liabilities and obligations under the FLSA with respect to an employee's principal activities?

The Portal Act does not change, in any way, an employer's liabilities regarding its employees' principal activities. Time devoted to these activities must be taken into account in computing hours worked to the same extent as if the Portal Act had not been enacted. [29 C.F.R. § 790.8(a)]

An employee's principal activities are the activities or duties that the employee is employed to perform. [Armour & Co. v. Wantock, 323 U.S. 126, 132–34 (1944)] The phrase *principal activities* means all activities that are indispensable to the performance of productive work. Thus, the phrase *principal activities* includes all activities that are an integral part of an individual's work. For example, a lathe operator's activities in oiling, greasing, or cleaning the lathe are integral parts of the operator's principal work activity. In addition, a worker's preparatory activities in distributing supplies to the work sites of other employees are part of the employee's principal activities. [29 C.F.R. § 790.8(a), (b)]

Q 12:5   Can an employee's otherwise noncompensable activities be made compensable by an express provision of a written or unwritten contract?

Yes. The Portal Act recognizes that employers can and do pay workers for activities performed outside the hours of the regular workday. The Portal Act's exclusion from compensability does not apply to preliminary or postliminary activities that are compensated under an express provision of a written or unwritten contract. The contract can be an individual or collective agreement, but it must be between an employer and a worker or an employer and the worker's agent or collective bargaining representative. A contract between any other parties (e.g., an employer and a government agency) does not render a preliminary or postliminary activity compensable. [29 U.S.C. § 254(b); 29 C.F.R. § 790.9]

A written contractual provision directing that compensation be paid for certain prework or postwork activities clearly establishes the employer's obligation to treat those activities as paid time. In the case of an unwritten contract, however, two factors must be established to make prework and postwork activity compensable: (1) the intent of the parties to contract for the specific activity in question and (2) the intent of the parties to pay the worker for engaging in that activity. To render the activity compensable, both factors must be apparent from the express terms of the agreement. [29 C.F.R. § 790.9]

Q 12:6   Can a prework or postwork activity be made compensable in the absence of an express provision of a written or unwritten contract?

Yes. A preliminary or postliminary activity can be made compensable by a custom or practice that is not inconsistent with the provisions of an existing contract in effect at the location where the worker is employed. This custom or practice scenario applies to situations in which an employer has voluntarily, as a matter of general practice, paid employees for certain prework or postwork activities performed. In addition to the requirement that the practice not be inconsistent with an existing contract, the following four conditions must be met for such activities to be compensable:

1. The custom or practice at issue must be observed or followed at the employer's workplace or place of business (i.e., an industry-wide or geographic practice is not sufficient).

2. The contract, custom, or practice must be in effect at the time that the activity is being performed (i.e., claims may not be based on provisions or practices that were either terminated before or adopted after the activity occurred).

3. The activity in question must be engaged in during the particular time of day envisioned by the contract, custom, or practice.

4. The custom or practice must apply to the specific activity in question (e.g., a practice of paying for wash-up time does not ensure the compensability of the travel time between the washroom and the facility's exit).

[29 C.F.R. §§ 790.10–790.12]

If a contract is silent as to whether an activity is compensable, a custom or practice to pay for the activity is not inconsistent with the contract.

The fact that certain preliminary or postliminary activities outside of the normal workday may be compensated pursuant to contract, custom, or practice in no way affects the compensability of activities performed within the workday proper. There is no requirement, however, as there is with regard to contracts, that the custom or practice be one "between such employee, his agent, or collective bargaining representative and his employer." [29 C.F.R. § 790.9(d)]

If an employer pays employees for preliminary or postliminary activities because of contract, custom, or practice, these hours count as hours worked under the FLSA. An exception applies to paid commuting time. Even if an employer agrees to compensate workers for ordinary travel time between home and work, that travel time need not be counted as hours worked under the FLSA. [29 C.F.R. §§ 785.34, 790.5]

A company with a contract requirement or custom of paying for prework or postwork activities does not have to pay for more time spent in these activities than is called for by the contract or custom. This is true even when the employee is required to and spends more time in the activity than is provided for in the custom or agreement. [Hoover v. Wyandotte Chems. Corp., 455 F.2d 387 (5th Cir. 1972)]

Q 12:7   Are there any provisions of the FLSA that are not directly affected by the provisions of the Portal Act?

Yes. For example, the provisions of the Portal Act do not directly affect FLSA Section 15(a)(1), which bans shipments in interstate commerce of "hot" goods—those goods produced by employees who are not paid in accordance with the FLSA's requirements. In addition, the Portal Act does not affect FLSA Section 11(c), which requires employers to keep records in accordance with the regulations prescribed by the Wage and Hour Division Administrator. Further, the Portal Act does not affect the provision in FLSA Section 15(a)(3) banning discrimination against employees who assert their rights under the FLSA. Finally, the Portal Act does not affect the provision in FLSA Section 12(a) banning from interstate commerce goods produced in establishments in which oppressive child labor is employed. [29 C.F.R. § 790.2]

Q 12:8   Is there a threshold amount of noncompensated time that must be spent on prework or postwork activities for an employee to receive compensation for that time under the FLSA?

Maybe. For federal employees, the Office of Personnel Management (OPM) has established a *de minimis* rule, providing that time spent on preliminary or postliminary activities is compensable only when it exceeds ten minutes. For example, a store cashier's preliminary activities, which consisted of receiving money and information and lasted no more than ten minutes, has been declared too insignificant to require compensation under the FLSA. The *de minimis* rule applies by analogy to FLSA cases in the private sector, because Congress gave both the Department of Labor (DOL) and the OPM substantive rule-making authority in this regard to achieve compatibility between the administration of the FLSA throughout the public and private sectors. [Riggs v. United States, 30 Wage & Hour Cas. (BNA) 84 (Cl. Ct. 1990)] Results in the private sector have been mixed, and some courts have held that if the time can be measured without an undue administrative burden, it is not *de minimis*. However, "the ability of the employer to maintain records is a factor. And, where the compensable preliminary work is truly minimal, it is the policy of the law to disregard it." [*See* Reich v. New York City Transit Auth., 45 F.3d 646 (2d Cir. 1995)] Under that rule, only a very few minutes would be considered *de minimis* (see also Q 7:85). [29 C.F.R. § 785.47]

Q 12:9   Can employees agree to waive their FLSA right to compensation for travel time that is a principal activity?

No. If employees' travel time is an integral and indispensable part of the principal activities for which they are hired, no mutual agreement can waive the application of the FLSA minimum and overtime wage provisions to that work. Such travel time constitutes a compensable principal activity rather than a noncompensable preliminary or postliminary task. Generally, FLSA rights cannot be abridged by contract or otherwise waived because doing so would nullify the purposes of the statute and thwart the legislative policies that it was designed to effectuate. If an employer attempts to rely on such a waiver of rights, it will be the employer's burden to prove (1) the existence of the contractual agreement in which the employee waived his or her right to compensation for travel time, and (2) the legality of the contractual agreement under the FLSA. [Baker v. Barnard Constr. Co., 146 F.3d 1214 (10th Cir. 1998)]

Q 12:10   Do the Portal Act amendments nullify employees' state law claims for the payment of minimum wages and overtime compensation?

No. For a federal statute to displace all state laws on a subject, there must be a clear and manifest purpose of Congress to supersede state laws. Under their police powers, states possess broad authority to regulate employment relationships for the protection of workers. Congressional intent to preempt state laws may be found in three ways. First, such intent may be expressed in the statute. Congress did not expressly state such an intent in the FLSA or the Portal Act amendments. Second, congressional intent to preempt state law may be inferred when the scheme of federal regulation is sufficiently comprehensive to infer that Congress left no room for supplementary state regulation. The FLSA's saving clause, which provides that state law requirements apply where they are more stringent than the provisions of the FLSA, reveals that Congress did not intend to occupy the field of wage and labor law exclusively. Finally, congressional intent to preempt state law may be inferred when the state law actually conflicts with the federal law. Such a conflict may exist either because it is impossible to comply with both the federal law and the state law, or because the state law stands as an obstacle to the fulfillment of Congress's purposes and objectives.

When dealing with a preemption issue, it is helpful to consider why the Portal Act was enacted. The Portal Act was enacted not in response to state actions, but in response to judicial interpretations of the FLSA that could have had devastating effects on employers. Before enactment of the Portal Act, courts interpreted the FLSA to require compensation for preliminary activities, such as walking and other travel. Thus, the Portal Act did not result from an excess of state wage claims that were more beneficial to employees. Significantly, when discussing the Portal Act's statute of limitations, congressional commentary expressly stated that the Portal Act's limitations period does not apply to actions brought to recover wages under state laws. Clearly, Congress envisioned that state-based claims for wages could be asserted and governed by separate procedures. [29 U.S.C. § 255]

Therefore, state wage actions, which sometimes may provide plaintiffs with more procedural advantages and remedies than those contained in the FLSA, do not frustrate the enforcement of the FLSA. In addition, state procedures and remedies apply to state wage actions, whereas federal procedures and remedies apply to federal wage actions. Consequently, the Portal Act does not preempt an employee's state law claims for the payment of minimum wages and overtime compensation. [Maccabees Mut. Life Ins. Co. v. Perez-Rosado, 641 F.2d 45, 46 (1st Cir. 1981); Aragon v. Bravo Harvesting, Inc., 1 Wage & Hour Cas. 2d (BNA) 982 (D. Ariz. 1993)]

Q 12:11   Can a plaintiff sue under the Portal Act and FLSA in either state or federal court?

Yes. Both state and federal courts have concurrent jurisdiction over Portal Act and FLSA wage actions brought by employees or by the Secretary of Labor for unpaid minimum wages and overtime pay. [29 U.S.C. § 216(b), (c)] The Secretary of Labor, however, may only seek an injunction against an employer in federal district court, not state court. Further, because such lawsuits are also within the original subject matter jurisdiction of federal district courts, most courts today allow a Portal Act and FLSA action to be removed from state court to federal district court as a matter of right and with no federal judge discretion to remand the matter to state court. [*See, e.g.*, Troutt v. Stavola Bros., 2 Wage & Hour Cas. 2d (BNA) 924, 925 (M.D.N.C. 1994)]

The United States Supreme Court held in May 2003 that a lawsuit brought under the FLSA can be removed as a matter of right from state to federal court, in *Breuer v. Jim's Concrete of Brevard*. [538 U.S. 691 (2003)] The Supreme Court held that language in the FLSA, which states that a case "may be maintained against any employer . . . in any federal or state court of competent jurisdiction," did not mean that a claim filed in state court could not be removed to federal court. The Court specifically rejected the plaintiff's pragmatic argument that many FLSA claims are for such small amounts that removal to federal court may make it less convenient and more expensive for employees to vindicate their rights effectively. The Court noted that this may be true, but it does not justify creating an exception to the removal statute for FLSA claims. The Court noted that other federal laws, such as the Age Discrimination in Employment Act, the Employee Polygraph Protection Act, and the Family and Medical Leave Act, incorporate or use the same language as used in the FLSA. The Court held that the plaintiff cannot have a removal exception for the FLSA without entailing exceptions for other statutory actions, to the point that it becomes just too hard to believe that a right to "maintain" an action was ever meant to displace the right to remove. Those involved in litigation under the FLSA or other federal laws will be relieved to know that the Court has reinforced the right of a defendant/employer to remove a case to federal court where appropriate.

Statute of Limitations

Q 12:12 Is there a time limit within which an employee must file a lawsuit under the FLSA?

Yes. The Portal Act establishes a two-year statute of limitations for unpaid minimum wages, overtime compensation, or liquidated damages running from the date an action is filed in court, except that a cause of action arising out of a willful violation is subject to a three-year statute of limitations. These are maximum periods for bringing such actions, measured from the time the employee's cause of action accrues until the time the employee's action is commenced. [29 U.S.C. § 255; 29 C.F.R. § 790.21(a)] The Portal Act provides that a cause of action is commenced:

1. In individual actions, on the date the complaint is filed; and
2. In collective or class actions, as to an individual claimant:
    a. On the date the complaint is filed, if the claimant is named in the complaint as a party plaintiff and his or her written consent to become a party plaintiff is filed along with the complaint, or
    b. On the date when the claimant's written consent to become a party plaintiff is filed with the court if it was not so filed with the complaint or if the claimant was not then named as a party plaintiff.

[29 C.F.R. § 790.21(b)]

Q 12:13 When is a cause of action deemed to accrue for purposes of the Portal Act and the FLSA?

Generally, an FLSA action accrues at each regular payday immediately following the workweek during which services are rendered and for which overtime compensation or minimum wages are claimed. The courts have held that an FLSA cause of action accrues when the employer fails to pay the required compensation for any workweek at the regular payday for the period in which the workweek ends. [Knight v. Columbus, 19 F.3d 579 (11th Cir. 1994); Karr v. City of Beaumont, 950 F. Supp. 1317, 1325 (E.D. Tex. 1997)] Thus, for an overtime or minimum wage violation that continues over several or many pay periods, a new cause of action accrues with each paycheck that contains less pay than it should.

When a plaintiff's complaint alleges that his or her employer violated the FLSA each time it issued a paycheck during the time period following a wage reduction (e.g., each paycheck issued biweekly over a five-year span), such a pay practice may constitute a continuing violation for purposes of the FLSA. Because each violation gives rise to a new cause of action, each failure to pay minimum or overtime wages begins a new statute of limitations period as to that particular event. In such a circumstance, the plaintiffs are entitled to recover overtime or minimum wages dating back to the beginning of the statute of limitations period, even if the original unlawful wage reduction occurred outside of the statute of limitations. To invoke this continuing-violation theory, a plaintiff's complaint should allege that the issuance of each paycheck constitutes a separate and distinct violation of the FLSA. [Knight v. Columbus, 19 F.3d 579 (11th Cir. 1994)]

The continuing-violation doctrine does not apply when the plaintiff's complaint is based on a single event that violates the FLSA. For example, if a plaintiff's complaint contends that an employer violated the FLSA through a one-time, unilateral wage reduction, the issuance of subsequent paychecks effectuating that reduction will not constitute a continuing violation of the FLSA. Consequently, only one unlawful act will be deemed to have occurred and the repetitive effects of that act are not continuing violations that renew the limitations period. Significantly, if the original unlawful act occurred outside the statute of limitations period, a plaintiff's claim based on that act will be timebarred. [Alldread v. City of Grenada, 988 F.2d 1425 (5th Cir. 1993); Dunn v. Cobb County, 760 F. Supp. 909 (N.D. Ga. 1991)] When resolving a continuing-violation issue, courts focus on a complaint's allegations of how an employer purportedly violated the FLSA.

In some instances, an employee may receive compensation in the form of incentive or bonus plans that do not permit computation and payment of such sums until after the pay period in which services are rendered. An employee's FLSA action based on such bonus or incentive payments will not accrue until the time when such payment should be made. [See, e.g., Oliver v. Layrisson, 3 Wage & Hour Cas. 2d (BNA) 316 (E.D. La. 1996) (cause of action for compensatory time payout did not accrue until termination of employment when payment became due)]

Q 12:14   Does the Portal Act's statute of limitations bar a plaintiff's discovery of documents or other material generated outside of the limitations period?

No. The statute of limitations does not bar relevant discovery. Thus, discovery that is related to valid claims is permitted, even if it extends to time periods outside of the statute of limitations period. [Smith v. K-Mart Corp., 3 Wage & Hour Cas. 2d (BNA) 156 (E.D. Wash. 1995). *But see* Boehm v. EF Hutton & Co.,

107 Lab. Cas. (CCH) ¶ 34,998 (S.D.N.Y. 1987) (discovery limited to statute of limitations period)]

Q 12:15   When does an employer have to raise the statute of limitations defense?

The Portal Act's statute of limitations serves as a procedural limit on available remedies. Accordingly, the statute of limitations defense must be pled as an affirmative defense in a responsive pleading, such as an answer to the complaint or a motion to dismiss. Such defense may not be raised for the first time at trial or on appeal. [Brock v. Wackenhut Corp., 662 F. Supp. 1482, 1487 (S.D.N.Y. 1987); Hodgson v. Humphries, 454 F.2d 1279 (10th Cir. 1972)]

Q 12:16   Can a plaintiff amend his or her pleading under the FLSA after the expiration of the statute of limitations period?

Generally yes, depending upon whether the plaintiff is doing so before or after a date set by court scheduling order to amend the pleadings, and if the amendment relates back to the date of the original pleading in accordance with Federal Rule of Civil Procedure 15. To establish that an amendment relates back, it is the plaintiff's burden to show that the same transaction is the basis of the original pleading and of the amendment, the same kind of evidence will prove the amendment, and the employer is not unfairly surprised by the amendment. [Rural Fire Prot. Co. v. Hepp, 366 F.2d 355, 362 (9th Cir. 1966)]

If the plaintiff attempts to amend the pleadings to add an FLSA claim before the deadline to amend the pleadings set by court scheduling order (but after the original complaint was answered), the plaintiff will typically be allowed to do so under the procedures of Rule of Civil Procedure 15(a) (which provides in this situation that the permission of the court to amend the pleadings "shall be freely given when justice so requires"). On the other hand, however, if a plaintiff waits to attempt to amend the pleadings to add an FLSA claim until after the expiration of the deadline to amend the pleadings as set by court order, plaintiff will be permitted to do so by the judge only upon a showing of good cause pursuant to Federal Rule of Civil Procedure 16(b). The good cause standard is a higher standard for plaintiff to overcome, especially if the plaintiff knew of or could readily have discovered the information supporting the additional allegations at the time the original lawsuit was filed. [Sosa v. Airprint Sys., Inc., 133 F.3d 1417 (11th Cir. 1998) (denying plaintiff's request to amend complaint after the time prescribed by the district court's scheduling order due to plaintiff's lack of diligence demonstrated in part by the fact that the information supporting the allegations in her amended complaint was known and/or readily available to her at the time the original complaint had been filed)]

Q 12:17   What types of events will toll (i.e., stop the running of) the Portal Act's statute of limitations?

The initiation of litigation will toll the statute of limitations for each party plaintiff and each representative party. FLSA class action suits are distinct from other federal class actions. Other class actions require prospective plaintiffs to affirmatively opt out of inclusion in the class and therefore the initiation of the class action tolls the statute of limitations for all members of the alleged class. In an FLSA class action, on the other hand, the prospective plaintiffs must opt in to the class and their statute of limitations will not be tolled until they do. In an FLSA class action lawsuit, the limitations period is tolled by the filing of the written consent of the party plaintiffs. A copy of a consent form for each named plaintiff must be attached to the original complaint and must contain each plaintiff's signature beneath a typewritten statement requesting legal action under the FLSA to secure minimum and overtime wages allegedly due. Unnamed plaintiffs' statutes of limitations are not tolled until they file their individual consent forms. [29 U.S.C. §§ 216(b), 257]

A plaintiff may also toll the statute of limitations by showing that the employer concealed its unlawful acts, thereby preventing the plaintiff from becoming aware of the acts and/or the resultant injury. [Udvari v. United States, 28 Fed. Cl. 137, 1 Wage & Hour Cas. 2d (BNA) 591 (Ct. Cl. 1993)] In addition, an employer's affirmative misrepresentations to employees regarding their pay or FLSA rights will equitably toll the statute of limitations, even if the representation was not made negligently or fraudulently. Further, an employer's failure to display a DOL poster advising employees of their FLSA rights can toll the running of the limitations period. [Kamens v. Summit Stainless, Inc., 586 F. Supp. 324 (E.D. Pa. 1984); *see also* Baba v. Grand Cent. P'ship, Inc., 142 Lab. Cas. (CCH) ¶ 34,181, 2000 U.S. Dist. LEXIS 17876 (S.D.N.Y. 2000)]

Q 12:18   What actions will not toll the running of the Portal Act's statute of limitations?

An employee's filing of an administrative claim does not toll or otherwise affect the limitations period. An employee is not required, however, to choose between pursuing either administrative or judicial relief, but, rather, may satisfy the requirements of the statute of limitations by filing a lawsuit and thereafter applying for a stay of such legal proceeding pending the outcome of his or her administrative remedies. [Aguilar v. Clayton, 452 F. Supp. 896 (E.D. Okla. 1978)] In addition, the limitations period is not tolled by an employer's delay in fulfilling its offer to make minimum or overtime wage payments when the plaintiffs had actual notice of their potential claims and failed to take appropriate legal action. Third, the limitations period is not tolled by an investigation conducted by the Wage and Hour Division, since such investigation does not prevent the filing of a complaint. Further, the limitations period is not equitably tolled by private settlement negotiations between the employee and employer, unless the employer acted in bad faith or deceitfully lured the plaintiff into settlement discussions to cause the employee to miss the appropriate filing date. [Pfister v. Allied Corp., 539 F. Supp. 224 (S.D.N.Y. 1982)] Negotiating parties may, however, execute a tolling agreement that serves to toll the statute of limitations until settlement negotiations have concluded.

Tolling of a statute of limitations based upon the employer's misconduct in causing a plaintiff to delay bringing suit is a limited concept. The statute of limitations will not be tolled indefinitely as a result of such misconduct. A plaintiff claiming equitable tolling of the statute of limitations on this basis must show that he or she brought his or her claim within a reasonable time after the facts giving rise to the equitable tolling have ceased. Thus, where plaintiffs waited three years after the alleged employer misconduct (which consisted of promises of enhanced benefits and threats) had stopped to bring their claim, there could be no equitable tolling based on that conduct. [Baba v. Grand Cent. P'ship, Inc., 142 Lab. Cas. (CCH) ¶ 34,181, 2000 U.S. Dist. LEXIS 17876 (S.D.N.Y. 2000)]

Q 12:19 Can an employee's agent or representative bring an FLSA lawsuit on behalf of the employee?

No. An FLSA complaint for underpayment of minimum or overtime wages may not be brought by an employee's agent or representative (such as in the name of a union). Rather, the employee is required to bring the action for himself or herself and others similarly situated, and all such employees must consent in writing to become parties to the lawsuit. The filing of the consent form may occur after the filing of the complaint, but the claim is not asserted for purposes of the statute of limitations until both the complaint and the individual's written consent are filed. [29 U.S.C. § 216(b); 29 C.F.R. § 790.20]

However, although a union is prohibited by the Portal Act from bringing a claim on behalf of employees seeking monetary relief under the FLSA, a union or association of employees could make the initial contact with the DOL concerning alleged FLSA violations and solicit and advise its members to bring suit. [Arrington v. Nat'l Broad. Co., 531 F. Supp. 498, 503, 25 Wage & Hour Cas. (BNA) 479 (D.D.C. 1982) (rejecting the argument that the action was really a representative action barred by the Portal Act where the union appeared to be the real (but unnamed) party in the litigation and was financing the lawsuit)]

Q 12:20 Is it possible for employees to sue anonymously under the FLSA?

Yes, although this should occur very rarely. For example, garment workers in the United States Commonwealth of Saipan were permitted to anonymously bring claims of gross underpayment of wages, unlawful deductions for forced purchases, and failure to keep adequate records based on their stated fears of physical retribution and reprisals. The court ruled that the plaintiffs' fears and need for anonymity outweighed any prejudice to the defendants. [Does I Thru XXIII v. Advanced Textile Corp., 214 F.3d 1058 (9th Cir. 2000)] It is possible that other anonymous cases could arise out of claims from workers in the garment industry, agriculture, or meat processing, where use of immigrant labor is high.

Q 12:21 When is a violation of the FLSA a willful violation?

A violation of the FLSA is willful when the evidence shows that the employer either knew that its actions violated the FLSA's regulations or showed reckless disregard for the FLSA's rules. The issue of whether an employer willfully violated the FLSA is a factual question. A willful violation extends the statute of limitations to three years for purposes of collecting back wages. [29 U.S.C. § 255]

In 1988, the Supreme Court adopted a fairly lenient willfulness standard favoring employers. The Supreme Court ruled that a violation of the FLSA is willful for purposes of triggering a third year of liability when the employer acts with actual knowledge or reckless disregard of whether its conduct was prohibited. The Court declared that the term *willful* is generally understood to refer to conduct that is not merely negligent. In other words, an employer does not act willfully merely because it knows that the FLSA is "in the picture," but rather must know or show reckless disregard for whether its conduct is prohibited by the FLSA. Thus, the Court's decision encourages employers to obtain legal guidance on their wage payment plans to bolster their defenses to employees' claims for a third year of wage and hour liability. [McLaughlin v. Richland Shoe Co., 486 U.S. 128 (1988)]

Q 12:22   How specific must an employee's complaint be regarding the employer's willful violation of the FLSA?

An employee is permitted to allege generally the employer's willful violation of the FLSA. Under Federal Rule of Civil Procedure 9(b), malice, intent, knowledge, and other conditions of a person's mind may be alleged generally. If this were not the case, it would be virtually impossible to allege willfulness without presenting all of the evidence bearing on the matter at issue. [Pfister v. Allied Corp., 539 F. Supp. 224, 228 (S.D.N.Y. 1982)]

Q 12:23   What type of employer conduct is considered willful under the FLSA?

An employer's awareness of the FLSA's provisions and amendments makes its failure to pay minimum and overtime wages a willful violation, thereby incurring a three-year statute of limitations. Similarly, an employer's practice of knowingly maintaining inaccurate time records combined with its failure to seek advice of legal counsel concerning the legality of its pay plan constitutes a willful violation of the FLSA. In addition, an employer that knowingly ignores impending changes in the FLSA's coverage of its employees will be found in willful violation of the FLSA. [Marshall v. Sam Dell's Dodge Corp., 451 F. Supp. 294 (N.D.N.Y. 1978)]

Evidence of a knowing failure to maintain accurate records combined with an employer's lack of rebuttal evidence will likely lead to a finding of willfulness. [Jarrett v. ERC Props., Inc., 211 F.3d 1078, 1083 (8th Cir. 2000) (employer failed to present any evidence or testimony to contradict employee's testimony and evidence that, despite her nonexempt classification, she was told to write only 40 hours on her timesheet and also told she would not be paid overtime)]

Q 12:24 What can an employer do to avoid a third year of liability under the FLSA?

If an employer acts reasonably in determining its legal obligations under the FLSA, its actions are not considered willful. For example, an employer should not be held in willful violation of the FLSA if it reviews the FLSA's requirements, relies on an opinion letter drafted by a responsible attorney, and acts in accordance with the reasonable advice contained in that opinion letter. [Dalheim v. KDFW-TV, 712 F. Supp. 533 (N.D. Tex. 1989), aff'd, 918 F.2d 1220 (5th Cir. 1990)] Further, an employer's actions will not be willful when the employer relies on an administrative ruling or opinion letter. In fact, an employer's liability may be completely excused when the employer actually relies on an applicable opinion letter or ruling. [See 29 U.S.C. § 259(a)]

(See also the more detailed discussion related to this good-faith defense in Qs 12:25, 12:36.)

Employer Defenses

Q 12:25 How can an employer avoid liability under the FLSA?

An employer can avoid liability for a violation of the FLSA when it can show that its act was taken in good-faith reliance on, and in conformity with, a written administrative regulation, order, ruling, approval or interpretation, or an administrative practice or enforcement policy with respect to the class of employers to which it belonged. To provide such a defense, the regulation, etc., must be that of the appropriately authorized government agency and it must be in writing. Further, the employer's act or omission must be both "in conformity with" and "in reliance on" the administrative regulation, order, ruling, approval, interpretation, practice, or enforcement policy. Finally, the employer's conformance and reliance must be made "in good faith." It is the employer's burden to both plead and prove all of the requirements of this defense. Thus, the employer's defense of good-faith reliance on an administrative regulation, etc., must be asserted as an affirmative defense. This defense is most often raised based on reliance on a Wage and Hour Division interpretative bulletin or on an official opinion letter issued by the Wage and Hour Administrator to an individual employer (some of which are published). [29 U.S.C. §§ 258, 259; 29 C.F.R. § 790.13]

Q 12:26 What must an employer do to be in conformity with the regulation, etc.?

An employer must actually conform to the regulation, opinion letter, etc., in question. An employer loses the benefit of the good-faith reliance defense if it cannot show that its actions being complained of actually were in accordance with the administrative regulation, etc. (i.e., the defense does not apply to an employer that failed to comply with advice contained in an opinion letter issued by the Wage and Hour Administrator). One example of an employer not acting in conformity with an administrative regulation, etc., is a situation in which an employer receives an opinion letter stating that its employees are exempt from the FLSA's coverage under certain specified circumstances and the employer relies on that opinion without meeting each of the circumstances listed in the letter. The employer might assume that one of the listed circumstances, which does not apply to the employees in question, is irrelevant. But by not meeting each of the circumstances in the letter, the employer could not be considered to be acting in conformity with the administrative ruling. [29 C.F.R. § 790.14]

Q 12:27   Is the good-faith requirement judged from an objective or subjective point of view?

Both. The legislative history of the Portal Act makes it clear that the employer's good faith is not to be determined merely from the employer's actual state of mind. The good-faith requirement also depends on an objective test to determine whether the employer, in acting or omitting to act and in relying on the regulation, etc., acted as a reasonably prudent person would have acted under the same or similar circumstances. The good-faith standard requires that the employer have honest intentions and no knowledge of circumstances that ought to put on it a duty of inquiry.

One example of this principle occurs where the Wage and Hour Administrator's ruling was expressly based on certain court decisions and the employer subsequently learns that those decisions have been reversed by a higher court. If the employer, after learning of this, makes no further inquiry and continues to pay its employees in violation of the FLSA based on its reliance on the Wage and Hour Administrator's earlier ruling, in a subsequent lawsuit it may not have a good-faith defense because it knew facts that would compel a reasonably prudent person to inquire further. Thus, if an employer fails to act on knowledge that would have caused a reasonable person to inquire further, the employer has not relied in good faith within the meaning of the Portal Act. [29 C.F.R. § 790.15]

Q 12:28   Is the good-faith reliance defense available to an employer that violates the FLSA while acting in conformity with a DOL opinion letter of which the employer was unaware?

No. In addition to acting in good faith and in conformity with an administrative regulation, etc., the employer must prove that it *actually* relied on it. If an employer has no previous knowledge of the Wage and Hour Administrator's opinion letter, such as one stating that similar employees are exempt from the provisions of the FLSA, the employer's failure to comply with the FLSA could not have been "in reliance on" that interpretation. Accordingly, the employer has no defense under the Portal Act. [29 C.F.R. § 790.16]

Q 12:29   What is meant by the phrase *administrative regulation, order, ruling, approval, interpretation, administrative practice, or enforcement policy?*

The terms *regulation* and *order* are used to refer to the authoritative rules of an administrative agency, issued pursuant to statute, which have the binding effect of law. The term *interpretation* is used to describe an advisory statement, which indicates merely the agency's present belief concerning the meaning of applicable statutory language. This term includes bulletins, releases, and other statements issued by an agency that interpret the provisions of a statute.

The term *ruling* refers to an interpretation made by an agency in response to an individual request for a ruling on particular questions. An agency's opinion letters, which express opinions on the application of the law to a particular set of facts, fall within this description.

The term *approval* includes the granting of licenses, permits, certificates, or other forms of permission by an agency pursuant to its statutory authority.

The terms *administrative practice* or *enforcement policy* refer to courses of conduct or policies which an agency has determined to follow in the administration and enforcement of a statute, either generally, or with respect to specific classes of situations. Administrative practices and enforcement policies differ from administrative regulations, orders, rulings, approvals or interpretations in that they are not limited to matters concerned with the meaning or legal effect of the statutes administered by the agency and may be based wholly or in part on other considerations. For example, the agency may issue a general statement indicating that in its opinion a certain class of employees comes within a specified FLSA exemption in any workweek when they do not engage in a substantial amount of nonexempt work. Such a statement is an "interpretation" within the meaning of Sections 9 and 10 of the Portal Act. In contrast, the agency may state that for purposes of enforcement, until further notice, such an employee will be considered as engaged in a substantial amount of nonexempt work in any workweek when he spends in excess of a specified percentage of his time in such nonexempt work. This latter type of statement announces an *administrative practice or enforcement policy* within the meaning of Sections 9 and 10 of the Portal Act. Furthermore, an administrative practice or enforcement policy may even be at variance under certain circumstances with the agency's current interpretation of the law. For example, the agency may announce an intention not to commence enforcement of a new court interpretation of a provision of the law until the expiration of a specified period, in order to give affected employers an opportunity to make the necessary adjustments to comply. (Many U.S. Department of Labor (DOL) Wage and Hour Division enforcement policies are written in its Field Operations Handbook (FOH) that is available in most part through a Freedom of Information Act (FOIA) request to the federal government, and is also available on the DOL Web site, www.dol. gov.)

The phrase *administrative regulation, order, ruling, approval, interpretation, administrative practice, or enforcement policy* refers to affirmative action by an agency. An administrative agency's failure to act or failure to reply to an inquiry does not constitute a regulation, order, ruling, approval, interpretation, practice, or enforcement policy within the meaning of the Portal Act. Thus, the Wage and Hour Administrator's silence in response to an employer's FLSA inquiry does not equate to agreement with the employer's perspective. If the employer thereafter acts on the mistaken belief that the silence indicated agreement, the employer's reliance is not a reliance on an administrative regulation, etc., within the meaning of the Portal Act and the employer will be held liable for violating the FLSA. [29 C.F.R. §§ 790.17, 790.18]

Q 12:30   Is the good-faith reliance defense available to an employer that unwittingly relies on a rescinded administrative regulation, etc.?

No. An employer does not have a defense unless the regulation, etc., on which it relies is in effect and operation at the time of the reliance. To the extent that it has been rescinded, modified, or determined to be invalid, it is no longer a regulation, etc., and, accordingly, an employer's subsequent reliance on it provides no defense. If an employer's good-faith reliance on a regulation, etc., occurs before the date on which it is rescinded, modified, or determined to be invalid, however, the employer has a legitimate good-faith defense for FLSA violations that occur before that date. [29 C.F.R. § 790.17(h)]

Q 12:31   Is the good-faith reliance defense available to an employer that does not receive actual notice of a Wage and Hour Administrator's interpretation letter rescinding or modifying an earlier interpretation?

No. Even if the employer did not receive actual notice of a published statement that an earlier interpretation was rescinded, the employer is afforded no defense. Once the Wage and Hour Administrator's initial interpretation is rescinded by a subsequent interpretation or statement, the original interpretation ceases to be an administrative regulation, etc., within the meaning of the Portal Act, notwithstanding the employer's lack of notice of the rescission. Accordingly, an employer that fails to comply with the new interpretation is in violation of the FLSA. [29 C.F.R. § 790.17(i)]

Q 12:32   What is meant by the term *administrative practice or enforcement policy* as used in the good-faith reliance defense?

The term *administrative practice or enforcement policy* refers to courses of conduct or policies that an agency has decided to follow in the administration and enforcement of a statute, either generally or with respect to certain classes of situations. Administrative practices and enforcement policies are often set forth in statements addressed by the agency to the public. Although administrative practices and enforcement policies are often based on decisions that the agency has set forth in its regulations, orders, etc., they are not limited to matters concerned with the meaning or legal effect of the statutes administered by the agency. Indeed, an administrative practice or enforcement policy may, under certain circumstances, be at odds with the agency's current interpretation of the law. For example, the Wage and Hour Administrator may respond to a court decision by announcing a change in the exempt status of a certain class of employees but may provide employers with a grace period in which to make necessary adjustments to ensure their compliance with the new interpretation. In such a circumstance, the Wage and Hour Division will not begin to enforce the FLSA on the basis of the new interpretation until the expiration of the grace period. [29 C.F.R. § 790.18]

Q 12:33 Under what circumstances is an employer relieved of liability by relying in good faith on an administrative practice or enforcement policy?

An employer may escape liability by relying in good faith on an administrative practice or enforcement only:

1. When the practice or policy was based on the ground that the specific act or omission in question was not a violation of the FLSA; or

2. When a practice or policy of not enforcing the FLSA with respect to acts or omissions led the employer to believe, in good faith, that the acts or omissions were not violations of the FLSA.

[29 C.F.R. § 790.18(d)]

Q 12:34 Can an employer in one industry rely in good faith on a practice or policy regarding an employer in another industry?

No. An employer has a defense for good-faith reliance on an administrative practice or enforcement policy only when the practice or policy is "with respect to the class of employers to which [the employer] belongs." Thus, a linen supply company serving industrial establishments may not rely in good faith on an enforcement policy pertaining to a window-washing service that serves industrial establishments. [29 C.F.R. § 790.18(g)]

Q 12:35 Can an employer assert the good-faith reliance defense on an administrative practice or enforcement policy based on the fact that Wage and Hour Division inspectors failed to investigate its business's pay practices?

No. Like administrative regulations, etc., administrative practices and enforcement policies require affirmative action by an administrative agency. An agency may have an administrative practice or policy to refrain from taking certain action, or some practice or policy contemplating positive acts of some kind. There must, however, be some evidence of an agency's adoption of such practice or policy through some affirmative action. A failure to investigate, without more, does not establish a policy or practice to treat the employer's action as in compliance with the FLSA. This is because a failure to inspect could be due to a number of reasons other than a policy or practice of nonenforcement. [29 C.F.R. § 790.18(h)]

Q 12:36   Can an employer rely in good faith on an administrative regulation, etc., issued by any agency of the United States?

No. The Portal Act expressly limits the meaning of the term *agency of the United States* to the official or officials actually vested with final authority under the statutes involved. Therefore, an employer is required to prove that the administrative regulation, etc., with which it conformed and on which it relied in good faith was actually that of the authority vested with the power to issue or adopt the regulation, etc., in question. The agencies vested with such final authority are as follows:

- In the case of the FLSA, the DOL Wage and Hour Administrator;
- In the case of the Walsh-Healey Public Contracts Act, the Secretary of Labor or any federal officer used by the Secretary of Labor in the administration of that Act; or
- In the case of the Davis-Bacon Act, the Secretary of Labor.

[29 U.S.C. § 259(b); 29 C.F.R. § 790.19]

Liquidated Damages

Q 12:37   What are *liquidated damages*, and when will an employer be required to pay liquidated damages to an employee under the FLSA?

Liquidated damages are double damages that may be assessed against an employer that violates the overtime or minimum wage provisions of the FLSA. FLSA Section 216(b) states that an employer that violates the FLSA's overtime or minimum wage provisions "shall be liable to the employee or employees affected in the amount of their unpaid minimum wages, or their unpaid overtime compensation . . . , and in an additional equal amount as liquidated damages." Standing alone, this provision would permit every successful employee-plaintiff to receive double damages in a successful FLSA lawsuit; however, the Portal Act provides employers with some relief from FLSA Section 216's liquidated damages provision. Portal Act Section 260 states: "[I]f the employer shows to the satisfaction of the court that the act or omission giving rise to such action was in good faith and that he had reasonable grounds for believing that his act or omission was not a violation of the Fair Labor Standards Act . . . , the court may, in its sound discretion, award no liquidated damages." Courts also have discretion to award liquidated damages in amounts less than

100 percent of the back wages won by successful employee-plaintiffs. [29 U.S.C. §§ 216, 260]

Q 12:38   Is an employer's ignorance of the FLSA a defense to liability for liquidated damages?

No. Courts have held that ignorance of the law is not a defense to liability for liquidated damages. The Portal Act's good-faith standard imposes some duty on the employer's part to investigate potential liability under the FLSA. "Apathetic ignorance is never the basis of a reasonable belief." [Barcellona v. Tiffany English Pub, Inc., 597 F.2d 464, 469 (5th Cir. 1979)]

Q 12:39   What are the consequences of an employer's failure to meet the good-faith and reasonable grounds standard?

If an employer fails to establish that the act or omission giving rise to court action was in good faith and that it had reasonable grounds for believing that its act or omission was not a violation of the FLSA, the court is given no discretion by the statute and is thus required to award liquidated damages. [29 C.F.R. § 790.22(b)]

Q 12:40   What constitutes good faith and reasonable grounds for purposes of the FLSA?

Good faith requires that the employer acted with the honest intention to discover what the FLSA requires and to act in accordance with it. [Brock v. Shirk, 833 F.2d 1326, 1330 (9th Cir. 1987)] Thus, good faith requires some duty to investigate potential liability under the FLSA. The test of whether an employer acted in good faith also has been interpreted to include the objective standard of whether the employer acted as a reasonably prudent person would have acted under similar circumstances. An employer that operates blindly without making an investigation of its responsibilities under the law cannot claim good faith. [Barcellona v. Tiffany English Pub, Inc., 597 F.2d 464, 469 (5th Cir. 1979)]

The requirement that the employer have reasonable grounds that its conduct complies with the FLSA also imposes an objective standard by which to judge the employer's behavior. For example, an employer that acts in accordance with prior DOL investigations and the advice of experienced legal counsel should have reasonable grounds for believing that its conduct complies with the FLSA to possibly avoid the award of liquidated damages, even if otherwise found liable for a violation of the FLSA. [See Dalheim v. KDFW-TV, 712 F. Supp. 533 (N.D. Tex. 1989), and the discussion under Q 12:41]

Q 12:41   Does a court's finding of good faith and reasonable grounds preclude an award of liquidated damages?

No. A court's determination that an employer acted in good faith and on reasonable grounds does not end the matter. The court still retains the discretion to award liquidated damages. An award of liquidated damages under such circumstances, however, is exceedingly rare. Courts have declined to award liquidated damages in the following circumstances (when the suits have been brought by individuals rather than the DOL):

1. The Wage and Hour Administrator was aware of the employer's practices and took no action. [Retail Store Employees Union, Local 400 v. Drug Fair—Community Drug Co., 307 F. Supp. 473, 480 (D.D.C. 1969)]

2. The DOL conducted an investigation that revealed no violation. [Dalheim v. KDFW-TV, 712 F. Supp. 533 (N.D. Tex. 1989)]

3. A regional office of the Wage and Hour Division classified as exempt employees who were later found to be entitled to overtime. [Giannini v. Standard Oil Co., 130 F. Supp. 740, 745 (N.D. Ind. 1955)]

4. A Wage and Hour Division investigator found no violation after inquiring into the employer's payroll. [Knudson v. Lee & Simmons, Inc., 89 F. Supp. 400, 406 (S.D.N.Y. 1949)]

Reasonableness in general is not what the Portal Act demands. An employer may have a good excuse for its mistake in underpaying minimum or overtime wages. In addition, an employer may have acted entirely in good faith. Liability for liquidated damages under the FLSA will attach, however, unless the employer has a certain kind of excuse—a reasonable belief that its acts or omissions did not violate the law. [Thomas v. Howard Univ. Hosp., 39 F.3d 370, 373 (D.C. Cir. 1994)]

Q 12:42   Does a finding of an employer's good faith and reasonable grounds preclude an award of attorneys' fees and court costs?

No. Portal Act Section 11 does not change the provisions of FLSA Section 16(b), under which attorneys' fees and court costs are recoverable when judgment is awarded to the plaintiff. [Luther v. Z. Wilson, Inc., 528 F. Supp. 1166 (S.D. Ohio 1981)]

Q 12:43   Does a finding that an employer did not willfully violate the FLSA for statute of limitations purposes prevent an award of liquidated damages?

No. A finding that an employer did not willfully violate the FLSA for statute of limitations purposes in no way forecloses a finding that the employer did *not* act in good faith for purposes of liquidated damages. Proof of an employer's intentional violation of the FLSA is not necessary to obtain an award of liquidated damages. [Troutt v. Stavola Bros., Inc., 905 F. Supp. 295, 302 (M.D.N.C. 1995)] The two issues are technically separate and subject to different burdens of proof, but obviously the background facts in a case could affect both.

However, it has been held that a finding of willfulness for purposes of the statute of limitations weighs extremely heavily against the possibility of a finding of good faith for purposes of reducing or avoiding liquidated damages. Thus, an employer faced with a three-year statute of limitations because of a finding of willfulness should expect that the plaintiff will also be awarded liquidated damages. [Jarrett v. ERC Props., Inc., 211 F.3d 1078, 1084 (8th Cir. 2000) (jury's finding that employer's actions in not paying overtime were willful weighed against any finding of good faith by the employer for purposes of reducing liquidated damages, particularly where employer offered no evidence of nonwillfulness or good faith in its failure to pay overtime)]

Q 12:44   Can an employer be ordered to pay liquidated damages for failure to keep proper wage records?

Yes. Courts have ordered liquidated damages based on an employer's failure to maintain and provide workers' proper wage records, failure to provide and maintain adequate housing for workers (in the case of migrant farm workers), and failure to post accurate signs informing workers of the terms and conditions of their employment. [Washington v. Miller, 721 F.2d 797 (11th Cir. 1983)]

Q 12:45   Can an employer be held liable for liquidated damages when it pays employees straight-time instead of time and one half for overtime hours worked?

Yes. No defensive good faith is established by an employer based on the fact that it paid only straight-time instead of time and a half for hours worked in excess of 40 hours per week. In such a situation, an award of liquidated damages to a successful plaintiff would likely be required. [*See* Kerew v. Emerson Radio & Phonograph Corp., 76 F. Supp. 197 (S.D.N.Y. 1947)]

Q 12:46   Under the FLSA, is an employer's good faith only relevant to the issue of liquidated damages?

No. Under the FLSA, an employer's good faith is relevant to two distinct issues. First, the employer may raise good faith under FLSA Section 259 (good-faith reliance on and conformity with a written administrative regulation, etc., from the appropriate government agency) as an absolute defense against an employee's claim for minimum or overtime wages. Second, the employer may raise good faith under FLSA Section 260 as a partial defense to the FLSA's liquidated damages provision. [29 U.S.C. §§ 259, 260; L&F Distribs., Inc. v. Cruz, 941 S.W.2d 274, 284 (Tex. App. 1996)]

Q 12:47   Will a court's determination that an employer willfully violated the FLSA result in a mandatory award of liquidated damages?

No. "A finding of willfulness for limitations purposes does not compel an award of liquidated damages." Although an employer's reliance on certain legal advice may not prevent a finding of willfulness for purposes of the statute of limitations, such reliance can insulate the employer from an award of liquidated damages when facts show the employer's good-faith basis for accepting the advice. [Hill v. JC Penney Co., 688 F.2d 370, 375 (5th Cir. 1982) (citing Coleman v. Jiffy June Farms, Inc., 458 F.2d 1139 (5th Cir.), *cert. denied*, 409 U.S. 948 (1972))]

Q 12:48   What should an employer do to avoid liability for liquidated damages?

An employer's best defense against liability for liquidated damages is to:

1. Send a written request for an administrative ruling governing the employer's factual situation to the Wage and Hour Division;

2. Act in conformity with the advice contained in that administrative ruling;

3. Seek the advice of experienced labor law counsel to determine coverage issues under the FLSA as interpreted by court decisions; and

4. Stay abreast of any and all administrative rulings, etc., and court decisions that may rescind, modify, or alter the status of the employees or hours of work in question.

Q 12:49   Must employees arbitrate their claims under the FLSA if they have signed a valid arbitration agreement with their employer?

Probably. In *Circuit City Stores, Inc. v. Adams* [532 U.S. 105 (2001)], the United States Supreme Court ruled that the Federal Arbitration Act applies to employment-related contracts (except those involving workers engaged in transportation of foreign or interstate commerce) and, therefore, employees who sign valid arbitration agreements may be compelled to arbitrate their claims against their employers, including statutory claims. Consistent with this opinion, the Southern District of New York has ruled that employees who sign valid and enforceable arbitration agreements with their employers may be compelled by the employer to arbitrate claims they subsequently bring under the Fair Labor Standards Act. [*See, e.g.,* Martin v. SCI Mgmt. L.P., 296 F. Supp. 2d 462 (S.D.N.Y. 2003); Ciago v. AmeriQuest Mortgage Co., 295 F. Supp. 2d 324 (S.D.N.Y. 2003)]

Chapter 13

Investigations by the Wage and Hour Division

This chapter deals with the practical aspects of why and how a Wage and Hour Division investigation comes about and is conducted. It also addresses possible employer responses and various points during an investigation at which labor counsel should be consulted.

Q 13:1   Who enforces the Fair Labor Standards Act (FLSA)?

The Wage and Hour Division of the Department of Labor (DOL) is responsible for enforcing the FLSA. It investigates alleged violations of the FLSA and inspects employers' records and premises. If it cannot obtain compliance, it may ask the DOL Solicitor to file suit against employers. In addition, individual employees can file lawsuits against their employers under the statute.

The Administrator of the Wage and Hour Division reports to the Assistant Secretary of Labor for Employment Standards Administration, who in turn reports to the Secretary of Labor.

The Wage and Hour Division operates through various branches. Inspection and field services are conducted through a system of regional field and district offices. The Wage and Hour Administrator has the authority to make general investigations and inspections with respect to minimum wage and overtime and investigations and inspections with respect to the employment of child labor. The Wage and Hour Administrator does not have general rule-making authority under FLSA but does issue interpretative bulletins explaining the law. Only the Secretary of Labor has authority to issue FLSA regulations, and only the Secretary can initiate proceedings for the purpose of enforcing the FLSA.

The Complaint

Q 13:2   How does a Wage and Hour Division investigation of an employer come about?

A Wage and Hour Division investigation of an employer usually comes about as a result of a complaint by an employee, a group of employees, or a labor union if the employees are represented. Most of the time, it is a former employee who complains. The Wage and Hour Division has the authority to conduct routine inspections and investigations, but seldom does so because of the large number of complaints it receives and a lack of resources. The reason for an investigation does not have to be disclosed and seldom is. Many investigators simply tell the employer that they are conducting a routine audit.

Q 13:3   Are complaints investigated in the order in which they are received?

No. According to the Wage and Hour Division's internal guidelines, it attempts to schedule investigations based on its assessment of which complaints will reveal the most significant violations.

The Investigation

Q 13:4   What is the scope of a Wage and Hour Division investigation?

It depends. Where the complaint appears to involve only a minor violation affecting one employee or a few employees, the Wage and Hour Division may attempt to conciliate the matter, usually through telephone contacts. In such cases, the investigator often asks the employer to look into the matter and get back to the investigator regarding what the employer discovers. If the employer takes the position that there has been no violation of the FLSA, the investigator may ask to have particular payroll records sent to him or her or ask for additional information. If the complaint cannot be resolved in this fashion, or if additional violations appear during the conciliation process, the Wage and Hour Division may turn this conciliation process into a full-scale investigation. In short, employers must take any contact with the Wage and Hour Division very seriously.

When the Wage and Hour Division intends to conduct a full-scale investigation, an investigator typically advises the employer that an investigation is being conducted and arranges a time to come to the establishment where the violation or violations supposedly occurred to start the investigation. Sometimes the investigator appears at the employer's place of business unannounced, but this is relatively rare because an employer often cannot stop what it is doing to participate in the investigation. Most investigators recognize this and are typically willing to arrange for a convenient time to start the investigation, as long as it does not involve too much delay. The investigation usually covers the establishment at which the violation or violations supposedly occurred, as well as any other operations of the employer in the immediate vicinity of that establishment. The geographic scope of any investigation can be broadened, however, if the Wage and Hour Division believes that practices that violate the FLSA are being used by the employer in operations elsewhere.

The Wage and Hour Division has the right to subpoena payroll records and other employment records that an employer is required to keep under the FLSA, so it is seldom in an employer's best interests to refuse to cooperate with an investigation. It is strongly recommended, however, that an employer that learns about an investigation consult with its labor counsel immediately to obtain further guidance regarding the employer's rights and approaches to use in particular situations.

Q 13:5   What should an employer do when the investigator appears at the employer's place of business?

First, the employer should make sure that the investigator is really an authorized representative of the DOL Wage and Hour Division. Although there are penalties for posing as a federal agent, there have been instances in which unscrupulous individuals acting on behalf of employees, labor unions, or others seeking confidential information about an employer have posed as representatives of some mythical labor board to gain access to information. Cooperating with an authorized representative of the Wage and Hour Division is one thing. Handing confidential employee information over to strangers is another.

Q 13:6   After the employer verifies the investigator's credentials, how does the investigation proceed?

Typically, a Wage and Hour Division investigator wants to meet with whoever at the employer is responsible for employee matters, including payroll. The investigator begins the investigation with an initial interview, in which he or she explains the purpose of the investigation and its scope and assesses whether the employer is covered by the FLSA. Typically, the investigator asks to review the payroll and time records for the two-year period immediately preceding the investigation on the premises. In some cases, it may be advisable for the records to be produced at the employer's attorney's office or another site away from the business operations.

Although the investigator may not review every time record or every payroll register requested, he or she typically spot-checks them looking for minimum wage, overtime, timekeeping, or other potential violations of the FLSA. Improper rounding, deductions from employees' pay that reduce wage rates below the minimum, alterations to time records that reduce hours worked and overtime, and failure to pay for recorded preshift, postshift, or meal-break (work) time are just some of the things investigators are looking for as they review an employer's records. This review may reveal actual violations, or areas that the investigator feels warrant further investigation. The point is, however, that these records are generally the first thing an investigator looks at in an investigation. The more complete and accurate these records are, the less the chance of an expanded and lengthy investigation.

Q 13:7   Does the employer have to give the investigator its payroll and employment records, or copies of them?

The Wage and Hour Division tells its investigators in internal guidelines not to take any records of the employer from the employer's place of business unless they are essential to the investigation and the employer consents. There may be times when the investigator asks for copies of records, and there may also be times when the employer wants to submit copies of certain records to support its position that no violations have occurred. If faced with a request by an investigator to take records, or for copies of these records, it is strongly recommended that the employer consult with its labor counsel regarding an appropriate response.

Q 13:8   Does the investigator check records relating to exempt employees?

Yes. An investigator conducting a full-scale audit almost always asks for the names and titles of anyone the employer claims is exempt under any provision of the FLSA. In reviewing payroll records relating to these individuals, the investigator typically looks to make sure that the individuals are being paid in accordance with whatever exemption is claimed. For example, if the employer claims that an employee is exempt under the executive, administrative, or professional exemption, the investigator usually checks to make sure that the employee has been paid his or her guaranteed salary in any workweek in which the employee performed any work. If the employee has not been paid his or her guaranteed salary, the investigator looks further to see if there is a violation of the "salary basis of payment" requirement for these exemptions. This, however, is not the end of the inquiry in most cases. When there is any question as to the applicability of an exemption, the investigator asks for additional information about the duties of the employees in question and often asks to interview the employees or their supervisors as well.

Q 13:9   Can the investigator interview anyone he or she wants at the employer's place of business?

No. An investigator does not have a "blank check" when it comes to interviewing. There are essentially two types of interview situations. In the first, the investigator asks to interview a manager or supervisor to obtain information about payroll practices or the duties of employees who work for the manager or supervisor. In other words, these employees are being interviewed as representatives of the employer, and anything they say is going to be taken by the Wage and Hour Division as a statement of the employer. For example, the investigator may ask to talk with the supervisor of a particular employee for whom the employer claims the executive exemption to obtain that supervisor's opinion as to the employee's job duties. The employer may provide this information in some other fashion or may be present when such an interview is being conducted. This is a situation that should be discussed with the employer's labor counsel at the time it occurs. Counsel is entitled to be present during an interview of a managerial employee.

In the second situation, the investigator asks to interview employees to verify the adequacy and accuracy of the employer's records or to further investigate alleged violations of the FLSA as applied to those employees. For example, an investigator may ask to talk to a particular supervisor to determine that supervisor's actual job duties or may ask to talk with nonexempt employees to verify that the times recorded on time records are accurate. The Wage and Hour Division tells its investigators that these interviews should be conducted under conditions that assure privacy and confidentiality of the information given. Thus, these interviews may be conducted on the employer's premises, by telephone, or at some other suitable location away from the employer's place of business. Although an employer does not have to make these employees available to be interviewed on its premises during working hours, it may be in its best interests to do so. Employers should discuss this with labor counsel at the time of any investigation. In some cases, counsel may seek affidavits from the employees in advance of any interviews.

Q 13:10　What happens if the employer refuses to cooperate with the Wage and Hour Division in an investigation?

Typically, the Wage and Hour Division issues an administrative subpoena for the employer's records. The Supreme Court has held that the Wage and Hour Division can inspect an employer's payroll records without a search warrant, and it is clear that the Secretary of Labor has broad authority to obtain information from any employer that is relevant to that employer's compliance with the FLSA. The Wage and Hour Division cannot, however, act arbitrarily or in excess of its statutory authority. In other words, information that is not relevant to investigating violations of the FLSA or is otherwise protected does not have to be disclosed. If the employer refuses to comply with a subpoena, the DOL asks a federal court to enforce the subpoena. Because of the scope of the Wage and Hour Division's investigative powers and the substantial penalties that may result from refusal to comply with a valid and enforceable subpoena, it is recommended that labor counsel be consulted before any such outright refusal is undertaken.

Q 13:11　What happens when the investigator completes the investigation?

The investigator has a conference with the employer's representatives to discuss his or her findings. If the investigator believes that there are violations, he or she tells the employer about them. The investigator also tells the employer what he or she believes will be necessary for the employer to bring itself into compliance with the FLSA. This is an important conference for the employer because, in most instances, the investigator attempts to obtain an agreement from the employer's representatives that the employer will bring itself into compliance with the FLSA in the future, and that it will remedy any past violations of the FLSA by payment of allegedly unpaid minimum wages and/or overtime premiums. Depending on the circumstances, actual calculations of back wages may be made by the investigator or may be left to the employer after agreement is reached on general terms for settlement and the method of calculation to be used. If there are factual discrepancies or omissions, or if the employer has other defenses or disagreements to assert, a number of conferences may be held in an effort to resolve these matters at the administrative level.

In calculating back wages due for the failure to pay minimum wage or overtime premiums, the investigator will typically require the employer to do so for all employees in an affected job classification for the preceding two years (unless this is a repeated violation cited in a previous investigation, which may also result in additional Civil Money Penalties (CMP), see Chapter 14 (Qs 14:32–14:36) for a detailed discussion of CMPs), whether the employees are currently employed or not. According to the Wage and Hour Division, an employer cannot simply avoid the payment of back wages to former employees who are unable to be located. For former employees entitled to back wage payments, the investigator will typically allow the employer a reasonable time to notify the former employees based on last address of record with the employer. If the employer is still unable to locate the employees in order to pay back wages owed, the investigator will assert that the employer should pay the money into the U.S. Treasury. The Wage and Hour Division views FLSA Section 16(c), which provides when the Secretary of Labor sues an employer and recovers monetary damages on behalf of employees and former employees to cover them into the U.S. Treasury as miscellaneous receipts after three years of failure to locate these employees, as giving them the same authority in an investigation for monies owed to unlocatable former employees. The Wage and Hour Division's authority to do so in investigations, however, is unclear. Employers may consider following their state law regarding unclaimed property for the monies owed to unlocatable former employees. Labor counsel should be consulted before an employer signs any agreement calling for payment to the U.S. Treasury, to discuss possible alternatives to paying these monies into the U.S. Treasury when unable to directly pay them to the former employees owed the back wages. [29 U.S.C. § 216(c)]

Q 13:12   What happens if the Wage and Hour Division claims violations, but the employer does not agree and refuses to settle?

In this situation, the Wage and Hour Division must decide whether to forward the matter to the DOL Solicitor for court action or merely to inform the employer's employees that it has found that they are owed unpaid minimum wages or overtime. In the latter situation, the Wage and Hour Division also informs employees that they have the right to file a court action to collect these sums. There is no requirement that employees file a complaint with the Wage and Hour Division before resorting to court action.

Q 13:13 If a settlement is finally reached with the Wage and Hour Division, does this protect the employer against lawsuits?

Yes. This is an important point. Under 29 U.S.C. Section 216(c), if back wage payments are made to employees, and accepted by them, where these payments have been reviewed and supervised by the Wage and Hour Division, then the employees' right to sue is extinguished. Likewise, under 29 U.S.C. Section 216(b), if the Department of Labor institutes a lawsuit on behalf of employees, then their rights to sue under FLSA Section 217 are cut off.

However, when an employer, on its own, privately pays employees what it believes to be back wages that are due and owed, there is no protection against lawsuits by either the Department of Labor or the employees, individually or in a class action, seeking additional back wages, liquidated damages, and attorneys' fees. Therefore, it becomes very important that employer interests are protected either by (1) making certain, in writing and even through agreements with the Wage and Hour Division where necessary, that payments have in fact been reviewed and are being supervised by the Wage and Hour Division, even if the employer is the one actually making the bulk of the calculations and/or payments, which is the normal course; (2) making certain that a settlement is reviewed and approved by a judge where the dispute is already in front of a court; or (3) where it is simply a private payment made by an employer, the settlement agreement and release must cover all possible claims that could be made by or on behalf of the employee, including not only minimum wages and overtime pay, but also liquidated damages, attorneys' fees, and costs. Private settlements that do not comport with each of the above could still be subject to attack if they have not been supervised by either the Wage and Hour Division or approved and entered by a court of law.

As long as the Wage and Hour Division is supervising a settlement, it will provide official receipt forms (Form WH-58) for employers to use in completing supervised payments to employees. These official receipt forms should not be provided to an employer unless the Wage and Hour Division has reviewed and agreed with the back wage calculations completed by either the investigator or the employer. In some instances, the Wage and Hour Division has taken the position that where it did not have its investigators review the records and interview employees at a particular location, but rather left the audit up to representatives of the employer, it could not give official receipt forms to the employer for use in paying the individuals, nor would the payments be "supervised," thereby leaving the employer exposed to additional lawsuits, claims, and liability if the matter was not resolved. If this occurs, it becomes imperative for the employer to obtain adequate Wage and Hour Division review and a written agreement that, in fact, the back wage calculations and payments are being supervised by the Wage and Hour Division. This review and agreement on the supervised status of the payments is especially important in cases involving large numbers of employees or large amounts of money, which otherwise could turn into expensive class actions brought in court by private plaintiffs' attorneys.

In a recent case, an employee claimed he had the right to sue for back wages even though he accepted a settlement payment from his employer. According to the employee, the settlement did not bar his right to sue because the DOL did not adequately supervise the payment of back wages. The employee also claimed that he did not waive his right to sue because the employer did not use Form WH-58. An appellate court concluded that the payment of back wages had been adequately supervised by a DOL Regional Director who spent many months negotiating with the employer, arranging for an independent accounting firm to determine the amount of back wages due to employees, and reviewing the determinations of the accounting firm. Moreover, the court said that use of Form WH-58 is not mandatory. The DOL can either authorize an employer to use the WH-58 *or* authorize other waiver language. [29 C.F.R. § 516.2(b)(2)] In this case, the DOL authorized the use of other waiver language that was included in payments to employees. Therefore, that language was sufficient to create an enforceable waiver of the employee's right to sue. [Niland v. Delta Recycling Corp., 377 F.3d 1244 (11th Cir. 2004)]

Chapter 14

Penalties for Violations of the FLSA

This chapter focuses on how the Fair Labor Standards Act (FLSA) is enforced and the penalties that can be imposed when violations of the FLSA are established and the FLSA is enforced. The Secretary of Labor has the authority under the FLSA to supervise the payment of minimum wages and overtime pay wrongfully withheld from employees' compensation and to sue to recover such back wages on behalf of the employees in certain circumstances. The Secretary may seek not only recovery of back wages but also an equal amount of liquidated damages. The Secretary is not limited to suing only on behalf of an employee who submitted a written request that the Secretary bring suit on the employee's behalf. In addition, individuals may bring private suits for themselves and for others similarly situated to recover unpaid minimum wages and overtime under the FLSA.

Recovery of Unpaid Wages and Liquidated Damages

Q 14:1　Who is entitled to enforce the provisions of the Fair Labor Standards Act (FLSA)?

The FLSA can be enforced via several different means:

1. The Department of Labor (DOL) through the Secretary of Labor, can sue to recover back wages and liquidated damages (see Q 14:4) on behalf of aggrieved employees, or can seek injunctive relief to restrain employers from violating the law or to prevent the sale, transportation, etc., of "hot goods" (see Qs 14:68–14:71). [29 U.S.C. §§ 216(c), 217] *Back wages* are minimum wages and/or overtime pay wrongfully withheld from an employee's compensation.

2. The Department of Justice can bring criminal actions for willful violations of the FLSA. [29 U.S.C. § 216(a)]

3. Employees can bring suits, either individually or as collective actions, to recover unpaid wages and liquidated damages on behalf of themselves and others "similarly situated." [29 U.S.C. § 216(b)]

The FLSA also prohibits discrimination or retaliation against employees who have filed a complaint, testified, instituted proceedings, or asserted coverage under the Act. A civil action can be filed individually or collectively alleging prohibited retaliation under the FLSA. [29 U.S.C. § 215(a)(3)]

Thus, the FLSA provides a cause of action both to the wronged employee and to the Secretary of Labor. If the Secretary brings a legal action against the employer, the employee's right of action is automatically terminated by the filing of the Secretary's lawsuit. Subsequently, the employee must depend on the Secretary's attorney to collect any unpaid wages due. [29 U.S.C. § 216(c)]

Q 14:2　What remedies are available if an employer fails to comply with minimum wage and overtime provisions?

An employer that fails to comply with federal or state minimum wage and overtime compensation laws can be ordered to change its pay practices to conform to legal standards. Additionally, the employer can be required to pay, as damages, the amount of minimum wages and overtime compensation that should have been, but was not, paid. An employer can also be required to pay additional damages (i.e., liquidated damages) as a penalty for noncompliance, usually in the same amount as the unpaid minimum or overtime wages. An action to recover such remedies can be maintained against any employer (including a public agency) in any federal or state court of competent jurisdiction by any one or more employees on behalf of themselves and other employees similarly situated. An employee who brings a wage action in federal court can also seek to include claims alleging breach of related state compensation laws. [29 U.S.C. § 216; 28 U.S.C. § 1367]

Q 14:3   How likely is it that an employer will be penalized for an FLSA violation?

Statistics point to an increased effort by the Department of Labor's Wage and Hour Division (WHD) to pursue these violations. In fiscal year 2006, more than 222,000 employees received a total of $135.7 million in minimum wage and overtime back wages as a result of FLSA violations. The WHD collected over $120.5 million in back wages for FLSA overtime violations and more than $15.2 million for FLSA minimum wage violations. Back wages for overtime violations represented roughly 89 percent of all FLSA back wages collected, and the number of employees due overtime back wages represented about 87 percent of all employees due FLSA back wages. Over a third of WHD enforcement resources are attributed to investigations in nine low-wage industries, which include day care, restaurants, janitorial services, and temporary help. In fiscal year 2006, the agency collected nearly $50.6 million in back wages for approximately 86,700 workers in low-wage industries—an increase of over 10 percent of back wages collected in the same low-wage industries during the previous fiscal year.

Q 14:4   What are *liquidated damages* under the FLSA?

Liquidated damages are damages awarded under the FLSA in addition to the back pay unlawfully withheld from the employee. Liquidated damages are assessed as a general rule at an amount equal to the minimum wage and overtime compensation wrongfully withheld. Thus, if an employer, in violation of federal or state wage laws, failed to pay an employee $2,000 in minimum wages and overtime, the employer can be liable to pay $4,000 in compensatory damages to the complaining employee, consisting of $2,000 in withheld compensation and $2,000 in liquidated damages.

FLSA Section 216 states that an employer that violates the overtime and minimum wage provisions of the FLSA "shall be liable to the employee or employees affected in the amount of their unpaid minimum wages, or their unpaid overtime compensation . . . and in an additional equal amount as liquidated damages." Standing alone, this provision would enable the successful employee-plaintiff to receive double damages in every successful lawsuit for back wages. In 1947, however, Congress passed the Portal Act, which provides employers with some relief from the FLSA's liquidated damages provision. Although double damages are intended to compensate the successful employee-plaintiff for the wait and difficulty of collecting the back wages due, FLSA Section 260 states:

> If the employer shows to the satisfaction of the court that the act or omission giving rise to such action was in good faith and that he had reasonable grounds for believing that his act or omission was not a violation of the FLSA, the court may, in its sound discretion, award no liquidated damages.

[29 U.S.C. § 260]

The court is also accorded discretion to award liquidated damages of less than 100 percent of the back wages won by the successful employee-plaintiff. An employer can avoid assessment of liquidated damages if it can demonstrate that it acted in good faith in failing to pay minimum wages or overtime and had a reasonable basis for believing that there was no violation of any federal or state regulation. The employer must show that it honestly intended to ascertain and follow the applicable wage laws. A plea of ignorance does not suffice. (The Portal Act is discussed in Chapter 12.) [29 U.S.C. § 260]

Examples of circumstances in which liquidated damages have been assessed include the following:

1. The employer gave men but not women in similar positions more severance pay; thus violating the Equal Pay Act ("EPA"), which became part of the FLSA in 1963. The court determined that liquidated damages for EPA violations were the "norm." [Rinaldi v. World Book, Inc., 2002 WL 172449 (N.D. Ill. 2002)]

2. The employer never questioned the legality of its pay practices or took any affirmative steps to determine the FLSA's requirements or verify that the FLSA applied to its employees. [See, e.g., Troutt v. Stavola Bros., Inc., 905 F. Supp. 295, 302 (M.D.N.C. 1995)]

3. The employer argued that its pay practices conformed to industry practice. [See, e.g., Martin v. Cooper Elec. Supply Co., 940 F.2d 896, 908 (3d Cir. 1991)]

4. The employer had a history of FLSA violations. [See, e.g., Avitia v. Metro. Club, 49 F.3d 1219, 1223 (7th Cir. 1995)]

5. The employer relied on the terms of a collective bargaining agreement with its workers and a lack of complaints for failing to pay overtime. [Ackler v. Cowlitz County, 2001 U.S. App. LEXIS 2672 (9th Cir. 2001)]

6. An employer that failed to pay an employee of a meat packing plant for time spent donning and doffing protective clothing did not take active steps to ensure that its practices complied with FLSA but instead engaged in "ex post explanation and justification" in an attempt to avoid liability for liquidated damages. [Alvarez v. IBP, Inc., 339 F.3d 894 (9th Cir. 2003), aff'd, 126 S. Ct. 514 (2005)]

7. An employer based its incorrect conclusion that an employee was exempt from overtime on reading it had done concerning the FLSA 20 years earlier. [Friedman v. S. Fla. Psychiatric Assocs., Inc. (11th Cir. 2005)]

Q 14:5 Are liquidated damages available under the FLSA and state law?

No. A successful plaintiff may recover liquidated damages under the FLSA or state law, not both. [Pascoe v. Mentor Graphics Corp., 145 Lab. Cas. ¶ 34,453 (D. Or. 2001)]

Q 14:6   What statute of limitations applies to collecting back pay pursuant to the FLSA?

The FLSA has a two-year statute of limitations on collecting back wages for nonwillful violations of the law. For willful violations, the statute of limitations on collecting back pay is extended to three years. [29 U.S.C. § 255(a)] The same two- or three-year limitations period has also been applied to private actions for retaliatory discharge under FLSA Section 15(a)(3) in which back wages are sought. [Crowley v. Pace Suburban Bus. Div., 938 F.2d 797, 800 (7th Cir. 1991)]

In 1988, the Supreme Court adopted the definition of a willful violation of the FLSA that most employers favor. In *McLaughlin v. Richland Shoe Company* [486 U.S. 128 (1988)], the Court ruled that an employer is guilty of a willful violation, thus triggering a three-year statute of limitations, only when it acts with actual knowledge or reckless disregard of whether its compensation scheme violates the FLSA.

Examples of circumstances in which willful violations were found and, thus, a three-year statute of limitations was applied include the following:

1. An employer with legal training was aware of the minimum wage requirements but had never investigated their potential application to his business. Once aware, the employer attempted to come into compliance by discharging all but one employee. [Ford v. Sharp, 758 F.2d 1018 (5th Cir. 1985)]

2. A company officer had actual notice of the FLSA requirements by virtue of the company's earlier violations, his agreement to pay unpaid overtime, and his assurance of future compliance. [Dole v. Elliott Travel & Tours, 942 F.2d 962, 967 (6th Cir. 1991)]

Employers should know that, while it is difficult for employees to waive their rights under the FLSA, employers may waive the statute of limitations as a defense to an action by employees. First, if the statute of limitations is not raised promptly as a defense, it is waived. Second, prior agreements with the DOL may contain waivers that act against the employer, including a waiver of the statute of limitations, if the DOL ultimately brings suit. For example, a nursing home company sued by the DOL after a prior agreement with the DOL did not work out compliance to the DOL's satisfaction (due to late payments) was held to have waived the statute of limitations as part of that prior agreement. As a result, the DOL could seek overtime going back almost four years. [Herman v. Hogar Praderas de Amor, Inc., 130 F. Supp. 2d 257 (D.P.R. 2001)] Limited waivers may sometimes be negotiated as part of a settlement with the DOL.

Q 14:7   How can an employer in an FLSA action have liquidated damages against it reduced?

An employer can have liquidated damages against it reduced if it shows to the court's satisfaction that its failure to pay minimum wages or overtime was in good faith, and that it had a reasonable ground for believing that it was not violating the FLSA. Indeed, if an employer shows that it acted in good faith and had reasonable grounds to believe its actions were not unlawful, a court can reduce or even eliminate liquidated damages. No specific reliance on an administrative ruling is required to establish this defense. [29 U.S.C. § 260]

An employer cannot rely on ignorance alone as a reasonable ground for believing that its actions were not in violation of the FLSA. The good-faith defense requires proof that the employer's failure to obey the FLSA was in good faith and that it would be unfair to award liquidated damages. [Elwell v. Univ. Hosp. Home Care Serv., 276 F.3d 832 (6th Cir. 2002)] A court has the discretion not to award liquidated damages if "the employer shows to the satisfaction of the court that the act or omission giving rise to such action was in good faith and that he had reasonable grounds for believing that his act or omission was not a violation of the Fair Labor Standards Act of 1938." [29 U.S.C. § 260] The FLSA imposes some affirmative duty to investigate potential liability under the FLSA. [Barcellona v. Tiffany English Pub, Inc., 597 F.2d 464 (5th Cir. 1979)]

Examples of situations in which no liquidated damages were assessed include the following:

1. In structuring its compensation plan, the employer sought the advice of counsel and consulted with the DOL, but the employer failed to implement the plan correctly. [Lee v. Coahoma County, 937 F.2d 220 (5th Cir. 1991), *reissued as amended*, 37 F.3d 1068 (5th Cir. 1993)]

2. The employer made an objective study of job classifications to determine exempt and nonexempt status and the regulations did not specifically address its employees. [Bratt v. County of L.A., 912 F.2d 1066, 1072 (9th Cir. 1990)]

3. A city employer relied on an administrative opinion that concluded that the salary test was not applicable to its fire lieutenants. [Atlanta Prof'l Firefighters Union v. City of Atlanta, 920 F.2d 800 (11th Cir. 1991)]

An example of a situation in which liquidated damages were assessed because of failure to prove good faith is as follows:

Employer's only evidence of good faith consisted of employer's vice president and administrator's testimony that she was surprised by an opinion letter the court relied on which concluded that home care nurses were not professionals, and employer did not rely on an expert opinion when it instituted its payment plan. [Elwell v. Univ. Hosp. Home Care Serv., 276 F.3d 832 (6th Cir. 2002)]

Q 14:8   What is the plaintiff's burden of proof to recover unpaid wages under the FLSA?

The plaintiff has the burden of proof on the issues of coverage under the FLSA and the existence of a violation of the statute. An employee suing for unpaid overtime meets his or her burden of proof if:

1. The employer's records are inadequate and do not reflect hours worked;

2. The employee can prove that he or she has done work for which he or she was not properly paid; *and*

3. The employee produces enough evidence to show the amount and extent of that work as a matter of just and reasonable inference.

It then becomes incumbent on the employer to disprove the employee's claim. [Anderson v. Mt. Clemens Pottery Co., 328 U.S. 680, 687 (1946)]

The Eighth Circuit has ruled that the *Mt. Clemens* decision requires plaintiffs in cases involving falsified records to present a prima facie case as to unpaid overtime hours worked before the burden of proof shifts to the employer. Further, this burden must be met by each plaintiff when different work situations make pattern evidence unpersuasive. [Murray v. Stuckey's, Inc., 939 F.2d 614 (8th Cir. 1991)] When, however, the issue is that the employer's records are inadequate, employees do not have to prove the precise extent of the un-compensated work. [Brock v. Normans Country Mkt., Inc., 835 F.2d 823 (11th Cir. 1988)]

For an employee to recover for uncompensated overtime work, the employee must also prove that the employer had knowledge, either actual or constructive, of the employee's overtime work in order to show that the employer "employed" the employee within the meaning of the FLSA's overtime provisions. [Davis v. Food Lion, 792 F.2d 1274 (4th Cir. 1986); *see also* Strickland v. MICA Info. Sys., 800 F. Supp. 1320 (M.D.N.C. 1992)]

Q 14:9   Is an employee's FLSA lawsuit barred by prior submission of the wage claim to arbitration proceedings?

No. A federal action alleging violation of the FLSA is not barred by the prior submission of the wage claim to arbitration based on the same underlying facts, although the arbitration decision has some weight in the FLSA action. [Barrentine v. Arkansas-Best Freight Sys., Inc., 450 U.S. 728 (1981)] It runs contrary to the FLSA's enforcement scheme to force employees to exhaust their contractual remedies before bringing an FLSA claim for unpaid minimum wages or overtime compensation. Consequently, it has been held that a trial court erred by granting an employer's motion to dismiss its employee's FLSA claim for overtime compensation on the ground that the employee failed to exhaust his administrative remedies as required by state law. [Laurence v. Colorado, 910 P.2d 73 (Colo. Ct. App. 1995)] On the other hand, it is possible that a court's determination of a wage suit would require the resolution of certain issues in contract arbitration under a collective bargaining agreement, in which instance it would be appropriate for the court to hold the civil suit pending the arbitration results, presuming the arbitration proceeded with diligence and efficiency. [*See* Vadino v. A Valey Engineers, 903 F.2d 253 (3d Cir. 1990)]

Significantly, since exhaustion of administrative remedies is not a prerequisite to filing an FLSA suit, the filing of the administrative claim does not toll the statute of limitations, even if the employer appears to want to resolve the dispute. [Nerseth v. United States, 29 Wage & Hour Cas. (BNA) 639 (Cl. Ct. 1989); *see also* Hartt v. United Constr. Co., 655 F. Supp. 937 (M.D. Mo. 1987)]

Q 14:10   Will a court compel an employee to arbitrate an FLSA dispute if the employee has signed an agreement to arbitrate?

A court can compel arbitration under the Federal Arbitration Act (FAA) [9 U.S.C. §§ 3 and 4] if an employee has signed a binding arbitration agreement.

Under the FAA, a written agreement to arbitrate is "valid, irrevocable, and enforceable, save upon such grounds as exist at law or in equity for the revocation of any contract."

For example, a court ordered mandatory arbitration of an FLSA dispute under an employer's written dispute resolution policy finding that it had all the hallmarks of a valid contract. The employer presented the policy to employees as an offer in return for their continued employment with the employer, and the employees accepted that offer. [Caley v. Gulfstream Aerospace Corp., 333 F. Supp. 2d 1367 (N.D. Ga. 2004)]

In another case, a court held that an employee was bound by an employer's standard arbitration agreement even though the employer could not produce a written agreement signed by the employee because it had lost the employee's file. Despite the missing document, the court concluded that an implied-in-fact arbitration agreement existed between the employer and the employee. [Johnson v. Long John Silver's Rests., Inc., 414 F.3d 583 (6th Cir. 2005)]

On the other hand, a court is unlikely to enforce an arbitration agreement if the agreement does not provide for effective vindication of an FLSA claim. For example, an appellate court concluded that arbitration agreements signed by restaurant employees were invalid because the selection of arbitrators was biased in favor of the restaurant employer. [Walker v. Ryan's Family Steak Houses, Inc., 400 F.3d 370 (6th Cir. 2005)]

Moreover, an employer must act promptly to enforce an arbitration agreement. A court refused to enforce an arbitration agreement when an employer waited more than 10 months after the beginning of an FLSA case to raise the issue of arbitration. [Robinson v. Food Serv. of Belton, Inc. 2005 U.S. Dist. LEXIS 17552 (D. Kan. 2005)]

Q 14:11   Will the Department of Labor defer to arbitration in wage-hour cases?

The Supreme Court has affirmed the government's ability to proceed with litigation on behalf of employees even when the employees have agreed to arbitrate employment disputes with their employers. [EEOC v. Waffle House, Inc., 534 U.S. 279 (2002)]

Nonetheless, a memorandum from the Department of Labor's Office of the Solicitor says that the Department of Labor will defer to arbitration in some instances. However, those instances may be rare in wage-hour cases. According to the memorandum, wage-hour cases typically involve numerous employees and as a consequence may have been the subject of time-consuming investigations and may be unwieldy for private parties to arbitrate. In those cases, moreover, court-ordered prospective compliance with the law often is an important DOL objective. Therefore, deferral to arbitration often will not be appropriate in wage-hour matters.

Here are some of the factors the DOL will consider in deciding whether to defer to an arbitration agreement:

- Is it a matter that calls for immediate injunctive relief (e.g., hot goods) or one in which prospective equitable relief will be particularly important?
- Is it likely that the violative conduct will recur absent intervention?
- Was the misconduct willful or egregious?
- Does the dispute involve a general policy or practice of the employer?
- Does the dispute involve a legal issue the DOL has made a priority of emphasizing or clarifying?
- Has the employer previously refused to arbitrate the dispute?
- Does the agreement to arbitrate appear valid and enforceable under applicable state law and the Federal Arbitration Act?
- Did the employer explain the key provisions of the agreement to the employee orally or in writing?
- Was the employee informed that by signing the agreement he or she waived the right to trial by jury?
- Did the employer give the employee time to consider the agreement before signing it?
- Did the employer inform the employee that he or she might want to discuss the agreement with an attorney before signing it?
- In light of arbitration expenses, is the arbitral forum in this particular case accessible financially? (Consideration should be given to the approximate amount of arbitration fees and costs, the extent to which fees and costs would be paid by the employer, and the estimated cost differential for the claimant between arbitration and private litigation.)
- Does the arbitrator have authority to provide for reimbursement of attorneys' fees?
- Does the arbitrator (or pool of available arbitrators) have an appropriate background, including experience in overseeing hearings, knowledge of the pertinent legal issues, and an understanding of employment relations?
- Is the arbitrator associated with a reputable arbitration or mediation service, particularly one with established rules of procedure?
- Is the pool of available arbitrators created in a nondiscriminatory manner so that it can be expected the parties' positions will be considered fairly?
- Does the arbitrator have a duty to inform the parties of any relationship that might reasonably create or be perceived as creating a conflict of interest?
- Is the employee (or an employee representative) afforded a meaningful role in selecting the arbitrator?

- Can the employee be represented by counsel in the arbitration?
- Is there provision for reasonable mutual discovery (e.g., pre-hearing disclosures, depositions) consistent with the expedited nature of the arbitration?
- Does the employee have access to the information reasonably relevant to the arbitration?
- Does the arbitrator have authority regarding the time and place of the hearing, the issuance of subpoenas, evidentiary matters, and the authority to issue an award resolving the dispute?
- Does the arbitration agreement set a limitations period shorter than that granted the employee by statute?
- Is any right the employee has to proceed through a collective action (such as under the FLSA) preserved?
- Is the employee required to travel a great distance to arbitrate the claim?
- Is the arbitrator provided the authority to award whatever relief would be available in a judicial forum?
- Is the employer prepared to arbitrate without delay?
- If the Department agrees to defer to the arbitration process, will the parties sign a tolling agreement that extends the period for bringing a court case?
- Does the arbitration agreement provide for (or the employer consent to) a written arbitration decision setting out not only the award but also the essential findings of fact and conclusions of law on which it is based?

[Memorandum on Consideration of Employment Arbitration Agreements (Aug. 9, 2002), *available at,* http://www.dol.gov/sol/media/memos/August9.htm]

While these guidelines govern the decisions of DOL attorneys when deciding whether to bring a court case on behalf of aggrieved employees, they can also serve as useful guidelines for employers drafting arbitration agreements.

Q 14:12   What sources do courts rely on in interpreting the FLSA?

In interpreting the FLSA, courts look not only to prior cases but also to rulings, opinions, and interpretations of the Secretary of Labor and Wage and Hour Administrator. Although most such rulings, opinions, and interpretations do not bind courts, they do constitute a body of experience and informed judgment to which courts and litigants may properly resort for guidance. [Dalheim v. KDFW-TV, 918 F.2d 1220, 1228 (5th Cir. 1990); *see also* Skidmore v. Swift & Co., 323 U.S. 134, 140 (1944)]

Q 14:13   Can an employee sue his or her employer for violating the FLSA by failing to keep proper records?

No. An employee's private right of action is limited in scope. It does not encompass the employer's failure to keep records, but is limited to the recovery of unpaid minimum wages and unpaid overtime compensation and to remedies for retaliatory discharge. [*See* East v. Bullock's, Inc., 34 F. Supp. 2d 1176 (D. Ariz. 1998); O'Quinn v. Chambers County, 636 F. Supp. 1388 (S.D. Tex. 1986)]

Q 14:14   Is an employer entitled to credit any costs or expenses against an award of back wages to an employee in an FLSA action?

Yes. If an employee is awarded back wages in an FLSA action, the employer may be entitled to credit against that award all or some of the costs expended by the employer for the employee's housing and food, because the FLSA permits the employer to include as part of an employee's wage the reasonable cost of furnishing board, lodging, or other facilities. This will usually be a limited credit, because no credit is allowed against overtime wages owed to an employee. The FLSA does not, however, provide for an independent legal action by the employer to recover these costs if no back pay has been awarded to the employee. [Morrisoe v. Goldsboro Milling Co., 884 F. Supp. 192 (E.D.N.C. 1994)] In that circumstance, the employer must recover such costs through a state contract action.

Q 14:15   When does an employee's cause of action for unpaid minimum wages or overtime compensation accrue for purposes of the FLSA?

An employer becomes liable for any unpaid minimum wages or overtime compensation on the next regular payday covering the period of employment during which the work at issue occurred. Further, a new cause of action accrues every time the employer fails to pay overtime compensation or minimum wages on each regular payday. Thus, when an employee's compensation is at a monthly rate and the employee is paid on the 25th day of each month, it is on this day each month that an FLSA cause of action accrues to the employee for salary due for the preceding month, together with any unpaid overtime compensation, and if applicable, liquidated damages. The employee's cause of action is not held in abeyance until the employment ends or until the employee demands overtime pay. [Knight v. City of Columbus, 19 F.3d 579 (11th Cir. 1994); Nerseth v. United States, 29 Wage & Hour Cas. (BNA) 639 (Cl. Ct. 1989)]

The failure to issue paychecks promptly when due has also been held to be a violation of the FLSA. The Ninth Circuit read a requirement of promptness into the FLSA and ruled that wages are "unpaid" for purposes of the FLSA unless they are paid on the employee's regular payday. [Biggs v. Wilson, 1 F.3d 1537 (9th Cir. 1993), *cert. denied*, 510 U.S. 1081 (1994)] Furthermore, some state statutes mandate prompt payment of wages to employees. [*See, e.g.,* Ky. Rev. Stat. Ann. § 337.020; Va. Code Ann. § 17.1-29]

Q 14:16   Can an employee's time limit for filing an FLSA action be equitably tolled?

Generally, no. The doctrine of equitable tolling (i.e., suspending the statute of limitations for reasons of fairness) applies only when a plaintiff is excusably unaware of the existence of a cause of action at the time of its accrual. Thus, when employees pursue administrative remedies to seek minimum wage or overtime payment, their time limit for filing an FLSA lawsuit continues to run because they were clearly aware that they were not being paid in compliance with the FLSA. It may be possible, however, for an employee to claim equitable tolling when there has been some affirmative misrepresentation or fraudulent concealment of facts by the employer that lulled the employee into inaction. [Hodgson v. Holden Hosp., Inc., 64 Lab. Cases (CCH) ¶ 32,442 (D. W. Va. 1970)]

Q 14:17   Does the joint employment doctrine apply to actions and penalties under the FLSA?

Yes. For example, an employer may not shield itself from liability by placing a recruiter-contractor between itself and laborers and giving the recruiter-contractor responsibility for direct oversight and supervision of the laborers. In such a situation, the joint employment doctrine may apply and the independent contractor status of the recruiter-contractor may not negate the effect of the joint employment doctrine. Under the joint employment doctrine, two employers that employ the same employee may be treated as one employer due to the employers' common or joint control over personnel matters or due to other factors such as common ownership or financial control. The result of a determination that two employers are joint with respect to an employee is that the employee's hours for each employer must be combined and both employers will be jointly responsible for unpaid wages, overtime, and any penalties that might be assessed. If employers are completely disassociated with respect to the employment of a particular employee, however, the joint employment situation may not exist. [Campbell v. Miller, 836 F. Supp. 827 (M.D. Fla. 1993)]

Significantly, the joint employment doctrine applies in situations in which a person's wages are paid by one company while his or her services are engaged on a temporary basis by another company. The key factor in these temporary-employee cases is whether the client company has the exclusive right to supervise the employee's work during the period of temporary service. Courts hold both employers liable for wage payments to shared employees when there is an arrangement to share an employee's services. Such a finding would permit FLSA liability to be shared among employers. Regulations promulgated under the Family and Medical Leave Act, which utilizes the FLSA's definitions of the terms employer and joint employer, support this analysis. [See 29 C.F.R. § 825.106]

In addition, companies that contract for services from another company may be deemed the joint employer of the employees of the second company if the second company is so economically dependent on the first company (the contracting company) that its employees are effectively controlled by the first company. This "economic reality" joint employment has been found in wage and hour suits brought over conditions in the garment industry on several occasions. These cases hold that the clothing manufacturer—usually a big name clothing brand label—is responsible for wage and hour violations committed by the garment factories with which the manufacturer usually does business. If the garment factory is getting the bulk of its work from one manufacturer, then that manufacturer may be the real "economic" employer of the factory's workers. For example, Donna Karan International, Inc. was held, by virtue of the "economic realities," to be the joint employer of garment workers at the garment factory making clothes for the Donna Karan label. [Liu v. Donna Karan Int'l, Inc., 6 Wage & Hour Cas. 2d (BNA) 1142 (S.D.N.Y. 2000)] Probably contributing to that decision was the fact that the garment factories that employed the workers had little money. The Wage and Hour Division takes the position that the manufacturer should use its economic power to put wage and hour compliance as a term in its contracts with garment factories. This position of the DOL is not the "norm" and probably would be applied primarily to "capture" supplier companies.

A group of New York city garment workers sued their employer, a garment industry contractor, for failing to pay them the required minimum wage. But they also sued the garment manufacturer whose products they worked on, claiming the manufacturer was their joint employer under the FLSA. A U.S. district court dismissed the workers' lawsuit on the grounds that the manufacturer did not meet the key tests for joint employer status. The employer did not:

1. Hire and fire the workers,
2. Supervise and control their work schedules or conditions of employment,
3. Determine the rate and method of payment, or
4. Maintain employment records.

However, the United States Court of Appeals for the Second Circuit reinstated the workers' lawsuit. The court concluded that the four factors relied on by the district court can be useful in joint employment cases because when an entity exercises those four prerogatives, that entity, in addition to any primary employer, must be considered a joint employer. However, the court said the four factors are not the *only* factors to be considered. Instead, the determination of joint employer status must be based on "the circumstances of the whole activity," viewed in light of "economic reality."

Factors to be considered in assessing the economic reality include:

1. Whether the putative joint employer's premises and equipment were used for the work;
2. Whether the contractor had a business that could or did shift as a unit from one putative joint employer to another;
3. The extent to which workers performed a discrete line-job that was integral to the putative joint employer's process of production;
4. Whether responsibility under the contracts could pass from one subcontractor to another without material changes;
5. The degree to which the putative joint employer or its agents supervised the workers' work; and
6. Whether the workers worked exclusively or predominantly for the putative joint employer.

[Zheng v. Liberty Apparel Co., 355 F.3d 61 (2d Cir. 2003)]

Q 14:18　Do federal courts have jurisdiction over FLSA actions against state employers for violation of the FLSA's minimum wage and overtime pay provisions?

Maybe. There is a decided split among the federal circuits as to whether federal courts have jurisdiction over actions against state employers for violating the FLSA's minimum wage and overtime pay provisions. The First, Second, Fourth, Sixth, Eighth, Tenth, and Eleventh Circuits have ruled that Congress, in enacting the FLSA, had no power to abrogate the states' 11th Amendment immunity under the Interstate Commerce Clause and, accordingly, that federal district courts do not have subject matter jurisdiction over FLSA actions brought by state employees against the state. [*See, e.g.,* Mills v. Maine, 118 F.3d 37 (1st Cir. 1997); Close v. New York, 125 F.3d 31 (2d Cir. 1997); Abril v. Virginia, 145 F.3d 182 (4th Cir. 1998); Wilson-Jones v. Caviness, 99 F.3d 203 (6th Cir. 1996), *modified on other grounds* 707 F.3d 358 (6th Cir. 1997) (*per curiam*); Moad v. Ark. State Police Dep't, 111 F.3d 585 (8th Cir. 1998); Aaron v. Kansas, 115 F.3d 813 (10th Cir. 1997); Powell v. Florida, 132 F.3d 677 (11th Cir. 1998)] According to these circuits, appropriate remedies in such circumstances include having state employees sue a state officer in federal court for an injunction requiring compliance with the FLSA, having the federal government sue in federal court for money damages on behalf of state employees, and having state employees sue in state court for money damages. In some states, statutes mirroring all or part of the FLSA can provide relief to state employees.

In contrast, the Ninth Circuit has ruled that Congress intended to abrogate the states' sovereign immunity from suit for violations of the FLSA. [*See* Hale v. Arizona, 993 F.2d 1387 (9th Cir. 1993)]

Q 14:19　Can wage claims initiated in state court be removed to federal court?

Yes. The United States Supreme Court held in May 2003 that a lawsuit brought under the FLSA can be removed as a matter of right from state to federal court, in *Breuer v. Jim's Concrete of Brevard.* [538 U.S. 691 (2003)] The Supreme Court held that language in the FLSA, which states that a case "may be maintained against any employer. . .in any federal or state court of competent jurisdiction," did not mean that a claim filed in state court could not be removed to federal court. The Court specifically rejected the plaintiff's pragmatic argument that many FLSA claims are for such small amounts that removal to federal court may make it less convenient and more expensive for employees to vindicate their rights effectively. The Court noted that this may be true, but it does not justify creating an exception to the removal statute for FLSA claims. The Court noted that other federal laws, such as the Age Discrimination in Employment Act, the Employee Polygraph Protection Act, and the Family and Medical Leave Act, incorporate or use the same language as used in the FLSA. The Court held that the plaintiff cannot have a removal exception for the FLSA without entailing exceptions for other statutory actions, to the point that it becomes just too hard to believe that a right to "maintain" an action was ever meant to displace the right to remove. Those involved in litigation under the FLSA or other federal laws will be relieved to know that the Court has reinforced the right of a defendant/employer to remove a case to federal court where appropriate.

The importance of removal lies in the differences between state court systems and the federal court system. Cases are more likely to proceed to the trial stage in state court than in federal court, while early resolution is more likely in federal court than in state court. And, while federal district court judges in general rely more on pleadings and written submissions from attorneys, many state court systems rely on in-person presentations through hearings. Finally, cases in federal court tend to take a great deal longer to reach resolution than cases in most state court systems. All of this, of course, will vary from state to state, but such considerations may affect an employer's initial actions when faced with wage litigation.

Q 14:20   Can an employer rely on an employment agreement, whereby the employee agrees to accept less than the minimum wage or to postpone overtime payments, to avoid a liquidated damages judgment?

No. An employer's reliance on an agreement to pay less than the FLSA requires does not avoid a judgment for liquidated damages. [Wright v. Carrigg, 275 F.2d 448 (4th Cir. 1960)] Indeed, it is no defense to a liquidated damages award that the employment contract between the plaintiff-employee and the defendant-employer calls for the accumulation of unpaid overtime to be used to make up for time lost in weeks when, because of sickness or for personal reasons, the employee works fewer than the required number of hours. [Brown v. Bouchard, 209 F. Supp. 130 (D. Mass. 1962)] Employees simply do not have the ability to prospectively waive rights under the FLSA.

Q 14:21   Can an employer avoid liability for unpaid wages by filing for bankruptcy?

No. The reorganization of a corporation under bankruptcy law does not cloak a debtor with immunity from its liabilities to its employees for unpaid wages under the FLSA, even during the pendency of the proceedings. [Plourde v. Mass. Cities Realty Co., 47 F. Supp. 668 (D. Mass. 1942)]

Q 14:22   Does the employer's good-faith defense to liquidated damages excuse its liability for unpaid wages?

No. An employer's good faith does not excuse its obligation to pay what is due under the FLSA. Additionally, an employer's good faith does not excuse its violations of the FLSA's recordkeeping provisions. The good-faith defense is a partial defense potentially excusing an employer from liability for liquidated damages only. [29 U.S.C. § 260]

An employer that asserts good faith as a defense to liquidated damages must demonstrate that it had an honest intention to ascertain that which the FLSA requires and to act in accordance with it. [Dalheim v. KDFW-TV, 712 F. Supp. 533

(N.D. Tex. 1989)] The good-faith defense is an affirmative defense that the employer must plead and prove, and if the employer fails to plead "good faith and reasonable grounds" in its answer to a complaint, the good-faith defense is waived.

Q 14:23 Do settlements between the employer and employee as to back wages preclude the employee's claim for liquidated damages?

No. Private settlements between the employer and employee as to back wages only cannot completely protect the employer against claims for liquidated damages. Indeed, it has been held that an employer's tender or payment to employees for overtime compensation due under the FLSA is not sufficient to avoid an award of liquidated damages. [Petrlik v. Cmty. Realty Co., 347 F. Supp. 638 (D. Md. 1972)]

The Secretary of Labor is authorized to supervise an employer's payment of any unpaid minimum wages or overtime compensation owed to employees under the FLSA. Employees, however, must consent to the amount of the employer's voluntary settlement. When employees agree to accept the back wages offered by the employer in such circumstances, they waive their rights to civil action against the employer. Thus, the employer, by participating in such a voluntary settlement, can limit its liability to the actual amount of wages or overtime compensation due and avoid the assessment of liquidated damages and attorneys' fees. [29 U.S.C. § 216(c)]

The Fifth Circuit held that when an employee signed a statement acknowledging that he agreed to accept the employer's payment in return for dropping his claim for overtime compensation, and the statement and check for the full amount were prepared and supervised by the Wage and Hour Division, the employee waived his right to sue the employer for statutory overtime compensation and liquidated damages. [Sneed v. Sneed's Shipbldg., Inc., 545 F.2d 537 (5th Cir. 1977)]

A settlement that is not supervised and approved by the DOL, however, can be rejected by a court. For instance, agreements between an employer and its employees under which the employees agreed to accept a reduced payment in return for a waiver of their rights under the FLSA to claim back pay were found to be invalid when the agreements were not supervised by the DOL and were not entered as a stipulated judgment in any action by the employees against the employer. [Lynn's Food Stores, Inc. v. United States, 679 F.2d 1350 (11th Cir. 1982)] Sums paid under such agreements, however, might be used as a setoff against liability assessed in subsequent litigation.

Q 14:24 Can an employee's waiver of his or her FLSA rights preclude a subsequent court action?

No. A release signed by an employee purporting to waive his or her right to unpaid minimum wages or overtime compensation under the FLSA does not bar him or her from taking subsequent action to recover what is due or to recover liquidated damages. The provisions of the law dealing with the payment of minimum wages and overtime compensation are mandatory and provide a public benefit; therefore, employees cannot waive these rights. Indeed, neither employees nor their union can waive the right to overtime or minimum wage payments under a collective bargaining agreement. [Lerwill v. Inflight Serv., Inc., 379 F. Supp. 690 (N.D. Cal. 1974)]

Q 14:25   When does the successorship theory of liability apply to the FLSA context?

The successorship theory of liability probably applies to the FLSA context when an employer's operations are bought and then operated by a new entity. The Ninth Circuit ruled that the successorship theory of liability applies to suits under the FLSA. Under this theory, a successor corporation or entity can be liable for wage violations of the predecessor. The Ninth Circuit ruled that the FLSA's fundamental purpose of protecting workers' standards of living justifies the application of the successorship theory of liability in the FLSA context. That court declined, however, to impose liability on a company that operated a bankrupt firm's business for only three to four months under a lease of assets. The failure to transfer the business "permanently" was controlling for the court, which noted that the policies underlying the FLSA and supporting the free transfer of capital would best be served by finding no liability. [Steinbach v. Hubbard, 51 F.3d 843 (9th Cir. 1995)]

Successorship liability would likely be applied, however, to a situation in which a company with a judgment against it transferred its assets to another company that then operated the same business. For example, in a migrant farmworker case where the farm's owner at the time of the violations transferred the farm to his sons, who then operated the farm, the migrant farmworkers would be permitted to execute their judgment against the new owners as bona fide successors to the original owner. [Herrera v. Singh, 118 F. Supp. 2d 1120 (E.D. Wash. 2000)]

Q 14:26   How can a court arrive at a total damage award for unpaid wages when precise records are unavailable?

To arrive at a total damage award for unpaid wages under the FLSA when precise records of hours worked are unavailable, it is permissible for the court to rule that each employee need only produce sufficient evidence to show the amount and extent of that work as a matter of just and reasonable inference. [LeCompte v. Chrysler Credit Corp., 780 F.2d 1260 (5th Cir. 1986)]

Q 14:27   Can employee bonuses and premium pay be credited against an employer's liability for back pay under the FLSA?

Generally, no. Annual bonuses based on earnings during the year that are voluntarily paid by the employer cannot be credited against liability for overtime. [Bable v. TW Phillips Gas & Oil Co., 287 F.2d 21 (3d Cir. 1961)]

Q 14:28   Can compensatory time off taken by employees be credited against an employer's liability for back pay under the FLSA?

As a general rule, private employers are not permitted to provide compensatory time off in lieu of overtime compensation (a narrow exception, rarely used, allows compensatory time off where the time given is one and one-half times the period that overtime was worked, and the time off is within the same pay period [Wage and Hour Opinion Letter, Dec. 27, 1968; DOL Field Operations Handbook, § 32j16b]). In the public sector, provided certain requirements are met, public agencies can provide compensatory time off at a rate of not less than one and one-half hours for each hour of employment for which overtime compensation is required under the FLSA. [29 U.S.C. § 207(o)(2)]

In a recent case, a group of police officers sued their city employer for back overtime, claiming that the city's compensatory time off plan did not meet the FLSA requirements. The city conceded that the compensatory time off plan was in violation of the FLSA and admitted liability for back overtime. However, the parties disputed how the back overtime should be computed.

The police officers contended that compensatory damages should equal the dollar value of the total amount of FLSA overtime accrued in the liability period, regardless of whether any of the overtime had been paid out in the form of compensatory time off (other than comp time that was actually used in the same workweek in which the comp time was earned).

The city claimed that such a computation would give the police officers a "gigantic windfall." The city argued that although the comp time scheme in this case was unlawful, the officers were paid when they took paid time off. Therefore, the proper measure of compensatory damages was limited to the amount of unused comp time that remained banked by the police officers.

The First Circuit Court of Appeals held that in computing compensatory damages, the city's liability under the FLSA could be offset by the used comp time hours. In other words, the city's liability (all hours for which comp time credits were granted but not used within the same week) minus offset for comp time paid out equals compensatory damages. [Lupien v. City of Marlborough, 387 F.3d 83 (1st Cir. 2004)]

Q 14:29   Can an employer rely on the terms of a collective bargaining agreement to avoid liability for back pay under the FLSA?

According to at least one appellate court, the terms of a collective bargaining agreement will not override the FLSA.

In the case before the court, a group of police officers sued the township that employed them, claiming that the township's method for calculating overtime shortchanged them, even though they agreed to that method in their collective bargaining agreement. Specifically, the police officers claimed that the FLSA required certain items of incentive and expense pay to be included in their regular rate of pay for calculating overtime. The township conceded that the items were technically required to be included in the regular rate of pay for calculating overtime, but it argued that in the collective bargaining agreement the officers traded the incentive and expense pay added to their base pay in exchange for the inclusion of nonwork pay, which is not required to be included under the FLSA. Therefore, the township claimed it should be allowed to offset the exclusion of incentive and expense pay from the base rate with a "credit" for including nonwork pay in the base rate.

The appellate court did not agree with the township's proposed credit. The court acknowledged that "the FLSA was not intended to limit [the] creativity of labor and management to make economically beneficial agreements." However, the court said the FLSA spells out what credits employers may take for extra compensation, and the credit the township claimed was not allowed by the FLSA. [Wheeler v. Hampton Township, 399 F.3d 238 (3d Cir. 2005)]

Q 14:30   Can prejudgment interest on back pay be awarded in FLSA cases?

Maybe. Since prejudgment interest awards serve some of the same purposes as awards of liquidated damages under the FLSA—that is, making the employee whole—employees who obtain liquidated damages are not also entitled to prejudgment interest. [*See* Reich v. Newspapers of New England, Inc., 834 F. Supp. 530 (D.N.H. 1993), *aff'd*, 44 F.3d 1060 (1st Cir. 1995)] Generally, however, courts deem that prejudgment interest is necessary, in the absence of liquidated damages, to offset the effect of wages being wrongfully withheld and to make prevailing parties whole. [Roy v. County of Lexington, 928 F. Supp. 1406 (D.S.C.), *vacated in part,* 948 F. Supp. 529 (D.S.C. 1996); Rushing v. Shelby County Gov't, 8 F. Supp. 2d 737 (W.D. Tenn. 1997)] Some courts hold that prejudgment interest should be awarded when liquidated damages are not awarded in the full amount or are denied because of an employer's good faith. [*See* McClanahan v. Mathews, 440 F.2d 320 (6th Cir. 1971)]

Q 14:31   Are court costs and attorneys' fees available to successful plaintiff-employees in FLSA actions?

Yes. The law provides that employees who are successful in a back-pay suit can recover the back wages, an equal additional amount as liquidated damages, "reasonable" attorneys' fees, and the cost of the action. An attorney representing an employee whose rights under the FLSA were violated can collect only the amount recognized by the court as reasonable under the circumstances.

Costs are awarded to the prevailing party, whether it is the plaintiff or the defendant. Costs include such items as court filing fees, witness fees, copy charges for necessary copies, and most deposition costs. Outlays for travel and related expenses by attorneys and paralegals may not be reimbursed as costs in FLSA actions; however, they may be reimbursable as part of an award for attorneys' fees, since travel and meal expenses are the sort of things that lawyers include in billing for professional services. [29 U.S.C. § 216(b); Calderon v.

Witvoet, 112 F.3d 275 (7th Cir. 1997)] Appropriate costs will be awarded to a prevailing party regardless of the limited nature of the party's success, but attorneys' fees to a prevailing plaintiff may be reduced in proportion to the plaintiff's limited success on his or her claims.

Costs are awarded to a prevailing party in federal litigation as a matter of course, but this right can be overridden by Federal Rules of Civil Procedure 68, the offer of judgment rule. That rule provides that a party that was offered a settlement must pay the costs incurred after an offer is made if the judgment finally obtained is not more favorable than the offer. [Fed. R. Civ. P. 68]

In determining attorneys' fees for plaintiffs who rejected their employer's settlement offer, such factors as the amount of the offer, the stage of litigation at which the offer was made, the services rendered after the offer, the amount obtained by judgment, and the reasonableness of continuing litigation after the offer must be considered. Although Federal Rules of Civil Procedure 68 enables the employer to cut off costs incurred after an offer of judgment is made if the judgment finally obtained is not more favorable than that offer, such offer or judgment would not bar an award of subsequent attorneys' fees under the FLSA. If an offer is rejected and the plaintiff recovers far less than the amount of the offer, however, the court can take that into consideration in determining the "reasonableness" of the fees demanded. [Haworth v. Nevada, 56 F.3d 1048 (9th Cir. 1995)]

Attorneys' fees can be awarded for appellate work as well. Courts consider whether such fees should be awarded on a case-by-case basis. When the court considers the original award adequate to compensate the attorney for any additional appellate services, however, no further award need be made. [U.S. Steel v. Burlett, 192 F.2d 489 (4th Cir. 1951)]

A prevailing *defendant* in an FLSA action is not, however, entitled to attorneys' fees, since the FLSA does not provide for plaintiffs to pay attorneys' fees to defendants. [Fegley v. Higgins, 19 F.3d 1126 (6th Cir. 1994)]

The amount of attorneys' fees to be awarded to an FLSA plaintiff is a matter of discretion with the court. Factors to be considered in determining the amount of attorneys' fees awarded include the following:

- Time and labor required;
- Novelty and difficulty of the questions presented;
- Skill requisite to perform the legal service properly;
- Preclusion of other employment by the attorney due to his or her acceptance of the case;
- The attorney's customary fee;
- Whether the fee is fixed or contingent;
- Time limitations posed by the client or the circumstances, the amount involved, and the results obtained;
- Experience, reputation, and ability of the attorney or attorneys in question;
- Desirability or undesirability of the case;

- Nature and length of the attorney's professional relationship with the client;
- Comparable awards in similar cases; and
- The plaintiff's financial resources.

[Kreager v. Solomon & Flanagan, PA, 775 F.2d 1541 (11th Cir. 1985) (citing Johnson v. Georgia Highway Express, Inc., 488 F.2d 714, 717 (5th Cir. 1974))]

Attorneys' fees to a prevailing plaintiff may be reduced to reflect the plaintiff's limited success. In *Shea v. Galaxie Lumber & Construction Co.* [221 F.3d 1339 (7th Cir. 2000)], the court reduced the plaintiff's attorneys' fee request by 40 percent because the plaintiff failed to win a significant award of back wages, although she did receive liquidated damages and a small punitive damages award from the jury.

Employers that are considering whether to contest an employee's lawsuit for back wages should carefully factor their potential liability for attorneys' fees into their decision making. In one case, an employee who sued her employer for failure to pay overtime received a compensatory damage award of $12,922 and an equal amount in liquidated damages—or a grand total of $25,844. However, the district court also ordered the employer to pay $85,822.75 in attorneys' fees and $589.25 in costs. In upholding the award of attorneys' fees, an appellate court noted that the employer made generalized statements that the time spent on the case was unreasonable but did not point to any specific time entries to support its argument. The appellate court also noted that the district court judge did not rubber stamp the fees submitted by employee's attorney, but reduced certain charges and eliminated charges spent on duplicative work. [Friedman v. S. Fla. Psychiatric Assocs., Inc., 2005 WL 1540129 (11th Cir. 2005)]

Civil Money Penalties

Q 14:32　What civil penalties can be assessed against an employer that violates the FLSA's minimum wage and overtime pay provisions?

The 1989 amendments to the FLSA amended FLSA Section 16(e) to subject any person who repeatedly or willfully violates the overtime or minimum wage provisions to a civil money penalty not to exceed $1,000 for each such violation. For violations that occur after January 7, 2002, the $1,000 civil money penalty increased to $1,100. [29 U.S.C. § 216(e); 29 C.F.R. §§ 578.1, 578.3]

An employer's violation of the FLSA's minimum wage or overtime pay provisions is deemed to be "repeated" for purposes of FLSA Section 16(e) when:

1. The employer has previously violated the FLSA's minimum wage or overtime pay provisions, provided that the employer has previously received notice from a responsible official of the Wage and Hour Division that it was in violation of the FLSA; or

2. A court or other tribunal has found that the employer has previously violated the FLSA's minimum wage or overtime pay provisions, unless an appeal from such decision is pending or unless the finding has been set aside or reversed by an appellate court.

[29 C.F.R. § 578.3(b)]

An employer's violation of the FLSA's minimum wage or overtime pay provisions is deemed to be "willful" when the employer knew that its conduct was prohibited or showed reckless disregard for the requirements of the FLSA. All of the facts and circumstances surrounding the violation are taken into account in determining whether a violation was willful. For purposes of imposing civil monetary penalties, an employer's conduct is deemed "knowing" if the employer received advice from the Wage and Hour Division to the effect that the conduct in question was not lawful. An employer's conduct is deemed to be in reckless disregard of the FLSA's requirements if the employer failed to make adequate further inquiry into whether its conduct was in compliance with the FLSA. [29 C.F.R. § 578.3(c)]

In determining the amount of penalty to be assessed for a repeated or willful violation of the FLSA's minimum wage or overtime pay provisions, the Wage and Hour Administrator considers the seriousness of the violations and the size of the employer's business. When appropriate, the Wage and Hour Administrator can also consider other relevant facts, including, but not limited to, the following:

- Whether the employer has made efforts in good faith to comply with the provisions of the FLSA;
- The employer's explanation for the violations, including whether the violations were the result of a bona fide dispute of doubtful legal certainty;
- Previous history of violations, including whether the employer is subject to injunction against future violations of the FLSA;
- The employer's commitment to future compliance;
- Time interval between violations;
- Number of employees affected by the employer's conduct; and
- Whether there is any established pattern to the employer's violations.

[29 C.F.R. § 578.4]

Q 14:33   May an employer's failure to pay overtime constitute grounds for a state law tort claim against the employer?

Probably not. In *Walsh v. Walgreen Eastern Co.*, 2004 WL 722226 (D. Conn. 2004), the plaintiff filed claims alleging, among other things: (1) failure to pay overtime in violation of the FLSA and state law; (2) that such failure constituted negligent infliction of emotional distress; and (3) that such failure resulted in constructive discharge in violation of the state public policy exemption to the at-will employment doctrine. The court granted defendant's motion to dismiss the negligent infliction of emotional distress and constructive discharge claims, explaining that, even assuming the employer did fail to pay required overtime, such failure does not rise to a claim for either cause of action. It should be noted, however, that different states may have different elements for these and other causes of action, and so it is theoretically possible that plaintiff could claim that a violation of a statutory right to overtime under the FLSA could, in some instances, support a tort claim under state law.

Q 14:34 What civil penalties can be assessed against an employer for violating the FLSA's child labor provisions?

Congress amended the FLSA in 1990 to increase the civil penalties for violations of the FLSA's child labor provisions from $1,000 to $10,000. The penalty amount increased to up to $11,000 for each employee for any violation occurring on or after January 7, 2002. Since the amendment bases the civil penalty on the number of employees whose employment has been in violation of the child labor provisions rather than on the number of separate violations, it can increase the liability of an employer that has only a few child labor violations but can limit the liability of an employer that has many child labor violations for each minor-employee. [29 U.S.C. § 216(e); 29 C.F.R. pt. 579]

Sums collected as civil penalties for child labor violations are returned to the Employment Standards Administration of the DOL as reimbursement for enforcement expenses. (The Wage and Hour Division is a division of the Employment Standards Administration.) [Marshall v. Jerrico, Inc., 446 U.S. 238 (1980) (upholding the constitutionality of this payment procedure)]

Although the death of or injury to a minor due to child labor violations can lead to the imposition of civil money penalties, nothing in the FLSA provisions creates a private cause of action against the employer for damages for the death of or injury to a child while the child is employed in a hazardous occupation in violation of the FLSA. [Breitwieser v. KMS Indus., Inc., 467 F.2d 1391 (5th Cir. 1972), *cert. denied,* 410 U.S. 969 (1973)]

Q 14:35 What constitutes a child labor violation for which civil penalties can be imposed?

Each of the following constitutes a child labor violation for which a civil penalty can be imposed under the FLSA:

- Each shipment or delivery for shipment in commerce by a producer, manufacturer, or dealer of any goods produced in an establishment situated in the United States in or about which, within 30 days before the removal of such goods from such establishment, any minor has been employed in violation of the FLSA.
- Each employment by an employer of a minor as described in the FLSA for any period in commerce or in the production of goods for commerce or in any enterprise engaged in commerce or in the production of goods for commerce.

- Failure by an employer employing a minor to maintain and preserve records concerning the date of the minor's birth and concerning proof of the minor's age.
- Failure by an employer to take or cause to be taken action necessary to ensure compliance with all requirements of the FLSA that are made conditions for lawful employment of minors.

[29 U.S.C. §§ 203(l), 213(c); 29 C.F.R. § 579.3(a)]

For further discussion of child labor requirements, see Chapter 9.

Q 14:36   In what manner can an FLSA child labor penalty be collected and recovered?

When finally determined, the amount of any child labor penalty under the FLSA can be:

1. Deducted from any sums owing by the United States to the person charged;
2. Recovered in a civil action brought by the Secretary of Labor in any court of competent jurisdiction, in which litigation the Secretary is represented by the Solicitor of Labor; or
3. Ordered by the court to be paid to the Secretary.

[29 U.S.C. § 216(e); 29 C.F.R. § 580.18]

An administrative determination by the Secretary of the amount of any child labor penalty is final unless, within 15 days after receipt of notice of the determination by certified mail, the person charged with the violation takes exception to the determination that the violations for which the penalty is imposed actually occurred. On receipt of an employer's timely exception to the Secretary's determination of a child labor penalty and a request for a hearing, the Wage and Hour Administrator refers the matter to the chief administrative law judge for determination in an administrative proceeding. Any party wanting review of the administrative law judge's decision must file an appeal with the Department of Labor Administrative Review Board. To be effective, the appeal must be received by the Board within 30 days of the date of the decision of the administrative law judge. [29 U.S.C. § 216(e); 29 C.F.R. §§ 580.3, 580.5, 580.6, 580.10, 580.13]

Injunctive Relief

Q 14:37   Who can bring an injunction action to enforce the FLSA?

The Secretary of Labor can bring an injunction action to enforce the FLSA. Pursuant to FLSA Sections 11(a) and 12(b) the DOL is given exclusive authority to seek injunctive relief under FLSA Section 17 to enjoin an employer's violation of the FLSA. In addition to prospective injunctions against minimum wage and overtime violations, the Secretary can seek to enjoin prospectively child labor and recordkeeping violations and those involving the transportation of hot goods. (See Q 9:5 for discussion of how the FLSA regulates hot goods.) Federal district courts also have the power to order the payment of back wages in injunction actions brought by the Secretary as a restitutionary injunction. Thus, FLSA injunction actions can compel the payment of past-due compensation to all employees, enjoin future violations of the FLSA, and/or prohibit the sale or distribution of goods that were manufactured with labor paid in violation of the FLSA. The DOL can also seek reinstatement with back pay for an individual who has been discharged for attempting to enforce the FLSA. [29 U.S.C. §§ 211(a), 212(b), 215, 217]

The Secretary is not so limited. Both the back pay and liquidated damages remedies provided in FLSA Section 216(c), and the injunctive remedies provided in FLSA Section 217, are available to the Secretary. [Reich v. Great Lakes Collection Bureau, 176 F.R.D. 81 (W.D.N.Y. 1997)] But if the Secretary seeks only a restitutionary injunction under FLSA Section 17, he or she cannot recover liquidated damages as in an action for wages under FLSA Section 16. [Brock v. Superior Care, Inc., 840 F.2d 1054, 1064 (2d Cir. 1988)]

Because injunctions are equitable in nature, actions for injunctive relief do not involve a jury trial and the DOL often seeks to avoid a jury trial.

Q 14:38   When may a private individual seek injunctive relief for violations of the FLSA?

A private individual may obtain injunctive relief for violations of the FLSA's anti-retaliation provision in Section 215(a)(3) [Bailey v. Gulf Coast Transp., Inc., 280 F.3d 1333 (11th Cir. 2002)]. In *Bailey,* the court determined that the "remedies" Section 216(b) provides to employees for violations of the FLSA's anti-retaliation provision are broader than those available for violations of the wage and overtime provisions. Therefore, a plaintiff may seek equitable relief (such as reinstatement) for violation of the anti-retaliation provision of the FLSA.

Q 14:39   What are the burdens of proof for the DOL and an employer in an FLSA injunction action?

The burdens of proof in an injunction action are the same as those in a wage suit (see Q 14:8). As the plaintiff, the DOL bears the burden of proving that additional wages in the form of overtime and minimum wage compensation are due. If applicable, an employer bears the burden of pleading and proving that an employee is exempt from the receipt of overtime or minimum wage compensation. The burden of proof as to the number of hours worked and amount of wages shifts to an employer if it has failed to keep records as required by the FLSA and employees testify to performing hours of work for which no compensation was provided. As a practical matter, when no records have been kept, it is exceptionally difficult to prove that an employee is exaggerating his or her wage claim. In such situations, uncertainty as to the amount of an employee's unpaid wages does not preclude an award for damages. [Anderson v. Mt. Clemens Potter Co., 328 U.S. 680 (1946)]

Q 14:40   In what situations have courts issued injunctions to enforce the FLSA?

Injunctions against future violations of the FLSA have been issued in the following circumstances:

1. Employees who were terminated shortly after bringing suit against their employer for failure to pay minimum wage were granted preliminary injunctive relief after amending the complaint subsequent to their termination of employment to include a claim for retaliation and a motion for a preliminary injunction to reinstate the employees whose employment was terminated. [Bailey v. Gulf Coast Transp., Inc., 280 F.3d 1333 (11th Cir. 2002)]

2. An employer that employed minor-employees was investigated for child labor violations at two different locations, was fined once for violations, and continued to have child labor issues at both locations despite ongoing investigations. [Martin v. Fun-time, Inc., 963 F.2d 110 (6th Cir. 1992)]

3. An employer unlawfully failed to record and pay for time employees spent in certain preliminary and postliminary shift activities and failed to enter into a compliance agreement with the Secretary of Labor to compensate or to record properly any compensable time following findings of violations that were confirmed by an appellate court. [Metzler v. IBP, Inc., 127 F.3d 959 (10th Cir. 1997)]

Injunctions are, as a practical matter, frequently sought by the DOL for the simple reason that, with an injunction in place, the DOL's enforcement job is made easier with respect to future violations. By seeking injunctions, however, the DOL makes it more difficult for employers to settle. This is because unless the injunction's language is carefully drafted to be limited, it will run in perpetuity, effectively eliminating the statute of limitations.

Injunctions are not always granted, however. For example, an injunction was denied when the employer's violations arose from its failure to understand the FLSA's requirements, which was careless but inadvertent, and the employer was currently in compliance with the FLSA. [Martin v. Coventry Fire Dist., 981 F.2d 1358 (1st Cir. 1982)] An injunction was denied on a similar rationale where the employer had corrected its pay practices, had received poor advice in the past, had complied with all requests and orders of the DOL once the DOL began investigating, and did not appear likely to violate the FLSA in the future. [Herman v. Hogar Praderas de Amor, Inc., 130 F. Supp. 2d 257 (D.P.R. 2001)]

Q 14:41   Can a corporate officer be a proper party-defendant to an FLSA injunction?

Yes. An injunction can be issued against an individual when he or she exercises some supervisory authority over employees (such as a corporate officer who actively administers daily business operations) and is at least partially responsible for the alleged violation or violations. In those circumstances, the injunction is issued against the corporation and the individual jointly. [Donovan v. Sabine Irrigation Co., 695 F.2d 190 (5th Cir.), *cert. denied*, 463 U.S. 1207 (1983)]

In contrast, an injunction should not be issued against an individual who does not have control over the management and operations of the employer that has violated the FLSA. [Hodgson v. Colonnades, Inc., 472 F.2d 42 (5th Cir. 1973) (corporate president not an appropriate subject of an injunction when daily operations and management were controlled by others)]

Q 14:42   What is significant about injunction actions and how are they enforced?

The significance of an injunction requiring an employer to obey the FLSA for the indefinite future lies in the fact that the injunction can be enforced through a civil or criminal contempt proceeding. An employer that violates an injunction can be subject to a fine or imprisonment, in addition to having to pay past-due wages and, possibly, attorneys' fees.

When an injunction is in effect, the DOL can return to court merely by filing a petition to hold an employer in contempt. In addition to an assessment of back wages, a contempt sanction includes an assessment against the employer of the DOL's costs of investigation and litigation incurred in pursuit of a contempt order. [*See* Mitchell v. Fiore, 470 F.2d 1149 (3d Cir. 1972), *cert. denied,* 411 U.S. 938 (1973)] Further, the petition for contempt can be based on alleged violations of the FLSA that were not part of the original investigation that led to the injunction.

In a civil contempt proceeding of this type, the fact that the employer's violations were not willful does not preclude a finding of contempt. [McComb v. Jacksonville Paper Co., 336 U.S. 187 (1949)] Moreover, the Portal Act's statute of limitations period for the filing of FLSA actions does not apply to such contempt proceedings. Courts have ruled that the application of the limitations period to injunction actions would be contrary to the purpose of the FLSA, would reward an employer whose violation of the injunction escaped immediate detection, and would limit the effectiveness of the injunction as prospective relief for FLSA violations. [Donovan v. Sureway Cleaners, 656 F.2d 1368 (9th Cir. 1981)]

Q 14:43   How long can an FLSA injunction run?

The duration of an injunction is a matter of court discretion: Injunctions can be permanent or for a specific term. If an employer complies with FLSA requirements after an injunction action has been filed, a court should be able to consider that in determining the length of the injunction. An injunction entered against an offending employer under the FLSA can remain in effect indefinitely;

however, injunctions can be dissolved or modified in a subsequent action, usually initiated by the employer.

In one case, the Fourth Circuit dissolved an injunction against an employer only after it complied with the law in good faith for nine years following the original issuance of the injunction and the injunction was shown to be interfering with a sale of the business. [Tobin v. Alma Mills, 192 F.2d 133 (4th Cir. 1951)] In another case, a consent injunction was dissolved after three and one-half years of continued compliance, where the original violation was small and there was evidence that the injunction was a continuing source of embarrassment to the employer that interfered with the orderly conduct of its business. [Brennan v. Thor, Inc., 516 F.2d 999 (4th Cir. 1975)]

Q 14:44   Can a court order an employer to purge a contempt action pursuant to an FLSA injunction?

Yes. If a company is subject to an injunction from a court not to violate the FLSA and is found to be in contempt of the injunction because of violations of the FLSA after the issuance of the injunction, the court can order the company to pay damages (i.e., back pay) to purge the contempt. These damages can be the amount equal to the unpaid minimum wages and overtime due to the employees in question. The Supreme Court has upheld the power of courts to assess such damages in civil contempt proceedings. No statute of limitations period applies to a court's order that the employer purge the contempt action by payment of back wages. [McComb v. Jacksonville Paper Co., 336 U.S. 187 (1949)]

Q 14:45   Can an employer be subject to criminal contempt for failure to comply with an injunction?

Yes. The Department of Justice, with the assistance of the Wage and Hour Administrator, can petition the court for criminal contempt sanctions when an employer fails to comply with an injunction. Civil contempt is designed to be remedial and bring an employer into compliance; criminal contempt is entirely punitive and is a reaction to an employer's defiance of the court's authority. [United Mine Workers of Am. v. Bagwell, 512 U.S. 821 (1994)] Criminal contempt is necessarily based on proof that the employer's continued violations are willful. [Wirtz v. Reyna Fashions, 17 Wage & Hour Cas. (BNA) 233 (S.D. Fla. 1966)] It is possible to be imprisoned for criminal contempt.

Q 14:46   Can prejudgment interest be awarded in an FLSA injunction action?

Yes. Interest generally is regarded as appropriate when no liquidated damages are sought or awarded. Prejudgment interest should generally be awarded on top of a back-pay award in an injunction action under FLSA Section 17, even if the underpayments were made in good faith. [Donovan v. Sovereign Sec., Ltd., 726 F.2d 55 (2d Cir. 1984)] Federal district courts have the jurisdiction to set the interest rate to be used in awarding prejudgment interest to employees under FLSA Section 17. [29 U.S.C. § 217]

Action by More Than One Plaintiff

Q 14:47   Can an FLSA action be brought on behalf of more than one plaintiff?

Yes. Pursuant to FLSA Section 216(b), an FLSA action can be maintained by one or more employees on behalf of themselves and any other employees similarly situated. Unlike traditional class action lawsuits, however, no employee can become a party-plaintiff to an FLSA collective action unless his or her consent to become a named party is given in writing and the consent is filed in the court in which the action is brought. Significantly, the FLSA's statute of limitations continues to run against an employee until the employee files such a consent form with the court. [29 U.S.C. § 216(b); Lee v. Vance Executive Prot., Inc., 7 Fed. Appx. 160, 2001 U.S. App. LEXIS 1849 (4th Cir. 2001) (holding that consents filed after the complaint do not relate back to the complaint)] The importance of stopping the statute of limitations by filing those consent forms lies in the fact that any recovery for a plaintiff suing under the FLSA dates back only as many as two years (or three years if the plaintiff can establish a willful violation). Thus, if the plaintiff no longer works for the employer being sued, each day that the statute of limitations continues to run cuts off a day of unpaid minimum wages or overtime pay liability that might have otherwise been ordered.

Indeed, for the last couple of years, FLSA claims have been targeted by plaintiffs' lawyer groups. FLSA collective actions are now the most frequently filed labor and employment claims. The plaintiffs' lawyers are attempting to use the collective "opt-in" class actions and three-year "willful" statute of limitations, as well as attorney's fees, to expand exposure for employers. The significant increase in collective actions by plaintiffs' lawyers is one primary cause of the congressional effort to revise the "white-collar" exemptions under 29 C.F.R. pt. 541 and reduce the amount of litigation occurring.

As an example of the type of cases some judges have considered an abuse of the provisions of the FLSA, consider Goss v. Killian Oaks House of Learning, 248 F. Supp. 2d 1162 (S.D. Fla. 2003), in which the judge explained that the plaintiff had an approximate $300 claim under the FLSA after having worked for approximately two weeks for the employer and subsequently going to the plaintiff's counsel, who pursued the litigation and ultimately claimed in excess of $16,000 in attorney's fees. Even though the plaintiff was viewed as the prevailing party, the judge viewed the plaintiff's counsel's actions and claim for fees as unreasonable with a pattern of activity to "churn" the file and that he engaged in a strategy of "shaking down" the defendant with nightmarishly expensive litigation solely in pursuit of attorney's fees, which shocked the conscience of the court. All fees as well as costs to the plaintiff were denied.

Q 14:48   Can an association bring a representative FLSA action on behalf of state employees?

No. An association of state employees, like a union, is barred from suing under the FLSA on behalf of its members. Each individual member of the association or union must file consent opt-in forms under the FLSA. [Nevada Employees' Ass'n, Inc. v. Bryan, 916 F.2d 1384 (9th Cir. 1990); *see also* OTR Drivers v. Frito-Lay, Inc., 160 F.R.D. 146 (D. Ky. 1995) (organization cannot bring FLSA action on behalf of members)]

Q 14:49   In a collective action suit under the FLSA, must all plaintiffs testify at trial?

No. At trial, the testimony of a representative group of employees can provide the basis of an award of back wages to nontestifying employees. It was held, however, that a district court abused its discretion when, for purposes of determining back pay and liquidated damages, in a case brought by the Secretary of Labor on behalf of more than 3,000 employees, it limited trial testimony to only 1.6 percent of the total employee population. Such a small ratio of testifying representative employees could not provide a sufficient basis to justify an award of back pay to nontestifying employees. In a collective action under the FLSA, discovery, whether conducted before or after class certification should be conducted on a class-wide level, except in the rarest of cases. [Reich v. S. Md. Hosp., 43 F.3d 949 (4th Cir. 1995)]

Q 14:50   What must a prospective plaintiff do to consent properly in writing to opt-in to an FLSA collective action?

The "consent in writing to become such a party" referred to in FLSA Section 216(b) is a document signed by the person whose consent it reports declaring that person's intent to become a named party-plaintiff in the action. Such a consent form must be filed with the court in which the action is pending. A document merely bearing the typewritten name of the proposed party-plaintiff does not satisfy the FLSA's requirement that a consent opt-in be filed with the court; the document must be signed by the proposed party-plaintiff. [29 U.S.C. § 216(b); *see* Montalvo v. Tower Life Bldg., 426 F.2d 1135, 1147–49 (5th Cir. 1970)]

Q 14:51   What are the differences between a class action as described by Rule 23 of the Federal Rules of Civil Procedure and a collective action provided for in FLSA Section 216(b)?

The most important difference relates to the effect of a judgment in the action. In a traditional Rule 23 class action, a person must opt out of the class to avoid being bound by the judgment rendered in the class action. Under an FLSA collective action, no person can become a party-plaintiff and be bound by a judgment in the case unless he or she has opted in to the class by his or her written filed consent. [29 U.S.C. § 216(b); Fed. R. Civ. P. 23] Most courts do not apply the requirements of Rule 23 of the Federal Rules of Civil Procedure to FLSA collective actions, because the procedures under each are fundamentally different from one another.

Q 14:52   What authority do courts have to supervise notification to potential class members of their right to opt in to an FLSA collective action?

Federal courts have discretionary authority to order or approve notification to potential class members of their right to opt in to an FLSA lawsuit as party-plaintiffs. [Braunstein v. E. Photographic Labs., Inc., 600 F.2d 335 (2d Cir. 1978), *cert. denied,* 441 U.S. 944 (1979)] Before determining to exercise such discretionary power, however, district courts should satisfy themselves that there are other employees of the employer who want to opt in and who are similarly situated with respect to their job requirements and with regard to their pay provisions. [Dybach v. Fla. Dep't of Corr., 942 F.2d 1562 (11th Cir. 1991)] Unsupported assertions by the plaintiff's counsel that FLSA violations were widespread and that additional plaintiff's would likely join the action are not sufficient to authorize the sending of court-supervised notice. [*See* Haynes v. Singer Co., 696 F.2d 884 (11th Cir. 1983)] According to the Supreme Court, trial courts have a managerial responsibility over collective actions to avoid a multiplicity of suits and to ensure efficiency. [Hoffmann-La Roche Inc. v. Sperling, 493 U.S. 165 (1989)]

The threshold issue in deciding whether to authorize class notice in an FLSA action is whether the plaintiffs have adequately demonstrated that the potential class members are similarly situated. When determining if persons are similarly situated under the FLSA, the persons must be similarly situated with respect to their job requirements and with regard to their pay provisions; however, the positions need not be identical, only similar. [Tucker v. Labor Leasing, Inc., 872 F. Supp. 941 (M.D. Fla. 1994)] (See Q 14:54.)

Once a court determines that plaintiffs may proceed as a collective group, as a class, the court may facilitate the provision of notice to potential class members. Whether or not the court decides to facilitate the provision of notice, the wording of the notice is a subject of concern to all parties. Plaintiffs will wish to give notice that is as broad as possible and which strongly presents their claims so that potential class members opt-in. Defendants will wish to have notice worded to limit the group of plaintiffs strictly to the group that has been determined to be "similarly situated," and will want to mention the possibility of fees and costs in order to discourage potential class members from opting-in to the action. More often than not, a court is going to step in to mediate this process of determining the wording for notice to potential class members. [*See, e.g.,* Jackson v. Go-Tane Servs. Inc., 6 Wage & Hour Cas. 2d (BNA) 679 (N.D. Ill. 2000) (wording of plaintiff's notice was acceptable, over defendant's objections)]

Q 14:53   When can a representative plaintiff discover the names and addresses of other employees?

Courts will usually allow a representative to discover the names and addresses of other employees when the representative plaintiff is able to make a showing that there are other employees of the defendant who are similarly situated to the representative. The practical effect of the notice aspects of an FLSA collective action is that a court will likely allow some limited discovery on the issue of whether there are categories of employees who are or might be similarly situated to the representative plaintiff. If that discovery yields results, the court can then proceed to class-wide discovery, including names and addresses, to facilitate notice. [*See* Tucker v. Labor Leasing, Inc., 155 F.R.D. 687 (M.D. Fla. 1994)]

Q 14:54   What is required for plaintiffs to attain class certification in the FLSA context?

The consequence of class certification in the FLSA context is that the court allows the suit to proceed as a collective action in accordance with the requirements of FLSA Section 216(b). To receive class certification, two conditions must be met:

1. The named representatives and members of the prospective class must be similarly situated; and

2. The action must be one of general effect, not one that is purely personal to the plaintiff.

[29 U.S.C. § 216(b); Wyatt v. Pride Offshore, Inc., 3 Wage & Hour Cas. 2d (BNA) 892 (E.D. La. 1996)]

The "similarly situated" requirement is the source of most litigation and dispute in this area, with employers seeking to avoid a class certification by arguing that plaintiffs are not similarly situated. Some courts state that to be similarly situated, plaintiffs must be or have been employed in the same division, department, and location, have similar claims, and seek substantially the same relief. Other courts are less stringent in the requirement that the plaintiffs have been employed in the same department and location, as long as they all are or were in the same job category and subject to the same pay practice or policy alleged to be in violation of the ADA.

The class certification inquiry under the FLSA is a two-tiered process in many courts. At the first stage, early in the litigation, the burden of establishing that plaintiffs are "similarly situated" is lighter, and if the plaintiffs make that showing, they are "conditionally certified" as a class. Courts apply different standards at this initial stage in determining whether the plaintiff has met the burden of establishing others are "similarly situated." Some courts have held that motions for preliminary certification and notice may be granted provided the plaintiff simply alleges that the putative class members were injured as a result of a single policy of the defendant employer. Other courts, however, apply a slightly more stringent test that requires the plaintiff to make a "modest factual showing" that the putative class members are similarly situated. [*See, e.g.,* Smith v. Sovereign Bankcorp, Inc., 2003 WL 22701017 (E.D. Pa. 2003), and discussion therein] If the plaintiff meets this initial burden of establishing others are similarly situated, notice is given to potential class members, which the court may facilitate in its discretion, that they may opt in to the class. Later, the second tier inquiry is reached by the filing by the defendant(s) of a motion to decertify. At the decertification stage, the burden to prove that the plaintiffs are "similarly situated" is more stringent in the sense that more information is available to the court to analyze whether the plaintiffs really are similarly situated. If the class is decertified, the opt-in plaintiffs are dismissed and the representative plaintiffs proceed to trial. If the class is not decertified, the class proceeds to trial. [*See* Felix de Asencio v. Tyson Foods, Inc., 130 F. Supp. 2d 660 (E.D. Pa. 2001) (class was conditionally certified because all plaintiffs worked in the same position, their claims were all based on the defendant's alleged failure to pay overtime and minimum wage, and all sought similar relief)]

The "similarly situated" determination truly rests on a determination that the same factual analysis for establishing a violation of the FLSA will apply to each of the group of plaintiffs. For this reason, the plaintiffs should be performing the same type(s) of jobs subject to the same pay practices. In one case, plaintiffs were challenging their employer's classification of them as exempt, but the court concluded the plaintiffs were not similarly situated. The court noted that the plaintiffs worked in different positions and performed different duties at different levels. In judging whether an employee is exempt or not, the analysis turns on a detailed review of the plaintiff's job duties and performance. Where this fact-intensive analysis is required for each plaintiff, the employer's argument would be that the inquiry itself cuts against a finding that the plaintiffs as a group were similarly situated. [Morisky v. Pub. Serv. Elec. & Gas Co., 111 F. Supp. 2d 493 (D.N.J. 2000) (class certification denied, because plaintiffs were not similarly situated)]

Criminal Penalties

Q 14:55   Can a person face criminal penalties for violating the FLSA's provisions?

Yes. Any person who willfully violates the FLSA is, on conviction, subject to a fine of up to $10,000 or to imprisonment for not more than six months, or both. No person is imprisoned for violating the FLSA, however, until he or she is found guilty of committing a second offense. [29 U.S.C. § 216(a)]

A violation must be willful to justify criminal action. A violation of the FLSA is willful if it is "deliberate, voluntary and intentional." [Nabob Oil Co. v. United States, 190 F.2d 478 (10th Cir.), *cert. denied,* 342 U.S. 876 (1951)] The standard used to determine whether a violation is willful in a criminal sense is much more stringent than that used to determine whether a violation is willful for the purpose of extending the FLSA's statute of limitations. A willful violation does not require an evil motive—"reckless indifference" to the FLSA's requirements may suffice. [United States v. Klinghoffer Bros. Realty Corp., 285 F.2d 487, 492 (2d Cir. 1960)] A violation is not willful, however, when it is "committed [merely] through inadvertence, accidentally or by ordinary negligence." [*Nabob Oil*, 190 F.2d at 480]

Q 14:56 Are criminal actions and actions for back wages under the FLSA mutually exclusive?

No. Criminal actions can be prosecuted in lieu of, or in conjunction with, a civil action to recover back wages or obtain an injunction under the FLSA. Thus, in cases involving willful overtime and minimum wage violations, it is possible for an employer to be assessed actual and liquidated damages and have criminal sanctions imposed. If willfulness is not proved but the violations are, the employer would be liable for back wages but not for criminal sanctions. The DOL does not have the authority to prosecute criminal actions. Criminal prosecutions under the FLSA are brought by the federal Department of Justice, with the assistance of and based on information uncovered by the Wage and Hour Division.

Q 14:57 How is criminal contempt under the FLSA initiated and enforced?

When a court has issued an order to a company to comply with the law, or the company has agreed to a "consent judgment" in court, a willful failure to comply with the court's order can be punished as criminal contempt of the court. As with criminal actions generally, criminal contempt cannot be prosecuted by the DOL. FLSA Section 16(a), which provides criminal penalties for violations of the FLSA but prohibits imprisonment for a first offense, does not prohibit imprisonment on the first conviction of the employer for criminal contempt of a court order directing compliance with the FLSA. The ability to imprison a person found to be in criminal contempt of a court's order directing compliance with the FLSA, even without a prior criminal conviction under the FLSA, is permitted because such contempt is an affront to the integrity of the court; thus, it is not the employer's substantive criminal violation that is being punished through such contempt action. [United States v. Fidanian, 465 F.2d 755 (5th Cir. 1972); 29 U.S.C. § 216(a)]

Q 14:58 Are there other circumstances under which a first-time offender of the FLSA can be imprisoned?

Yes. A first-time offender who is convicted under the criminal provisions of the FLSA, though punishable only by a fine, can be placed on probation, with the possible condition of probation being that the offender make reparation for losses caused by the FLSA violation (i.e., make payment of wages due to employees). Thus, a first-time offender who violates the conditions of his or her probation can be imprisoned. Further, courts have the authority to commit a first-time offender until the fine imposed is paid or he or she is otherwise discharged of such obligations according to the law. [United States v. Ridgewood Garment Co., 44 F. Supp. 435 (E.D.N.Y. 1942)]

Manager of Business as Employer

Q 14:59   Who can be held liable for an employer's violations of the FLSA?

A company, as well as its officers, can be convicted of and fined for a violation of the FLSA. An employer "includes any person acting directly or indirectly in the interest of an employer in relation to an employee." [29 U.S.C. § 203(d)] An employer can be any individual or company that hires help or any individual or company supervising employees or managing labor at a work site. Therefore, the definition of *employer* under the FLSA includes the following:

- Individuals, such as agents or managers of a company or corporate officers
- Corporations
- Partnerships
- Associations
- Government agencies or branches
- Government contractors
- Religious enterprises

Labor unions are expressly excluded from the FLSA's definition of employer in relation to their members. Although labor organizations are not employers of their members, they are employers of the individuals hired to administer the organization's business. [29 U.S.C. § 203(d)]

An individual member of management who actively participates in the running of a business may be held to be an employer and therefore liable for unpaid wages and subject to court injunctions for violation of the FLSA. Thus, an officer of the company who hires and fires, sets hours of work, directs work activities, and sets wages can be individually liable for wage and hour violations. [Herman v. Hogar Praderas de Amor, Inc., 130 F. Supp. 2d 257 (D.P.R. 2001); *see also* Reich v. Circle C Invest., Inc., 998 F.2d 324, 329 (5th Cir. 1993) (definition of employer under the FLSA is broad enough to encompass individuals who lack a possessory interest in the business but who exercise significant control over the employees)]

The key factor in fixing liability on a corporate officer or manager is that individual's operational control of the enterprise and not necessarily any ownership interest held by that person. A corporate officer or manager who is deemed to be an employer for FLSA purposes is liable in his or her individual, not simply representative, capacity. [Donovan v. Grim Hotel Co., 747 F.2d 966 (5th Cir. 1984)]

Q 14:60   Can FLSA liability extend to partners and stockholders?

Yes. Partners are jointly liable with the partnership for FLSA plaintiffs' damages when they are jointly liable for the partnership's debts under state law. [Fegley v. Higgins, 19 F.3d 1126 (6th Cir. 1994)] In addition, stockholders receiving assets of a corporation on its dissolution, who are subject to payment of corporate liabilities, can be liable to the extent that assets received must be allocated to overtime or minimum wage compensation liabilities of the corporation before the dissolution.

Prohibition of Reprisals Against Employees

Q 14:61   Does the FLSA prohibit retaliation by employers against employees who become involved in FLSA proceedings?

Yes. FLSA Section 215(a)(3) prohibits any person from discharging or discriminating in other ways against any employee because the employee has filed a complaint or instituted a proceeding under the FLSA, has testified or is about to testify in such proceeding, or has served on an industry committee. The provisions of FLSA Section 215(a)(3) also apply to a state, political subdivision of a state, or an interstate government agency. Thus, any employer or person who violates the FLSA's anti-retaliation provision is liable for the legal or equitable relief appropriate to effectuate the purposes of the FLSA, including, without limitation, employment, reinstatement, promotion, payment of lost wages, and an additional equal amount as liquidated damages. [29 U.S.C. §§ 215(a)(3), 216(b)]

An action to recover damages for prohibited retaliation can be maintained against any employer (including a public agency) in any federal or state court of competent jurisdiction by any one or more employees on behalf of themselves and other employees similarly situated. An employee discharged in retaliation for claiming that his or her employer violated the FLSA's minimum wage or overtime pay provisions is entitled to an award of back pay (including the amount that would have been earned if employment had continued through time of trial), minus earnings from other employment and any unemployment benefits received in the interim, and including any reasonable prospect that the employee would have been promoted or would have received pay increases in light of his or her employment history before the discharge. [29 U.S.C. § 216(b); see Johnston v. Specialty Rests. Corp., 628 F. Supp. 32 (W.D. Mo. 1985)]

Q 14:62   What must an employee prove in an FLSA retaliatory discharge case?

To establish retaliation under FLSA Section 215(a)(3), an employee must prove that he or she engaged in protected activity (such as a complaint about overtime wages), that he or she was then subjected to an adverse employment action, and that the adverse employment action was in retaliation for the protected activity. Plaintiffs can assert that the fact that an adverse employment action occurs shortly after a complaint is proof of retaliation, and temporal proximity may indeed raise an inference of retaliation. Unless an employee's termination is very closely connected in time to the protected conduct in issue, however, the plaintiff-employee will need to rely on additional evidence beyond mere temporal proximity to establish the requisite causation necessary for such action. [Conner v. Schnuck Mkts., Inc., 121 F.3d 1390 (10th Cir. 1997) (four months between complaint and discharge is insufficient to establish causal connection)] The protected activity—that is, the complaint about a real or suspected violation of the FLSA, or testimony in a proceeding—must precede the adverse employment action in order for a retaliation claim to succeed. For example, one plaintiff's claim of retaliation failed because the plaintiff failed to produce evidence that she engaged in protected activity (i.e., complained) before her termination. [Wolf v. Coca-Cola Co., 200 F.3d 1337 (11th Cir. 2000)]

If an employee establishes a case for retaliation, but the employer claims that there were other reasons for discharging the employee or taking some other adverse employment action, the employee must show that those reasons were pretextual. That is, the employee must prove that reasons put forth by the employer were not the true reasons for the discharge or adverse employment action but merely excuses for retaliating against the employee. For example, in one case, the short period of time between the filing of an FLSA lawsuit by an employee and his firing, coupled with evidence suggesting that the employer was looking for and creating reasons to justify the employee's termination was a strong indication that the employer's explanations for the employee's termination were pretextual. [Krieg v. Pell's, Inc., 2001 WL 548394 (S.D. Ind. 2002)]

In other cases, employees have been less successful in casting doubt on the employer's justifications for termination. For example, when an employee who worked in the packaging department of a chicken feather processing plant discovered that employees in the shipping department received overtime while she did not, she asked one of the bosses if packaging department employees could also receive overtime. The boss seemed uncomfortable with the question but said he would look into it. He later explained that employees in the packaging department were considered "agricultural" and exempt from overtime, while employees in the shipping department were not. The employee said "okay" and went back to work. She never mentioned overtime to any of the bosses again. About two months later, after the employee disregarded direct orders of her supervisor, which resulted in a large backlog of products, she was fired. The employee brought suit under the FLSA claiming retaliatory discharge. A U.S. district court concluded that the employee did not show that the employer's reason for firing her—failure to follow reasonable instructions causing a product backlog—was pretextual, and an appellate court agreed. According to the appeals court, an employee demonstrates pretext with evidence that the employer's proffered reasons are so weak, implausible, or inconsistent a reasonable jury would not believe them. However, in this case, the employee did not offer *any* evidence on which a reasonable jury could infer retaliatory motive or disbelieve the employer's claimed reason for terminating her employment. [Pacheco v. Whiting Farms, Inc., 365 F.3d 1199 (10th Cir. 2004)]

Q 14:63   What is the extent of the FLSA's anti-retaliation prohibition?

FLSA Section 215(a)(3) prohibits retaliatory conduct by any person against employees who engage in any protected conduct under the statute. Prohibited retaliation includes any retaliatory discharge or alteration in the terms or conditions of employment, including a reduction in wages or a demotion. Retaliation can occur after the employment relationship has ended. Thus, it has been found that a former employee, even though voluntarily separated from his job, was protected from discrimination by his former employer, who caused a prospective employer to refuse to hire the employee because he had filed a complaint against the former employer under the FLSA. [Dunlop v. Carriage Carpet Co., 548 F.2d 139 (6th Cir. 1977)]

Job applicants who are neither current nor former employees of the accused do not qualify as "any employee" for purposes of the FLSA's anti-retaliation provision, and, accordingly, cannot sue under the Act. [Glover v. City of N. Charleston, 942 F. Supp. 243 (D.S.C. 1996)]

Q 14:64   What types of employee conduct are protected under the FLSA's anti-retaliation provision?

Although the FLSA by its terms protects only employee conduct that rises to the level of a complaint or proceeding, or an employee who has testified in such a proceeding, in reality courts have interpreted the anti-retaliation provision to include internal or informal complaints about wage and hour issues, or refusals to give up rights under the FLSA. [*See, e.g.*, Valerio v. Putnam Assocs. Inc., 173 F.3d 35 (1st Cir. 1999)] According to the courts, the anti-retaliation protections would be worthless if the employee could be discharged for declining to give up the benefits to which he or she is entitled pursuant to the FLSA. [*See, e.g.*, Brock v. Casey Truck Sales, Inc., 839 F.2d 872 (2d Cir. 1988) (employer violated anti-retaliation provision when it discharged employees because they pressed for—and refused to waive—their right to overtime pay)]

There are limits to what informal activities constitute protected activity. For example, a company's personnel director did not engage in protected activity under the FLSA when she discussed with the company attorney and its president her concerns that employees were not receiving proper overtime compensation. It was part of the personnel director's job to evaluate wage and hour issues for her employer. The court held that to engage in protected activity, an employee must step outside his or her role of representing the employer and either file or threaten to file an action adverse to the employer, actively help other employees to assert their rights, or otherwise engage in activities that reasonably could be perceived as directed toward the assertion of FLSA rights. Internal company complaints that are consistent with an employee's duties do not constitute protected activities under the FLSA. [McKenzie v. Renberg's Inc., 94 F.3d 1478 (10th Cir. 1996), *cert. denied*, 520 U.S. 1186 (1997)]

In another case, an employee whose job responsibilities included monitoring security guards and approving their invoices for payment sent a letter to his employer indicating that he had concluded the guards were not being properly compensated for overtime. At a meeting with attorneys, it was determined that the guards were not employees of the employer and that the employer was not responsible for seeing that the guards were properly paid for overtime work. However, the employer indicated that it would inform the contractor who supplied the guards of the potential overtime violations the employee detected. At the conclusion of the meeting, the employee was told that, in the meantime, he should approve the guards' invoices. The employee refused to do so and was terminated from employment. The employee sued for retaliatory discharge, but a district court ruled in favor of the employer. The U.S. Court of Appeals affirmed the district court's decision. According to the court, when the employee first informed the employer of the potential overtime violations he did so in furtherance of his job responsibilities, which included approving invoices for the guards' pay. He "never crossed the line from being an employee merely performing his job. . .to an employee lodging a personal complaint" and, therefore, did not engage in a protected activity. Moreover, the employee's subsequent refusal to sign the guards' invoices did not amount to the filing of a complaint under the FLSA. The FLSA anti-retaliation provision protects an employee's lawful efforts to secure rights afforded by the FLSA. However, the refusal to sign the invoices occurred after the whistle had been blown and after corrective actions were being taken to remedy any FLSA violations. [Claudio Gotay v. Becton Dickinson Caribe, Ltd., 375 F.3d 99 (1st Cir. 2004)]

There are also limits to what constitutes "testimony" for purposes of claiming retaliation on the basis of "testimony" given or about to be given in support of a proceeding. For example, one court held that, in the case of one employee who was terminated after telling the president of the company that if he was called to testify in a lawsuit being threatened by a former employee, his testimony would not support the president's version of events, the employee did not engage in protected activity. Because there was no "proceeding" at that time, only an internal complaint by another employee, the court held that the termination was not prohibited retaliation under the FLSA. The "proceeding" required by the anti-retaliation provision refers to a judicial or administrative procedure, not an internal complaint. [Ball v. Memphis Bar-B-Q Co., 228 F.3d 360 (4th Cir. 2000)]

Moreover, a recent case raised the interesting question of whether helping a fellow employee institute a wage claim against an employer constitutes protected activity. The employee in the case had informed a coworker about federal and state overtime requirements and helped him draft two letters to institute a claim against the employer for failure to pay him proper overtime compensation. When the employer received notice of the coworker's claim, the employer's management became angry over the employee's involvement. A few days later, he was fired. The employee claimed his firing was illegal retaliation for engaging in a protected activity. However, the employer argued that helping a coworker file a claim is not protected activity under the FLSA and asked the court to dismiss the employee's lawsuit. However, the court concluded that the issue was not quite that cut-and-dried. The FLSA prohibits an employer from discharging an employee because the employee "caused to be instituted any proceeding" related to the assertion of wage rights. And there was some evidence that the employee *caused* the coworker to file his wage claim—in which case, the employee's activity would be protected. Therefore, the court ordered a trial for a determination of that issue. [Onken v. W.L. May Co., 300 F. Supp. 2d 1066 (D. Ore. 2004)]

Q 14:65 What remedies are available to an employee who can prove that the employer violated the FLSA's anti-retaliation provisions?

If it is found that an employee has been illegally fired or disciplined for asserting his or her rights under the FLSA, several remedies are available. A "willful or flagrant" violation of the FLSA can be punished by fine or imprisonment or both, and the court can order the company to stop violating the law. In addition, the FLSA's anti-retaliation provision provides for legal or equitable relief that is appropriate, including, without limitation, employment reinstatement, promotion, payment of lost wages, and an additional amount as liquidated damages. Thus, plaintiffs can recover damages because of retaliation, including back pay and damages for mental anguish. Moreover, the court can order an employer to reinstate the employee. In the event that reinstatement is inappropriate, front pay can be awarded to an employee who is discharged for filing an FLSA overtime or minimum wage claim. [29 U.S.C. § 216(b); Avitia v. Metro. Club of Chicago, Inc., 49 F.3d 1219 (7th Cir. 1995)] Finally, it has been held that punitive damages can be awarded on FLSA retaliation claims, even without a separate award of compensatory damages. [Shea v. Galaxie Lumber & Constr. Co., 152 F.3d 729 (7th Cir. 1998)]

Q 14:66 Are emotional distress damages available to an employee who can prove that the employer violated the FLSA's anti-retaliation provisions?

Yes, according to the Sixth and Seventh Circuits. Those circuits have ruled that the FLSA damages provision for anti-retaliation claims is broad enough to include damages for mental and emotional distress caused by the employer's retaliation. [Moore v. Freeman, 355 F.3d 558 (6th Cir. 2004); Travis v. Gary Cmty. Health Ctr., Inc., 921 F.2d 108 (7th Cir. 1990)] Moreover, as the *Moore* court pointed out, "both the Eighth and Ninth Circuits have allowed damages for emotional distress to stand without directly addressing the issue." [*Moore,* 355 F.3d at 564 (citing Broadus v. O.K. Indus., Inc., 238 F.3d 990 (8th Cir. 2001); Lambert v. Ackerley, 180 F.3d 997 (9th Cir. 1999))] Other circuits have not yet addressed this issue.

Punitive Damages

Q 14:67 Are punitive damages available under the FLSA?

Generally, no. The FLSA does not provide for exemplary (punitive) damages. Several courts have held that exemplary damages are not available in light of the liquidated damages provision of FLSA Section 216(b) and are not available for claims based on a failure to pay overtime. However, like other legal relief provisions, the FLSA's provision for legal relief in cases involving retaliation or discrimination under FLSA Section 215(a)(3) may support an award for emotional distress and punitive damages. [Marrow v. Allstate Sec. & Investigative Serv., Inc., 167 F. Supp. 2d 838 (E.D. Pa. 2001) (holding that the scope of "legal or equitable relief" provided for in the FLSA's anti-retaliation provisions includes punitive damages); Shea v. Galaxie Lumber & Constr. Co., 152 F.3d 729 (7th Cir. 1998); Travis v. Gary Cmty. Mental Health Ctr., Inc., 921 F.2d 108 (7th Cir. 1990)] At least one court, however, has held that punitive damages are not available as "legal relief" for retaliation. [Snapp v. Unltd. Concepts, Inc., 208 F.3d 928 (11th Cir. 2000) (the court specifically disagreed with the *Travis* decision on this issue)]

Hot Goods

Q 14:68   What are *hot goods* for purposes of the FLSA?

For purposes of the FLSA, *hot goods* are goods that are ineligible for shipment because child labor, minimum wage, or overtime standards of the FLSA were not observed in the production of the goods. FLSA Sections 12(a) and 15(a)(1) contain prohibitions against putting hot goods into interstate or foreign commerce. The DOL has the power to bring a lawsuit to enjoin interstate shipments of such hot goods; however, this injunction power need not be directed solely at the manufacturer that violated the FLSA. The Supreme Court has held that the DOL can bring an injunction action against secured creditors of the manufacturer of the goods. [Citicorp Indus. Credit, Inc. v. Brock, 483 U.S. 27 (1987)] In such a situation, the secured creditor can ship the hot goods only after the manufacturer's employees have been paid the wages they are owed under the FLSA. In that case, in return for the restitution of back wages and a promise of future compliance with the FLSA, the Wage and Hour Division agreed not to tie up the company's goods by enforcing the ban on hot goods. [29 U.S.C. §§ 212(a), 215(a)(1)]

The FLSA does not prohibit the acquisition or sale of goods when reasonable value is paid for the goods, the acquirer of the goods relied on a written representation from the manufacturer that the goods were produced in accordance with the FLSA, and the acquirer of the goods had no knowledge of any violation of the FLSA. [29 U.S.C. § 215(a)(1)]

However, a United States district court has ruled that the good-faith purchaser exemption does not apply to a manufacturer that acquires goods prior to their being worked on by a contractor's employees in violation of the minimum wage and overtime provisions of the FLSA. According to the court, when a manufacturer already has a proprietary interest in goods when work on them is done by employees employed in violation of the FLSA, the manufacturer cannot be said to *acquire* the goods in good-faith *reliance* on assurances that the goods *were* produced in compliance with the FLSA. Therefore, selling or shipping the goods in commerce violates the hot goods ban even if the manufacturer did not know that the work by the contractor's employees was performed in violation of the FLSA. [Chao v. Fashion Etoile, 2002 WL 31947202, 147 Lab. Cas. ¶ 34,634 (C.D. Cal. 2003)]

There is no private right of action to enforce the ban on hot goods. As a result, employees may not add a claim for a hot goods injunction in an action to recover unpaid minimum wages or overtime. On the other hand, the Department of Labor can intervene in private suits to seek such injunctions as they deem necessary, or bring a separate suit against the offending employer.

Q 14:69 What is a *hot-goods injunction*?

A *hot-goods injunction* is an injunction against the shipment of hot goods. A hot-goods injunction usually comes in the form of a temporary restraining order or a preliminary injunction, which are forms of injunctions that can be obtained quickly, with little or no notice to the employer. A hot-goods injunction prohibits an employer from shipping, moving, or selling the offending goods.

Courts will generally grant a hot-goods injunction on short notice based on the FLSA's prohibition against the shipment of any goods produced by workers paid or assigned to work in violation of the FLSA. Hot-goods injunctions can affect more than just the enjoined employer. The Supreme Court affirmed injunctions against a hosiery manufacturer that failed to pay employees and agreed that the hot-goods prohibitions also apply to creditors of the manufacturer that acquired a security interest in the goods. [Citicorp Indus. Credit, Inc. v. Brock, 483 U.S. 27 (1987)]

Q 14:70 Can an employer avoid the effects of a hot-goods injunction by filing for bankruptcy?

No. For instance, the Eleventh Circuit found that a hot-goods injunction was exempted from the Bankruptcy Code's automatic stay provision and "that Congress intended to prevent the sale of hot goods in interstate commerce even when the manufacturer has filed for bankruptcy." [Brock v. Rusco Indus., Inc., 842 F.2d 270, 274 (11th Cir. 1988)]

Q 14:71 What can an employer be ordered to or prevented from doing pursuant to a hot-goods injunction?

First and foremost, a hot-goods injunction orders an employer to comply with the FLSA and to refrain from shipping any goods produced in violation of the FLSA. When an employer's business is one that relies on the labor of a contractor—such as when a garment manufacturer contracts with contractors for the production of certain items—a hot-goods injunction can also require the manufacturer to ensure its contractor's compliance with the FLSA. Thus, a manufacturer can be ordered to refrain from transporting contractor-produced goods that the DOL has determined are hot goods. Second, the manufacturer can be ordered to review with its contractor the economic feasibility of proposed price terms in light of the FLSA's requirements, the contractor's willingness and ability to comply with the FLSA, and the contractor's obligation to inform the manufacturer if it cannot so comply. Third, the manufacturer can be ordered to require its contractor to make payroll records available on request and to respond within certain time limits to a DOL request for records. Finally, a manufacturer can be required to notify the DOL if it finds a contractor in violation of the FLSA and to refrain from shipping or selling the affected goods until the DOL lifts any objection to shipping or selling the affected goods. [Herman v. Fashion Headquarters, Inc., 992 F. Supp. 677 (S.D.N.Y. 1998)]

Chapter 15

Migrant and Seasonal Agricultural Worker Protection Act

The Migrant and Seasonal Agricultural Worker Protection Act (MSPA) provides worker protections to migrant and seasonal agricultural workers. MSPA applies to agricultural employment only. As a complicated and difficult statute, it is troublesome for employers. This chapter presents a general overview of MSPA's provisions. MSPA protects most migrant and seasonal agricultural workers in their interactions with farm labor contractors, agricultural employers, agricultural associations, and providers of migrant housing. The primary issues of concern under MSPA for agricultural employers include: using the services of properly registered farm labor contractors; understanding the likelihood of a joint employment claim by the Department of Labor when using farm labor contractors; disclosing specially required information to workers in the prescribed manner; maintaining payroll and time records as required; paying wages owed when due; not requiring purchases by employees; adhering to the terms of the working agreement; ensuring that each vehicle used to transport workers is safe, insured, and operated by a licensed driver; and ensuring that migrant housing complies with safety and health standards. These areas of concern are covered in this chapter.

General Concepts

Q 15:1   What is the Migrant and Seasonal Agricultural Worker Protection Act?

The Migrant and Seasonal Agricultural Worker Protection Act (MSPA) is a 1983 Act that repeals and replaces the Farm Labor Contractor Registration Act of 1963. MSPA is a federal law providing certain worker protections to migrant and seasonal agricultural workers in their employment by farm labor contractors, agricultural employers, and agricultural associations. All persons and organizations subject to MSPA must observe certain rules when recruiting, soliciting, hiring, employing, furnishing, transporting, or housing migrant or seasonal agricultural workers or when furnishing them to other employers. MSPA applies to most field workers working in agricultural employment of a seasonal or other temporary nature. [29 U.S.C. §§ 1801–1872; 29 C.F.R. §§ 500.0, 500.1]

Q 15:2   What is a *migrant agricultural worker* under MSPA?

Under MSPA, a *migrant agricultural worker* is "an individual who is employed in agricultural employment of a seasonal or other temporary nature, and who is required to be absent overnight from his permanent place of residence." This does not include any immediate family member of an agricultural employer or a farm labor contractor, nor does it include any temporary nonimmigrant alien who is authorized to work in agricultural employment in the United States under provisions of the immigration laws. [29 U.S.C. § 1802(8)]

Q 15:3   What is a *seasonal agricultural worker* under MSPA?

Under MSPA, a *seasonal agricultural worker* is "an individual who is employed in agricultural employment of a seasonal or other temporary nature and is not required to be absent overnight from his permanent place of residence—(i) when employed on a farm or ranch performing field work related to planting, cultivating, or harvesting operations; or (ii) when employed in canning, packing, ginning, seed conditioning or related research, or processing operations, and transported or caused to be transported to and from the place of employment by means of a day-haul operation." The definition of *seasonal agricultural worker* does not include "any migrant agricultural worker"; any immediate family member of an agricultural employer or a farm labor contractor; or "any temporary nonimmigrant alien who is authorized to work in agricultural employment in the United States" under provisions of the immigration laws. [29 U.S.C. § 1802(10)]

Q 15:4   What does MSPA require with respect to farm labor contracting?

MSPA requires that an agricultural employer utilize the services of only those farm labor contractors who are registered with the U.S Department of Labor

(DOL). MSPA requires persons-other than agricultural employers and agricultural associations who engage in contracting farm labor activity for a fee to register with the DOL as a farm labor contractor. In addition to these registration requirements, a separate authorization to transport workers, to drive vehicles transporting workers, and to house workers must also be obtained if any of these activities are performed by the farm labor contractor. [29 C.F.R. § 500.1]

Q 15:5   What is a *farm labor contractor* under MSPA?

A *farm labor contractor* is "any person, other than an agricultural employer, an agricultural association, or an employee of an agricultural employer or agricultural association, who, for any money or other valuable consideration paid or promised to be paid, performs any farm labor contracting activity." Agricultural employers and agricultural associations are specifically exempted from the definition of a *farm labor contractor*. [29 U.S.C. § 1802(7); 29 C.F.R. § 500.20(j)]

Q 15:6   What is an agricultural employer or agricultural association for purposes of MSPA?

An *agricultural employer* is "any person who owns or operates a farm, ranch, processing establishment, cannery, gin, packing shed or nursery, or who produces or conditions seed, and who recruits, solicits, hires, employs, furnishes, or transports any migrant or seasonal agricultural worker." [29 U.S.C. § 1802(2)]

An *agricultural association* is "any nonprofit or cooperative association of farmers, growers, or ranchers, incorporated or qualified under applicable State law, which recruits, solicits, hires, employs, furnishes, or transports any migrant or seasonal agricultural worker." [29 U.S.C. § 1802(1)]

Q 15:7   What is farm labor contracting activity under MSPA?

Under MSPA, *farm labor contracting activity* is "recruiting, soliciting, hiring, employing, furnishing, or transporting any migrant or seasonal agricultural worker" for farm labor. [29 U.S.C. § 1802(6); 29 C.F.R. § 500.20(i)]

Q 15:8   Are farm labor contractors required to register as such under MSPA?

Yes. Farm labor contractors (FLCs) are required to register as FLCs with the Secretary of Labor and, under MSPA, must carry proof of that registration and show it to any worker or other person they deal with in their capacity as a farm labor contractor. In addition, any employee of a farm labor contractor who will assist in the performance of farm labor contracting activity must register either as a farm labor contractor individually or as the employee of a farm labor contractor. [29 U.S.C. § 1811; 29 C.F.R. §§ 500.60, 500.61] A person who performs "farm labor contracting activity" on an incidental basis only is not subject to the registration requirements of MSPA. The Department of Labor has said that activity is "incidental" if it does not exceed 20 percent of the person's working time. [Wage & Hour Opinion Letter, FLSA1555 (Dec. 1979)]

The application for a farm labor contractor certificate of registration must include all of the following:

1. The applicant's sworn declaration stating the applicant's permanent place of residence, the farm labor contracting activities for which the certificate is requested, and any other relevant information requested on the application;

2. A statement identifying each vehicle to be used to transport any migrant or seasonal agricultural worker and, if the vehicle is owned or will be owned or controlled by the applicant, documentation establishing the safety (such as by maintenance record) and the insurance coverage for the vehicle;

3. A statement identifying each facility or real property to be used to house any migrant or seasonal agricultural worker and, if the facility or real property is owned or will be owned or controlled by the applicant, documentation establishing that applicable safety and health standards have been met;

4. The applicant's fingerprints; and

5. The applicant's sworn declaration that the Secretary may accept service of process on behalf of the applicant in any action against the applicant, if the applicant has left the jurisdiction or is unavailable.

[29 U.S.C. § 1812]

A certificate may be refused or revoked by the Secretary of Labor if the applicant for or holder of the certificate:

1. Has knowingly misrepresented information in the application;

2. Applied for the certificate on behalf of someone who has been refused a certificate where that other person is the real party in interest of the application;

3. Has failed to comply with the MSPA;

4. Has failed to pay any outstanding judgment obtained for a violation of the MSPA or to comply with any final order issued as a result of a violation of the MSPA;

5. Has been convicted within the past 5 years of certain criminal activities; or

6. Has been found to have violated paragraph (1) or (2) of Section 1324a(a) of Title 8, regarding the unlawful employment of aliens.

[29 U.S.C. § 1813(a)]

Certificates of registration as an FLC or an FLC employee may not be transferred or assigned to another person and are good for 12-month periods. [29 U.S.C. § 1814]

Q 15:9 Are there any exemptions from the MSPA?

Yes. The provisions of MSPA do not apply to a number of different persons, businesses, partnerships, and other entities, as outlined in the statute. MSPA is inapplicable to the following persons and entities:

1. Family-owned farms and businesses as long as the farm labor contracting activities are performed on behalf of that family-owned farm, processing establishment, cannery, packing shed or nursery;

2. Small businesses that did not use more than 500 man-days of agricultural labor in the previous calendar year;

3. Common carriers used for transporting migrant or seasonal agricultural workers;

4. Labor organizations, such as unions;

5. Nonprofit charitable organizations or public or private nonprofit educational institutions;

6. Persons who engage in farm labor contracting activity solely within a 25-mile radius of the person's permanent place of residence and for not more than 13 weeks per year;

7. Custom combine, hay harvesting, or sheep-shearing operations;

8. Custom poultry operations provided the employees of the operations are not regularly required to be away from their permanent place of residence other than during their normal working hours;

9. Seed production or shade-grown tobacco operations when supplying or supplied with full-time students or other nonagricultural workers provided these full-time students and other nonagricultural workers are not required to be away from their permanent place of residence overnight and persons under the age of 18 are not providing the transportation; and

10. Employees of any of the above.

[29 U.S.C. § 1803(a); 29 C.F.R. § 500.30]

There is also a limited exemption for agricultural employers and associations. They are not required to register under MSPA as FLCs, but they are otherwise subject to the provisions of MSPA, including those requirements relating to worker disclosures, recordkeeping, and antidiscrimination.

Q 15:10 What must agricultural employers do before utilizing the services of an FLC?

An agricultural employer must take reasonable steps to ensure that all FLCs providing workers to the employer for farm labor have certificates of registration that are valid for the specific activities to be performed (transporting, driving, and housing). [29 U.S.C. § 1842; 29 C.F.R. § 500.71] The employer must also verify the specific authorizations of the FLC. For example, if the FLC is to provide housing to the workers supplied, the employer must verify not only that the FLC is specifically authorized to provide housing, but must also verify the specific location of the housing listed on the FLC's certificate. [Howard v. Malcolm, 852 F.2d 101 (4th Cir. 1988)]

Q 15:11   What are the consequences for an agricultural employer of dealing with an FLC?

The DOL often claims there is joint employment between an agricultural employer and the FLC providing workers to that employer when determining responsibility for issues of noncompliance with the MSPA requirements. This means the agricultural employer may be held responsible for MSPA violations created by a farm labor contractor. The factors that the DOL considers as significant in this regard include, but are not limited to the following:

1. The nature and degree of control of the workers;
2. The degree of supervision, direct or indirect, of the work;
3. The power to determine the pay rates or methods of payment of the workers;
4. The right, directly or indirectly, to hire, fire, or modify the employment conditions of the workers; and
5. Preparation of payroll and the payment of wages.

[29 C.F.R. § 500.20(h)(5)(iv)(A)–(G); *see* Gonzalez-Sanchez v. Int'l Paper Co., 346 F.3d 1017 (11th Cir. 2003) (upheld summary judgment for manufacturers finding they were not joint employers with FLC as manufacturers did not exercise control over migrant workers)]

Additionally, if an employer chooses to deal with an FLC outside its jurisdiction, it may be subjecting itself to a lawsuit in the FLC's jurisdiction. For example, if the employer resides in New York and elects to contract with an FLC in Texas, and that FLC recruits from a labor pool within Texas, the employees who sign their contracts in Texas may be able to sue the employer under the MSPA in Texas, thus exposing the New York employer to liability in Texas. [Gonzalez Moreno v. Milk Train, Inc., 182 F. Supp. 2d 590 (W.D. Tex. 2002); *see also* Elias Moreno v. Poverty Point Produce, Inc., 2007 U.S. Dist. LEXIS 27260 (S.D. Tex. 2007) (denied Louisiana corporation's motion to dismiss for lack of jurisdiction and venue or alternatively to transfer venue where Louisiana corporation contracted with Texas FLC and Texas FLC recruited and provided Texas resident migrant workers to work in Louisiana)]

Employer Obligations

Q 15:12   What are some of the employer obligations under MSPA?

There are certain positive actions that an employer subject to the provisions of the MSPA must accomplish in order to be in full compliance when soliciting, recruiting, transporting, hiring, or employing migrant and seasonal agricultural workers. The purpose of MSPA is to provide certain protections to migrant and seasonal agricultural workers. As such, most of the positive obligations imposed by MSPA are designed to provide this protection. Employers must, under MSPA:

1. Disclose conditions of employment, in writing, to each migrant worker at the time the migrant is recruited and to each seasonal worker, in writing, upon request. [29 U.S.C. §§ 1821(a), 1831(a); 29 C.F.R. §§ 500.75, 500.76]

2. Post a poster, at the work site, setting forth the basic protections of MSPA. [29 U.S.C. §§ 1821(b), 1831(b); 29 C.F.R. §§ 500.75, 500.76]

3. Provide each worker an itemized statement outlining the basis on which wages are paid, hours worked, gross pay, deductions from pay and basis for deduction each payday. [29 U.S.C. §§ 1821(d)(2), 1831(c)(2); 29 C.F.R. § 500.80]

4. Pay each worker the wages promised, not less than the federal minimum wage, and pay on the date promised, no less frequently than semimonthly. [29 U.S.C. § 1832; 29 C.F.R. § 500.81]

Additionally, if applicable, an employer must:

1. Post a poster in a conspicuous place disclosing the terms and conditions of housing provided. [29 U.S.C. § 1821(c); 29 C.F.R. § 500.75]

2. Ensure housing meets substantive safety and health standards prior to and during occupancy. A preoccupancy certification that standards are met must be obtained each season. [29 U.S.C. § 1823; 29 C.F.R. § 500.130]

3. Ensure that workers are transported in safe vehicles, by licensed drivers, and in properly insured vehicles. [29 U.S.C. § 1841; 29 C.F.R. §§ 500.100–500.128]

Common Mistakes

Q 15:13   What are some common disclosure violations of MSPA?

Agricultural employers often fail to provide the required disclosure notifications to their employees. According to the regulations governing employers and FLCs under MSPA:

> Each farm labor contractor, agricultural employer and agricultural association shall make all required written disclosures to the worker, including the written disclosures of the terms and conditions of occupancy of housing to be provided to any migrant worker, in English or, as necessary and reasonable, in Spanish or another language common to migrant or seasonal agricultural workers who are not fluent or literate in English. The Department of Labor shall make forms available in English, Spanish, Haitian-Creole, and other languages, as necessary, which may be used in providing workers with such information. [29 C.F.R. § 500.78]

Migrant and seasonal day-haul workers must be provided a written disclosure at the time of recruitment containing the terms and conditions of employment. Other seasonal workers must be provided such disclosure upon request when offered employment. The required disclosures should be made on Form WH-516, available from the U.S. DOL, Wage and Hour Division. This form can be downloaded from the DOL's Web site at http://www.dol.gov/libraryforms/go-us-dol-form.asp?FormNumber = 41&OMBNumber = 1215-0187. The required disclosures include such information as the place of employment; the wage rates to be paid; the crops and the kind of activities on which the worker may be employed; the period of employment; the transportation and any other employee benefit to be provided, if any, and any costs to be charged for those benefits; the existence of any strike or other concerted work stoppage, slowdown, or interruption of operations at the place of employment; the existence of any arrangements with any owner or agent of any establishment in the area of employment under which the FLC or the agricultural employer is to receive a commission or other benefit from sales at the establishment; and information about state workers' compensation insurance provided, if any. [29 U.S.C. §§ 1821(a), 1831(a); 29 C.F.R. §§ 500.75, 500.76]

An agricultural employer must also post in a conspicuous place at the job site a poster, provided by the DOL, setting out the rights and protections afforded by MSPA. The federal MSPA poster informs workers that they have rights to disclosure of information, timely payment of wages, and to have safe transportation and housing, if those things are provided as part of the job. The poster also informs workers how to file complaints and assures them that the law prohibits retaliation against them for filing a complaint. If requested by a worker, employers must provide a written statement of this information to the worker. [29 U.S.C. §§ 1821(b), 1831(b); 29 C.F.R. §§ 500.75, 500.76; WH Publication 1376]. This poster can be downloaded from the DOL's Web site in either English/Spanish or English/Haitian; *see* http://www.dol.gov/osbp/sbrefa/poster/main.htm.

If housing is provided, a statement of the terms and conditions of occupancy must be either posted or presented to the workers. Wage and Hour Division Form WH-521 can be used to satisfy this requirement. Form WH-521 provides information about the housing, including who is providing the housing, who are the individuals in charge of the housing, the mailing address and phone (if any) of the housing facility, and the conditions of occupancy at the housing (such as who may live there, any charges to be imposed, any meals provided, and any charges for utilities or otherwise). [29 U.S.C. § 1821(c); 29 C.F.R. § 500.75; Form WH-521]

Q 15:14 What are some common information and recordkeeping violations of MSPA?

MSPA, unlike the Fair Labor Standards Act (FLSA), prescribes specific payroll information that must be retained and also provided to agricultural workers. MSPA requires that farm payroll records reflect the basis on which wages were paid, the number of piecework units earned if paid on a piecework basis, number of hours worked, total pay for each pay period, amount and reason for any deductions, and the net pay. In addition, each employee must be provided with an itemized statement each pay period and these records must be kept and preserved by the employer for three years. If a farm labor contractor performs the payroll function, a copy of all of the required information must be provided to the agricultural employer to whom the workers are provided. [29 U.S.C. §§ 1821(d), (e), 1831(c), (d)]

Additionally, according to the regulations under MSPA:

> (d) In addition to making records of this payroll information, the farm labor contractor, agricultural employer and agricultural association shall provide each migrant or seasonal agricultural worker employed with an itemized written statement of this information at the time of payment for each pay period which must be no less often than every two weeks (or semi-monthly). Such statement shall also include the employer's name, address, and employer identification number assigned by the Internal Revenue Service. This responsibility does not require needless duplication such as would occur if each provided the worker with a written itemized statement for the same work. [29 C.F.R. § 500.80(d)]

With all of this very specific information that must be maintained and provided to workers, employers and FLCs often fail to maintain all of the appropriate information, in the appropriate format, for the appropriate length of time. In addition, agricultural employers and agricultural associations that permit an FLC to do payroll for workers being provided by that FLC must be sure to obtain and maintain a copy of all of the FLC's records. Agricultural employers and FLCs must be very careful to follow the recordkeeping obligations, because a failure to maintain the required records with all of the required information is a violation of MSPA.

Q 15:15 What are some common wage and working arrangement violations under MSPA?

MSPA requires that workers be paid all wages owed when due, but no less often than every two weeks. Employers that attempt to pay less often than every two weeks are in violation of the MSPA requirements. According to Section 500.81 of the regulations:

> Each farm labor contractor, agricultural employer and agricultural association which employs any migrant or seasonal agricultural worker must pay the wages owed such worker when due. In meeting this responsibility, the farm labor contractor, agricultural employer and agricultural association shall pay the worker no less often than every two weeks (or semi-monthly). [29 C.F.R. § 500.81]

Additionally, employees may not be required to purchase goods or services solely from an employer or FLC, or any person acting as an agent to them. [29 C.F.R. § 500.73]

The employer must not violate the terms of any working arrangement without adequate justification, and an FLC must comply with the terms of any written agreement entered into with an agricultural employer. [29 U.S.C. §§ 1822(c), 1832(c); 29 C.F.R. § 500.72]

Q 15:16 What are some common transportation and housing violations under MSPA?

Any agricultural employer involved in furnishing transportation and/or housing should study the regulations carefully, because violations of these provisions are commonly cited during federal investigations by the Wage and Hour Division. Under MSPA, vehicles used to transport migrant or seasonal agricultural workers must be properly insured, operated by properly licensed drivers, and meet federal and state safety standards. Migrant housing may not be occupied until it has been inspected and certified to meet applicable safety and health standards. The certification of occupancy must be posted at the housing site. Employers and FLCs commonly make mistakes in this area. [29 U.S.C. §§ 1823, 1841; 29 C.F.R. §§ 500.100–500.135]

It does not take much to come under the scrutiny of DOL's transportation regulators. If an FLC or its employee collects rent money from a migrant worker even if the FLC gains no personal benefit, this will be considered enough by the DOL. [29 C.F.R. § 500.130] Likewise, if an FLC or its employee innocently gives or loans a migrant worker gas money for his or her car, which is likely to occur in a car pool situation, that is "transportation." [29 C.F.R. §§ 500.100, 500.102, 500.103] Higher level "prime" contractors or even agricultural employers may be cited for these same violations as joint employers. [*See* Charles v. Burton, 169 F.3d 1322 (11th Cir. 1999)]

Miscellaneous Additional Provisions

Q 15:17 Does MSPA contain a prohibition on discrimination?

Yes. An employer may not "intimidate, threaten, restrain, coerce, blacklist, discharge, or in any manner discriminate against any migrant or seasonal agricultural worker because such worker has, with just cause, filed any complaint or instituted, or caused to be instituted, any proceeding under or related to [MSPA]." This prohibition also extends to workers testifying, or exercising any other right or protection afforded by MSPA. [*See* Centeno-Bernuy v. Perry, 302 F. Supp. 2d 128 (W.D.N.Y. 2003) (to establish retaliation under the MSPA, a plaintiff must demonstrate that he or she engaged in protected activity and that the defendant intimidated, threatened, restrained, coerced, blacklisted, discharged, or in any manner discriminated against the plaintiff)]

If DOL determines that these provisions have been violated, the Secretary of Labor may bring an action to restrain such violations and order all appropriate relief, including rehiring or reinstatement of the worker, with back pay and/or damages. [29 U.S.C. § 1855]

Q 15:18   May an employee waive his or her MSPA rights?

No. Agreements by employees purporting to waive or to modify their rights under MSPA will be held to be void, except that a waiver or modification of rights in favor of the Secretary of Labor shall be valid for purposes of enforcement of MSPA. [29 U.S.C. § 1856]

Q 15:19   Does the Department of Labor have authority to investigate businesses for MSPA compliance?

Yes. With or without a complaint, the DOL, as may be appropriate, can investigate, enter and inspect places (including housing and vehicles) and records, question persons, and gather information to determine compliance with the provisions of MSPA. Investigations are to be conducted in a manner that protects the confidentiality of any complainant. It is a violation of MSPA for any person to unlawfully resist, oppose, impede, intimidate, or interfere with any DOL official assigned to perform an investigation pursuant to MSPA during the performance of their duties. [29 U.S.C. § 1862]

The DOL will issue proposed civil money penalty ("CMP") assessments for each separate type of violation, and the amounts increase with the occurrence of any subsequent violations. [29 C.F.R. § 500.143] The employer cited must timely file a notice of contest if it desires to preserve the right to appeal and have an administrative hearing, which may ultimately be appealed to the Secretary of Labor and even possibly heard by the Federal Courts of Appeals. [29 U.S.C. § 1853] After filing a notice of contest, negotiations with the DOL to settle the CMP assessment on reasonable terms are often held.

Q 15:20   Who enforces MSPA and what are the court remedies available in the event of a violation?

Under MSPA, either an employee or the DOL can bring legal action to correct violations. DOL has the authority to file for either civil or criminal relief. Criminal convictions carry fines ranging from $1,000 to $10,000 plus the possibility of a prison sentence of up to three years, depending on the nature of the violation. In private actions brought by an employee a court may order up to $500 per worker per violation for statutory damages or an amount equal to the actual damages. Workers may combine to bring collective suits under MSPA, but a limit of $500,000 is established for any single class action. The Secretary of Labor may petition any appropriate district court of the United States for temporary or permanent injunctive relief. [29 U.S.C. §§ 1851–1854]

Appendix A

General Information and Publications

Publications

The DOL Office of Public Affairs maintains a listing of publications available from the Department, some of which are available at Wage and Hour Offices.

Office of Public Affairs
Department of Labor
200 Constitution Ave., N.W., Room S-1032
Washington, DC 20210
(202) 693-4650

A number of DOL publications are available electronically on the DOL Internet site at http://www.dol.gov. The DOL Internet site also provides access to the United States Code, Federal Regulations, administrative opinions, texts of speeches, DOL reports, and information about various divisions within the Department of Labor.

The Employment and Training Administration [www.doleta.gov] issues periodicals, including Area Trends in Employment and Unemployment. Employers can become subscribers by contacting the Superintendent of Documents, Government Printing Office, Washington, DC 20402.

Wage and Hour Division Offices

The DOL Wage and Hour Division is a branch of the Employment Standards Administration. The Wage and Hour Division is responsible for planning, directing, and administering programs dealing with federal labor issues such as the FLSA, administering and enforcing immigration-related programs (along with the Immigration and Naturalization Service), and determining prevailing wage rates for federal construction contracts and public works subject to the Davis-Bacon Act, to name a few. The Wage and Hour Division also is primarily responsible for enforcing contractor compliance with the Davis-Bacon Act.

The headquarters of the Wage and Hour Division is:

200 Constitution Ave., N.W., Room S-3502
Washington, DC 20210
(202) 693-0051 or 1-866 – 4- USWAGE (1-866-487-9243)

Following are the addresses for the Regional and District Offices of the U.S. Department of Labor, ESA Wage and Hour Division for the 50 states, the District of Columbia, and Puerto Rico. Regional offices are located in Atlanta, Chicago, Philadelphia, and San Francisco.

Alabama
950 22nd St. North, Suite 656
Birmingham, AL 35203-3711
4001 Carmichael Road, Suite 215
Montgomery, AL 36106

Alaska: See Seattle, WA

Arizona
230 N. First Avenue, Suite 4021
Phoenix, AZ 85003-1725

Arkansas
TCBY Building, Suite 725
10810 Executive Center Drive
Little Rock, AR 72221

California
East Los Angeles District Office
100 N. Barranca, Suite #850
West Covina, CA 91791

Los Angeles District Office
915 Wilshire Blvd., Suite 960
Los Angeles, CA 90017-3446

Sacramento District Office
2800 Cottage Way, Room W-1836
Sacramento, CA 95825-1886

San Diego District Office
5675 Ruffin Rd., Suite 310
San Diego, CA 92123-1362

San Francisco District Office
90 7th Street, Suite 18-300
San Francisco, CA 94103-6719

Orange Area Office
770 The City Drive South
Suite 5710
Orange, CA 92868-4954

San Jose Area Office
60 South Market Street, Suite 420
San Jose, CA 95113-2354

Colorado
1999 Broadway, Suite 2445
PO Box 46550
Denver, CO 80202-3025

Connecticut
Hartford District Office
135 High Street, Room 210
Hartford, CT 06103-1111

New Haven Area Office
150 Court Street, Room 423
New Haven, CT 06510

Delaware: See Baltimore, MD

District of Columbia: See Baltimore, MD

Florida
Fort Lauderdale Area Office
Federal Building, Room 408
299 East Broward Blvd.
Ft. Lauderdale, FL 33301-1976

Jacksonville District Office
400 West Bay Street, Room 956
Jacksonville, FL 32202

Miami District Office
Sunset Center
10300 Sunset Drive, Room 255
Miami, FL 33173-3038

Orlando Area Office
1001 Executive Center Drive, #103
Orlando, FL 32803-3712

Tampa District Office
Austin Laurel Building
4905 W. Laurel Ave., Suite 300
Tampa, FL 33607-3838

Georgia
Atlanta District Office
Atlanta Federal Center
61 Forsyth St., SW, Room 7 M10
Atlanta, GA 30303

Savannah Area Office
Juliette Gordon Low Federal Building Complex
124 Barnard St., Suite B-210
Savannah, GA 31401-3648

Hawaii
300 Ala Moana Blvd., Room 7225
Honolulu, HI 96850

Idaho
Northern Panhandle (Coeurd'Alene, Lewiston):
See Seattle, WA

Remainder of State: See Portland, OR

Illinois
Calhoun, Jersey, Madison, Monroe, Randolph and St. Clair Counties: See
St. Louis, MO
Chicago District Office
230 South Dearborn Street, Room 412
Chicago, IL 60604-1591

Springfield District Office
509 West Capitol Avenue, Suite 205
Springfield, IL 62704-1929

Indiana
Indianapolis District Office
U.S. Courthouse
46 E. Ohio Street, Room 413
Indianapolis, IN 46204

South Bend Area Office
501 E. Monroe St., Room 160
South Bend, IN 46601-1615

Iowa
Des Moines District Office
Federal Building
210 Walnut St., Room 643
Des Moines, IA 50309-2407

Kansas
Kansas City District Office
Gateway Tower II
400 State Avenue, Suite 1010
Kansas City, KS 66101-2414

Kentucky
Louisville District Office
Gene Snyder U.S. Courthouse & Customhouse
601 West Broadway, Room 31
Louisville, KY 40202-9570

Louisiana
New Orleans District Office
600 South Maestri Place
Room 615
New Orleans, LA 70130

Maine: See Manchester, NH

Maryland
Baltimore District Office
Appraisers-Stores Building, Room 207
103 South Gay Street
Baltimore, MD 21202-4061

Massachusetts
Boston District Office
JFK Federal Building, Room 525
Boston, MA 02203

Taunton Area Office
17 Broadway, Room 308
Taunton, MA 02780

Michigan
Detroit District Office
211 W. Fort St., Room 1317
Detroit, MI 48226-3237

Grand Rapids Area Office
800 Monroe Ave., N.W., Suite 315
Grand Rapids, MI 49503-1451

Minnesota
Minneapolis District Office
Tri-Tech Center, Suite 920
331 Second Ave. South
Minneapolis, MN 55401-1321

Mississippi
Northeast Quadrant: See Birmingham, AL

Remainder of State:
Jackson Area Office
McCoy Federal Building
100 W. Capitol Street, Suite 608
Jackson, MS 39269

Missouri:
Eastern Half:
St. Louis District Office
1222 Spruce Street, Room 9.102B
St. Louis, MO 63103-2830

Western Half: See Kansas City, KS

Montana: See Salt Lake City, UT

Nebraska
Omaha Area Office
111 South 18th Plaza, Suite 2238
Omaha, NE 68102-1615

Nevada
Clark, Lincoln & Nye Counties (Las Vegas):
See Phoenix, AZ

Remainder of State: See Sacramento, CA

New Hampshire
Manchester District Office
1750 Elm Street, Suite 111
Manchester, NH 03104-2907

New Jersey
Southern NJ:
Southern New Jersey District Office
3131 Princeton Pike, Building 5, Room 216
Lawrenceville, NJ 08648

Northern NJ:
Northern New Jersey District Office
200 Sheffield Street, Room 102
Mountainside, NJ 07092

New Mexico
Albuquerque District Office
500 Fourth Street, Suite 403
Albuquerque, NM 87102

New York
Albany District Office
Leo W. O'Brien Federal Building, Room 822
Albany, NY 12207

Brooklyn Area Office
625 Fulton Street, 7th Floor
Brooklyn, NY 11201

Buffalo Area Office
111 West Huron Street, Rm 1512
Buffalo, NY 14202

New York City District Office
26 Federal Plaza, Room 3700
New York, NY 10278

Syracuse Area Office
100 South Clinton Street
FOB Room 1373
Syracuse, NY 13260

Long Island District Office
1400 Old Country Road, Suite 410
Westbury, NY 11590-5119

Hudson Valley Area Office
140 Grand Street, Suite 304
White Plains, NY 10601

North Carolina
Charlotte District Office
800 Briar Creek Road, Suite CC-412
Charlotte, NC 28205-6903

Raleigh District Office
Somerset Bank Building
4407 Bland Road, Suite 260
Raleigh, NC 27609-6296

North Dakota: See Denver, CO

Ohio
Cincinnati Area Office
550 Main Street, Room 10-409
Cincinnati, OH 45202-5208

Cleveland District Office
Federal Office Building
1240 East Ninth Street, Room 817
Cleveland, OH 44199-2054

Columbus District Office
200 North High Street, Room 646
Columbus, OH 43215-2408

Oklahoma: See Little Rock, AR

Oregon
Portland District Office
1515 S.W. Fifth Ave., Suite 1040
Portland, OR 97201-5445

Pacific Territories: See San Francisco, CA

Pennsylvania
Philadelphia District Office
U.S. Custom House, Room 400
Second & Chestnut Streets
Philadelphia, PA 19106

Pittsburgh District Office
Federal Building
1000 Liberty Avenue, Room 313
Pittsburgh, PA 15222

Wilkes Barre District Office
Stegmaier Building, Suite 373 M
7 N. Wilkes-Barre Blvd.
Wilkes-Barre, PA 18702-5284

Puerto Rico
Caribbean District Office
7 Tabonuco Street
San Patricio Office Center, 4th Fl.
Guaynabo, PR 00968

Rhode Island
Providence Area Office
380 Westminster Mall, Room 546
Providence, RI 02903

South Carolina
Columbia District Office
Federal Building, Room 1072
1835 Assembly Street
Columbia, SC 29201-9863

South Dakota: See Denver, CO

Tennessee
Nashville District Office
1321 Murfreesboro Road, Suite 511
Nashville, TN 37217-2626

Knoxville Area Office
John J. Duncan Federal Building
710 Locust Street, Room 101
Knoxville, TN 37902-2557

Texas
Dallas District Office
The Offices @ Brookhollow
1701 E. Lamar Blvd., Suite 270, Box 22
Arlington, TX 76006-7303

Houston District Office
8701 S. Gessner Drive, Suite 1164
Houston, TX 77044-2944

San Antonio District Office
Northchase 1 Office Bldg.
10127 Morocco, Suite 140
San Antonio, TX 78216

West Texas Panhandle and Northwest Quadrant:
See Albuquerque, NM

Utah
Salt Lake City District Office
150 East Social Hall Avenue, Suite 695
Salt Lake City, UT 84111

Vermont: See Manchester, NH

Virginia

Northern VA: See Baltimore, MD

Southwestern VA: See Charleston, WV

Remainder of State:
Richmond District Office
Federal Building
400 N. 8th Street, Room 416
Richmond, VA 23219-4815

Virgin Islands: See Guaynabo, PR

Washington
Wahkiakum and Klickitat Counties: See Portland, OR

Remainder of State and Alaska:
1111 Third Avenue, Suite 755
Seattle, WA 98101-3212

West Virginia
Eastern Panhandle: See Baltimore, MD

Remainder of State:
Charleston Area Office
500 Quarrier Street, Suite 120
Charleston, WV 25301-2130

Wisconsin
Madison District Office
740 Regent Street, Suite 102
Madison, WI 53715-1233

Wyoming: See Salt Lake City, UT

Solicitor of Labor

The Office of the Solicitor serves as the legal branch of the DOL and is responsible for civil litigation to enforce the FLSA, the Employment Retirement Income Security Act of 1971, and the Migrant Seasonal Agricultural Worker Protection Act. The Solicitor also represents the DOL in hearings under the Occupational and Safety Health Act of 1970, the Black Lung Benefits Reform Act, Federal Mine Safety and Health Act of 1977, and the government contract labor standards laws.

The Office of the Solicitor is headquartered at:

Frances Perkins Building
200 Constitution Ave., N.W.
Washington, DC 20210
(202) 693-5260

The regional offices of the U.S. Department of Labor, Office of the Solicitor are:

Atlanta, Boston, Chicago, Dallas, Kansas City, New York, Philadelphia, and San Francisco.
Sam Nunn Atlanta Federal Center
61 Forsyth Street, Room 7T10
Atlanta, GA 30303
(404) 562-2057

Branch offices:
Nashville
618 Church Street, Suite 230
Nashville, TN 37219-2456
(615) 781-5330

Connecticut, Maine, Massachusetts, New Hampshire, Rhode Island, and Vermont
John F. Kennedy Federal Office Building, Room E-375
Boston, MA 02203
(617) 565-2500

Illinois, Indiana, Michigan, Minnesota, Ohio, and Wisconsin
230 S. Dearborn St., Room 844
Chicago, IL 60604-1502
(312) 886-5260

Branch office:
Federal Office Building
1240 E. Ninth Street, Room 881
Cleveland, OH 44199
(216) 522-3870

Arkansas, Louisiana, New Mexico, Oklahoma, and Texas
525 S. Griffin St., Suite 501
Dallas, TX 75202-5020
(972) 850-3100

Colorado, Iowa, Kansas, Missouri, Montana, Nebraska, North Dakota, South Dakota, Utah, and Wyoming
City Center Square
1100 Main St., Suite 1210
Kansas City, MO 64105
(816) 426-6441

Branch office:
1999 Broadway, Suite 1600
P.O. Box 46550
Denver, CO 80201-6550
(303) 844-1745

New Jersey, New York, Puerto Rico, and the U.S. Virgin Islands
201 Varick St., Room 983
New York, NY 10014
(212) 337-2078

Delaware, the District of Columbia, Maryland, Pennsylvania, Virginia, and West Virginia
The Curtis Center, Suite 630 East
170 S. Independence Mall West
Philadelphia, PA 19106-3306
(215) 861-5121

Branch office:
1100 Wilson Blvd., 22nd Floor, West
Arlington, VA 22209-2247
(202) 693-9393

Alaska, Arizona, California, Hawaii, Idaho, Nevada, Oregon, and Washington
90 7th Street, Suite 3-700
San Francisco, CA 94103-1516
(415) 625-7740

Branch offices:
World Trade Center, Suite 370
350 S. Figueroa St.
Los Angeles, CA 90071-1202
(213) 894-4980

1111 Third Ave., Suite 945
Seattle, WA 98101-3212
(206) 553-0940

State Agencies Responsible for Wage and Hour or Labor Matters

Alabama
Alabama Department of Labor
P.O. Box 303500
Montgomery, AL 36130-3500
(334) 242-3460
www.alalabor.state.al.us

Alaska
Department of Labor
P.O. Box 11149
Juneau, AK 99822-2249
(907) 465-2700
www.labor.state.ak.us

Arizona
Industrial Commission
P.O. Box 19070
Phoenix, AZ 85005-9070
(602) 542-4411
www.ica.state.az.us

Arkansas
Department of Labor & Workforce Development
10421 West Markham
Little Rock, AR 72205
(501) 682-4541
www.arkansas.gov/labor

California
Department of Industrial Relations
455 Golden Gate Ave., 10th Floor
San Francisco, CA 94102
(415) 703-5050
www.dir.ca.gov

Colorado
Department of Labor and Employment
633 17th Street, Suite 200
Denver, CO 80202-3660
(303) 318-8000
www.coworkforce.com

Connecticut
Wage and Workplace Standards Division
200 Folly Brook Blvd.
Wethersfield, CT 06109-1114
(860) 263-6505
www.ct.gov/dol

Delaware
Department of Labor
4425 N. Market Street, 4th Floor
Wilmington, DE 19802
(302) 761-8000
www.delawareworks.com

District of Columbia
Department of Employment Services
Employment Security Building
614 New York Ave., NE
Suite 300
Washington, DC 20002
(202) 671-1900
www.does.dc.gov

Florida
Agency for Workforce Innovation
Caldwell Bldg., Suite 100
107 East Madison St.
Tallahassee, FL 32399-4120
(850) 245-7105
www.floridajobs.org or www.MyFlorida.com

Georgia
Department of Labor
148 International Blvd., NE
Sussex Place, Room 600
Atlanta, GA 30303
(404) 656-3011
www.dol.state.ga.us

Hawaii
Department of Labor and Industrial Relations
830 Punchbowl Street, Room 321
Honolulu, HI 96813
(808) 586-8842
www.Hawaii.gov/labor

Idaho
Department of Labor
317 W. Main Street
Boise, ID 83735-0001
(208) 332-3579
www.labor.state.id.us

Illinois
Department of Labor
160 North LaSalle Street
13th Floor, Suite C-1300
Chicago, IL 60601
(312) 793-1808
www.state.il.us/agency/idol

Indiana
Department of Labor
402 W. Washington Street, Room W195
Indianapolis, IN 46204-2739
(317) 232-2655
www.in.gov/dol

Iowa
Workforce Development
1000 East Grand Ave.
Des Moines, IA 50319-0209
(515) 281-5365
www.iowaworkforce.org/labor

Kansas
Department of Human Resources
401 SW Topeka Blvd.
Topeka, KS 66603-3182
(785) 296-4062
www.dol.ks.gov

Kentucky
Labor Cabinet
1047 US Highway 127 South, Suite 4
Frankfort, KY 40601-4381
(502) 564-3070
www.labor.ky.gov

Louisiana
Department of Labor
P.O. Box 94094
Baton Rouge, LA 70804-9094
(225) 342-3011
www.laworks.net

Maine
Department of Labor
19 Union St.
P.O. Box 259
Augusta, ME 04332-0259
(207) 287-3787
www.state.me.us/labor

Maryland
Department of Labor, Licensing, and Regulation
Division of Labor and Industry
500 N. Calvert Street, Suite 401
Baltimore, MD 21202
(410) 230-2060
www.dllr.state.md.us

Massachusetts
Department of Labor & Workforce Development
1 Ashburton Place, Room 2112
Boston, MA 02108
(617) 626-7122
www.mass.Gov/dlwd

Michigan
Department of Labor and Economic Growth
P.O. Box 30004
Lansing, MI 48909
(517) 373-3034
www.michigan.gov/cis

Minnesota
Department of Labor and Industry
443 Lafayette Road
St. Paul, MN 55155
(651) 284-5010
www.doli.state.mn.us

Mississippi
Employment Security Commission
1235 Echelon Parkway
Jackson, MS 39215-1699
(601) 321-6000
www.mesc.state.ms.us

Missouri
Labor and Industrial Relations Commission
P.O. Box 599
3315 W. Truman Boulevard
Jefferson City, MO 65102-0599
(573) 751-2461
www.dolir.state.mo.gov/lirc

Montana
Department of Labor and Industry
P.O. Box 1728
Helena, MT 59624-1728
(406) 444-9091
http://www.mt.gov

Nebraska
Department of Labor
550 South 16th Street
Box 94600
Lincoln, NE 68509-4600
(402) 471 3405
www.nebraskaworkforce.gov

Nevada
Department of Business and Industry
555 E. Washington Ave., Suite 4100
Las Vegas, NV 89101-1050
(702) 486-2650
www.LaborCommissioner.com

New Hampshire
Department of Labor
95 Pleasant Street
Concord, NH 03301
(603) 271-3171
www.labor.state.nh.us

New Jersey
Department of Labor
John Fitch Plaza, 13th Floor, Suite D
P.O. Box 110
Trenton, NJ 08625-0110
(609) 292-2323
www.state.nj.us/labor

New Mexico
Department of Labor
401 Broadway, NE
P.O. Box 1928
Albuquerque, NM 87103-1928
(505) 841-8409
www.dol.state.nm.us

New York
Department of Labor
NY State Campus, Building 12
Albany, NY 12240-0003
(518) 457-2741
www.labor.state.ny.us

North Carolina
Department of Labor
4 West Edenton Street
Raleigh, NC 27601-1092
(919) 733-0359
www.nclabor.com

North Dakota
Department of Labor
State Capitol Building
600 East Boulevard Avenue, Dept. 406
Bismarck, ND 58505-0340
(701) 328-2660
www.state.nd.us/labor

Ohio
Division of Labor and Worker Safety
50 West Broad St., 28th Fl.
Columbus, OH 43215
(614) 644-2239
www.state.oh.us/ohio/agency.htm

Oklahoma
Department of Labor
4001 N. Lincoln Blvd.
Oklahoma City, OK 73105
(405) 528-1500, ext. 200
www.state.ok.us/ ~ okdol

Oregon
Bureau of Labor and Industries
800 N.E. Oregon Street, Suite #32
Portland, OR 97232
(503) 731-4070
www.oregon.gov/boli

Pennsylvania
Department of Labor and Industry
1700 Labor and Industry Bldg.
7th and Forster Streets
Harrisburg, PA 17120
(717) 787-5279
www.dli.state.pa.us

Puerto Rico
Department of Labor and Human Resources
Edificio Prudencia Rivera Martinez
505 Munoz Rivera Ave.
G.P.O. Box 3088
Hato Rey, PR 00918
(787) 754-2119
www.dtrh.gobierno.pr

Rhode Island
Department of Labor and Training
1511 Pontiac Avenue
Cranston, RI 02920
(401) 462-8870
www.dlt.state.ri.us

South Carolina
Department of Labor, Licensing & Regulations
Synergy Center, King Street Building
110 Center View Drive
P.O. Box 11329
Columbia, SC 29211-1329
(803) 896-4300
www.llr.state.sc.us

South Dakota
Department of Labor
700 Governors Drive
Pierre, SD 57501
(605) 773-3101
www.state.sd.us/

Tennessee
Department of Labor
Andrew Johnson Tower
710 James Robertson Parkway, 8th Floor
Nashville, TN 37243-0655
(615) 741-6642
www.state.tn.us/labor-wfd

Texas
Texas Workforce Commission
101 East 15th St., Room 618
Austin, TX 78778
(512) 463-2829
www.twc.state.tx.us

Utah
Labor Commission
P.O. Box 146610
Salt Lake City, UT 84114-6610
(801) 530-6680
Laborcommission.utah.gov

Vermont
Department of Labor and Industry
5 Green Mountain Drive
P.O. Box 488
Montpelier, VT 056020-0488
(802) 828-4000
www.labor.vermont.gov

Virginia
Department of Labor and Industry
Powers-Taylor Bldg.
13 South 13th St.
Richmond, VA 23219
(804) 786-2377
www.doli.virginia.gov

Washington
Department of Labor and Industries
P.O. Box 44001
Olympia, WA 98504-4001
(360) 902-4203
www.lni.wa.gov

West Virginia
Division of Labor
Bureau of Commerce
State Capitol Complex, Building #6, Room B749
Charles, WV 25305
(304) 558-7890
www.labor.state..wv.us

Wisconsin
Department of Workforce Development
201 East Washington Avenue, # A400
P.O. Box 7946
Madison, WI 53707-7946
(608) 267-9692
www.dwd.state.wi.us

Wyoming
Department of Employment
1510 E. Pershing Blvd, West Wing
Cheyenne, WY 82002
(307) 777-7672
wydoe.state.wy.us

Congress

In the Senate, wage and hour matters are under the purview of the Labor and Human Resources Committee. In the House of Representatives, the Education and Workforce Committee handles responsibility for wage and hour policies.

Appendix B

Fair Labor Standards Act

TITLE 29 B LABOR
CHAPTER 8—FAIR LABOR STANDARDS

(c) Repealed.

(d) Prohibition of sex discrimination.

(e) Employees of employers providing contract services to United States.

(f) Employees in domestic service.

(g) Newly hired employees who are less than 20 years old.

207. Maximum hours.

(a) Employees engaged in interstate commerce; additional applicability to employees pursuant to subsequent amendatory provisions.

(b) Employment pursuant to collective bargaining agreement; employment by independently owned and controlled local enterprise engaged in distribution of petroleum products.

(c), (d) Repealed.

(e) "Regular rate" defined.

(f) Employment necessitating irregular hours of work.

(g) Employment at piece rates.

(h) Extra compensation creditable toward overtime compensation.

(i) Employment by retail or service establishment.

(j) Employment in hospital or establishment engaged in care of sick, aged, or mentally ill.

(k) Employment by public agency engaged in fire protection or law enforcement activities.

(l) Employment in domestic service in one or more households.

(m) Employment in tobacco industry.

(n) Employment by street, suburban, or interurban electric railway, or local trolley or motorbus carrier.

(o) Compensatory time.

(p) Special detail work for fire protection and law enforcement employees; occasional or sporadic employment; substitution.

(q) Maximum hour exemption for employees receiving remedial education.

208. Wage orders in American Samoa. (Section stricken by Fair Minimum Wage Act of 2007, Pub. L. No. 110-28 (Title VIII).)

209. Attendance of witnesses.

210. Court review of wage orders in Puerto Rico and the Virgin Islands.

211. Collection of data.

(a) Investigations and inspections.

(b) State and local agencies and employees.

(c) Records.

(d) Homework regulations.

212. Child labor provisions.

    (a) Restrictions on shipment of goods; prosecution; conviction.

    (b) Investigations and inspections.

    (c) Oppressive child labor.

    (d) Proof of age.

213. Exemptions.

    (a) Minimum wage and maximum hour requirements.

    (b) Maximum hour requirements.

    (c) Child labor requirements.

    (d) Delivery of newspapers and wreathmaking.

    (e) Maximum hour requirements and minimum wage employees.

    (f) Employment in foreign countries and certain United States territories.

    (g) Certain employment in retail or service establishments, agriculture.

    (h) Maximum hour requirement: fourteen workweek limitation.

    (i) Cotton ginning.

    (j) Processing of sugar beets, sugar beet molasses, or sugar cane.

214. Employment under special certificates.

    (a) Learners, apprentices, messengers.

    (b) Students.

    (c) Handicapped workers.

    (d) Employment by schools.

215. Prohibited acts; prima facie evidence.

216. Penalties.

    (a) Fines and imprisonment.

    (b) Damages; right of action; attorney's fees and costs; termination of right of action.

    (c) Payment of wages and compensation; waiver of claims; actions by the Secretary; limitation of actions.

    (d) Savings provisions.

    (e) Civil penalties for child labor violations.

216a. Repealed.

216b. Liability for overtime work performed prior to July 20, 1949.

217. Injunction proceedings.

218. Relation to other laws.

219. Separability.

Sec. 201. Short title

This chapter may be cited as the "Fair Labor Standards Act of 1938."

-SOURCE-
(June 25, 1938, ch. 676, Sec. 1, 52 Stat. 1060.)

Sec. 202. Congressional finding and declaration of policy

(a) The Congress finds that the existence, in industries engaged in commerce or in the production of goods for commerce, of labor conditions detrimental to the maintenance of the minimum standard of living necessary for health, efficiency, and general well-being of workers (1) causes commerce and the channels and instrumentalities of commerce to be used to spread and perpetuate such labor conditions among the workers of the several States; (2) burdens commerce and the free flow of goods in commerce; (3) constitutes an unfair method of competition in commerce; (4) leads to labor disputes burdening and obstructing commerce and the free flow of goods in commerce; and (5) interferes with the orderly and fair marketing of goods in commerce. That Congress further finds that the employment of persons in domestic service in households affects commerce.

(b) It is declared to be the policy of this chapter, through the exercise by Congress of its power to regulate commerce among the several States and with foreign nations, to correct and as rapidly as practicable to eliminate the conditions above referred to in such industries without substantially curtailing employment or earning power.

-SOURCE-
(June 25, 1938, ch. 676, Sec. 2, 52 Stat. 1060; Oct. 26, 1949, ch. 736, Sec. 2, 63 Stat. 910; Pub. L. 93-259, Sec. 7(a), Apr. 8, 1974, 88 Stat. 62.)

Sec. 203. Definitions

As used in this chapter—

(a) "Person" means an individual, partnership, association, corporation, business trust, legal representative, or any organized group of persons.

(b) "Commerce" means trade, commerce, transportation, transmission, or communication among the several States or between any State and any place outside thereof.

(c) "State" means any State of the United States or the District of Columbia or any Territory or possession of the United States.

(d) "Employer" includes any person acting directly or indirectly in the interest of an employer in relation to an employee and includes a public agency, but does not include any labor organization (other than when acting as an employer) or anyone acting in the capacity of officer or agent of such labor organization.

(e) (1) Except as provided in paragraphs (2), (3), and (4), the term "employee" means any individual employed by an employer.

(2)In the case of an individual employed by a public agency, such term means—

(A) any individual employed by the Government of the United States—

(i) as a civilian in the military departments (as defined in section 102 of title 5),

(ii) in any executive agency (as defined in section 105 of such title),

(iii) in any unit of the judicial branch of the Government which has positions in the competitive service,

(iv) in a nonappropriated fund instrumentality under the jurisdiction of the Armed Forces,

(v) in the Library of Congress, or

(vi) the Government Printing Office;

(B) any individual employed by the United States Postal Service or the Postal Rate Commission; and

(C) any individual employed by a State, political subdivision of a State, or an interstate governmental agency, other than such an individual—

(i) who is not subject to the civil service laws of the State, political subdivision, or agency which employs him; and

(ii) who—

(I) holds a public elective office of that State, political subdivision, or agency,

(II) is selected by the holder of such an office to be a member of his personal staff,

(III) is appointed by such an officeholder to serve on a policymaking level,

(IV) is an immediate adviser to such an officeholder with respect to the constitutional or legal powers of his office, or

(V) is an employee in the legislative branch or legislative body of that State, political subdivision, or agency and is not employed by the legislative library of such State, political subdivision, or agency.

(3) For purposes of subsection (u) of this section, such term does not include any individual employed by an employer engaged in agriculture if such individual is the parent, spouse, child, or other member of the employer's immediate family.

(4) (A) The term "employee" does not include any individual who volunteers to perform services for a public agency which is a State, a political subdivision of a State, or an interstate governmental agency, if—

(i) the individual receives no compensation or is paid expenses, reasonable benefits, or a nominal fee to perform the services for which the individual volunteered; and

(ii) such services are not the same type of services which the individual is employed to perform for such public agency.

(B) An employee of a public agency which is a State, political subdivision of a State, or an interstate governmental agency may volunteer to perform services for any other

State, political subdivision, or interstate governmental agency, including a State, political subdivision or agency with which the employing State, political subdivision, or agency has a mutual aid agreement.

(5) The term "employee" does not include individuals who volunteer their services solely for humanitarian purposes to private non-profit food banks and who receive from the food banks groceries.

(f) "Agriculture" includes farming in all its branches and among other things includes the cultivation and tillage of the soil, dairying, the production, cultivation, growing, and harvesting of any agricultural or horticultural commodities (including commodities defined as agricultural commodities in section 1141j(g) of Title 12), the raising of livestock, bees, fur-bearing animals, or poultry, and any practices (including any forestry or lumbering operations) performed by a farmer or on a farm as an incident to or in conjunction with such farming operations, including preparation for market, delivery to storage or to market or to carriers for transportation to market.

(g) "Employ" includes to suffer or permit to work.

(h) "Industry" means a trade, business, industry, or other activity, or branch or group thereof, in which individuals are gainfully employed.

(i) "Goods" means goods (including ships and marine equipment), wares, products, commodities, merchandise, or articles or subjects of commerce of any character, or any part or ingredient thereof, but does not include goods after their delivery into the actual physical possession of the ultimate consumer thereof other than a producer, manufacturer, or processor thereof.

(j) "Produced" means produced, manufactured, mined, handled, or in any other manner worked on in any State; and for the purposes of this chapter an employee shall be deemed to have been engaged in the production of goods if such employee was employed in producing, manufacturing, mining, handling, transporting, or in any other manner working on such goods, or in any closely related process or occupation directly essential to the production thereof, in any State.

(k) "Sale" or "sell" includes any sale, exchange, contract to sell, consignment for sale, shipment for sale, or other disposition.

(l) "Oppressive child labor" means a condition of employment under which (1) any employee under the age of sixteen years is employed by an employer (other than a parent or a person standing in place of a parent employing his own child or a child in his custody under the age of sixteen years in an occupation other than manufacturing or mining or an occupation found by the Secretary of Labor to be particularly hazardous for the employment of children between the ages of sixteen and eighteen years or detrimental to their health or well-being) in any occupation, or (2) any employee between the ages of sixteen and eighteen years is employed by an employer in any occupation which the Secretary of Labor shall find and by order declare to be particularly hazardous for the employment of children between such ages or detrimental to their health or well-being; but oppressive child labor shall not be deemed to exist by virtue of the employment in any occupation of any person with respect to whom the employer shall have on file an unexpired certificate issued and held pursuant to regulations of the Secretary of Labor certifying that such person is above the oppressive child-labor age. The Secretary of Labor shall provide by regulation or by order that the employment of employees between the ages of fourteen and sixteen years in occupations other than manufacturing and mining shall not be deemed to constitute oppressive child labor if and to the extent that the Secretary of Labor determines that such employment is confined to periods which will not interfere with their schooling and to conditions which will not interfere with their health and well-being.

(m) "Wage" paid to any employee includes the reasonable cost, as determined by the Administrator, to the employer of furnishing such employee with board, lodging, or other facilities, if such board, lodging or other facilities are customarily furnished by such employer to his employees: Provided, That the cost of board, lodging, or other facilities shall not be included as a part of the wage paid to any employee to the extent it is excluded therefrom under the terms of a bona fide collective-bargaining agreement applicable to the particular employee: Provided further, That the Secretary is authorized to determine the fair value of such board, lodging, or other facilities for defined classes of employees and in defined areas, based on average cost to the employer or to groups of employers similarly situated, or average value to groups of employees, or other appropriate measures of fair value. Such evaluations, where applicable and pertinent, shall be used in lieu of actual measure of cost in determining the wage paid to any employee. In determining the wage an employer is required to pay a tipped employee, the amount paid such employee by the employee's employer shall be an amount equal to—

(1) the cash wage paid such employee which for purposes of such determination shall be not less than the cash wage required to be paid such an employee on August 20, 1996; and

(2) an additional amount on account of the tips received by such employee which amount is equal to the difference between the wage specified in paragraph (1) and the wage in effect under section 206(a)(1) of this title.

The additional amount on account of tips may not exceed the value of the tips actually received by an employee. The preceding 2 sentences shall not apply with respect to any tipped employee unless such employee has been informed by the employer of the provisions of this subsection, and all tips received by such employee have been retained by the employee, except that this subsection shall not be construed to prohibit the pooling of tips among employees who customarily and regularly receive tips.

(n) "Resale" shall not include the sale of goods to be used in residential or farm building construction, repair, or maintenance: Provided, That the sale is recognized as a bona fide retail sale in the industry.

(o) Hours Worked.—In determining for the purposes of sections 206 and 207 of this title the hours for which an employee is employed, there shall be excluded any time spent in changing clothes or washing at the beginning or end of each workday which was excluded from measured working time during the week involved by the express terms of or by custom or practice under a bona fide collective-bargaining agreement applicable to the particular employee.

(p) "American vessel" includes any vessel which is documented or numbered under the laws of the United States.

(q) "Secretary" means the Secretary of Labor.

(r) (1) "Enterprise" means the related activities performed (either through unified operation or common control) by any person or persons for a common business purpose, and includes all such activities whether performed in one or more establishments or by one or more corporate or other organizational units including departments of an establishment operated through leasing arrangements, but shall not include the related activities performed for such enterprise by an independent contractor. Within the meaning of this subsection, a retail or service establishment which is under independent ownership shall not be deemed to be so operated or controlled as to be other than a separate and distinct enterprise by reason of any arrangement, which includes, but is not necessarily limited to, an agreement, (A) that it will sell, or sell only, certain goods specified by a particular manufacturer, distributor, or advertiser, or (B) that it will join with other such establishments in the same industry for the purpose of collective purchasing, or (C) that it will have the exclusive right to sell the goods or use the brand name of a manufacturer, distributor, or advertiser within a specified area, or by reason of the fact that it occupies premises leased to it by a person who also leases premises to other retail or service establishments.

(2) For purposes of paragraph (1), the activities performed by any person or persons—

(A) in connection with the operation of a hospital, an institution primarily engaged in the care of the sick, the aged, the mentally ill or defective who reside on the premises of such institution, a school for mentally or physically handicapped or gifted children, a preschool, elementary or secondary school, or an institution of higher education (regardless of whether or not such hospital, institution, or school is operated for profit or not for profit), or

(B) in connection with the operation of a street, suburban or interurban electric railway, or local trolley or motorbus carrier, if the rates and services of such railway or carrier are subject to regulation by a State or local agency (regardless of whether or not such railway or carrier is public or private or operated for profit or not for profit), or

(C) in connection with the activities of a public agency, shall be deemed to be activities performed for a business purpose.

(s) (1) "Enterprise engaged in commerce or in the production of goods for commerce" means an enterprise that—

(A) (i) has employees engaged in commerce or in the production of goods for commerce, or that has employees handling, selling, or otherwise working on goods or materials that have been moved in or produced for commerce by any person; and

(ii) is an enterprise whose annual gross volume of sales made or business done is not less than $500,000 (exclusive of excise taxes at the retail level that are separately stated);

(B) is engaged in the operation of a hospital, an institution primarily engaged in the care of the sick, the aged, or the mentally ill or defective who reside on the premises of such institution, a school for mentally or physically handicapped or gifted children, a preschool, elementary or secondary school, or an institution of higher education (regardless of whether or not such hospital, institution, or school is public or private or operated for profit or not for profit); or

(C) is an activity of a public agency.

(2) Any establishment that has as its only regular employees the owner thereof or the parent, spouse, child, or other member of the immediate family of such owner shall not be considered to be an enterprise engaged in commerce or in the production of goods for commerce or a part of such an enterprise. The sales of such an establishment shall not be included for the purpose of determining the annual gross volume of sales of any enterprise for the purpose of this subsection.

(t) "Tipped employee" means any employee engaged in an occupation in which he customarily and regularly receives more than $30 a month in tips.

(u) "Man-day" means any day during which an employee performs any agricultural labor for not less than one hour.

(v) "Elementary school" means a day or residential school which provides elementary education, as determined under State law.

(w) "Secondary school" means a day or residential school which provides secondary education, as determined under State law.

(x) "Public agency" means the Government of the United States; the government of a State or political subdivision thereof; any agency of the United States (including the United States Postal Service and Postal Rate Commission), a State, or a political subdivision of a State; or any interstate governmental agency.

(y) "Employee in fire protection activities" means an employee, including a firefighter, paramedic, emergency medical technician, rescue worker, ambulance personnel, or hazardous materials worker, who—

(1) is trained in fire suppression, has the legal authority and responsibility to engage in fire suppression, and is employed by a fire department of a municipality, county, fire district, or State; and

(2) is engaged in the prevention, control, and extinguishments of fires or response to emergency situations where life, property, or the environment is at risk.

-SOURCE-
(June 25, 1938, ch. 676, Sec. 3, 52 Stat. 1060; 1946 Reorg. Plan No. 2, Sec. 1(b), eff. July 16, 1946, 11 F.R. 7873, 60 Stat. 1095; Oct. 26, 1949, ch. 736, Sec. 3, 63 Stat. 911; Pub. L. 87-30, Sec. 2, May 5, 1961, 75 Stat. 65; Pub. L. 89-601, Title I, Sec. 101-103, Title II, Sec. 215(a), Sept. 23, 1966, 80 Stat. 830-832, 837; Pub. L. 92-318, Title IX, Sec. 906(b)(2), (3), June 23, 1972, 86 Stat. 375; Pub. L. 93-259, Sec. 6(a), 13(e), Apr. 8, 1974, 88 Stat. 58, 64; Pub. L. 95-151, Sec. 3(a), (b), 9(a)-(c), Nov. 1, 1977, 91 Stat. 1249, 1251; Pub. L. 99-150, Sec. 4(a), 5, Nov. 13, 1985, 99 Stat. 790; Pub. L. 101-157, Sec. 3(a), (d), 5, Nov. 17, 1989, 103 Stat. 938, 939, 941; Pub. L. 104-1, Title II, Sec. 203(d), Jan. 23, 1995, 109 Stat. 10; Pub. L. 104-188, (Title II), Sec. 2105(b), Aug. 20, 1996, 110 Stat. 1929.)

Sec. 204. Administration

(a) Creation of Wage and Hour Division in Department of Labor; Administrator

There is created in the Department of Labor a Wage and Hour Division which shall be under the direction of an Administrator, to be known as the Administrator of the Wage and Hour Division (in this chapter referred to as the "Administrator"). The Administrator shall be appointed by the President, by and with the advice and consent of the Senate.

(b) Appointment, selection, classification, and promotion of employees by Administrator

The Administrator may, subject to the civil-service laws, appoint such employees as he deems necessary to carry out his functions and duties under this chapter and shall fix their compensation in accordance with chapter 51 and subchapter III of chapter 53 of Title 5. The Administrator may establish and utilize such regional, local, or other agencies, and utilize such voluntary and uncompensated services, as may from time to time be needed. Attorneys appointed under this section may appear for and represent the Administrator in any litigation, but all such litigation shall be subject to the direction and control of the Attorney General. In the appointment, selection, classification, and promotion of officers and employees of the Administrator, no political test or qualification shall be permitted or given consideration, but all such appointments and promotions shall be given and made on the basis of merit and efficiency.

(c) Principal office of Administrator; jurisdiction

The principal office of the Administrator shall be in the District of Columbia, but he or his duly authorized representative may exercise any or all of his powers in any place.

(d) Biennial report to Congress; studies of exemptions to hour and wage provisions and means to prevent curtailment of employment opportunities

(1) The Secretary shall submit biennially in January a report to the Congress covering his activities for the preceding two years and including such information, data, and recommendations for further legislation in connection with the matters covered by this chapter as he may find advisable. Such report shall contain an evaluation and appraisal by the Secretary of the minimum wages and overtime coverage established by this chapter, together with his recommendations to the Congress. In making such evaluation and appraisal, the Secretary shall take into consideration any changes which may have occurred in the cost of living and in productivity and the level of wages in manufacturing, the ability of employers to absorb wage increases, and such other factors as he may deem pertinent. Such report shall also include a summary of the special certificates issued under section 214(b) of this title.

(2) The Secretary shall conduct studies on the justification or lack thereof for each of the special exemptions set forth in section 213 of this title, and the extent to which such exemptions apply to employees of establishments described in subsection (g) of such section and the economic effects of the application of such exemptions to such employees. The Secretary shall submit a report of his findings and recommendations to the Congress with respect to the studies conducted under this paragraph not later than January 1, 1976.

(3) The Secretary shall conduct a continuing study on means to prevent curtailment of employment opportunities for manpower groups which have had historically high incidences of unemployment (such as disadvantaged minorities, youth, elderly, and such other groups as the Secretary may designate). The first report of the results of such study shall be transmitted to the Congress not later than one year after the effective date of the Fair Labor Standards Amendments of 1974. Subsequent reports on such study shall be transmitted to the Congress at two-year intervals after such effective date. Each such report shall include suggestions respecting the Secretary's authority under section 214 of this title.

(e) Study of effects of foreign production on unemployment; report to President and Congress

Whenever the Secretary has reason to believe that in any industry under this chapter the competition of foreign producers in United States markets or in markets abroad, or both, has resulted, or is likely to result, in increased unemployment in the United States, he shall undertake an investigation to gain full information with respect to the matter. If he determines such increased unemployment has in fact resulted, or is in fact likely to result, from such competition, he shall make a full and complete report of his findings and determinations to the President and to the Congress: Provided, That he may also include in such report information on the increased employment resulting from additional exports in any industry under this chapter as he may determine to be pertinent to such report.

(f) Employees of Library of Congress; administration of provisions by Office of Personnel Management

The Secretary is authorized to enter into an agreement with the Librarian of Congress with respect to individuals employed in the Library of Congress to provide for the carrying out of the Secretary's functions under this chapter with respect to such individuals. Notwithstanding any other provision of this chapter, or any other law, the Director of the Office of Personnel Management is authorized to administer the provisions of this chapter with respect to any individual employed by the United States (other than an individual employed in the Library of Congress, United States Postal Service, Postal Rate Commission, or the Tennessee Valley Authority). Nothing in this subsection shall be construed to affect the right of an employee to bring an action for unpaid minimum wages, or unpaid overtime compensation, and liquidated damages under section 216(b) of this title.

-SOURCE-
(June 25, 1938, ch. 676, Sec. 4, 52 Stat. 1061; Oct. 26, 1949, ch. 736, Sec. 4, 63 Stat. 911; Oct. 28, 1949, ch. 782, Title XI, Sec. 1106(a), 63 Stat. 972; Aug. 12, 1955, ch. 867, Sec. 2, 69 Stat. 711; Pub. L. 87-30, Sec. 3, May 5, 1961, 75 Stat. 66; Pub. L. 93-259, Sec. 6(b), 24(c), 27, Apr. 8, 1974, 88 Stat. 60, 72, 73; 1978 Reorg. Plan No. 2, Sec. 102, eff. Jan. 1, 1979, 43 F.R. 36037, 92 Stat. 3783; Pub. L. 104-66, Title I, Sec. 1102(a), Dec. 21, 1995, 109 Stat. 722.)

Sec. 205. Special industry committees for American Samoa (section striken by Fair Minimum Wage Act of 2007, Pub. L. No. 110-28 (Title VIII))

Sec. 206. Minimum wage

(a) Employees engaged in commerce; home workers in Puerto Rico and Virgin Islands; employees in American Samoa; seamen on American vessels; agricultural employees

Every employer shall pay to each of his employees who in any workweek is engaged in commerce or in the production of goods for commerce, or is employed in an enterprise engaged in commerce or in the production of goods for commerce, wages at the following rates:

(1) except as otherwise provided in this section, not less than $4.25 an hour during the period ending on September 30, 1996, not less than $4.75 an hour during the year beginning on October 1, 1996, and not less than $5.15 an hour beginning September 1, 1997;

(2) if such employee is a home worker in Puerto Rico or the Virgin Islands, not less than the minimum piece rate prescribed by regulation or order; or, if no such minimum piece rate is in effect, any piece rate adopted by such employer which shall yield, to the proportion or class of employees prescribed by regulation or order, not less than the applicable minimum hourly wage rate. Such minimum piece rates or employer piece rates shall be commensurate with, and shall be paid in lieu of, the minimum hourly wage rate applicable under the provisions of this section. The Administrator, or his authorized representative, shall have power to make such regulations or orders as are necessary or appropriate to carry out any of the provisions of this paragraph, including the power without limiting the generality of the foregoing, to define any operation or occupation which is performed by such home work employees in Puerto Rico or the Virgin Islands; to establish minimum piece rates for any operation or occupation so defined; to prescribe the method and procedure for ascertaining and promulgating minimum piece rates; to prescribe standards for employer piece rates, including the proportion or class of employees who shall receive not less than the minimum hourly wage rate; to define the term "home worker;" and to prescribe the conditions under which employers, agents, contractors, and subcontractors shall cause goods to be produced by home workers;

(3) if such employee is employed as a seaman on an American vessel, not less than the rate which will provide to the employee, for the period covered by the wage payment,

wages equal to compensation at the hourly rate prescribed by paragraph (1) of this subsection for all hours during such period when he was actually on duty (including periods aboard ship when the employee was on watch or was, at the direction of a superior officer, performing work or standing by, but not including off-duty periods which are provided pursuant to the employment agreement); or

(4) if such employee is employed in agriculture, not less than the minimum wage rate in effect under paragraph (1) after December 31, 1977.

(b) Additional applicability to employees pursuant to subsequent amendatory provisions

Every employer shall pay to each of his employees (other than an employee to whom subsection (a)(5) of this section applies) who in any workweek is engaged in commerce or in the production of goods for commerce, or is employed in an enterprise engaged in commerce or in the production of goods for commerce, and who in such workweek is brought within the purview of this section by the amendments made to this chapter by the Fair Labor Standards Amendments of 1966; title IX of the Education Amendments of 1972 (20 U.S.C. 1681 et seq.), or the Fair Labor Standards Amendments of 1974, wages at the following rate: Effective after December 31, 1977, not less than the minimum wage rate in effect under subsection (a)(1) of this section.

(c) Repealed. Pub. L. 104-188, Sec. 2104(c), Aug. 20, 1996, 110 Stat. 1929

(d) Prohibition of sex discrimination

(1) No employer having employees subject to any provisions of this section shall discriminate, within any establishment in which such employees are employed, between employees on the basis of sex by paying wages to employees in such establishment at a rate less than the rate at which he pays wages to employees of the opposite sex in such establishment for equal work on jobs the performance of which requires equal skill, effort, and responsibility, and which are performed under similar working conditions, except where such payment is made pursuant to (i) a seniority system; (ii) a merit system; (iii) a system which measures earnings by quantity or quality of production; or (iv) a differential based on any other factor other than sex: Provided, That an employer who is paying a wage rate differential in violation of this subsection shall not, in order to comply with the provisions of this subsection, reduce the wage rate of any employee.

(2) No labor organization, or its agents, representing employees of an employer having employees subject to any provisions of this section shall cause or attempt to cause such an employer to discriminate against an employee in violation of paragraph (1) of this subsection.

(3) For purposes of administration and enforcement, any amounts owing to any employee which have been withheld in violation of this subsection shall be deemed to be unpaid minimum wages or unpaid overtime compensation under this chapter.

(4) As used in this subsection, the term "labor organization" means any organization of any kind, or any agency or employee representation committee or plan, in which employees participate and which exists for the purpose, in whole or in part, of dealing with employers concerning grievances, labor disputes, wages, rates of pay, hours of employment, or conditions of work.

(e) Employees of employers providing contract services to United States

(1) Notwithstanding the provisions of section 213 of this title (except subsections (a)(1) and (f) thereof), every employer providing any contract services (other than linen supply services) under a contract with the United States or any subcontract thereunder shall pay to each of his employees whose rate of pay is not governed by the Service Contract Act of

1965 (41 U.S.C. §§ 351-357) or to whom subsection (a)(1) of this section is not applicable, wages at rates not less than the rates provided for in subsection (b) of this section.

(2) Notwithstanding the provisions of section 213 of this title (except subsections (a)(1) and (f) thereof) and the provisions of the Service Contract Act of 1965 (41 U.S.C. 351 et seq.) every employer in an establishment providing linen supply services to the United States under a contract with the United States or any subcontract thereunder shall pay to each of his employees in such establishment wages at rates not less than those prescribed in subsection (b) of this section, except that if more than 50 per centum of the gross annual dollar volume of sales made or business done by such establishment is derived from providing such linen supply services under any such contracts or subcontracts, such employer shall pay to each of his employees in such establishment wages at rates not less than those prescribed in subsection (a)(1) of this section.

(f) Employees in domestic service

Any employee—

(1) who in any workweek is employed in domestic service in a household shall be paid wages at a rate not less than the wage rate in effect under subsection (b) of this section unless such employee's compensation for such service would not because of section 209(a)(6) of the Social Security Act (42 U.S.C. § 409(a)(6)) constitute wages for the purposes of title II of such Act (42 U.S.C. § 401 et seq.), or

(2) who in any workweek—

(A) is employed in domestic service in one or more households, and

(B) is so employed for more than 8 hours in the aggregate,

shall be paid wages for such employment in such workweek at a rate not less than the wage rate in effect under subsection (b) of this section.

(g) Newly hired employees who are less than 20 years old

(1) In lieu of the rate prescribed by subsection (a)(1) of this section, any employer may pay any employee of such employer, during the first 90 consecutive calendar days after such employee is initially employed by such employer, a wage which is not less than $4.25 an hour.

(2) No employer may take any action to displace employees (including partial displacements such as reduction in hours, wages, or employment benefits) for purposes of hiring individuals at the wage authorized in paragraph (1).

(3) Any employer who violates this subsection shall be considered to have violated section 215(a)(3) of this title.

(4) This subsection shall only apply to an employee who has not attained the age of 20 years.

-SOURCE-
(June 25, 1938, ch. 676, Sec. 6, 52 Stat. 1062; June 26, 1940, ch. 432, Sec. 3(e), (f), 54 Stat. 616; Oct. 26, 1949, ch. 736, Sec. 6, 63 Stat. 912; Aug. 12, 1955, ch. 867, Sec. 3, 69 Stat. 711; Aug. 8, 1956, ch. 1035, Sec. 2, 70 Stat. 1118; Pub. L. 87-30, Sec. 5, May 5, 1961, 75 Stat. 67; Pub. L. 88-38, Sec. 3, June 10, 1963, 77 Stat. 56; Pub. L. 89-601, Title III, Sec. 301-305, Sept. 23, 1966, 80 Stat. 838, 839, 841; Pub. L. 93-259, Sec. 2-4, 5(b), 7(b)(1), Apr. 8, 1974, 88 Stat. 55, 56, 62; Pub. L. 95-151, Sec. 2(a)-(d)(2), Nov. 1, 1977, 91 Stat. 1245, 1246; Pub. L. 101-157, Sec. 2, 4(b), Nov. 17, 1989, 103 Stat. 938, 940; Pub. L. 101-239, Title X, Sec. 10208(d)(2)(B)(i), Dec. 19, 1989, 103 Stat. 2481; Pub. L. 104-188, (Title II), Sec. 2104(b), (c), 2105(c), Aug. 20, 1996, 110 Stat. 1928, 1929.)

Sec. 207. Maximum hours

(a) Employees engaged in interstate commerce; additional applicability to employees pursuant to subsequent amendatory provisions

(1) Except as otherwise provided in this section, no employer shall employ any of his employees who in any workweek is engaged in commerce or in the production of goods for commerce, or is employed in an enterprise engaged in commerce or in the production of goods for commerce, for a workweek longer than forty hours unless such employee receives compensation for his employment in excess of the hours above specified at a rate not less than one and one-half times the regular rate at which he is employed.

(2) No employer shall employ any of his employees who in any workweek is engaged in commerce or in the production of goods for commerce, or is employed in an enterprise engaged in commerce or in the production of goods for commerce, and who in such workweek is brought within the purview of this subsection by the amendments made to this chapter by the Fair Labor Standards Amendments of 1966—

(A) for a workweek longer than forty-four hours during the first year from the effective date of the Fair Labor Standards Amendments of 1966,

(B) for a workweek longer than forty-two hours during the second year from such date, or

(C) for a workweek longer than forty hours after the expiration of the second year from such date,

unless such employee receives compensation for his employment in excess of the hours above specified at a rate not less than one and one-half times the regular rate at which he is employed.

(b) Employment pursuant to collective bargaining agreement; employment by independently owned and controlled local enterprise engaged in distribution of petroleum products

No employer shall be deemed to have violated subsection (a) of this section by employing any employee for a workweek in excess of that specified in such subsection without paying the compensation for overtime employment prescribed therein if such employee is so employed—

(1) in pursuance of an agreement, made as a result of collective bargaining by representatives of employees certified as bona fide by the National Labor Relations Board, which provides that no employee shall be employed more than one thousand and forty hours during any period of twenty-six consecutive weeks; or

(2) in pursuance of an agreement, made as a result of collective bargaining by representatives of employees certified as bona fide by the National Labor Relations Board, which provides that during a specified period of fifty-two consecutive weeks the employee shall be employed not more than two thousand two hundred and forty hours and shall be guaranteed not less than one thousand eight hundred and forty-hours (or not less than forty-six weeks at the normal number of hours worked per week, but not less than thirty hours per week) and not more than two thousand and eighty hours of employment for which he shall receive compensation for all hours guaranteed or worked at rates not less than those applicable under the agreement to the work performed and for all hours in excess of the guaranty which are also in excess of the maximum workweek applicable to such employee under subsection (a) of this section or two thousand and eighty in such period at rates not less than one and one-half times the regular rate at which he is employed; or

(3) by an independently owned and controlled local enterprise (including an enterprise with more than one bulk storage establishment) engaged in the wholesale or bulk distribution of petroleum products if—

(A) the annual gross volume of sales of such enterprise is less than $1,000,000 exclusive of excise taxes,

(B) more than 75 per centum of such enterprise's annual dollar volume of sales is made within the State in which such enterprise is located, and

(C) not more than 25 per centum of the annual dollar volume of sales of such enterprise is to customers who are engaged in the bulk distribution of such products for resale,

and such employee receives compensation for employment in excess of forty hours in any workweek at a rate not less than one and one-half times the minimum wage rate applicable to him under section 206 of this title,

and if such employee receives compensation for employment in excess of twelve hours in any workday, or for employment in excess of fifty-six hours in any workweek, as the case may be, at a rate not less than one and one-half times the regular rate at which he is employed.

(c), (d) Repealed. Pub. L. 93-259, Sec. 19(e), Apr. 8, 1974, 88 Stat. 66

(e) "Regular rate" defined

As used in this section the "regular rate" at which an employee is employed shall be deemed to include all remuneration for employment paid to, or on behalf of, the employee, but shall not be deemed to include—

(1) sums paid as gifts; payments in the nature of gifts made at Christmas time or on other special occasions, as a reward for service, the amounts of which are not measured by or dependent on hours worked, production, or efficiency;

(2) payments made for occasional periods when no work is performed due to vacation, holiday, illness, failure of the employer to provide sufficient work, or other similar cause; reasonable payments for traveling expenses, or other expenses, incurred by an employee in the furtherance of his employer's interests and properly reimbursable by the employer; and other similar payments to an employee which are not made as compensation for his hours of employment;

(3) Sums paid in recognition of services performed during a given period if either, (a) both the fact that payment is to be made and the amount of the payment are determined at the sole discretion of the employer at or near the end of the period and not pursuant to any prior contract, agreement, or promise causing the employee to expect such payments regularly; or (b) the payments are made pursuant to a bona fide profit-sharing plan or trust or bona fide thrift or savings plan, meeting the requirements of the Administrator set forth in appropriate regulations which he shall issue, having due regard among other relevant factors, to the extent to which the amounts paid to the employee are determined without regard to hours of work, production, or efficiency; or (c) the payments are talent fees (as such talent fees are defined and delimited by regulations of the Administrator) paid to performers, including announcers, on radio and television programs;

(4) contributions irrevocably made by an employer to a trustee or third person pursuant to a bona fide plan for providing old-age, retirement, life, accident, or health insurance or similar benefits for employees;

(5) extra compensation provided by a premium rate paid for certain hours worked by the employee in any day of workweek because such hours are hours worked in excess of

eight in a day or in excess of the maximum workweek applicable to such employee under subsection (a) of this section or in excess of the employee's normal working hours or regular working hours, as the case may be;

(6) extra compensation provided by a premium rate paid for work by the employee on Saturdays, Sundays, holidays, or regular days of rest, or on the sixth or seventh day of the workweek, where such premium rate is not less than one and one-half times the rate established in good faith for like work performed in nonovertime hours on other days;

(7) extra compensation provided by a premium rate paid to the employee, in pursuance of an applicable employment contract or collective-bargaining agreement, for work outside of the hours established in good faith by the contract or agreement as the basic, normal, or regular workday (not exceeding eight hours) or workweek (not exceeding the maximum workweek) applicable to such employee under subsection (a) of this section, where such premium rate is not less than one and one-half times the rate established in good faith by the contract or agreement for like work performed during such workday or workweek; or

(8) any value or income derived from employer-provided grants or rights provided pursuant to a stock option, stock appreciation right, or bona fide employee stock purchase program which is not otherwise excludable under any of paragraphs (1) through (7) if—

(A) grants are made pursuant to a program, the terms and conditions of which are communicated to participating employees either at the beginning of the employee's participation in the program or at the time of the grant;

(B) in the case of stock options and stock appreciation rights, the grant or right cannot be exercisable for a period of at least 6 months after the time of grant (except that grants or rights may become exercisable because of an employee's death, disability, retirement, or a change in corporate ownership, or other circumstances permitted by regulation), and the exercise price is at least 85 percent of the fair market value of the stock at the time of grant;

(C) exercise of any grant or right is voluntary; and

(D) any determinations regarding the award of, and the amount of, employer-provided grants or rights that are based on performance are—

(i) made based upon meeting previously established performance criteria (which may include hours of work, efficiency, or productivity) of any business unit consisting of at least 10 employees or of a facility, except that, any determinations may be based on length of service or minimum schedule of hours or days of work; or

(ii) made based upon the past performance (which may include any criteria) of one or more employees in a given period so long as the determination is in the sole discretion of the employer and not pursuant to any prior contract.

(f) Employment necessitating irregular hours of work

No employer shall be deemed to have violated subsection (a) of this section by employing any employee for a workweek in excess of the maximum workweek applicable to such employee under subsection (a) of this section if such employee is employed pursuant to a bona fide individual contract, or pursuant to an agreement made as a result of collective bargaining by representatives of employees, if the duties of such employee necessitate irregular hours of work, and the contract or agreement (1) specifies a regular rate of pay of not less than the minimum hourly rate provided in subsection (a) or (b) of section 206 of this title (whichever may be applicable) and compensation at not less than one and one-half times such rate for all hours worked in excess of such maximum workweek, and (2) provides a weekly guaranty of pay for not more than sixty hours based on the rates so specified.

(g) Employment at piece rates

No employer shall be deemed to have violated subsection (a) of this section by employing any employee for a workweek in excess of the maximum workweek applicable to such employee under such subsection if, pursuant to an agreement or understanding arrived at between the employer and the employee before performance of the work, the amount paid to the employee for the number of hours worked by him in such workweek in excess of the maximum workweek applicable to such employee under such subsection—

(1) in the case of an employee employed at piece rates, is computed at piece rates not less than one and one-half times the bona fide piece rates applicable to the same work when performed during nonovertime hours; or

(2) in the case of an employee performing two or more kinds of work for which different hourly or piece rates have been established, is computed at rates not less than one and one-half times such bona fide rates applicable to the same work when performed during nonovertime hours; or

(3) is computed at a rate not less than one and one-half times the rate established by such agreement or understanding as the basic rate to be used in computing overtime compensation thereunder: Provided, That the rate so established shall be authorized by regulation by the Administrator as being substantially equivalent to the average hourly earnings of the employee, exclusive of overtime premiums, in the particular work over a representative period of time;

and if (i) the employee's average hourly earnings for the workweek exclusive of payments described in paragraphs (1) through (7) of subsection (e) of this section are not less than the minimum hourly rate required by applicable law, and (ii) extra overtime compensation is properly computed and paid on other forms of additional pay required to be included in computing the regular rate.

(h) Credit toward minimum wage or overtime compensation of amounts excluded from regular rate

(1) Except as provided in paragraph (2), sums excluded from the regular rate pursuant to subsection (e) of this section shall not be creditable toward wages required under section 206 of this title or overtime compensation required under this section.

(2) Extra compensation paid as described in paragraphs (5), (6), and (7) of subsection (e) of this section shall be creditable toward overtime compensation payable pursuant to this section.

(i) Employment by retail or service establishment

No employer shall be deemed to have violated subsection (a) of this section by employing any employee of a retail or service establishment for a workweek in excess of the applicable workweek specified therein, if (1) the regular rate of pay of such employee is in excess of one and one-half times the minimum hourly rate applicable to him under section 206 of this title, and (2) more than half his compensation for a representative period (not less than one month) represents commissions on goods or services. In determining the proportion of compensation representing commissions, all earnings resulting from the application of a bona fide commission rate shall be deemed commissions on goods or services without regard to whether the computed commissions exceed the draw or guarantee.

(j) Employment in hospital or establishment engaged in care of sick, aged, or mentally ill

No employer engaged in the operation of a hospital or an establishment which is an institution primarily engaged in the care of the sick, the aged, or the mentally ill or defective who reside on the premises shall be deemed to have violated subsection (a) of this section if, pursuant to an agreement or understanding arrived at between the employer and the employee before performance of the work, a work period of fourteen consecutive days is accepted in lieu of the workweek of seven consecutive days for purposes of overtime computation and if, for his employment in excess of eight hours in any workday and in excess of eighty hours in such fourteen-day period, the employee receives compensation at a rate not less than one and one-half times the regular rate at which he is employed.

(k) Employment by public agency engaged in fire protection or law enforcement activities

No public agency shall be deemed to have violated subsection (a) of this section with respect to the employment of any employee in fire protection activities or any employee in law enforcement activities (including security personnel in correctional institutions) if—

(1) in a work period of 28 consecutive days the employee receives for tours of duty which in the aggregate exceed the lesser of (A) 216 hours, or (B) the average number of hours (as determined by the Secretary pursuant to section 6(c)(3) of the Fair Labor Standards Amendments of 1974) in tours of duty of employees engaged in such activities in work periods of 28 consecutive days in calendar year 1975; or

(2) in the case of such an employee to whom a work period of at least 7 but less than 28 days applies, in his work period the employee receives for tours of duty which in the aggregate exceed a number of hours which bears the same ratio to the number of consecutive days in his work period as 216 hours (or if lower, the number of hours referred to in clause (B) of paragraph (1)) bears to 28 days,

compensation at a rate not less than one and one-half times the regular rate at which he is employed.

(l) Employment in domestic service in one or more households

No employer shall employ any employee in domestic service in one or more households for a workweek longer than forty hours unless such employee receives compensation for such employment in accordance with subsection (a) of this section.

(m) Employment in tobacco industry

For a period or periods of not more than fourteen workweeks in the aggregate in any calendar year, any employer may employ any employee for a workweek in excess of that specified in subsection (a) of this section without paying the compensation for overtime employment prescribed in such subsection, if such employee—

(1) is employed by such employer—

(A) to provide services (including stripping and grading) necessary and incidental to the sale at auction of green leaf tobacco of type 11, 12, 13, 14, 21, 22, 23, 24, 31, 35, 36, or 37 (as such types are defined by the Secretary of Agriculture), or in auction sale, buying, handling, stemming, redrying, packing, and storing of such tobacco,

(B) in auction sale, buying, handling, sorting, grading, packing, or storing green leaf tobacco of type 32 (as such type is defined by the Secretary of Agriculture), or

(C) in auction sale, buying, handling, stripping, sorting, grading, sizing, packing, or stemming prior to packing, of perishable cigar leaf tobacco of type 41, 42, 43, 44, 45, 46, 51, 52, 53, 54, 55, 61, or 62 (as such types are defined by the Secretary of Agriculture); and

(2) receives for—

(A) such employment by such employer which is in excess of ten hours in any workday, and

(B) such employment by such employer which is in excess of forty-eight hours in any workweek, compensation at a rate not less than one and one-half times the regular rate at which he is employed.

An employer who receives an exemption under this subsection shall not be eligible for any other exemption under this section.

(n) Employment by street, suburban, or interurban electric railway, or local trolley or motorbus carrier

In the case of an employee of an employer engaged in the business of operating a street, suburban or interurban electric railway, or local trolley or motorbus carrier (regardless of whether or not such railway or carrier is public or private or operated for profit or not for profit), in determining the hours of employment of such an employee to which the rate prescribed by subsection (a) of this section applies there shall be excluded the hours such employee was employed in charter activities by such employer if (1) the employee's employment in such activities was pursuant to an agreement or understanding with his employer arrived at before engaging in such employment, and (2) if employment in such activities is not part of such employee's regular employment.

(o) Compensatory time

(1) Employees of a public agency which is a State, a political subdivision of a State, or an interstate governmental agency may receive, in accordance with this subsection and in lieu of overtime compensation, compensatory time off at a rate not less than one and one-half hours for each hour of employment for which overtime compensation is required by this section.

(2) A public agency may provide compensatory time under paragraph (1) only—

(A) pursuant to—

(i) applicable provisions of a collective bargaining agreement, memorandum of understanding, or any other agreement between the public agency and representatives of such employees; or

(ii) in the case of employees not covered by subclause (i), an agreement or understanding arrived at between the employer and employee before the performance of the work; and

(B) if the employee has not accrued compensatory time in excess of the limit applicable to the employee prescribed by paragraph (3).

In the case of employees described in clause (A)(ii) hired prior to April 15, 1986, the regular practice in effect on April 15, 1986, with respect to compensatory time off for such employees in lieu of the receipt of overtime compensation, shall constitute an agreement or understanding under such clause (A)(ii). Except as provided in the previous sentence, the provision of compensatory time off to such employees for hours worked after April 14, 1986, shall be in accordance with this subsection.

(3) (A) If the work of an employee for which compensatory time may be provided included work in a public safety activity, an emergency response activity, or a seasonal activity, the employee engaged in such work may accrue not more than 480 hours of compensatory time for hours worked after April 15, 1986. If such work was any other work, the employee engaged in such work may accrue not more than 240 hours of compensatory time for hours

worked after April 15, 1986. Any such employee who, after April 15, 1986, has accrued 480 or 240 hours, as the case may be, of compensatory time off shall, for additional overtime hours of work, be paid overtime compensation.

> (B) If compensation is paid to an employee for accrued compensatory time off, such compensation shall be paid at the regular rate earned by the employee at the time the employee receives such payment.

(4) An employee who has accrued compensatory time off authorized to be provided under paragraph (1) shall, upon termination of employment, be paid for the unused compensatory time at a rate of compensation not less than—

> (A) the average regular rate received by such employee during the last 3 years of the employee's employment, or

> (B) the final regular rate received by such employee, whichever is higher

(5) An employee of a public agency which is a State, political subdivision of a State, or an interstate governmental agency—

> (A) who has accrued compensatory time off authorized to be provided under paragraph (1), and

> (B) who has requested the use of such compensatory time,

shall be permitted by the employee's employer to use such time within a reasonable period after making the request if the use of the compensatory time does not unduly disrupt the operations of the public agency.

(6) The hours an employee of a public agency performs court reporting transcript preparation duties shall not be considered as hours worked for the purposes of subsection (a) of this section if—

> (A) such employee is paid at a per-page rate which is not less than—

> > (i) the maximum rate established by State law or local ordinance for the jurisdiction of such public agency,

> > (ii) the maximum rate otherwise established by a judicial or administrative officer and in effect on July 1, 1995, or

> > (iii) the rate freely negotiated between the employee and the party requesting the transcript, other than the judge who presided over the proceedings being transcribed, and

> (B) the hours spent performing such duties are outside of the hours such employee performs other work (including hours for which the agency requires the employee's attendance) pursuant to the employment relationship with such public agency.

For purposes of this section, the amount paid such employee in accordance with subparagraph (A) for the performance of court reporting transcript preparation duties, shall not be considered in the calculation of the regular rate at which such employee is employed.

(7) For purposes of this subsection—

> (A) the term "overtime compensation" means the compensation required by subsection (a), and

> (B) the terms "compensatory time" and "compensatory time off" mean hours during which an employee is not working, which are not counted as hours worked during the applicable workweek or other work period for purposes of overtime compensation, and for which the employee is compensated at the employee's regular rate.

(p) Special detail work for fire protection and law enforcement employees; occasional or sporadic employment; substitution

(1) If an individual who is employed by a State, political subdivision of a State, or an interstate governmental agency in fire protection or law enforcement activities (including activities of security personnel in correctional institutions) and who, solely at such individual's option, agrees to be employed on a special detail by a separate or independent employer in fire protection, law enforcement, or related activities, the hours such individual was employed by such separate and independent employer shall be excluded by the public agency employing such individual in the calculation of the hours for which the employee is entitled to overtime compensation under this section if the public agency—

(A) requires that its employees engaged in fire protection, law enforcement, or security activities be hired by a separate and independent employer to perform the special detail,

(B) facilitates the employment of such employees by a separate and independent employer, or

(C) otherwise affects the condition of employment of such employees by a separate and independent employer.

(2) If an employee of a public agency which is a State, political subdivision of a State, or an interstate governmental agency undertakes, on an occasional or sporadic basis and solely at the employee's option, part-time employment for the public agency which is in a different capacity from any capacity in which the employee is regularly employed with the public agency, the hours such employee was employed in performing the different employment shall be excluded by the public agency in the calculation of the hours for which the employee is entitled to overtime compensation under this section.

(3) If an individual who is employed in any capacity by a public agency which is a State, political subdivision of a State, or an interstate governmental agency, agrees, with the approval of the public agency and solely at the option of such individual, to substitute during scheduled work hours for another individual who is employed by such agency in the same capacity, the hours such employee worked as a substitute shall be excluded by the public agency in the calculation of the hours for which the employee is entitled to overtime compensation under this section.

(q) Maximum hour exemption for employees receiving remedial education

Any employer may employ any employee for a period or periods of not more than 10 hours in the aggregate in any workweek in excess of the maximum workweek specified in subsection (a) of this section without paying the compensation for overtime employment prescribed in such subsection, if during such period or periods the employee is receiving remedial education that is—

(1) provided to employees who lack a high school diploma or educational attainment at the eighth grade level;

(2) designed to provide reading and other basic skills at an eighth grade level or below; and

(3) does not include job specific training.

-SOURCE-
(June 25, 1938, ch. 676, Sec. 7, 52 Stat. 1063; Oct. 29, 1941, ch. 461, 55 Stat. 756; July 20, 1949, ch. 352, Sec. 1, 63 Stat. 446; Oct. 26, 1949, ch. 736, Sec. 7, 63 Stat. 912; Pub. L. 87-30, Sec. 6, May 5, 1961, 75 Stat. 69; Pub. L. 89-601, Title II, Sec. 204(c), (d), 212(b), Title IV,

Sec. 401-403, Sept. 23, 1966, 80 Stat. 835-837, 841, 842; Pub. L. 93-259,Sec. 6(c)(1), 7(b)(2), 9(a), 12(b), 19, 21(a), Apr. 8, 1974, 88 Stat. 60, 62, 64, 66, 68; Pub. L. 99-150, Sec. 2(a), 3(a)-(c)(1), Nov. 11, 1985, 99 Stat. 787, 789; Pub. L. 101-157, Sec. 7, Nov. 17, 1989, 103 Stat. 944; Pub. L. 104-26, Sec. 2, Sept. 6, 1995, 109 Stat. 264.)

Sec. 208. Wage orders in American Samoa (section striken by Fair Minimum Wage Act of 2007, Pub. L. No. 110-28 (Title VIII))

Sec. 209. Attendance of witnesses

For the purpose of any hearing or investigation provided for in this chapter, the provisions of sections 49 and 50 of title 15 (relating to the attendance of witnesses and the production of books, papers, and documents), are made applicable to the jurisdiction, powers, and duties of the Administrator, the Secretary of Labor, and the industry committees.

-SOURCE-
(June 25, 1938, ch. 676, Sec. 9, 52 Stat. 1065; 1946 Reorg. Plan No. 2, Sec. 1(b), eff. July 16, 1946, 11 F.R. 7873, 60 Stat. 1095.)

Sec. 210. Court review of wage orders in Puerto Rico and the Virgin Islands

(a) Any person aggrieved by an order of the Secretary issued under section 208 of this title may obtain a review of such order in the United States Court of Appeals for any circuit wherein such person resides or has his principal place of business, or in the United States Court of Appeals for the District of Columbia, by filing in such court, within 60 days after the entry of such order a written petition praying that the order of the Secretary be modified or set aside in whole or in part. A copy of such petition shall forthwith be transmitted by the clerk of the court to the Secretary, and thereupon the Secretary shall file in the court the record of the industry committee upon which the order complained of was entered, as provided in section 2112 of title 28. Upon the filing of such petition such court shall have exclusive jurisdiction to affirm, modify (including provision for the payment of an appropriate minimum wage rate), or set aside such order in whole or in part, so far as it is applicable to the petitioner. The review by the court shall be limited to questions of law, and findings of fact by such industry committee when supported by substantial evidence shall be conclusive. No objection to the order of the Secretary shall be considered by the court unless such objection shall have been urged before such industry committee or unless there were reasonable grounds for failure so to do. If application is made to the court for leave to adduce additional evidence, and it is shown to the satisfaction of the court that such additional evidence may materially affect the result of the proceeding and that there were reasonable grounds for failure to adduce such evidence in the proceedings before such industry committee, the court may order such additional evidence to be taken before an industry committee and to be adduced upon the hearing in such manner and upon such terms and conditions as to the court may seem proper. Such industry committee may modify the initial findings by reason of the additional evidence so taken, and shall file with the court such modified or new findings which if supported by substantial evidence shall be conclusive, and shall also file its recommendation, if any, for the modification or setting aside of the original order. The judgment and decree of the court shall be final, subject to review by the Supreme Court of the United States upon certiorari or certification as provided in section 1254 of title 28.

(b) The commencement of proceedings under subsection (a) of this section shall not, unless specifically ordered by the court, operate as a stay of the Administrator's order. The court shall not grant any stay of the order unless the person complaining of such order shall file in court an undertaking with a surety or sureties satisfactory to the court for the payment to the employees affected by the order, in the event such order is affirmed, of the amount by which the compensation such employees are entitled to receive under the order exceeds the compensation they actually receive while such stay is in effect.

-SOURCE-
(June 25, 1938, ch. 676, Sec. 10, 52 Stat. 1065; Aug. 12, 1955, ch. 867, Sec. 5(f), 69 Stat. 712; Pub. L. 85-791, Sec. 22, Aug. 28, 1958, 72 Stat. 948; Pub. L. 93-259, Sec. 5(c)(2), Apr. 8, 1974, 88 Stat. 58.)

Sec. 211. Collection of data

(a) Investigations and inspections

The Administrator or his designated representatives may investigate and gather data regarding the wages, hours, and other conditions and practices of employment in any industry subject to this chapter, and may enter and inspect such places and such records (and make such transcriptions thereof), question such employees, and investigate such facts, conditions, practices, or matters as he may deem necessary or appropriate to determine whether any person has violated any provision of this chapter, or which may aid in the enforcement of the provisions of this chapter. Except as provided in section 212 of this title and in subsection (b) of this section, the Administrator shall utilize the bureaus and divisions of the Department of Labor for all the investigations and inspections necessary under this section. Except as provided in section 212 of this title, the Administrator shall bring all actions under section 217 of this title to restrain violations of this chapter.

(b) State and local agencies and employees

With the consent and cooperation of State agencies charged with the administration of State labor laws, the Administrator and the Secretary of Labor may, for the purpose of carrying out their respective functions and duties under this chapter, utilize the services of State and local agencies and their employees and, notwithstanding any other provision of law, may reimburse such State and local agencies and their employees for services rendered for such purposes.

(c) Records

Every employer subject to any provision of this chapter or of any order issued under this chapter shall make, keep, and preserve such records of the persons employed by him and of the wages, hours, and other conditions and practices of employment maintained by him, and shall preserve such records for such periods of time, and shall make such reports therefrom to the Administrator as he shall prescribe by regulation or order as necessary or appropriate for the enforcement of the provisions of this chapter or the regulations or orders thereunder. The employer of an employee who performs substitute work described in section 207(p)(3) of this title may not be required under this subsection to keep a record of the hours of the substitute work.

(d) Homework regulations

The Administrator is authorized to make such regulations and orders regulating, restricting, or prohibiting industrial homework as are necessary or appropriate to prevent the circumvention or evasion of and to safeguard the minimum wage rate prescribed in this chapter, and all existing regulations or orders of the Administrator relating to industrial homework are continued in full force and effect.

-SOURCE-
(June 25, 1938, ch. 676, Sec. 11, 52 Stat. 1066; 1946 Reorg. Plan No. 2, Sec. 1(b), eff. July 16, 1946, 11 F.R. 7873, 60 Stat. 1095; Oct. 26, 1949, ch. 736, Sec. 9, 63 Stat. 916; Pub. L. 99-150, Sec. 3(c)(2), Nov. 14, 1985, 99 Stat. 789.)

Sec. 212. Child labor provisions

(a) Restrictions on shipment of goods; prosecution; conviction

No producer, manufacturer, or dealer shall ship or deliver for shipment in commerce any goods produced in an establishment situated in the United States in or about which within thirty days prior to the removal of such goods therefrom any oppressive child labor has been employed: Provided, That any such shipment or delivery for shipment of such goods by a purchaser who acquired them in good faith in reliance on written assurance from the producer, manufacturer, or dealer that the goods were produced in compliance with the requirements of this section, and who acquired such goods for value without notice of any such violation, shall not be deemed prohibited by this subsection: And provided further, That a prosecution and conviction of a defendant for the shipment or delivery for shipment of any goods under the conditions herein prohibited shall be a bar to any further prosecution against the same defendant for shipments or deliveries for shipment of any such goods before the beginning of said prosecution.

(b) Investigations and inspections

The Secretary of Labor or any of his authorized representatives, shall make all investigations and inspections under section 211(a) of this title with respect to the employment of minors, and, subject to the direction and control of the Attorney General, shall bring all actions under section 217 of this title to enjoin any act or practice which is unlawful by reason of the existence of oppressive child labor, and shall administer all other provisions of this chapter relating to oppressive child labor.

(c) Oppressive child labor

No employer shall employ any oppressive child labor in commerce or in the production of goods for commerce or in any enterprise engaged in commerce or in the production of goods for commerce.

(d) Proof of age

In order to carry out the objectives of this section, the Secretary may by regulation require employers to obtain from any employee proof of age.

-SOURCE-
(June 25, 1938, ch. 676, Sec. 12, 52 Stat. 1067; 1946 Reorg. Plan No. 2, Sec. 1(b), eff. July 16, 1946, 11 F.R. 7873, 60 Stat. 1095; Oct. 26, 1949, ch. 736, Sec. 10, 63 Stat. 917; Pub. L. 87-30, Sec. 8, May 5, 1961, 75 Stat. 70; Pub. L. 93-259, Sec. 25(a), Apr. 8, 1974, 88 Stat. 72.)

Sec. 213. Exemptions

(a) Minimum wage and maximum hour requirements

The provisions of sections 206 (except subsection (d) in the case of paragraph (1) of this subsection) and section 207 of this title shall not apply with respect to—

(1) any employee employed in a bona fide executive, administrative, or professional capacity (including any employee employed in the capacity of academic administrative personnel or teacher in elementary or secondary schools), or in the capacity of outside salesman (as such terms are defined and delimited from time to time by regulations of the Secretary, subject to the provisions of subchapter II of chapter 5 of Title 5, except that an employee of a retail or service establishment shall not be excluded from the definition of employee employed in a bona fide executive or administrative capacity because of the number of hours in his workweek which he devotes to activities not directly or closely related to the performance of executive or administrative activities, if less than 40 per centum of his hours worked in the workweek are devoted to such activities); or

(2) Repealed. Pub. L. 101-157, Sec. 3(c)(1), Nov. 17, 1989, 103 Stat. 939.

(3) any employee employed by an establishment which is an amusement or recreational establishment organized camp, or religious or non-profit educational conference center, if (A) it does not operate for more than seven months in any calendar year, or (B) during the preceding calendar year, its average receipts for any six months of such year were not more than 331/3 per centum of its average receipts for the other six months of such year, except that the exemption from sections 206 and 207 of this title provided by this paragraph does not apply with respect to any employee of a private entity engaged in providing services or facilities (other than, in the case of the exemption from section 206 of this title, a private entity engaged in providing services and facilities directly related to skiing) in a national park or a national forest, or on land in the National Wildlife Refuge System, under a contract with the Secretary of the Interior or the Secretary of Agriculture; or

(4) Repealed. Pub. L. 101-157, Sec. 3(c)(1), Nov. 17, 1989, 103 Stat. 939.

(5) any employee employed in the catching, taking, propagating, harvesting, cultivating, or farming of any kind of fish, shellfish, crustacea, sponges, seaweeds, or other aquatic forms of animal and vegetable life, or in the first processing, canning or packing such marine products at sea as an incident to, or in conjunction with, such fishing operations, including the going to and returning from work and loading and unloading when performed by any such employee; or

(6) any employee employed in agriculture

(A) if such employee is employed by an employer who did not, during any calendar quarter during the preceding calendar year, use more than five hundred man-days of agricultural labor,

(B) if such employee is the parent, spouse, child, or other member of his employer's immediate family,

(C) if such employee (i) is employed as a hand harvest laborer and is paid on a piece rate basis in an operation which has been, and is customarily and generally recognized as having been, paid on a piece rate basis in the region of employment, (ii) commutes daily from his permanent residence to the farm on which he is so employed, and (iii) has been employed in agriculture less than thirteen weeks during the preceding calendar year,

(D) if such employee (other than an employee described in clause (C) of this subsection) (i) is sixteen years of age or under and is employed as a hand harvest laborer, is paid on a piece rate basis in an operation which has been, and is customarily and generally recognized as having been, paid on a piece rate basis in the region of employment, (ii) is employed on the same farm as his parent or person standing in the place of his parent, and (iii) is paid at the same piece rate as employees over age sixteen are paid on the same farm, or

(E) if such employee is principally engaged in the range production of livestock; or

(7) any employee to the extent that such employee is exempted by regulations, order, or certificate of the Secretary issued under section 214 of this title; or

(8) any employee employed in connection with the publication of any weekly, semi-weekly, or daily newspaper with a circulation of less than four thousand the major part of which circulation is within the county where published or counties contiguous thereto; or

(9) Repealed. Pub. L. 93-259, Sec. 23(a)(1), Apr. 8, 1974, 88 Stat. 69.

(10) any switchboard operator employed by an independently owned public telephone company which has not more than seven hundred and fifty stations; or

(11) Repealed. Pub. L. 93-259, Sec. 10(a), Apr. 8, 1974, 88 Stat. 63.

(12) any employee employed as a seaman on a vessel other than an American vessel; or

(13) , (14) Repealed. Pub. L. 93-259, Sec. 9(b)(1), 23(b)(1), Apr. 8, 1974, 88 Stat. 63, 69.

(15) any employee employed on a casual basis in domestic service employment to provide babysitting services or any employee employed in domestic service employment to provide companionship services for individuals who (because of age or infirmity) are unable to care for themselves (as such terms are defined and delimited by regulations of the Secretary); or

(16) a criminal investigator who is paid availability pay under section 5545a of Title 5; or

(17) any employee who is a computer systems analyst, computer programmer, software engineer, or other similarly skilled worker, whose primary duty is—

(A) the application of systems analysis techniques and procedures, including consulting with users, to determine hardware, software, or system functional specifications;

(B) the design, development, documentation, analysis, creation, testing, or modification of computer systems or programs, including prototypes, based on and related to user or system design specifications;

(C) the design, documentation, testing, creation, or modification of computer programs related to machine operating systems; or

(D) a combination of duties described in subparagraphs (A), (B), and (C) the performance of which requires the same level of skills, and

who, in the case of an employee who is compensated on an hourly basis, is compensated at a rate of not less than $27.63 an hour.

(b) Maximum hour requirements

The provisions of section 207 of this title shall not apply with respect to—

(1) any employee with respect to whom the Secretary of Transportation has power to establish qualifications and maximum hours of service pursuant to the provisions of section 31502 of Title 49; or

(2) any employee of an employer engaged in the operation of a rail carrier subject to part A of subtitle IV of Title 49; or

(3) any employee of a carrier by air subject to the provisions of title II of the Railway Labor Act (45 U.S.C. 181 et seq.); or

(4) Repealed. Pub. L. 93-259, Sec. 11(c), Apr. 8, 1974, 88 Stat. 64.

(5) any individual employed as an outside buyer of poultry, eggs, cream, or milk, in their raw or natural state; or

(6) any employee employed as a seaman; or

(7) Repealed. Pub. L. 93-259, Sec. 21(b)(3), Apr. 8, 1974, 88 Stat. 68.

(8) Repealed. Pub. L. 95-151, Sec. 14(b), Nov. 1, 1977, 91 Stat. 1252.

(9) any employee employed as an announcer, news editor, or chief engineer by a radio or television station the major studio of which is located

(A) in a city or town of one hundred thousand population or less, according to the latest available decennial census figures as compiled by the Bureau of the Census, except where such city or town is part of a standard metropolitan statistical area, as defined and designated by the Office of Management and Budget, which has a total population in excess of one hundred thousand, or

(B) in a city or town of twenty-five thousand population or less, which is part of such an area but is at least 40 airline miles from the principal city in such area; or

(10) (A)any salesman, partsman, or mechanic primarily engaged in selling or servicing automobiles, trucks, or farm implements, if he is employed by a nonmanufacturing establishment primarily engaged in the business of selling such vehicles or implements to ultimate purchasers; or

(B) any salesman primarily engaged in selling trailers, boats, or aircraft, if he is employed by a nonmanufacturing establishment primarily engaged in the business of selling trailers, boats, or aircraft to ultimate purchasers; or

(11) any employee employed as a driver or driver's helper making local deliveries, who is compensated for such employment on the basis of trip rates, or other delivery payment plan, if the Secretary shall find that such plan has the general purpose and effect of reducing hours worked by such employees to, or below, the maximum workweek applicable to them under section 207(a) of this title; or

(12) any employee employed in agriculture or in connection with the operation or maintenance of ditches, canals, reservoirs, or waterways, not owned or operated for profit, or operated on a sharecrop basis, and which are used exclusively for supply and storing of water, at least 90 percent of which was ultimately delivered for agricultural purposes during the preceding calendar year; or

(13) any employee with respect to his employment in agriculture by a farmer, notwithstanding other employment of such employee in connection with livestock auction operations in which such farmer is engaged as an adjunct to the raising of livestock, either on his own account or in conjunction with other farmers, if such employee (A) is primarily employed during his workweek in agriculture by such farmer, and (B) is paid for his employment in connection with such livestock auction operations at a wage rate not less than that prescribed by section 206(a)(1) of this title; or

(14) any employee employed within the area of production (as defined by the Secretary) by an establishment commonly recognized as a country elevator, including such an

establishment which sells products and services used in the operation of a farm, if no more than five employees are employed in the establishment in such operations; or

(15) any employee engaged in the processing of maple sap into sugar (other than refined sugar) or syrup; or

(16) any employee engaged (A) in the transportation and preparation for transportation of fruits or vegetables, whether or not performed by the farmer, from the farm to a place of first processing or first marketing within the same State, or (B) in transportation, whether or not performed by the farmer, between the farm and any point within the same State of persons employed or to be employed in the harvesting of fruits or vegetables; or

(17) any driver employed by an employer engaged in the business of operating taxicabs; or

(18), (19) Repealed. Pub. L. 93-259, Sec. 15(c), 16(b), Apr. 8, 1974, 88 Stat. 65.

(20) any employee of a public agency who in any workweek is employed in fire protection activities or any employee of a public agency who in any workweek is employed in law enforcement activities (including security personnel in correctional institutions), if the public agency employs during the workweek less than 5 employees in fire protection or law enforcement activities, as the case may be; or

(21) any employee who is employed in domestic service in a household and who resides in such household; or

(22) Repealed. Pub. L. 95-151, Sec. 5, Nov. 1, 1977, 91 Stat. 1249.

(23) Repealed. Pub. L. 93-259, Sec. 10(b)(3), Apr. 8, 1974, 88 Stat. 64.

(24) any employee who is employed with his spouse by a nonprofit educational institution to serve as the parents of children—

(A) who are orphans or one of whose natural parents is deceased, or

(B) who are enrolled in such institution and reside in residential facilities of the institution, while such children are in residence at such institution, if such employee and his spouse reside in such facilities, receive, without cost, board and lodging from such institution, and are together compensated, on a cash basis, at an annual rate of not less than $10,000; or

(25), (26) Repealed. Pub. L. 95-151, Sec. 6(a), 7(a), Nov. 1, 1977, 91 Stat. 1249, 1250.

(27) any employee employed by an establishment which is a motion picture theater; or

(28) any employee employed in planting or tending trees, cruising, surveying, or felling timber, or in preparing or transporting logs or other forestry products to the mill, processing plant, railroad, or other transportation terminal, if the number of employees employed by his employer in such forestry or lumbering operations does not exceed eight;

(29) any employee of an amusement or recreational establishment located in a national park or national forest or on land in the National Wildlife Refuge System if such employee

(A) is an employee of a private entity engaged in providing services or facilities in a national park or national forest, or on land in the National Wildlife Refuge System, under a contract with the Secretary of the Interior or the Secretary of Agriculture, and

(B) receives compensation for employment in excess of fifty-six hours in any workweek at a rate not less than one and one-half times the regular rate at which he is employed; or

(30) a criminal investigator who is paid availability pay under section 5545a of Title 5.

(c) Child labor requirements

(1) Except as provided in paragraph (2) or (4), the provisions of section 212 of this title relating to child labor shall not apply to any employee employed in agriculture outside of school hours for the school district where such employee is living while he is so employed, if such employee—

(A) is less than twelve years of age and (i) is employed by his parent, or by a person standing in the place of his parent, on a farm owned or operated by such parent or person, or (ii) is employed, with the consent of his parent or person standing in the place of his parent, on a farm, none of the employees of which are (because of subsection (a)(6)(A) of this section) required to be paid at the wage rate prescribed by section 206(a)(5) of this title,

(B) is twelve years or thirteen years of age and (i) such employment is with the consent of his parent or person standing in the place of his parent, or (ii) his parent or such person is employed on the same farm as such employee, or

(C) is fourteen years of age or older.

(2) The provisions of section 212 of this title relating to child labor shall apply to an employee below the age of sixteen employed in agriculture in an occupation that the Secretary of Labor finds and declares to be particularly hazardous for the employment of children below the age of sixteen, except where such employee is employed by his parent or by a person standing in the place of his parent on a farm owned or operated by such parent or person.

(3) The provisions of section 212 of this title relating to child labor shall not apply to any child employed as an actor or performer in motion pictures or theatrical productions, or in radio or television productions.

(4) (A)An employer or group of employers may apply to the Secretary for a waiver of the application of section 212 of this title to the employment for not more than eight weeks in any calendar year of individuals who are less than twelve years of age, but not less than ten years of age, as hand harvest laborers in an agricultural operation which has been, and is customarily and generally recognized as being, paid on a piece rate basis in the region in which such individuals would be employed. The Secretary may not grant such a waiver unless he finds, based on objective data submitted by the applicant, that—

(i) the crop to be harvested is one with a particularly short harvesting season and the application of section 212 of this title would cause severe economic disruption in the industry of the employer or group of employers applying for the waiver;

(ii) the employment of the individuals to whom the waiver would apply would not be deleterious to their health or well-being;

(iii) the level and type of pesticides and other chemicals used would not have an adverse effect on the health or well-being of the individuals to whom the waiver would apply;

(iv) individuals age twelve and above are not available for such employment; and

(v) the industry of such employer or group of employers has traditionally and substantially employed individuals under twelve years of age without displacing substantial job opportunities for individuals over sixteen years of age.

(B) Any waiver granted by the Secretary under subparagraph (A) shall require that—

(i) the individuals employed under such waiver be employed outside of school hours for the school district where they are living while so employed;

(ii) such individuals while so employed commute daily from their permanent residence to the farm on which they are so employed; and

(iii) such individuals be employed under such waiver (I) for not more than eight weeks between June 1 and October 15 of any calendar year, and (II) in accordance with such other terms and conditions as the Secretary shall prescribe for such individuals' protection.

(5) (A) In the administration and enforcement of the child labor provisions of this chapter, employees who are 16 and 17 years of age shall be permitted to load materials into, but not operate or unload materials from, scrap paper balers and paper box compactors—

(i) that are safe for 16- and 17-year-old employees loading the scrap paper balers or paper box compactors; and

(ii) that cannot be operated while being loaded.

(B) For purposes of subparagraph (A), scrap paper balers and paper box compactors shall be considered safe for 16- or 17-year-old employees to load only if—

(i) (I) the scrap paper balers and paper box compactors meet the American National Standards Institute's Standard ANSI Z245.5-1990 for scrap paper balers and Standard ANSI Z245.2-1992 for paper box compactors; or

(II) the scrap paper balers and paper box compactors meet an applicable standard that is adopted by the American National Standards Institute after August 6, 1996, and that is certified by the Secretary to be at least as protective of the safety of minors as the standard described in subclause (I);

(ii) the scrap paper balers and paper box compactors include an on-off switch incorporating a key-lock or other system and the control of the system is maintained in the custody of employees who are 18 years of age or older;

(iii) the on-off switch of the scrap paper balers and paper box compactors is maintained in an off position when the scrap paper balers and paper box compactors are not in operation; and

(iv) the employer of 16- and 17-year-old employees provides notice, and posts a notice, on the scrap paper balers and paper box compactors stating that—

(I) the scrap paper balers and paper box compactors meet the applicable standard described in clause (i);

(II) 16- and 17-year-old employees may only load the scrap paper balers and paper box compactors; and

(III) any employee under the age of 18 may not operate or unload the scrap paper balers and paper box compactors. The Secretary shall publish in the Federal Register a standard that is adopted by the American National Standards Institute for scrap paper balers or paper box compactors and certified by the Secretary to be protective of the safety of minors under clause (i)(II).

(C) (i) Employers shall prepare and submit to the Secretary reports—

(I) on any injury to an employee under the age of 18 that requires medical treatment (other than first aid) resulting from the employee's contact with a scrap paper baler or paper box compactor during the loading, operation, or unloading of the baler or compactor; and

(II) on any fatality of an employee under the age of 18 resulting from the employee's contact with a scrap paper baler or paper box compactor during the loading, operation, or unloading of the baler or compactor.

(ii) The reports described in clause (i) shall be used by the Secretary to determine whether or not the implementation of subparagraph (A) has had any effect on the safety of children.

(iii) The reports described in clause (i) shall provide—

(I) the name, telephone number, and address of the employer and the address of the place of employment where the incident occurred;

(II) the name, telephone number, and address of the employee who suffered an injury or death as a result of the incident;

(III) the date of the incident;

(IV) a description of the injury and a narrative describing how the incident occurred; and

(V) the name of the manufacturer and the model number of the scrap paper baler or paper box compactor involved in the incident.

(iv) The reports described in clause (i) shall be submitted to the Secretary promptly, but not later than 10 days after the date on which an incident relating to an injury or death occurred.

(v) The Secretary may not rely solely on the reports described in clause (i) as the basis for making a determination that any of the employers described in clause (i) has violated a provision of section 212 of this title relating to oppressive child labor or a regulation or order issued pursuant to section 212 of this title. The Secretary shall, prior to making such a determination, conduct an investigation and inspection in accordance with section 212(b) of this title.

(vi) The reporting requirements of this subparagraph shall expire 2 years after August 6, 1996.

(6) In the administration and enforcement of the child labor provisions of this chapter, employees who are under 17 years of age may not drive automobiles or trucks on public roadways. Employees who are 17 years of age may drive automobiles or trucks on public roadways only if—

(A) such driving is restricted to daylight hours;

(B) the employee holds a State license valid for the type of driving involved in the job performed and has no records of any moving violation at the time of hire;

(C) the employee has successfully completed a State approved driver education course;

(D) the automobile or truck is equipped with a seat belt for the driver and any passengers and the employee's employer has instructed the employee that the seat belts must be used when driving the automobile or truck;

(E) the automobile or truck does not exceed 6,000 pounds of gross vehicle weight;

(F) such driving does not involve—

(i) the towing of vehicles;

(ii) route deliveries or route sales;

(iii) the transportation for hire of property, goods, or passengers;

(iv) urgent, time-sensitive deliveries;

(v) more than two trips away from the primary place of employment in any single day for the purpose of delivering goods of the employee's employer to a customer (other than urgent, time-sensitive deliveries);

(vi) more than two trips away from the primary place of employment in any single day for the purpose of transporting passengers (other than employees of the employer);

(vii) transporting more than three passengers (including employees of the employer); or

(viii) driving beyond a 30 mile radius from the employee's place of employment; and

(G) such driving is only occasional and incidental to the employee's employment.

For purposes of subparagraph (G), the term "occasional and incidental" is no more than one-third of an employee's worktime in any workday and no more than 20 percent of an employee's worktime in any workweek.

(d) Delivery of newspapers and wreathmaking

The provisions of sections 206, 207, and 212 of this title shall not apply with respect to any employee engaged in the delivery of newspapers to the consumer or to any homeworker engaged in the making of wreaths composed principally of natural holly, pine, cedar, or other evergreens (including the harvesting of the evergreens or other forest products used in making such wreaths).

(e) Maximum hour requirements and minimum wage employees

The provisions of section 207 of this title shall not apply with respect to employees for whom the Secretary of Labor is authorized to establish minimum wage rates as provided in section 206(a)(3) of this title, except with respect to employees for whom such rates are in effect; and with respect to such employees the Secretary may make rules and regulations providing reasonable limitations and allowing reasonable variations, tolerances, and exemptions to and from any or all of the provisions of section 207 of this title if he shall find, after a public hearing on the matter, and taking into account the factors set forth in section 206(a)(3) of this title, that economic conditions warrant such action.

(f) Employment in foreign countries and certain United States territories

The provisions of sections 206, 207, 211, and 212 of this title shall not apply with respect to any employee whose services during the workweek are performed in a workplace within a foreign country or within territory under the jurisdiction of the United States other than the following: a State of the United States; the District of Columbia; Puerto Rico; the Virgin Islands; outer Continental Shelf lands defined in the Outer Continental Shelf Lands Act (ch. 345, 67 Stat. 462) (43 U.S.C. 1331 et seq.); American Samoa; Guam; Wake Island; Eniwetok Atoll; Kwajalein Atoll; and Johnston Island.

(g) Certain employment in retail or service establishments, agriculture

The exemption from section 206 of this title provided by paragraph (6) of subsection (a) of this section shall not apply with respect to any employee employed by an establishment (1) which controls, is controlled by, or is under common control with, another establishment the activities of which are not related for a common business purpose to, but materially support the activities of the establishment employing such employee; and (2) whose annual gross volume of sales made or business done, when combined with the annual gross volume of sales made or business done by each establishment which controls, is controlled by, or is under common control with, the establishment employing such employee, exceeds $10,000,000 (exclusive of excise taxes at the retail level which are separately stated).

(h) Maximum hour requirement: fourteen workweek limitation

The provisions of section 207 of this title shall not apply for a period or periods of not more than fourteen workweeks in the aggregate in any calendar year to any employee who—

(1) is employed by such employer—

(A) exclusively to provide services necessary and incidental to the ginning of cotton in an establishment primarily engaged in the ginning of cotton;

(B) exclusively to provide services necessary and incidental to the receiving, handling, and storing of raw cotton and the compressing of raw cotton when performed at a cotton warehouse or compress-warehouse facility, other than one operated in conjunction with a cotton mill, primarily engaged in storing and compressing;

(C) exclusively to provide services necessary and incidental to the receiving, handling, storing, and processing of cottonseed in an establishment primarily engaged in the receiving, handling, storing, and processing of cottonseed; or

(D) exclusively to provide services necessary and incidental to the processing of sugar cane or sugar beets in an establishment primarily engaged in the processing of sugar cane or sugar beets; and

(2) receives for—

(A) such employment by such employer which is in excess of ten hours in any workday, and

(B) such employment by such employer which is in excess of forty-eight hours in any workweek,

compensation at a rate not less than one and one-half times the regular rate at which he is employed.

Any employer who receives an exemption under this subsection shall not be eligible for any other exemption under this section or section 207 of this title.

(i) Cotton ginning

The provisions of section 207 of this title shall not apply for a period or periods of not more than fourteen workweeks in the aggregate in any period of fifty-two consecutive weeks to any employee who—

(1) is engaged in the ginning of cotton for market in any place of employment located in a county where cotton is grown in commercial quantities; and

(2) receives for any such employment during such workweeks—

(A) in excess of ten hours in any workday, and

(B) in excess of forty-eight hours in any workweek,

compensation at a rate not less than one and one-half times the regular rate at which he is employed. No week included in any fifty-two week period for purposes of the preceding sentence may be included for such purposes in any other fifty-two week period.

(j) Processing of sugar beets, sugar beet molasses, or sugar cane

The provisions of section 207 of this title shall not apply for a period or periods of not more than fourteen workweeks in the aggregate in any period of fifty-two consecutive weeks to any employee who—

(1) is engaged in the processing of sugar beets, sugar beet molasses, or sugar cane into sugar (other than refined sugar) or syrup; and

(2) receives for any such employment during such workweeks—

(A) in excess of ten hours in any workday, and

(B) in excess of forty-eight hours in any workweek,

compensation at a rate not less than one and one-half times the regular rate at which he is employed. No week included in any fifty-two week period for purposes of the preceding sentence may be included for such purposes in any other fifty-two week period.

-SOURCE-
(June 25, 1938, ch. 676, Sec. 13, 52 Stat. 1067; Aug. 9, 1939, ch. 605, 53 Stat. 1266; Oct. 26, 1949, ch. 736, Sec. 11, 63 Stat. 917; Aug. 8, 1956, ch. 1035, Sec. 3, 70 Stat. 1118; Pub. L. 85-231, Sec. 1(1), Aug. 30, 1957, 71 Stat. 514; Pub. L. 86-624, Sec. 21(b), July 12, 1960, 74 Stat. 417; Pub. L. 87-30, Sec. 9, 10, May 5, 1961, 75 Stat. 71, 74; Pub. L. 89-601, Title II, Sec. 201-204(a), (b), 205-212(a), 213, 214, 215(b), (c), Sept. 23, 1966, 80 Stat. 833-838; Pub. L. 89-670, Sec. 8(e), Oct. 15, 1966, 80 Stat. 943; 1970 Reorg. Plan No. 2, Sec. 102, eff. July 1, 1970, 35 F.R. 7959, 84 Stat. 2085; Pub. L. 92-318, Title IX, Sec. 906(b)(1), June 23, 1972, 86 Stat. 375; Pub. L. 93-259, Sec. 6(c)(2), 7(b)(3), (4), 8, 9(b), 10, 11, 12(a), 13(a)-(d), 14-18, 20(a)-(c), 21(b), 22, 23, 25(b), Apr. 8, 1974, 88 Stat. 61-69, 72; Pub. L. 95-151, Sec. 4-8, 9(d), 11, 14, Nov. 1, 1977, 91 Stat. 1249, 1250-1252; Pub. L. 96-70, Title I, Sec. 1225(a), Sept. 27, 1979, 93 Stat. 468; Pub. L. 101-157, Sec. 3(c), Nov. 17, 1989, 103 Stat. 939; Pub. L. 103-329, Title VI, Sec. 633(d), Sept. 30, 1994, 108 Stat. 2428; Pub. L. 104-88, Title III, Sec. 340, Dec. 29, 1995, 109 Stat. 955; Pub. L. 104-174, Sec. 1, Aug. 6, 1996, 110 Stat. 1553; Pub. L. 104-188, Sec. 2105(a), Aug. 20, 1996, 110 Stat. 1929; Pub. L. 105-78, Sec. 105, Nov. 13, 1997, 111 Stat. 1477.)

Sec. 214. Employment under special certificates

(a) Learners, apprentices, messengers

The Secretary, to the extent necessary in order to prevent curtailment of opportunities for employment, shall by regulations or by orders provide for the employment of learners, of apprentices, and of messengers employed primarily in delivering letters and messages, under special certificates issued pursuant to regulations of the Secretary, at such wages lower than the minimum wage applicable under section 206 of this title and subject to such limitations as to time, number, proportion, and length of service as the Secretary shall prescribe.

(b) Students

(1) (A) The Secretary, to the extent necessary in order to prevent curtailment of opportunities for employment, shall by special certificate issued under a regulation or order provide, in accordance with subparagraph (B), for the employment, at a wage rate not less than 85 per centum of the otherwise applicable wage rate in effect under section 206 of this title or not less than $1.60 an hour, whichever is the higher, of full-time students (regardless of age but in compliance with applicable child labor laws) in retail or service establishments.

(B) Except as provided in paragraph (4)(B), during any month in which full-time students are to be employed in any retail or service establishment under certificates issued under this subsection the proportion of student hours of employment to the total hours of employment of all employees in such establishment may not exceed—

(i) in the case of a retail or service establishment whose employees (other than employees engaged in commerce or in the production of goods for commerce) were covered by this chapter before the effective date of the Fair Labor Standards Amendments of 1974—

(I) the proportion of student hours of employment to the total hours of employment of all employees in such establishment for the corresponding month of the immediately preceding twelve-month period,

(II) the maximum proportion for any corresponding month of student hours of employment to the total hours of employment of all employees in such establishment applicable to the issuance of certificates under this section at any time before the effective date of the Fair Labor Standards Amendments of 1974 for the employment of students by such employer, or

(III) a proportion equal to one-tenth of the total hours of employment of all employees in such establishment,

whichever is greater;

(ii) in the case of retail or service establishment whose employees (other than employees engaged in commerce or in the production of goods for commerce) are covered for the first time on or after the effective date of the Fair Labor Standards Amendments of 1974—

(I) the proportion of hours of employment of students in such establishment to the total hours of employment of all employees in such establishment for the corresponding month of the twelve-month period immediately prior to the effective date of such Amendments,

(II) the proportion of student hours of employment to the total hours of employment of all employees in such establishment for the corresponding month of the immediately preceding twelve-month period, or

(III) a proportion equal to one-tenth of the total hours of employment of all employees in such establishment,

whichever is greater; or

(iii) in the case of a retail or service establishment for which records of student hours worked are not available, the proportion of student hours of employment to the total hours of employment of all employees based on the practice during the immediately preceding twelve-month period in (I) similar establishments of the same employer in the same general metropolitan area in which such establishment is located, (II) similar establishments of the same or nearby communities if such establishment is not in a metropolitan area, or (III) other establishments of the same general character operating in the community or the nearest comparable community.

For purpose of clauses (i), (ii), and (iii) of this subparagraph, the term "student hours of employment" means hours during which students are employed in a retail or service establishment under certificates issued under this subsection.

(2) The Secretary, to the extent necessary in order to prevent curtailment of opportunities for employment, shall by special certificate issued under a regulation or order provide for the employment, at a wage rate not less than 85 per centum of the wage rate in effect

under section 206(a)(5) of this title or not less than $1.30 an hour, whichever is the higher, of full-time students (regardless of age but in compliance with applicable child labor laws) in any occupation in agriculture.

(3) The Secretary, to the extent necessary in order to prevent curtailment of opportunities for employment, shall by special certificate issued under a regulation or order provide for the employment by an institution of higher education, at a wage rate not less than 85 per centum of the otherwise applicable wage rate in effect under section 206 of this title or not less than $1.60 an hour, whichever is the higher, of full-time students (regardless of age but in compliance with applicable child labor laws) who are enrolled in such institution. The Secretary shall by regulation prescribe standards and requirements to insure that this paragraph will not create a substantial probability of reducing the full-time employment opportunities of persons other than those to whom the minimum wage rate authorized by this paragraph is applicable.

(4) (A) A special certificate issued under paragraph (1), (2), or (3) shall provide that the student or students for whom it is issued shall, except during vacation periods, be employed on a part-time basis and not in excess of twenty hours in any workweek.

(B) If the issuance of a special certificate under paragraph (1) or (2) for an employer will cause the number of students employed by such employer under special certificates issued under this subsection to exceed six, the Secretary may not issue such a special certificate for the employment of a student by such employer unless the Secretary finds employment of such student will not create a substantial probability of reducing the full-time employment opportunities of persons other than those employed under special certificates issued under this subsection. If the issuance of a special certificate under paragraph (1) or (2) for an employer will not cause the number of students employed by such employer under special certificates issued under this subsection to exceed six—

(i) the Secretary may issue a special certificate under paragraph (1) or (2) for the employment of a student by such employer if such employer certifies to the Secretary that the employment of such student will not reduce the full-time employment opportunities of persons other than those employed under special certificates issued under this subsection, and

(ii) in the case of an employer which is a retail or service establishment, subparagraph (B) of paragraph (1) shall not apply with respect to the issuance of special certificates for such employer under such paragraph.

The requirement of this subparagraph shall not apply in the case of the issuance of special certificates under paragraph (3) for the employment of full-time students by institutions of higher education; except that if the Secretary determines that an institution of higher education is employing students under certificates issued under paragraph (3) but in violation of the requirements of that paragraph or of regulations issued thereunder, the requirements of this subparagraph shall apply with respect to the issuance of special certificates under paragraph (3) for the employment of students by such institution.

(C) No special certificate may be issued under this subsection unless the employer for whom the certificate is to be issued provides evidence satisfactory to the Secretary of the student status of the employees to be employed under such special certificate.

(D) To minimize paperwork for, and to encourage, small businesses to employ students under special certificates issued under paragraphs (1) and (2), the Secretary shall, by regulation or order, prescribe a simplified application form to be used by employers in applying for such a certificate for the employment of not more than six full-time students. Such an application shall require only—

(i) a listing of the name, address, and business of the applicant employer,

(ii) a listing of the date the applicant began business, and

(iii) the certification that the employment of such full-time students will not reduce the full-time employment opportunities of persons other than persons employed under special certificates.

(c) Handicapped workers

(1) The Secretary, to the extent necessary to prevent curtailment of opportunities for employment, shall by regulation or order provide for the employment, under special certificates, of individuals (including individuals employed in agriculture) whose earning or productive capacity is impaired by age, physical or mental deficiency, or injury, at wages which are—

(A) lower than the minimum wage applicable under section 206 of this title,

(B) commensurate with those paid to nonhandicapped workers, employed in the vicinity in which the individuals under the certificates are employed, for essentially the same type, quality, and quantity of work, and

(C) related to the individual's productivity.

(2) The Secretary shall not issue a certificate under paragraph (1) unless the employer provides written assurances to the Secretary that—

(A) in the case of individuals paid on an hourly rate basis, wages paid in accordance with paragraph (1) will be reviewed by the employer at periodic intervals at least once every six months, and

(B) wages paid in accordance with paragraph (1) will be adjusted by the employer at periodic intervals, at least once each year, to reflect changes in the prevailing wage paid to experienced nonhandicapped individuals employed in the locality for essentially the same type of work.

(3) Notwithstanding paragraph (1), no employer shall be permitted to reduce the hourly wage rate prescribed by certificate under this subsection in effect on June 1, 1986, of any handicapped individual for a period of two years from such date without prior authorization of the Secretary.

(4) Nothing in this subsection shall be construed to prohibit an employer from maintaining or establishing work activities centers to provide therapeutic activities for handicapped clients.

(5) (A) Notwithstanding any other provision of this subsection, any employee receiving a special minimum wage at a rate specified pursuant to this subsection or the parent or guardian of such an employee may petition the Secretary to obtain a review of such special minimum wage rate. An employee or the employee's parent or guardian may file such a petition for and in behalf of the employee or in behalf of the employee and other employees similarly situated. No employee may be a party to any such action unless the employee or the employee's parent or guardian gives consent in writing to become such a party and such consent is filed with the Secretary.

(B) Upon receipt of a petition filed in accordance with subparagraph (A), the Secretary within ten days shall assign the petition to an administrative law judge appointed pursuant to section 3105 of Title 5. The administrative law judge shall conduct a hearing on the record in accordance with section 554 of Title 5 with respect to such petition within thirty days after assignment.

(C) In any such proceeding, the employer shall have the burden of demonstrating that the special minimum wage rate is justified as necessary in order to prevent curtailment of opportunities for employment.

(D) In determining whether any special minimum wage rate is justified pursuant to subparagraph (C), the administrative law judge shall consider—

(i) the productivity of the employee or employees identified in the petition and the conditions under which such productivity was measured; and

(ii) the productivity of other employees performing work of essentially the same type and quality for other employers in the same vicinity.

(E) The administrative law judge shall issue a decision within thirty days after the hearing provided for in subparagraph (B). Such action shall be deemed to be a final agency action unless within thirty days the Secretary grants a request to review the decision of the administrative law judge. Either the petitioner or the employer may request review by the Secretary within fifteen days of the date of issuance of the decision by the administrative law judge.

(F) The Secretary, within thirty days after receiving a request for review, shall review the record and either adopt the decision of the administrative law judge or issue exceptions. The decision of the administrative law judge, together with any exceptions, shall be deemed to be a final agency action.

(G) A final agency action shall be subject to judicial review pursuant to chapter 7 of Title 5. An action seeking such review shall be brought within thirty days of a final agency action described in subparagraph (F).

(d) Employment by schools

The Secretary may by regulation or order provide that sections 206 and 207 of this title shall not apply with respect to the employment by any elementary or secondary school of its students if such employment constitutes, as determined under regulations prescribed by the Secretary, an integral part of the regular education program provided by such school and such employment is in accordance with applicable child labor laws.

-SOURCE-
(June 25, 1938, ch. 676, Sec. 14, 52 Stat. 1068; Oct. 26, 1949, ch. 736, Sec. 12, 63 Stat. 918; Pub. L. 87-30, Sec. 11, May 5, 1961, 75 Stat. 74; Pub. L. 89-601, Title V, Sec. 501, Sept. 23, 1966, 80 Stat. 842; Pub. L. 93-259, Sec. 24(a), (b), Apr. 8, 1974, 88 Stat. 69, 72; Pub. L. 95-151, Sec. 12, 13, Nov. 1, 1977, 91 Stat. 1252; Pub. L. 99-486, Oct. 16, 1986, 100 Stat. 1229; Pub. L. 101-157, Sec. 4(d), Nov. 17, 1989, 103 Stat. 941.)

Sec. 215. Prohibited acts; prima facie evidence

(a) After the expiration of one hundred and twenty days from June 25, 1938, it shall be unlawful for any person—

(1) to transport, offer for transportation, ship, deliver, or sell in commerce, or to ship, deliver, or sell with knowledge that shipment or delivery or sale thereof in commerce is intended, any goods in the production of which any employee was employed in violation of section 206 or section 207 of this title, or in violation of any regulation or order of the Secretary issued under section 214 of this title; except that no provision of this chapter shall impose any liability upon any common carrier for the transportation in commerce in the regular course of its business of any goods not produced by such common carrier, and no provision of this chapter shall excuse any common carrier from its obligation to accept

any goods for transportation; and except that any such transportation, offer, shipment, delivery, or sale of such goods by a purchaser who acquired them in good faith in reliance on written assurance from the producer that the goods were produced in compliance with the requirements of this chapter, and who acquired such goods for value without notice of any such violation, shall not be deemed unlawful;

(2) to violate any of the provisions of section 206 or section 207 of this title, or any of the provisions of any regulation or order of the Secretary issued under section 214 of this title;

(3) to discharge or in any other manner discriminate against any employee because such employee has filed any complaint or instituted or caused to be instituted any proceeding under or related to this chapter, or has testified or is about to testify in any such proceeding, or has served or is about to serve on an industry committee;

(4) to violate any of the provisions of section 212 of this title;

(5) to violate any of the provisions of section 211(d) of this title, or any regulation or order made or continued in effect under the provisions of section 211(d) of this title, or to make any statement, report, or record filed or kept pursuant to the provisions of such section or of any regulation or order thereunder, knowing such statement, report, or record to be false in a material respect.

(b) For the purposes of subsection (a)(1) of this section proof that any employee was employed in any place of employment where goods shipped or sold in commerce were produced, within ninety days prior to the removal of the goods from such place of employment, shall be prima facie evidence that such employee was engaged in the production of such goods.

-SOURCE-
(June 25, 1938, ch. 676, Sec. 15, 52 Stat. 1068; Oct. 26, 1949, ch. 736, Sec. 13, 63 Stat. 919; 1950 Reorg. Plan No. 6, Sec. 1, 2, eff. May 24, 1950, 15 F.R. 3174, 64 Stat. 1263.)

Sec. 216. Penalties

(a) Fines and imprisonment

Any person who willfully violates any of the provisions of section 215 of this title shall upon conviction thereof be subject to a fine of not more than $10,000, or to imprisonment for not more than six months, or both. No person shall be imprisoned under this subsection except for an offense committed after the conviction of such person for a prior offense under this subsection.

(b) Damages; right of action; attorney's fees and costs; termination of right of action

Any employer who violates the provisions of section 206 or section 207 of this title shall be liable to the employee or employees affected in the amount of their unpaid minimum wages, or their unpaid overtime compensation, as the case may be, and in an additional equal amount as liquidated damages. Any employer who violates the provisions of section 215(a)(3) of this title shall be liable for such legal or equitable relief as may be appropriate to effectuate the purposes of section 215(a)(3) of this title, including without limitation employment, reinstatement, promotion, and the payment of wages lost and an additional equal amount as liquidated damages. An action to recover the liability prescribed in either of the preceding sentences may be maintained against any employer (including a public agency) in any Federal or State court of competent jurisdiction by any one or more employees for and in behalf of himself or themselves and other employees similarly situated. No employee shall be a party plaintiff to any such action unless he gives his consent in writing to become such a party and such consent is filed in the court in which such action is brought. The court in such action shall, in addition to any judgment awarded to the plaintiff or plaintiffs, allow a reasonable attorney's fee to be paid by the defendant, and costs of the action. The right provided by this subsection to bring an action by or on behalf of any employee, and the right of any employee to become a party plaintiff to any such action, shall terminate upon the filing of a complaint by the Secretary of Labor in an action under section 217 of this title in which (1) restraint is sought of any further delay in the payment of unpaid minimum wages, or the amount of unpaid overtime compensation, as the case may be, owing to such employee under section 206 or section 207 of this title by an employer liable therefor under the provisions of this subsection or (2) legal or equitable relief is sought as a result of alleged violations of section 215(a)(3) of this title.

(c) Payment of wages and compensation; waiver of claims; actions by the Secretary; limitation of actions

The Secretary is authorized to supervise the payment of the unpaid minimum wages or the unpaid overtime compensation owing to any employee or employees under section 206 or section 207 of this title, and the agreement of any employee to accept such payment shall upon payment in full constitute a waiver by such employee of any right he may have under subsection (b) of this section to such unpaid minimum wages or unpaid overtime compensation and an additional equal amount as liquidated damages. The Secretary may bring an action in any court of competent jurisdiction to recover the amount of unpaid minimum wages or overtime compensation and an equal amount as liquidated damages. The right provided by subsection (b) of this section to bring an action by or on behalf of any employee to recover the liability specified in the first sentence of such subsection and of any employee to become a party plaintiff to any such action shall terminate upon the filing of a complaint by the Secretary in an action under this subsection in which a recovery is sought of unpaid minimum wages or unpaid overtime compensation under sections 206 and 207 of this title or liquidated or other damages provided by this subsection owing to such employee by an employer liable under the provisions of subsection (b) of this section, unless such action is dismissed without prejudice on motion of the Secretary. Any sums thus recovered by the Secretary of Labor on behalf of an employee pursuant to this subsection shall be held in a special deposit account and shall be paid, on order of the Secretary of Labor, directly to the employee or employees affected. Any such sums not paid to an employee because of inability to do so within a period of three years shall be covered into the Treasury of the United States as miscellaneous receipts. In determining when an action is commenced by the Secretary of Labor under this subsection for the purposes of the statutes of limitations provided in section 255(a) of this title, it shall be considered to be commenced in the case of any individual claimant on the date when the complaint is filed if he is specifically named as a party plaintiff in the complaint, or if his name did not so appear, on the subsequent date on which his name is added as a party plaintiff in such action.

(d) Savings provisions

In any action or proceeding commenced prior to, on, or after August 8, 1956, no employer shall be subject to any liability or punishment under this chapter or the Portal-to-Portal Act of 1947 (29 U.S.C. § 251 et seq.) on account of his failure to comply with any provision or provisions of this chapter or such Act (1) with respect to work heretofore or hereafter performed in a workplace to which the exemption in section 213(f) of this title is applicable, (2) with respect to work performed in Guam, the Canal Zone or Wake Island before the effective date of this amendment of subsection (d), or (3) with respect to work performed in a possession named in section 206(a)(3) of this title at any time prior to the establishment by the Secretary, as provided therein, of a minimum wage rate applicable to such work.

(e) Civil penalties for child labor violations

Any person who violates the provisions of section 212 of this title or section 213(c)(5) of this title, relating to child labor, or any regulation issued under section 212 of this title or section 213(c)(5) of this title, shall be subject to a civil penalty of not to exceed $10,000 for each employee who was the subject of such a violation. Any person who repeatedly or willfully violates section 206 or 207 of this title shall be subject to a civil penalty of not to exceed $1,000 for each such violation. In determining the amount of any penalty under this subsection, the appropriateness of such penalty to the size of the business of the person charged and the gravity of the violation shall be considered. The amount of any penalty under this subsection, when finally determined, may be—

(1) deducted from any sums owing by the United States to the person charged;

(2) recovered in a civil action brought by the Secretary in any court of competent jurisdiction, in which litigation the Secretary shall be represented by the Solicitor of Labor; or

(3) ordered by the court, in an action brought for a violation of section 215(a)(4) of this title or a repeated or willful violation of section 215(a)(2) of this title, to be paid to the Secretary.

Any administrative determination by the Secretary of the amount of any penalty under this subsection shall be final, unless within fifteen days after receipt of notice thereof by certified mail the person charged with the violation takes exception to the determination that the violations for which the penalty is imposed occurred, in which event final determination of the penalty shall be made in an administrative proceeding after opportunity for hearing in accordance with section 554 of Title 5, and regulations to be promulgated by the Secretary. Except for civil penalties collected for violations of section 212 of this title, sums collected as penalties pursuant to this section shall be applied toward reimbursement of the costs of determining the violations and assessing and collecting such penalties, in accordance with the provisions of section 9a of this title. Civil penalties collected for violations of section 212 of this title shall be deposited in the general fund of the Treasury.

-SOURCE-
(June 25, 1938, ch. 676, Sec. 16, 52 Stat. 1069; May 14, 1947, ch. 52, Sec. 5(a), 61 Stat. 87; Oct. 26, 1949, ch. 736, Sec. 14, 63 Stat. 919; 1950 Reorg. Plan No. 6, Sec. 1, 2, 15 F.R. 3174, 64 Stat. 1263; Aug. 8, 1956, ch. 1035, Sec. 4, 70 Stat. 1118; Pub. L. 85-231, Sec. 1(2), Aug. 30, 1957, 71 Stat. 514; Pub. L. 87-30, Sec. 12(a), May 5, 1961, 75 Stat. 74; Pub. L. 89-601, Title VI, Sec. 601(a), Sept. 23, 1966, 80 Stat. 844; Pub. L. 93-259, Sec. 6(d)(1), 25(c), 26, Apr. 8, 1974, 88 Stat. 61, 72, 73; Pub. L. 95-151, Sec. 10, Nov. 1, 1977, 91 Stat. 1252; Pub. L. 101-157, Sec. 9, Nov. 17, 1989, 103 Stat. 945; Pub. L. 101-508, Title III, Sec. 3103, Nov. 5, 1990, 104 Stat. 1388-29; Pub. L. 104-174, Sec. 2, Aug. 6, 1996, 110 Stat. 1554.)

Sec. 216a. Repealed. Oct. 26, 1949, ch. 736, Sec. 16(f), 63 Stat. 920

Sec. 216b. Liability for overtime work performed prior to July 20, 1949

No employer shall be subject to any liability or punishment under this chapter (in any action or proceeding commenced prior to or on or after January 24, 1950), on account of the failure of said employer to pay an employee compensation for any period of overtime work performed prior to July 20, 1949, if the compensation paid prior to July 20, 1949, for such work was at least equal to the compensation which would have been payable for such work had subsections (d)(6), (7) and (g) of section 207 of this title been in effect at the time of such payment.

-SOURCE-
(Oct. 26, 1949, ch. 736, Sec. 16(e), 63 Stat. 920.)

Sec. 217. Injunction proceedings

The district courts, together with the United States District Court for the District of the Canal Zone, the District Court of the Virgin Islands, and the District Court of Guam shall have jurisdiction, for cause shown, to restrain violations of section 215 of this title, including in the case of violations of section 215(a)(2) of this title the restraint of any withholding of payment of minimum wages or overtime compensation found by the court to be due to employees under this chapter (except sums which employees are barred from recovering, at the time of the commencement of the action to restrain the violations, by virtue of the provisions of section 255 of this title).

-SOURCE-
(June 25, 1938, ch. 676, Sec. 17, 52 Stat. 1069; Oct. 26, 1949, ch. 736, Sec. 15, 63 Stat. 919; Pub. L. 85-231, Sec. 1(3), Aug. 30, 1957, 71 Stat. 514; Pub. L. 86-624, Sec. 21(c), July 12, 1960, 74 Stat. 417; Pub. L. 87-30, Sec. 12(b), May 5, 1961, 75 Stat. 74.)

Sec. 218. Relation to other laws

(a) No provision of this chapter or of any order thereunder shall excuse noncompliance with any Federal or State law or municipal ordinance establishing a minimum wage higher than the minimum wage established under this chapter or a maximum workweek lower than the maximum workweek established under this chapter, and no provision of this chapter relating to the employment of child labor shall justify noncompliance with any Federal or State law or municipal ordinance establishing a higher standard than the standard established under this chapter. No provision of this chapter shall justify any employer in reducing a wage paid by him which is in excess of the applicable minimum wage under this chapter, or justify any employer in increasing hours of employment maintained by him which are shorter than the maximum hours applicable under this chapter.

(b) Notwithstanding any other provision of this chapter (other than section 213(f) of this title) or any other law—

（1) any Federal employee in the Canal Zone engaged in employment of the kind described in section 5102(c)(7) of title 5, or

(2) any employee employed in a nonappropriated fund instrumentality under the jurisdiction of the Armed Forces,

shall have his basic compensation fixed or adjusted at a wage rate that is not less than the appropriate wage rate provided for in section 206(a)(1) of this title (except that the wage rate provided for in section 206(b) of this title shall apply to any employee who performed services during the workweek in a work place within the Canal Zone), and shall have his overtime compensation set at an hourly rate not less than the overtime rate provided for in section 207(a)(1) of this title.

-SOURCE-
(June 25, 1938, ch. 676, Sec. 18, 52 Stat. 1069; Pub. L. 89-601, Title III, Sec. 306, Sept. 23, 1966, 80 Stat. 841; Pub. L. 90-83, Sec. 8, Sept. 11, 1967, 81 Stat. 222.)

Sec. 219. Separability

If any provision of this chapter or the application of such provision to any person or circumstance is held invalid, the remainder of this chapter and the application of such provision to other persons or circumstances shall not be affected thereby.

-SOURCE-
(June 25, 1938, ch. 676, Sec. 19, 52 Stat. 1069.)

CHAPTER 9—PORTAL-TO-PORTAL PAY ACT

Sec.

Sec. 251. Congressional findings and declaration of policy

(a) The Congress finds that the Fair Labor Standards Act of 1938, as amended (29 U.S.C. 201 et seq.), has been interpreted judicially in disregard of long-established customs, practices, and contracts between employers and employees, thereby creating wholly unexpected liabilities, immense in amount and retroactive in operation, upon employers with the results that, if said Act as so interpreted or claims arising under such interpretations were permitted to stand, (1) the payment of such liabilities would bring about financial ruin of many employers and seriously impair the capital resources of many others, thereby resulting in the reduction of industrial operations, halting of expansion and development, curtailing employment, and the earning power of employees; (2) the credit of many employers would be seriously impaired; (3) there would be created both an extended and continuous uncertainty on the part of industry, both employer and employee, as to the financial condition of productive establishments and a gross inequality of competitive conditions between employers and between industries; (4) employees would receive windfall payments, including liquidated damages, of sums for activities performed by them without any expectation of reward beyond that included in their agreed rates of pay; (5) there would occur the promotion of increasing demands for payment to employees for engaging in activities no compensation for which had been contemplated by either the employer or employee at the time they were engaged in; (6) voluntary collective bargaining would be interfered with and industrial disputes between employees and employers and between employees and employees would be created; (7) the courts of the country would be burdened with excessive and needless litigation and champertous practices would be encouraged; (8) the Public Treasury would be deprived of large sums of revenues and public finances would be seriously deranged by claims against the Public Treasury for refunds of taxes already paid; (9) the cost to the Government of goods and services heretofore and hereafter purchased by its various departments and agencies would be unreasonably increased and the Public Treasury would be seriously affected by consequent increased cost of war contracts; and (10) serious and adverse effects upon the revenues of Federal, State, and local governments would occur.

The Congress further finds that all of the foregoing constitutes a substantial burden on commerce and a substantial obstruction to the free flow of goods in commerce.

The Congress, therefore, further finds and declares that it is in the national public interest and for the general welfare, essential to national defense, and necessary to aid, protect, and foster commerce, that this chapter be enacted.

The Congress further finds that the varying and extended periods of time for which, under the laws of the several States, potential retroactive liability may be imposed upon employers, have given and will give rise to great difficulties in the sound and orderly conduct of business and industry.

The Congress further finds and declares that all of the results which have arisen or may arise under the Fair Labor Standards Act of 1938, as amended, as aforesaid, may (except as to liability for liquidated damages) arise with respect to the Walsh-Healey (41 U.S.C. § 35 et seq.) and Bacon-Davis (40 U.S.C. § 276a et seq.) Acts and that it is, therefore, in the national public interest and for the general welfare, essential to national defense, and necessary to aid, protect, and foster commerce, that this chapter shall apply to the Walsh-Healey Act and the Bacon-Davis Act.

(b) It is declared to be the policy of the Congress in order to meet the existing emergency and to correct existing evils (1) to relieve and protect interstate commerce from practices which burden and obstruct it; (2) to protect the right of collective bargaining; and (3) to define and limit the jurisdiction of the courts.

-SOURCE-
(May 14, 1947, ch. 52, Sec. 1, 61 Stat. 84.)

Sec. 252. Relief from certain existing claims under the Fair Labor Standards Act of 1938, as amended, the Walsh-Healey Act, and the Bacon-Davis Act

(a) Liability of employer

No employer shall be subject to any liability or punishment under the Fair Labor Standards Act of 1938, as amended (29 U.S.C. § 201 et seq.) the Walsh-Healey Act (41 U.S.C. § 35 et seq.), or the Bacon-Davis Act (40 U.S.C. § 276a et seq.) (in any action or proceeding commenced prior to or on or after May 14, 1947), on account of the failure of such employer to pay an employee minimum wages, or to pay an employee overtime compensation, for or on account of any activity of an employee engaged in prior to May 14, 1947, except an activity which was compensable by either—

(1) an express provision of a written or nonwritten contract in effect, at the time of such activity, between such employee, his agent, or collective-bargaining representative and his employer; or

(2) a custom or practice in effect, at the time of such activity, at the establishment or other place where such employee was employed, covering such activity, not inconsistent with a written or nonwritten contract, in effect at the time of such activity, between such employee, his agent, or collective-bargaining representative and his employer.

(b) Compensable activity

For the purposes of subsection (a) of this section, an activity shall be considered as compensable under such contract provision or such custom or practice only when it was engaged in during the portion of the day with respect to which it was so made compensable.

(c) Time of employment

In the application of the minimum wage and overtime compensation provisions of the Fair Labor Standards Act of 1938, as amended (29 U.S.C. § 201 et seq.), of the Walsh-Healey Act (41 U.S.C. § 35 et seq.), or of the Bacon-Davis Act (40 U.S.C. § 276a et seq.), in determining the time for which an employer employed an employee there shall be counted all that time, but only that time, during which the employee engaged in activities which were compensable within the meaning of subsections (a) and (b) of this section.

(d) Jurisdiction

No court of the United States, of any State, Territory, or possession of the United States, or of the District of Columbia, shall have jurisdiction of any action or proceeding, whether instituted prior to or on or after May 14, 1947, to enforce liability or impose punishment for or on account of the failure of the employer to pay minimum wages or overtime compensation under the Fair Labor Standards Act of 1938, as amended (29 U.S.C. § 201 et seq.), under the Walsh-Healey Act (41 U.S.C. § 35 et seq.), or under the Bacon-Davis Act (40 U.S.C. § 276a et seq.), to the extent that such action or proceeding seeks to enforce any liability or impose any punishment with respect to an activity which was not compensable under subsections (a) and (b) of this section.

(e) Assignment of actions

No cause of action based on unpaid minimum wages, unpaid overtime compensation, or liquidated damages, under the Fair Labor Standards Act of 1938, as amended (29 U.S.C. § 201 et seq.), the Walsh-Healey Act (41 U.S.C. § 35 et seq.), or the Bacon-Davis Act (40 U.S.C. § 276a et seq.), which accrued prior to May 14, 1947, or any interest in such cause of action, shall hereafter be assignable, in whole or in part, to the extent that such cause of action is based on an activity which was not compensable within the meaning of subsections (a) and (b) of this section.

-SOURCE-
(May 14, 1947, ch. 52, Sec. 2, 61 Stat. 85.)

Sec. 253. Compromise and waiver

(a) Compromise of certain existing claims under the Fair Labor Standards Act of 1938, the Walsh-Healey Act, or the Bacon-Davis Act; limitations

Any cause of action under the Fair Labor Standards Act of 1938, as amended (29 U.S.C. § 201 et seq.), the Walsh-Healey Act (41 U.S.C. § 35 et seq.), or the Bacon-Davis Act (40 U.S.C. § 276a et seq.), which accrued prior to May 14, 1947, or any action (whether instituted prior to or on or after May 14, 1947) to enforce such a cause of action, may hereafter be compromised in whole or in part, if there exists a bona fide dispute as to the amount payable by the employer to his employee; except that no such action or cause of action may be so compromised to the extent that such compromise is based on an hourly wage rate less than the minimum required under such Act, or on a payment for overtime at a rate less than one and one-half times such minimum hourly wage rate.

(b) Waiver of liquidated damages under Fair Labor Standards Act of 1938

Any employee may hereafter waive his right under the Fair Labor Standards Act of 1938, as amended (29 U.S.C. § 201 et seq.), to liquidated damages, in whole or in part, with respect to activities engaged in prior to May 14, 1947.

(c) Satisfaction

Any such compromise or waiver, in the absence of fraud or duress, shall, according to the terms thereof, be a complete satisfaction of such cause of action and a complete bar to any action based on such cause of action.

(d) Retroactive effect of section

The provisions of this section shall also be applicable to any compromise or waiver heretofore so made or given.

(e) "Compromise" defined

As used in this section, the term "compromise" includes "adjustment," "settlement," and "release."

-SOURCE-
(May 14, 1947, ch. 52, Sec. 3, 61 Stat. 86.)

Sec. 254. Relief from liability and punishment under the Fair Labor Standards Act of 1938, the Walsh-Healey Act, and the Bacon-Davis Act for failure to pay minimum wage or overtime compensation

(a) Activities not compensable

Except as provided in subsection (b) of this section, no employer shall be subject to any liability or punishment under the Fair Labor Standards Act of 1938, as amended (29 U.S.C. § 201 et seq.), the Walsh-Healey Act (41 U.S.C. § 35 et seq.), or the Bacon-Davis Act (40 U.S.C. § 276a et seq.), on account of the failure of such employer to pay an employee minimum wages, or to pay an employee overtime compensation, for or on account of any of the following activities of such employee engaged in on or after May 14, 1947—

(1) walking, riding, or traveling to and from the actual place of performance of the principal activity or activities which such employee is employed to perform, and

(2) activities which are preliminary to or postliminary to said principal activity or activities,

which occur either prior to the time on any particular workday at which such employee commences, or subsequent to the time on any particular workday at which he ceases, such principal activity or activities. For purposes of this subsection, the use of an employer's vehicle for travel by an employee and activities performed by an employee which are incidental to the use of such vehicle for commuting shall not be considered part of the employee's principal activities if the use of such vehicle for travel is within the normal commuting area for the employer's business or establishment and the use of the employer's vehicle is subject to an agreement on the part of the employer and the employee or representative of such employee.

(b) Compensability by contract or custom

Notwithstanding the provisions of subsection (a) of this section which relieve an employer from liability and punishment with respect to any activity, the employer shall not be so relieved if such activity is compensable by either—

(1) an express provision of a written or nonwritten contract in effect, at the time of such activity, between such employee, his agent, or collective-bargaining representative and his employer; or

(2) a custom or practice in effect, at the time of such activity, at the establishment or other place where such employee is employed, covering such activity, not inconsistent with a written or nonwritten contract, in effect at the time of such activity, between such employee, his agent, or collective-bargaining representative and his employer.

(c) Restriction on activities compensable under contract or custom

For the purposes of subsection (b) of this section, an activity shall be considered as compensable under such contract provision or such custom or practice only when it is engaged in during the portion of the day with respect to which it is so made compensable.

(d) Determination of time employed with respect to activities

In the application of the minimum wage and overtime compensation provisions of the Fair Labor Standards Act of 1938, as amended (29 U.S.C. § 201 et seq.), of the Walsh-Healey Act (41 U.S.C. § 35 et seq.), or of the Bacon-Davis Act (40 U.S.C. § 276a et seq.), in determining the time for which an employer employs an employee with respect to walking, riding, traveling, or other preliminary or postliminary activities described in subsection (a) of this section, there shall be counted all that time, but only that time, during which the employee engages in any such activity which is compensable within the meaning of subsections (b) and (c) of this section.

-SOURCE-
(May 14, 1947, ch. 52, Sec. 4, 61 Stat. 86; Pub. L. 104-188, Sec. 2102, Aug. 20, 1996, 110 Stat. 1928.)

Sec. 255. Statute of limitations

Any action commenced on or after May 14, 1947, to enforce any cause of action for unpaid minimum wages, unpaid overtime compensation, or liquidated damages, under the Fair Labor Standards Act of 1938, as amended (29 U.S.C. § 201 et seq.), the Walsh-Healey Act (41 U.S.C. § 35 et seq.), or the Bacon-Davis Act (40 U.S.C. § 276a et seq.)—

(a) if the cause of action accrues on or after May 14, 1947—may be commenced within two years after the cause of action accrued, and every such action shall be forever barred unless commenced within two years after the cause of action accrued, except that a cause of action arising out of a willful violation may be commenced within three years after the cause of action accrued;

(b) if the cause of action accrued prior to May 14, 1947—may be commenced within whichever of the following periods is the shorter: (1) two years after the cause of action accrued, or (2) the period prescribed by the applicable State statute of limitations; and, except as provided in paragraph (c) of this section, every such action shall be forever barred unless commenced within the shorter of such two periods;

(c) if the cause of action accrued prior to May 14, 1947, the action shall not be barred by paragraph (b) of this section if it is commenced within one hundred and twenty days after May 14, 1947 unless at the time commenced it is barred by an applicable State statute of limitations;

(d) with respect to any cause of action brought under section 216(b) of this title against a State or a political subdivision of a State in a district court of the United States on or before April 18, 1973, the running of the statutory periods of limitation shall be deemed suspended during the period beginning with the commencement of any such action and ending one hundred and eighty days after the effective date of the Fair Labor Standards Amendments of 1974, except that such suspension shall not be applicable if in such action judgment has been entered for the defendant on the grounds other than State immunity from Federal jurisdiction.

-SOURCE-
(May 14, 1947, ch. 52, Sec. 6, 61 Stat. 87; Pub. L. 89-601, Title VI, Sec. 601(b), Sept. 23, 1966, 80 Stat. 844; Pub. L. 93-259, Sec. 6(d)(2)(A), Apr. 8, 1974, 88 Stat. 61.)

Sec. 256. Determination of commencement of future actions

-STATUTE-

(a) In determining when an action is commenced for the purposes of section 255 of this title, an action commenced on or after May 14, 1947 under the Fair Labor Standards Act of 1938, as amended (29 U.S.C. § 201 et seq.), the Walsh-Healey Act (41 U.S.C. § 35 et seq.), or the Bacon-Davis Act (40 U.S.C. § 276a et seq.), shall be considered to be commenced on the date when the complaint is filed; except that in the case of a collective or class action instituted under the Fair Labor Standards Act of 1938, as amended, or the Bacon-Davis Act, it shall be considered to be commenced in the case of any individual claimant—

(a) on the date when the complaint is filed, if he is specifically named as a party plaintiff in the complaint and his written consent to become a party plaintiff is filed on such date in the court in which the action is brought; or

(b) if such written consent was not so filed or if his name did not so appear—on the subsequent date on which such written consent is filed in the court in which the action was commenced.

-SOURCE-
(May 14, 1947, ch. 52, Sec. 7, 61 Stat. 88.)

Sec. 257. Pending collective and representative actions

The statute of limitations prescribed in section 255(b) of this title shall also be applicable (in the case of a collective or representative action commenced prior to May 14, 1947 under the Fair Labor Standards Act of 1938, as amended (29 U.S.C. § 201 et seq.)) to an individual claimant who has not been specifically named as a party plaintiff to the action prior to the expiration of one hundred and twenty days after May 14, 1947. In the application of such statute of limitations such action shall be considered to have been commenced as to him when, and only when, his written consent to become a party plaintiff to the action is filed in the court in which the action was brought.

-SOURCE-
(May 14, 1947, ch. 52, Sec. 8, 61 Stat. 88.)

Sec. 258. Reliance on past administrative rulings, etc.

In any action or proceeding commenced prior to or on or after May 14, 1947 based on any act or omission prior to May 14, 1947, no employer shall be subject to any liability or punishment for or on account of the failure of the employer to pay minimum wages or overtime compensation under the Fair Labor Standards Act of 1938, as amended (29 U.S.C. § 201 et seq.), the Walsh-Healey Act (41 U.S.C. § 35 et seq.), or the Bacon-Davis Act (40 U.S.C. § 276a et seq.), if he pleads and proves that the act or omission complained of was in good faith in conformity with and in reliance on any administrative regulation, order, ruling, approval, or interpretation, of any agency of the United States, or any administrative practice or enforcement policy of any such agency with respect to the class of employers to which he belonged. Such a defense, if established, shall be a bar to the action or proceeding, notwithstanding that after such act or omission, such administrative regulation, order, ruling, approval, interpretation, practice, or enforcement policy is modified or rescinded or is determined by judicial authority to be invalid or of no legal effect.

-SOURCE-
(May 14, 1947, ch. 52, Sec. 9, 61 Stat. 88.)

Sec. 259. Reliance in future on administrative rulings, etc.

-STATUTE-

(a) In any action or proceeding based on any act or omission on or after May 14, 1947, no employer shall be subject to any liability or punishment for or on account of the failure of the employer to pay minimum wages or overtime compensation under the Fair Labor Standards Act of 1938, as amended (29 U.S.C. § 201 et seq.), the Walsh-Healey Act (41 U.S.C. § 35 et seq.), or the Bacon-Davis Act (40 U.S.C. § 276a et seq.), if he pleads and proves that the act or omission complained of was in good faith in conformity with and in reliance on any written administrative regulation, order, ruling, approval, or interpretation, of the agency of the United States specified in subsection (b) of this section, or any administrative practice or enforcement policy of such agency with respect to the class of employers to which he belonged. Such a defense, if established, shall be a bar to the action or proceeding, notwithstanding that after such act or omission, such administrative regulation, order, ruling, approval, interpretation, practice, or enforcement policy is modified or rescinded or is determined by judicial authority to be invalid or of no legal effect.

(b) The agency referred to in subsection (a) of this section shall be—

(1) in the case of the Fair Labor Standards Act of 1938, as amended (29 U.S.C. § 201 et seq.)—the Administrator of the Wage and Hour Division of the Department of Labor;

(2) in the case of the Walsh-Healey Act (41 U.S.C. § 35 et seq.)—the Secretary of Labor, or any Federal officer utilized by him in the administration of such Act; and

(3) in the case of the Bacon-Davis Act (40 U.S.C. § 276a et seq.)—the Secretary of Labor.

-SOURCE-
(May 14, 1947, ch. 52, Sec. 10, 61 Stat. 89.)

Sec. 260. Liquidated damages

In any action commenced prior to or on or after May 14, 1947 to recover unpaid minimum wages, unpaid overtime compensation, or liquidated damages, under the Fair Labor Standards Act of 1938, as amended (29 U.S.C. § 201 et seq.), if the employer shows to the satisfaction of the court that the act or omission giving rise to such action was in good faith and that he had reasonable grounds for believing that his act or omission was not a violation of the Fair Labor Standards Act of 1938, as amended, the court may, in its sound discretion, award no liquidated damages or award any amount thereof not to exceed the amount specified in section 216 of this title.

-SOURCE-
(May 14, 1947, ch. 52, Sec. 11, 61 Stat. 89; Pub. L. 93-259, Sec. 6(d)(2)(B), Apr. 8, 1974, 88 Stat. 62.)

Sec. 261. Applicability of area of production regulations

No employer shall be subject to any liability or punishment under the Fair Labor Standards Act of 1938, as amended (29 U.S.C. § 201 et seq.), on account of the failure of such employer to pay an employee minimum wages, or to pay an employee overtime compensation, for or on account of an activity engaged in by such employee prior to December 26, 1946, if such employer—

(1) was not so subject by reason of the definition of an "area of production", by a regulation of the Administrator of the Wage and Hour Division of the Department of Labor, which regulation was applicable at the time of performance of the activity even though at that time the regulation was invalid; or

(2) would not have been so subject if the regulation signed on December 18, 1946 (Federal Register, Vol. 11, p. 14648) had been in force on and after October 24, 1938.

-SOURCE-
(May 14, 1947, ch. 52, Sec. 12, 61 Stat. 89.)

Sec. 262. Definitions

(a) When the terms "employer," "employee," and "wage" are used in this chapter in relation to the Fair Labor Standards Act of 1938, as amended (29 U.S.C. § 201 et seq.), they shall have the same meaning as when used in such Act of 1938.

(b) When the term "employer" is used in this chapter in relation to the Walsh-Healey Act (41 U.S.C. § 35 et seq.) or Bacon-Davis Act (40 U.S.C. § 276a et seq.) it shall mean the contractor or subcontractor covered by such Act.

(c) When the term "employee" is used in this chapter in relation to the Walsh-Healey Act (41 U.S.C. § 35 et seq.) or the Bacon-Davis Act (40 U.S.C. § 276a et seq.) it shall mean any individual employed by the contractor or subcontractor covered by such Act in the performance of his contract or subcontract.

(d) The term "Wash-Healey Act" (FOOTNOTE 1) means the Act entitled "An Act to provide conditions for the purchase of supplies and the making of contracts by the United States, and for other purposes," approved June 30, 1936 (49 Stat. 2036), as amended (41 U.S.C. § 35 et seq.); and the term "Bacon-Davis Act" means the Act entitled "An Act to amend the Act approved March 3, 1931, relating to the rate of wages for laborers and mechanics employed by contractors and subcontractors on public buildings," approved August 30, 1935 (49 Stat. 1011), as amended (40 U.S.C. Sec. 276a et seq.).

(FOOTNOTE 1) So in original. Probably should be "Walsh-Healey Act."

(e) As used in section 255 of this title the term "State" means any State of the United States or the District of Columbia or any Territory or possession of the United States.

-SOURCE-
(May 14, 1947, ch. 52, Sec. 13, 61 Stat. 90.)

Appendix C

White-Collar Regulations

PART 541—DEFINING AND DELIMITING THE EXEMPTIONS FOR EXECUTIVE, ADMINISTRATIVE, PROFESSIONAL, COMPUTER AND OUTSIDE SALES EMPLOYEES

Authority: 29 U.S.C. 213; Public Law 101-583, 104 Stat. 2871; Reorganization Plan No. 6 of 1950 (3 CFR 1945-53 Comp. p. 1004); Secretary's Order No. 4-2001 (66 FR 29656).

Subpart A—General Regulations

Sec. 541.0 Introductory statement

(a) Section 13(a)(1) of the Fair Labor Standards Act, as amended, provides an exemption from the Act's minimum wage and overtime requirements for any employee employed in a bona fide executive, administrative, or professional capacity (including any employee employed in the capacity of academic administrative personnel or teacher in elementary or secondary schools), or in the capacity of an outside sales employee, as such terms are defined and delimited from time to time by regulations of the Secretary, subject to the provisions of the Administrative Procedure Act. Section 13(a)(17) of the Act provides an exemption from the minimum wage and overtime requirements for computer systems analysts, computer programmers, software engineers, and other similarly skilled computer employees.

(b) The requirements for these exemptions are contained in this part as follows: executive employees, subpart B; administrative employees, subpart C; professional employees, subpart D; computer employees, subpart E; outside sales employees, subpart F. Subpart G contains regulations regarding salary requirements applicable to most of the exemptions, including salary levels and the salary basis test. Subpart G also contains a provision for exempting certain highly compensated employees. Subpart H contains definitions and other miscellaneous provisions applicable to all or several of the exemptions.

(c) Effective July 1, 1972, the Fair Labor Standards Act was amended to include within the protection of the equal pay provisions those employees exempt from the minimum wage and overtime pay provisions as bona fide executive, administrative, and professional employees (including any employee employed in the capacity of academic administrative personnel or teacher in elementary or secondary schools), or in the capacity of an outside sales employee under section 13(a)(1) of the Act. The equal pay provisions in section 6(d) of the Fair Labor Standards Act are administered and enforced by the United States Equal Employment Opportunity Commission.

Sec. 541.1 Terms used in regulations

Act means the Fair Labor Standards Act of 1938, as amended.

Administrator means the Administrator of the Wage and Hour Division, United States Department of Labor. The Secretary of Labor has delegated to the Administrator the functions vested in the Secretary under sections 13(a)(1) and 13(a)(17) of the Fair Labor Standards Act.

Sec. 541.2 Job titles insufficient

A job title alone is insufficient to establish the exempt status of an employee. The exempt or nonexempt status of any particular employee must be determined on the basis of whether the employee's salary and duties meet the requirements of the regulations in this part.

Sec. 541.3 Scope of the section 13(a)(1) exemptions

(a) The section 13(a)(1) exemptions and the regulations in this part do not apply to manual laborers or other "blue collar" workers who perform work involving repetitive operations with their hands, physical skill and energy. Such nonexempt "blue collar" employees gain the skills and knowledge required for performance of their routine manual and physical work through apprenticeships and on-the-job training, not through the prolonged course of specialized intellectual instruction required for exempt learned professional employees such as medical doctors, architects and archeologists. Thus, for example, non-management production-line employees and non-management employees in maintenance, construction and similar occupations such as carpenters, electricians, mechanics, plumbers, iron workers, craftsmen, operating engineers, longshoremen, construction workers and laborers are entitled to minimum wage and overtime premium pay under the Fair Labor Standards Act, and are not exempt under the regulations in this part no matter how highly paid they might be.

(b) (1) The section 13(a)(1) exemptions and the regulations in this part also do not apply to police officers, detectives, deputy sheriffs, state troopers, highway patrol officers, investigators, inspectors, correctional officers, parole or probation officers, park rangers, fire fighters, paramedics, emergency medical technicians, ambulance personnel, rescue workers, hazardous materials workers and similar employees, regardless of rank or pay level, who perform work such as preventing, controlling or extinguishing fires of any type; rescuing fire, crime or accident victims; preventing or detecting crimes; conducting investigations or inspections for violations of law; performing surveillance; pursuing, restraining and apprehending suspects; detaining or supervising suspected and convicted criminals, including those on probation or parole; interviewing witnesses; interrogating and fingerprinting suspects; preparing investigative reports; or other similar work.

(2) Such employees do not qualify as exempt executive employees because their primary duty is not management of the enterprise in which the employee is employed or a customarily recognized department or subdivision thereof as required under Sec. 541.100. Thus, for example, a police officer or fire fighter whose primary duty is to investigate crimes or fight fires is not exempt under section 13(a)(1) of the Act merely because the police officer or fire fighter also directs the work of other employees in the conduct of an investigation or fighting a fire.

(3) Such employees do not qualify as exempt administrative employees because their primary duty is not the performance of work directly related to the management or general business operations of the employer or the employer's customers as required under Sec. 541.200.

(4) Such employees do not qualify as exempt professionals because their primary duty is not the performance of work requiring knowledge of an advanced type in a field of science or learning customarily acquired by a prolonged course of specialized intellectual instruction or the performance of work requiring invention, imagination, originality or talent in a recognized field of artistic or creative endeavor as required under Sec. 541.300. Although some police officers, fire fighters, paramedics, emergency medical technicians and similar employees have college degrees, a specialized academic degree is not a standard prerequisite for employment in such occupations.

Sec. 541.4 Other laws and collective bargaining agreements

The Fair Labor Standards Act provides minimum standards that may be exceeded, but cannot be waived or reduced. Employers must comply, for example, with any Federal, State or municipal laws, regulations or ordinances establishing a higher minimum wage or lower maximum workweek than those established under the Act. Similarly, employers, on their own initiative or under a collective bargaining agreement with a labor union, are not precluded by the Act from providing a wage higher than the statutory minimum, a shorter workweek than the statutory maximum, or a higher overtime premium (double time, for example) than provided by the Act. While collective bargaining agreements cannot waive or reduce the Act's protections, nothing in the Act or the regulations in this part relieves employers from their contractual obligations under collective bargaining agreements.

Subpart B—Executive Employees

Sec. 541.100 General rule for executive employees

(a) The term "employee employed in a bona fide executive capacity" in section 13(a)(1) of the Act shall mean any employee:

(1) Compensated on a salary basis at a rate of not less than $455 per week (or $380 per week, if employed in American Samoa by employers other than the Federal Government), exclusive of board, lodging or other facilities;

(2) Whose primary duty is management of the enterprise in which the employee is employed or of a customarily recognized department or subdivision thereof;

(3) Who customarily and regularly directs the work of two or more other employees; and

(4) Who has the authority to hire or fire other employees or whose suggestions and recommendations as to the hiring, firing, advancement, promotion or any other change of status of other employees are given particular weight.

(b) The phrase "salary basis" is defined at Sec. 541.602; "board, lodging or other facilities" is defined at Sec. 541.606; "primary duty" is defined at Sec. 541.700; and "customarily and regularly" is defined at Sec. 541.701.

Sec. 541.101 Business owner

The term "employee employed in a bona fide executive capacity" in section 13(a)(1) of the Act also includes any employee who owns at least a bona fide 20-percent equity interest in the enterprise in which the employee is employed, regardless of whether the business is a corporate or other type of organization, and who is actively engaged in its management. The term "management" is defined in Sec. 541.102. The requirements of Subpart G (salary requirements) of this part do not apply to the business owners described in this section.

Sec. 541.102 Management

Generally, "management" includes, but is not limited to, activities such as interviewing, selecting, and training of employees; setting and adjusting their rates of pay and hours of work; directing the work of employees; maintaining production or sales records for use in supervision or control; appraising employees' productivity and efficiency for the purpose of recommending promotions or other changes in status; handling employee complaints and grievances; disciplining employees; planning the work; determining the techniques to be used; apportioning the work among the employees; determining the type of materials, supplies, machinery, equipment or tools to be used or merchandise to be bought, stocked and sold; controlling the flow and distribution of materials or merchandise and supplies; providing for the safety and security of the employees or the property; planning and controlling the budget; and monitoring or implementing legal compliance measures.

Sec. 541.103 Department or subdivision

(a) The phrase "a customarily recognized department or subdivision" is intended to distinguish between a mere collection of employees assigned from time to time to a specific job or series of jobs and a unit with permanent status and function. A customarily recognized department or subdivision must have a permanent status and a continuing function. For example, a large employer's human resources department might have subdivisions for labor relations, pensions and other benefits, equal employment opportunity, and personnel management, each of which has a permanent status and function.

(b) When an enterprise has more than one establishment, the employee in charge of each establishment may be considered in charge of a recognized subdivision of the enterprise.

(c) A recognized department or subdivision need not be physically within the employer's establishment and may move from place to place. The mere fact that the employee works in more than one location does not invalidate the exemption if other factors show that the employee is actually in charge of a recognized unit with a continuing function in the organization.

(d) Continuity of the same subordinate personnel is not essential to the existence of a recognized unit with a continuing function. An otherwise exempt employee will not lose the exemption merely because the employee draws and supervises workers from a pool or supervises a team of workers drawn from other recognized units, if other factors are present that indicate that the employee is in charge of a recognized unit with a continuing function.

Sec. 541.104 Two or more other employees

(a) To qualify as an exempt executive under Sec. 541.100, the employee must customarily and regularly direct the work of two or more other employees. The phrase "two or more other employees" means two full-time employees or their equivalent. One full-time and two half-time employees, for example, are equivalent to two full-time employees. Four half-time employees are also equivalent.

(b) The supervision can be distributed among two, three or more employees, but each such employee must customarily and regularly direct the work of two or more other full-time employees or the equivalent. Thus, for example, a department with five full-time nonexempt workers may have up to two exempt supervisors if each such supervisor customarily and regularly directs the work of two of those workers.

(c) An employee who merely assists the manager of a particular department and supervises two or more employees only in the actual manager's absence does not meet this requirement.

(d) Hours worked by an employee cannot be credited more than once for different executives. Thus, a shared responsibility for the supervision of the same two employees in the same department does not satisfy this requirement. However, a full-time employee who works four hours for one supervisor and four hours for a different supervisor, for example, can be credited as a half-time employee for both supervisors.

Sec. 541.105 Particular weight

To determine whether an employee's suggestions and recommendations are given "particular weight," factors to be considered include, but are not limited to, whether it is part of the employee's job duties to make such suggestions and recommendations; the frequency with which such suggestions and recommendations are made or requested; and the frequency with which the employee's suggestions and recommendations are relied upon. Generally, an executive's suggestions and recommendations must pertain to employees whom the executive customarily and regularly directs. It does not include an occasional suggestion with regard to the change in status of a co-worker. An employee's suggestions and recommendations may still be deemed to have "particular weight" even if a higher level manager's recommendation has more importance and even if the employee does not have authority to make the ultimate decision as to the employee's change in status.

Sec. 541.106 Concurrent duties

(a) Concurrent performance of exempt and nonexempt work does not disqualify an employee from the executive exemption if the requirements of Sec. 541.100 are otherwise met. Whether an employee meets the requirements of Sec. 541.100 when the employee performs concurrent duties is determined on a case-by-case basis and based on the factors set forth in Sec. 541.700. Generally, exempt executives make the decision regarding when to perform nonexempt duties and remain responsible for the success or failure of business operations under their management while performing the nonexempt work. In contrast, the nonexempt employee generally is directed by a supervisor to perform the exempt work or performs the exempt work for defined time periods. An employee whose primary duty is ordinary production work or routine, recurrent or repetitive tasks cannot qualify for exemption as an executive.

(b) For example, an assistant manager in a retail establishment may perform work such as serving customers, cooking food, stocking shelves and cleaning the establishment, but performance of such nonexempt work does not preclude the exemption if the assistant manager's primary duty is management. An assistant manager can supervise employees and serve customers at the same time without losing the exemption. An exempt employee can also simultaneously direct the work of other employees and stock shelves.

(c) In contrast, a relief supervisor or working supervisor whose primary duty is performing nonexempt work on the production line in a manufacturing plant does not become exempt merely because the nonexempt production line employee occasionally has some responsibility for directing the work of other nonexempt production line employees when, for example, the exempt supervisor is unavailable. Similarly, an employee whose primary duty is to work as an electrician is not an exempt executive even if the employee also directs the work of other employees on the job site, orders parts and materials for the job, and handles requests from the prime contractor.

Subpart C—Administrative Employees

Sec. 541.200 General rule for administrative employees

(a) The term "employee employed in a bona fide administrative capacity" in section 13(a)(1) of the Act shall mean any employee:

(1) Compensated on a salary or fee basis at a rate of not less than $455 per week (or $380 per week, if employed in American Samoa by employers other than the Federal Government), exclusive of board, lodging or other facilities;

(2) Whose primary duty is the performance of office or non-manual work directly related to the management or general business operations of the employer or the employer's customers; and

(3) Whose primary duty includes the exercise of discretion and independent judgment with respect to matters of significance.

(b) The term "salary basis" is defined at Sec. 541.602; "fee basis" is defined at Sec. 541.605; "board, lodging or other facilities" is defined at Sec. 541.606; and "primary duty" is defined at Sec. 541.700.

Sec. 541.201 Directly related to management or general business operations

(a) To qualify for the administrative exemption, an employee's primary duty must be the performance of work directly related to the management or general business operations of the employer or the employer's customers. The phrase "directly related to the management or general business operations" refers to the type of work performed by the employee. To meet this requirement, an employee must perform work directly related to assisting with the running or servicing of the business, as distinguished, for example, from working on a manufacturing production line or selling a product in a retail or service establishment.

(b) Work directly related to management or general business operations includes, but is not limited to, work in functional areas such as tax; finance; accounting; budgeting; auditing; insurance; quality control; purchasing; procurement; advertising; marketing; research; safety and health; personnel management; human resources; employee benefits; labor relations; public relations, government relations; computer network, internet and database administration; legal and regulatory compliance; and similar activities. Some of these activities may be performed by employees who also would qualify for another exemption.

(c) An employee may qualify for the administrative exemption if the employee's primary duty is the performance of work directly related to the management or general business operations of the employer's customers. Thus, for example, employees acting as advisers or consultants to their employer's clients or customers (as tax experts or financial consultants, for example) may be exempt.

Sec. 541.202 Discretion and independent judgment

(a) To qualify for the administrative exemption, an employee's primary duty must include the exercise of discretion and independent judgment with respect to matters of significance. In general, the exercise of discretion and independent judgment involves the comparison and the evaluation of possible courses of conduct, and acting or making a decision after the various possibilities have been considered. The term "matters of significance" refers to the level of importance or consequence of the work performed.

(b) The phrase "discretion and independent judgment" must be applied in the light of all the facts involved in the particular employment situation in which the question arises. Factors to consider when determining whether an employee exercises discretion and independent judgment with respect to matters of significance include, but are not limited to: whether the employee has authority to formulate, affect, interpret, or implement management policies or operating practices; whether the employee carries out major assignments in conducting the operations of the business; whether the employee performs work that affects business operations to a substantial degree, even if the employee's assignments are related to operation of a particular segment of the business; whether the employee has authority to commit the employer in matters that have significant financial impact; whether the employee has authority to waive or deviate from established policies and procedures without prior approval; whether the employee has authority to negotiate and bind the company on significant matters; whether the employee provides consultation or expert advice to management; whether the employee is involved in planning long- or short-term business objectives;

whether the employee investigates and resolves matters of significance on behalf of management; and whether the employee represents the company in handling complaints, arbitrating disputes or resolving grievances.

(c) The exercise of discretion and independent judgment implies that the employee has authority to make an independent choice, free from immediate direction or supervision. However, employees can exercise discretion and independent judgment even if their decisions or recommendations are reviewed at a higher level. Thus, the term "discretion and independent judgment" does not require that the decisions made by an employee have a finality that goes with unlimited authority and a complete absence of review. The decisions made as a result of the exercise of discretion and independent judgment may consist of recommendations for action rather than the actual taking of action. The fact that an employee's decision may be subject to review and that upon occasion the decisions are revised or reversed after review does not mean that the employee is not exercising discretion and independent judgment. For example, the policies formulated by the credit manager of a large corporation may be subject to review by higher company officials who may approve or disapprove these policies. The management consultant who has made a study of the operations of a business and who has drawn a proposed change in organization may have the plan reviewed or revised by superiors before it is submitted to the client.

(d) An employer's volume of business may make it necessary to employ a number of employees to perform the same or similar work. The fact that many employees perform identical work or work of the same relative importance does not mean that the work of each such employee does not involve the exercise of discretion and independent judgment with respect to matters of significance.

(e) The exercise of discretion and independent judgment must be more than the use of skill in applying well-established techniques, procedures or specific standards described in manuals or other sources. See also Sec. 541.704 regarding use of manuals. The exercise of discretion and independent judgment also does not include clerical or secretarial work, recording or tabulating data, or performing other mechanical, repetitive, recurrent or routine work. An employee who simply tabulates data is not exempt, even if labeled as a "statistician."

(f) An employee does not exercise discretion and independent judgment with respect to matters of significance merely because the employer will experience financial losses if the employee fails to perform the job properly. For example, a messenger who is entrusted with carrying large sums of money does not exercise discretion and independent judgment with respect to matters of significance even though serious consequences may flow from the employee's neglect. Similarly, an employee who operates very expensive equipment does not exercise discretion and independent judgment with respect to matters of significance merely because improper performance of the employee's duties may cause serious financial loss to the employer.

Sec. 541.203 Administrative exemption examples

(a) Insurance claims adjusters generally meet the duties requirements for the administrative exemption, whether they work for an insurance company or other type of company, if their duties include activities such as interviewing insureds, witnesses and physicians; inspecting property damage; reviewing factual information to prepare damage estimates; evaluating and making recommendations regarding coverage of claims; determining liability and total value of a claim; negotiating settlements; and making recommendations regarding litigation.

(b) Employees in the financial services industry generally meet the duties requirements for the administrative exemption if their duties include work such as collecting and analyzing information regarding the customer's income, assets, investments or debts; determining which financial products best meet the customer's needs and financial circumstances; advising the customer regarding the advantages and disadvantages of different financial products; and marketing, servicing or promoting the employer's financial products. However, an employee whose primary duty is selling financial products does not qualify for the administrative exemption.

(c) An employee who leads a team of other employees assigned to complete major projects for the employer (such as purchasing, selling or closing all or part of the business, negotiating a real estate transaction or a collective bargaining agreement, or designing and implementing productivity improvements) generally meets the duties requirements for the administrative exemption, even if the employee does not have direct supervisory responsibility over the other employees on the team.

(d) An executive assistant or administrative assistant to a business owner or senior executive of a large business generally meets the duties requirements for the administrative exemption if such employee, without specific instructions or prescribed procedures, has been delegated authority regarding matters of significance.

(e) Human resources managers who formulate, interpret or implement employment policies and management consultants who study the operations of a business and propose changes in organization generally meet the duties requirements for the administrative exemption. However, personnel clerks who "screen" applicants to obtain data regarding their minimum qualifications and fitness for employment generally do not meet the duties requirements for the administrative exemption. Such personnel clerks typically will reject all applicants who do not meet minimum standards for the particular job or for employment by the company. The minimum standards are usually set by the exempt human resources manager or other company officials, and the decision to hire from the group of qualified applicants who do meet the minimum standards is similarly made by the exempt human resources manager or other company officials. Thus, when the interviewing and screening functions are performed by the human resources manager or personnel manager who makes the hiring decision or makes recommendations for hiring from the pool of qualified applicants, such duties constitute exempt work, even though routine, because this work is directly and closely related to the employee's exempt functions.

(f) Purchasing agents with authority to bind the company on significant purchases generally meet the duties requirements for the administrative exemption even if they must consult with top management officials when making a purchase commitment for raw materials in excess of the contemplated plant needs.

(g) Ordinary inspection work generally does not meet the duties requirements for the administrative exemption. Inspectors normally perform specialized work along standardized lines involving well-established techniques and procedures which may have been catalogued and described in manuals or other sources. Such inspectors rely on techniques and skills acquired by special training or experience. They have some leeway in the performance of their work but only within closely prescribed limits.

(h) Employees usually called examiners or graders, such as employees that grade lumber, generally do not meet the duties requirements for the administrative exemption. Such employees usually perform work involving the comparison of products with established standards which are frequently catalogued. Often, after continued reference to the written standards, or through experience, the employee acquires sufficient knowledge so that reference to written standards is unnecessary. The substitution of the employee's memory for a manual of standards does not convert the character of the work performed to exempt work requiring the exercise of discretion and independent judgment.

(i) Comparison shopping performed by an employee of a retail store who merely reports to the buyer the prices at a competitor's store does not qualify for the administrative exemption. However, the buyer who evaluates such reports on competitor prices to set the employer's prices generally meets the duties requirements for the administrative exemption.

(j) Public sector inspectors or investigators of various types, such as fire prevention or safety, building or construction, health or sanitation, environmental or soils specialists and similar employees, generally do not meet the duties requirements for the administrative exemption because their work typically does not involve work directly related to the management or general business operations of the employer. Such employees also do not qualify for the administrative exemption because their work involves the use of skills and technical abilities in gathering factual information, applying known standards or prescribed procedures, determining which procedure to follow, or determining whether prescribed standards or criteria are met.

Sec. 541.204 Educational establishments

(a) The term "employee employed in a bona fide administrative capacity" in section 13(a)(1) of the Act also includes employees:

(1) Compensated for services on a salary or fee basis at a rate of not less than $455 per week (or $380 per week, if employed in American Samoa by employers other than the Federal Government) exclusive of board, lodging or other facilities, or on a salary basis which is at least equal to the entrance salary for teachers in the educational establishment by which employed; and

(2) Whose primary duty is performing administrative functions directly related to academic instruction or training in an educational establishment or department or subdivision thereof.

(b) The term "educational establishment" means an elementary or secondary school system, an institution of higher education or other educational institution. Sections 3(v) and 3(w) of the Act define elementary and secondary schools as those day or residential schools that provide elementary or secondary education, as determined under State law. Under the laws of most States, such education includes the curriculums in grades 1 through 12; under many it includes also the introductory programs in kindergarten. Such education in some States may also include nursery school programs in elementary education and junior college curriculums in secondary education. The term "other educational establishment" includes special schools for mentally or physically disabled or gifted children, regardless of any classification of such schools as elementary, secondary or higher. Factors relevant in determining whether post-secondary career programs are educational institutions include whether the school is licensed by a state agency responsible for the state's educational system or accredited by a nationally recognized accrediting organization for career schools. Also, for purposes of the exemption, no distinction is drawn between public and private schools, or between those operated for profit and those that are not for profit.

(c) The phrase "performing administrative functions directly related to academic instruction or training" means work related to the academic operations and functions in a school rather than to administration along the lines of general business operations. Such academic administrative functions include operations directly in the field of education. Jobs relating to areas outside the educational field are not within the definition of academic administration.

(1) Employees engaged in academic administrative functions include: the superintendent or other head of an elementary or secondary school system, and any assistants, responsible for administration of such matters as curriculum, quality and methods of instructing, measuring and testing the learning potential and achievement of students, establishing and maintaining academic and grading standards, and other aspects of the teaching program; the principal and any vice-principals responsible for the operation of an elementary or secondary school; department heads in institutions of higher education responsible for the administration of the mathematics department, the English department, the foreign language department, etc.; academic counselors who perform work such as administering school testing programs, assisting students with academic problems and advising students concerning degree requirements; and other employees with similar responsibilities.

(2) Jobs relating to building management and maintenance, jobs relating to the health of the students, and academic staff such as social workers, psychologists, lunch room managers or dietitians do not perform academic administrative functions. Although such work is not considered academic administration, such employees may qualify for exemption under Sec. 541.200 or under other sections of this part, provided the requirements for such exemptions are met.

Subpart D—Professional Employees

Sec. 541.300 General rule for professional employees

(a) The term "employee employed in a bona fide professional capacity" in section 13(a)(1) of the Act shall mean any employee:

(1) Compensated on a salary or fee basis at a rate of not less than $455 per week (or $380 pe r week, if employed in American Samoa by employers other than the Federal Government), exclusive of board, lodging, or other facilities; and

(2) Whose primary duty is the performance of work:

(i) Requiring knowledge of an advanced type in a field of science or learning customarily acquired by a prolonged course of specialized intellectual instruction; or

(ii) Requiring invention, imagination, originality or talent in a recognized field of artistic or creative endeavor.

(b) The term "salary basis" is defined at Sec. 541.602; "fee basis" is defined at Sec. 541.605; "board, lodging or other facilities" is defined at Sec. 541.606; and "primary duty" is defined at Sec. 541.700.

Sec. 541.301 Learned professionals

(a) To qualify for the learned professional exemption, an employee's primary duty must be the performance of work requiring advanced knowledge in a field of science or learning customarily acquired by a prolonged course of specialized intellectual instruction. This primary duty test includes three elements:

(1) The employee must perform work requiring advanced knowledge;

(2) The advanced knowledge must be in a field of science or learning; and

(3) The advanced knowledge must be customarily acquired by a prolonged course of specialized intellectual instruction.

(b) The phrase "work requiring advanced knowledge" means work which is predominantly intellectual in character, and which includes work requiring the consistent exercise of discretion and judgment, as distinguished from performance of routine mental, manual, mechanical or physical work. An employee who performs work requiring advanced knowledge generally uses the advanced knowledge to analyze, interpret or make deductions from varying facts or circumstances. Advanced knowledge cannot be attained at the high school level.

(c) The phrase "field of science or learning" includes the traditional professions of law, medicine, theology, accounting, actuarial computation, engineering, architecture, teaching, various types of physical, chemical and biological sciences, pharmacy and other similar occupations that have a recognized professional status as distinguished from the mechanical arts or skilled trades where in some instances the knowledge is of a fairly advanced type, but is not in a field of science or learning.

(d) The phrase "customarily acquired by a prolonged course of specialized intellectual instruction" restricts the exemption to professions where specialized academic training is a standard prerequisite for entrance into the profession. The best prima facie evidence that an employee meets this requirement is possession of the appropriate academic degree. However, the word "customarily" means that the exemption is also available to employees in such professions who have substantially the same knowledge level and perform substantially the same work as the degreed employees, but who attained the advanced knowledge through a combination of work experience and intellectual instruction. Thus, for example, the learned professional exemption is available to the occasional lawyer who has not gone to law school, or the occasional chemist who is not the possessor of a degree in chemistry. However, the learned professional exemption is not available for occupations that customarily may be performed with only the general knowledge acquired by an academic degree in any field, with knowledge acquired through an apprenticeship, or with training in the performance of routine mental, manual, mechanical or physical processes. The learned professional exemption also does not apply to occupations in which most employees have acquired their skill by experience rather than by advanced specialized intellectual instruction.

(e)(1) Registered or certified medical technologists. Registered or certified medical technologists who have successfully completed three academic years of pre-professional study in an accredited college or university plus a fourth year of professional course work in a school of medical technology approved by the Council of Medical Education of the American Medical Association generally meet the duties requirements for the learned professional exemption.

(2) Nurses. Registered nurses who are registered by the appropriate State examining board generally meet the duties requirements for the learned professional exemption. Licensed practical nurses and other similar health care employees, however, generally do not qualify as exempt learned professionals because possession of a specialized advanced academic degree is not a standard prerequisite for entry into such occupations.

(3) Dental hygienists. Dental hygienists who have successfully completed four academic years of pre-professional and professional study in an accredited college or university approved by the Commission on Accreditation of Dental and Dental Auxiliary Educational Programs of the American Dental Association generally meet the duties requirements for the learned professional exemption.

(4) Physician assistants. Physician assistants who have successfully completed four academic years of pre-professional and professional study, including graduation from a physician assistant program accredited by the Accreditation Review Commission on Education for the Physician Assistant, and who are certified by the National Commission on Certification of Physician Assistants generally meet the duties requirements for the learned professional exemption.

(5) Accountants. Certified public accountants generally meet the duties requirements for the learned professional exemption. In addition, many other accountants who are not certified public accountants but perform similar job duties may qualify as exempt learned professionals. However, accounting clerks, bookkeepers and other employees who normally perform a great deal of routine work generally will not qualify as exempt professionals.

(6) Chefs. Chefs, such as executive chefs and sous chefs, who have attained a four-year specialized academic degree in a culinary arts program, generally meet the duties requirements for the learned professional exemption. The learned professional exemption is not available to cooks who perform predominantly routine mental, manual, mechanical or physical work.

(7) Paralegals. Paralegals and legal assistants generally do not qualify as exempt learned professionals because an advanced specialized academic degree is not a standard prerequisite for entry into the field. Although many paralegals possess general four-year advanced degrees, most specialized paralegal programs are two-year associate degree programs from a community college or equivalent institution. However, the learned professional exemption is available for paralegals who possess advanced specialized degrees in other professional fields and apply advanced knowledge in that field in the performance of their duties. For example, if a law firm hires an engineer as a paralegal to provide expert advice on product liability cases or to assist on patent matters, that engineer would qualify for exemption.

(8) Athletic trainers. Athletic trainers who have successfully completed four academic years of pre-professional and professional study in a specialized curriculum accredited by the Commission on Accreditation of Allied Health Education Programs and who are certified by the Board of Certification of the National Athletic Trainers Association Board of Certification generally meet the duties requirements for the learned professional exemption.

(9) Funeral directors or embalmers. Licensed funeral directors and embalmers who are licensed by and working in a state that requires successful completion of four academic years of pre-professional and professional study, including graduation from a college of mortuary science accredited by the American Board of Funeral Service Education, generally meet the duties requirements for the learned professional exemption.

(f) The areas in which the professional exemption may be available are expanding. As knowledge is developed, academic training is broadened and specialized degrees are offered in new and diverse fields, thus creating new specialists in particular fields of science or learning. When an advanced specialized degree has become a standard requirement for a particular occupation, that occupation may have acquired the characteristics of a learned profession. Accrediting and certifying organizations similar to those listed in paragraphs (e)(1), (e)(3), (e)(4), (e)(8) and (e)(9) of this section also may be created in the future. Such organizations may develop similar specialized curriculums and certification programs which, if a standard requirement for a particular occupation, may indicate that the occupation has acquired the characteristics of a learned profession.

Sec. 541.302 Creative professionals

(a) To qualify for the creative professional exemption, an employee's primary duty must be the performance of work requiring invention, imagination, originality or talent in a recognized field of artistic or creative endeavor as opposed to routine mental, manual, mechanical or physical work. The exemption does not apply to work which can be produced by a person with general manual or intellectual ability and training.

(b) To qualify for exemption as a creative professional, the work performed must be "in a recognized field of artistic or creative endeavor." This includes such fields as music, writing, acting and the graphic arts.

(c) The requirement of "invention, imagination, originality or talent" distinguishes the creative professions from work that primarily depends on intelligence, diligence and accuracy. The duties of employees vary widely, and exemption as a creative professional depends on the extent of the invention, imagination, originality or talent exercised by the employee. Determination of exempt creative professional status, therefore, must be made on a case-by-case basis. This requirement generally is met by actors, musicians, composers, conductors, and soloists; painters who at most are given the subject matter of their painting; cartoonists who are merely told the title or underlying concept of a cartoon and must rely on their own creative ability to express the concept; essayists, novelists, short-story writers and screen-play writers who choose their own subjects and hand in a finished piece of work to their employers (the majority of such persons are, of course, not employees but self-employed); and persons holding the more responsible writing positions in advertising agencies. This requirement generally is not met by a person who is employed as a copyist, as an "animator" of motion-picture cartoons, or as a retoucher of photographs, since such work is not properly described as creative in character.

(d) Journalists may satisfy the duties requirements for the creative professional exemption if their primary duty is work requiring invention, imagination, originality or talent, as opposed to work which depends primarily on intelligence, diligence and accuracy. Employees of newspapers, magazines, television and other media are not exempt creative professionals if they only collect, organize and record information that is routine or already public, or if they do not contribute a unique interpretation or analysis to a news product. Thus, for example, newspaper reporters who merely rewrite press releases or who write standard recounts of public information by gathering facts on routine community events are not exempt creative professionals. Reporters also do not qualify as exempt creative professionals if their work product is subject to substantial control by the employer. However, journalists may qualify as exempt creative professionals if their primary duty is performing on the air in radio, television or other electronic media; conducting investigative interviews; analyzing or interpreting public events; writing editorials, opinion columns or other commentary; or acting as a narrator or commentator.

Sec. 541.303 Teachers

(a) The term "employee employed in a bona fide professional capacity" in section 13(a)(1) of the Act also means any employee with a primary duty of teaching, tutoring, instructing or lecturing in the activity of imparting knowledge and who is employed and engaged in this activity as a teacher in an educational establishment by which the employee is employed. The term "educational establishment" is defined in Sec. 541.204(b).

(b) Exempt teachers include, but are not limited to: regular academic teachers; teachers of kindergarten or nursery school pupils; teachers of gifted or disabled children; teachers of skilled and semi-skilled trades and occupations; teachers engaged in automobile driving instruction; aircraft flight instructors; home economics teachers; and vocal or instrumental music instructors. Those faculty members who are engaged as teachers but also spend a considerable amount of their time in extracurricular activities such as coaching athletic teams or acting as moderators or advisors in such areas as drama, speech, debate or journalism are engaged in teaching. Such activities are a recognized part of the schools' responsibility in contributing to the educational development of the student.

(c) The possession of an elementary or secondary teacher's certificate provides a clear means of identifying the individuals contemplated as being within the scope of the exemption for teaching professionals. Teachers who possess a teaching certificate qualify for the exemption regardless of the terminology (e.g., permanent, conditional, standard, provisional, temporary, emergency, or unlimited) used by the State to refer to different kinds of certificates. However, private schools and public schools are not uniform in requiring a certificate for employment as an elementary or secondary school teacher, and a teacher's certificate is not generally necessary for employment in institutions of higher education or other educational establishments. Therefore, a teacher who is not certified may be considered for exemption, provided that such individual is employed as a teacher by the employing school or school system.

(d) The requirements of Sec. 541.300 and Subpart G (salary requirements) of this part do not apply to the teaching professionals described in this section.

Sec. 541.304 Practice of law or medicine

(a) The term "employee employed in a bona fide professional capacity" in section 13(a)(1) of the Act also shall mean:

(1) Any employee who is the holder of a valid license or certificate permitting the practice of law or medicine or any of their branches and is actually engaged in the practice thereof; and

(2) Any employee who is the holder of the requisite academic degree for the general practice of medicine and is engaged in an internship or resident program pursuant to the practice of the profession.

(b) In the case of medicine, the exemption applies to physicians and other practitioners licensed and practicing in the field of medical science and healing or any of the medical specialties practiced by physicians or practitioners. The term "physicians" includes medical doctors including general practitioners and specialists, osteopathic physicians (doctors of osteopathy), podiatrists, dentists (doctors of dental medicine), and optometrists (doctors of optometry or bachelors of science in optometry).

(c) Employees engaged in internship or resident programs, whether or not licensed to practice prior to commencement of the program, qualify as exempt professionals if they enter such internship or resident programs after the earning of the appropriate degree required for the general practice of their profession.

(d) The requirements of Sec. 541.300 and subpart G (salary requirements) of this part do not apply to the employees described in this section.

Subpart E—Computer Employees

Sec. 541.400 General rule for computer employees

(a) Computer systems analysts, computer programmers, software engineers or other similarly skilled workers in the computer field are eligible for exemption as professionals under section 13(a)(1) of the Act and under section 13(a)(17) of the Act. Because job titles vary widely and change quickly in the computer industry, job titles are not determinative of the applicability of this exemption.

(b) The section 13(a)(1) exemption applies to any computer employee compensated on a salary or fee basis at a rate of not less than $455 per week (or $380 per week, if employed in American Samoa by employers other than the Federal Government), exclusive of board, lodging or other facilities, and the section 13(a)(17) exemption applies to any computer employee compensated on an hourly basis at a rate not less than $27.63 an hour. In addition, under either section 13(a)(1) or section 13(a)(17) of the Act, the exemptions apply only to computer employees whose primary duty consists of:

> (1) The application of systems analysis techniques and procedures, including consulting with users, to determine hardware, software or system functional specifications;

> (2) The design, development, documentation, analysis, creation, testing or modification of computer systems or programs, including prototypes, based on and related to user or system design specifications;

> (3) The design, documentation, testing, creation or modification of computer programs related to machine operating systems; or

> (4) A combination of the aforementioned duties, the performance of which requires the same level of skills.

(c) The term "salary basis" is defined at Sec. 541.602; "fee basis" is defined at Sec. 541.605; "board, lodging or other facilities" is defined at Sec. 541.606; and "primary duty" is defined at Sec. 541.700.

Sec. 541.401 Computer manufacture and repair

The exemption for employees in computer occupations does not include employees engaged in the manufacture or repair of computer hardware and related equipment. Employees whose work is highly dependent upon, or facilitated by, the use of computers and computer software programs (e.g., engineers, drafters and others skilled in computer-aided design software), but who are not primarily engaged in computer systems analysis and programming or other similarly skilled computer-related occupations identified in Sec. 541.400(b), are also not exempt computer professionals.

Sec. 541.402 Executive and administrative computer employees

Computer employees within the scope of this exemption, as well as those employees not within its scope, may also have executive and administrative duties which qualify the employees for exemption under subpart B or subpart C of this part. For example, systems analysts and computer programmers generally meet the duties requirements for the administrative exemption if their primary duty includes work such as planning, scheduling, and coordinating activities required to develop systems to solve complex business, scientific or engineering problems of the employer or the employer's customers. Similarly, a senior or lead computer programmer who manages the work of two or more other programmers in a customarily recognized department or subdivision of the employer, and whose recommendations as to the hiring, firing, advancement, promotion or other change of status of the other programmers are given particular weight, generally meets the duties requirements for the executive exemption.

Subpart F—Outside Sales Employees

Sec. 541.500 General rule for outside sales employees

(a) The term "employee employed in the capacity of outside salesman" in section 13(a)(1) of the Act shall mean any employee:

(1) Whose primary duty is:

(i) making sales within the meaning of section 3(k) of the Act, or

(ii) obtaining orders or contracts for services or for the use of facilities for which a consideration will be paid by the client or customer; and

(2) Who is customarily and regularly engaged away from the employer's place or places of business in performing such primary duty.

(b) The term "primary duty" is defined at Sec. 541.700. In determining the primary duty of an outside sales employee, work performed incidental to and in conjunction with the employee's own outside sales or solicitations, including incidental deliveries and collections, shall be regarded as exempt outside sales work. Other work that furthers the employee's sales efforts also shall be regarded as exempt work including, for example, writing sales reports, updating or revising the employee's sales or display catalogue, planning itineraries and attending sales conferences.

(c) The requirements of Subpart G (salary requirements) of this part do not apply to the outside sales employees described in this section.

Sec. 541.501 Making sales or obtaining orders

(a) Section 541.500 requires that the employee be engaged in:

(1) Making sales within the meaning of section 3(k) of the Act, or

(2) Obtaining orders or contracts for services or for the use of facilities.

(b) Sales within the meaning of section 3(k) of the Act include the transfer of title to tangible property, and in certain cases, of tangible and valuable evidences of intangible property. Section 3(k) of the Act states that "sale" or "sell" includes any sale, exchange, contract to sell, consignment for sale, shipment for sale, or other disposition.

(c) Exempt outside sales work includes not only the sales of commodities, but also "obtaining orders or contracts for services or for the use of facilities for which a consideration will be paid by the client or customer." Obtaining orders for "the use of facilities" includes the selling of time on radio or television, the solicitation of advertising for newspapers and other periodicals, and the solicitation of freight for railroads and other transportation agencies.

(d) The word "services" extends the outside sales exemption to employees who sell or take orders for a service, which may be performed for the customer by someone other than the person taking the order.

Sec. 541.502 Away from employer's place of business

An outside sales employee must be customarily and regularly engaged "away from the employer's place or places of business." The outside sales employee is an employee who makes sales at the customer's place of business or, if selling door-to-door, at the customer's home. Outside sales does not include sales made by mail, telephone or the Internet unless such contact is used merely as an adjunct to personal calls. Thus, any fixed site, whether home or office, used by a salesperson as a headquarters or for telephonic solicitation of sales is considered one of the employer's places of business, even though the employer is not in any formal sense the owner or tenant of the property. However, an outside sales employee does not lose the exemption by displaying samples in hotel sample rooms during trips from city to city; these sample rooms should not be considered as the employer's places of business. Similarly, an outside sales employee does not lose the exemption by displaying the employer's products at a trade show. If selling actually occurs, rather than just sales promotion, trade shows of short duration (i.e., one or two weeks) should not be considered as the employer's place of business.

Sec. 541.503 Promotion work

(a) Promotion work is one type of activity often performed by persons who make sales, which may or may not be exempt outside sales work, depending upon the circumstances under which it is performed. Promotional work that is actually performed incidental to and in conjunction with an employee's own outside sales or solicitations is exempt work. On the other hand, promotional work that is incidental to sales made, or to be made, by someone else is not exempt outside sales work. An employee who does not satisfy the requirements of this Subpart may still qualify as an exempt employee under other Subparts of this rule.

(b) A manufacturer's representative, for example, may perform various types of promotional activities such as putting up displays and posters, removing damaged or spoiled stock from the merchant's shelves or rearranging the merchandise. Such an employee can be considered an exempt outside sales employee if the employee's primary duty is making sales or contracts. Promotion activities directed toward consummation of the employee's own sales are exempt. Promotional activities designed to stimulate sales that will be made by someone else are not exempt outside sales work.

(c) Another example is a company representative who visits chain stores, arranges the merchandise on shelves, replenishes stock by replacing old with new merchandise, sets up displays and consults with the store manager when inventory runs low, but does not obtain a commitment for additional purchases. The arrangement of merchandise on the shelves or the replenishing of stock is not exempt work unless it is incidental to and in conjunction with the employee's own outside sales. Because the employee in this instance does not consummate the sale nor direct efforts toward the consummation of a sale, the work is not exempt outside sales work.

Sec. 541.504 Drivers who sell

(a) Drivers who deliver products and also sell such products may qualify as exempt outside sales employees only if the employee has a primary duty of making sales. In determining the primary duty of drivers who sell, work performed incidental to and in conjunction with the employee's own outside sales or solicitations, including loading, driving or delivering products, shall be regarded as exempt outside sales work.

(b) Several factors should be considered in determining if a driver has a primary duty of making sales, including, but not limited to: a comparison of the driver's duties with those of other employees engaged as truck drivers and as salespersons; possession of a selling or solicitor's license when such license is required by law or ordinances; presence or absence of customary or contractual arrangements concerning amounts of products to be delivered; description of the employee's occupation in collective bargaining agreements; the employer's specifications as to qualifications for hiring; sales training; attendance at sales conferences; method of payment; and proportion of earnings directly attributable to sales.

(c) Drivers who may qualify as exempt outside sales employees include:

(1) A driver who provides the only sales contact between the employer and the customers visited, who calls on customers and takes orders for products, who delivers products from stock in the employee's vehicle or procures and delivers the product to the customer on a later trip, and who receives compensation commensurate with the volume of products sold.

(2) A driver who obtains or solicits orders for the employer's products from persons who have authority to commit the customer for purchases.

(3) A driver who calls on new prospects for customers along the employee's route and attempts to convince them of the desirability of accepting regular delivery of goods.

(4) A driver who calls on established customers along the route and persuades regular customers to accept delivery of increased amounts of goods or of new products, even though the initial sale or agreement for delivery was made by someone else.

(d) Drivers who generally would not qualify as exempt outside sales employees include:

(1) A route driver whose primary duty is to transport products sold by the employer through vending machines and to keep such machines stocked, in good operating condition, and in good locations.

(2) A driver who often calls on established customers day after day or week after week, delivering a quantity of the employer's products at each call when the sale was not significantly affected by solicitations of the customer by the delivering driver or the amount of the sale is determined by the volume of the customer's sales since the previous delivery.

(3) A driver primarily engaged in making deliveries to customers and performing activities intended to promote sales by customers (including placing point-of-sale and other advertising materials, price stamping commodities, arranging merchandise on shelves, in coolers or in cabinets, rotating stock according to date, and cleaning and otherwise servicing display cases), unless such work is in furtherance of the driver's own sales efforts.

Subpart G—Salary Requirements

Sec. 541.600 Amount of salary required

(a) To qualify as an exempt executive, administrative or professional employee under section 13(a)(1) of the Act, an employee must be compensated on a salary basis at a rate of not less than $455 per week (or $380 per week, if employed in American Samoa by employers other than the Federal Government), exclusive of board, lodging or other facilities. Administrative and professional employees may also be paid on a fee basis, as defined in Sec. 541.605.

(b) The $455 a week may be translated into equivalent amounts for periods longer than one week. The requirement will be met if the employee is compensated biweekly on a salary basis of $910, semimonthly on a salary basis of $985.83, or monthly on a salary basis of $1,971.66. However, the shortest period of payment that will meet this compensation requirement is one week.

(c) In the case of academic administrative employees, the compensation requirement also may be met by compensation on a salary basis at a rate at least equal to the entrance salary for teachers in the educational establishment by which the employee is employed, as provided in Sec. 541.204(a)(1).

(d) In the case of computer employees, the compensation requirement also may be met by compensation on an hourly basis at a rate not less than $27.63 an hour, as provided in Sec. 541.400(b).

(e) In the case of professional employees, the compensation requirements in this section shall not apply to employees engaged as teachers (see Sec. 541.303); employees who hold a valid license or certificate permitting the practice of law or medicine or any of their branches and are actually engaged in the practice thereof (see Sec. 541.304); or to employees who hold the requisite academic degree for the general practice of medicine and are engaged in an internship or resident program pursuant to the practice of the profession (see Sec. 541.304). In the case of medical occupations, the exception from the salary or fee requirement does not apply to pharmacists, nurses, therapists, technologists, sanitarians, dietitians, social workers, psychologists, psychometrists, or other professions which service the medical profession.

Sec. 541.601 Highly compensated employees

(a) An employee with total annual compensation of at least $100,000 is deemed exempt under section 13(a)(1) of the Act if the employee customarily and regularly performs any one or more of the exempt duties or responsibilities of an executive, administrative or professional employee identified in Subparts B, C or D of this part.

(b)(1) "Total annual compensation" must include at least $455 per week paid on a salary or fee basis. Total annual compensation may also include commissions, nondiscretionary bonuses and other nondiscretionary compensation earned during a 52-week period. Total annual compensation does not include board, lodging and other facilities as defined in Sec. 541.606, and does not include payments for medical insurance, payments for life insurance, contributions to retirement plans and the cost of other fringe benefits.

(2) If an employee's total annual compensation does not total at least the minimum amount established in paragraph (a) of this section by the last pay period of the

52-week period, the employer may, during the last pay period or within one month after the end of the 52-week period, make one final payment sufficient to achieve the required level. For example, an employee may earn $80,000 in base salary, and the employer may anticipate based upon past sales that the employee also will earn $20,000 in commissions. However, due to poor sales in the final quarter of the year, the employee actually only earns $10,000 in commissions. In this situation, the employer may within one month after the end of the year make a payment of at least $10,000 to the employee. Any such final payment made after the end of the 52-week period may count only toward the prior year's total annual compensation and not toward the total annual compensation in the year it was paid. If the employer fails to make such a payment, the employee does not qualify as a highly compensated employee, but may still qualify as exempt under Subparts B, C or D of this part.

(3) An employee who does not work a full year for the employer, either because the employee is newly hired after the beginning of the year or ends the employment before the end of the year, may qualify for exemption under this section if the employee receives a pro rata portion of the minimum amount established in paragraph (a) of this section, based upon the number of weeks that the employee will be or has been employed. An employer may make one final payment as under paragraph (b)(2) of this section within one month after the end of employment.

(4) The employer may utilize any 52-week period as the year, such as a calendar year, a fiscal year, or an anniversary of hire year. If the employer does not identify some other year period in advance, the calendar year will apply.

(c) A high level of compensation is a strong indicator of an employee's exempt status, thus eliminating the need for a detailed analysis of the employee's job duties. Thus, a highly compensated employee will qualify for exemption if the employee customarily and regularly performs any one or more of the exempt duties or responsibilities of an executive, adminis- trative or professional employee identified in Subparts B, C or D of this part. An employee may qualify as a highly compensated executive employee, for example, if the employee custom- arily and regularly directs the work of two or more other employees, even though the employee does not meet all of the other requirements for the executive exemption under Sec. 541.100.

(d) This section applies only to employees whose primary duty includes performing office or non-manual work. Thus, for example, non-management production-line workers and non-management employees in maintenance, construction and similar occupations such as carpenters, electricians, mechanics, plumbers, iron workers, craftsmen, operating engineers, longshoremen, construction workers, laborers and other employees who perform work involving repetitive operations with their hands, physical skill and energy are not exempt under this section no matter how highly paid they might be.

Sec. 541.602 Salary basis

(a) General rule. An employee will be considered to be paid on a "salary basis" within the meaning of these regulations if the employee regularly receives each pay period on a weekly, or less frequent basis, a predetermined amount constituting all or part of the employee's compensation, which amount is not subject to reduction because of variations in the quality or quantity of the work performed. Subject to the exceptions provided in paragraph (b) of this section, an exempt employee must receive the full salary for any week in which the employee performs any work without regard to the number of days or hours worked. Exempt employees need not be paid for any workweek in which they perform no work. An employee is not paid on a salary basis if deductions from the employee's predetermined compensation are made for absences occasioned by the employer or by the operating requirements of the business. If the employee is ready, willing and able to work, deductions may not be made for time when work is not available.

(b) Exceptions. The prohibition against deductions from pay in the salary basis requirement is subject to the following exceptions:

(1) Deductions from pay may be made when an exempt employee is absent from work for one or more full days for personal reasons, other than sickness or disability. Thus, if an employee is absent for two full days to handle personal affairs, the employee's salaried status will not be affected if deductions are made from the salary for two full-day absences. However, if an exempt employee is absent for one and a half days for personal reasons, the employer can deduct only for the one full-day absence.

(2) Deductions from pay may be made for absences of one or more full days occasioned by sickness or disability (including work-related accidents) if the deduction is made in accordance with a bona fide plan, policy or practice of providing compensation for loss of salary occasioned by such sickness or disability. The employer is not required to pay any portion of the employee's salary for full-day absences for which the employee receives compensation under the plan, policy or practice. Deductions for such full-day absences also may be made before the employee has qualified under the plan, policy or practice, and after the employee has exhausted the leave allowance thereunder. Thus, for example, if an employer maintains a short-term disability insurance plan providing salary replacement for 12 weeks starting on the fourth day of absence, the employer may make deductions from pay for the three days of absence before the employee qualifies for benefits under the plan; for the twelve weeks in which the employee receives salary replacement benefits under the plan; and for absences after the employee has exhausted the 12 weeks of salary replacement benefits. Similarly, an employer may make deductions from pay for absences of one or more full days if salary replacement benefits are provided under a State disability insurance law or under a State workers' compensation law.

(3) While an employer cannot make deductions from pay for absences of an exempt employee occasioned by jury duty, attendance as a witness or temporary military leave, the employer can offset any amounts received by an employee as jury fees, witness fees or military pay for a particular week against the salary due for that particular week without loss of the exemption.

(4) Deductions from pay of exempt employees may be made for penalties imposed in good faith for infractions of safety rules of major significance. Safety rules of major significance include those relating to the prevention of serious danger in the workplace or to other employees, such as rules prohibiting smoking in explosive plants, oil refineries and coal mines.

(5) Deductions from pay of exempt employees may be made for unpaid disciplinary suspensions of one or more full days imposed in good faith for infractions of workplace conduct rules. Such suspensions must be imposed pursuant to a written policy applicable to all employees. Thus, for example, an employer may suspend an exempt employee without pay for three days for violating a generally applicable written policy prohibiting sexual harassment. Similarly, an employer may suspend an exempt employee without pay for twelve days for violating a generally applicable written policy prohibiting workplace violence.

(6) An employer is not required to pay the full salary in the initial or terminal week of employment. Rather, an employer may pay a proportionate part of an employee's full salary for the time actually worked in the first and last week of employment. In such

weeks, the payment of an hourly or daily equivalent of the employee's full salary for the time actually worked will meet the requirement. However, employees are not paid on a salary basis within the meaning of these regulations if they are employed occasionally for a few days, and the employer pays them a proportionate part of the weekly salary when so employed.

(7) An employer is not required to pay the full salary for weeks in which an exempt employee takes unpaid leave under the Family and Medical Leave Act. Rather, when an exempt employee takes unpaid leave under the Family and Medical Leave Act, an employer may pay a proportionate part of the full salary for time actually worked. For example, if an employee who normally works 40 hours per week uses four hours of unpaid leave under the Family and Medical Leave Act, the employer could deduct 10 percent of the employee's normal salary that week.

(c) When calculating the amount of a deduction from pay allowed under paragraph (b) of this section, the employer may use the hourly or daily equivalent of the employee's full weekly salary or any other amount proportional to the time actually missed by the employee. A deduction from pay as a penalty for violations of major safety rules under paragraph (b)(4) of this section may be made in any amount.

Sec. 541.603 Effect of improper deductions from salary

(a) An employer who makes improper deductions from salary shall lose the exemption if the facts demonstrate that the employer did not intend to pay employees on a salary basis. An actual practice of making improper deductions demonstrates that the employer did not intend to pay employees on a salary basis. The factors to consider when determining whether an employer has an actual practice of making improper deductions include, but are not limited to: the number of improper deductions, particularly as compared to the number of employee infractions warranting discipline; the time period during which the employer made improper deductions; the number and geographic location of employees whose salary was improperly reduced; the number and geographic location of managers responsible for taking the improper deductions; and whether the employer has a clearly communicated policy permitting or prohibiting improper deductions.

(b) If the facts demonstrate that the employer has an actual practice of making improper deductions, the exemption is lost during the time period in which the improper deductions were made for employees in the same job classification working for the same managers responsible for the actual improper deductions. Employees in different job classifications or who work for different managers do not lose their status as exempt employees. Thus, for example, if a manager at a company facility routinely docks the pay of engineers at that facility for partial-day personal absences, then all engineers at that facility whose pay could have been improperly docked by the manager would lose the exemption; engineers at other facilities or working for other managers, however, would remain exempt.

(c) Improper deductions that are either isolated or inadvertent will not result in loss of the exemption for any employees subject to such improper deductions, if the employer reimburses the employees for such improper deductions.

(d) If an employer has a clearly communicated policy that prohibits the improper pay deductions specified in Sec. 541.602(a) and includes a complaint mechanism, reimburses employees for any improper deductions and makes a good faith commitment to comply in the future, such employer will not lose the exemption for any employees unless the employer willfully violates the policy by continuing to make improper deductions after receiving employee complaints. If an employer fails to reimburse employees for any improper deductions or continues to make improper deductions after receiving employee complaints, the exemption is lost during the time period in which the improper deductions were made for employees in the same job classification working for the same managers responsible for the actual improper deductions. The best evidence of a clearly communicated policy is a written policy that was distributed to employees prior to the improper pay deductions by, for example, providing a copy of the policy to employees at the time of hire, publishing the policy in an employee handbook or publishing the policy on the employer's Intranet.

(e) This section shall not be construed in an unduly technical manner so as to defeat the exemption.

Sec. 541.604 Minimum guarantee plus extras

(a) An employer may provide an exempt employee with additional compensation without losing the exemption or violating the salary basis requirement, if the employment arrangement also includes a guarantee of at least the minimum weekly-required amount paid on a salary basis. Thus, for example, an exempt employee guaranteed at least $455 each week paid on a salary basis may also receive additional compensation of a one percent commission on sales. An exempt employee also may receive a percentage of the sales or profits of the employer if the employment arrangement also includes a guarantee of at least $455 each week paid on a salary basis. Similarly, the exemption is not lost if an exempt employee who is guaranteed at least $455 each week paid on a salary basis also receives additional compensation based on hours worked for work beyond the normal workweek. Such additional compensation may be paid on any basis (e.g., flat sum, bonus payment, straight-time hourly amount, time and one-half or any other basis), and may include paid time off.

(b) An exempt employee's earnings may be computed on an hourly, a daily or a shift basis, without losing the exemption or violating the salary basis requirement, if the employment arrangement also includes a guarantee of at least the minimum weekly required amount paid on a salary basis regardless of the number of hours, days or shifts worked, and a reasonable relationship exists between the guaranteed amount and the amount actually earned. The reasonable relationship test will be met if the weekly guarantee is roughly equivalent to the employee's usual earnings at the assigned hourly, daily or shift rate for the employee's normal scheduled workweek. Thus, for example, an exempt employee guaranteed compensation of at least $500 for any week in which the employee performs any work, and who normally works four or five shifts each week, may be paid $150 per shift without violating the salary basis requirement. The reasonable relationship requirement applies only if the employee's pay is computed on an hourly, daily or shift basis. It does not apply, for example, to an exempt store manager paid a guaranteed salary of $650 per week who also receives a commission of one-half percent of all sales in the store or five percent of the store's profits, which in some weeks may total as much as, or even more than, the guaranteed salary.

Sec. 541.605 Fee basis

(a) Administrative and professional employees may be paid on a fee basis, rather than on a salary basis. An employee will be considered to be paid on a "fee basis" within the meaning of these regulations if the employee is paid an agreed sum for a single job regardless of the time required for its completion. These payments resemble piecework payments with the important distinction that generally a "fee" is paid for the kind of job that is unique rather than for a series of jobs repeated an indefinite number of times and for which payment on an identical basis is made over and over again. Payments based on the number of hours or days worked and not on the accomplishment of a given single task are not considered payments on a fee basis.

(b) To determine whether the fee payment meets the minimum amount of salary required for exemption under these regulations, the amount paid to the employee will be tested by determining the time worked on the job and whether the fee payment is at a rate that would amount to at least $455 per week if the employee worked 40 hours. Thus, an artist paid $250 for a picture that took 20 hours to complete meets the minimum salary requirement for exemption since earnings at this rate would yield the artist $500 if 40 hours were worked.

Sec. 541.606 Board, lodging or other facilities

(a) To qualify for exemption under section 13(a)(1) of the Act, an employee must earn the minimum salary amount set forth in Sec. 541.600, "exclusive of board, lodging or other facilities." The phrase "exclusive of board, lodging or other facilities" means "free and clear" or independent of any claimed credit for non-cash items of value that an employer may provide to an employee. Thus, the costs incurred by an employer to provide an employee with board, lodging or other facilities may not count towards the minimum salary amount required for exemption under this part 541. Such separate transactions are not prohibited between employers and their exempt employees, but the costs to employers associated with such transactions may not be considered when determining if an employee has received the full required minimum salary payment.

(b) Regulations defining what constitutes "board, lodging, or other facilities" are contained in 29 CFR part 531. As described in 29 CFR 531.32, the term "other facilities" refers to items similar to board and lodging, such as meals furnished at company restaurants or cafeterias or by hospitals, hotels, or restaurants to their employees; meals, dormitory rooms, and tuition furnished by a college to its student employees; merchandise furnished at company stores or commissaries, including articles of food, clothing, and household effects; housing furnished for dwelling purposes; and transportation furnished to employees for ordinary commuting between their homes and work.

Subpart—H Definitions and Miscellaneous Provisions

Sec. 541.700 Primary duty

(a) To qualify for exemption under this part, an employee's "primary duty" must be the performance of exempt work. The term "primary duty" means the principal, main, major or most important duty that the employee performs. Determination of an employee's primary duty must be based on all the facts in a particular case, with the major emphasis on the character of the employee's job as a whole. Factors to consider when determining the primary duty of an employee include, but are not limited to, the relative importance of the exempt duties as compared with other types of duties; the amount of time spent performing exempt work; the employee's relative freedom from direct supervision; and the relationship between the employee's salary and the wages paid to other employees for the kind of nonexempt work performed by the employee.

(b) The amount of time spent performing exempt work can be a useful guide in determining whether exempt work is the primary duty of an employee. Thus, employees who spend more than 50 percent of their time performing exempt work will generally satisfy the primary duty requirement. Time alone, however, is not the sole test, and nothing in this section requires that exempt employees spend more than 50 percent of their time performing exempt work. Employees who do not spend more than 50 percent of their time performing exempt duties may nonetheless meet the primary duty requirement if the other factors support such a conclusion.

(c) Thus, for example, assistant managers in a retail establishment who perform exempt executive work such as supervising and directing the work of other employees, ordering merchandise, managing the budget and authorizing payment of bills may have management as their primary duty even if the assistant managers spend more than 50 percent of the time performing nonexempt work such as running the cash register. However, if such assistant managers are closely supervised and earn little more than the nonexempt employees, the assistant managers generally would not satisfy the primary duty requirement.

Sec. 541.701 Customarily and regularly

The phrase "customarily and regularly" means a frequency that must be greater than occasional but which, of course, may be less than constant. Tasks or work performed "customarily and regularly" includes work normally and recurrently performed every work-week; it does not include isolated or one-time tasks.

Sec. 541.702 Exempt and nonexempt work

The term "exempt work" means all work described in Secs. 541.100, 541.101, 541.200, 541.300, 541.301, 541.302, 541.303, 541.304, 541.400 and 541.500, and the activities directly and closely related to such work. All other work is considered "nonexempt."

Sec. 541.703 Directly and closely related

(a) Work that is "directly and closely related" to the performance of exempt work is also considered exempt work. The phrase "directly and closely related" means tasks that are related to exempt duties and that contribute to or facilitate performance of exempt work. Thus, "directly and closely related" work may include physical tasks and menial tasks that arise out of exempt duties, and the routine work without which the exempt employee's exempt work cannot be performed properly. Work "directly and closely related" to the performance of exempt duties may also include recordkeeping; monitoring and adjusting machinery; taking notes; using the computer to create documents or presentations; opening the mail for the purpose of reading it and making decisions; and using a photocopier or fax machine. Work is not "directly and closely related" if the work is remotely related or completely unrelated to exempt duties.

(b) The following examples further illustrate the type of work that is and is not normally considered as directly and closely related to exempt work:

(1) Keeping time, production or sales records for subordinates is work directly and closely related to an exempt executive's function of managing a department and supervising employees.

(2) The distribution of materials, merchandise or supplies to maintain control of the flow of and expenditures for such items is directly and closely related to the performance of exempt duties.

(3) A supervisor who spot checks and examines the work of subordinates to determine whether they are performing their duties properly, and whether the product is

satisfactory, is performing work which is directly and closely related to managerial and supervisory functions, so long as the checking is distinguishable from the work ordinarily performed by a nonexempt inspector.

(4) A supervisor who sets up a machine may be engaged in exempt work, depending upon the nature of the industry and the operation. In some cases the setup work, or adjustment of the machine for a particular job, is typically performed by the same employees who operate the machine. Such setup work is part of the production operation and is not exempt. In other cases, the setting up of the work is a highly skilled operation which the ordinary production worker or machine tender typically does not perform. In large plants, non-supervisors may perform such work. However, particularly in small plants, such work may be a regular duty of the executive and is directly and closely related to the executive's responsibility for the work performance of subordinates and for the adequacy of the final product. Under such circumstances, it is exempt work.

(5) A department manager in a retail or service establishment who walks about the sales floor observing the work of sales personnel under the employee's supervision to determine the effectiveness of their sales techniques, checks on the quality of customer service being given, or observes customer preferences is performing work which is directly and closely related to managerial and supervisory functions.

(6) A business consultant may take extensive notes recording the flow of work and materials through the office or plant of the client; after returning to the office of the employer, the consultant may personally use the computer to type a report and create a proposed table of organization. Standing alone, or separated from the primary duty, such note-taking and typing would be routine in nature. However, because this work is necessary for analyzing the data and making recommendations, the work is directly and closely related to exempt work. While it is possible to assign note-taking and typing to nonexempt employees, and in fact it is frequently the practice to do so, delegating such routine tasks is not required as a condition of exemption.

(7) A credit manager who makes and administers the credit policy of the employer, establishes credit limits for customers, authorizes the shipment of orders on credit, and makes decisions on whether to exceed credit limits would be performing work exempt under Sec. 541.200. Work that is directly and closely related to these exempt duties may include checking the status of accounts to determine whether the credit limit would be exceeded by the shipment of a new order, removing credit reports from the files for analysis, and writing letters giving credit data and experience to other employers or credit agencies.

(8) A traffic manager in charge of planning a company's transportation, including the most economical and quickest routes for shipping merchandise to and from the plant, contracting for common-carrier and other transportation facilities, negotiating with carriers for adjustments for damages to merchandise, and making the necessary rearrangements resulting from delays, damages or irregularities in transit, is performing exempt work. If the employee also spends part of the day taking telephone orders for local deliveries, such order-taking is a routine function and is not directly and closely related to the exempt work.

(9) An example of work directly and closely related to exempt professional duties is a chemist performing menial tasks such as cleaning a test tube in the middle of an original experiment, even though such menial tasks can be assigned to laboratory assistants.

(10) A teacher performs work directly and closely related to exempt duties when, while taking students on a field trip, the teacher drives a school van or monitors the students' behavior in a restaurant.

Sec. 541.704 Use of manuals

The use of manuals, guidelines or other established procedures containing or relating to highly technical, scientific, legal, financial or other similarly complex matters that can be understood or interpreted only by those with advanced or specialized knowledge or skills does not preclude exemption under section 13(a)(1) of the Act or the regulations in this part. Such manuals and procedures provide guidance in addressing difficult or novel circumstances and thus use of such reference material would not affect an employee's exempt status. The section 13(a)(1) exemptions are not available, however, for employees who simply apply well-established techniques or procedures described in manuals or other sources within closely prescribed limits to determine the correct response to an inquiry or set of circumstances.

Sec. 541.705 Trainees

The executive, administrative, professional, outside sales and computer employee exemptions do not apply to employees training for employment in an executive, administrative, professional, outside sales or computer employee capacity who are not actually performing the duties of an executive, administrative, professional, outside sales or computer employee.

Sec. 541.706 Emergencies

(a) An exempt employee will not lose the exemption by performing work of a normally nonexempt nature because of the existence of an emergency. Thus, when emergencies arise that threaten the safety of employees, a cessation of operations or serious damage to the employer's property, any work performed in an effort to prevent such results is considered exempt work.

(b) An "emergency" does not include occurrences that are not beyond control or for which the employer can reasonably provide in the normal course of business. Emergencies generally occur only rarely, and are events that the employer cannot reasonably anticipate.

(c) The following examples illustrate the distinction between emergency work considered exempt work and routine work that is not exempt work:

(1) A mine superintendent who pitches in after an explosion and digs out workers who are trapped in the mine is still a bona fide executive.

(2) Assisting nonexempt employees with their work during periods of heavy workload or to handle rush orders is not exempt work.

(3) Replacing a nonexempt employee during the first day or partial day of an illness may be considered exempt emergency work depending on factors such as the size of the establishment and of the executive's department, the nature of the industry, the consequences that would flow from the failure to replace the ailing employee immediately, and the feasibility of filling the employee's place promptly.

(4) Regular repair and cleaning of equipment is not emergency work, even when necessary to prevent fire or explosion; however, repairing equipment may be emergency work if the breakdown of or damage to the equipment was caused by accident or carelessness that the employer could not reasonably anticipate.

Sec. 541.707 Occasional tasks

Occasional, infrequently recurring tasks that cannot practicably be performed by nonexempt employees, but are the means for an exempt employee to properly carry out exempt functions and responsibilities, are considered exempt work. The following factors should be considered in determining whether such work is exempt work: Whether the same work is performed by any of the exempt employee's subordinates; practicability of delegating the work to a nonexempt employee; whether the exempt employee performs the task frequently or occasionally; and existence of an industry practice for the exempt employee to perform the task.

Sec. 541.708 Combination exemptions

Employees who perform a combination of exempt duties as set forth in the regulations in this part for executive, administrative, professional, outside sales and computer employees may qualify for exemption. Thus, for example, an employee whose primary duty involves a combination of exempt administrative and exempt executive work may qualify for exemption. In other words, work that is exempt under one section of this part will not defeat the exemption under any other section.

Sec. 541.709 Motion picture producing industry

The requirement that the employee be paid "on a salary basis" does not apply to an employee in the motion picture producing industry who is compensated at a base rate of at least $695 a week (exclusive of board, lodging, or other facilities). Thus, an employee in this industry who is otherwise exempt under Subparts B, C or D of this part, and who is employed at a base rate of at least $695 a week is exempt if paid a proportionate amount (based on a week of not more than 6 days) for any week in which the employee does not work a full workweek for any reason. Moreover, an otherwise exempt employee in this industry qualifies for exemption if the employee is employed at a daily rate under the following circumstances:

(a) The employee is in a job category for which a weekly base rate is not provided and the daily base rate would yield at least $695 if 6 days were worked; or

(b) The employee is in a job category having a weekly base rate of at least $695 and the daily base rate is at least one-sixth of such weekly base rate.

Sec. 541.710 Employees of public agencies

(a) An employee of a public agency who otherwise meets the salary basis requirements of Sec. 541.602 shall not be disqualified from exemption under Sec. 541.100, 541.200, 541.300 or 541.400 on the basis that such employee is paid according to a pay system established by statute, ordinance or regulation, or by a policy or practice established pursuant to principles of public accountability, under which the employee accrues personal leave and sick leave and which requires the public agency employee's pay to be reduced or such employee to be placed on leave without pay for absences for personal reasons or because of illness or injury of less than one work-day when accrued leave is not used by an employee because:

(1) Permission for its use has not been sought or has been sought and denied;

(2) Accrued leave has been exhausted; or

(3) The employee chooses to use leave without pay.

(b) Deductions from the pay of an employee of a public agency for absences due to a budget-required furlough shall not disqualify the employee from being paid on a salary basis except in the workweek in which the furlough occurs and for which the employee's pay is accordingly reduced.

Index

[References are to question numbers and appendices.]